BY TH

STRAVI
Volume I

STRAVI
(with Ve

CURRE

PREJUD

CHRON

STRAVINSKY

SELECTED CORRESPONDENCE

ALFRED A. KNOPF   NEW YORK   1984

STRAVINSKY

SELECTED CORRESPONDENCE
VOLUME II

EDITED AND
WITH COMMENTARIES BY
ROBERT CRAFT

This is a Borzoi Book published by Alfred A. Knopf, Inc.

Copyright © 1984 by Robert Craft

All rights reserved under International and Pan-American Copyright Conventions.

Published in the United States by Alfred A. Knopf, Inc., New York.

Distributed by Random House, Inc., New York.

Published in England by Faber and Faber Limited, London.

Letters and other copyright material

from the Stravinsky Archive are published

by kind permission of the Paul Sacher Foundation.

Library of Congress Cataloging in Publication Data

(Revised for volume 2)

Stravinsky, Igor, 1882–1971.   Stravinsky, selected correspondence, volume II.

Includes index.

1. Stravinsky, Igor, 1882–1971.   2. Composers—
Correspondence.   I. Craft, Robert.   II. Title.

ML410.S932A395   1982   780'.92'4 [B]   81-47495

ISBN 0-394-51870-5 (v. 1)

ISBN 0-394-52813-1 (v. 2)

Manufactured in the United States of America

First American Edition

Igor Stravinsky—grand dans mon temps. (Saint-John Perse, Washington, D.C., 1947)

Igor et Véra Stravinsky, qui détiennent, à eux deux, de plus miraculeuses clés. (Saint-John Perse, Washington, D.C., December 15, 1962)

I quite understand why you feel this need to pursue, physically, the destiny of your work, even to the ultimate corps-à-corps *with conducting. So, go right on being prodigal. Artistic creation was not invented, as woman is said to have been, for the hero's repose. Artistic creation is war itself. And you are a warrior. (Saint-John Perse, Washington, D.C., January 25, 1962)*

CONTENTS

II

III

IV

ACKNOWLEDGMENTS

I am indebted to Eva Resnikova, Phyllis Crawford, Elbert Lenrow, Lawrence Morton, Robert Gottlieb, and Patrick Carnegy for valuable suggestions and improvements. The Russian letters were translated by Lucia Davidova, Mary Brown, Malcolm Macdonald, and Helen and Franklin Reeve. Mrs. Reeve also translated the letters and documents in German in the *Firebird* chapter. The translations of the French letters are the work of Eva Resnikova, Kristin Crawford, and myself.

R. C.

I

CORRESPONDENCE WITH

1911 ~ 1928

SERGE DE DIAGHILEV

SERGE DE DIAGHILEV TO STRAVINSKY[1]

St. Petersburg
February 10, 1911
[Telegram]

1, avenue Anglais
Beaulieu-sur-Mer

Today I took *Firebird* score from Jurgenson.[2] When will I have Fourth Tableau *Petrushka*?   Diaghilev

STRAVINSKY TO DIAGHILEV

Clarens
April 11, 1912

Riviera Palace
Monte Carlo

[The text, in Stravinsky's carbon copy, is illegible.]

DIAGHILEV TO STRAVINSKY

London
June 20, 1912
[Telegram]

Ustilug

Congratulations great success *Firebird* [in the] press. Very best wishes.
Diaghilev, Savoy

---

[1] Russian is the original language of the letters, French the language of the one post-card (February 2, 1916) and of all but two of the telegrams, the exceptions being written in an invented language of Latin-letter Russian. The texts of Stravinsky's tele-grams are drafts and not necessarily final. Stravinsky and Diaghilev referred to them-selves as "cousins." Natalya Furman, a sister of Stravinsky's great-grandfather, mar-ried Admiral F. P. Litke, the president of the Russian Academy of Sciences and the brother of Diaghilev's great-grandmother. Two sons of the marriage, the counts Litke—second cousins of Stravinsky's mother—stood watch at Tchaikovsky's death-bed.

[2] The Russian music-publishing firm, run since the death (1904) of its founder, Pyotr Ivanovich Jurgenson, by his son Boris, assisted by his brother Grigory.

DIAGHILEV TO STRAVINSKY

Santa Elisabetta (Lido)
Venice
September 21, 1912
[Telegram]

Ustilug

[I] find [the] participation of Maeterlinck desirable. Through whom [was] the proposal made? Could discuss it with Maeterlinck next week. Telegraph details.   Diaghilev

DIAGHILEV TO STRAVINSKY

Santa Elisabetta (Lido)
Venice
September 22, 1912
[Telegram]

Ustilug

Telegraph me Paris [Hôtel] Crillon immediately[3] [or at Théâtre] des Champs [Elysées].   Diaghilev

DIAGHILEV TO STRAVINSKY

Santa Elisabetta (Lido)
Venice
October 5, 1912
[Telegram]

Ustilug

I will try to see Maeterlinck. Leaving Monday [for] Paris Hôtel Crillon. Diaghilev

DIAGHILEV TO STRAVINSKY

Munich
November 11, 1912
[Telegram]

Hôtel Châtelard
Clarens

We begin the Berlin performances on the 16th. *Firebird* premiere 21st. I will be in Berlin tomorrow Adlon[4] Hotel.   Diaghilev

DIAGHILEV TO STRAVINSKY

Vier Jahreszeiten Hotel
Munich
November 11, 1912
[Telegram]

Hôtel Châtelard
Clarens

Have you finished *Sacre?* Can you come Berlin again November 20? Diaghilev

---

[3] This virtually illegible word resembles the Polish for "immediately."

[4] Stravinsky has underscored the name of the hotel and written: "Please be so kind as to check this word. It is incomprehensible." He stayed at the Adlon himself on this trip, as well as in later years.

DIAGHILEV TO STRAVINSKY

Berlin
December 18, 1912
[Telegram]

Hôtel Châtelard
Clarens

Rehearsals have not begun [yet]. We do not have the designs. No need for pianola arrangement.   Diaghilev

DIAGHILEV TO STRAVINSKY

Budapest
January 2, 1913
[Telegram]

Hôtel Châtelard
Clarens

If you do not come here immediately for fifteen days *Sacre* will not be given. Roerich's presence is unnecessary. Sets not [yet] received. Struve[5] has been paid. Jurgenson will be [paid] soon. Telegraph the date of your arrival. Diaghilev, Hungaria Hotel

STRAVINSKY TO DIAGHILEV

Clarens
January 3, 1913
[Telegram]

Budapest

I arrive Sunday night. Impossible to obtain reservation before Saturday. If you leave Budapest Monday [it is] preferable to come directly to Vienna. Telegraph.[6]

DIAGHILEV TO STRAVINSKY

Vienna
January 17, 1913
[Telegram]

Hôtel Châtelard
Clarens
Montreux

Second performance of *Petrushka* great success. Four unanimous curtain calls.[7] Write immediately Florent Schmitt [asking him to] telegraph me. Reply Petersburg 22 quai Anglais.   Serge

---

[5] Nicolas G. Struve, director of the Edition Russe de Musique.

[6] Before sending this telegram, Stravinsky drafted and canceled two others: 1. "I can reserve a ticket for Saturday arriving Sunday at 11:30 Hungaria Hotel." 2. "Is it worth my while to come to Budapest?"

[7] On January 24, the *Petersburg Gazette* published a news item under the headline "Members of the Diaghilev Troupe Report an Incident": "From the artists of Diaghilev's troupe comes news of a disturbing incident that occurred in Vienna involving the orchestra of the Royal Opera there and the composer Stravinsky. When the rehearsals for Stravinsky's ballet *Petrushka* got under way, the composer, not satisfied with the sonority of the orchestra, requested that it be increased in size. This request on the

DIAGHILEV TO STRAVINSKY

Hôtel Châtelard
Clarens

Petersburg
February 1, 1913
[Telegram]

Ask Florent Schmitt to come by [on] Monday seven o'clock to the Hôtel Crillon. Cable him the address. When can you come to London? *Petrushka* premiere is Tuesday.   Diaghilev

DIAGHILEV TO STRAVINSKY

Savoy Hotel
London

Paris
[February 6, 1913]
[Telegram]

Arriving tomorrow evening [the] 7th. Counting on you for performance tonight.[8]   Serge

DIAGHILEV TO STRAVINSKY

Pension [*sic*] Châtelard
Clarens

London
March 2, 1913
[Telegram]

Think about coming to Paris Sunday for one day.   Serge

DIAGHILEV TO STRAVINSKY

Hôtel Châtelard
Clarens

Petersburg
March 23, 1913
[Telegram]

Send immediately Roerich's books, designs.[9]   Diaghilev

---

part of Stravinsky evidently offended the members of the orchestra, who protested that
they had performed even Wagner with the present number of players, that never before had anyone complained about the sound of the Vienna orchestra, and that they
could not agree to increase the orchestra's size under any circumstances. Stravinsky
then became insistent, and the entire orchestra left the rehearsal and refused to play
Petrushka. S. P. Diaghilev took great pains to settle the matter, though he was not successful in increasing the orchestra's size."

[8] The Ballets Russes evening in London. Stravinsky had been in London since the beginning of the month.

[9] For *Le Sacre du printemps*. Serge Grigoriev, Diaghilev's régisseur, had written to
Stravinsky on December 18, 1912: "We are still waiting for the costumes for your new
work. . . . *Firebird* was performed nine times in Berlin, *Petrushka* seven times."

DIAGHILEV TO STRAVINSKY

Petersburg
April 4, 1913
[Telegram]

Hôtel Châtelard

Clarens

[I] beg you to come to Monte Carlo the Riviera Palace [Hôtel] on Tuesday with finished chorus.[10] I leave tonight.   Diaghilev

DIAGHILEV TO STRAVINSKY

Beausoleil
April 19, 1913
[Telegram]

Clarens

Cable to Sanine[11] that you will give [him] the answer. In a month I will have to discuss some serious matters with you.   Serge

---

[10] The *Petersburg Gazette* for February 17, 1913, had printed a letter from Diaghilev concerning his choice of the young composer Igor Stravinsky to compose and orchestrate the final chorus of *Khovanshchina:* "To the Editor: In reference to the article that appeared in your newspaper concerning the restorations in *Khovanshchina,* I consider it my duty to reply to the attacks directed at my friend Stravinsky. He is planning neither to rewrite nor to reorchestrate Rimsky-Korsakov's work; but as everyone knows, Rimsky-Korsakov based the final chorus of the unfinished opera on a theme by Mussorgsky. At my request, Stravinsky is now writing a new finale on this same theme. Which of the two will prove the better is a matter for those who have heard both versions to decide. As for the orchestration of those pages of *Khovanshchina* that are as yet unpublished and unorchestrated, this is the first time I have heard it suggested that to familiarize oneself with the work of the brilliant Mussorgsky might be considered a sad development. London, February 12, 1913. Serge Diaghilev."

The letter was written in response to a lengthy article on the subject in the St. Petersburg *Commercial News* (*Birzhevyie Vedomosti*), February 3, 1913. This states that "in the Imperial Library, Diaghilev found manuscripts of material for *Khovanshchina* that Mussorgsky did not use." The article includes the opinions of eight "experts" on the matter, but the only one worth quoting is that of César Cui: "If new material of Mussorgsky's has indeed been found, why not use it?! Let the public and the music world see and hear the new material and deliver its own verdict. I find Diaghilev's decision to commission Stravinsky to orchestrate this material entirely logical. The latter was a pupil of Rimsky and is a magnificent orchestrator. As for Diaghilev's intention to recompose the final chorus, I must say that I cannot understand it. Would Stravinsky really set about correcting his own teacher? It would be incredibly impudent on his part to undertake such a mission. I am inclined to think that Stravinsky would never agree to redo the final chorus for Diaghilev's purposes."

[11] Alexander Aksimovich Sanine (1868–1956), theatre director.

DIAGHILEV TO STRAVINSKY   *Beausoleil*
                                                          April 21, 1913
Stravigor   *[Telegram]*
Clarens

Decline St. Petersburg [Sanine, *The Nightingale*] in general phrase saying
that terms are not suitable. Send Shaklovity and [*Khovanshchina*] chorus.
[*Original in transliterated Russian*]

DIAGHILEV TO STRAVINSKY   *Monte Carlo*
                                                          April 27, 1913
Stravigor   *[Telegram]*
Clarens

The chorus has been received. You will have the money tomorrow. Fondly,
Serge

DIAGHILEV TO STRAVINSKY   *Paris*
                                                          May 6, 1913
Stravigor   *[Telegram]*
Clarens

When do you plan to come?   Serge, Hôtel Crillon

STRAVINSKY TO DIAGHILEV   *Berlin*
                                                          July 12, 1913
Hotel Savoy   *[Cable]*
London

Regret having caused trouble but did not understand your diplomatic position.[12] Cable to Ustilug.

DIAGHILEV TO STRAVINSKY   *Paris*
                                                          August 14, 1913[13]
Ustilug   *[Cable]*

When do you expect to finish the opera [*The Nightingale*]? Best wishes,
Serge, Crillon

---

[12] See the section on Stravinsky, Diaghilev, and Misia Sert in *Stravinsky in Pictures
and Documents* (New York, 1978), pp. 514–522 (hereafter referred to as *S.P.D.*).
[13] Léon Bernstein, Stravinsky's representative in Paris, had written to the composer in
Ustilug, July 28: "I have only just returned from London today. . . . I spoke at length
with Sergei Pavlovich there, and of course met with energetic resistance on his
part. . . . He is not prepared to pay you anything for performances outside of Paris and
Monte Carlo. I pointed out that it is hardly fair to pay Russian composers only in those

DIAGHILEV TO STRAVINSKY

Hôtel Châtelard
Clarens

I will be at the Beau Rivage in Lausanne tomorrow morning. [I] embrace [you]. Seriozha

DIAGHILEV TO STRAVINSKY

Hôtel Châtelard
Clarens

Come to Montreux around 10:15. Serge

DIAGHILEV TO STRAVINSKY

Hôtel Châtelard
Clarens

Yes I plan to present *The Nightingale* [in] Paris and London. I could come to Montreux if absolutely necessary. Cable me. Serge

DIAGHILEV TO STRAVINSKY

Hôtel Châtelard
Clarens

I arrive tomorrow morning. Serge

DIAGHILEV TO STRAVINSKY

Stravigor
Clarens

Send a letter to Messager via Misia.[14] Serge

---

cases in which, owing to the peculiar conditions of the Société des Auteurs, it is impossible to avoid doing so. The unfairness of this is even more obvious when one considers that Sergei Pavlovich is obliged to pay non-Russian composers, such as Debussy. . . . I discussed the question with lawyers in London, and they said that it might be impossible to use compulsory means, but I have not lost hope that Sergei Pavlovich will agree to pay your author's rights. . . . Since he will be in Paris in a few days, please write a letter to me (in French) listing the terms of your agreement with him for each of your works."

[14] André Messager was to have conducted the first performance of *The Nightingale*.

DIAGHILEV TO STRAVINSKY   *Petersburg*
                                                    December 29, 1913
Hôtel Châtelard   *[Telegram]*
Clarens

Come to Paris the 1st of January French [style]. Cable reply to the Continental
Hotel Berlin. Important.   Serge

DIAGHILEV TO STRAVINSKY   *Paris*
                                                      January 6, 1914
Hôtel Châtelard   *[Telegram]*
Clarens

Thank Messager for accepting [the invitation] to conduct *Nightingale*. How is
your wife's health? Did you finish the piano score?   Serge, Crillon

DIAGHILEV TO STRAVINSKY   *Paris*
                                                     January 17, 1914
Hôtel Châtelard   *[Telegram]*
Clarens

Sincere congratulations. A thousand best wishes.   Serge

DIAGHILEV TO STRAVINSKY   *Paris*
                                                     January 18, 1914
Clinique Mont-Riant   *[Telegram]*
Avenue de la Gare
Lausanne

Best wishes to all three of you.[15] Enraptured by the Chinese melodies.[16] With
great fondness,   Misia Sert, Serge

---

[15] Stravinsky's wife had given birth to a second daughter, Milene, on January 15.

[16] Stravinsky's *Three Japanese Lyrics* had been presented by the Société Musicale
Indépendante on January 13 at the Salle Erard, but Diaghilev had not been present.
(See M. D. Calvocoressi's letter to Stravinsky of January 16, 1914.) Stravinsky wrote
to his wife that he dined alone with Debussy on January 21, Diaghilev, who was also
invited, having left for Moscow. But on January 23 Stravinsky wrote to his wife in Lausanne that Diaghilev was still in Paris. Stravinsky telegraphed again the next day to
say that he would be in Lausanne on the morning of the 25th.

DIAGHILEV TO STRAVINSKY

Milan
September 21, 1914
[Telegram]

Hôtel Châtelard
Clarens

Need to see you. I will gladly cover your traveling expenses. Definitely come. Reply Florence 4 viale Torricelli.   Serge

STRAVINSKY TO DIAGHILEV

Clarens
September 22, 1914
[Telegram]

Florence

I beg you come here [instead]. If not I will come to Florence. Send 200 francs. Otherwise impossible [for me] to budge.

DIAGHILEV TO STRAVINSKY

Florence
September 28, 1914
[Telegram]

Hôtel Châtelard
Clarens

I am sending 200 francs right away.[22] I embrace you.   Diaghilev

DIAGHILEV TO STRAVINSKY

Florence
September 29, 1914
[Telegram]

Hôtel Châtelard
Clarens

Bring all of your music and everything you have of the French [composers] including [*Le Martyre de*] *Saint-Sébastien.*   Diaghilev

DIAGHILEV TO STRAVINSKY

Florence
October 13, 1914
[Telegram]

Hôtel Châtelard
Clarens

The contract for America signed by Meštrović awaits us in Rome. I embrace you.   Diaghilev

---

[22] On the following day Diaghilev wired 185 francs to the composer.

DIAGHILEV TO STRAVINSKY

4 *viale Torricelli*
Florence
November 1, 1914

La Pervenche
Clarens

You awful pig! I wire you, saying that I have signed the American contract, that Meštrović telegraphed and is expecting me in Rome in November, yet not a peep out of you! You force me, an old man, to take up my pen!

We[23] stay here until November 10, then go to Rome. We were overwhelmed in Ravenna by this magnificent cemetery. I received a mad telegram from Misia to the effect that she will not leave Paris because it is *now* the most beautiful city in the world! I received a telegram from Nijinsky saying that he cannot come right now because he *still* does not have an exit visa! Prokofiev is working with Gorodyetsky and also finishing the piano concerto. Koussevitzky is conducting in Rome, and I shall see him. I also received an amicable inquiry about my affairs from your M. Fokine. He and his wife are in Biarritz. Well, and what scene of *Noces* have you reached? Write, dog.

Yours,   Sergei Diaghilev

DIAGHILEV TO STRAVINSKY

Rome
November 14, 1914
[Telegram]

Hôtel Châtelard
Clarens

Why do you not answer the telegram and letters? I have arranged a concert for you at the Augusteo [in] Rome. San Martino[24] should be writing to you. [I] suppose you [should] consider asking 1,000 francs and travel expenses. You could conduct *Scherzo fantastique, Fireworks,* [and the] *Petrushka* and *Firebird* suites.   Diaghilev, Grand Hotel

STRAVINSKY TO DIAGHILEV

Clarens
November 15, 1914
[Telegram]

Grand Hotel
Rome

Think [I] will be able to accept. [I] tremble [at the thought]. I embrace you. Letter follows. Telegraph the date of the concert.

---

[23] Diaghilev was with Léonide Massine.
[24] Count Enrico San Martino di Valperga was president of the Accademia di Santa Cecilia.

DIAGHILEV TO STRAVINSKY

Hôtel Châtelard
Clarens

Dear Igor,

Unfortunately, at the last minute, our concert did not materialize. When I first proposed it to San Martino, he jumped on the sofa in excitement and shouted, "But I will welcome Stravinsky with open arms!" When I saw him next, he told me how good it is to be an autocrat: "In half an hour you can invite Stravinsky without having to ask anyone's permission." All details were settled and the concert arranged for January 3; suddenly I received a letter with the following statement: ". . . as for the fee, you can imagine how embarrassed the Academy is to find itself facing a season like this with so few resources. But Stravinsky is young, and since it is not his aim to make a career as a conductor, I hope he will be satisfied with a very modest sum, between 600 and 700 francs."

I ran to San Martino and explained that the train ticket alone costs 240 francs, and your sojourn in Rome for seven days, at 50 francs a day, 350, *id est* 600 francs, the sum he proposed. All that I can do now is invite you to stay with me, so you will have no hotel expenses, and convince you to accept 1,200 francs. [San Martino] agrees with this and says that in order for the concert to take place, he will shrink his budget (!!) (he has also invited Strauss, Debussy, Koussevitzky from Moscow, and others). I even spoke with him and with their conductor about the schedule, insisting that they give all of you twelve rehearsals. Then I received this note: "My dear friend, I regret very much that we have to cancel Stravinsky's concert for reasons that I will explain to you on my return." He went to Turin for three days, and I will not see him before Sunday's concert. Now I will propose to pay your traveling expenses myself if he will pay you 1,000 francs. If this fails, to hell with him.

But we absolutely must see each other. You must come here for two weeks—the best time would be beginning December 20. If you spend the holidays here, you can have a quiet little room in our apartment; and the food is not bad. But you must come: our business with Meštrović is progressing rapidly. He is shy, sickly, proud, suspicious of everything. He has genius in his work, his intentions are always good, and he is brimming with ideas, but his criticisms are mediocre. We must attend to everything ourselves. He and Massine are working together, and I have given Massine my blessing. I want him to stage this ballet!

Nijinsky behaves so stupidly. He did not even answer my detailed, and, in my opinion, fair, letter; then in reply to the humble telegram I sent subsequently, asking whether he had received my letter, he answered only: "Letter received. Cannot come." (I even paid for the reply.)

I am certain that his wife is busy making him into the first ballet master of the Budapest Opera! As for *Noces,* do not worry, for I shall write a second, less modest, and less correct letter, after which this miserable person will understand that the joke has gone too far. The invention of movement in *Noces* is definitely a job for Nijinsky, but I will not discuss this with him for several months yet. Massine is still too young, but each day he becomes more and more ours, and this is important.

I cannot tell you about the subject in any detail, but let me say that what I have in mind is a performance of the Mass in six or seven short scenes. The epoch will be Byzantine, which Meštrović will arrange in his own way. The music, a series of *a cappella* sacred choruses, should perhaps be inspired by Gregorian chant, but of that more later. When you come you will meet a great connoisseur of these matters—Meštrović.

The frescoes in the Roman underground churches of the first century are really astonishing.

For the moment that is all. I hope you approve. The main thing is that you come. Please answer me immediately at the Grand Hotel. I embrace you.

Serge

DIAGHILEV TO STRAVINSKY

Rome
January 1, 1915
[Telegram]

Hôtel Châtelard
Clarens

January 18 I leave for Africa until May. I understand nothing of your telegram. Your immediate arrival is indispensable. You must meet with Meštrović. Come quickly. Wire me.   Diaghilev

---

STRAVINSKY TO DIAGHILEV

Château-d'Oex
January 2, 1915
[Telegram]

Rome

Impossible [for me to come] now. I will try to come January 15.

DIAGHILEV TO STRAVINSKY

Rome
January 3, 1915
[Telegram]

Château-d'Oex

I will postpone my departure until February 1. Come January 15 for 10 days. Meštrović is leaving at the end of January. [I will] explain what has happened by letter.   Diaghilev

---

DIAGHILEV TO STRAVINSKY

Rome
January 13, 1915
[Telegram]

Hôtel Victoria
Château-d'Oex

Best wishes. We look forward to Friday.   Diaghilev, Massine

DIAGHILEV TO STRAVINSKY

Hôtel Victoria
Château-d'Oex

Rome
January 13, 1915
[Telegram]

No danger but come Friday. If not you will once again [have] disrupted all my plans.

DIAGHILEV TO STRAVINSKY

Hôtel Victoria
Château-d'Oex

Rome
January 16, 1915
[Telegram]

[I] am infinitely disgusted. All my plans [for] my trip disrupted. Have wasted time for nothing. Wire immediately if you can come January 25 for 8 or 10 days. We must work very seriously.   Diaghilev

DIAGHILEV TO STRAVINSKY

Hôtel Victoria
Château-d'Oex

[End of January 1915]
[Telegram]

Received [your] letter. Understand situation but insist you come for a few days given the agreement with Meštrović, the alliance with Marinetti, and other very serious questions. Let us be strong and energetic.

DIAGHILEV TO STRAVINSKY

Hôtel Victoria
Château-d'Oex

Rome
February 6, 1915
[Telegram]

I have wired to Marinetti and Pratella to come to Rome Tuesday morning. Remember to bring Liadov's *Dumka* and evening clothes.   Diaghilev

DIAGHILEV TO STRAVINSKY

Hôtel Victoria
Château-d'Oex

Rome
February 24, 1915[25]
[Telegram]

Misia 20. Send me [the] polka. Cable how much you would charge, all joking aside.   Diaghilev

---

[25] Stravinsky had been in Rome from February 8 to 17, lionized by Diaghilev, the Futurists, and the personnel of the Russian Embassy, including Vasily Khvoshchinsky and his wife. The composer met Rodin as well as Meštrović. On February 14, Casella conducted *Petrushka* in the Augusteo. Alexander Amfiteatrov reviewed the concert for

DIAGHILEV TO STRAVINSKY   *Grand Hotel (until March 8)*
                                                      March 3, 1915

Hôtel Victoria
Château-d'Oex

Dear,

You are a little mad. San Martino buy something? His wife would choke to
death first. They will never do it. The American [*sic*] Russell was here; he
found the price very high, though he did say he would try to do something, if
you send him a manuscript [of *Firebird*]. He has gone to America: Henry Russell, Esq., Metropolitan Opera, New York. I hesitate to send him the manuscript, because someone could print it in America without paying you a penny;
if you want to send it, do so yourself. For my part, I will speak to Ricordi, although I am not optimistic. As for the score and parts of *The Nightingale*, you
are not so much mad as ridiculous. If Telyatina[26] stages it at all, he will not do
so earlier than 1917, when everybody will have forgotten about the war. Why in
hell should Prokofiev (who is coming today) drag the music with him so that it
can lie around for two years in Petrogrrrrrad? Tell me whether we are obliged to
fulfill this foolish order.

Now about us. We are going to Naples and Palermo on March 8 for ten to
twelve days, and afterward coming to you to fetch *Les Noces*. It must be finished
by that time. Then, with or without you, we will go to Spain for about three
weeks. And after that, I do not know what we will be doing and where we will
be, but we will be working and not twiddling our thumbs as some people do. So
expect us about March 20, and have a big ballet ready—without that I shall be
very angry. Before speaking with Dalcroze we must see what scores he has.

Everybody sends his regards and remembers you fondly. You left an unde-
niable impression, as they say here.

                                                      Serge D.

P.S. Khvoshchinsky leaves for the war, drafted in Russia.[27]
P.P.S. It is as hot as summer here, and the sun beats down full force.

---

the St. Petersburg newspaper the *New Russian Word* (February 15), under the headline "Stravinsky Success in Rome and Geneva": "Despite poor conducting by Casella,
Stravinsky had an enormous success.... The ovation was somewhat spoiled by Marinetti, who wanted to get in on Stravinsky's triumph."

[26] Vladimir Teliakovsky, director of the Imperial Theatres in St. Petersburg. *Teliatina*
means veal.

[27] Vasily Khvoshchinsky was in the Russian diplomatic service in Rome. Shortly after
Diaghilev's letter, Madame Khvoshchinskaya sent Stravinsky a postcard from Capri:
"The sun is splendidly bright and warm, and there are millions of flowers. I hope to see
you soon.... My husband has already left for Russia." But Khovshchinsky evidently
returned from Russia to Rome (see fn. 39 below).

DIAGHILEV TO STRAVINSKY

Rome
March 4, 1915
[Telegram]

Hôtel Victoria
Château-d'Oex

Try to arrange for Prokofiev to play his second concerto, lasting 30 minutes, Saturday, March 20, in Geneva without charging a fee.   Diaghilev, Grand Hotel

DIAGHILEV TO STRAVINSKY

Rome
March 8, 1915

Hôtel Châtelard
Clarens

Dear Igor,

A number of new questions. First of all, Prokofiev. Yesterday he played in the Augusteo, with considerable success. But that is not the point. He brought me a ballet. The subject is a St. Petersburg confection, fit for a Maryinsky Theatre production of ten years ago. As he puts it, the score is "just plain music, devoid of any attempt at 'Russianness.' " And that is an apt description: it is plain music and quite awful, so that everything will have to be done over again. For that reason [the score] will have to be ... left with us for a while (two or three months), and I am counting on you. [Prokofiev] is talented, but what do you want when the most cultured man he sees is Gorodyetsky, who astounds him with his trust? [Prokofiev] yields to influences and is evidently more naive than his former arrogance would indicate. I will bring the piece to you, for it needs a complete overhaul; otherwise we will never be able to present it.

Now something else, even more important: we have had a brilliant idea. After 32 rehearsals for *Liturgy,* we have concluded that absolute silence is Death, and that there is and can be no absolute silence in any air space. Thus the action must have some accompaniment, not musical accompaniment but, rather, sounds. The source of the sounds must not be revealed, and the passage from one to another must not be noticeable to the ear, i.e., they must flow into each other. No rhythm should exist at all, because the beginning and end of sound should be imperceptible. The proposed instruments are: *guzli* (psalters), bells with tongues wrapped in felt, aeolian harps, sirens, tops, and so on. Of course, this all has to be worked over. Marinetti urges us to plan a meeting in Milan, if just for a day, in order to discuss matters with the orchestra's representatives and to examine all of their instruments. In addition, he is going to send Pratella to Milan to acquaint us with his latest works, which are, as he puts it, stunning. All this could be done between March 15 and 20. Cable me, Naples, Hotel Vesuvius, telling me whether you could come with us to Milan for a day; you will see a lot of new workshops, and we will go from there to Montreux. Please do this, as it is extremely important for the future. I am sending this off right away.

As for Prokofiev's concert in Geneva, if the 20th is not possible, he can play for the benefit of the Serbs.

And so, until our imminent meeting, I embrace you.

Seriozha

P.S. Work on *Noces,* for I am in love with it.

DIAGHILEV TO STRAVINSKY

Hôtel Châtelard
Clarens

Rome
March 22, 1915
[Telegram]

I hope to see you Milan at the end of this week. [I] will cable.   Diaghilev

---

DIAGHILEV TO STRAVINSKY

Hôtel Châtelard
Clarens

Rome
March 28, 1915[28]
[Telegram]

Come to Milan, Hotel Continental, Wednesday morning. Bring all of your music.   Diaghilev

---

DIAGHILEV TO STRAVINSKY

Hôtel Châtelard
Clarens

Rome
March 29, 1915
[Telegram]

I have been delayed for a day. We will be in Milan Thursday morning. Diaghilev

---

DIAGHILEV TO STRAVINSKY

Hôtel Châtelard
Clarens

Milan
April 1, 1915
[Telegram]

Did you receive the money [and] my two telegrams? We await you here. Why have you not arrived yet? Send a cable.   Diaghilev, Continental Hotel

---

[28] Diaghilev had wired 90 francs to Stravinsky from Rome the previous day, together with the following message: "Money [has been] sent. Wait for my dispatch. Diaghilev."

DIAGHILEV TO STRAVINSKY

Rome
April 18, 1915
[Telegram]

Hôtel Châtelard
Clarens

I will be in Montreux at the end of this week. I embrace you.   Diaghilev

Poster for a Red Cross benefit performance, attended by the king and queen of England and the president of France, Paris, December 29, 1915. Stravinsky conducted Firebird—*his first appearance as a conductor in Paris.*

DIAGHILEV TO STRAVINSKY

Milan
April 25, 1915
[Telegram]

Hôtel Châtelard
Clarens

We will be in Montreux tonight at nine o'clock.   Diaghilev

DIAGHILEV TO STRAVINSKY

Morges

Diaghilev, Massine embrace you [from the] Plaza Hotel.

Stravinsky's postcard of February 2, 1916, sent to Diaghilev in New York and returned to the composer in Morges.

STRAVINSKY TO DIAGHILEV

Plaza Hotel
New York

Very dear one,

Your telegram gave me double pleasure, but already a week has passed, and I have not received the money you promised in the cable. Have you already wired that sum, or did you mail it instead? If you have not yet sent it, please do so by cable, and add [five?] hundred francs to that amount, as we agreed in Paris. I embrace you as well as Massine.

Igor

I am revolted to read in C. Von [*sic*] Vechten's rag about our ballets (just published by G. Schirmer) that I am Jewish. I implore you to deny that I am a *boche,* or a Jew, or a Social Democrat.

DIAGHILEV TO STRAVINSKY

Blackstone Hotel
Chicago
February 21, 1916
[Cable]

Morges

The payment to Jurgenson has been made. Have you received the money? I embrace you.   Diaghilev, Blackstone Hotel

STRAVINSKY TO DIAGHILEV

Morges
February 22, 1916
[Cable]

New York

Received only 2,500 Swiss francs. To avoid losing in the exchange [send] the 2,500 francs for March through B[anque] F[édérale] Zürich.   Stravinsky

DIAGHILEV TO STRAVINSKY

Milwaukee
March 2, 1916
[Cable]

Morges

See Nijinsky right away in the Grand Hotel Bern. Tell him of the pains [we have taken] to obtain papers for him. Guide him in the right direction [i.e., of] devotion to our enterprise. Discourage him from dancing in Europe without us, even for charity.   Diaghilev

DIAGHILEV TO STRAVINSKY

Cleveland
March 17, 1916
[Cable]

Villa Rogivue
Morges

Russell telegraphed [Otto] Kahn [that] Nijinsky was ready to leave but [that] you spoiled everything by opposing his departure. You terrified him and preju-diced the Bern legation against the idea. Kahn is disgusted. I am dismayed. Your future in America is at stake. Nijinsky must come immediately, following the instructions in the cable to Devaux. Otherwise the Metropolitan will lose confidence in all of us. Reply [to the] William Penn Hotel, Pitts-burgh.   Diaghilev

STRAVINSKY TO DIAGHILEV

Morges
March 18, 1916
[Cable]

William Penn Hotel
Pittsburgh

Profoundly indignant [about] false accusations of Devaux and Russell. Ni-jinsky decided to leave for America only after the Russian military government judged him unfit [for service].   Stravinsky

DIAGHILEV TO STRAVINSKY

Pittsburgh
March 22, 1916
[Cable]

Villa Rogivue
Morges

The Metropolitan is convinced that I am [blocking] Nijinsky's trip and that I have arranged for you to detain him in Switzerland. I warn you that if Nijinsky does not depart immediately relations with the Metropolitan will be broken for good. I find Nijinsky's pretenses utterly absurd, and the "unexecutable" instructions [which were] given to Devaux are clear. I beseech you to accompany Nijinsky to Bordeaux immediately and to settle the tiny formality at the Paris prefecture, with the assistance of [the Countess] Greffuhle.   Diaghilev

STRAVINSKY TO DIAGHILEV

Morges
March 26, 1916
[Cable]

Metropolitan Opera House
New York

I continue begging you to transfer 2,500 francs [to my account] . Can wait [no] longer.

DIAGHILEV TO STRAVINSKY

Philadelphia
March 30, 1916
[Cable]

Villa Rogivue
Morges

I am sending you 2,000 francs.[29] I embrace you.   Diaghilev

STRAVINSKY TO DIAGHILEV

Morges
April 17, 1916

Metropolitan Opera House
New York

Very dear one,

I just received an official telegram from the Edition Russe de Musique in Moscow. They advise that it would be to my advantage to renew the *Petrushka* contract for one year only, on the condition that you pay the rental of the orchestra parts for all of the American performances of this season and next directly to Moscow (Kuzentsky, Most, 6), in Russian money. Myself, I will charge you

---

[29] A document dated March 21, 1916, from the Banque Fédérale in Zürich shows that Diaghilev sent the 2,000 francs via American Express from New York. A memo in Stravinsky's hand says: "All the money that I received from S. P. Diaghilev during the war is listed in a letter of mine to him dated April 7, 1916. . . . After that I received 1,500 fr., which were transferred from Madrid to Katya [Catherine] in Morges in June 1916."

10,000 Swiss francs for this new year. In order to facilitate your payments, I propose the following. Unless I am mistaken,* you had already paid me 3,500 Swiss francs for *Firebird;* after that you sent me 3,000 francs via Argutinsky,[30] and, recently (March), you sent another 2,000 francs, which brings the total to 8,500 francs. Thus you still owe me 4,500 francs.[31] I propose that you send me the 17,500 (which is to say 7,500 more for *Firebird* and the 10,000 for *Petrushka*) in twelve installments of 1,458 francs a month. It is unnecessary for me to remind you that the money I earn from my works is my only income, *my only means of existence,* and I think that you will not object to my terms, for they are infinitely more modest than many others you accept. Please reply quickly. The Edition Russe is impatient because they wish to begin negotiations with the Imperial Theatres. I just received a letter on this subject from Siloti, who still wants *Petrushka* for the Imperial Theatres. I embrace you and Massine warmly.

Your   Igor Stravinsky

* Look at the receipt I gave you at the Hôtel Edward VII in Paris when you were leaving for America.

DIAGHILEV TO STRAVINSKY   *Paris*
                                                    July 5, 1916
Morges   *[Telegram]*

I am sending you 1,000 francs.[32] Excuse the delay. [I] embrace you.
Diaghilev

STRAVINSKY TO DIAGHILEV   *Morges*
                                                    July 7, 1916
Hôtel Edward VII   *[Telegram]*
Paris

Received 885 francs. Unfortunately two weeks too late. Edition Russe de Musique demands your immediate reply concerning the *Petrushka* ballet and payment in rubles for all of the American performances. Telegraph me your opinion.   Stravinsky

---

[30] Prince Vladimir Argutinsky-Dolgurokov (1874–1941), of the Russian Foreign Ministry, was a close friend of Stravinsky.

[31] Boris Petrovich Jurgenson, the publisher of *Firebird,* had meanwhile complained to Stravinsky that Diaghilev had not sent any payments from America. Stravinsky wrote to Jurgenson in an undated letter advising him to address Diaghilev in care of the Metropolitan Opera in New York, "so that it is not said that he is the only Russian there who is skillfully and successfully propagandizing Russian art. . . . I thank you for your patience with regard to Diaghilev's tardiness and carelessness."

[32] Stravinsky has written: "That makes 885 Swiss francs."

DIAGHILEV TO STRAVINSKY

San Sebastián
July 13, 1916
[Telegram]

Villa Rogivue
Morges

Following your promise that the agreement will be renewed I consent to continue exclusivity for the ballet *Petrushka* for one year. Let me know to what address in Russia I am to send the money. Diaghilev, Continental Hotel

STRAVINSKY TO DIAGHILEV

Morges
July 14, 1916
[Telegram]

Continental Hotel
San Sebastián

Address of the Edition Russe de Musique [is] Pont des Maréchaux 6, Moscow. Stravinsky

DIAGHILEV TO STRAVINSKY

San Sebastián
July 21, 1916
[Telegram]

Villa Rogivue
Morges

Give the painter Kochinsky of Chemin de Jurigoz, Villa la Roseraie, Lausanne, 200 francs [so he can] leave immediately for San Sebastián. I will send that sum by wire. How is the new little ballet [*Renard*] coming along? I embrace you. Diaghilev, Continental

STRAVINSKY TO DIAGHILEV

Morges
July 24, 1916
[Telegram]

Continental Hotel
San Sebastián

I beg you to send 2,000 francs[33] apart from what I paid to Kochinsky. I am obliged first to conclude the work for Polignac, who awaits its delivery. Stravinsky

---

[33] According to a letter from the Banque Russe to Diaghilev, September 14, 1916: "In reference to your order of July 28 to transfer 200 francs to M. Igor Stravinsky in Morges, we have just received word from the Banque Cantonale Vaudoise to the effect that M. Stravinsky did not present himself to pick up the money and his address is unknown." In the margin of this letter the composer has written: "The sum was picked up by M. Stravinsky as soon as I returned from Paris on September 13."

DIAGHILEV TO STRAVINSKY

Villa Rogivue
Morges

[I will send the money] as soon as I receive the American advance, I hope next week. [The] contract is not yet signed, but the affair has been agreed upon in principle.   Diaghilev

STRAVINSKY TO DIAGHILEV

Continental Hotel
San Sebastián

My dear,

On July 24 I informed you by telegram that I had paid the painter Kochinsky 200 francs and asked you to send 2,000 in addition to the 200 (which I have not received, despite the phrase in your telegram "am wiring you the sum"!!). It is now August 18. In twelve days you will owe me 2,000 francs more, for the month of August. Please tell me how I am to live and support such a large family on the 2,385 francs that you have paid me over this three-month period. You gave me 1,500 francs in Madrid, for the month of June, and 885 francs in Paris, for the month of July. Thus I ask you to send me 2,200 francs now and another 2,000 francs at the beginning of September.

Be considerate of your old friend; do not force him to look for employment elsewhere.

Your   Igor Stravinsky

DIAGHILEV TO STRAVINSKY

Villa Rogivue
Morges

What [does] Thévenaz[35] reply? Important to arrange [this matter].
Diaghilev

---

[34] On August 12, 1916, Ansermet had written to Stravinsky from Madrid: "I encountered Diaghilev in Paris, and we traveled to San Sebastián together. . . . Diaghilev was unhappy because the decor Sert made for [Fauré's] *Pavane* was bad, and he could not be induced to change it. Diaghilev and Madame [Misia] Edwards spent an afternoon discussing the bitterness and ingratitude which this or that country has shown them. Naturally you were included among the ingrates, and Diaghilev described the exchange of letters between Madame Edwards and yourself. I pretended to know nothing about it, but Diaghilev's version differed greatly from yours, and I was not prepared to deal with his lies."

[35] Paul Thévenaz's name is found in Stravinsky's correspondence from 1914 until the

STRAVINSKY TO DIAGHILEV

San Sebastián

Morges
September 22, 1916
[Telegram]

Thévenaz [will be] returning to Paris soon. [He] claims that everything is settled concerning his departure for America at the beginning of November to earn his living as a painter. Attempted to see him in Paris nevertheless. I await the money we agreed on.   Stravinsky

DIAGHILEV TO STRAVINSKY

Villa Rogivue
Morges

Rome
November 3, 1916
[Telegram]

Money [has been] sent.[36] I beg you to come to Rome right away. The matter is very urgent.   Diaghilev, via [del] Parlamento 9

DIAGHILEV TO STRAVINSKY

Morges

Rome
via del Parlamento 9
November 16, 1916

Request that Misia: (1) have Erik Satie immediately send me his "Piccadilly March" by express mail, in either the piano or the orchestral version; (2) arrange permission from Ravel for us to present his "Feria"; (3) telephone Bakst and tell him that Massine and Tommasini[37] have already completed more than half of the Scarlatti ballet.

Changes in *The Nightingale:* (1) recompose the singing for the Nightingale, reducing the number of measures on page 49; (2) page 51: cut the first 3 measures in the last line; (3) page 60: cut the first 5 measures; (4) page 62: go back from the last measure to page 40, which must be recomposed; (5) page 49: after the first measure, make a transition to the 4th measure of page 67,

---

young man's death in 1921. According to the following undated letter from Colette to Stravinsky, from the early summer of 1914, Thévenaz seems to have been connected with the incipient *L'Enfant et les sortilèges:* "M. Jacques Rouché will send you the scenario of my ballet. If you would consent to write the music, this little [scenario] would become a marvel. Thévenaz would dance the role of the Fire—the speeches could be removed here and wherever they are in the way—the Fire, the Squirrel, anything he wishes. Please find here the testimony to my admiration for you. I miss *The Nightingale* terribly. Colette de Jouvenel (previously Colette Willy), 57, rue Cortambert."

[36] Stravinsky received the 2,000 francs on September 30. On the 29th, he had received from Diaghilev the program of a concert that had taken place in the Gran Casino on the 20th, in which Fernández Arbós had conducted the *Firebird* Suite.

[37] Vincenzo Tommasini (1878–1950), Italian composer.

thus cutting pages 63–66 and the first three measures of page 67; (6) page 67: transpose the entire remainder of the page (the last 4 lines); (7) page 70: cut the first 4 measures of page 71 and recompose the following 6 measures; (8) cut pages 78–79; (9) page 80: recompose the first three measures, keeping the tremolo in the accompaniment; cut the 7th and 8th measures; (10) page 82: compose a good accompaniment from the 3rd through the 8th measures; (11) page 83: cut the 5th and 6th measures, recompose the 7th, 8th, and 9th measures, and from the 9th make a transition to the 3rd measure of page 90; (12) page 93: consolidate measures 3 and 4 into one measure.

Both of the Nightingale's songs must be abbreviated and tedious places eliminated. And there is no reason for anyone to go off into a temper about this! I am a man of the theatre and not, thank God, a composer.

DIAGHILEV TO STRAVINSKY   *Rome*
                                                       November [20], 1916
Morges

Dear Igor,

I am sending you some clippings about the scandal that arose when Toscanini was prevented from finishing the concert.[38] I am very glad that the tactlessness of that whole company has been avenged. In connection with, and during, this incident, I had quite a quarrel with Khvoshchinsky,[39] who loudly defended the performance of Wagner. Our fight ended when we called in our seconds, and

---

[38] While conducting Siegfried's Funeral March in Rome on November 19, Toscanini was interrupted by a shout from the balcony protesting the performance of German music "to bury Italian warriors." On February 11, Madame Khvoshchinskaya had written to Stravinsky: "Toscanini presented *Petrushka* in a concert hall filled to the very last seat, and the audience liked the music so much that he decided to repeat the concert." Stravinsky replied by telegraph: "Wire me when Toscanini will perform *Petrushka* the second time. Would like to come to Rome. Friendly greetings, Stravinsky."

[39] Best known as the author of books on the Tuscan painters, Vasily Khvoshchinsky was a competent pianist who founded a string quartet in Rome (his wife had written to Stravinsky on January 12 requesting his quartet pieces for this ensemble). Only a month before the incidents referred to in Diaghilev's letter, Khvoshchinsky had come to Leysin, where his wife was in a sanitarium. He had written to Stravinsky from there on October 9 and 18 thanking him for the books and music he had sent to Madame Khvoshchinskaya, announcing an imminent return to Rome, and asking Stravinsky to telephone, or, if possible, to meet the train at Aigle. Stravinsky did not fulfill either request. To judge from a card from Madame Khvoshchinskaya in Leysin to Madame Stravinsky in Morges, postmarked November 6 and asking the composer to give regards to Balla in Rome, Stravinsky answered in Rome on November 8 or 9. Khvoshchinsky wrote to him there, at the Hotel Splendide: "The consulate will provide a

the affair was settled peacefully, but with great difficulty. Thus you should keep in mind that he and I have broken off relations. I am telling you this because he mentioned a letter he wrote to you concerning a somewhat different matter, but on the same theme. We will discuss it all in detail when we meet.

I have concluded a contract with [Fortunato] Depero [for *The Song of the Nightingale*], and he is doing marvelous work; the decorations are splendid, and Massine is dreaming about presenting the ballet.

Why haven't I had a word from you? This is the third time I have written to you. Once again, we embrace you.

Serge Diaghilev

STRAVINSKY TO DIAGHILEV   *Morges*
                                              November 21, 1916
Rome

Dear Seriozha,

I received your telegram in the Hôtel Meurice [Paris] and your registered letter to me in Morges. I, too, regretted that I did not say proper farewells to you and Massine. I left [Rome] in great turmoil and, I must admit, with an ominous feeling about our financial dealings. I honestly would like to avoid such discus-

---

passport, but you must go yourself to the Palazzo Farnese, since the French Consulate there must have a photograph of you. If you do not have one, get one taken on the Corso San Carlo. . . . You do not need a tourist visa here in Rome, but you must let the police know that you will be here for three days. . . . I shall expect you tomorrow at one o'clock."

Stravinsky scandalized the Russian Embassy when he visited it. The story is found in Khvoshchinsky's letter to Stravinsky, dated November 16: "I dropped in to see you at the Hotel Splendide, but you were not in, which upset me because now I shall have to write down what would have been much easier to discuss face to face: I consider it my duty to say something to you about your extremely tactless phrase, uttered in the consul's office, 'Are there any other Russian names in the Embassy besides Khvoshchinsky's?' . . . The Kurbersky sheet that was given to you (and thanks to which you managed to extricate yourself intact from Italy), and the sending of your notes and sketches in an official packet—all of that was possible owing exclusively to the kindness of our first secretary, Vasily Nikolayev-Shtrandtman; I can assure you that if, instead of him, someone else with a bureaucratic Russian name had been in charge, you would never have received the document. If you get another paper in our Embassy in Paris, that too will be due to the kindness of the first secretary there, Baron Ungern-Shternberg. I fear that now, in order to obtain exclusive services in the Embassy in Rome, you are going to have to wait until all of the members are to your liking; perhaps that will coincide with the moment when you take leave of your German governess, the one who reared you and who is now rearing your children. Devotedly yours, Vasily Khvoshchinsky."

sions in the future . . . and therefore will let you know my stipulations concerning my trips in advance; you will always be free to accept or reject.

I received the first installment for *The Nightingale,* but unfortunately with a deduction of 90 francs—i.e., 910 Swiss francs instead of 1,000, as agreed. You should have specified Swiss francs in your telegram of instructions to the bank; they sent French francs. Please correct your mistake. When you send the monthly 2,000 (Swiss) francs, on November 25, add 90 more Swiss francs.

Now to other matters.

I am sending you the nice little note I received from V. Khvoshchinsky in Rome. I will not comment on it, but it fell on me like a shadow [illegible]. It concerns our conversation at the Embassy. . . . Remember, we good-naturedly sent [illegible] and here Khvoshchinsky bursts out with this belligerent letter.

I answered him that his sanctimonious outrage should be divided between you and me, hence I said that I would send you a copy . . . of his letter. . . . Tell me, what is behind all of this? Such letters simply are not written, even when a certain lack of manners is in evidence. Imagine [that in Rome] he left a note for me: "Dear Igor Fyodorovich, I did not go to the rehearsal and stopped by to wish you all the best and a happy journey. Khvoshchinsky."

As I see it, he has gone mad.[40]

1. I did the errands [in Paris], as you asked. I saw Bakst and told him that he should hurry, but he just keeps grinning. . . .

2. [I saw] Erik Satie [and?] Cocteau. . . .

3. I saw Ravel at the rehearsal of the Colonne, where they played his *Rapsodie espagnole* and Debussy's *Saint-Sébastien.* Debussy was also present; he feels much better but has lost a lot of weight. There are two extraordinary bits in *Saint-Sébastien,* but the rest is boring and insignificant. My delight in the *Rapsodie espagnole* was not unmitigated, but the "Feria" sounds very good.

I immediately asked, in your name, as per your instructions, for permission to present a choreographic version of this "Feria," and Ravel agreed to arrange for a contract with payment against 1,000 (Swiss) francs. He wants to keep his author's rights for French-speaking countries, however. He says only [illegible].

Polignac wrote: "You know, Stravinsky, I have decided not to present *Renard* in Rome," to which I replied that "this was already clear when Diaghilev

---

[40] Khvoshchinsky's letter is such as to suggest that the stated provocation may not be the only one. Since Diaghilev's jealousy of Massine's interest in women first became evident when the dancer failed to hide his interest in Madame Khvoshchinskaya, it is conceivable that Stravinsky was also attracted to her. In any case, the tone of the Stravinsky-Khvoshchinskaya correspondence is unusually affectionate. She gave him a "keepsake," with a tender note, when he was in Rome in February 1915. And one of her letters (April 15, 1916) begins: "I have not heard anything from you in a long time, and I have begun missing you. I hope that you will not have forgotten me."

came to see you about the matter in Versailles and you did not breathe a word to him about it."

Misia is in bed and will remain there for another two weeks. She feels fine. Everybody comes to see her, they smoke, . . . eat, and sit in the W.C.

Yours,   I. Stravinsky

DIAGHILEV TO STRAVINSKY   *Rome*
                                            December 3, 1916
Morges

Dear friend Igor,

I want to return briefly to our conversation in Rome regarding the rights to *Petrushka*. Having noted that this involves nearly 12,000 francs, i.e., 6,000 rubles per year, I still want to say . . . "have pity." . . . After all, I am neither Astruc nor an American swindler. From Telyakovsky, or, in other words, from the budget of the Imperial Theatres, you will receive money for three years for *The Nightingale*, and you will admit that this is good money. But for me, who commissioned *Petrushka*—which I have not presented for a year because of the war—you are driving a hard bargain. If not for the war, after all, I would already have presented it in Russia and thus would not need exclusive rights: I would have presented it as I did everything else. The war, which is suffocating us all, has destroyed my plans; now I must either pay money that I cannot afford or cancel this trip to Russia, which I have dreamed about and gone to such pains to arrange during these ten years abroad. All the same, I feel that you must not treat me like some Limin [?] or Rabunov [?]; bear in mind that I could prove useful to you in the future, and that I feel closer to you and understand you better than all of those who appeal to you as belated relatives of your admirers. I myself despise cretinous discussions about money, like the petty one in Rome; nevertheless, you are mistaken in your belief that I "returned from America and consequently. . . ."

There is no "consequently," and I am nearing my last gasp precisely because of America, which was supposed to give us breathing room, and because of the war. I have spent the whole of this past week in terrible trances. Our affairs in America have become so thoroughly unglued that the situation is scarcely believable. I have received three cables signed "Vatza" [Nijinsky], and addressed in the familiar *"tu,"* begging me to come to America immediately, since he now is convinced that the only salvation (for him!!!) is "for us to work together." Better late than never. In order to send such a cable he must have had "a knife at his throat."

I did everything that I could to settle, or at least to postpone, the disaster. But the main thing is that I have not received a single cent from America in three months. There are "profitable American enterprises" for you! . . . [Otto] Kahn put our whole business, as you might have expected, into the hands of the most inveterate Germans—Hänckel, Teligsberg, Mandelkern, Elsler, Kopikstein, and Goetze, the new director of the Russian Ballet, who led the company all over America. All of them are lackeys to Gatti-Casazza, a self-confessed *boche*-lover and my mortal enemy. I see from daily letters that to propagandize Russian art, Hänckel is putting together exclusively German programs—*Carnaval, Rose, Papillons,* and *Till Eulenspiegel.* Moreover, he speaks loudly on stage with Madame Nijinsky in German. After the first performance, Nijinsky announced *in print* that the decorator Augustus John is a much better colorist than Bakst and that *Till Eulenspiegel* is going to be very successful in Paris! You see what a madhouse I am describing to you.

We continue to work here. Massine has almost finished the Scarlatti [*Les Femmes de bonne humeur*], and after the short *Triana* by Albéniz, he will begin *The Nightingale.* Depero is brilliant.

But my spirit has been depressed. That awful business with Khvoshchinsky is over, but it will be better to talk about that in person. I will be coming to Paris when you are there. I am writing all of this to you because of our friendship, and you likewise should understand that in this life friends are few; I value friendship and expect the same of others.

Regards to your loved ones. Until our imminent meeting, I embrace you.

Your   Seriozha

P.S. There can be no question of paying more for *Petrushka* than for *Firebird,* nor is there any reason for doing so. Be accommodating and try to see other people's points of view.

DIAGHILEV TO CATHERINE STRAVINSKY   *Rome*
                                                          December 17, 1916
Villa Rogivue
Morges

Dear Ekaterina Gavrilovna,

My first impulse, when I received your letter, was to board a train and go to you, but unfortunately my American affairs require my constant presence here for a while longer. If Igor has decided not to go to Paris—and any trip there now involves a great number of risks and could be most injurious to him—then I shall come to you.

It would be very good for you to have a change of air. If you plan to come with Igor to Italy for a month, I promise to find you very comfortable accommodations and to see to it that your stay is an agreeable one. Igor likes ballet, rehearsals, discussions, walks, and, in general, he is an inexhaustible sightseer of this divine Italy. If the question is really one of nerves, it would do you a world of good to get away for a short while from that damp, gray lake weather. We have only sunshine all day, so you can enjoy a thorough rest.

If you need me for anything urgent, please let me know.

I shall give the bank instructions about the money. As for *Nightingale,* tell Igor not to worry. He will have time to reorchestrate later.[41] It is a question only of the Nightingale's new songs [cadenzas] . . . but I cannot offer [*The Song of the*] *Nightingale* before February 25 anyway, so there is still time.

Tell Igor that Massine has finished [his] Scarlatti [ballet]. As an involved colleague, it is hard for me to judge, but I think it is a small masterpiece—all merriment and liveliness from beginning to end.

The Futurists are working a great deal and, so far, very amusingly. I do not know how people are going to move around in Futuristic costumes, but in any case the *quality* of their movements must change totally, i.e., movement must be renewed.

I shake your hand. Until our imminent meeting.

Yours,   S. Diaghilev

P.S. Please embrace Igor for me, and tell him that we have all begun to show signs of aging. Recently, I too had a fainting spell, which lasted two hours. I am well now, but "damned old age, the devil take it!"

DIAGHILEV TO STRAVINSKY   *Paris*
                                                  January 7, 1917
Morges   *[Telegram]*

Ravel just lost his mother.   Diaghilev

DIAGHILEV TO STRAVINSKY   *Rome*
                                              [March 1917][42]
Morges   *[Telegram]*

Would you like to conduct charity concerts of *Firebird* and *Fireworks* in Rome, Naples, Milan from April 9 to 26? Italian ambassador in Bern would facilitate your passage.   Diaghilev

---

[41] Stravinsky, suffering from nicotine poisoning, could not work; Diaghilev's letter is evidence that *The Song of the Nightingale* was written in the first three months of 1917 and that he intended to stage it in Rome.

[42] Ansermet wrote to Stravinsky from Rome, March 26: "Diaghilev arrived from Paris today shortly after I did. I cannot have a serious conversation with him anymore, but I plan to conduct three evenings in Rome, some in Naples, and six in Paris. He has already announced your concerts in Paris. Then Spain and South America. Nijinsky is not coming here or to Paris. . . . The program here, as in Paris, will be *Firebird, Fireworks,* and some old ballets, Scarlatti, Liadov, Satie. Cocteau, Picasso, and Bakst are here, along with a certain Semenov. Diaghilev received a telegram signed by some of the biggest names in Russian art, Gorky, Chaliapin, Benois, Bilibin, et al., asking him to go to Petrograd and take charge of artistic affairs there. He is flattered but seems hesi-

DIAGHILEV TO STRAVINSKY

Morges

Dear friend,

Massine, Depero, and I were late at the railroad station and could not see you off, and all of the great Italian composers told us that you had neglected to see them. I regret not having embraced you, and I await a word from you. The idea of composing new *Nightingale* arias for choreography enchanted Massine, and he no longer has any hesitation about the ballet. You know very well what is needed for choreographic movement, and we are certain to receive some new masterpieces.

I embrace you as I love you.

Your   Serge Diaghilev

P.S. I paid Balla and Depero 100 lire.

DIAGHILEV TO STRAVINSKY

Morges

The money has been sent. We await you. I have cabled to Bibikov.   Diaghilev

Stravinsky's next message to Diaghilev was indirect, via an unidentified friend in Rome, probably Lord Berners.

Please tell Diaghilev that I could go to South America only with my family. I will explain everything when I see him. A thousand fond regards.

Stravinsky[43]

STRAVINSKY TO DIAGHILEV

Lido [Venice]

I have taken all the necessary steps for the Italian [contract?]. My plans will have to be altered if I do not receive authorization now, since next week I am too busy. I beg you to cable if you have taken action [as well].   Stravinsky

---

tant, desiring something more definite and more modest. I think that above all he is afraid of the trip. We would both be very happy if you could come as soon as possible. From now until April 9, I must prepare the orchestra in Naples and here."

[43] Stravinsky cabled to Soloviev at the Russian Embassy in Madrid, May 30, 1917: "I beg you to notify Diaghilev that I categorically refuse to go to South America given the circumstances of the war [which have] totally changed since January."

An excerpt from Stravinsky's arrangement for pianola of Petrushka, *dated "winter 1918, Morges."*

DIAGHILEV TO STRAVINSKY   *Lido*
                                                         August 28, 1919
Morges   *[Telegram]*

Absolutely essential that I see you in Paris September 8. Make plans immediately. We have urgent issues to discuss.[44]   Serge Diaghilev

DIAGHILEV TO STRAVINSKY   *London*
                                                         October 13, 1919
Morges   *[Cable]*

Have never changed terms payment *Noces*. Ask only [that you] count rights
beginning next autumn when [I] want to give premiere London. Unnecessary
to make contracts through Kling[45] when [you] can write to me directly. Have
sent 4,000 as agreed.   Diaghilev

STRAVINSKY TO DIAGHILEV   *Morges*
                                                         October 18, 1919
Savoy Hotel   *[Cable]*
London

Receiving no reply [to] my October 13 telegram [I] have refused to accept
4,000 that has just arrived.[46]   Stravinsky

---

[44] This allusion is to the pending contract, of which a typed copy exists in the Stravinsky archives: "The undersigned has received 10,000 Swiss francs—via M. Ansermet—in exchange for which he gives M. Serge de Diaghilev the right to present the
ballets *Petrushka* and *Firebird* as many times as desired during the period April 30,
1919, through April 29, 1920. This agreement does not prohibit the undersigned from
receiving payment for rights from the Société des Auteurs in those countries in which
[the works?] are given without the intervention of the author or the editor, which is to
say in French-speaking countries. This agreement is renewable annually as you desire,
until April 29, 1922. In this case, the sum of 10,000 Swiss francs is payable each year
in the following manner: 5,000 Swiss francs on August 1. Geneva, August 27, 1919.
Read and approved, Serge Diaghilev."

On the handwritten draft of the agreement, which Ansermet had sent to Stravinsky on August 21, the conductor wrote: "Diaghilev attached a note to this, asking
me to be in London beginning September 1 for a month. I am going to write to him on
the off chance [that it will reach him, saying that I will] stay here for a while because I
must conclude some business. I will telephone you tomorrow. Maybe you could come
here."

[45] Otto Marius Kling, director of J. & W. Chester, Ltd., London (with a branch in Geneva), one of Stravinsky's publishers. Chester was the English representative of Jurgenson, Stravinsky's publisher in Russia of *Firebird, Zvezdoliki,* and other pieces.

[46] Stravinsky has written on the envelope that contained the money-order from Dia-

DIAGHILEV TO STRAVINSKY

Morges

Savoy Hotel
London
November 19, 1919
[Cable]

Why no news from you? Have you received 800 francs? How is Pergolesi work
going?   Diaghilev

STRAVINSKY TO DIAGHILEV

Savoy Hotel
London

Morges
November 22, 1919
[Telegram]

My wife and I were both ill. Received 8,000. Still working [on] *Pulcinella*. Kling
will give you a copy of the already completed section.   Stravinsky

DIAGHILEV TO STRAVINSKY

Morges

London
December 3, 1919
[Cable]

Grovlez[47] comes tomorrow to London to study the repertory. I fear there will not
be time to go to Lausanne. I count on your presence in Paris in January for the
premiere of *The [Song of the] Nightingale*. Massine is doing marvelously. I am
sending you 4,000 francs.   Diaghilev

DIAGHILEV TO STRAVINSKY

Garches
(Versailles)

Rome
January 1920

Dear one,

Did you receive my note, addressed to the Russian consul in [Lausanne?]?
What did you do in Paris? What does old Polignac say, and what date has been
set for the Paris performance? How did Misia seem to you? Did you take care of
the little business matters for me? We continue to work.

    I would like to come to Paris, directly to the Opéra, when you are there. . . .
Goncharova and Larionov came to talk to me about *The Nightingale*. They are
enraptured by the music but nervous that the choreographic version will not
have sufficient movement, especially because of the Nightingale's arias, which

---

ghilev: "From the Banque Cantonale Vaudoise, notifying me of the arrival of 4,000
francs. The two documents inside were returned to the bank by me personally along
with my refusal to accept them, accompanied by a note with my signature. Lausanne,
October 17, 1919."

[47] Gabriel Grovlez (1879–1944), conductor at the Paris Opéra from 1914 to 1933.

are not danced. I am still counting on the new parts that you promised to compose for me. I embrace you.

Serge Diaghilev

Pulcinella's funeral music (1920). The Russian words at the beginning of Stravinsky's manuscript say "after troika."

DIAGHILEV TO STRAVINSKY

Monday [July 1921]
Savoy Hotel
London

My dear Igor,

I am sending you an article written by one of your Jewish friends.[48] As your close friend, I advise you to avoid having much to do with these Jewish musicians, since you are only *beginning* to understand what such relationships can cost you. I shook with fury when I read this article. In my view, Russians living abroad, especially now, have no right to settle accounts among themselves. [Koussevitzky] will have to take responsibility for his *felonious* letter. He cannot be given a *direct* reply, but I will stand up for you in my new letter to the

---

[48] Koussevitzky, who had written to *The Times* in answer to the denunciation of his performance of the Symphonies of Wind Instruments by the composer.

English public, as I did in my last article as well. It will be very brief, but I shall try to make it clear.

I embrace you and look forward to seeing you soon.

Yours, Seriozha

P.S. Make yourself translate *every* word.

DIAGHILEV TO STRAVINSKY   *Paris*
                                                     April 23, 1922
Hôtel de Paris
Monte Carlo

Marseille probably impossible. If so it will be necessary to reduce the fees. I fear that in the inauguration of our theatre in the autumn, we will have to sacrifice *Noces*. Are you certain you and Bronia [Nijinska] will be ready? If *Noces* is postponed, would you and Boris [Kochno] then prefer to cede the premiere of *Mavra* to Raoul?[49] I hope to come to Monte Carlo Thursday.

Diaghilev

STRAVINSKY TO DIAGHILEV   *Monte Carlo*
                                                     April 24, 1922
Paris

I am sure that Bronia will never manage to arrange *Noces* in a month. Deal with Chester for *Renard*.

STRAVINSKY TO DIAGHILEV   *Nice*
                                                      April 6, 1926
Dear Serge,

In the hope that these few lines reach you in time, I write to you with the certainty that you will recognize the good faith of what I have to say to you here.

I have not been a Communicant in twenty years, and it is because of an extreme spiritual need that I am going to take Communion now. In the next days I will go to Confession, and before the Confession, I want, as far as is possible, to ask the forgiveness of everyone. I ask this of you also, dear Serge, with whom I have worked for such a long time, to forgive me the transgressions of all of these years that have passed without repentance before God, and to repent sincerely and with all my heart, as I ask of you today.

I beg you to answer me by a single word that I will receive in time. I beg you not to speak to anyone about this letter; better still would be for you to destroy it. I embrace you as a brother.

---

[49] Raoul Guinsbourg, director of the Monte Carlo Opera.

DIAGHILEV TO STRAVINSKY

Hôtel de Paris
Monte Carlo
April 7, 1926

My dear Igor,

I read your letter through my own tears, for I have never, not for a single moment, ceased to regard you as a brother, and that is why I felt such pleasure and joy that you sent me "a brotherly embrace" in your letter. I remember the letter you wrote after the death of your brother Gury,[50] and I remember another letter that I wrote to you not so long ago, in which I said that in moments of great depression, I think about the fact that you exist in this same world, and life becomes a little easier.

I think that only God can forgive, because only He can judge. And we, the little prodigal children, must be strong enough, both in moments of joy and in moments of repentance, always to have a brotherly embrace for others and to forget everything that causes others to desire forgiveness. If you are the victim of such a desire, of course you must turn to me, and though I am not fasting, I shall nevertheless ask you to forgive *me* for all of the conscious and unconscious sins that I have committed against you, and to preserve in your heart only those feelings of brotherly love that I also feel for you.

Your   Seriozha[51]

STRAVINSKY TO DIAGHILEV

167, blvd. Carnot
Nice
[April 1927]
[Telegram]

Hôtel de Paris
Monte Carlo

Cocteau writes that Chanel returned from trip. [She] offers [the] necessary sums [which will] also [be available] to you if you would like to stage *Oedipus*. Give me your opinion through Nouvel. [I] embrace [you]. Stravigor

---

[50] In 1917.

[51] Diaghilev and Stravinsky were together in London in July 1926. The *Daily Sketch* reported, July 9: "Dropping out of the clouds at Croydon yesterday, Stravinsky fell into the arms of Diaghilev. That might be a broad way of describing the advent to these shores of the great composer and the manner of his reception at the Croydon aerodrome. There was an exchange of kisses and then exuberant conversation. . . . Stravinsky, who does not fulfill the popular idea of what a composer should look like, breathlessly discoursed on the wonders of air travel. 'It is my first trip,' he said, 'and I enjoyed it immensely.' He found it difficult to express himself in English, but with a wealth of French eloquence he said he was going to spend a busy three days in London, seeing friends as well as attending to business." Stravinsky was in London for the English premiere of *Les Noces*. He had flown from Le Bourget with his agent, Robert Lyon, director of Pleyel.

DIAGHILEV TO STRAVINSKY

167, blvd. Carnot
Nice

All arranged with Polignac in concert form. I have telegraphed Zereteli[52] to engage the singers [and] chorus. [I] beg you [to inform?] Païchadze.[53] [I] embrace [you].   Serge

STRAVINSKY TO DIAGHILEV

My dear,

I am writing to you this time about a wholly different matter. Knowing of your piety, but also knowing that, for many reasons, you do not attend religious services during these holy days, I think of you often and, as I pray for you, I would like you to join even indirectly in this spiritual union, by act if not by your personal presence. Something very simple is involved through our Father Nikolai.[54] On the day of Christ's Resurrection, I am arranging for a distribution of alms among the poor, among all those who waste away in destitution. I will participate personally, and I am seeking people who might respond to my appeal. If you would like to give something yourself, and take up a small collection among those around you, you would be performing an act of charity. But do it right away (if possible), so that I have the money on Sunday to give to Father Nikolai.

I embrace you and send you all my best wishes on this holiday eve.

---

[52] Prince Alexis Zereteli was the director of Zerbason, the Paris concert agency with which Stravinsky had entrusted the organization of the *Oedipus* production.

[53] Stravinsky's financial discussions with Gavril Gavrilovich Païchadze of the Edition Russe de Musique *about* Diaghilev are probably as voluminous as the composer's correspondence *with* Diaghilev. For instance, on April 8, 1928, Stravinsky wrote to Païchadze from Rome: "In principle I am in complete agreement with you concerning Diaghilev. Still, I would like some guarantee, and, accordingly, I proposed terms that are both easy and modest for him. . . . But if these conditions are not to his liking, then we should dismiss the question of exclusive rights and simply move on to per-performance payment, which I do not want to do with Diaghilev because he is so unpunctual. On the other hand, the countries for which he is now requesting exclusivity on *Apollo* are precisely those in which he can already play it gratis. . . . But since I know Diaghilev, I would rather talk about everything very plainly and deal in figures and dates, not in shares."

[54] Nikolai Podosenov, of the Russian Church in Nice. His letters to Stravinsky are the principal source for the study of the composer's religious life at the time.

STRAVINSKY TO DIAGHILEV

Monte Carlo

Nice
January 21, 1928
[Telegram]

Come tomorrow at four with Balanchine.[55]

DIAGHILEV TO STRAVINSKY

Hotel Europa
Venice
August 10, 1928

Only now can I answer your letter, which came while I was frantically busy preparing to leave London.

The season ended very well, thanks largely to the energetic assistance of our London friends, who made our performances places of rendezvous for English society. This is very important for the future, since we proved that we can exist without Rothermere and have once again joined Beecham, who is full of the most grandiose yet practical plans. We will make a tour with him through England in the fall—which will be dull but well arranged, and, I hope, profitable. Speaking of Beecham's plans, you and I will have to talk about *Mavra*. Where can we meet this fall, at the end of October?

Apollon went well, and it was performed with success twelve times. (But what is this that I hear about your offer of *Apollon* to Ida Rubinstein?) I think that it was liked in England, and, in any event, it has gained a new group of enthusiastic admirers. I am thinking of *Firebird* for my English tour, since the [same] orchestra will be traveling with us to all five cities. Beecham very much wants to play the *Sacre* with us in London in the spring, and I think it will be good, because he has become a first-class conductor. There is no one like him in Paris, including the great Ansermet.

How are you coming along in your composition? I would like to see you and get your advice on many matters. I will stay here for about another month. Then—and this will probably surprise you—I will go to Athos. Yes! Do you want me to bring you anything back from there?

---

[55] Stravinsky played *Apollon Musagète* at this meeting. Dining with Balanchine, September 18, 1977, the present writer asked him if he had any recollections of the occasion, and he replied as follows: "Igor Fyodorovich read the score at the piano, repeating the tempi over and over for me. Diaghilev later changed them, but, then, he never understood the music. . . . Nobody will believe me, of course, but Diaghilev did not know anything about dancing. His real interest in ballet was sexual. He could not bear the sight of Danilova and would say to me, 'Her tits make me want to vomit.' Once when I was standing next to him at a rehearsal for *Apollo*, he said 'How beautiful.' I agreed, thinking that he was referring to the music, but he quickly corrected me: 'No, no. I mean Lifar's ass; it is like a rose.' "

I gave your Russian typewriter to Païchadze.[56] It was difficult to find a very good one, because they all have the Bolshevik spelling.

Yours, Serg. Diaghilev

STRAVINSKY TO DIAGHILEV   *Echarvines*
                                                                    August 15, 1928
Hotel Europa
Venice

Dear Serge,

I thank you and Boris [Kochno] very much for the Russian typewriter, but since I have not yet picked it up at Païchadze's, I am typing these lines in French—in answer to your handwritten letter.

I am happy for you and for the Ballets that you have found someone [Beecham] to replace the late Rothermere. But to put Beecham above the "great Ansermet" makes me think of Gogol's "Although Alexander of Macedonia was a great man . . ." So much so that I find considerable difference between the King of Macedonia, who never improvised his battles, and Beecham, who only improvises the movements of the works of others. But if you recognize genius in Beecham, why not in Koussevitzky?

I go to Holland toward the end of August for my concert at Scheveningen, then, after ten days, return to Nice, where I will finish my work for Ida Rubinstein. This will take from mid-September through all of October; hence it will be possible for me to see you only in Nice.

You ask about my "offer of *Apollon* to Ida Rubinstein." It is a question neither of "business" nor of "an offer," unless you are referring to inquiries addressed to my publisher concerning my ballets. But since you seem to be particularly interested in this case, I can tell you that Rubinstein, like many other theatrical entrepreneurs, has made inquiries to Païchadze about *Apollon*. I myself never offer my works to anyone, directly or indirectly.

When do you leave for Mount Athos?[57] I must tell you that your trip to this

---

[56] Boris Kochno had written to Stravinsky from Albemarle Court, London, July 25: "Dear Igor Fyodorovich, Seriozha has only just relayed your request to me concerning the typewriter. I will take care of it today. The only complication is that the typewriters in London, so far as I know, are for Soviet texts, i.e., they do not have [certain letters] . . . . I had to send my own typewriter to the shop for two weeks in order to have these symbols fitted on. As you know, we will be leaving London on the 29th, so write immediately—or, better yet, telegraph me—as to whether or not I should buy you a typewriter without the above-mentioned letters if I do not manage to find one with the orthodox alphabet. I think the typewriter costs £12. . . . I cannot forgive myself for my disgraceful oversleeping (though in fairness I should add that I had been exhausted for some time before) and consequently my late arrival at the station."

[57] Stravinsky sent money to Father Gerasim, Monastery of Bogoslov, St. John the

holy place interests me more than anything else. I would like you to bring several icons (oleographs) for me, and a wooden cross, and to have them blessed at the same place. Since I know that your main reason for going to Athos is to search for books, I would also be grateful if you would bring me a catalogue of every book for sale there in Russian and Slavonic. . . .

Embrace Lifar for his kind letter, which gave me great pleasure, and tell him that I am sending the *Saintes Ecritures*[58] that I promised. He will receive it in a few days.

Apostle, Mount Athos, until the mid-1930s. On November 15, 1932, the monastery sent a receipt to the composer for a 100-franc gift. This was in response to a letter from Stravinsky to Father Gerasim, asking him to "pray for the health and well-being of Archpriest Nikolai and for the long life of Father Superior Sergei, for Anna, Ekaterina, and Igor and their children; Yury and Elena and children; Lyudmila and Gregory and their children; Vera; . . . Sergei; Nikolai [Yelachich]; and Archpriest Vasily." (Stravinsky probably meant to write "Alexis" rather than "Sergei," who had died two years earlier.)

[58] In a letter to Stravinsky sent from the Hotel Europa, Venice, August 23, Lifar thanks the composer for "the Gospel, the Acts of the Apostles, and the Apocalypse" sent from Paris. The letter also says that Diaghilev hopes to see Stravinsky in Nice.

LETTERS FROM

1 9 1 3

VASLAV NIJINSKY

VASLAV NIJINSKY TO STRAVINSKY[1]

Petrushka was very successful in Vienna. I embrace you.   Vatza

NIJINSKY TO STRAVINSKY

Petrushka [February] 4th. Serge arrives later. Embrace you.   Vatza

NIJINSKY TO STRAVINSKY

Ustilug[2]

Dear Igor,

Since we parted company in Vienna, I have managed to have five rehearsals [for *Le Sacre du printemps*]. Of course that is not very many, considering what remains to be done. But given the load of work we have right now and the strain of moving from one city to another, staying only two or three days in any one place, it has not been possible to do more. I have profited from these few rehearsals, squeezing as much out of them as possible. If all goes well, I should be able to complete everything without jeopardizing my health or lowering my standards for my own current performances.

We have [the *Sacre*] perfectly arranged up to the dances and games in the ring and the abduction. So far I am very pleased with the way everything has turned out. If the work continues like this, Igor, it will really be splendid.

Once we have everything the way you and I want it, I know that the *Sacre du printemps* will be something astounding. The ordinary spectator will be stunned, and for the others, new and vast horizons, flooded with different illu-

---

[1] Both letters from Nijinsky are in Russian, and the three telegrams are in transliterated Russian.

[2] Someone has written on the envelope: "Please forward from Ustilug to Clarens, Switzerland, Hôtel Châtelard . . . before departure there."

minations, will open up. People will see new, diverse colors and lines. Everything will be different, new, and beautiful.

Today I leave for Dresden, where I will not be able to rehearse, since I will be there for only one day. From Dresden I proceed to London, Savoy Hotel. Good-bye for now. Regards to your wife. I kiss you affectionately.

Vatza

NIJINSKY TO STRAVINSKY

London
February 1, 1913
[Telegram]

Serge arrives morning of 4th.   Vatza

NIJINSKY TO STRAVINSKY

Budapest
December 1, 1913[3]

Dear Igor,

I cannot conceal from you what I have been going through lately. You know that I was away from Europe for four months, in South America. These four months cost me a great deal of money, as well as my health. For a room and my meals I paid 150 francs per day. I had not yet collected that money from Seriozha, so I was obliged to pay it out of my own pocket. I do not know what Seriozha was doing while I was in America. I wrote to him often and did not receive a reply to a single letter, even though I desperately needed instructions regarding the new ballets on which I was working (*Till Eulenspiegel* by Strauss, and one to music by Bach). All of the preparatory work was completed, and only the rehearsals remained, but thanks to the frightful heat in America, which nearly finished us, I was not able to rehearse these ballets. I cannot imagine how I managed to stay well through the final performance. I was lucky, but upon my return to Europe I fell ill for two weeks. Now I am well again.

I did not send you an invitation to my wedding because I knew you would not be able to come. And I did not write you any letters because I already had far too much to do. Please forgive me.

My wife and I went to visit her parents in Budapest, and I immediately cabled Seriozha, asking where and when we might meet. I received a reply from Grigoriev to the effect that I would not be given work on any ballet production this season, nor would I be needed as an artist. Please tell me whether or not this is true. I cannot believe that Seriozha would do me such a foul turn. He owes me a great deal of money. For two years I was not paid a sou, neither for my dancing nor for the new productions of *Faune, Jeux,* or *Sacre du printemps.*

---

[3] This letter, addressed to Stravinsky in Ustilug, was forwarded to Clarens, where it arrived on December 27.

I worked without a contract. Indeed, if Seriozha no longer wants to work with me, then I have lost everything. You see the situation in which I now find myself.

I cannot explain Seriozha's behavior. Ask him what has happened, and write to me. All the magazines in Germany, Paris, London, etc., report that I am no longer working with Diaghilev, and the whole press is coming out against him. In addition, they say that I am assembling a troupe. I receive offers from far and wide. The most significant one came from a certain astute and wealthy dealer who proposes to give me about a million francs with which to establish a new enterprise *similar to Diaghilev's Ballets Russes.* I would direct the entire artistic side of it, which would be very lucrative for me. I would also handle the sets, the music, etc. But I will not give a definite acceptance until I hear from you.

My many friends send me letters expressing indignation at Diaghilev's behavior and offering to assist and support me in any endeavor I undertake.

I hope that you will not forget me and will answer my letter immediately.

I remain fondly yours.

Vatza

Regards to your wife and to all of your loved ones.

The Monteux correspondence is the only one that extends from Stravinsky's pre–World War I to his American period, though, of course, the 1912–14 letters are incomparably more valuable than the later ones, and that of March 30, 1913, remains the most consequential that the composer ever received from a musician.

    The first letter in the collection records the effects of one of the young Stravinsky's explosions of temperament. And if he seems to have been harsh in 1913, he is remarkably so in the 1930 letters, partly because Monteux's performances and recordings of Stravinsky's early pieces were more highly praised than the composer's own. When Monteux conducted Petrushka *in Paris in the 1930s, and the Russian émigré newspaper* Renaissance *lavished compliments on him, Stravinsky filled the margins of the review with exclamation and question marks. For instance, Stravinsky underlined the statement that Monteux had been the first to "decipher" the score and questioned the remark in the margin, though the meaning is not clear, since Monteux was incontestably the first to conduct the piece. Then, too, next to the reviewer's assertion that "in yesterday's performance of* Petrushka, *Monteux exhibited all of the general qualities of a great conductor as well as one uniquely his own, spirituality," Stravinsky expressed his deepest doubts. Yet not long after writing these criticisms, he informed Alexis Kall: "I would be very pleased if Monteux would conduct the [Los Angeles] performance of* Les Noces, *for he is a good musician and conscientious." (December 27, 1937)*

    In truth, Stravinsky was contemptuous of, and could be remarkably rude to, conductors, even in person, as the present writer, having seen him with Stokowski, Koussevitzky, Reiner, and others, can testify. If Ansermet appears to have been an exception, this is partly for the reason that he, unlike Monteux, could be manipulated. Stravinsky knew, of course, that Monteux was a far more technically skilled conductor than Ansermet; but Stravinsky needed Ansermet.

    From the mid-1930s to the early 1950s, Monteux loyally and regularly invited Stravinsky to conduct the San Francisco Symphony, then one of the four or five finest American orchestras. Monteux gave Stravinsky generous fees and abundant rehearsal time, and a vieux ami *affection flourished between the two musicians. More than that, Stravinsky began to discover Monteux's virtues as a conductor, especially cherishing his recording of Beethoven's Eighth Sym-*

phony and his performances of Fidelio. *Indeed, after one presentation of the opera in Los Angeles, Stravinsky made a special visit to Monteux's hotel to leave a message of appreciation for the* maître.

In May 1952, Monteux conducted the Sacre *at the Théâtre des Champs-Elysées. The present writer, seated next to the composer, heard him unreservedly praise the performance—which is mentioned here only because Stravinsky had not heard Monteux conduct the piece in more than two decades and in the interim had heard many stories of how he had regrouped the measures. Neither audible nor visual evidence of such tampering could be detected; but, then, Monteux's semaphoring was never displayed to the audience.*

On May 29, 1963, Stravinsky heard Monteux, then nearly ninety years old, conduct from memory a fiftieth-anniversary performance of the Sacre *in the Albert Hall. The ensemble was ragged, as the result of an echo in the hall, which caused the front and back halves of the orchestra to interpret Monteux's beat differently. Afterward the two men embraced publicly. Stravinsky did not withhold some critical remarks, but he was deeply moved, as he was the following year by Monteux's death.*

STRAVINSKY TO PIERRE MONTEUX   *Clarens*
                                                     April 5, 1912

Monte Carlo[1]

Dear friend,

My publisher (Edition Russe de Musique) asks the administration of the Ballets Russes to return the orchestra parts used for last year's stagings of *Petrushka* in exchange for the new parts that he sent you a few days ago. I write to you and not Diaghilev, dear friend, since you have the orchestra score. The Edition Russe understands that the score is my personal property, for which reason I ask you to keep it until my arrival. Wishing you happy holidays and all good things, and asking you favorably to receive (as is said in such cases) "the assurances of my very cordial friendship."

                            All best wishes,   Igor Stravinsky

MONTEUX TO STRAVINSKY   *Berlin*
                                                November 16, 1912
Clarens   *[Telegram]*

We are beginning rehearsals Monday, performances Thursday, come Wednesday. Friendly greetings,   Monteux

---

[1] Monteux was chief conductor of the Ballets Russes from 1911 to 1914, when he joined the French army and was replaced by Ansermet. French is the original language of all the correspondence.

MONTEUX TO STRAVINSKY

Hotel Hungaria
Budapest

Hotel Europa
Budapest
January 5, 1913

My dear friend,

Appearances can be misleading. Underneath my cold and indifferent exterior, I am so sensitive that a simple remark can sometimes make me ill. Perhaps it seemed to you that I was indifferent to the criticisms you addressed to me a while ago, but I was so stunned by them that I have just sent my resignation to M. Diaghilev.

You hold me responsible for having played *Firebird* under bad conditions. But what can I do when my contract with M. Diaghilev obliges me to conduct all performances required by him? I can do only one thing: I can work without interruption, divide the orchestra, take one group and then the other separately, then rehearse all together and, without a moment of rest, put all my heart and all my devotion into a score that I love, at the same time trying, as a man who is an artist and who dreams only of art, to avoid the deadening weariness.

In thanks, I receive criticisms from you, who are my friend, but who says that I am too weak because I did what I had to do. I cannot endure what I consider to be unjust, and I gave up my position. I have tried in this letter to justify myself in your eyes, since I was not able to do it in person, after the event.

Believe, my dear friend, in my regrets at having received your censure, and accept the assurances of my keen sympathy and my profoundest feelings of admiration.

Pierre Monteux[2]

MONTEUX TO STRAVINSKY

Clarens

Adelphi Hotel
London
February 22, 1913

Dear friend,

I received your letter and was upset not to have said good-bye to you before your departure.

On the subject of the score of the *Sacre,* I have not clearly understood precisely what you want me to do. Should I make the orchestra score conform to the 2-hand piano score in Nijinsky's possession, or should the 2-hand piano score be corrected according to the orchestra score? Since I received your letter, I have not been able to get together with Nijinsky, but on the day of your departure, he showed me certain passages in the piano score that are not in agreement with the orchestra score, and he told me that the orchestra score is

---

[2] Stravinsky's response to this letter, if any, is not known, though obviously Diaghilev did not accept Monteux's resignation.

correct. I therefore corrected the piano score according to the orchestra score, as he requested, but I believe that you are now asking me to do the contrary. I cannot do this, however, nor can anyone but you, since it affects the orchestration. I await your reply before doing what is necessary.

Everything is going very well here, and I am sorry that you cannot hear the performances of *Petrushka* and *Firebird* that we are giving now, since they are much better than the first ones. As for success, *Petrushka* has more each time. *L'Après-midi d'un faune* is a great success and much discussed in the newspapers. We have presented *Dieu bleu*!!! There, my dear friend, you have all the news. My wife is doing wonderfully, and I thank you for so kindly asking about her.

Present my respects to Madame Stravinsky, I beg you, and believe me, my friend, your very cordially and affectionately devoted

Pierre Monteux

MONTEUX TO STRAVINSKY

Clarens

Adelphi Hotel
London
March 5, 1913

Dear friend,

I have the pleasure of announcing to you and to Madame Stravinsky the birth of a daughter, Denise, on March 1. The little girl must like your music, because she took advantage of the only program that did not have a single one of your works on it and chose to come into the world at that time. This allowed me to leave London without doing any harm to your music! My wife and the baby are as well as can be expected, and they ask me to convey their best wishes to you and Madame Stravinsky.

I leave London on Saturday morning, and I would be much obliged if you would send your score of the *Sacre* to me in Paris as soon as possible; I would like to begin work on it at the very beginning of next week. I can count on you, can't I, dear [illegible]?

What a novelty here! We did *Le Dieu Bleu*. The press found that this work should have been presented before, but certainly not after, *Firebird* and *Petrushka* were made known.

Please accept the expression of my most cordial feelings of devotion, my dear friend.

Pierre Monteux

MONTEUX TO STRAVINSKY

Dear friend,

8, rue Denis-Poisson
Paris
March 30, 1913

From my first telegram you will have understood that, not having rehearsed in the hall of the Théâtre [des Champs-Elysées], I cannot tell you what the *Sacre* will produce once the orchestra is in place. Nevertheless, and in comparison with *Firebird* and *Petrushka,* which I have rehearsed in the same hall, the *Sacre* sounds at least as good as your two elder children. The passages to which I refer and which perhaps will need to be slightly altered are the following:

At **28**, beginning with measure 5 (4-hand piano score, p. 22, first measure), I do not hear the horns loudly enough (unless the rest of the orchestra plays pp), and if I make a little crescendo, I do not hear them at all.

At **37**, measures 3 and 4 (4-hand piano score, p. 25, measure 3), it is impossible to hear a single note of the flute accompanied by four horns and four trumpets FF, and first and second violins, also FF. The first flute plays the theme alone in the middle of all this noise.

At **41**, measures 1 and 2 (4-hand piano score, p. 27, measure 1), you have, first, the *tubas,* which, in spite of FF, produce only a very weak sound; second, the seventh and eighth horns, which one does not hear at all in the low register; third, the trombones, which are extremely loud; fourth, the first six horns, which one hears only moderately in comparison with the trombones. I have added the fourth horn to the seventh and eighth, but without achieving an equilibrium for the four groups. One hears:

1. mf
2. nothing
3. FF
4. F

At **65**, measure 3 (4-hand piano score, p. 39, measure 10), the first four horns have FF, but they play with mutes, and I can hear them only with difficulty.

This is all that seems to me not to sound the way you want it, and nothing here is of great importance.

When you are in Paris, I will ask you for some instructions concerning the mutes for the brasses in certain places; the markings seem not always to be correct (which is to say that I believe the word "mutes" is sometimes missing). Furthermore, it is possible that the four passages I have listed will sound better when the orchestra is in place, though this would surprise me, because the proportions remain the same.

I think that you have the numbers in your original score, but if not, send me a telegram and I will copy the passages for you on a sheet of music paper. I doubt that I will have more rehearsals until our return from Monte Carlo, because the Théâtre [des Champs-Elysées] opens tomorrow, and I leave on Friday. I have done a lot of work during my stay here, nevertheless: for *Firebird,* two separate rehearsals for the strings, and two for the winds, then one rehearsal together; the same for *Petrushka;* and for *Sacre,* two string rehearsals, three wind, and two with full orchestra. Finally, yesterday afternoon I had a full rehearsal of each piece. I think I have accomplished something with this work, and I will return to it. What a pity that you could not come to these rehearsals, above all for the *Sacre,* and that you did not attend the revelation of your work. I have thought about you a great deal and regretted your absence, but I know that you have much work to do. Now it is for the month of May. I await news of you, and I ask you to present my most respectful greetings to Madame Stravinsky (who must deeply envy my knowing the first part of your *Sacre*). Your very affectionately devoted

Pierre Monteux

Would you kindly present my friendly greetings to Ravel and tell him that I am thinking of preparing *Daphnis* during my stay in Paris? I took the parts to the theatre, but the ten rehearsals that had been given to me have now been taken away, and I did not even have a chance to begin.

MONTEUX TO STRAVINSKY

8, rue Denis-Poisson
Paris

Dear friend,

April 2, 1913

I am sending you the score that I used for the rehearsals. I received another one this morning from your publisher. It lacks the last twenty measures!!, but since I have no more rehearsals until my return from Monte Carlo, that is of no importance. In any case, I will bring all of the parts to Monte Carlo so that if you wish to make any changes, we can do it there. Please send to Monte Carlo the measures that were newly added—no one will be at my Paris address—and I will enter them immediately into all of the parts.

    A thousand best wishes. I hope to have the pleasure of seeing you again soon.

Faithfully yours,   Pierre Monteux

P.S. We will begin with *Firebird* in Monte Carlo. I hope that the orchestra will play it better than last year!!

MONTEUX TO STRAVINSKY

Théâtre du Casino
Monte Carlo

My dear friend,

April 15, 1913

It would be very helpful if, right away, you would send the *Sacre* score containing the changes to be copied into the parts. I would like to take advantage of my stay here to complete the work on all of the parts, in order not to lose time doing it when I return to Paris.

    I already gave the copyist the four added measures to be inserted, as soon as I received them from Berlin. I count on you, my dear friend, and I thank you in advance.

    Petrushka will be done tomorrow. The orchestra plays it without spirit, like everything else. Thanks to all of the music of *amateurs* that they are obliged to play all year long, they like only that!!, and when they are given real music, they are out of their element, bewildered. What is to be done?

My respects to Madame Stravinsky, I beg you, and a cordial handshake to you from your faithful

Pierre Monteux

MONTEUX TO STRAVINSKY[3]   *8, rue Denis-Poisson*
                                                           [May 25?], 1913
Dear friend,

I came to your hotel on the chance that I would be able to work with you. Since you are out, I am going to the theatre library to enter in the parts the changes that we decided on yesterday. Will you be free this evening after dinner, and can we work together? A word will give me great pleasure. Your very affectionately devoted

Pierre Monteux

MONTEUX TO STRAVINSKY   *Adelphi Hotel*
                                                           London
My dear friend,   *July 7, 1913*

You can be absolutely certain that on Friday the *Sacre* will be played in its entirety, preceded by a lecture by M. Evans[4] (I think this is a very good idea). I will conduct the premiere, and Rhené Baton[5] is sharing all of the rehearsals with me. He works with the strings in Part One while I rehearse the winds in Part Two, and vice versa. This is to say that he will know the piece as well as I do. Furthermore, we are staying in the same hotel, and we work together as much as we can.

The second performance will take place on Monday, and between Friday and Monday Rhené Baton will have enough time for six rehearsals if he wishes. You see that there is no reason to be uneasy.

As for returning the *Sacre* parts to your publisher, Rhené Baton will take care of that after the last performance.

Petrushka enjoyed its usual success, and Delage must have told you how

---

[3] This note is written on stationery of the Hôtel Splendide, avenue Carnot, Paris. Monteux had gone there hoping to find Stravinsky in his room.

[4] Edwin Evans (1874–1945), music critic for the *Pall Mall Gazette*. See the correspondence with Evans in the present volume.

[5] Rhené Baton (1879–1940), assistant to Pierre Monteux as conductor of the Ballets Russes, then chief conductor of the Concerts Pasdeloup. The name is hyphenated in many dictionaries, but not by Baton himself in his correspondence with Stravinsky, and not on programs of the time.

well the orchestra plays! Tonight is *Firebird*. I am happy to know that you are recovering, and I am convinced that in a few days you will be completely cured. My respects to Madame Stravinsky and to you, dear friend. An affectionate handshake from your devoted

Pierre Monteux

MONTEUX TO STRAVINSKY   *Casino Municipal*
                                              Dieppe
My dear friend,   *July 31, 1913*

Do not mistake my long silence for indifference. The reason is that I left London the morning after the *Sacre* premiere and that endless work awaited me here. I had entrusted someone to send me the newspapers that reviewed the *Sacre,* but since this was not done right away, a long time was spent retrieving the few papers from which I send you the enclosed clippings. Forgive me, please, for taking so long to write.

We did not have many rehearsals—seven!—but the *Sacre* went very well with that fine orchestra. The London audience, much more polite than the Parisian, at least heard your work from beginning to end, and the success was considerable, with six or seven curtain calls. I was sorry that you were not with us, for you would have had great joy as well as compensation for the rude reception offered you by my compatriots, of whom I am really not proud!!

Rhené Baton conducted the work after my departure, and I know that he did it well, having heard from some of the musicians.

I hope, my dear friend, that you are fully recovered and have resumed your work once again in the midst of your children. My wife and I send our best wishes to Madame Stravinsky, and be assured of the sincere affection of your devoted

Pierre Monteux

A note from you would give me great pleasure.

MONTEUX TO STRAVINSKY   *8, rue Denis-Poisson*
                                              Paris
My dear friend,   *October 31, 1913*

Thank you for your friendly note. Everyone is well here, and our little girl grows like a mushroom. I wait patiently for the Ballets Russes to return from Argentina and to resume their tours in Europe. Meanwhile, I have returned to certain jobs, and since I am remaining in Paris for some time, my pupils are delighted.

I have news of you from Diaghilev, whom I saw recently, and he told me that by now you have already finished your opera.[6] I greatly hope, dear friend, that it will be me, and not someone else, who leads your new work to the light of

---

[6] *The Nightingale.*

day. I am very impatient to know the answer to this, and when will I have the pleasure of seeing you again? A note from you from time to time would always give me great pleasure.

I ask you to pay my respects to Madame Stravinsky and to receive yourself affectionate thoughts from both of us. Your very devoted

Pierre Monteux

MONTEUX TO STRAVINSKY   8, *rue Denis-Poisson*
                                                                    Paris
Dear friend,   *January 1, 1914*

How are you? And Madame Stravinsky? I hear that you are expecting a baby. Has it arrived? And, as I hope, is everything well?

No doubt you know that I left the Ballets Russes. Now I will give Sunday-afternoon concerts in Paris with a very good orchestra, and I intend to play *Petrushka* and *Sacre*. Would you kindly send me the music as quickly as possible, since I plan to play you soon, in my first concerts. I begin February 8, in a wonderful hall with more than 2,000 seats.[7] Ravel promised me the premiere of *Valses nobles et sentimentales,* and I will also play Florent Schmitt, Casella, Debussy, Delage. I plan to do a great deal for modern music. I also plan to invite Koussevitzky to come and conduct one of my concerts.

My dear friend, send me a note quickly, since I am very actively engaged in planning my programs and I want to reserve a good place for you. Also, send me news of you and your family. My wife joins me in sending you and Madame Stravinsky our most sympathetic thoughts. Your very cordially devoted

Pierre Monteux

MONTEUX TO STRAVINSKY   8, *rue Denis-Poisson*
                                                                    Paris
My dear friend,   *February 11, 1914*

I gave my first concert last Sunday. The public was wildly enthusiastic, the success was huge, and I am delighted. I have a very good orchestra, and I hope to do interesting things.

On March 1, I will perform *Petrushka* for the first time in a concert, and I am asking you to add to the brilliance I want to give this event by playing the piano part yourself. Show me this great act of friendship. Although *The Nightingale* is to be conducted by Messager, I have agreed to conduct the other works at the Opéra (except those that [Richard] Strauss will conduct himself). Here is a good opportunity to show the Parisian public that I have not lost your confidence, that in spite of everything I am still the conductor chosen by you to present your works. I count on a favorable reply, my dear friend, and I rejoice in

---

[7] The Casino de Paris, on the rue de Clichy.

advance thinking of the productive years that lie ahead of you. My respectful greetings to Madame Stravinsky, I beg you, and believe me [to be] your very affectionate and sincerely devoted

Pierre Monteux

P.S. I will probably play *Petrushka* in two concerts and *Sacre* also twice.

MONTEUX TO STRAVINSKY   *8, rue Denis-Poisson*
                                               March 14, 1914

My dear friend,

Yes, your *Petrushka* had an enormous success at the concert, so great, in fact, that I am playing it again tomorrow, March 15. You cannot have any idea how much this music gains in concert performance. Every detail is heard throughout the hall, and the musicians who knew the score in the theatre found that they had never heard it so well before. The success for you was truly enormous, and I am expecting the same tomorrow.

I must also tell you that my orchestra is really the one that plays your works best, because I am at home with it and can do with it what I want. I am sorry that you could not come to hear us, because I believe that you would have been pleased.

Now I very much want to give the *Sacre,* but Struve does not send me the parts, as he promised to do more than a month ago. It seems that Koussevitzky is playing *Sacre* in Russia and that I should receive it after him, but nothing has come, and time passes. I have only four more concerts, and I would like to give the first performance on April 5, then play it again at my last concert, April 26. I will telegraph Struve. Do the same, to make him move. You know that one must have time to present this work!!

I hope that your next letter will give me good news of Madame Stravinsky. Here everyone is well. My wife sends you and Madame Stravinsky her sympathetic greetings, and I, my dear friend, shake your hand very affectionately. I will thank you, dear friend, for reserving the premiere of the Three Dances for me.[8] Nothing would please me more. When will this take place? I am in a hurry to know. Thank you again, and very affectionate greetings to you.

Pierre Monteux

MONTEUX TO STRAVINSKY   *8, rue Denis-Poisson*
                                               Paris
Dear friend,   *March 18, 1914*

First of all, I must tell you that the second performance of *Petrushka* had as great a success as the first. Also, while the newspapers did not pay much atten-

---

[8] The Three Pieces for String Quartet, of which the first piece is a dance. Stravinsky must have mentioned to Monteux a plan to compose three dances.

tion to the work the first time, they gave it a great deal of space after the second. What a pity you could not come to hear us! You know that I wrote to Struve to tell him that we played *Petrushka* twice and will probably play the *Sacre* twice, and I asked him not to make me pay the high fee of 100 francs per performance. We are not rich, after all, and you know how costly are all the supplementary players that *Sacre* requires. His answer was that he was mistaken in asking me for 100 francs per performance and that the price is 150 francs!! Please be kind enough to write to him and make him understand that if he insists on these fees, we will be obliged to cancel the *Sacre* performances. We simply do not have the means to pay nearly 1,000 francs for the additional players and 300 francs for the rental of the music. Thank you in advance, my dear friend.

I am happy to hear that Madame Stravinsky's health has improved. Present my respects to her, along with my wife's best greetings, and believe me [to be] your affectionately devoted

Pierre Monteux

STRAVINSKY TO MONTEUX[9] *Paris*
April 5, 1914

My dear Monteux,

I am happy to be able to give you here my impression of your performance [*exécution*][10] of *Sacre du printemps*. To tell you that it was excellent is not sufficient, for you have merited this praise since the last Russian Season. Like myself, everyone can appreciate your zeal and your probity in regard to the contemporary works of various tendencies that you have had occasion to defend.

But today I am touched to see you spontaneously placing your mastery in the service of works that, though obscure, seem to you to represent an artistic effort. And you do this voluntarily, without fear of the reactionary critics, who will attack you, perhaps openly.

After such an artistic performance of my work, I also wish to express to you not only my own recognition, but also that of my French colleagues, who are aware of your comparable efforts and care [in behalf of their music].

I attach the greatest importance to the devoted and attentive collaboration of the remarkable artists of the orchestra whom you guide so intelligently in the interpretation [*interprétation*] of music of whose great difficulty I am well

---

[9] This letter, published in *Comoedia*, April 6, 1914, was written by Stravinsky just before he left on the night train for Switzerland. The concert took place at 2:30 p.m. in the hall of the Casino de Paris. Stravinsky was acclaimed by the audience as no other living composer had ever been in the history of music, and the scandal of the first performance, the year before, was forgotten in the triumph. Stravinsky was carried from the hall on the shoulders of the crowd.

[10] The French terms of the original, *exécution* and *interprétation,* are given here because of Stravinsky's distinction between them in the letters of March 31 and April 3, 1930.

aware. It is precisely because I consider all of the instrumentalists to be equally important that I write difficult music for each one of them.

Once again, thank you for the most beautiful performance that I have had of the *Sacre du printemps*.[11]

MONTEUX TO STRAVINSKY   *Villa du Midi*
                                                              Monte Carlo
Dear friend,   *April 20, 1914*

Certainly I will return to Paris to conduct the *Sacre* [on the 26th], and I gave the order by telegram to send you tickets for a loge.[12] We played *Petrushka* here, and we will repeat it tomorrow, after which I leave for Paris. Looking forward to the pleasure of seeing you again, I am your very affectionately devoted

                                                    Pierre Monteux

My greetings to Madame Stravinsky, I beg you.

MONTEUX TO STRAVINSKY   *Paris*
                                                          May 13, 1914[13]
Hôtel du Châtelard   *[Telegram]*
Clarens

Learned this moment Messager will not conduct *Nightingale*. I count on your friendship so that no one else but myself presents your work. Thank you. Monteux

STRAVINSKY TO MONTEUX[14]   *Paris*
                                                          May 29, 1914
My dear Monteux,

As I left the theatre after the second performance of *The Nightingale*, I felt the desire to thank you warmly for your interpretation [*interprétation*] of my work. You and the orchestra of the Opéra truly surpassed yourselves in the so-rapid study of this score, which I have had the honor to present to the public on the stage of the Académie Nationale de Musique. Your intelligent devotion to the limits of the possible has truly touched me, and in asking you to convey my

---

[11] This was the *first* complete performance that Stravinsky had heard.

[12] Stravinsky did not attend.

[13] This telegram implies that on May 13 Monteux had not yet seen the *Nightingale* score, though he conducted the premiere on the 26th.

[14] The letter was published in *Gil Blas*, May 30, 1914.

profound thanks to the valiant players, I assure you of my most sympathetic and devoted feelings.

Igor Stravinsky

MONTEUX TO STRAVINSKY

My dear friend,

35th *Territorial Regiment*
Compagnie hors rang
[Censored by] Postal Reader #93
December 30, 1914

Your thoughtful card reached me here in the front line of the troops and gave me the greatest pleasure. I have been in uniform for five months!! My last performance in London took place on July 25, and on August 5 I left for the war with the rank of private.

Recently I spent a month in the forest between the Germans and some other French; then I was kept on alert for a fortnight some kilometers in the rear.

I was very happy to receive news of you and to know that you are calm amid this torment. I am also happy to know that you were able to save the parts of *Petrushka,* and, above all, those of the *Sacre.* Never again, after all this, will we negotiate with a German publisher. I hope that the sets and costumes of the Ballets Russes are not lost in the bombardments of the cities and the railroad stations, and in the universal disruption of the railroads. I will be pleased to have news of Diaghilev's affairs, and of our other friends, and I hope that it will not be a German who conducts the Ballets Russes. As for me, I do not need to tell you how much I am losing in this war, all of the money that I was able to save during these last years. In addition, I fear that I have lost my concerts, since nearly all my musicians are, like myself, at the front, and many of them have been killed or wounded. It is horrible. What consoles me is the thought that my wife and children are well and that I will be happy to find them if I return (which is probable), even if it means beginning my career all over again. My wife is in Paris, and she writes to me every day. I hope that Madame Stravinsky and your children are in good health. I would love to have news of you from time to time. You must also be losing a great deal with this war. Happily, you are still safe and can continue to give us many *Sacres* and *Nightingales.*

To you, dear friend, very affectionately and in friendship, your wholly devoted

Pierre Monteux

MONTEUX TO STRAVINSKY

Hotel Victoria
Château-d'Oex

35th *Territorial Regiment*
Compagnie hors rang
[Censored by] Postal Reader #93
January 16, 1915
[Postcard]

Thank you, my dear friend, for your friendly postcard. But yes, here I am, a soldier for six months already! I spent an unspeakable month and a half but at the

moment am away from it all. I do not know for how long, and what makes me
suffer the most, as you cannot doubt, is the interminable separation from my
wife, whom I took with me on all of my tours! Let us hope that all of this will
quickly come to an end and that we will once again find each other and make
music together, Russian music above all. Oh! When will I feel the joy of conducting your works? Our dear *Petrushka!* Our *Sacre!!* Let us hope that the
whole world will know them soon. My respects to Madame Stravinsky, and to
you, dear friend, my affectionate accolades. Your wholly devoted

Pierre Monteux

MONTEUX TO STRAVINSKY   *Boston*[15]
October 4, 1922

My dear friend,

Infinite thanks for your friendly letter, and for sending the score of your first
Pulcinella Suite.[16] It arrived in very good condition, and I immediately gave it to
be copied. You will tell me when I may conduct the first performance.

Would you tell me if you have seen Hammond about the question of these
two suites, or do you want me to see him on your behalf?[17] If he purchases the
work from you, he will naturally pay for the copying, while we pay your author's
rights and the rental of the parts to him. If not, I will send you, as agreed, $25
per performance for the one or the other suite, with the understanding that we
will play one or the other ten times in all (which is to say, a total of $250).

I received your card with the address of Madame Brooks,[18] to whom I
wrote immediately. She has not replied. I will write to her again and, in addition, visit her on my next trip to New York (in December). You might write to
her yourself saying that your friend Monteux, on your instructions, will come to
fetch your score from her. Otherwise it is quite possible that she will not give it
to me.

Good-bye, my dear friend. I am very happy to be able to present this *Pulcinella* Suite, which is not so difficult for me to play as *Sacre*. We will also perform the [*Song of the*] *Nightingale* this winter. My respects to Madame Stravinsky. (Tell her that I send her my compliments for her admirable copy!!) And
believe me [to be] your very faithful and affectionately devoted

Pierre Monteux

---

[15] Monteux was music director of the Boston Symphony Orchestra from 1919 to 1924.
[16] Stravinsky had originally extracted eight movements from the ballet *Pulcinella* and
divided them into two suites. Only after Monteux's performances did the composer
consider the two as a single piece.
[17] See *Stravinsky: Selected Correspondence,* Volume I (hereafter referred to as
S.S.C. I), p. 155.
[18] Germaine Brooks, one of Stravinsky's first American friends, was in correspondence, in French, with the composer from 1919 to 1923.

MONTEUX TO STRAVINSKY

My dear friend,

I completed the rehearsals of the first suite, and the performance will take place tomorrow. I will send you the program and the reviews next week. I hope that it will be a success.

Have you finally received the money sent on October 20? On this subject, you should know that my board of directors, who paid $135 to have the parts of the first suite copied, want to deduct this sum from the performance fees—if the parts are returned to you. Otherwise, they wish to keep the parts in the library as orchestra property, in which case they will pay you $25 for each performance in addition to the $250 you have already received. Since the second suite has not yet been copied, and since I am not certain to be able to play it this season, the board asks you, or at least asks me to ask you, to let me perform this second suite next year and to take into consideration that they have already paid for five performances in advance and therefore should not have to pay anything additional. This way you will be able to realize $125 for five performances this season and $125 for five next season.

Would you kindly reply to me on all of these questions? It is understood that the two orchestra scores are your property and that they will be returned to you as soon as the performances are over. I count on your answer as soon as possible. The best and friendliest wishes of my wife and myself to you and Madame Stravinsky for 1923. Your affectionately devoted

                                                    Pierre Monteux

I have your *Firebird* score [from Madame Brooks]. Do you want me to send it, or to bring it with me in May?

MONTEUX TO STRAVINSKY

My dear friend,

It seemed to me that your last letter did not require a reply on any question other than that of bringing the parts of the two *Pulcinella* suites with me on my return in May. Darius Milhaud asked me for your *Firebird* score on your behalf, saying that he would bring it to you. I hope that he has done so.

I counted on your making an exception for the second suite, which was not copied and therefore not played. My directors persist in their point of keeping the music if they pay to have it copied. Now I have decided to pay for the copying of the first suite myself. Since I made this unacceptable agreement, the responsibility to rectify it is mine. This leaves the question of $125 for the performance rights to the second suite, the one that has not been played, and I am the one who loses the $125, since you do not agree to postpone the performances to next season.

On the subject of the sale of the *Pulcinella* suites, after the success in New

York of the first suite, I expected that Hammond would come himself to speak to me. He has done nothing. I wrote to him, and he answered that the only advantage for the publisher of a work excerpted from an orchestra piece was the sale of the piano score. But since the piano score of *Pulcinella* was published by Chester, Hammond does not see anything for himself except to publish the orchestra score. At least, I am afraid that he will reply in this way. Why not ask Chester to publish the suites?

Certainly the first suite had a great success. I played it in Boston, New York, Cambridge, Providence, and Brooklyn. Some critics, expecting a complete deformation of the work and deceived by the simplicity, regretted that there was not more "Stravinsky" in the arrangement. Others said that they preferred Pergolesi without Stravinsky or Stravinsky without Pergolesi!! But what surprised me is that no other orchestra asked me how to obtain the music.

A *bientôt*, dear friend, and believe in my very affectionate devotion.

Pierre Monteux

MONTEUX TO STRAVINSKY   *Etretat*
                                                                July 17, 1923

My dear friend,

Would you read this prospectus and this letter from Salzedo and tell me what to reply? How far have you gotten with Stokowski?[19] I hope to meet up with you in Boston. My respects to Madame Stravinsky, and believe me [to be] your very faithfully devoted

Pierre Monteux

MONTEUX TO STRAVINSKY   *Etretat*
                                                                July 27, 1923

Dear friend,

Would you be kind enough to send me Diaghilev's address? Do you know where, at present, I can write to him? A thousand thanks in advance.

Very cordially yours,   Pierre Monteux

MONTEUX TO STRAVINSKY   *The Biltmore*
                                                                  New York
My dear friend,   *Friday, February 1, 1924*

I want to tell you that I played the *Sacre* in Boston last week and here in New York last night with enormous success in both cities. My wife will send you the

---

[19] See Appendix J, "Stravinsky, Stokowski, and Madame Incognito," in *S.S.C.* I.

Boston reviews.[20] I am sending you the ones from the principal newspapers in New York. I will send those that appear in the evening as well. But you must understand that the success was as great as it was ten years ago on the rue de Clichy, except that here it was *unanimous.* I regret only one thing, dear friend, that you were not present to hear your work as you have certainly never heard it before. I myself do not recall having given a performance of the *Sacre* even approaching these. I must tell you that this orchestra has no equal, that it worked on your score with the *desire* to play it well, and that we rehearsed a great deal. The orchestra has now given more than five hundred concerts conducted by me, and the players know me so well that I can achieve what I want!! A pity that you were not here to take your part in the success. By popular request, I will play the *Sacre* again March 15 in New York and April 11 in Boston, which will make four performances instead of the three [specified] in my agreement with M. Oeberg.

My dear friend, I am very happy. It is my greatest triumph since I came to America, and this with your piece. I embrace you.

Pierre Monteux

In 1929, the Compagnie Française du Gramophone issued a press release calling the attention of its customers to the following points:

1. That the interpretation of the *Sacre* created by M. Monteux in his memorable premiere of 1913 has been approved and sanctioned by the composer.

2. That without the perseverance of M. Monteux, who repeated the *Sacre* in concert in 1914, the work would perhaps be forgotten today.

3. That the interpretation of M. Monteux is now considered as a classic, the only model on which all conductors base their performances.

In December 1929, Stravinsky issued the following advertisement in response, some of it at the request of Columbia Records (France):

I am happy to state that the *Sacre du printemps* just recorded under my direction by Columbia is a masterpiece of phonographic realization. To be specific, the dynamic element (which is the play of relationships, not the intensity of the sound), as well as the *timbre* of the *Sacre,* is conveyed by these new records in a way that could not be more evident. The result is a model of recording that renders a true service to all those who would like to learn the performance tradition of my work.

---

[20] On February 11, Germaine Monteux wrote to Stravinsky from St. Jean de Luz, asking him to write or telephone indicating when he would be in Biarritz in order to receive the clippings.

Monteux responded to this printed notice as follows.

MONTEUX TO STRAVINSKY   *Hôtel Majestic*
                                                                Paris
Dear Stravinsky,   *February 3, 1930*

Enclosed you will find a letter from the Brussels Société Philharmonique offering me a concert of your works next season, with your participation. Since you are no longer satisfied with my interpretations, I naturally refused this offer, and I leave to you to designate the conductor of your choice directly to the Société. My dear Stravinsky, believe in my best wishes.

                                                        Pierre Monteux

STRAVINSKY TO MONTEUX   *Nice*
                                                         March 4, 1930
My dear Monteux,

I have been on tour these last weeks and your letter of February 3 trailed after me. Not until today have I been able to answer you.

     I am astonished by what you tell me. *Who* told you that I am no longer satisfied with your performances of my works? On the contrary, five years ago, if you remember, I asked you to come to Barcelona, where you conducted my Symphony and accompanied me in my Concerto. That must prove my confidence in you rather than the opposite. Since then, your attitude toward me has undergone a radical change, for reasons that remain completely unknown to me. As these are surely not of a musical order, and since I have no reason to complain of your performances, I really do not know why I should not play under your direction in the concert that was proposed to us in Brussels, and why I should no longer hear you conduct my works.

     By the same mail, therefore, I am sending a letter to the Brussels Société Philharmonique accepting their offer to play my Capriccio under your direction and expressing my hope that you will reconsider your decision. I send you, my dear Monteux, my best greetings.

                                                                I. Str.

P.S. Meanwhile, I have learned from the Brussels Philharmonique (through M. Païchadze of the Edition Russe de Musique) that this concert will take place on December 13, 1930, under the direction of Ansermet. Since I saw Ansermet some days ago and told him of my desire to have you conduct this concert, and since he was delighted and declared himself in complete agreement, I will write to Brussels as I have already told you.

MONTEUX TO STRAVINSKY

Hôtel Majestic
Paris
March 31, 1930

My dear friend,

Your letter deeply touched me, and I ask you to excuse me for this tardy reply. I want to explain to you what led me to suppose that I no longer have your confidence in the performance of your works.

First, you no longer entrust me with first performances of your works. Second, last spring, when I gave a festival of your music, you did not attend, telling me that you would not be in Paris; but I believe that you did not want to be seen at this concert. Third, the publicity pertaining to your recording of the *Sacre* says frankly that you do not approve of my "interpretations" of your works. These are the factors that led to my refusal of the Brussels concert.

You affirm that you have nothing to complain about in my performances, and you recommend me as a conductor for this concert. I am very appreciative of this, and as proof of my sincerity I have included the *Sacre du printemps* in my Salle Pleyel program next Friday, April 4 (my birthday). We began [rehearsals] this morning, and I have every reason to believe that it will go very well. And now, hoping that the misunderstanding is over, I ask you to believe, my dear Stravinsky, in the most devoted feelings of your old collaborator and friend,

Pierre Monteux

STRAVINSKY TO MONTEUX

April 3, 1930

My dear Monteux,

Since it is only today that you let me know your answer to the questions set forth in my letter (of a month ago) concerning my concert in Brussels, I presume that the Philharmonique has long since negotiated with Ansermet—after having addressed themselves to him on receiving your refusal. I hope that you are in direct contact with him or with the Philharmonique concerning the receipt of my letter. I do not know this, and your letter does not make it clear.

As for your reproaches to me, (a) for no longer giving you first performances of my works, and (b) concerning the publicity for my own recordings, publicity that you believe to be slighting to you, I want to hope, like yourself, that these misunderstandings are over—if only these reproaches could be taken for misunderstandings.

In effect, the phrase in my letter to Columbia, for which you reproach me, puts aside all question of "interpretations," beautiful as they may be, and speaks only of performances, which, in the present case, is the only question that interests me. It is more than understandable that the author of the work, satisfied with the results obtained, states that these records can render a true service to those who would like to have the performance tradition of the *Sacre* from my own hands. Can anyone contest that I have this right? Again, if my conducting were in question, the matter would be different, but I believe that I possess sufficient technique to make the public understand what I want.

Your "interpretation" of the *Sacre,* perhaps very beautiful in itself (apart from the sonority, which I do not like at all, in all Gramophone records), is not questioned in my letter, but only the performance of my score, pure and simple. Therefore I do not see by what logic you write to me: "The publicity made for your *Sacre* recordings says frankly that you do not approve of my 'interpretation' of this work." In my letter to Columbia I do not criticize what is generally called interpretation, I only contrast the two ideas, primary and secondary, performances and interpretations. Since the legitimate interpretation (the secondary idea only in the chronological sense) of a work can occur only if the conductor knows the performance traditions of the score (the primary idea). This is what I tried to make the readers of my letter understand. But instead of understanding, I encounter in you wounded pride. If there is any allusion in my letter, it is to the Compagnie du Gramophone, when I speak of volumes and sonorities, and not to you, who are the victim of this vulgar technique of recording.

The reproaches that you direct against me for no longer giving you the first performances of my works are groundless. For eight years now, I have been conducting my first performances myself, conducting them and playing them at the piano (the first of my piano concertos, commissioned by Kussevitzky, and the second, requested by the O.S.P. [Orchestre Symphonique de Paris], which is conducted by Ansermet). I must hope that you will consider your reproaches as misunderstandings and that you will rid yourself of your suspicions toward me. As always, I send you, my dear Monteux, my sincerest wishes for your birthday.

Igor Stravinsky

MONTEUX TO STRAVINSKY

April 11, 1930
[Telegram]

Would you be willing to play your Capriccio May 2 contemporary music concert O.S.P.? Hope favorable reply.   Monteux

STRAVINSKY TO MONTEUX

April 11, 1930
[Telegram]

Accept with pleasure your proposition. Ask you same time to advance date my recording Capriccio with O.S.P. and Ansermet requested by Couesnon.[21] Friendly greetings,   Stravinsky

---

[21] Jean-Félix Couesnon was the French representative of Columbia-Couesnon, the English branch of Columbia Records.

STRAVINSKY TO MONTEUX

Astonished your failure to reply to my cable Friday.

MONTEUX TO STRAVINSKY

Delighted to have your participation May 2. Hope be able to study Capriccio with you soon. Have found solution to recording. Letter follows.   Monteux

MONTEUX TO STRAVINSKY   *April 17, 1930*

My dear Stravinsky,

Since your telegram accepting participation in our May 2 concert, we have been on tour in Belgium and Holland. On my return yesterday I found your telegram, to which I replied immediately. What delayed my reply to Columbia was that it seemed to me unflattering that this company asks for my orchestra without me. There is no such thing as recording an orchestra with a conductor other than its own. I still don't see a record from the Concertgebouw without Mengelberg, from the Berlin Philharmonic without Furtwängler, from the Concerts Colonne without Pierné, from the Concerts Pasdeloup without Baton!! etc., etc. You must understand that [being obliged to take] Ansermet is disagreeable to me; he is making a recording with the O.S.P. without me.

Anyway, I am prepared to allow you to have my orchestra for this recording on condition that the name of the orchestra is not mentioned, and I hope that this solution will settle the matter. As for your participation in our concert of May 2, I would be obliged if you would tell me your terms, since I must convey them to the committee that assures the existence of the orchestra, and since the responsibility for the matter is now mine alone.

Thank you in advance for what you will do, and in the expectation of the pleasure of working with you once again, believe me, my dear Stravinsky, [to be] your entirely devoted

Pierre Monteux

The Brussels concert has been announced, in the program of the concert that I have just given in that city, as being under the direction of Ansermet.

STRAVINSKY TO MONTEUX   *April 19, 1930*

My dear Monteux,

Thank you for your letter. I have just sent you a telegram with my terms, which I thought you already knew, since I had supposed that the administration of the O.S.P. had told you. I wait for your answer by telegram, being myself the slave of my time and of my engagements. I must know as soon as possible if I should reserve May 2 for you.

Concerning the question of the recording, I must tell you that I never had any intention of putting the name of the orchestra on the records: your proposal is therefore irrelevant. Neither in the case of *Petrushka,* nor in those of *Firebird* and *Sacre,* which I recorded with the Orchestre Straram, did the question of mentioning or not mentioning the name of the orchestra arise. As for Ansermet, ever since the premiere of the Capriccio, I have been proposing to him to record the piece with me, and I do not think that I committed a blunder in asking him, and not you, to conduct the orchestral accompaniment. After all, he created the orchestra of which you are today the conductor, and he continues again this year to work with this orchestra: he can hardly be considered an outsider to the O.S.P.

Pardon me once again if I have wounded your pride, but you can and must understand that any other attitude on my part vis-à-vis Ansermet or any other artist in a similar circumstance—i.e., who would have my "word"—would be misjudged by you; of this I am convinced. In the hope that you receive these lines as they are meant, I beg you to believe, dear Monteux, in my friendly feelings.

Igor Stravinsky

P.S. I hope that you received my letter of April 3. You do not refer to it in your letter of today.

MONTEUX TO STRAVINSKY

Hotel Empire
San Francisco[22]
February 5, 1939[23]

My dear and great friend,

First, I would be happy if you would give me news of Madame Stravinsky, who was so ill at the time of my last visit to you. Since my departure I have no idea what has happened, but I hope that you have some peace of mind now regarding her health and that you have surmounted your sorrow with the courage that I know you possess.[24]

Here we have not wanted to replace you with another soloist or composer,[25] and I have taken the position that your contract should remain valid.

I have given the *Sacre,* which was new to San Francisco and was a triumph. We rehearsed it very well, and the orchestra played admirably. We managed to find all of the extra players, even the tubas and the bass trumpet, the

---

[22] Monteux had been music director of the San Francisco Symphony Orchestra since 1936.

[23] Stravinsky noted on the letter, in Russian, that his answer, written on February 17, went on the *Queen Mary* the next day.

[24] Stravinsky's elder daughter, Lyudmila, had died of tuberculosis in November 1938.

[25] Stravinsky had just canceled his spring 1939 American tour.

flute in G, the contrabassoon, the bass clarinets, and the guero. I am sending you the reviews a little indirectly, by way of Nancie (who has remained in Paris to work); after reading them, she will forward them to you. I was handsomely rewarded with the success accorded me by the public, the orchestra, and the press.

Naturally, my dear friend, concerning our business here in San Francisco, your engagement is simply postponed until next year. A note from you on this subject, but above all on Madame Stravinsky, would give me great pleasure. Please give her my greetings. Believe, my dear friend, in my very affectionate and faithfully devoted feelings.

Pierre Monteux

MONTEUX TO STRAVINSKY

My dear friend,

Cathedral Apartments
1201 California Street
San Francisco
November 24, 1939

I was happy to receive your letter on my return from a little vacation that I have just taken in the country, and I beg your pardon for this late reply for this reason.

Our rehearsals will take place on Sunday, December 10, from 10:00 to 1:00, and Tuesday, Wednesday, and Thursday at the same time. Monday, unfortunately, is the orchestra's free day. As for the parts, our manager tells me that according to your contract, you or your agent leaves it to us to procure them, and we have nothing here except Tchaikovsky's Second Symphony, for which we have a complete set except for three string parts and the full score.

I am happy at the thought of seeing you soon, and I will reserve your two rooms at the Empire Hotel. You will have noticed that we are no longer at the hotel. We now have an apartment with our own furniture, and we hope to have you with us there often during your sojourn. *A bientôt,* dear friend. Believe always in the most faithful feelings of admiration of your devoted

Pierre Monteux

My wife and Nancie join me in sending you our most friendly greetings.

MONTEUX TO STRAVINSKY

1201 California Street
San Francisco
May 8, 1941

Thank you, dear friend, for your kind reply. I am happy that you have accepted, and I think that your program is perfect: Symphony [in C], *Le Baiser de la fée,* and *Sacre.* If I may advise you, I suggest that you do not play the whole *Baiser de la fée,* but only a few excerpts, so that the program will not be too long. The

Symphony is unknown to the orchestra, and *Sacre* is always difficult, even for an orchestra that has already played it.

I conveyed your acceptance to Mrs. Armsby, our president, who is delighted. Our manager will write to Paul Stoes,[26] and you may be assured that everything will be arranged according to your wishes. With all our affectionate greetings to Vera and to you, and with my faithful friendly greetings.

Your devoted   Pierre Monteux

STRAVINSKY TO MONTEUX   *November 7, 1941*

My dear Monteux,

Thank you for your kind note. I give you my answer to each question.

I understand the reasons that it is embarrassing to give *Sacre,* but I am afraid I am unable to play the old *Firebird* Suite because of the limited number of rehearsals that I have at my disposal. My Symphony will require two and a half rehearsals in itself, which leaves me only one and a half for the Divertimento [from *Le Baiser de la fée*] and *Firebird.* The old suite is difficult and will take much time. It seems to me that the only solution is to perform the suite that I play regularly and that your orchestra knows very well. This lasts 20 minutes, the Divertimento 20, and the Symphony 30 minutes. To open the program, I will play my arrangement of "The Star-Spangled Banner," which I harmonized and instrumentated (normal-size orchestra) not long ago. It was performed in a patriotic concert by the W.P.A. of Los Angeles a month ago, and I will bring the parts myself. Here is the program:

1. "Star-Spangled Banner"
2. Symphony in C

   INTERMISSION

3. Divertimento
4. *Firebird*

Send me your agreement quickly, my friend, since I see no other possible solution.

Very happy to see both of you soon. I send you both, from the both of us, our faithful friendly greetings.

P.S. For the parts to my Symphony, you must write to Associated Music Publishers in New York. They have them on rental. And for the Divertimento and *Firebird,* Galaxy Music Corporation in New York.

---

[26] Stravinsky's New York concert agent at the time.

STRAVINSKY TO MONTEUX   *December 25, 1941*

My dear Monteux,

Do not be surprised to have my reply to your letter of December 10 only today. In the first place, you mailed the letter on the 15th, according to the postmark, and it arrived the 17th and was forwarded to me in St. Louis, where I had a week of guest-conducting. I have just returned, and your letter, readdressed to me from St. Louis, has come only this minute.

   With the best will in the world, I do not see any way of adding to the program as agreed upon (my Symphony in C, Divertimento, *Firebird* Suite). I am also of the opinion that the program is a little short, but what am I to do if the unions will not permit us more than four rehearsals for the concert? My Symphony alone requires from two and a half to three full rehearsals, to judge from my experience with other orchestras, and I assure you that I do not lose a minute of time in the rehearsals. Calculate for yourself what this leaves me for the Divertimento, which the orchestra does not know (and which is not an easy piece), and the *Firebird* Suite, which, nevertheless, must be played through at least once (20 minutes).

   Because of the delay in receiving your letter, I ignored the rehearsal question, which is to say the schedule, and I do not know if it is possible for you to arrange one rehearsal on Tuesday afternoon and two on Wednesday, which I prefer, since the rehearsal on Sunday [and a free day Monday] makes me lose too much time. I have very little time at present, being occupied with urgent work that must be finished for a deadline. Be an angel and arrange this for me.

   I hope that your administration has done everything to procure the parts for my Divertimento and Symphony in time. After I played my Symphony in St. Louis, the parts had to be returned to New York. As for the Divertimento and *Firebird,* the parts are in your Symphony library, but we must be clear that the suite that I am going to play is the one orchestrated in 1919 and that if you do not have it, you must request it from New York.

   On the subject of the parts, I have just received a strange letter from Mr. Gerald C. Rosse (who exactly is this?). This gentleman is probably not in touch with the situation concerning the parts and does not know that, according to the correspondence between Mr. Skinner and my agent, Mr. Stoes, I really have nothing to do with the matter. Stoes's letter of September 25 informed me that the question of the parts was settled "once and for all." The only ones that I will bring are those of my version of "The Star-Spangled Banner." I count on you, dear friend, so as not to have any surprises in this area. Reassure me and drop me a note by return mail. Thank you. Good holidays and a thousand faithful thoughts in this time of anguish through which we are living.

STRAVINSKY TO MONTEUX   *December 29, 1941*

My dear friend,

A thousand thanks for the prompt reply and also for having put everything in order. I am certain that to carry out my program would really have been impossible without you. Understood for rehearsals: be assured that you will have your half-hours. May I ask you to reserve a large suite with bath at the Empire Hotel (like last time), and for a good price? Excuse me for disturbing you with this request, but after all the confusion with the orchestra parts, I no longer have any confidence in the punctilio of administrations. A brief note will reassure me on this question and greatly oblige me. Thank you in advance.

We will be traveling overnight and arrive Tuesday, January 6, in the morning. A thousand best wishes for the New Year to you both from the two of us. Do not forget to put your telephone number on your letter, since I do not know it.

STRAVINSKY TO MONTEUX   *1260 N. Wetherly Drive*
                                               Hollywood 46, California
My dear Monteux,   *December 30, 1947*

First of all, a good and happy New Year to both of you from the two of us.

And now, a few lines concerning the program for my concerts with your orchestra in February. Before proposing the program, however, I would like to know if it would be possible for you to give me one supplementary rehearsal for the strings alone, on Saturday, February 7—in addition to the regular rehearsals on Tuesday, Wednesday, and Thursday (February 10, 11, and 12). I can come as early as February 6. This extra rehearsal would be very useful to me because I intend to conduct a new work of mine, the String Concerto in D, composed for the twentieth anniversary of the Basler Kammerorchester—where this Concerto had its world premiere a year ago under the direction of its conductor, Paul Sacher. In two weeks, Fritz Reiner will play the piece for the first time in the United States, in Pittsburgh.

Even though the Concerto is composed in the modest dimensions of the Brandenburgs (about 12 minutes), it requires quite a lot of work, and an entire rehearsal is necessary for the players to become familiar with the music. Will you give me this rehearsal? After receiving your answer, I will send you my suggestions for the rest of the program.

Meanwhile, I send you, my dear Monteux, all my faithful and always admiring thoughts.

MONTEUX TO STRAVINSKY

Fairmont Hotel
San Francisco
January 6, 1948

My dear friend,

First of all, forgive the delay in my reply to your letter, which I received only during my rehearsal this morning. Thank you for your New Year's wishes, and accept those of Doris and myself for Vera and you.

The Saturday rehearsal is not possible, because the orchestra has a concert in the morning and a ballet performance in the evening. But we will do everything possible to give you this rehearsal on Sunday morning, February 8, even though the orchestra must also play a ballet matinee that day, and though, in principle, they are not supposed to rehearse in the morning before a matinee.

We are all very happy at the thought of seeing you again soon and of hearing your new work. Believe, dear friend, in my always faithfully devoted feelings, and do not forget to remember me to Vera.

> Your old friend,   Pierre Monteux

STRAVINSKY TO MONTEUX

January 8, 1948

My dear Monteux,

How to thank you for this extra string rehearsal, which is so necessary? All of my gratitude to you. Sunday, February 8, is more convenient for me than the Saturday. Thank you, thank you, thank you.

I permit myself (in view of your strong support) to consider this rehearsal as definite, and I now give you my program:

Apollo (strings only)		28–29 min.
Four Norwegian Moods	(orchestra)	8 min.
Circus Polka		4 min.

INTERMISSION

Concerto in D (strings only)	12 min.
Divertimento	23 min.

To save time, may I ask you to communicate this program to Alfred Frankenstein, who already asked me some time ago, as well as today by telegram, for notes for his newspaper. Thank you in advance, and believe me [to be] your cordially devoted

MONTEUX TO STRAVINSKY

Westbury
New Bond Street
London W1
April 27, 1955

My very dear friend,

How to thank you for your so-touching idea to compose this so-*amusant* Prelude for my eightieth birthday? I had great joy hearing it conducted by

[Charles] Munch at the end of my birthday concert. I intend to copy the score so that I can have a permanent memory of this little masterpiece.

Thank you. Thank you a thousand times, dear friend. I am very proud to have inspired this gesture of sympathy from you, and I am very thankful to you.

Your old friend and devoted interpreter,   Pierre Monteux

Doris and I send our affectionate wishes to Vera.

MONTEUX TO STRAVINSKY   *Albergo Sirmione*
                                                  Lago di Garda
            (For Igor Stravinsky on his seventy-fifth birthday)   *May 23, 1957*

My dear great friend,

I do not want to let this date of June 17 [*sic*] pass without sending you my most sincere and affectionate wishes for the good health that will enable you to continue to give us masterpieces.

I will not write you a fugue on "Happy Birthday,"[27] but I want you to know that I do not forget what you did for my career in having me conduct your *Petrushka* and your *Sacre*. It was with these that I rose from the ranks, and I owe this to you. You have all of my gratitude, my dear friend.

I wish you long years of work and of success, and I send you, on Doris's part and on mine, our most affectionate thoughts for you and for Vera.

Pierre Monteux

---

[27] Stravinsky's "Greeting Prelude," composed in honor of Monteux's eightieth birthday, consists of canons on "Happy Birthday."

LETTERS FROM

1913 ✣ 1918

ÉMILE JAQUES-DALCROZE

ÉMILE JAQUES-DALCROZE[1] TO STRAVINSKY

Dresden-Hellerau
January 7, [1913]

Monsieur Igor Stravinsky
Compositeur de Musique
Russisches Ballett
Vienna

Dear sir,

I am determined to write to you, when at the same time I strive to remain completely indifferent to anything to do with the theatre, with which I was impassioned not long ago, while today the run-of-the-mill theatre disillusions me and fills me with despair. I write to you because you hold in your hands the future of the dance, for you were born to compose works that are capable of being danced and that are not common—and base—crowd-pleasers, but a synthesis of our yearnings, an overwhelming outpouring of our emotions capable of being translated into movement. You contribute already at present to the regeneration of the ballet, but there is more! And it is in this connection that I allow myself to write to you.

You have in the Russian dancers a wonderful interpretive instrument. But they do not yet understand music. You yourself perhaps do not yet know all of the resources that this instrument can have at its disposal—excuse me—but you are surely the man of genius who can—through an inspired music—re-

---

[1] Emile Jaques-Dalcroze (1865–1950), Swiss composer and originator of eurhythmics, a method for developing musical sensitivity by translating rhythms into bodily movements. Jaques-Dalcroze founded a school at Hellerau, near Dresden, which Diaghilev and Nijinsky visited in the hope of finding help with the complex rhythms of *Le Sacre du printemps.* Diaghilev employed Jaques-Dalcroze's disciple, Miriam Ramberg (1888–1981), who became Dame Marie Rambert of the Ballet Rambert, London.

The present publication is incomplete because of illegibility, absence of dates, and Jaques-Dalcroze's impenetrable style. Nevertheless, Dalcroze is a figure of some importance in Stravinsky's life in the Swiss years, and Stravinsky seems to have thought well enough of Dalcroze's music to recommend it to Diaghilev. French is the original language of all the letters.

store to the human body its expressive omnipotence. M. Nijinsky too is a man of very rare and powerful talent, who can contribute effectively to the rebirth of the dance. In certain works I find him wonderful, in others (like *Le Spectre de la rose,* in which he dances *next to* and *against* the music), he fills me with despair. But obviously he is an individual who inspires admiration, and if I were able to converse with him, I am certain that he would understand me, as I am certain that he would be able to retrain himself completely and to create, with your help, definitive works. Plastique in motion is a great deal, expressive dance music is also a great deal. What is necessary to create a consummate work of art is an intimate coupling of one with the other. It is an art of sacrifice that requires in addition a special technique, a *natural* one, one of the mastering of oneself in the expression of simple emotions, one of the control of the body in *all the nuances* of time and space. As soon as—in the Russian ballet—the sacrosanct frenzy of movement intervenes, the dancers are as admirable as can be. As soon as the situation demands poses, gestures, outbursts of pure *feeling,* the conventional ballet technique paralyzes the emotions and substitutes virtuosity for the spontaneous externalization of inner states.

Now, it is certain that if, here at Hellerau, we do not possess the art of the dance in the technical sense of the term, we are beginning to gain an inkling of that of the total transformation of feelings into equivalent movements. And this is why—I come to the point of my letter—I would like to ask you to spend a fortnight here with us, to attend our classes regularly. I have a deep-seated conviction that, for your composing, the fortnight would not be wasted, and that the rebirth of the dance would be hastened because of it. You could also at that time make use of the knowledge of my dear Mlle Ramberg, who knows thoroughly the principles of my rhythmic system but *who cannot do without* an essentially musical collaborator in order to put them into practice. Now, this musical collaborator must know the system! . . . Dilemma!

It seems to me that a collaboration is called for among all those who dream of conferring a new virginity on expressive bodily movement. I think that you must be of my opinion, for there are in you and in your music yearnings that are so fresh, such foresight into natural musico-plastique art, that—obviously— our desires are the same, as are our wills.[2]

Believe me, dear sir, to be your very sympathetically devoted and sincere admirer.

Jaques-Dalcroze

P.S. The problem is even more complicated: the plastic art means a purely decorative one, free of any display of emotion; the music must regulate it, must create for it an environment; but as soon as there is a decorative art, there are styles, and as soon as there is style, the literary aspect, pantomime, must disap-

---

[2] In his *Journal des années de guerre,* Romain Rolland reported that Stravinsky "is in favor of stage movement of a more artistic kind than the rhythmic gymnastics of Dalcroze."

pear. Debussy would have written *L'Après-midi d'un faune* completely differently had he dreamed of a plastic realization of his music. I understand a plastic rendering of a musical work when it draws its inspiration directly from the music. But when one invents a poetic action for six movements, one must insist upon a music that regulates this action. In some cases, accordingly, the body calls for a music equivalent to its movement. In others, it is the music that demands bodily movement equivalent to its essence. Conclusion: the musician must know the human body, and the human body must be impregnated with music. It is this interpenetration of the two elements that I seek to obtain, and I feel that it is absolutely necessary that you understand *thoroughly* my working methods, for in the Russian ballet of Nijinsky I see only inspired intuition often paralyzed by a lack of method and resulting in the constant recourse to conventional means at variance with the very laudable desires for progress and even for revolution. It is essential to create a new technique, unencumbered by convention.

DALCROZE TO STRAVINSKY   *71, chemin Channel*
                                                                  Geneva
My dear colleague,   *June 21, [1914]*

Will you come to Geneva for our festivities, July 2 to 12?[3] I would like for you to be present. . . . We have 350 eurhythmicians who have studied for only six months, and their performance is convincing.

Write to me as to whether you can come and when. Very sympathetically,

your   Jaques-Dalcroze

DALCROZE TO STRAVINSKY   *Geneva*
                                              Saturday [January 23, 1915]
Dear friend,

I say "dear friend," and at the same time I loathe the French manner of saying "dear friend" to slight acquaintances. But I say "dear friend," although I have [met] you only two or three times, because I know you—through your music—as though I had once rocked you on my knees, and in my spirit ever since. Your music makes occult fibers vibrate in me; I can guess what you mean, and I know what you sing. And the life which is in you flows deep into me. I would like to see you up close, far from the newspapers, far from the intellectuals, far from the snobs. This whole world horrifies me, because it only *pretends* to understand! Living people understand your life and the ways in which you express it, transcending theories. Theory is our enemy—analysts are our enemies. They must be fought with works whose dazzling magnificence

---

[3] The celebration of the hundredth anniversary of Geneva's entrance into the Helvetian Confederation.

violates their intellect. Oh, how I detest what is written, and how I love what I feel. And discrepancies between theories are nothing, less than nothing, and words are nothing, and schools are nothing, and everything, everything, everything lies in personality. I learned that tomorrow is your wedding anniversary. Is that true? If so, a firm handshake for you from me, to begin the day. To live with a mate is to live according to natural religion. A man needs the antagonism and harmony a woman grants. Be happy, you deserve to be, for you emanate life. I still await the expression of calm life from you. Perhaps you have already externalized it? I still am familiar with only a few of your works, and these excite me: *Le Sacre du printemps,* among others. But it is not out of snobbery that I admire you, and I am intent upon making you realize this. I am surprised at finding myself in the middle of writing to you, because I am modest about my impressions. But life is so short. It is essential to let certain people know that you admire, love, and appreciate them, so that Death does not seal us in a foolish posture of indifference.

. . . May tomorrow be a [blessed?] day for you and your family, and may it be followed by myriad radiances, people, and masterpieces. Yours, with all my heart,

Jaques-Dalcroze

DALCROZE TO STRAVINSKY   *Geneva*
                                              Saturday night [January 23, 1915]
Dear friend,

I was overwhelmed with joy, emotion, and human pride at your concert. Such a plethora of . . . primitive, eternal sentiments, such a revelation of the power of sounds, of the intensity and dynamism of nuances. This is testimony to the ever-changing and renewing eternity which is opening for the art of music. After so many centuries of developmental exercise, a sudden genius, yours, makes . . . vibrant emotions spring forth from the depths of sensibility.

Your music not only resounds in my ears but makes my whole organism vibrate, and I thank you for this . . . magnificent and rare power that you communicate to your listeners, penetrating them with strength, enthusiasm, and courage for the struggle.

I shake your hand sincerely and cordially.

Jaques-Dalcroze

After the first complete performance of Petrushka *in Geneva, Jaques-Dalcroze wrote in* La Tribune de Genève, *February 8, 1915:*

Many of the young people in my entourage were profoundly touched by the essentially human side of Stravinsky's music. . . . Music capable of producing a manifest emotion in people merits performance as pure music [apart from visual associations] . . . . The musical movement in *Petrushka* is identical to the bodily movement, and anyone endowed with an ordinary musical sense should be able to perceive all of the propulsive intentions in the work. . . . If in hearing this lively, gripping score, with its actively suggestive rhythms, we do not feel the fundamental drama vibrating in our whole organism, it can only mean that our imaginative faculties are of a singular indigence.

DALCROZE TO STRAVINSKY

S. A. Institute
Jaques-Dalcroze
44, Terrassière
[No date]

Dear friend,

Would you like to come and see our June performance, the 24th and 28th at 4:30 and the 25th at 8:30 in the evening? The number of seats is very limited, and I must know if you will accept my invitation. Jacques Chenerier's poem is very beautiful.

In all admiration, cordially yours,

Jaques-Dalcroze

DALCROZE TO STRAVINSKY

Geneva
January 15, 1917

My dear friend,

I call you "friend," although I never see you, but my students know that I love your music, which is "you," and they love you as I do. I saw you again yesterday and enjoyed seeing you again, for to me you embody youth, ardor, sensibility, and the superb genius of discovery in the—alas—unexplored realm of musical sensation. You probably do not know that your music—which is you—is the subject of almost all of my conversations with my disciples—to a much greater degree than that of Debussy, or especially Ravel. I single out your music because it exposes a state of the soul and a nervous psychic receptivity that anyone concerned with human movement needs to comprehend. (I think you understand me.) I know your scores, I have studied them. . . . I have no reason to reproach myself in your regard. You occupy my thoughts, and I, in every instant of my time, seek to consecrate your thoughts, to scrutinize them, and to deepen them. Moreover, I seek to imprint your ideas, which I understand and love, upon my own [work].

Permit me, my dear friend, to state bluntly that I regret that you have no inclination to make a special study of my ideas, such as I have made of your work. I am sure that [my ideas] would . . . influence yours in the realm of plastic realization, and, since you frequently compose for human movement, it is your duty to explore my method. I am convinced that I have discovered many absolutely new rhythms over the past three years and, finally, found the way to sculpt *plastic silences*. . . . How is it that as close to Geneva as you are, you, the audacious, enthusiastic explorer, do not seek to [incorporate] my research in your singular penetration and to propel music toward completely new voices? Granted, you would see in my lessons that my students are not yet capable of embodying my will. Man of genius that you are, though, I believe that you could penetrate my secret, intimate feelings, and . . . my still amorphous attempts at creating an ameliorization of contemporary ballet. . . . These sonorous harmonies, which you use as the base of a new sonorous art, . . . [could be] introduced into the musical art as various imperceptible elements of temporal sensibility.

In those deliciously full experiments (from the point of view of Debussy's sensibility), the nuances of timing are, for me, the natural consummation of the treasure of musical effects. In all musical works with which I am familiar, the nuance of timing, the science of duration . . . is simply architectural. . . . Why don't you want to research these elements, which could surely contribute something positive and new [to music]? . . .

You, dear, are the only man to whom I would dare to write in this manner. I flee all publicity. The thought of propagandizing repels me. I am resigned to living in my corner . . . because I detest drawing attention to my name and my efforts, and I have [subordinated] my will, which is enormous, to create a love and comprehension of my desires in my students. Also, I beg of you to keep this letter confidential. You are—I promise you—the only artist to whom I have written in this way. If I were not certain of my rhythmic [ideas], which are a step ahead by nature, I would not write to you at all. Undoubtedly it is impossible to judge my ideas from public recitals. But a prolonged contact with my rhythm classes would reveal new horizons to you. . . . I attain a singular joy . . . when I see that I am considered a master of the dance, but you do not know what a joy it would give me to demonstrate [this] to you personally. . . .

Obviously, in order to demonstrate my intentions you should follow my courses regularly . . . but to submit you to such a constraint is far from what I have in mind. . . . Here in my corner I seek to work for the art of tomorrow, and I am convinced that certain of my rhythmic discoveries will contribute to the progress of music.

Be assured, my dear friend, that I am your loyal and affectionate admirer.

Jaques-Dalcroze

DALCROZE TO STRAVINSKY   *Geneva*
                                                    September 26, 1918[4]

Morges

My dear colleague and friend,

I would have been very happy to attend the dress rehearsal of your new work [*Histoire du soldat*]: you know the unique admiration that I have for your ge-

---

[4] Although this is apparently the last letter between Dalcroze and Stravinsky, the two

nius. I was to have given a lecture on the night of your premiere in Lausanne, and have switched the talk to tonight, but it is impossible to avoid twice in the same week the lectures that I give at my Institute. I am with you in thought, however, and with your collaborator [Ramuz] and your performers, to whom I beg you to convey my good wishes. I have the most sincere interest, and it is not too late to come and to applaud.

Cordially yours,   Jaques-Dalcroze

---

men saw each other at a concert in the Hostel des Etudiants, Lausanne, March 5, 1919, when Dalcroze's song "Avril" was performed on a program with Stravinsky's Eight Easy Pieces, played by the composer and Bela Petchitch.

1 9 1 2 ᴗᴄ 1 9 1 7

LÉON BAKST

The tone of the letters of Léon Bakst[1] to Stravinsky—rough, coarse, affectionate—is difficult to capture in translation. But the content of the correspondence makes clear that the two friends had little in common artistically. Bakst had wanted to do the decor for Mavra—*one of his designs for the opera, a water color with gouache and gold point, can be seen in the Victoria and Albert Museum—and he was mistaken in thinking that Stravinsky had influenced Diaghilev to commission Léopold Survage instead.[2] Bakst wrote to Diaghilev, April 26, 1922:*

I have learned that you have assigned the decor and costumes of *Mavra* to someone else. . . . Through my lawyer, therefore, I claim 10,000 francs, and I suggest that you deduct this sum from Stravinsky's honorarium.

Diaghilev replied that he had not made any such assignment, though if this were true, he must have done so soon after. Following the premiere of the opera on June 3, 1922, Bakst wrote to Diaghilev with unconcealed delight about "the fiasco of the new work by the 'Yankel Shtravinsky.' " The reference is to the character in Gogol's Taras Bulba, *and by giving a Yiddish spelling to Stravinsky's name,[3] Bakst was, in effect, calling him a shylock. Stravinsky, who was never told about Bakst's reaction, was shocked and saddened two years later when, en route from France to America, he heard of his former friend's death.*

LÉON BAKST TO STRAVINSKY

112, blvd. Malesherbes
Paris
Dear Igor,
November 17, 1912

Thanks for remembering me. I have just come from St. Petersburg. Things are as bad there as before. At least the music scene is alive, though, whereas the world of painting is as lifeless as the sons of bitches who populate it and who do

[1] Born Lev Samoilovich Rosenberg (1866–1924). Russian is the original language of all the correspondence.

[2] See *S.S.C.* I, p. 173.

[3] On December 21, 1931, Stravinsky wrote to the *Revue de Paris* pointing out certain inaccuracies in their October 1, 1931, issue: "I am not Jewish, and there is no Jewish

nothing but quarrel among themselves, play foul tricks on each other, and, in general, lead utterly useless existences. When at an 8:30 a.m. rehearsal you see a concert hall almost filled to capacity with noblemen, already dressed and groomed (and the ladies made-up and radiant), come to listen, despite the threat of bad weather—well, then you understand that the Petersburgers are a musical people. In contrast, when you see a handful of individuals dragging themselves despondently through an exhibition of Cubist rot, you want to complain to someone, and to call out the law against those who charge money to see such shit! And when you see the exhibitions themselves—and they are spreading—trying so hard to demonstrate that they are keeping up with that "progress" about which the newspapers write, you want to run as far away as you can. Then, too, you finally understand what Serge Diaghilev was talking about when he said: "There has never been and never will be a Russian school of painting."

I was delighted, at rehearsal, with the excerpts from Steinberg's[4] *Metamorphoses;* the instrumentation is exciting and fresh, and the originality and talent are abundant. I liked the music a great deal when I first heard it on the piano, especially the finale, even though I had not studied any of it. But Seriozha spoiled my impression with some sarcastic remarks. At the second hearing, I was alone. Steinberg and I became completely caught up in it, and I thoroughly enjoyed it. I told Seriozha, and he cursed my "understanding of music." Generally nothing belittles me more easily than a challenge to my interpretation of music, but this time I did not give in. Then when I heard the score performed by a full orchestra, I was enraptured. . . . I assure you that you cannot even imagine the potential effect from a piano rendition. I am happy for Steinberg, because he worked so hard in Paris. He is a quiet man who seems to have fallen in love with his art, as if that art were a blossoming young maiden who, seduced by tender conversation and by enterprising caresses, is drawn into the arms of a sweetheart who casts a firm arm around her, lifts her shift, and crawls under it—despite the hot blood, and the shouts, mixed in with the suffering and the ecstatic maiden's apologetic kisses. In truth, dear Igor, if you don't apply your art, how can you live with it?

I will not go to Berlin, because I have very little money. Seriozha has paid me only half of what he owes me for last year, and, what is more, I have many expenses. I await news from you, my dear friend, from Clarens and Berlin.

I have made up with Shura [Benois]; or, rather, he has made up with me. I did not start the quarrel, after all, and when Seriozha told me that Shura had recently told him that he had been "ill for three years because of Bakst," I was goggle-eyed. How do you like that?! It seems that I fell from the sky like a

---

ancestry in my family. I do not have red hair. I wear glasses, not a pince-nez. For your information, I bring to your attention the fact that the late Bakst, my former friend from the Ballets Russes, had red hair, was Jewish, and wore a pince-nez."

[4] Maximilian Oseyevich Steinberg (1883–1946), Russian composer and son-in-law of Nikolai Rimsky-Korsakov. See *S.S.C.* I, pp. 43–44, fn. 5.

plague. Well, everything is fine now, and Shura even seems to have found some of his former fondness for me.

I was expelled from St. Petersburg for being a Jew, but thanks to Siloti, Tolstoy (from the Alexander III Museum), and Sozopov, I was allowed to stay in a hotel. . . .

Keep well. I kiss you affectionately.

Your loyal friend,   Lev Bakst

BAKST TO STRAVINSKY

Paris
March 6, 1913
[Postcard]

Hôtel Châtelard
Clarens

Dear Igor,

You have set me such a difficult task that I am sorry, good friend, I cannot do it.

Léon Bakst

BAKST TO STRAVINSKY

112, blvd. Malesherbes
December 4, 1913

Dear Igor,

Thank you for your note and for the photographs. I am very touched and have added them to my collection. I especially like the Swiss Christ. I did not know that he had been so pretty. How you can stand the Swiss nation I will never know. I find the Swiss utterly detestable.

The young ladies of the art schools always draw men in the image of the Swiss. They draw a girl and then stick on some whiskers, and the outcome is a whore with a mustache! That's your Swiss "man" for you! Remember how on languid "white nights" on the Nevsky, the thickly made-up whores sway and call hoarsely after you: "Man, give me a cigarette." Here is revenge for you: I am sending you a Swiss man.

The new Hodler[5] is shit. I wouldn't give a fart for his huge exhibition here. It is brilliantly done, to such an extent that one is almost suspicious. I find it boring. . . . London (on the other hand) is a paradise that young people have built here on earth (the clever British!). I would like to walk around in the city with you. What suits, what things, what trousers—as good as your checked ones! I kiss you affectionately.

L. Bakst

---

[5] Ferdinand Hodler (1853–1918), Swiss painter. (Stephanie Guerzoni, mother-in-law of Theodore Stravinsky, was a pupil of Hodler. One of her frescoes includes a portrait of Stravinsky.)

Diaghilev finally took Fokine back. Otherwise [the Ballets Russes] might have gone bankrupt.

STRAVINSKY TO BAKST   *Clarens*
                                                September 20, 1914

Dear Lyovushka,

How I would love to see you. Make yourself known! I was very surprised when I heard that you were in our neighborhood (and even, it seems, spent the summer in Montreux). I am here in Clarens for the whole winter, and probably longer. I have become involved in householdery and have rented a villa, "La Pervenche."

I embrace you; I would be happy to see you, speak with you! Lord, what a terrible and at the same time magnificent period we are living through. I am not one of those lucky ones—how I envy them—who can rush into battle without a backward glance. My hatred for the Germans grows not by the day but by the hour, and I burn with even more envy when I see our friends, Ravel, Delage, Schmitt, all at war. That's all!

                                        Your   I. Stravinsky

BAKST TO STRAVINSKY   *January 24, 1915*

I would not have believed that such a success was possible in this hole, Geneva. . . .[6] I hope to see you in Rome. Tell that fat spider Diaghilev.

BAKST TO STRAVINSKY   *Hôtel Beau Rivage*
                                                      Lausanne
Dear Igor,   *April 20, 1915*

Bruni, the director of the Geneva Opera, wishes to study the *Nightingale* piano score and would like you to send it to him. I spoke with him and found him to be objective and well disposed, although reserved. I think that Moser has proposed [*Prince*] *Igor*, so perhaps Bruni ought to be informed about *Nightingale* soon. You might go there yourself, but speak to him on the telephone first: "Grand Théâtre, Genève." I embrace you.

                                              Lev Bakst

It is heavenly here—so quiet, warm sunshine, and everywhere the fragrance of spring flowers. I spent the whole morning working, coatless, in the garden.

---

[6] This refers to a performance of *Petrushka* conducted by Ansermet.

BAKST TO STRAVINSKY   *December 25, 1915*

Dear Igor,

When you receive this note, please call M. Schneider, Wagram 86-94. He is the man who will be making arrangements for your modern-music interview with the American reporter (representing the large New York newspaper). Schneider will be expecting your call.

I am very disappointed that ultimately it was impossible to put on *Firebird*,[7] since I am so fond of it, but I take comfort in the knowledge that as soon as it becomes available, Sasha Siloti is going to arrange to let me have it for the Maryinsky.

Let me hear from you, dear friend, before Misia.[8] I have to finish *Shéhérazade*. I embrace you affectionately.

                                                        Lev Bakst

BAKST TO STRAVINSKY   *August 17, 1916*

Dear Igor,

Please take part in this publication; you will be in good company.[9]

BAKST TO STRAVINSKY   *Paris*
                                                       August 25, 1916
Dear Igor,

The Americans are waiting for you to finish your music. They will return your manuscript a few days later. In case it is necessary to fetch your manuscript in Geneva, I will write to you again. . . . I embrace you with all my heart.

                                          Your   Léon Bakst

---

[7] This seems to imply that *Firebird* would not be performed at the Opéra on December 29, 1915, and it is true that on December 24–25, the performance was in doubt. Ansermet telegraphed from Paris to Diaghilev at the Hôtel Beau Rivage in Geneva that the orchestra was bad and rehearsals were insufficient: "Situation dangerous for Stravinsky though [Rhené] Baton could probably manage." But Stravinsky did conduct; a statement to him from Marcel Ballot of the Société des Auteurs, January 12, 1916, shows that Stravinsky received no royalties for the performance but 1,000 francs for expenses.

[8] Stravinsky was to play *Les Noces* for a gathering of friends at Misia Sert's.

[9] The reference is to Edith Wharton's anthology *Le Livre des sans foyer*. She wrote to Stravinsky, August 12, 1915, asking for some music, and mentioning Bakst. In response, Stravinsky composed the "Souvenir d'une marche boche," which was eventually published in facsimile in the book. Bakst's August 25, 1916, note to Stravinsky

BAKST TO STRAVINSKY   *November 17, 1916*

Dear Igor,

Violette Murat is in such a state of excitement about your [Three Pieces for String] Quartet that she wants me to tell you that she is offering to have the score engraved.[10] I pass on her kind suggestion. (I myself understand nothing in the music.)

Léon Bakst

Paris
January 8, 1917
BAKST TO STRAVINSKY   *[Postcard]*[11]

I send you heartiest New Year's greetings. On the other side is a charming subject for a waltz.

Léon Bakst

BAKST TO STRAVINSKY   *112, blvd. Malesherbes*
June 12, 1917
Dear Igor,

I do not know whether you are aware that Ida Rubinstein and I are doing a production of Shakespeare's *Antony and Cleopatra,* which is to say that I am designing the costumes and sets. She has asked André Gide to provide a literal translation of the text (the first in French), and now she wants to ask you to write the music, specifically the introduction and incidental pieces—as you see fit and feel inspired to compose them, much in the way that Debussy wrote for her in *Saint-Sébastien.* You would be entirely free so far as the music is concerned, but, if possible, do not use voices. She has asked me to get a decision from you one way or the other and to tell you that she would need the music in six months, if that is possible. So, dear Igor, write to me giving your decision and intention, as well as your terms. Personally, I believe that the production will be extraordinary; she is thinking of engaging [Firmin] Gémier as the

---

reveals that he had not yet sent the music. Since 1941, the manuscript has been in the Library of Congress, a bequest of Nicolas Nabokov.

[10] A letter to Stravinsky, February 22, 1933, from Jeanne Gautier thanks him for his compliments on her performance of Prokofiev's Violin Concerto at a Lamoureux concert two months earlier and reminds him that they had met before, "at one of Princess Murat's musicales, where I had the honor to play your Quartet under your direction." This suggests that, returning from Rome to Switzerland via Paris in November 1916, Stravinsky coached the players of his Three Pieces for String Quartet at Princess Murat's. Jeanne Gautier was then eighteen years old.

[11] Picture postcard of a young woman dreaming of her engagement.

director. I began preparing for it a long time ago, but the plans were stalled. Keep this to yourself, though the secret is hers, not mine. I await your prompt reply. I kiss you affectionately.

Lev Bakst

My regards to your wife!

Morges
June 18, 1917
STRAVINSKY TO BAKST   *[Telegram]*

Would like to compose music for you but can decide nothing before seeing you and cannot come to Paris.

BAKST TO STRAVINSKY   *112, blvd. Malesherbes*
                                           June 21, 1917

Dear Igor,

I have your telegram and am very glad that you give your in-principle agreement. Unfortunately, I cannot leave Paris now, not until I finish the hundred-odd things I have to do . . . in other words, not for another month. When I read your telegram to Ida Rubinstein, she said that she has always communicated by letter, even concerning the finer details. On the basis of her experience with the productions of *Sébastien* and *Salomé* (for which she commissioned Glazunov to write the music), she thinks that you ought to take into account the lack of resonance offstage. Debussy had miscalculated this and the part that was done offstage was messy and ineffective; he was eventually obliged to move the orchestra into the pit. All of this assumes, of course, that you decide to set any portion of the various scenes to music. She would very much like to have parallel music during Cleopatra's death scene. You know the scene, which is one of the greatest works of human inspiration. But she leaves everything up to you—the length of the music, its importance, and its distribution. The Biumina and Milsky translation, in the Efron edition of Shakespeare, is the best and most complete. The French translations are abridged and cut, but in Switzerland perhaps you can find a good translation in another language. Write to me with all of your questions, and I will answer immediately, also any doubts you might have. And send me your estimates concerning time and money, and your choice of conductor. I think that the production will open in the Paris Opéra, but this is a secret. Let me know also about the dates for the installments and other related conditions. The more garrulous you are, the better. I kiss you affectionately.

Lev Bakst

Regards to your wife.

STRAVINSKY TO BAKST

If you want me to compose music for Shakespeare absolutely indispensable you come here. Categorically refuse to discuss questions in writing. I await you. Stravinsky

BAKST TO STRAVINSKY

In three weeks André Gide will come to see you. Powerful artistic and financial means available. Rubinstein will write to you. Answer her.   Bakst

STRAVINSKY TO BAKST

Dear Lyovushka!

I have just received your telegram of July 7 about André Gide coming here in three weeks for talks with me!!! I find that you are wasting a terrible lot of time. Your first telegram says that the music must be finished in six months. An entire month has already gone for discussions, but I must still wait for Gide, who, according to your telegram, will arrive only in August.

A still more important question. Since I am definitely not in a position to take a direct part in your *Antony and Cleopatra,* my role will naturally amount to composing a certain quantity of musical numbers. Here I must talk seriously with either you or Gide, for I want to find out how you intend to present Shakespeare. If you are going to put him on in the way I suppose, in the light spirit and sumptuous settings of *Saint-Sébastien* or *Helen of Sparta,* then I definitely cannot imagine a link between such a treatment of Shakespeare and the music I would be interested in writing. I do not feel capable of composing "mood" music (like that of Debussy's *Saint-Sébastien*), and therein lies the most important question.[12] Give this a lot of thought and hurry with the answer, for time flies, and letters and telegrams take terribly long, especially from France.

This Saturday (July 14) we are all going to the mountains and will remain there until the beginning of September. My address will be: "Les Fougères," Diablerets, Canton de Vaud, Stravinsky. Tell Gide.

I embrace you warmly.

Your   Igor Stravinsky

For telegrams: Stravinsky, "Les Fougères," Diablerets, Switzerland.

---

[12] In a draft of this letter, Stravinsky wrote: "Since my role must be confined strictly to the composition of a specific number of pieces (and I am most insistent on complete autonomy in determining the *character* of these pieces), either you and I, or Gide and I, must meet, so that I can ascertain the general character of the production."

Paris
July 30, 1917
[Telegram]

BAKST TO STRAVINSKY

Will have eight months to compose the music. Staging will be realistic and synthetic at the same time.   Bakst

Les Fougères
July 30, 1917
[Telegram]

STRAVINSKY TO BAKST

Difficult to perceive appearance of production. Notions of synthetic realism too vague. Await Gide for clear answers to my questions.   Stravinsky

BAKST TO STRAVINSKY

112, blvd. Malesherbes
August 3, 1917

Dear Igor,

I received your letter in which you express fear that my production of *Antony and Cleopatra* will be like *Saint-Sébastien* and *Helen of Sparta*. But these two productions have absolutely nothing in common. So far from being "light," *Sébastien* is, instead, profound and mystical, and it is one of my best productions. I always remain faithful to the author, so naturally D'Annunzio's showiness *had* to be reflected in the production. Take as an example the recent, bitter failure of Seriozha's *Contes russes* with Larionov's decor. Thanks to Larionov, this enjoyed no success whatever, and to this day Seriozha still complains that "even Picasso refuses to listen to Larionov." Judging from your afterthoughts, however, I think that you would like this *Russian Tales,* for you would find that it was "the last word." The example itself best illustrates what I mean: The *Tales* production was the *"dernier cri"* of Martin's toys and colors, with a smattering of ultimate Modernism. All of the press observed and remarked this, as well as all of the artists, including the most progressive ones, and however disdainfully. Larionov set himself the goal of delivering this superficial progressive work, and he succeeded, as did Massine with his splendid choreography. If Shakespeare's masterpiece had to be portrayed in the same "progressive" terms, obviously I would have to do without the honor and pleasure of your collaboration.

But let me give you another, quite disarming example: Ida Rubinstein and I put on *Phèdre* in a single act at the Opéra and were rewarded with positively stunning success. Seriozha was expecting a failure, but the production actually enjoyed its greatest and clearest success among the Cubists, as well as the most progressive literary and musical figures!!! Seriozha could not believe his ears when Misia argued passionately with him, as Ida might have done, that there was nothing in the world more artistic or new than Ida's own performance and her production of *Phèdre*. I have purposely saved the enthusiastic letters of the Cubists (of whom you are so fond). So what should you do in this particular case? . . . I know that you are full of prejudices, that often you form notions about people and their work off-handedly. . . . If I refused to go along with Satie's participation in *Antony and Cleopatra* and have inner reservations about his participation in a ballet of mine that Seriozha is planning to produce, this is because I am not one to be caught with chaff, no matter how progressive, and because I value genuine inspiration and authentic talent above all else. As for the production, I believe that one must relate the essence of the play and the author's creation, leaving its time-period intact, however unwillingly.

Let me say a few general words about my production of *Antony*. It consists of roughly twenty-five scenes. I found that the drama is divided along the lines of two worlds in juxtaposition, the hard, military world of Rome and that of the more gentle and sensitive Egypt. This is my starting point; A. Gide will tell you more about it. The antithesis will be made very clear in the production, for I plan to unsheathe Shakespeare's own terrifying sword.

Did you know that I am producing the entire opera *Sadko* at the Opéra? This will be a brilliant re-creation of *Firebird*. You will see that the first Russian landscape painter *might* have been Levitan.[13]

Sasha Siloti wrote to me yesterday that he has been appointed director of the Maryinsky Theatre. *A nous "Orphée" alors! Je t'embrasse.*

Ton   Léon Bakst

Morges
September 9, 1917
[Telegram]

BAKST TO STRAVINSKY

You will receive long letter. Embrace you,   Bakst

September 26, 1917
[Telegram]

BAKST TO STRAVINSKY

Will come to Morges beginning of October. Embrace you,   Bakst

October 17, 1917
[Telegram]

STRAVINSKY TO BAKST

After medical examination Russian consulate denies [me] passport to travel anywhere [for] reasons of health. Impossible to join you. Urgent that you come here.   Stravinsky

---

[13] Isaac I. Levitan (1860?–1900), Russian painter.

STRAVINSKY TO BAKST   *October 31, 1917*

Dear Lyovushka,

Just a note of explanation to the telegram I sent you. . . . I *agree* to compose the music to your production of Shakespeare, since you have consented to give me the full freedom that I would require to write the accompaniment, which is the fundamental condition of my participation. I am very pleased about this, and I do not think you will be sorry you chose to meet that condition. As for my financial terms, I would expect the following: in addition to the advance of 5,000 Swiss francs, which I mentioned in my cable, I want to receive the second payment of 5,000 Swiss francs on December 1, the third payment of 5,000 on December 20, the fourth payment of 5,000 on February 1, and the final payment of 5,000 upon completion of the orchestra score. Also, I retain the right to play the music in concert after the first performance of the play, and I retain the right to grant or refuse performance rights to the music in America (where I wish to be the music's sole proprietor). Obviously, all printing rights and royalties are entirely mine.

On the other hand, I grant you the right to play the music, without special compensation to me, wherever and whenever you see fit. (Reciprocal royalties also belong automatically to me, following the practice of the Société des Auteurs et Compositeurs.)

A legal contract will have to be drawn up, since this letter cannot be considered as such.

Lyudmila Botkina, who is going to Paris today, will give you this letter. I kiss you affectionately.

Yours,   I. Str.

Give me the date by which everything must be finished.

BAKST TO STRAVINSKY   *112, blvd. Malesherbes*
                                                              October 25, 1917

Dear Igor,

I have seen Madame Rubinstein and André Gide, and spoken endlessly with them about the production; now I am writing to tell you of their consent and approval, and of my own thoughts regarding your plans. But first, and most important, it is *absolutely impossible* for me to come to Switzerland, for the same reasons that you cannot come here, even though I would love to visit my sister and her family, whom I have not seen for more than three years! Since it is physically impossible for us to discuss the details of the production in person, the only alternative is to come to a mutual agreement through correspondence. We must either do it this way or call off the whole affair. It is a pity that you spoke so little with Gide, for he is a man full of life and power. But there is nothing to be done.

Your idea for a modernist interpretation of the staging of *Antony and Cleopatra* has been unanimously rejected, and for the following, carefully considered reasons: First and most important is the effect on the audience of "modern" sets, modern at least in relation to the actual figures of Roman and Egyptian history: the result would be that the hall would resound with continuous Homeric laughter. Even if I myself believed this interpretation of Shakespeare's tragedy to be a good and valid one, I would not try to defend your point of view, because I am morally responsible for making the show an opportunity for Rubinstein to display her rare dramatic talent; my sets and costumes would therefore be completely inconsistent with her work, as well as with Gide's and Shakespeare's. We would be all alone, you and I. But I do not want that. Think about it a minute. Clearly there are two antithetical worlds in this brilliant Shakespeare tragedy, the Egyptian and the Roman, and for you and for me this might be the starting point of our work. But imagine De Max dressed up as a modern Italian general, in a most colorful uniform (with decorations!). . . . How, then, would Cleopatra be dressed? If you were going to be a modernist, if you were going to preserve the local color (and you would *have* to), then you would be obliged to dress her as the wife of an Egyptian sheik, and her court would have to be half English, half Turkish. And what about her palace? Contemporary Egyptian, you say, but that means in a false Moorish style, with furniture from Maple and Co.; that is what the furnishing of modern Egyptian palaces resembles these days. Cleopatra's suite will look something like those of Cairo belly dancers. And how would this go with phrases about triremes and galleys?! Can you imagine? Gide would justifiably object that Shakespeare's text coming from the lips of an Italian soldier and a modern Egyptian "girl" would sound horribly theatrical and like pure rhetoric. At best the whole thing would look like a rehearsal, the actors not yet having received their costumes.

The hardest fact for me to swallow, and the most disappointing, is that I would be working against my wishes, without any intuition or excitement. I do not believe in doing that, nor do I believe in this production, which, as a result, would be nothing more for me than the cold and tiresome fulfillment of a commission.

You are in the best position, because to write modernist music comes easily enough to you, and because you have decided and established as a condition that you are not obligated to attend either the rehearsals or the performance itself. You also have the best role because your music (which, I am certain, is excellent) will remain for everyone to enjoy long after the performance. But what remains of a show when the din of the scandal—and I have had enough of that kind of notoriety—has died down? The damage is done! I cannot consent, therefore, because, above and beyond all else, I love Shakespeare's tragedy and will do everything I can to ensure its success as a tragedy. I also think that Rubinstein's extraordinary dramatic talent, so new and fresh, will delight all lovers of literature and art, even Cubists.* The play simply must have a good setting, which is exactly the reason why I was so insistent upon your participation.

So I say to you in complete frankness: it is better to call off the production if you adopt a selfish attitude toward it and expect it to serve the interests of just one or two of the many participants. After all, the public in Paris is not that of Shakespeare's time, when it was enough simply to hang out a sign saying "forest" for the audience to imagine a forest. No, the Paris public consists of aesthetes, rotten through and through, and they will regard your ideas as part not of a serious production but of an extremely amusing and caustic one. Three-quarters of the audience will laugh, create a scandal, and demand "their money back." . . . Thus not for anything will I see the show ruined.

But if you try to follow my view, which does not strive to be historically or archeologically accurate, at least not obsessively, but instead is an expression of *my* understanding of this tragedy of Shakespeare's, then the question is really answered very simply: each of us must try to express himself through the play. The essential criteria for such expression are that it be authentic, unique, and alive (the highest of my ideals). As I see it, we have two worlds, the Egyptian and the Roman. One is sly, voluptuous, spicy, tender, and arrogant; the other is strongly military . . . Rome *über alles.* Antony's rise and fall is also Rome's. Egypt is everything to him, the love of his life, the country of Cythère, and it is in this sense that he says, as he is leaving, "farewell Egypt." At the moment of death, however, both he and Cleopatra discover *human* love, stronger than either Egypt or Rome, and remain ever after mystical lovers. That is all.

It will be obvious to anyone who is not nearsighted that I have used some historical material in the set design. I am very little concerned with archeology, though I play with it, purposely mixing styles, but ultimately creating an authentic impression, a sincere portrait. I would not dream of creating a modern death scene that might provoke someone close up to run out onstage with a stomach pump or an enema. I can already hear the hysterical laughter that would result from some such prank in Cleopatra's death scene.

I could write for years on end pointing out ways of sabotaging this wonderful work, in each scene and each act, with modernist interpretations. But instead I simply ask you to put yourself in my place and try to imagine how a modernist might have staged each of the scenes. You will come to the same conclusions I did; it is simply that you had not yet pictured such an interpretation of the tragedy sculpturally.

But if you cannot accept my view, the problem is still easily resolved in three or four letters. Madame Rubinstein has left the composition and distribution of the music to you. She thinks (and so do I) that it would be good to have an overture to each act,** then music for the appearance of the Roman camps, on the ramparts and in the private chambers, and, finally, for the "death of Cleopatra." All of this would be evoked in the pit, not on the stage, for reasons about which I have already written to you—performance complications, the muffling of the sound, etc. . . .

Decide how much music you want to write and for what scenes—the duration is important to me—and your approximate needs in terms of the orchestra, the numbers and kinds of instruments. Then, when you have made up your mind, let us know immediately how much time you will require, give us a detailed account of your fee, and tell us how and when we can get the music, and so on.

It would be best if you yourself made up a draft of a contract. Depending on whether changes are to be made, Madame Rubinstein will sign it through her business representatives.[14] If you start immediately, the contract can be signed in three or four weeks. Then you will be able to begin your work. You could conceivably wait to write to me about your ideas and their connection with my production until after you have begun to compose. There will be plenty of time to take everything into account. Gide will not be finished for five or six months either.

This is all that I can tell you now. It is my great and sincere wish to see our plans jointly realized!

I embrace you affectionately.

Sincerely and fondly yours,   Lev Bakst

* Remember how furiously I argued with Debussy and Seriozha for an airplane in the music and on stage in *Jeux*? Seriozha and Debussy laughed, but then Cocteau stole my idea for *Parade*. Still, *Jeux* was modernist.
** Four overtures, since we have joined the fourth and fifth acts.

	December 3, 1917
STRAVINSKY TO BAKST	*[Telegram]*

Please tell Rubinstein that it is already one month that I have been awaiting her reply. Should I do the music for her production? Demand reply immediately.   Stravinsky[15]

---

[14] On November 26, Bakst wrote to Charles Péquin, Rubinstein's agent: "I forwarded Stravinsky's terms to Madame Rubinstein, who said that she would negotiate directly with Stravinsky. I wrote this to Mlle Botkina, who was to have telegraphed this to Stravinsky immediately. Any delay will depend entirely on Madame Rubinstein." Botkina had written to Stravinsky from Montpellier on November 10: "I received a letter from Bakst with only these words, 'Madame Rubinstein has just telephoned me that in the next few days she will consider with her business adviser Igor Stravinsky's terms on the subject of the music for *Antony and Cleopatra*. By about Thursday she will send her reply through him.'" On November 18, Stravinsky telegraphed to Ramuz, who was in Paris, at the Hôtel Monsigny, rue Monsigny: "If advance not yet received ask Bakst send it Banque Cantonale."
[15] Before renouncing the project, Stravinsky telegraphed to Péquin on December 6 and 16, modifying the terms.

CORRESPONDENCE WITH

1912 ~ 1914

M. D. CALVOCORESSI

STRAVINSKY TO M. D. CALVOCORESSI[1]

[Paris]

Very dear friend,

Am a dirty pig, anyway you know it. But I must say that I have not heard from you in a long time. That is why [illegible]. One of these days I will leave Clarens and go to Monte Carlo, where my two ballets are going to be performed. Otherwise, are you back from our charming capital [St. Petersburg]? Did you like it? Were you seriously influenced by our poor friend [Maximilian] Steinberg, who seems to me to have plunged totally into academicism [two words illegible]? In his last few letters he declares that he understands nothing in my most recent compositions—which remark must of course remain between you and me. Write to me, dear friend, what you thought of him. Is there still a possibility of saving him?

Always my greatest friendship for you—I do not forget you, and I send my regards to your mother.

Your   Igor Stravinsky

Petrushka

which awaits you in Monte Carlo. Go to see it in Paris, all right? *Le Sacre* is actually almost finished. I will have the pleasure of playing it for my friends, of whom you are one of the foremost! See you soon! My wife asks that you convey her [illegible] best wishes to Madame Calvocoressi.

---

[1] French is the original language of all the correspondence.

CALVOCORESSI TO STRAVINSKY   *May 31, 1913*
                                                   [Pneumatique]

Hôtel Splendide
1 bis, avenue Carnot

Old friend,

Excuse me for not having come. . . .[2] It went well . . . perhaps a bit of. . . . Finally we heard the complete work [*Sacre*].

    See you tomorrow at 2:00 at the Théâtre [des Champs-Elysées]. Rehearsal of *Petrushka*. Did you know?

    Respects to Madame Stravinsky.

                            Embrace you,   M. D.

CALVOCORESSI TO STRAVINSKY   *London*
                                                   Tuesday [July 5?], 1913
Villa Borghese   *[Postcard]*[3]
29, blvd. Victor Hugo
Neuilly (Seine)

Magnificent performance yesterday of *Petrushka*. What a wonderful orchestra, my old friend!

    Svetlov[4] told me he sent you a telegram.

    Respects to Madame Stravinsky. See you soon.

                        Affectionately,   M. D.

CALVOCORESSI TO STRAVINSKY   *London*
                                                   July 14, 1913
[Ustilug]

Dear Igor,

Here is all that I have found.[5] The music magazines will appear in a week. In short, several big newspapers proclaim the success. Three—and it is a shame!—don't bother to speak of music. Readers of the *Morning Post,* in which I said good things about the *Sacre,* must be astounded by the attitude of my colleagues in London. But who cares?—"the truth can arise" only from the conflict of opinions (M. D. Calvocoressi, in various articles, one more wonderful than the next).

    How are you? We send a thousand affectionate regards. I am in the midst

---

[2] Text missing because the stamp has been cut out.

[3] Picture postcard of Ludgate Circus, London.

[4] Valerian Svetlov (1860–1934), Russian ballet critic and husband of the ballerina Vera Trefilova.

[5] Newspaper reviews of the *Sacre* in London.

of preparing the course for Oxford. My address from August 8 to 20 (say, for mailing, from the 4th to the 16th, New Style), 24 Wellington Square, Oxford. After that, from September 13 to 28 (for mailing, four days), The Musician's Holiday, Red House, Port Ballintrae, Ireland. There I will give a lecture with recital on the *Sacre*. Don't forget, dear friend, Koussevitzky for Viñes!!![6]

Very cordially yours,   M. Calvocoressi

CALVOCORESSI TO STRAVINSKY

London
Sunday, July 20, 1913

Ustilug

Dear Igor,

I ask your forgiveness on bended knees: a forced absence delayed me concerning you. I find this sheet on which are listed the principal newspapers of London, I send it to you to allay your justifiable impatience and my remorse. On Tuesday I will have the newspapers themselves and will send them to you.

How are you? I hope to have excellent news of you; and we send you our fondest remembrances. Present my respects to your mother and to Madame Stravinsky, and believe me to be

yours sincerely,   M. Calvocoressi

CALVOCORESSI TO STRAVINSKY

Oxford
August 19, 1913
[Postcard][7]

Ustilug

Dear old friend,

The lectures are over. Everything went very well at the university. How are you?

Respects to Madame Stravinskaya and to your mother. My mother sends you her best wishes.

Affectionately, your   M. Calvocoressi

CALVOCORESSI TO STRAVINSKY

164, rue de Courcelles
Paris
October 16, 1913

Dear Igor,

I was almost certain of the response, despite the peremptory authority of the newspapers. But I must have misaddressed the telegram, since there was no reply for forty-eight hours. Thank you for the answer and the postcard. We are all delighted.

---

[6] Ricardo Viñes (1875–1943), Spanish pianist.

[7] Picture postcard of Queen Street, Oxford.

I have some rather interesting details to give you about England. Some interesting and serious musicians told me that the newspapers greatly exaggerated the public's displeasure at the *Sacre;* on the contrary, they ignored the great satisfaction of a considerable majority at *every* performance. Two young musicians came to the music camp and played [the 4-hand version] several times. It would have made your ears tingle.

Enclosed are some clippings. I have not yet written a special article on the *Sacre* in English. I must do that, and the same for Russia, etc., but I do not have the spare time these days in which to collect my thoughts enough to do it *well.*

The treatise by R. K. [Rimsky-Korsakov] being nearly translated (I will have finished, quite exhausted, on the 25th), I await *The Nightingale*[8] with doubled impatience. Have you and the RMV [Russischer Musik Verlag] decided on someone for the English translation?

Have you thought about pressuring Koussevitzky *finally* to have our dear Viñes play in Russia? You know that this is my dream!

A thousand kind and affectionate thoughts and good wishes to all of you from my mother as well as from me.

Your   M. Calvocoressi

CALVOCORESSI TO STRAVINSKY

164, rue de Courcelles
Paris
November 5, 1913

Dear Igor,

Thank you for your postcard. This solution is the best one, and you know that I simply wanted to avoid your dealing *with another Parisian theatre,** fearing the result, which has, in any case, come to pass, as you no doubt know. I am intrigued by the announcement of your children's poems.[9] Bravo!

Enclosed is a new clipping on Stravinsky. Delage is well—Ravel too, following a mild cold. I am lazy these days, having finished the Korsakov [treatise].

I am always glad to have good news of you, as of Madame Stravinsky and the children. My respects to her, I beg of you, and best wishes from my mother to everyone.

Cordially, your   M. Calvocoressi

* Théâtre des Champs-Elysées (Astruc)[10] [*in Stravinsky's hand*]

---

[8] Underlined in red by Stravinsky.

[9] *Recollections of My Childhood.*

[10] Gabriel Astruc (1884–1938), impresario who presented Diaghilev's pre–World War I seasons in Paris.

CALVOCORESSI TO STRAVINSKY   *January 16, 1914*

Dear Igor,

We impatiently await good news of Madame Stravinsky and all of you. . . . Delage must have written to you about the triumphant success of your songs with
Nikitina at the SMI [Société Musicale Indépendante]. Today at the Ecole des
Hautes Etudes Sociales, she sang these songs no less admirably at a lecture
given by yours truly, with Casella at the piano, splendid. And again huge success, the third being encored despite the late hour. There were also calls for an
encore at the SMI, but the program was too long and they were ignored.

Nikitina is a splendid interpreter from every point of view, I dream of her
for the Nightingale, about which I have already spoken to the Op[éra]
Com[ique]. You must support me in this. Gheusi and I might [go] to Moscow
to hear her at the premiere.

I must also tell you that you ought to recommend her for the role to
Diaghilev, dear friend.

Received the second act for translation.*

Also had Schoenberg's opus 16 pieces played for me today, which [I]
liked.

Very affectionately, your   M. Calvocoressi

* *Rossignol* [*in Stravinsky's hand*].

CALVOCORESSI TO STRAVINSKY   *164, rue de Courcelles*
                                                                Paris
Dear Igor,   *[January 1914]*

All my thanks for your kind postcard and also for the latest photograph, of
which, thoughtlessly, I have not yet acknowledged receipt.

I have the pleasure of announcing to you:

(a) the first scene of *Nightingale* is translated and delivered
(b) today I finished correcting the proofs of the Korsakov treatise
(c) on January 1 I become editor in chief, with M. Vuillermoz,[11] of *La
Revue Française de Musique,* a handsome periodical, independent,
liberal, with which I hope to do some good for all of our own people
and to uphold our views. If you could advise me concerning how to
promote this review a bit in Russia and among your friends, I would
be most grateful.

When are you coming? I will be gone from the 20th to the 30th, Berlin and

---

[11] Emile Vuillermoz (1878–1960), French music critic, one of the founders of the
Société Musicale Indépendante.

Stockholm. Present my respects to Madame Stravinsky, accept all my mother's best wishes, and believe me to be, dear [illegible].

Very affectionately, your   M. Calvocoressi

I am dying of impatience to see the second scene . . . the last product of [two words in Russian].*

* *Rossignol en russe* [*in Stravinsky's handwriting, referring to the second word*].

CALVOCORESSI TO STRAVINSKY   [*January 1914*]

Dear Igor,

The nomination *this morning* of Gheusi (Isola Vistal) at the Op[éra]-Comique is extremely important. If *The Nightingale* is not contractually committed in France, I think that it is *essential* to reserve it for them. I know that this would interest them and would be good for the work. So, my old friend, while I wait to see my friend Vidal, try not to let anything happen, and give me your thoughts. I am *very* impatient to have an answer to this letter.

Affectionately,   M. Calvocoressi

FLORENT SCHMITT

STRAVINSKY TO FLORENT SCHMITT[1]

Ustilug
November 2, 1911

Dear, and very dear friend,

When will your work of genius *Salomé* finally appear so that I can spend happy hours playing it from beginning to end *à la folie*? I confess that it has given me greater joy than any work I have heard in a long time. This is without flattery! Believe me! I am proud that the piece is dedicated to me. During my last visit to Paris, I drew Diaghilev's attention to it, conveying my ecstasy. Since then I have had no news of him and do not know if he intends to play my "choreographics" in St. Petersburg, which was to have happened in February. All of this is very painful for me! As for myself, I have almost completed Part One of the *Sacres* [*sic*], including the instrumentation. From time to time I receive news of Maurice Delage, who is so far from us and who does not seem to be tormenting himself over the great distance that separates us. I send you my nude body, which is not to be seen elsewhere.[2] If you want to see it, I will send you another print.

Very cordially and affectionately, your   Igor Stravinsky

STRAVINSKY TO SCHMITT

Ustilug
September 18, 1912

My dear friend,

I received your letter, which was a new proof of your friendship for me. Thank you. I could not reply immediately, because I was away from August 15 to September 15.

---

[1] The composer Florent Schmitt (1870–1958) is best known for *La Tragédie de Salomé*, which Serge Sudeikin designed for Diaghilev. Stravinsky and Schmitt became friends in June 1910. Schmitt was so enthusiastic about *Firebird* that he changed the name of his home to "Villa *Oiseau de feu*." Stravinsky's true opinion of Schmitt's music, in contrast to the statements about it in this letter, is unprintable, but Stravinsky's March 29, 1912, letter to Diaghilev (at the Riviera Palace, Monte Carlo) about Schmitt and *Salomé* seems to have survived only in an illegible carbon copy. The friendship between the two musicians did not endure, and by the 1930s Schmitt was openly hostile to Stravinsky's music. In later years, the former friends met only once, at a reception for Stravinsky at the American Embassy in Paris, in October 1957 (see photograph). French is the original language of all the correspondence.

[2] This three-quarter-view nude photograph of Stravinsky, taken in the summer of 1911

What can I tell you concerning your question about Rhené Baton? You know very well that I am not esteemed in my admirable country. Even [Alexander] Siloti, who protected me at first, has at last declared that my music has not had the desired success—for which reason he advises me to compose a more digestible kind of music. Again this summer he wrote to me that *Petrushka,* which he heard during his stay in Paris, interested him very much. Contradictory opinions (!!! completely unexpected). Is this not polite? After all of this, what do you expect me to do with Siloti? The critics, who are irritated by my success abroad, declare that I am without originality, that I am not at the head of the avant-garde (which is malicious), but that, on the contrary, I am at the tail end of the snobbist theories, and all this after having heard the works that precede *Petrushka* (which has not yet been played in Russia, even in concert). After this, what do you expect me to do? My old friend, it disturbs me to refuse your small request, all the more so because it concerns Rhené Baton, to whom I owe the perfect performance of *Firebird.* Also, he saved us from the great embarrassment that we suffered at the beginning of our London season. Write to me, therefore, that I am not a dirty pig. This will be sufficient to convince me that you have understood the situation. I am working hard to complete the music of the *Sacre* and the orchestration, as well as the instrumentation of the "chorus," proofreading, travels, etc., etc. . . .

SCHMITT TO STRAVINSKY

Hôtel du Châtelard
Clarens

10, rue des Girondins
St.-Cloud
Seine-et-Oise
November 15, 1912
[Postcard]

Dear friend [illegible],

Many thanks again. Thanks, too, for having finished the *Sacres* [*sic*], with all the joys it holds for us. If *Salomé* is eventually given in the theatre, which is something that would be easy to do, I will pay a little visit to Clarens and have the double pleasure of seeing you and your kind family again and discussing old memories in the country where I had good times in the past. Perhaps you are coming here? *A bientôt.*

Very affectionately yours,   and from Jeanne[3] also

---

on the east bank of the Bug River, is reproduced in *Igor and Vera Stravinsky: A Photograph Album* (London, 1982). Stravinsky sent a print of the picture to Delage as well as to Schmitt.

[3] Schmitt's wife.

SCHMITT TO STRAVINSKY   *[End of 1912]*
                                              [On the back of a calling card]

Dear friend,

Here are two or three lines for you, until a better opportunity. *A bientôt*, Stravinsky, respects to Madame Stravinsky; I speak of you often with [Gabriel] Pierné, who asked me again about the *Sacre*.

STRAVINSKY TO SCHMITT   *Hôtel du Châtelard*
                                                              Clarens
Dear old friend,   *January [17?], 1913*[4]

I have just returned from Vienna, where the "famous" orchestra of the Opera, like the dirtiest of pigs, sabotaged my *Petrushka*. They said that ugly and dirty music such as mine could not be played better than they played it. My old friend!! You cannot imagine the problems and the insults this orchestra gave me.

    Now something else. Diaghilev has fallen in love with your *Salomé*, and he definitely wants to stage it this year (in May). I know very well that Astruc, influenced by Madame [Misia] Edwards, wants to give it. He has not spoken about it since, for which reason I am certain that he plans to do it. . . . Telegraph me your in-principle agreement. I will telegraph this to Diaghilev in St. Petersburg. He will come to Paris soon, see you there, and discuss the matter with you.

                                    Your   Igor Stravinsky

SCHMITT TO STRAVINSKY   *10, rue des Girondins*
                                                           St.-Cloud
Dear friend,   *January [19], 1913*

Yes, I received the Japanese melody, and I enjoyed it so much that I resolved to thank you at length. As a result of a succession of annoying events, I put off this [response] from day to day. But do not believe that I have not thought of you. My wife and I and my friends speak of you daily, and from time to time I indulge myself by sounding off about you.

    I must go to Monte Carlo next month for *Pénélope*.[5] Will you be there then? And where might you be found? Would you please have Delage keep me up-to-date on his stints in the country and his whereabouts in general?

    Here we attended the dress rehearsal of [Vincent d'Indy's] *Fervaal*. For three days now Ravel and I have combed through the newspapers in an attempt to find the most objective reviews. But I cannot go to Geneva. Too many concerns hold me here—unfortunately.

---

[4] The performance of *Petrushka* at the Vienna Hofoper that Stravinsky attended took place on January 15.

[5] The premiere of Fauré's *Pénélope* took place in Monte Carlo on March 4, 1913.

I cannot wait to hear the *Sacre.* I envy you, being able to work in peace, away from all distractions. Someday we must take your great courage to heart and leave Paris for good. My life is squandered here.

I hope your whole family is well. My wife joins me in sending our most affectionate regards to all of you, Maurice [Delage] included.

A bientôt, and until Monaco, definitely.

Florent Schmitt

Attached find two articles from *La France.* These brutes need a good lecture. Furthermore, I never miss a chance to cite you.

SCHMITT TO STRAVINSKY

10, rue des Girondins
St.-Cloud
January 20, 1913 (Monday)

Hôtel du Châtelard
Clarens

Very dear friend,

I am distressed by what you told me about Vienna. [The Viennese] have not changed! In this respect, I congratulate myself on being French; the reception my compatriots have always given you singularly reconciles me with my country. When your letter arrived, I was in the process of writing your name, along with Schoenberg's, in an article for *La France,* and my [distrust] of the Viennese is all that restrained me from chastising them. But do not be discouraged, my dear Igor. You are young. You will witness your universal triumph. I predict it. In the meantime, all of us here are eager and anxious for the *Sacre,* and we are busy preparing the spirit of the masses [for the event] .

Thank you, my dear, for *Salomé,* since I am certain that I owe Diaghilev's "whim" to you. Tell him that it is agreed that he may make all the desired changes. I am thrilled, as is my wife. What pleases me most is to think that you will hear it, for you will be in Paris then. One day—if life allows me—I aspire to complete my mystery of Proserpina.

For the question of author's rights, I am obliged to give 20 percent to S'Hunière's and 15 percent (which I find hateful and unjust) to Loie Fuller. But I will try to convince them to reduce [these percentages] . The important thing is that Diaghilev be the one to present [*Salomé*] .

Thank you again, my dear friend. Respectful regards to Madame Stravinsky, and affectionate greetings from Jeanne and me.

Florent Schmitt

You neglected to tell me whether you will be in Monte Carlo on February 27.

[The manuscript of] your Japanese song is with the framer!

It is difficult for me to reply to your letter by telegram. Besides, you will have this by tomorrow morning, and no time will have been lost.

January 21, 1913
[Telegram]

SCHMITT TO STRAVINSKY

Agreed for the changes. Best thanks.   Schmitt

SCHMITT TO STRAVINSKY   *January 21, 1913*

Dear friend,

Pardon me, I did not think that a telegram was indispensable. I did not want you to assume the costs, which would have been rather excessive! I hasten to send you the French stamps, for you to use soon, I hope—in France.

I dined last night with some friends: Ravel, Grovlez, Aubert, Casella, Vuillermoz, to whom I told your tale of Vienna, to their great interest. This led to a discussion of the destiny of the S [ociété] M [usicale] I [ndépendante], and we resolved to place Schoenberg's *Pierrot Lunaire* and Béla Bartók's quartet on the upcoming programs. Let me know quickly if you have something that could be done in a chamber-music concert. Perhaps your *Japanese Lyrics*? But you would undoubtedly want to be in Paris for the performance.

Aubert was very moved by your score. We discussed you at length with the pianists Lazare-Lévy and Dumesnil, whom I attempted to convince of the necessity of a Stravinskian Bayreuth. They are not yet convinced beyond all doubt, but will be after the *Sacre*.

A bientôt, dear friend. Thanks again.

Affectionately yours,   Florent Schmitt

Best regards from [Ravel?].

I wrote to you yesterday, Monday; undoubtedly you will have received that . . . letter this morning, Tuesday. Incidentally, tell me whether you will be on the soil of Monte Carlo around February 27.

Hôtel du Châtelard
Clarens
January 22, 1913

STRAVINSKY TO SCHMITT

It was a real pleasure for me to read my letter (edited) in *La France* [of January 21] and good that it was placed in your article—you are truly wonderful!!?!!? I flatter myself meanwhile that somehow the Viennese will be aware of your lines.

I am happy that I have succeeded in interesting you (also Ravel) in Schoenberg and in making you play his prodigious *Pierrot Lunaire*. Bravo! Certainly you are going to tell me that this is not to say that you like it; but, speaking for myself, I am convinced that, in time, this will come, too. I feel it! As for my *Japanese Lyrics*, I have just finished the third (dedicated to Ravel). All three are at your disposal, if you would like them. Perhaps I can come on my return from London, and even, *horribile dictu*, play the piano part (because there is a piano at bottom—naturally) in this huge orchestra, which, besides this instrument and the human voice, consists of a piccolo, a flute, two clarinets (the second doubling on bass clarinet), and a string quartet.

SCHMITT TO STRAVINSKY   *Nice*
                                                March 9, 1913
My old friend,   *[Postcard]*[6]

Delage and I have spoken about you a great deal, and you are very much missed here.

    Affectionately; respects to Madame Stravinsky.

                                                Florent Schmitt

Will I perhaps see you for a few hours on Wednesday? This is not definite, so do not wait for me. If you will not be in Clarens, send me a note to that effect in Lyon (general delivery) on Tuesday.

[At the bottom of the letter] Very happy to have found Father Schmitt. I am slightly demoralized.   Maurice Delage

SCHMITT TO STRAVINSKY   *Avignon*
                                                March 11, 1913
Dear friend,   *[Postcard]*[7]

Do not expect me. I realized that it would be better for me to go directly home, since I have work to do. I would nevertheless have been delighted to see you and to hear some of the *Sacre*.

    Affectionately, and see you soon, I hope.

                                                Florent Schmitt

SCHMITT TO STRAVINSKY   *St.-Cloud*
                                                [March 26], 1913
Dear friend,   *[Postcard]*[8]

Certainly, nothing [prevents] the postponement of the Japanese songs until spring. I regret that you will not be coming through [Paris], where many friends await you. But I understand that your work takes priority. Saturday I go to Monte Carlo. Delage is still in Nice, and I will attempt to see him. I saw Diaghilev, and I think that preparations for *Salomé* are going smoothly. Thank you again, my dear friend.

    Best to all. Respects to Madame Stravinsky.

                                                Florent Schmitt

You left an inkwell and a pen here. Shall I send them to you?

---

[6] Picture postcard of a view of the Alpes-Maritimes.

[7] Picture postcard of the tomb of Pope John XXII, Avignon.

[8] Picture postcard of St.-Flour, Cantal.

SCHMITT TO STRAVINSKY   *St.-Cloud*
June 22, 1913

Villa Borghese
29, blvd. Victor Hugo
Neuilly-sur-Seine

Dear friend,

Jeanne[9] and I plan to visit you on Wednesday around six o'clock. I hope that we
will not disturb you.

       Respects to Madame Stravinsky. I embrace you, my old and great friend.

            Florent Schmitt

[*At the bottom of the letter*] Dear friend, I asked Delage and Ravel to express
my congratulations, my regrets at not having seen you, and my best wishes for
your prompt recovery. Find here all of that along with one more bravo for the
marvelous *Sacre*. Best to you,   Abbé Petit

SCHMITT TO STRAVINSKY   *St.-Cloud*
December 14, 1913
Clarens   *[Postcard]*

Dear friend,

I will be conducting a concert in Bordeaux on February 8. I proposed *Fireworks*. They prefer the Berceuse from *Firebird*—it is easier. Would you please
have Madame Stravinsky send me a few lines of commentary about the Berceuse? Also, would Jurgenson like to rent (or sell?) the orchestra parts of the
Berceuse separately, without the rest of the work? Excuse this business letter. I
will not bother you anymore. Will you be in Clarens on January 12? This because I thought of passing through on my return from Lyon, where I must be
on the 11th for my *Psalm*.

       Best to all,

            Florent Schmitt

SCHMITT TO STRAVINSKY   *December 17, 1913*

Clarens

Dear friend,

Thank you for the nice letter. I neglected to ask you for Jurgenson's address in
Moscow or Leipzig. Tell me quickly, for now it is urgent. Also tell me whether I

---

[9] On September 21, Jeanne Schmitt sent a postcard (of the early-twelfth-century
church of Notre-Dame at St.-Dié) to Catherine Stravinsky in Ustilug (forwarded to
Clarens): "Dear Madame, Florent and I are sad that we have had no news from your

must send the money at the same time (of course the Société de Bordeaux will assume the costs)—although, good point, I do not know how much to send.

There are eighteen firsts [violins], sixteen seconds, but, alas, only six violas, eight cellos, and six basses. So please remember to send me a note about the Berceuse (Madame Stravinsky would be kind to do me this favor, which I do not wish to ask of you, for you are hard at work!).

Affectionately,   F. S.

I will write to let you know whether I am coming.

SCHMITT TO STRAVINSKY   *[February 1914]*

Dear friend,

What has become of you? How is Madame Stravinsky? We would greatly appreciate a little note, for we are all dismayed to learn that she was ill, and would like to know that your worries are over.

The Société de Bordeaux asked me how much they owe for the score and parts of the Berceuse from *Firebird*. Would you inform me of that at the same time?

A bientôt, my dear Igor. Very affectionate regards from the three of us.

Florent Schmitt

I am overjoyed, looking forward to hearing *The Nightingale* (I read the second act, but that did not suffice for me).

Has [Leo] Ornstein spoken to you about his *Danse sauvage?*

I attach a few lines about *Petrushka* by Carraud (*La Liberté* of February 16).

Would you like to have your Four Etudes (Opus 7) played at the S.M.I.?

SCHMITT TO STRAVINSKY   37, *rue du Calvaire*
                                                          St.-Cloud
Clarens[10]   *March 18, 1914*

Dear friend,

By now you have perhaps received word from the Société Chaptal.[11] I did not forget. Twice I went to see [Garifand?], with whom I had wanted to speak,

---

husband—the apaches have a conspiracy of silence. We would like some assurance that Stravinsky is happy, as he was after emerging from his convalescence, and working in Poland [Ustilug] to the delight of you all. Please be so kind as to send news, and believe in our profound friendship. . . ."

[10] Forwarded to Leysin.

[11] The office of the Société des Auteurs et Compositeurs Dramatiques was on the rue Chaptal.

thinking that maybe all of these lawyers still extend a closed hand to music. He was not in. Finally, the third time, I left a note, asking him to spare you all of these ridiculous formalities—I did not say "ridiculous," since these people take themselves very seriously—and giving him your address, so that he could write to you directly. I hope he did so. If not, tell me, and I will confront him energetically.

A *bientôt,* dear friend. Jeanne joins me in sending best regards to you and yours.

Florent Schmitt

I was thrilled by the good afternoon the other day. That has not happened to me in so long. The musicians did not know one another. They are not enemies, not even a little bit.

Would you like to come to the S.M.I. on Thursday? My sonata will be given, along with some new pieces by Casella. Only if you intend to be in Paris, since I know that otherwise it is a bothersome trip.

SCHMITT TO STRAVINSKY

Clarens[12]

My old friend,

Name: *Florent Schmitt*
Rank: *Homme de base*
Regiment: *41st*
Company: *16th*

Toul
January 2, 1915

I was touched to see—in a Swiss newspaper—that you attended the concert of the Borodin symphony in Geneva. But I would be delighted to have more direct news, from you and your brothers from the *"rouleau compresseur."*[13]

A *bientôt* . . .

Florent Schmitt

[*At the bottom of the letter*] Your portrait, my dear Stravinsky, will be ready for the next Salon d'Automne, and then you will be in Schmitt's company. We are in Toul, where we make war, rather a more aesthetic war. Returning to Paris and to the pleasure of seeing you again. My best compliments, Albert Gleizes[14]

---

[12] Forwarded to Château-d'Oex.

[13] Steam roller? Russia?

[14] Gleizes's Cubist portrait of Stravinsky was completed that year.

SCHMITT TO STRAVINSKY

Morges

37, rue du Calvaire
St.-Cloud
November 28, 1919

Dear Igor,

Here is a letter for you that was delivered to Durand's. I took it, since I know your address. Do not upset yourself. I recognized the handwriting, for I have seen it addressed to me in the past, and so has Ravel. In the end, one must please the passionate young girls, for there are so many indifferent ones.

I hope that you and Madame Stravinsky are well. I have heard news about you frequently—from, among others, Madame Errazuriz,[15] whom I encountered in London, and from Diaghilev, who spoke marvels about your *Noces villageoises,* which I cannot wait to hear.

A bientôt, dear friend. I hope that we shall finally see each other again, after so long. I am starting to regain my composure after two less-than-amusing years of militarism.

I heard your *Pribaoutki* and liked it infinitely, and the other day, for the nth time, *Petrushka,* which is always a joy. Besides, Pierné did not do such a bad job of conducting it.

Best wishes to you and your whole family. My wife joins me in this. A short note from you would give me great pleasure.

Florent Schmitt

SCHMITT TO STRAVINSKY

"Bel Respiro"
avenue Alphonse de Neuville
Garches

37, rue du Calvaire
St.-Cloud
January 31, 1921

Dear friend,

Could I have a few words with you, on either Sunday or Monday afternoon in Paris, or Tuesday or Wednesday in Garches? . . .

A bientôt, and best regards to Madame Stravinsky.

Florent Schmitt

---

[15] Eugenia Errazuriz, the Chilean patroness of Picasso and Stravinsky. She gave Stravinsky a stipend from 1916 to 1919. See the correspondence with Errazuriz in the present volume.

SCHMITT TO STRAVINSKY   *January 21, [?]*

Dear friend,

This note follows the second performance of *Petrushka* in Lyon. Admirably done, even one of the best concert performances I have heard. There was movement, life, atmosphere, and the audience, still so good here, showed enthusiasm.

Witkowski[16] put a lot into it. I think that he would be happy and touched if you were to send him a note of recognition. Would you do that for him, and for me? I would be grateful: Witkowski, 28, cours Morand, Lyon.

Thank you, dear friend. Very affectionately yours,

Florent Schmitt

I saw Ansermet in Geneva one night and we spoke about you for long hours.

---

[16] Georges Witkowski (1867–1943), conductor, composer, student of d'Indy.

CORRESPONDENCE WITH

1913 ✍ 1937

EDWIN EVANS

EDWIN EVANS[1] TO STRAVINSKY

31 Coleherne Road
Earl's Court
London SW10
February 4, 1913

Sir,

My friend Delage wrote me a letter from Nice which has only just been delivered to me now, because of a change of address.

It seems that he mentioned me to you, and probably in terms that are far too flattering, and that I shall have difficulty living up to. Nevertheless, if you would like to risk an almost certain disillusionment, I would be very happy to make your acquaintance.

I have heard the delicious music of the *Firebird* many times, but I have not yet heard *Petrushka*. I am not even certain that I will hear it tonight, because the administration of Covent Garden has the bad habit of reserving the premieres for the daily papers, while my journal [*Pall Mall Gazette*] is a weekly. I will probably be able to obtain a seat only at the second performance, unless you would like to take the matter into your own hands.

You are probably very busy at this time, but if you would like to indicate to me your free hours, I would not miss the opportunity to take advantage of this—or even to abuse it, because musical discussion is a penchant that I have a hard time resisting.

Please send me a note at your convenience. In the meantime, I am grateful to Delage for having done me the favor of making possible my introduction to an artist whom I have admired for a long time.

I offer you my best wishes.

Edwin Evans

EVANS TO STRAVINSKY

Earl's Court
February 6, 1913

Dear sir,

I went out early this morning, before your message arrived, and have just returned, too late to go and find you. Would it be convenient for you if I were to

---

[1] The British musicologist Edwin Evans (1874–1945) was an early friend of Stravinsky in London. Evans's early writings about Stravinsky had the composer's endorsement. French is the original language of all the correspondence.

come at the same time (2:00 to 3:00) tomorrow, that is, Friday? For the reply, I can be reached by telephone tomorrow morning from 11:30 to 12:30 at Regent 1534. If you do not telephone, I shall take it to mean that you expect me.

My congratulations for *Petrushka!* What you have done there is something entirely new. I especially like your ingenious way of protecting your motifs against the ravages of too-compact polyphony. Someone else would have woven a fabric in which the individual value of the motifs would have been diminished in the interest of their musical combinations. I would very much like to examine the score.

Best wishes,   Edwin Evans

EVANS TO STRAVINSKY   *February 27, 1913*[2]

. . . Nijinsky was a great success in *L'Après-midi d'un faune*. . . . The audience, not for the first time, proved itself to be much more intelligent than the press. Some of the important reviewers were good, especially those who were inspired in advance by Diaghilev and company! . . . The critic who astonished me with his praise of *Petrushka* found [*L'Après-midi*] comical! . . . The pianist was indeed Madame Herbert Withers, as I told you. . . . Do not forget [to inscribe] her *Petrushka* [score]—you owe her that much. . . .

EVANS TO STRAVINSKY   *February 5, 1914*

. . . Delage told me that he explained my problems to you. . . . Did he also tell you of my efforts in behalf of the *Sacre*? . . . Our anxiety was unnecessary; the audience responded very well. The reviews were slightly negative, but what does that matter? . . . Of course, the critics wrote their reports on the night of the premiere, and by the last performance many already regretted their first impressions. . . . Most important, you made a very great conquest in the artistic, intellectual world.

I am thinking of doing a detailed study of your music, which I would then submit to one of our more serious reviews. Would you be willing to give me some biographical facts . . . and also to have your publisher send me those works that I do not possess? I have: the piano reductions of *Firebird, Petrushka, Sacre;* the two [Gorodyetsky] poems (Opus 6); the two Balmont [poems]; and the full score of the *Japanese,* for which I need the piano and vocal scores as well; I have made an English translation and need to try it out with a singer. . . .

---

[2] On February 12, Evans had invited Stravinsky to dinner at Hamilton's (?) with Cyril Scott ("the composer of that sonata which you read") and asked Stravinsky to bring along "those delicious Japanese poems"—i.e., his just-completed *Three Japanese Lyrics.*

Delage says that you intended to speak to Diaghilev about me. . . . His publicity is attended to in the most careless manner; rather, it doesn't exist. Last year everything was done at the last minute (after my return from Paris). On the eve of the premiere, the public barely knew the subject. London is a slow-moving town. They say that the first six weeks of a new production do not count, because only after that do people begin to realize what is being performed! Newspaper publicity is essential. My idea would be to present a press agency with a season ticket . . . and as soon as I noticed that no publicity about the Ballets Russes had appeared in some time, I would provide the agency with some copy. . . . Naturally, I would have to be given day-to-day documentation, but M. Diaghilev's secretary could take charge of that. . . . I could also circulate news about his new productions and intentions constantly. . . . Moreover, I could become his official representative, because I have a great deal of experience. . . . But you know all of that, and I need only to activate negotiations with Diaghilev. . . .

At one time you mentioned a St. Petersburg journal for which I could write in French or in English, to be translated there. Can something be done about it? . . .

Your devoted   Evans

EVANS TO STRAVINSKY   *September 22, 1917*

. . . I have not heard from you in a long time. Are you by chance still sulking because my approaches to Beecham at the beginning of the war did not turn out well? . . .

Recently I saw some little pieces of yours, published by [Adolphe] Henn in Geneva, which I would like to have sent to me. I have not received any of your works since *The Nightingale* and the *Japanese,* and it is time to begin performing you in England again. . . .

I had an interesting discussion with the director of Pianola. I explained to him that the issue is not to make pianola arrangements of existing piano or orchestral scores, but rather to invite modern composers to create an independent, pianolistic style. . . . Since Casella is here now, I obtained permission to have him compose something. . . . Reflect on the possibilities of this instrument a bit, and if you are interested, I will take charge of the rest. I also proposed to the [director] that he invite composers to make pianola adaptations of their works. . . .

STRAVINSKY TO EVANS   *Morges*
                                                  October 28, 1917

London

Dear friend,

Along with these lines I am sending you a copy of my new work, the Etude for Pianola. Would you be so kind as to tell the director of the Orchestrelle Company that I am prepared to sell [Orchestrelle] the work on the following conditions: (1) In exchange for five hundred (500) Swiss francs, I cede all rights for use of this work on pianola or other mechanical instruments. . . . (2) I renounce my author's rights . . . in regard to performance of this work in public places on pianola or other mechanical instruments. . . . (3) On the other hand, I reserve the right to arrange this work for any ensemble of instruments (chamber or orchestral) and all author's rights thereof. (4) I also cede to the aforementioned company the right to publish a pianola part of this work such as it is in the manuscript (or the copy). . . .

I would like to say two words about *Petrushka* and *Le Sacre du printemps* (for pianola). I do not understand a single word of the Orchestrelle Company's reply about these works. . . . Through the intermediary of my lawyer (M. Philippe Dunant, Geneva), I accepted their conditions (!!!). I informed them that I disagree only with the question of giving an English company control of my author's rights (and this only for the time being, because I will surely do so later). Nevertheless, this point is not even included in the contract. For this reason I will send [Orchestrelle] the control stamps each time they place the rolls up for sale (they need only refer to their copies of our correspondence and my lawyer's replies). Thus I was in complete agreement with their offer and proposed only certain minor modifications that would in no way alter the principal points of the contract. They proposed—according to the new English law—2½ percent for each roll of *Petrushka* and 5 percent for *Sacre*, and agreed to provide me with all of the particulars and the number of rolls of each work. I accepted all of that, because they told me that another arrangement (a lump sum) would be impossible, given the new English law, which accords everyone the right to cut the work into rolls once it is published.

Let me tell you frankly that I would prefer a lump sum, rather than having to scrutinize every penny in executing control. Besides (in response to your letter), I do not think that I will have time to arrange *Petrushka* and *Sacre* for pianola. Still, time is money . . . and these gentlemen surely will not want to spend the sums that this task will require.

Give me your advice quickly, my dear, as well as good news of yourself. Best to you.

                                                  Igor Stravinsky

EVANS TO STRAVINSKY   *November 11, 1917*

. . . The manuscript [of the Etude for Pianola] has not yet been delivered to me,[3] and I suppose that the censor still has it, which does not surprise me at all, since the *boches* now mistrust even their own music.

EVANS TO STRAVINSKY   *November 17, 1917*

. . . Apparently [under English law] a lump sum can be paid only if the work was composed specifically for pianola. . . . As you say, the agreement with [Orchestrelle] was complete, but one question remains. You must send your 96 control stamps, half at 2½ percent and half at 5 percent, and the rolls will be ready as soon as possible.

Concerning your Etude for Pianola, [Orchestrelle] agrees to pay you 500 Swiss francs, provided that the [company] is not bound necessarily to [pay the same amount] in the future (depending on the success of this experimental venture). . . . Thus the only obstacle arises because of the absurd law. . . .

Cordially yours,   Edwin Evans

STRAVINSKY TO EVANS   *November 24, 1917*

Thank you, dear friend, for your great zeal. I think that I could give in on the question of the arrangement of this music, which I had wanted to retain for myself. The contract should therefore read: "In exchange for the sum of five hundred (500) Swiss francs, I cede to the Orchestrelle Company (London) *all of my rights* to my work entitled 'Etude for Pianola,' reserving author's rights for performances of the aforementioned work in public. On the other hand, the Orchestrelle Company agrees not to make arrangements of this work for instruments other than pianola (or [other] mechanical piano[s and] the phonograph).* . . .

Your   Igor Stravinsky

* I.e., the Orchestrelle Company's rights include these instruments.

EVANS TO STRAVINSKY   *December 11, 1917*

. . . The new conditions proposed in your last letter create new difficulties. . . . I think that to retain the right [for performance in public] would yield minimum results. . . . You would do best to cede this point and to receive the agreed sum directly from the company with a simple contract. Obviously, if we succeed in

---

[3] The manuscript arrived two days later.

establishing this kind of [pianolistic] music . . . you could profit by demanding
more advantageous conditions, but for that you must wait a bit. . . .

> Cordially yours,   Edwin Evans

STRAVINSKY TO EVANS

[No date]
[Draft of a letter]

. . . Thus Aeolian must [illegible] in the limits of the 4-hand (20-finger) parts,
which the company possesses, and the few pages of special arrangement that I
am in the process of making. I will send you these pages in ten days. I will also
send you a little list of metronomic mistakes and other things I have noticed in
Petrushka.

> Cordially yours,   I. Stravinsky

EVANS TO STRAVINSKY   *April 30, 1918*

. . . I have made several attempts but can do nothing with your *Ragtime* without
having the music at hand. Everyone likes the idea of it, but they all request to
see it. . . . I am convinced that I could place this composition favorably. . . .

Pribaoutki, sung by Mrs. Olga Haley, was a great success. She will sing it
again this season. . . .

STRAVINSKY TO EVANS

Morges
November 19, 1918

London

Dear Evans,

Here are the exact details that you request of me in your telegram of the
15th, and which you might convey, if need be, to the editor who addressed himself to you.

Histoire du soldat, recently completed and performed, is eminently suitable for theatrical and musical exploitation, and it should interest a serious publisher. He should be informed that my terms (and Ramuz's), for performing
rights and an edition of the music, are the following:

1. The authors demand the sum of 600 francs an evening (the length of
the piece) and that the publisher notify me each time he undertakes to negotiate for a presentation.

2. The authors agree to relinquish all editorial rights (Russia excepted)
for the lump sum of 15,000 francs. Please call the publisher's attention to the
fact that the piece would be commercially very advantageous for him, since the
music, without any special changes, can be played perfectly well in concert as a
suite. In addition, arranged for piano, or for various instruments, this suite it-

self can be broken down into several pieces—marches, violin arias, piano solos, dances, etc.

Then again, the publisher must be told that we (Ramuz and I) are negotiating with a publisher here for a deluxe edition of the piece, a *very limited* edition that would sell for not less than 100 francs a copy. This business would not harm his interests, but, on the contrary, it *could be useful to him* in case he would like to take a certain number of copies on consignment. The deluxe edition would appear in *facsimile,* that is, Ramuz's entire text in manuscript, my piano reduction (only piano) in manuscript, and the sketches of the painter René Auberjonois—all would be reproduced just as they are.

In the event that this proposition does not suit the publisher, *but only in that event,* mention *Les Noces villageoises,* [whose rights] I would cede to him (only with the French text, with the right to translate into English*) for 22,000 francs (Russia excepted), with 800 francs for staged performances, retaining for me [the right] to demand a higher price for premieres. As in the case of *Histoire du soldat,* the publisher must likewise notify me of any negotiations that he expects to have with producers.

1.   Quite apart from all of this, I would like to sell the Four Russian Songs for children (French text by Ramuz, with the right to translate into English**), songs with piano, of which I have already spoken to you.

2.   Three pieces for solo clar [inet]

3.   Four a cappella choruses [Podblyudnye]

(1)   Children's songs (Russia excepted)—2,000 francs

(2)   Three pieces for clarinet (Russia excepted)—1,000 francs

(3)   A cappella choruses (Russia excepted)—1,000 francs

It is understood that I retain all performance rights, as well as my reproduction rights for mechanical instruments, for all of my works.

As for the *Ragtime,* do not mention it, since I am in the process of selling it elsewhere. If this does not work out, I will speak to you about it again.

There you have it, my dear Evans, that is all at the moment. I await your response.

Cordially, your   Igor Stravinsky

* Or other language except Russian
** Or other language except Russian

STRAVINSKY TO EVANS   *April 1, 1929*

My dear Evans,

Thank you for your kind letter.

I will be in London to record with Aeolian on May 15, 16, 17, and 18. At the same time, I may do a BBC broadcast concert, unless they insist on the date they proposed (in June). I must settle this question before I can offer a date for my appearance with Goossens.[4]

As you see, I give an in-principle acceptance of your proposition. I say in-principle because I do not yet know if it will be possible for the Goossens venture to pay my customary fee of 100 guineas. I must tell you frankly that even if the sum seems too high, it is not possible for me to lower it; this is a condition that I would not change for anything in the world. Another condition of mine is to give 10 percent to the person who obtains an engagement for me. Consequently, I would give you 10 percent of my honorarium if the concert takes place.

Perhaps you could arrange with Clark[5] to group the two engagements (BBC and Goossens) in June. As you see, I have come back to Clark's idea of the month of June. I fear that I will not have the necessary time in May, since I must be in Paris on the 19th, 20th, etc.

In awaiting your reply, I send you, my dear Evans, my faithful and fond regards.

STRAVINSKY TO EVANS

London

Maison Pleyel
252, rue du Faubourg St.-Honoré
Paris
December 13, 1929

My dear Evans,

What you have been asked to request of me is completely contrary to my beliefs. The first request—for a few words of greeting—is inoffensive and can be satisfied. But the second is a subject that, in my opinion, should never be touched upon. In effect, what can I think of the future (which does not exist, because it *is* the future)? Also, I prefer not to make pronouncements on the past, because it no longer exists. As for the present, since I am part of it myself, I refrain from talking about it, not being certain of the soundness of my opinions. Try, my dear Evans, to make these gentlemen understand my embarrassment, and beg them not to ask me to reconsider my refusal.

For the greeting, be kind enough to send me the text (which you will certainly do better than I can). I will sign it and send it to them; only do not forget to give me the address of the *Musical Courier*. I am here until Saturday, then leave for Nice.

Yours very cordially,   Igor Stravinsky

---

[4] Eugene Goossens (1893–1962), conductor and composer.
[5] Edward Clark (1888–1962), conductor, personal friend of Stravinsky.

EVANS TO STRAVINSKY

Earl's Court
London SW10
December 30, 1930

My dear friend,

I have been commissioned to write the program notes for the radio concert on January 28,[6] as well as for the one on March 3 at Madame Courtauld's, and I ask for your assistance. I scarcely know two of the pieces, the Capriccio and the Four Etudes, and I have never heard another, the overture to *Mavra* (I only have the piano reduction). Furthermore, I am not at all satisfied with the notes on the Piano Concerto that I did for Goossens, and, with the aid of your instructions, I want to rewrite them. I have the piano reductions only of the Concerto and *Apollon*. Numerous musical examples can be used for the radio, but not for Madame Courtauld's.

No doubt you have notes that have already appeared in programs of concerts in which these works were played, in which case I beg you to send them to me. If not, please come to my aid and give me any details that occur to you. It is evident that, with the little I have now, I will not be able to do the job adequately.

Also, if it does not disturb you too much, I ask you to send me the book, or books, about you that have recently been published in France. . . .

The Music Club would like to give an evening in your honor when you are here for the Courtauld concert. The four hundred members are the elite of our musicians and include as many professionals as amateurs. I recommend that you accept in good grace. Happy New Year.

Friendly greetings,   Edwin Evans

---

[6] This concert was conducted by Ernest Ansermet, who had assisted Stravinsky a few days before at one of the most unusual recording sessions of the composer's life. In May 1930, the jazz musician Jack Hylton had asked Stravinsky for permission to arrange parts of *Mavra*, including the duet and quartet (numbers 6 and 8), for the Hylton Band, substituting instruments for vocal parts. Hylton wrote to Stravinsky from London, September 10, 1930: "I am coming to Paris next week for a few days, and I am writing to ask you if it is possible for us to meet and discuss the music which you honored me by asking me to play." In the December 23 issue of *Le Petit Marseillais*, Hector Fraggi noted that Hylton was "preparing his arrangement of *Mavra*," interpreting this as a sign of rapprochement between serious and popular music. On January 6, 1931, G. G. Païchadze, Stravinsky's publisher, informed him: "I immediately made arrangements to have the [*Mavra*] score sent to Berlin, and I have had a letter from Hylton confirming that he has received it." In a letter to Arthur Brooks of Columbia Gramophone, London, February 6, 1931, Stravinsky denied that he knew anything about Hylton's recording but admitted that Hylton had been given permission to make the arrangement: "My agreement was simply to listen to his arrangement, which I did, recently, in London, and to give J. Hylton certain necessary instructions before the final recording of the excerpt, so that the arrangement would conform to the original version of the work." On February 12, Stravinsky wrote to Hylton, warning him that

EVANS TO STRAVINSKY

1 St. Nicholas Road
London SW17
August 26, 1937

My dear Stravinsky,

I see that on October 18 you are conducting the [English] premiere of *Jeu de cartes* [at the BBC], and I remind you that it is my job to write the program notes. As you know, I want these to be according to your wishes; hence you would be very kind (1) to ask your publisher to send me the music, and (2) to tell me what you think is important to be said. If a review that you find good has appeared in America or elsewhere, perhaps you could send it to me; I will certainly return it.

   We see each other very rarely nowadays.

Friendly greetings,   your devoted Edwin Evans

P.S. Musical examples are included in these programs.[7]

STRAVINSKY TO EVANS

Sancellemoz
Haute-Savoie
September 4, 1937

My dear friend,

I am immediately sending a note to my publisher, B. Schotts, asking them to give you the *Jeu de cartes* pocket score and piano reduction, as well as a clipping, from the American press, on my new ballet and on its performance under my direction (April 27 and 28, 1937) at the Metropolitan Opera House in New York.

   In a few days I will go to Venice to conduct a concert performance of the work—like the one in London—at the Biennale (September 12).

   I will be very happy to see you again. The last time [I was in London], when I conducted *Perséphone,* you did not come to see me, and I was saddened; I hope that this time it will not be the same.

   With my faithful regards to you.

Igor Stravinsky

---

the recording, soon to be released, "must not use my name otherwise than as the composer of the original." No doubt Stravinsky reworked the arrangement, and he appears to have conducted some portion of the recording. (See photograph.)

[7] Evans printed *Jeu de carte*'s quotation from Rossini in music type but failed to identify it. Stravinsky wrote in the margin: "I thought he was going to tell us about the *Barbiere.*"

ALFREDO CASELLA[1] TO THE STRAVINSKYS

Villa Borghese
29, blvd. Victor Hugo
Neuilly-sur-Seine

Here we are, in a deliciously serene spot. Soon we hope to hear (1) that your convalescence is coming along as well as possible, and (2) what the Lausanne doctor has to say.[3] Many best wishes from both of us.

A. Casella

CASELLA TO THE STRAVINSKYS

Ustilug

We know that you are in Russia, dear friends. How was the trip? How are you both? We are eager to know. We are here in absolute solitude and tranquility, a very good place for working.

Many best wishes.

Casella

P.S. Don't forget the portrait that you promised.

---

[1] The composer Alfredo Casella (1883–1947) was one of the first and most active champions of Stravinsky's music, as conductor, pianist, and critic. Casella's support continued throughout the 1930s (on April 21, 1939, the editor of *La Revue Musicale* wrote to Stravinsky that "Casella would be happy to collaborate" in the forthcoming special Stravinsky number) and during World War II (Stravinsky's friend Yuri Schleiffer-Ratkov wrote from Rome, May 7, 1942: "*Histoire du soldat* and *Renard* have been given, both of them staged, at the Theatre of the Arts, and the *Sacre* at the Opera, with ballet, as well as *Mavra*, in my translation; this spring Casella conducted *Noces*, with ballet. . . . Send me a few words in care of the Baroness de Steiger, Hotel Blockenhof, Zürich"). French is the original language of all the correspondence.

[2] Picture postcard of the Château de l'Aunay.

[3] Stravinsky returned from Paris to Russia via Switzerland.

[4] Picture postcard of the dolmen of the Grotte des Fées, Nettray.

CASELLA TO STRAVINSKY   *Vouvray*
                                                    August 19, 1913
Ustilug

Dear friend,

I have wanted to write to you for three weeks now, but the sky and countryside of Touraine encourage an epistolary sluggishness. Do not hold it against me. We had news about you via a letter from Madame Stravinsky, promising a letter from you shortly, which is much desired. I would like to have fresh news about the health of the entire S. family, as well as about your work.

We have been here in solitude for six weeks. Friday we go to the Vendée for two weeks, and we will spend the month of September in Florence and Venice.

I have worked hard here. I composed a song for solo voice and orchestra, based on a wonderful poem by my compatriot Carducci, entitled "Notte di Maggio." It is 11–12 minutes long. I am pleased, for I consider it my best piece. Certain spots bear a slight resemblance to *Sacre*. . . .

I think you will like this piece. I hope to have it orchestrated by my return. The *Sacre* keeps us company. We cherish it more each day.

Send news; do not be lazy. Write to Paris; our mail will be forwarded. Many affectionate thoughts from your friend

                                                          Casella

CASELLA TO STRAVINSKY   *Paris*
                                                  January 18, 1914
Clinique Mont-Riant   *[Telegram]*
Lausanne

Congratulations on your little daughter [Milene. We] have written today [about the] triumph [of your Japanese] melodies. Best,   Casella

CASELLA TO STRAVINSKY   *May 26, 1915*
                                                       [Postcard]
Clarens

Dear old friend,

Monteux is presenting four concerts at the Odéon in June, in an attempt to secure engagements for the summer, which promises to be a devastating one for the poor musicians. . . . I will conduct two of those concerts. In view of the favors that this orchestra has done for you, could you make a fraternal gesture? Could you authorize me to use the *Petrushka* parts in the concert of June 27 without paying the rental fee? I assure you that the poor musicians are really in a miserable way, and I hope that you will want to render them this service. And I will be glad to conduct *Petrushka* in Paris!

I have not yet been called to active duty, but that could happen later.
And Ricordi? And Diaghilev?
Long live Russia! Long live Italy!

Yours,   Casella

CASELLA TO STRAVINSKY

Morges

Prascorsano
Turin
July 13, 1915
[Postcard]

Dear old friend,

I have been officially nominated to the Accademia di Santa Cecilia. Write to congratulate me, if for no other reason. You have not written since March. What do you have against me?

I am working hard. And my piano piece, is it on the way?[5] We are very well. Send news.

Our best to you both.

Yours,   Casella

CASELLA TO STRAVINSKY

Dear old friend,

Prascorsano
Turin
September 3, 1915
[Postcard]

Today I am sending you my piano pieces. Excuse me for sending them separately; I have only one copy. In a few days we leave for Paris, where we will stay until October 12 or 15, before going to Rome. The Rome address will be: Liceo Musicale S. Cecilia, via dei Greci 18.

Write soon. What are you doing? I have done a lot of work. Four big songs on the Tagore-Gide *Gitanjali;* then four *Films,* inspired by cinematographic views of the war, for piano 4-hands. And my piano piece. When will you send it? What shall I do with the *Petrushka* score that I have?

Your affectionate   Casella

CASELLA TO STRAVINSKY

Morges

via Basilicata 13
Rome
March 17, 1916
[Postcard]

Dear Igor,

This morning I gave instructions to send the money due you [for performing *Petrushka*] directly to you. I hope that you will receive it soon. I think that the amount is 125 francs, correct? But must an additional sum be paid for the second performance, which took place five days later? In that case, you must ad-

---

[5] The March, dedicated to Casella, from Stravinsky's Three Easy Pieces.

dress yourself to the administrator of the Accademia, M. Martinez, via Vittoria.

I have the parts at my house. I am thinking of conducting it in Milan in the spring. I am working hard. Write more often, you naughty boy.

Many best regards.

Your   Casella

CASELLA TO STRAVINSKY   *via Basilicata 13*
                                                                    Rome
Morges   *April 3, 1916*
                                                              [Postcard]

Dear Igor,

M. Martinez will send you the fee for the second rental. I will conduct three concerts in Milan, April 16, 17, and 19. Try to make a little detour there.

Is is true that [Leo] Ornstein played some new pieces by you in New York? If so, how can they be obtained? R.S.V.P. He also played five of my *"nove pezzi."*

I am writing a sonatina, which you might enjoy.

In Milan I will play the Berceuse from *Firebird*. Marinetti is supposed to give *Petrushka* there soon. If you continue, your popularity in Italy will outshine Verdi's. Write promptly. Come to Milan.

Affectionately,   Casella

CASELLA TO STRAVINSKY   *Milan*
                                                          April 15, 1916
Morges   *[Telegram]*

I conduct *Petrushka* here Scala orchestra night of Wednesday 19th. Come. Casella

CASELLA TO STRAVINSKY   *Milan*
                                                          April 20, 1916
Morges   *[Postcard]*

Dear Igor,

Petrushka (conducted by the undersigned) enjoyed an enthusiastic success yesterday at the Concerti Sinfonica. The Scala orchestra took an extraordinary pleasure in playing it.

Did you receive the communication that I sent Saturday asking you to come to Milan? Why didn't you come?

I embrace you.

Casella

I am returning to Rome.

CASELLA TO STRAVINSKY   *Rome*
                                                  April 29, 1916
Morges

Dear Igor,

Thank you for the nice letter; I am sad to learn that an operation prevented you from witnessing the triumph of *Petrushka*. I have asked the Augusteo to send you the package and money. You will definitely receive them, but you know that we are never in a rush here (not even to be paid). Tell me one thing: could you have a copy made for me of your Polka and March [from Three Easy Pieces], 4-hands? I would so love to have them! Thank you in any case. I sent you my *Films*. Soon you will receive other 4-hand pieces (*Pupazzetti*).
    Many best regards.

                                                      Casella

CASELLA TO STRAVINSKY   *Rome*
                                               November 29, 1916
Morges   *[Postcard]*

Dear old friend,

Do you have the orchestra parts of your arrangement of the Berceuse and Finale from *Firebird*? Could you give them to Molinari?[6] Reply quickly.
    I work hard and embrace you.

                                              Your   Casella

CASELLA TO STRAVINSKY   *Rome*
                                               November 29, 1916
Morges   *[Postcard]*

Dear old friend,

I forgot to ask whether you could also lend Molinari the parts for *Scherzo fantastique*. Reply quickly.
    Here we need: eight first violins, eight second violins, five violas, six cellos, five basses.

                                              Yours,   Casella

---

[6] The conductor Bernardino Molinari (1880–1952), highly regarded by Stravinsky.

CASELLA TO STRAVINSKY   *Rome*
                                                  February 22, 1917

Morges

Dear Igor,

My Italian Music Society is giving six concerts of music by young Italian and
Allied [composers] in March–April. During the second two weeks, I would love
to present your 4-hand music. Could you give it to me? That would be a great
joy for us. Perhaps you will be coming to Rome at that time and will play it with
me? R.S.V.P. (quickly). How is your health?

                          Affectionately yours,   Casella

CASELLA TO STRAVINSKY   *Rome*
                                                   March 4, 1917

Morges

Dear Igor,

Our Italian Music Society concert, in which I wanted to play your 4-hand
pieces, has been advanced to the 23rd of this month. Diaghilev tells me that he
has the Polka. If you consent to this performance, would you, as I hope, send
me your music through the diplomatic channel, i.e., Khvoshchinsky? I feel certain that it would arrive too late via ordinary mail.

    I hope to have the manuscript soon. Thanks, and many best wishes.

                                                        Casella

                                            Società Italiana di Musica
CASELLA TO STRAVINSKY   *via Ennio Quirino Visconti 2*
                                                         Rome
Dear old friend,   *April 22, [1917]*

Our friend Malipiero, who is going to Switzerland for a month, will deliver this
letter, containing our fondest thoughts. We are happy that our friend's trip will
afford us some news about you, of which we have been deprived for so long. We
hope that the news will be good. What are you doing? What are you working
on? Malipiero will give you the details of my activities here in Rome, and on the
increasing importance of our movement to renew Italy.

    May I ask you to send me—via Malipiero—a signed photograph of your-
self? I have only an old and mediocre one, and I surely deserve a new one.
Thank you.

    See you soon, I hope. I would like to go to Switzerland next winter, as a pi-
anist, composer, conductor, lecturer, etc. You have influence there; try to obtain some engagements for me. . . .

    I embrace you.

                                          Your   Casella

At the last minute Malipiero's plans have changed, and he is not going. But I send this letter all the same, asking you to reply.

CASELLA TO STRAVINSKY

Morges

Dear old friend,

Thank you for the pieces, which have already given me a great deal of pleasure. I await the other Stravinsky publications impatiently.

What are you and yours doing? I am working hard, composing a poem for piano, orchestrating my *Films*, etc. We go to France on August 5.

A bientôt, and many fond wishes.

Your   Casella

Best to Tyrwhitt,[7] if he is there.

CASELLA TO STRAVINSKY

Dear friend,

I have not had news from you directly in a century. How are you and yours? We are well enough, after spending a few months in France and England. I am working steadily. This summer I completed a poem for piano (12 minutes), and now I am arranging the future pieces, *Siciliana e burlesca,* for piano and string trio. I am also finishing the orchestration of my *Films* [originally] for [piano] 4-hands.

This winter our Society plans to do a rather large number of concerts. We intend to present your *Japanese Lyrics,* and also your 4-hand [pieces]. When is the new series due to appear? Also, do you have any new chamber music that you would entrust to us? Reply without delay, telling me, in addition, whether you have the parts for the *Japanese Lyrics.*

I learned with pleasure that you have written some music for pianola; while in London, I was invited to do some [pianola] pieces, and I am enjoying the work.

I am sending you the first issue of our *Ars Nova;* I hope that it will interest you. We wish to create an interesting and objective voice for the arts. In the next issue we will publish your portrait, along with an article about you by Vuillermoz. Would you be so kind as to write a short article on a subject of your choice (for publication in our review), and in the language most convenient for you (even Russian; I would have it translated)? A brief article concerning contemporary Russia and its musical future, as you see it, would be opportune at the moment, when, unfortunately, Russophiles are rare!!!

[7] See the following chapter.

Write soon. And please share our fondest regards with Madame Stravinsky.

Your   Casella

CASELLA TO STRAVINSKY   *Cincinnati, Ohio*
April 6, 1923

Dear friend,

The International Composers' Guild, a New York society for modern music, would like to include your name on its list of members. Since I am a member of the committee myself, I ask you to accept. The society is infinitely serious and does good work for us.

My second American tour was a great success. I have been re-engaged for five similar tours. Did I tell you that this winter I played your Piano-Rag Music—which I like enormously—in Vienna, Prague, Berlin, Milan, Rome, Paris, New York, and Chicago? But I would like some compensation for this propaganda. Send me a photograph of yourself, more recent than the ancient one that I have in my studio. Thank you.

We will leave America on the 14th and be in Rome on the 24th. My address is still via Ennio Quirino Visconti 2, Rome. I have a new chamber-music society. At the beginning of May we are having many concerts, in which we will give the Italian premieres of your *Berceuses du chat* and your Concertino (played by the Brussels Pro Arte). It seems that Part One of the *Sacre,* conducted by Molinari, enjoyed a magnificent success at the Augusteo.

A thousand best wishes from my wife. I embrace you.

Casella

STRAVINSKY TO CASELLA   *167, blvd. Carnot*
Nice
A. Casella   *Cable address: Stravigor, Nice*
Presidente   *August 31, 1925*
"Corporazione della nuove musiche"
Liceo Benedetto Marcello
Venice

Mr. President,

I thank you for your letter of August 25 and for the information it contains.

I want to take this opportunity to tell you how much I appreciate the efforts on the part of the Swiss and Italian sectors to ensure my personal participation in the Venice festival. My conscience would be troubled for accepting their generosity if I were not, on my part, making an equivalent gesture by requesting only one-half of the fee that I charge everywhere else in Europe.*

Thus we are in agreement, and I will come to Venice on September 6.

I would ask you to do whatever is necessary with regard to the Ministry of Foreign Affairs to ensure that my passport, as well as that of Mlle Vera Sudeikina, who will be accompanying me, are stamped with visas at the Italian Consulate in Nice. If for any reason this request cannot be satisfied, I would unfortunately be obliged to cancel my trip to Venice.

In anticipation of a cabled confirmation concerning these two visas, please accept this expression of my sincere respect.

> Igor Stravinsky,
> Composer of Music

P.S. I would appreciate it if you would mention in your cable whether my concert will be taking place during the afternoon or the evening.

* My regular fee is 10,000 francs (regardless of the number of works I perform).

CASELLA TO STRAVINSKY

Voreppe

Milan
May 12, 1932
[Postcard] [8]

Dear friend,

Saturday night (the 14th) I will conduct the Symphony of Psalms here at the Scala (with choruses and orchestra of the theatre). I hope to give a good performance. I studied the work with your records. Come and hear it. It would be a joy for you.

> Your   Casella [9]

CASELLA TO STRAVINSKY

21, rue Viète (near the Lycée Carnot)

Dear Igor,

Osborne Hôtel
4 et 6, rue St.-Roch
Paris
February 3, 1934
[Pneumatique]

My Concerto will be presented tomorrow by the O [rchestre] S [ymphonique de] P [aris] around 5:45. Here are two tickets. I hope with all my heart to have the chance to see you and especially that the work will please you.

> Affectionate regards from your   Casella

---

[8] Picture postcard of Mantegna's *Judith*.

[9] The postcard was also signed by Virgilio Mortari (b. 1902, composer), Guido Agosto, and Domenico de' Paoli (author of a monograph on Stravinsky), who noted that the card was written "after a rehearsal of the Symphony of Psalms."

CASELLA TO STRAVINSKY   *Rome*
                                                  October 28 [1930s]

Dear Stravinsky,

My friend Pellegrini is the percussionist for the E.I.A.R. [Italian Radio] orchestra of Rome and has played your *Noces* with me throughout Italy. He is also
the brother of the percussionist who is currently with the Scala of Milan and
formerly played *Histoire du soldat* in Rome and elsewhere. The Luigi Pellegrini
who will give you this letter would like to have . . . a signed photograph of you,
for, it seems, he was very dejected to have been deprived of what his colleagues
in the orchestra received. If it would be possible for you to gratify his desire, you
will at the same time have given real pleasure to your old friend Casella, who
embraces you.

Luigi Pellegrini
viale Angelico 67
Rome

CORRESPONDENCE WITH

1916 ⚜ 1939

GERALD TYRWHITT *(Lord Berners)*

GERALD TYRWHITT[1] TO STRAVINSKY

British Embassy
Rome[2]
May 13, 1916

Dear M. Stravinsky,

I was overjoyed to learn, through Madame Khvoshchinsky,[3] that you will consent to see me and give me some guidance if I come to Switzerland for a few days. I fear that I will be a nuisance to you; nevertheless, I do not hesitate to accept your kind offer, for a half hour of conversation with you will undoubtedly mean more to me than a century of [lessons with academics].

I could come to Switzerland at the beginning of June, probably around the 10th. Please inform me as to whether that date is convenient for you.

Balla[4] asked me to give you his best regards. I also relay to you his cry: *"Viva l'Italia!,"* but you must take care in unwrapping this [exclamation], because it is deafeningly loud.

With a thousand thanks for the kindness you have shown me.

Gerald Tyrwhitt

TYRWHITT TO STRAVINSKY

June 26, 1916
[Telegram]

Morges

Thanks [for your] telegram. Hope to see you next Monday. Friendly greetings, Tyrwhitt

---

[1] Gerald Tyrwhitt (1883–1950), composer, painter, writer, succeeded to the Barony of Berners in 1918. Stravinsky and he were good friends before World War II. Tyrwhitt's letters are the first to reveal that Diaghilev stayed in Viareggio for a time in the summer of 1917. French is the original language of all the correspondence.

[2] Tyrwhitt was an official in the Embassy. Unless otherwise noted, all of his letters come from this address.

[3] Wife of Vasily Khvoshchinsky. See Diaghilev's letters to Stravinsky of March 3, 1915, and November 20, 1916, and Stravinsky's letter to Diaghilev of November 21, 1916, in the present volume.

[4] Giacomo Balla (1871–1958), the Futurist painter.

TYRWHITT TO STRAVINSKY   *August 16, [1916]*

Dear M. Stravinsky,

The first letter I write on returning to Rome is this one, to thank you once again for your kindness during my stay in Morges. I recall with joy our charming strolls together.

    I just saw Vasily Khvoshchinsky; he leaves tonight for San Sebastián, where his wife has fallen ill. For an entire month now she has had a fever and is not even ambulatory. He informed me that Diaghilev and the whole company will come to Rome this winter and stay until spring, when they go to America. I hope that this is true, but their plans are always subject to change.

    The other day I was in Milan and saw San Martino. I told him that you never received the money for the second performance of *Petrushka*.[5] He replied that this is Toscanini's business and that I should discuss it with Casella. At the moment, Casella is not in Rome, but when he returns I shall speak to him. San Martino affirmed that he definitely wants you to conduct in Rome. I suggested (very politely, of course) that in this case he should accept your conditions without haggling![6]

    I hope that your excursions to Bern and Lucerne were successful and salu-

---

[5] Toscanini's second performance, at the Augusteo in Rome.

[6] San Martino had written to Stravinsky, August 26, 1915: "I am writing to remind you of the promise you made last year that you would conduct here in the 1915–16 season. . . . I am certain that . . . you will try to fulfill this promise, which is very precious to us, and . . . I would be grateful if you would inform me as to when you would be available to come to Rome." San Martino wrote again on September 29: "I am infinitely appreciative of your kind letter, and we are all very happy about your acceptance. So much sympathy and admiration surrounds your name here that you will undoubtedly enjoy an enormous success. The pieces that you propose make up a good program. Before replying in detail, however, I would like to know: (1) Whether you want to conduct only your compositions or the other half of the program as well. You did say that you wanted us to reserve only the first part of the program for you, but we are in doubt as to whether you meant only in your capacity as composer, or as conductor, too. (2) Is November 28 the only date you have free? I ask you not because this date is impossible, but because the Roman season will be better two or three weeks later." A month later, San Martino wrote to Diaghilev: "M. Stravinsky wrote requesting an honorarium of 2,000 francs, plus travel expenses, to conduct half a concert. You are well aware of my strong desire to have Stravinsky conduct in Rome, but the conditions he proposes are absolutely unacceptable. In the past twenty years we have never paid anyone a similar honorarium. . . . Always and without exception, we have paid a set fee. Besides, Stravinsky's value is in his composing, not in his conducting. . . . Nonetheless, we are so eager to have Stravinsky conduct here that we will make an exception and offer him 1,500 francs for the concert, everything included. Since I would be somewhat embarrassed to have this discussion directly with M. Stravinsky, . . . with whom you are much more intimate, I take the liberty of asking you to

tary. Here in Rome the overwhelming heat seems to have passed, and the weather is now magnificent.

Apparently the war is progressing. I really think that the *Autres Chiens*[7] are skewered (not to use the word of which your son is so fond!) and that the Germans soon will be as well.

This afternoon I see Balla, who will be happy to have news of you. We search for wonderful postcards to send you.

My best to Madame Stravinsky . . . and to [René] Morax and Madame [Henri] Bischoff.[8] *Mit herzlichen, hochwohlgeborenen Gruss!!* Good-bye, *à bientôt* in Rome, I hope.

Gerald Tyrwhitt

How sorry I am that the eau de vie [that we drank in Morges] cannot be found here!

TYRWHITT TO STRAVINSKY   *October 9, [1916]*

Dear M. Stravinsky,

Count San Martino has asked that I invite you to . . . conduct a concert of your works at the Augusteo, sometime between Christmas and Easter, at a date convenient for you.

If you accept (here I attach my personal wishes that you will reply affirmatively), he would like you to do *Le Sacre du printemps,* which has yet to be presented in Rome, and perhaps the Symphony [in E flat] as well. Would it also be possible to play the Chinese March from *The Nightingale?*

I had some news from the Khvoshchinskys in Leysin: I think you are the one who recommended Kurt Ort to them. I regret that Madame Khvoshchinsky will not return to Rome this year, but evidently she is feeling much better now.

Casella is in Paris and will come home at the end of the month. Imagine, he was accepted for military service then was promptly released when they discovered that the measure of his bust was off by some centimeters!

Please send me a note concerning the proposed concert, and please say yes.

---

act as my intermediary." (October 28) San Martino wrote to Diaghilev again on November 4: "I received your telegram. . . . I refuse to accept M. Stravinsky's conditions, which I deem unacceptable for all of the reasons I already gave you, which I can only reconfirm. The instructions for renting the parts, evidently intended as a joke, are somewhat belated. Under these conditions I can only beg your pardon for having caused you needless bother, and once again I thank you cordially for having taken this matter into your hands."

[7] I.e., *Autrichiens* (Austrians).

[8] Friends of Stravinsky in his Morges period. See the correspondence with C.-F. Ramuz in *S.S.C.* III.

As for the finances, San Martino assures me that he will not try to bargain you down. In any case, please give me your terms. If I recall correctly, you told me 2,000 [francs] in Morges, but since I am rather vague on these questions, you had better send confirmation. . . .

Friendly greetings,   Gerald Tyrwhitt

STRAVINSKY TO TYRWHITT   *Morges*
                                                        October 13, 1916

Dear friend Tyrwhitt,

Thank you for your kind letter. For the moment, I accept Count San Martino's proposition *in principle*—because the date, the program, and many other things must be decided. As for my honorarium, it is still the same in wartime: 2,000 Swiss francs, plus travel expenses, Lausanne–Rome, in first-class (*wagon-lit*). These are my terms for conducting a whole concert, not a half concert, as was the case last year (for which reason I lowered my fee for [the Accademia] Santa Cecilia).

I think that I will be able to obtain the Symphony, but not the *Sacre*, because it is in Berlin, the *boche* capital. Nevertheless, since I am in Switzerland, I will have someone try to get the orchestra parts of the work, for the full score is here with me—that is my advantage over the *boches*!!! San Martino, were he so inclined, could pay to have the parts copied. But these would have to be returned to me after the performance, since my publisher would not permit the parts of a rental work to remain permanently in the hands of a concert society.* If San Martino would agree to this, I could give the job to my copyist right away. Otherwise, I propose to do the *Firebird* Suite with the Berceuse and the Finale, which also have not been done in Rome, or *Fireworks*, which can be found in Geneva. The *Scherzo fantastique* presents a difficulty because the parts are in Russia, and Diaghilev has the orchestra score. The piece was printed by Jurgenson in Moscow,[9] and the supply of copies in Europe has been exhausted. But perhaps San Martino could obtain the work from J. & W. Chester (11 Great Marlborough Street, London). O. M. Kling is the proprietor of that company and the English representative of Jurgenson; Kling might also be able to furnish San Martino with the complete parts of the *Scherzo*, which would please me very much indeed!

1. The Symphony = ¾ hour
2. *Scherzo fantastique* = ¼ hour
3. *Fireworks* = 6 minutes
4. *Firebird* Suite = 30 minutes

---

[9] Less than three months after this letter, the *Scherzo* was presented as a ballet, *Les Abeilles,* at the Paris Opéra, with choreography by Léo Staats and conducted by Gabriel Grovlez.

I still have the orchestra score (Acts two and three) of *The Nightingale*. Conceivably, something could be done with that, but again the question of the parts arises. Reply quickly, and give my regards to Count San Martino. The two of us send our best wishes.

Igor Stravinsky

P.S. Please ask San Martino to inform the border patrol that I will be crossing into Italy carrying all of the music (so that Customs will not make trouble).

* In addition, [San Martino] would have to pay a performance fee of 125 Swiss francs, as [he did] for *Petrushka*.

TYRWHITT TO STRAVINSKY   *[November 1916]*

Dear friend,

I hope that you received the implements for packing tobacco. I spoke to Mlle Pecci[10] about facilitating your entry into Italy, and she will gladly see to it. She awaits word from you; write to Donna Anna Pecci, Château des Appénins, Montetan, Lausanne.

Try to advise her of your departure a week before, and she will write immediately to the Italian Legation in Bern and obtain a pass for you. You will still have to show your passport to the Italian authorities.

I leave tomorrow morning. Good-bye, and thank you again for the proofs. Regards to Madame Stravinsky and the children. Give my best to Queen Wilhelmina—formerly *Mouche*.

Your devoted   Gerald Tyrwhitt

P.S. Find enclosed one perfectly *boche* and idiotic postcard.[11]

STRAVINSKY TO TYRWHITT   *December 2, 1916*
                                                    [Draft of a telegram]

Please ask Diaghilev to send me [the] money. Have you received letters for him and Larionov? Friendly greetings,   Stravinsky

---

[10] Later, Countess Mimi Pecci-Blunt, a friend of Stravinsky from 1915 until after World War II, when she sponsored chamber-music concerts in her palace in Rome.
[11] The card shows a painting of Brahms with nude women in the clouds behind him. Tyrwhitt has added: "Why all of these nude women? I was always assured that Brahms was chaste."

TYRWHITT TO STRAVINSKY   *January 2, 1917*
                                                          [Telegram]

Morges

Diaghilev left for Paris, returning Rome soon. Friendly greetings,   Gerald Tyrwhitt

TYRWHITT TO STRAVINSKY   *February 11, [1917]*

Dear friend,

I gave your first telegram—about [South] America—to Diaghilev, and I hope
that you received mine.

    Diaghilev has left for Paris and will stay there ten days or so. Lately he has
been overwhelmed with work, and a little under the weather as well, which
probably explains his failure to write to you.

    Have you by chance heard anything from Klukovsky? As you know, he has
been in a sanitarium in Davos for the past two years. The Marchesa Casati sent
him several telegrams, inviting him to visit her in Rome: suddenly she received
a telegram from the [management of the] sanitarium stating that [Klukovsky]
had left for parts unknown, and since then no one has been able to discover
what he is doing or where he has gone. The director of the [Eden] Sanitarium
is German, and despite the admiration we all share for that charming nation, I
suspect some maleficence on his part. So if [Klukovsky] has contacted you,
please let me know. . . . I hope to see you soon in Rome.

                    Your devoted   Gerald Tyrwhitt

I was very impressed by your nomination of *"accademico onorario"* [to the Accademia di Santa Cecilia] !! I, too, am *"onorario"* but unfortunately not *"accademico"!!*

TYRWHITT TO STRAVINSKY   *March 13, 1917*

Dear friend,

Thank you for the letter. In accordance with your request, I told Diaghilev to
send you the money and to inform you of his plans. "Yes, yes," he replied, with
a benevolent smile, and I can't imagine why he does not capitulate. He is *very*
busy now, I know, and his plans are somewhat disorganized because of [the]
America[n tour]. The remainder of the company is returning from [South
America]. Diaghilev went to Naples, and I think that he will now proceed to
Spain and meet the company at [the boat]. They are working hard on a new
production for Rome, but the arrangements are not yet definite.

    Jean Cocteau and Picasso are in Rome. (At the moment they are in Naples
with Diaghilev, but I suppose that they will return to Rome in a few days.)
Larionov and Madame Goncharova have a big studio near the Riviera and are in

the process of painting the sets for Liadov's five little ballets [*Contes russes*]: *Baba-Yaga, Khorovod,* etc. (I have been there several times to help paint the sets!) A great Deperesque[12] work is also being prepared for your [*Song of the*] *Nightingale:* I saw the sets and costumes, which are very, very pretty. Balla is working for you as well and has already made some gigantic constructions.[13] Diaghilev promised to show them to me when they are completed. Bakst, also in Rome, has a studio in the same building as Larionov and is working on the Scarlatti ballet [*Les Femmes de bonne humeur*]. You are probably already aware of all of this, but you asked about what is going on here, so I have told you!

As soon as I know Diaghilev's plans I will write to you, but most likely he will have written to you himself before then. I hope to see you here soon. The spring weather is magnificent. Near my house I have discovered a tiny, dirty little theatre–music hall, which I want you to see when you come. They have a variety program and an orchestra *à tout crever.* I took Picasso and Cocteau there the other night, and they were thrilled. . . .

A bientôt, I hope. With friendly greetings,

your   Gerald Tyrwhitt

TYRWHITT TO STRAVINSKY *March 27, 1917*
[Telegram]

Morges

Ballets Russes premiere April 9. Diaghilev begs you to come immediately. Friendly greetings.   Gerald Tyrwhitt

March 28, 1917
[Telegram]

STRAVINSKY TO TYRWHITT

Have asked Diaghilev to send [the] money through Ansermet. When I receive it, will go to Bern to arrange passport.

TYRWHITT TO STRAVINSKY *April [?], 1917*
[Telegram]

Dear friend,

I hope that you enjoyed yourself in Naples and that the premiere[14] was successful. Best wishes to Picasso. Friendly greetings,   Gerald Tyrwhitt. I sent the telegram to Madame Stravinsky.

---

[12] Fortunato Depero (1892–1960), Futurist painter.

[13] For *Fireworks,* performed at the Teatro Costanzi on April 12.

[14] At the Teatro San Carlo. The evening had begun with Stravinsky's orchestration of "The Song of the Volga Boatmen" (to replace the hymn of the recently abdicated

TYRWHITT TO STRAVINSKY   *April 25, [1917]*

Dear friend,

Enclosed is the packet of letters that you left at my house. I will send the music,
dolls for the children, and other items by various means, but everything will arrive shortly. I hope that . . . the trip to Morges was not too unpleasant.

   The ballet comes to Rome today. I have not seen Diaghilev yet. I will ask
him for your *frac,* etc. I was so happy to have you here with me for those two
days; I only regret that you could not stay longer. . . .

                                                Your   Gerald Tyrwhitt

TYRWHITT TO STRAVINSKY   *May 18, [1917]*

Dear friend,

A box of cigarettes has been delivered here mysteriously, bearing no [return]
address. I think I remember that you were expecting some cigarettes. If so,
shall I send them to Morges right away, or wait until I come myself in June? To
send them might be a little complicated, but maybe I could do so one at a
time—not one cigarette at a time!!, which would be a protracted venture, but
perhaps one pack at a time (there are four altogether). Tell me your wishes. By
now all of your other things (the music I gave to Diaghilev, the dolls, etc.)
should have arrived.

   What happened in Paris?[15] I saw only one review, in *Le Figaro,* about the
first matinee, and from this I learned with dismay that Bakst's designs were not
well liked. Have your 4-hand pieces and songs appeared yet? I await them impatiently. . . .

                                          Your devoted   Gerald Tyrwhitt

TYRWHITT TO STRAVINSKY   *May 21, 1917*
                                                         [Telegram]

Morges

Delivered music and [Picasso's] portrait [to] Diaghilev. Friendly greetings,
Tyrwhitt

---

tsar), and the program consisted of *Las Meninas, Soleil de nuit,* and *Les Femmes de
bonne humeur.*

[15] Diaghilev had presented *Firebird* at the Théâtre du Châtelet on May 11, 14, and 16.
Abel Hermant reported in *Les Temps,* May 18, that in the Finale, "Prince Ivan, draped
in red, brandished a red standard."

TYRWHITT TO STRAVINSKY   *June 6, [1917]*

Dear friend,

Apparently the Marchese Durazzo is in Italy. If I find him, I will give him the cigarettes—if not, I will bring them to you myself.

I wrote to Madrid for the recordings you wanted, but since my friend has not replied, I fear that he is on vacation. If the records arrive in time, I will hand-deliver them to you. I expect to be in Switzerland around the 20th and hope that you will not already have left for the mountains.

I also hope that you received everything I entrusted to Diaghilev.

I left my apartment and now live in a little country house on the grounds of the Embassy. It is delicious, like living in the country.

Good-bye, dear friend. *A bientôt,* I hope. . . .

                                                        Gerald Tyrwhitt

TYRWHITT TO STRAVINSKY   *Thursday [July 1917]*

Dear friend,

I am very, very happy to have the proofs that you sent [of the *Pribaoutki*], and I cannot thank you enough. To receive them gave me great pleasure.

So, until next Sunday; I will be at the station in Aigle at 10:30. The train from Lausanne probably has a connection to Diablerets. Unless you instruct me otherwise, I will be at the Aigle depot at 10:30. Another train arrives in Aigle at 1:30. Would that perhaps be more convenient for you?

Morax informed me that you arrived without complications. I hope that Madame Stravinsky and the children are not suffering from the difference in atmospheric pressure. Best wishes to [all] . . . .

                                              Your   Gerald Tyrwhitt

TYRWHITT TO STRAVINSKY   *Saturday [July 1917]*

Dear friend,

I deeply regret that I will not be able to see you on Sunday. I must be in Lausanne in the evening and thus will not have time to go to Diablerets, but perhaps I could do so on the day I leave here. I will spend the night in Aigle, Saturday the 26th or 27th, and catch the train for Italy the next day.

I have not yet received the packages from [Adolphe] Henn; if they do not arrive soon, I will telephone him.

I do not know the name of Diaghilev's hotel, and Viareggio, like Lausanne, is nothing *but* hotels. If you wish to write to him, it would be easiest just to give me the letter, and I could find out his address upon my arrival in Italy.

Many thanks for the proofs; I am immensely pleased to have them. The *timbre* is beautiful and turned out very well, compensating for all of the annoyance that it caused.

Best wishes to Madame Stravinsky. I hope that the children are well and happy in their new abode [in Les Diablerets].

I will write to you when I have time to go up to Diablerets, I think Sunday the 27th.

Friendly greetings,   Gerald Tyrwhitt

TYRWHITT TO STRAVINSKY   *July 21, 1917*
                                                        [Telegram]

Diablerets

Regret impossible to visit Diablerets Sunday. Will arrange to do so later. Will write to you. Friendly greetings,   Gerald Tyrwhitt

---

TYRWHITT TO STRAVINSKY   *[July 1917]*
                                                        [Telegram]

Diablerets

I leave on the 27th. Will certainly see you before leaving. Friendly greetings, Tyrwhitt

---

TYRWHITT TO STRAVINSKY   *July 24, 1917*
                                                        [Telegram]

Diablerets

Will come to Diablerets Thursday if convenient [for you]. Friendly greetings, Tyrwhitt

---

TYRWHITT TO STRAVINSKY   *August 4, [1917]*

Dear friend,

Upon my return to Rome this morning I found a letter from Lady Cunard. She discussed *The Nightingale* designs with Beecham, who said that he would consider [lending them], although he intended to give *The Nightingale* in London soon and would therefore prefer not to part with them. But nothing is definite, and perhaps he will consent in the end.

I sent all of the packages of music to their respective destinations,[16] but I still have not managed to locate Diaghilev. Evidently he rented a

---

[16] Stravinsky had given several copies of his 4-hand pieces to Tyrwhitt "for distribution

house. I will wait until I have the exact address before forwarding your letter to him.

An extremely nice letter arrived from M. Kling—on the strength of your recommendation, no doubt. He has already sent me the proofs, which he printed without even waiting for the contract to be signed. I therefore find myself in an advantageous position and could wrangle over percentages for author's rights!

Best wishes . . . to all, and thanks again for your hospitality.

Your devoted   Gerald Tyrwhitt

TYRWHITT TO STRAVINSKY   *August 13, 1917*

Diablerets

Dear friend,

I wrote to the Orchestrelle Company and hope within a few days to have their reply, which I will forward to you by express mail. I enclosed your letter as well, so that they could examine the details.

Several days ago I saw Diaghilev, who was in Rome for one day. He is waiting for Madame Edwards at Viareggio and has not yet decided whether to spend the winter here or in Monte Carlo. When are you going [to Viareggio]? I gave [Diaghilev] your cigarettes, so that you will have them upon your arrival. I hope that Mlle Pecci will be able to facilitate the border-crossing and that you will not leave Italy without spending at least one day in Rome! . . .

Your devoted   Gerald Tyrwhitt

TYRWHITT TO STRAVINSKY   *August 28, [1917]*

Diablerets

Dear friend,

Only today did I receive the Orchestrelle Company's reply, which, though gratifying, certainly took them long enough.

Diaghilev was here twice, and I think that he went to Naples. When are you coming to Viareggio? It is still hot here, but I have a pretty little house in

---

in Italy," and a list in Stravinsky's hand names "Casella and Torrefranco," among other recipients. The copy for Madame Odescalchi is inscribed:

O - de - scal - chi   Cour La - ssan - ne   Vil - la   le Cè - dre Can - ton de   Vaud

the garden, and the heat does not affect me so. I hope that you will come soon. I am sending this letter to Diablerets, assuming that you are still there. . . .

Your   Gerald Tyrwhitt

TYRWHITT TO STRAVINSKY   *September 6, 1917*

Villa Rogivue
Morges

Dear friend,

A thousand thanks for the Five [Easy] Pieces—I am very happy to have them. I wrote immediately to Diaghilev, as you requested, but I have since learned that he left Viareggio (thanks to a microbe that Massine spotted on the beach).[17] Apparently [Diaghilev] has gone south, to Naples or Sorrento, but I suppose that his mail will be forwarded.

I hope you received the answer from the Orchestrelle Company that I sent to you.

When will you descend to the plains, and when will you come to Italy? It is very pleasant here now. . . .

How shall I answer the Orchestrelle [Company], or will you do so yourself?

Friendly greetings,   Gerald Tyrwhitt

As soon as I know Diaghilev's whereabouts I will attempt to send him another letter.

TYRWHITT TO STRAVINSKY   *September 15, 1917*

Dear friend,

I am truly sorry to learn of the loss that you have suffered.[18] You have all of my sympathy.

I already sent Diaghilev a telegram in regard to the money, but he is still off somewhere. He was in Naples and is now in Sorrento, I believe. I wrote to both places and am also sending a cable to Sorrento, I hope not in vain.

Your letter distressed me, and I am heartbroken to think that you have all of these annoyances on top of your grief.

Your predictions about Khvoshchinsky came true, and now, since I was the only one left with whom he had not quarreled, he started a quarrel with me! But, as you might imagine, I remain tranquil enough. I still sleep at night. . . .

Your devoted   Gerald Tyrwhitt

---

[17] Diaghilev had a morbid fear of germs.
[18] The death of Stravinsky's younger brother, Gury.

Queen's Hotel, Nice, end of September 1924.

Diaghilev (at table) and Nijinsky
(left, in straw hat), Stresa, August 1912. Photograph by Stravinsky.

Diaghilev and Massine,
Bellerive (Ouchy), September 1915. Photograph by Stravinsky.

With Lydia Lopokova, Bordeaux, September 8, 1916.

With Arthur Rubinstein and Alice Nikitina, England, June 1921.

Opposite: Vera Sudeikina as the Queen in *The Sleeping Princess,*
London, November 1921.
Above: London, November 1921. Photograph by Langdon Coburn.

Nice, 1925.

Anglet, August 1921.

With Grigory and Ganya Beliankin, Biarritz, 1926.

Father Nikolai Podosenov, Stravinsky's confessor, Nice, 1927.

Ganya Beliankin at the entrance to the Château Basque.

With Catherine, his first wife, Nice, 1925.

Amsterdam, 1930.

With Catherine in Montboron (Nice), 1930.

With Edwin Evans, London Zoo, October 1927. Photograph by Vera Sudeikina.

With Lord Berners at Faringdon, 1937. Photograph by Vera Sudeikina.

Darmstadt, 1930.
Photographs by
Hermann Collmann.

TYRWHITT TO STRAVINSKY

Diaghilev will send you 5,000 [francs] October 1. He had great financial difficulties. Will explain everything by letter. Friendly greetings, Gerald Tyrwhitt

TYRWHITT TO STRAVINSKY

Dear friend,

I finally saw Diaghilev, who stopped in Rome on his way to Paris. He wanted me to relay to you that he has just undergone a real financial ordeal: he was obliged to spend large sums restoring his costumes, which caught fire in a [railway] car in Brazil.

This circumstance explains his tardiness in making the payment to you. As I said in my telegram . . . he will send you 5,000 [francs] on October 1. He also wanted me to say that he expects you to spend a fortnight or so with him in Paris (from the middle of October) and to go to Barcelona, where the company will be in a few days.

Diaghilev is off to London now to arrange a very important project with Beecham. I hope that it can be realized, for it would be truly magnificent: a series of ballet and opera seasons, Russian, Italian, and French. Diaghilev is optimistic about the future and, as always, eager to organize new projects, despite all the failures he has had recently. . . . I think that you will be glad to hear about all of this directly from him. . . .

Pardon this rather breathless and incoherent communication; I simply wanted to transmit everything to you as quickly as possible. I hope that the money will already have arrived when you receive this letter. . . .

Your devoted   Gerald Tyrwhitt

STRAVINSKY TO TYRWHITT

My last letter crossed with your telegram. Say nothing [to] Diaghilev. [I] will write.   Stravinsky

TYRWHITT TO STRAVINSKY

Dear friend,

I am really shocked that Diaghilev, after his proclamation, has sent you nothing. He promised, emphatically, that he would pay 5,000 [francs] at the beginning of October and asked me to assure you of this by telegram right away, which I did.

I no longer know where he is; probably in Paris, since he should be back from England. In any case, he will soon have to write to you about the proposed trip to Spain (which I mentioned to you).

I vividly remember that old house in front of the church. I always liked it and hope that you will be very comfortable there.[19] I also think that it will be warmer there in the winter than at the Villa Rogivue.

I, too, plan to move soon. I have found an apartment near the Villa Borghese. I hope that you will visit me there this winter. . . .

> Your   Gerald Tyrwhitt

TYRWHITT TO STRAVINSKY   *October 20, [1917]*

Dear friend,

I was away from Rome and found your telegram on my return today. You will already have received my letter informing you that no one here knows where to find Diaghilev. I think he may be in Paris. Try writing to him at the Ritz; or perhaps Larionov would know. I really do not understand why [Diaghilev] has sent nothing, and why he has not written to you about the trip to Spain. . . . Something must have happened to change his whole itinerary. I regret not having been able to discover his hiding place, but if I do, I will telephone you right away. Aside from all of these problems, I hope that you are well. . . .

> Your   Gerald Tyrwhitt

TYRWHITT TO STRAVINSKY   *December 4, [1917]*

Enclosed is a letter from Diaghilev. I hope that you received my telegram; I received yours. I spoke to Diaghilev about sending you the monthly payment. . . .

> Friendly greetings,   Gerald Tyrwhitt

TYRWHITT TO STRAVINSKY   *December 10, [1917]*

Dear friend,

I enclose [Edwin] Evans's reply. The Swiss border is probably closed, but I think that you will receive my letter eventually. And it is not terribly urgent, after all.

How are you? And Diaghilev? Have you heard from him? Rumor has it that he is in Spain. . . .

> Your devoted   Gerald Tyrwhitt

---

[19] At the beginning of October, Stravinsky had moved, still in Morges, to the Maison Bornand, 2, place St. Louis, where he lived until June 8, 1920.

Dear friend,

Your letter came this morning and gave me enormous pleasure.

I would so love to hear the *Ragtime*. Will it be published soon?

I have already ordered the Etude [for Pianola] from Aeolian,[20] as well as your [pianola] roll, which I will mail to you.

Depero, the Futurist (whom you know), wanted me to ask you a favor. He is planning to do a little charity show at the Teatro dei Piccoli (with marionettes that he has constructed) and would like your permission to use the Five Easy Pieces as an accompaniment to one of the scenes. Would you please send me a postcard giving your reply?

Alas! I fear that it will be impossible for me to come to Switzerland for the concerts. I am very sorry to miss them but cannot budge from Rome at the moment. Everything must be done through the Embassy now, and it is everyone else's turn for a vacation. Will *Renard* be presented in stage or concert form?

I am in complete agreement with you about the review [*Ars Nova*]: moreover, everything that proclaims itself to be "art" and "new" automatically arouses my suspicion, since that combination is lethal. "I am very modern and very artistic!" . . .

Your   Gerald Tyrwhitt

Dear friend,

I have been sick in bed since the end of December, which is the reason why I did not write sooner to thank you for the card and to wish you a Happy New Year.[21] I just got up a few days ago and still feel somewhat weak.

I hope that you and Madame Stravinsky are well. I would so much like to hear from you and to know what you are doing. If you have a moment, write me a note, I beg of you.

Life here is very peaceful, not to say monotonous. The Countess San Martino is still very beautiful, and Casella continues to be very pleased with Casella. The Marchesa Casati presented a Futurist show, with works by Balla, Depero, Boccioni. In the Augusteo they play nothing but modern Italian music, wedging in a Saint-Saëns symphony from time to time.

I have had news—but very indirectly—about Diaghilev. He is in Madrid, but I have no idea what he is doing or intends to do.

Has the Etude for Pianola been released yet?

---

[20] The score of the Etude was never published, and the only manuscript that Stravinsky had after 1917 is not in his hand.

[21] Tyrwhitt must have forgotten that he had written on January 8.

The other day I saw the whole Massine collection[22] at Semenov's,[23] where it is being stored. . . .

Your very devoted   Gerald Tyrwhitt

TYRWHITT TO STRAVINSKY   *June 11, [1918]*

Dear friend,

How are you? I have not had news from Switzerland in ages. The last word that I heard about you came through the poor Marchesa Casati, who broke her arm while riding *à la* Valkyrie in the Villa Borghese and has been bedridden for a month. The other day I received a letter from Madame Goncharova in Paris. [She and Larionov] claim to be working hard but offer me no details. They go frequently to the country. Have you heard from Diaghilev? I suppose that he is still in Spain.

Did you finish the *Ragtime?* How I would love to hear it! Do you intend to publish it soon?

I plan to go to the seashore for a bit next week—to Sorrento, I think.

I wonder if you have met Princess Dorothy Radziwill, a charming and beautiful woman, who is now in Lausanne. How are all of the Morges-ians, [René] Morax et al., and where is [René] Auberjonois? If you see him, remind him of his promise to send me the book about his painting, which was due to appear. I await it impatiently.

The other day some pieces of mine, scored for small orchestra, were played at the Teatro dei Piccoli. This was the first time that I heard an orchestra perform my music, and I was pleased by the sonority. (I sound like Casella—but he would have said *"very* pleased.") . . .

Friendly greetings,   Gerald Tyrwhitt

TYRWHITT TO STRAVINSKY   *July 14, [1918]*

Dear friend,

Alas! I cannot go to Switzerland after all. I am very sorry. The complications are tremendous, and I have only three weeks [of vacation]. I have had to settle for a short excursion to the gulf of Naples—where I am now. I deeply regret that I will not be able to see you in Morges. I recently saw Yougine,[24] who passed on

---

[22] Including works by Braque, Picasso, Balla, Depero, Carrà, and Goncharova.

[23] Mikhail Semenov, a Russian living in Rome and Positano. He remained a good friend of Stravinsky throughout the 1930s.

[24] Probably Vladimir Vasilievich Yuzhin, to whom Stravinsky dedicated the 1918 piano transcription of *Firebird*.

some news about you. Please let me know whether you have published the *Ragtime* that you mentioned.

Have you heard from Diaghilev? He is probably still in Madrid. Will you go to Diablerets this year? . . .

Your   Gerald Tyrwhitt

TYRWHITT TO STRAVINSKY   *August 22, [1918]*

Dear friend,

I was very happy to receive your letter. My God, how I would love to attend the performance that you are organizing for October![25] Unfortunately, I am nailed down here, with no possibility of an escape from Rome for the time being.

I was shrewd and followed your suggestion: I asked [J. & W.] Chester to send me the *Ragtime,* adding that I was under the impression that they were about to release it. I always forget to ask your opinion of Chester's editions of my works (cover, print, etc.). Please tell me whether they meet with your approval, or if you think that improvements should be made, because I must now decide on a cover for a new work. Frankly, I think that the editions are simple enough, unostentatious, and not at all German! What is Diaghilev doing in London? Is the company with him?

Rome is pleasant now, not too hot, and I am working hard.

Apparently Beecham is going bankrupt! *Che notizia strabiliante!!* I don't know if this is true. I must verify it. . . .

Your devoted   Gerald Tyrwhitt

TYRWHITT TO STRAVINSKY   *September 11, 1918*

Dear friend,

I just saw Mlle Pecci, who came here directly from Lausanne. She said that you had written to me about sending some [ballet] slippers from Milan for the [*Histoire du soldat*] performance. I never received your letter, and I am sorry not to have been able to help you. It seems that the Swiss border has been closed for several weeks and that nothing is allowed to cross now, but if there is still time, telegraph, telling me exactly what you need, and I will try to send it to you via the Swiss courier.

When will the performance take place? I am very interested in it, as you might imagine. Please send me the program or libretto when it is printed. I wish you all possible success and satisfaction with the performance.

Friendly greetings, your devoted   Gerald Tyrwhitt

---

[25] The premiere of *Histoire du soldat,* which took place at the Théâtre de Lausanne on September 28.

TYRWHITT TO STRAVINSKY   *November 27, [1918]*

Dear friend,

I sent the prospectus and brochure to [Edwin] Evans. Would you please send other catalogues of your works for distribution among musicians here? Have the *Sacre* and *Petrushka* already appeared in pianola form?

I am astonished that Diaghilev has not written to you. Where could he be?

Larionov and Goncharova are expected here in Rome—in fact, they were due to arrive a few days ago. But they have not been in touch [with me] either, so I do not know whether they are really coming or not.

I hope that you are still happy with your house and that Madame Stravinsky and the children are well.

What did you think of the edition that Chester sent me? I find it discreet and not at all ostentatious.

International catastrophes and other minutiae aside, I am well and hope that you are too.

Would you please give me Auberjonois's address? I would like to send him a note.

P.S. My illness was complicated: infection, inflammation, followed by an abscess—prelude, chorale, and fugue!

                                                    Faringdon House
                                                       Faringdon
                                                       Berkshire
TYRWHITT TO STRAVINSKY   *January 9, [1919]*

To think that for several months I have been bombarding you with letters and postcards from Rome in vain. The Swiss border has been villainously obstructed. Perhaps you received my communications, but I certainly never received any response. Meanwhile, Carlo Placci,[26] whom I saw briefly in Paris, passed on some news about you. He was enthusiastic about the *Ragtime,* which you played for him. I spent a few days in London and saw Diaghilev and the ballet numerous times. We celebrated the New Year together. I think that he will stay in London until March, then return to Monte Carlo. I saw Lady Cunard and Beecham as well, who spoke about you at length. Beecham would like to present *The Nightingale;* has he discussed this with you? His head is always in the clouds!

Not long ago I composed three little pieces for orchestra: *Chinoiserie, Valse sentimentale, Kasachok,* which will be played in Manchester on March 8. I am pleased, because at present that is the best orchestra in England. . . .

I plan to stay in England until March, when I go back to Rome.

---

[26] Carlo Placci was an Italian diplomat.

Did you know that I changed my name—I am no longer Tyrwhitt! This thanks to my aunt—or, rather, to the death of my uncle, whose title I have now inherited. Unfortunately, though, it seems that this and plenty of taxes are all that I have inherited.

I would so much like to see you again. Send me a note, I beg of you, and tell me what you are doing. . . .

Your very devoted   Berners

TYRWHITT TO STRAVINSKY

Woodcote, Newport
Shropshire
February 15, 1919

Dear friend,

I am truly sorry to learn that poor Mika[27] has been so ill; you must be in anguish over her. I hope that she is better by now. Please give my best wishes to Madame Stravinsky and the little one.

I would like to stop in Morges on my return to Rome and would do anything to be able to visit you. But travel across Switzerland is still very difficult, even with diplomatic privileges.

Did you know that I too underwent an operation, yet another consequence of the illness I had in Rome? I would like to be rid of this once and for all. Fortunately, the operation was not very serious, but I have been bedridden since my last letter to you and got up only a few days ago. For this reason I have not written sooner.

The day after tomorrow I hope to go to London, where I will immediately look up Evans and speak to Lady Cunard as well. I suppose you know that Beecham declared bankruptcy—who would ever have expected that! This will complicate the extraction of a yes or no answer from him on our question, but I will do my best.

I deeply regret having missed your [Three Pieces for String] Quartet, given in London the day before yesterday. But since the work will be repeated twice more, I will certainly hear it later.

My address has not changed. I am here at my uncle's home. I go the day after tomorrow to London; then I return to my house at Faringdon.

I am so sorry to hear about all of your troubles, and for poor Mika to fall ill on top of everything is really dreadful. For us, too, this is a grave moment, and the menace of revolution all the time is no consolation. I will write and tell you the outcome of my actions.

Your very devoted   Berners

---

[27] Stravinsky's elder daughter, Lyudmila.

June 24, 1919
[Censor's stamp]

TYRWHITT TO STRAVINSKY

How are you? I have been sick and lazy, which is why I haven't written in so long! From time to time people coming from Switzerland have given me news about you, and I think of you very, very often. I hope that your daughter has completely recovered.

Perhaps you will recall my little piece for piano, the *Poisson d'or,* which you said was your favorite when I played it for you. Madame Goncharova designed a colorful cover for the piece, and I dedicated it to you. I hope that you will not mind. I told Chester to send you a copy as soon as it is printed.

Did you know that the CASELLAS ARE DIVORCING? I think that such an event merits capital letters. What effect do you suppose this will have on ARS NOVA?

Rome is very hot. The Futurist activities become increasingly futile, and the Marchesa Casati is in Capri. That is all the Roman news I can offer you. . . .

Your devoted   Berners

TYRWHITT TO STRAVINSKY   *July 25, [1919]*

Dear friend,

On my way to England, I hope to pass through Morges around August 4 or 5. Will you be there? I hope so, because I would love to see you and to speak to you. I will cable from Milan to be sure that you will be available. I could spend two or three days in Switzerland; I must be in London about August 10. . . .

Your devoted   Berners

Paris
August 16, 1919
[Postcard] [28]

TYRWHITT TO STRAVINSKY

Friendly greetings—I will write to you from London.

Ravello
[?], 1920
[Postcard] [29]

TYRWHITT TO STRAVINSKY

Carantec

We only regret that you are not here with us in the "Magic Garden"!

Berners, Werner Reinhart[30]

---

[28] Picture postcard of Ogata Korin's *Wave Screen.*

[29] A facsimile of Wagner's inscription: "Richard Wagner and wife and family. Klingsor's Magic Garden is found! May 26, 1880."

[30] Werner Reinhart (1884–1951), Stravinsky's patron from Winterthur, also sent the

TYRWHITT TO STRAVINSKY

40 Half Moon Street
London W1
December 7, [1920][31]

Dear friend,

I expect to be in Paris next Tuesday or Wednesday. I will be delighted to see you again—it has been a century. Nevertheless, I have had news about you often, and recently through Mlle Chanel, who was here the other day. She will inform you that I went to see the director of Aeolian regarding the [pianola] roll. I hope to be able to bring it to you next week.

Please tell me when the *Sacre* will be given. I would like to see it as soon as I arrive in Paris, if possible. Send me a few lines if you have a moment. . . .

Friendly greetings,   Berners

TYRWHITT TO STRAVINSKY

3 Chesham Place
London SW1
February 24, 1924

Dear friend,

I was so happy to see your handwriting and to have news about Madame Picabia,[32] who is a charming person. We really had to battle with Chester over the *Soldat*—they are very tight—but Madame Picabia finally managed to obtain a satisfactory contract. I was glad to be of some assistance in this battle!

I would so much like to have the recordings of the Octet.[33] Could you tell me where I must write to order them? In London they make it difficult to obtain French records; to write directly to France is easier.

I will probably be in Paris in mid-March. Will you by chance be there as well? I would so love to see you.

Friendly greetings,   Berners

---

composer a postcard from Positano. See the correspondence with Reinhart in S.S.C. III.

[31] Stravinsky has added "1921," but the year could only be 1920, since the *Sacre* was given in Paris several times in December 1920, while on December 7, 1921, Berners would recently have seen Stravinsky in London (at a performance—possibly the premiere—of *The Sleeping Princess*).

[32] Gabrielle-Buffet Picabia shared an apartment with Vera Sudeikina at 82, rue des Petits-Champs in Paris, both women having left their husbands. Stravinsky had given Madame Picabia a contract to negotiate for stage performances of *Histoire du soldat*.

[33] In November 1923 Stravinsky recorded the Octet in the *"salle d'enregistrement"* at Pleyel, 24, rue Rochechouart, and a number of copies were distributed, The sides are numbered 796–797 and 798.

TYRWHITT TO STRAVINSKY   *via Varese 8*
                                                             Rome
Dear friend,   *[May 1924]*

A brief note to tell you that I will be in Paris (I hope) on the 21st and that I eagerly await the night of the 22nd to hear the [Piano] Concerto.

With all the worries concerning the theatre, I fear that I did not tell you how beautiful I found this work. Perhaps you care little about my opinion, but it is sincere, and a sincere opinion is always something!

The Concerto made such a strong impression on me that I feel a rush of enthusiasm whenever I think of it. That, in turn, rejuvenates me. I thought that I would lose the violence of my enthusiasm with age; this work has demonstrated, though, that [my enthusiasm] can still be revived when [I am] confronted with beautiful things.

Pardon this effusion, and do not think me sentimental and ridiculous to write to you like this. What I say is sincere, and it gives me great pleasure to be able to convey this to you.

                    Friendly greetings, your devoted friend   Berners

TYRWHITT TO STRAVINSKY   *August 2, 1925*

Dear friend,

The address is S. Mario Pansa, Ministero degli Esteri, Rome, and it would be best to write *"Far seguire"* on the envelope, since chances are he could be away from Rome at the moment. But he could still arrange for your passport. I am writing him an explanatory note as well.

Tomorrow I leave for Salzburg, where I will stay until the end of August. I will be at the Hotel Europa.

My best to Madame Stravinsky and the whole family. I hope to see you soon.

                              Your devoted   Berners

TYRWHITT TO STRAVINSKY   *Faringdon House*
                                                             Berkshire
Dear friend,   *October 11, 1937*

I wait for you and Madame Sudeikina with joy—on the 15th, at 3 Halkin Street. Send a card telling me the time of your arrival in London, and I will come to the station.

I have been suffering from rheumatism and have been in bed nearly a week. Now I am better and hope to be completely cured in a few days.

I am going to London on Thursday. I hope that you can come here and see my country house, which is very pretty.[34] If you have a rehearsal Saturday

---

[34] The *Daily Express* printed a notice by William Hickey, Wednesday, October 20: "I

morning, perhaps we can come in the afternoon and return to London on Sunday evening. If not, then after the concerts. How long can you stay in England?

Friendly greetings, your devoted   Berners

Faringdon House
Berkshire
November 25, 1937[35]

TYRWHITT TO STRAVINSKY

I thank you kindly for your letters and the charming photographs. I hope that you still intend to come here in January. I will spend Christmas in Ireland, but I will return here at the beginning of January and await you with the greatest pleasure. When is your radio concert? Send me a postcard with the date. Announcements of radio concerts are hard to find in English newspapers.

Would you please thank Madame Sudeikina on my behalf for having sent the colors for the pigeons. They are magnificent and add a tropical touch to this wintry country. I hope that Madame Stravinsky is better. I beg you to say hello to her for me, and I hope to see you here in January.

Friendly greetings from   Gerald Berners

TYRWHITT TO STRAVINSKY

London
December 21, 1937

25, rue du Faubourg St.-Honoré
Paris

Dear friend,

Many good wishes for Christmas and the New Year. I listened to your concert with great pleasure: I also heard the Symphony of Psalms under Ansermet a few nights ago. I hope that you will be able to come to Faringdon in January or February—or whenever you wish. Sir Thomas Beecham just recorded the Suite from [*The Triumph of*] *Neptune*. I will send you the recordings as soon as they are released. I hope that you are well and that I will see you soon.

Friendly greetings from your devoted   Berners

---

lunched with [Stravinsky] yesterday. . . . He is staying at the London house of . . . Lord Berners and will go to . . . Berners's Berkshire house, Faringdon, where Berners . . . sprays his pigeons with different colours. Red, blue, orange colored flocks now flutter about the grey 1760 house. . . . The colours are harmless—cochineal, laundresses' blue, saffron."

[35] Stravinsky answered on November 29 but did not keep a copy.

TYRWHITT TO STRAVINSKY

Faringdon House
Berkshire
October 8, 1938

My dear friend,

Now that the danger is past, I hope that your personal unhappiness has also diminished and that Madame Stravinsky is better. It was a great pleasure and consolation to have seen you during my sad stay in Paris.

The [Channel crossing] was horrible. I was supposed to leave right away the next morning for Dieppe—I had been told that on the following day there would be a mobilization, making it impossible for me to transport my automobile. I arrived just in time and spent a dreadful night on a bench! Even with the most agreeable thoughts, that wasn't much fun! At the same time, I was greatly consoled by reading the Concerto.[36] I like it enormously. It is very, very good, and I hope that I will be able to hear it [in concert] as soon as possible, or that recordings will be made. I plan to come to Paris in November, and to see you again would be an immense joy.

Your devoted   Berners

TYRWHITT TO STRAVINSKY

3 Halkin Street
London SW1
November 5, 1938

Dear friend,

A brief note to tell you how much I love the magnificent Concerto, which Nadia Boulanger played last night with the BBC [Orchestra]. It is a superb work.

I expect to arrive in Paris next Wednesday and stay four or five days. . . .

Nadia Boulanger relayed the bad news about your daughter's [Mika's] health, which deeply saddened me. I hope that her condition is improving. The last time I was in Paris she seemed much better. *A bientôt, d*ear friend.

Your devoted   Berners

TYRWHITT TO STRAVINSKY

3 Halkin Street
[December 1938]

Dear friend,

I am writing to tell you of my sadness on hearing the terrible news of the death of your daughter. I learned about it only yesterday from your niece;[37] I have been in Faringdon and see no one—the reason for my not knowing. I send you all my sympathy.

---

[36] Stravinsky has written *"Dumbarton Oaks"* in the margin.

[37] Ira Beliankina, who used the stage name Ira Belline. She had been a member of the original cast of the Massine–Nicolas Nabokov ballet *Ode,* presented by Diaghilev in Paris in 1928. See the correspondence with the Beliankin family in the present volume.

Your niece will be making the costumes for my ballet, *Cupid and Psyche.*[38] I am very pleased that she wished to take part in this and that she likes the designs—which are the work of a young English painter [Francis Rose]. But I believe that she has already told you this.

I hope to come to see you in Paris soon. I think a great deal about you in your great sorrow. I send you my greatest sympathy.

Your always devoted   Berners

TYRWHITT TO STRAVINSKY   *London*
                                                      March 7, 1939

My dear friend,

I send you all of my most sincere sympathy for this second terrible loss that you have had to endure.[39] My dear friend, I cannot express how deeply I feel for you. I think of you and your great sorrow all the time. I shall see Mlle Belline, who will give me news about you, as soon as she returns to London.

I would very much like for you to come and spend some time at my home in Faringdon as soon as you feel up to it. The tranquility of the countryside and the change of air would perhaps do you some good.

With all the sympathy of a good friend, I am,

your ever-devoted   Berners

---

[38] Presented by the Vic-Wells Ballet on April 27, 1939, with choreography by Frederick Ashton.

[39] The death of Stravinsky's wife on March 2.

CORRESPONDENCE WITH

1916 ✣ 1945

MANUEL DE FALLA

MANUEL DE FALLA[1] TO STRAVINSKY
Ponzano 24
Madrid
July 7, 1916

Villa Les Sapins
Morges

My dear friend,

By the same mail I am sending you the photograph of our table at the banquet, which I finally found in the most recent issue of *Mundo Gráfico.* They promised me a copy of the photograph, which I will forward to you as soon as I receive it.

Our trip to Andalusia was magnificent, and, needless to say, we talked about you constantly. What a pity that you could not be with us! In Granada we had two nocturnal gypsy feasts. The first, which took place in a garden (as in *Carmen*) beneath the Alhambra, looking out over the adjoining neighborhood, was tremendous. The second . . . was with a troupe of gypsies. Afterward we visited the Alhambra in the starlight. . . . The evening before our departure, the Madrid orchestra played my *Nocturnes* at the Palacio Carlos V. According to our conductor, this music should be adapted to a tragic subject. . . .

I am now busy making corrections. The music . . . you did not like has already been replaced and the dance developed a little. Diaghilev and Massine[2] left on Saturday for San Sebastián and Paris. They were unconditionally enthusiastic about my "Andalusiz" [one of the Four Piano Pieces], and I am very proud! . . .

Will you come in October? The Marquise of Salamanca told me that you have a railway pass for the whole of Spain. So come! I would like to be in Granada at the end of September to go to Alpujarra. . . .[3]

---

[1] Stravinsky was very fond of Manuel de Falla (1876–1946) and of at least one of his pieces, the Harpsichord Concerto. French is the original language of all the correspondence.

[2] In an interesting note to Stravinsky from Córdoba, Léonide Massine describes "the organ in the cathedral at Seville, the altar dances with castanets, and the orchestra in front of the altar. The entire dance is accompanied by singing, by little boys, who are also dancing. The singing is really shouting; the dance consists of various steps involving swaying from side to side, and many figures."

[3] A network of valleys in the Sierra Nevada, described by Alarcón (in *La Alpujarra*).

I have not forgotten your *Noces villageoises*. What a profound impression! Send news about yourself. My greetings to Madame Stravinsky.

In friendship,   Manuel de Falla

STRAVINSKY TO FALLA   *Morges*
                                        August 11, 1916
Ponzano 24   *[Postcard]*[4]
Madrid

Forgive me for these few lines in reply to your kind letter (which reached me after an incredible delay!). They express with the greatest sincerity how much I love your art, yourself, and how dear to me is your sympathy for my art and for me. I embrace you cordially.

Your   Igor Stravinsky

FALLA TO STRAVINSKY   *Madrid*
                                        December 31, 1916
Morges   *[Postcard]*[5]

All my best wishes, dear friend, for 1917! Your *Japanese Lyrics* were sung by Madame Lajeune [?] at the Sociedad Nacional, accompanied by me on the piano.[6] A real success, especially the second piece. When will you make the trip to Spain?

A warm handshake from your   Manuel de Falla

STRAVINSKY TO FALLA   *Morges*
                                     [Postmark: Helvétia]
Ponzano 24   *[1917]*
Madrid   *[Postcard]*[7]

All our best wishes for the New Year. Your friend Igor Stravinsky embraces you.

---

[4] Picture postcard of El Greco's *Cristo abrazado a la Cruz*.

[5] Picture postcard of Goya's *Gallina Ciega*.

[6] Adolfo Salazar (1890–1958), a pupil of Falla and later a music critic, had written to Stravinsky on December 26: "Falla will have written to tell you that the first two of your *Japanese Lyrics* were sung at the Sociedad Nacional and experienced a great triumph. Let me express my most profound joy at this. I will send you the program."

[7] Picture postcard of Raphael's *Second Hour of the Day*.

FALLA TO STRAVINSKY   *Madrid*
                                                                  May 1, 1918

Dear friend,

Arthur Rubinstein has entrusted me to send you the enclosed letter of exchange of 5,000 francs (through the Agence de Crédit Lyonnais in Geneva).

Time was short, and [Rubinstein] was unable to send it himself before his departure from Madrid. He also asked me to relay his best wishes and to inform you that he is at your disposal, at the Plaza Hotel, Buenos Aires, until August, should you come to some decision about the composition [Piano-Rag Music] (which he leaves entirely up to you).

How I regret not seeing you in Madrid this spring! Meanwhile, I hope that the project with the Cercle des Beaux Arts and the Sociedad Nacional will be realized this year. Unfortunately, your reply, which they eagerly awaited, arrived too late. Rubinstein had wanted to appear in the festival as well. You know already that your good friend [Rubinstein] had a veritable triumph in Spain, and his popularity increases every day. Now he will spend several months in the Argentine Republic.

I heard that you wrote to the Cercle des Beaux Arts, although I have not yet seen your letter. I will keep you up-to-date on this matter.

We just paid homage to the memory of Debussy at the Ateneo and are preparing another concert at the Sociedad Nacional for the month of October. In the penultimate concert we devoted two parts of the program to his piano works. Arthur played them there, as well as at the Ateneo. . . .

The death of Debussy is really distressing to us all. Be assured, my dear, of my great friendship. I shake your hand cordially.

                                                        Manuel de Falla

My new address is: Lagasca 119.

I forgot something: Manuel Abríl, a Spanish writer, . . . has asked me to send you this ballet libretto . . . to see if it would interest you.

FALLA TO STRAVINSKY   *January 25, 1921*
                                                              [Postcard][8]

"Bel Respiro"
avenue Alphonse de Neuville
Garches

All of my best wishes, dear friend, for the coming year.

                                        Yours truly,   Manuel de Falla

New address: Alhambra, Granada.

I cannot wait to see the continuation of the symphonies that you are composing in memory of Debussy.

---

[8] Picture postcard of the Moorish Palace in the Alhambra.

STRAVINSKY TO FALLA   *[Postmark: Paris]*
                                                       [April 1921] [9]

Alhambra
Granada

Dear Falla,

You would be an angel if you would give me the address of Salvador and of Salazar. The former sent me a pretty souvenir, and I have lost his address, so it is
impossible for me to thank him. As for the latter, by chance I carried off the
music that he asked me to sign. Could you write a note to both of them about
these matters? I am very upset about what they must think of me. I embrace
you and await your response.

                                                       I. Stravinsky

FALLA TO STRAVINSKY   *Granada*
                                                         April 21, 1921
Garches   *[Postcard]*

Here, my dear, are the addresses that you wanted: Miguel Salvador, Velazquez
7; Adolfo Salazar, Abascal 7. I will convey your apologies to them. I have only a
fragment of your address, so would you, in turn, be an angel and send me your
complete address, as well as that of Massine? I would be extremely grateful! *A
bientôt;* I will be in Paris on May 10. In the meantime, many fond regards from
your Manuel de Falla, admirer of *Histoire du soldat* and *Ragtime!*

FALLA TO STRAVINSKY   *Granada*
                                                      January 2, 1924 [10]
Paris   *[Postcard]*

All of my best wishes, dear friend, for a magnificent year! Would you please tell
me whether a slide trombone is essential for your *Pulcinella?* I ask you because
only valve trombones are available in Seville, unfortunately. For when is your
trip to Spain scheduled? Remember our conversation on this subject.

                              Your ever-faithful   Manuel de Falla

---

[9] Marked by Falla: "received April 15, 1921."

[10] Stravinsky had seen Falla in Paris, at a concert at the Salle des Agriculteurs on May
29, 1923, in which Falla accompanied Vera Janacopulos in ten of his songs. The same
singer performed several Stravinsky songs, including—accompanied by Pleyela roll—
"Tilimbom."

STRAVINSKY TO FALLA

Pleyel
Paris

Antequeruela Alta
Granada

January 18, 1924
[Postcard] [11]

Dear one,

Just a word to tell you that you can perform *Pulcinella* with a valve trombone. I will be doing *Pulcinella* myself when I conduct in Barcelona in March, after which time the parts will be at your disposal. I have just had two triumphs, in Antwerp and in Brussels. I am on my way back to Biarritz. Write to me there. I embrace you.

I. Stravinsky

FALLA TO STRAVINSKY

Granada
February 21, 1924
[Aerogram]

Very dear friend,

What is the date next month of your Barcelona concert? Will you come to Granada afterward? I certainly hope so. Would you like me to make inquiries about a possible concert in Madrid? I should be going there toward the end of March, but until then I will be in Granada, where I await a note from you on this subject.

To hear of your two triumphs in Belgium (a great honor to that country) gave me immense joy.

The *Pulcinella* concerts in Seville will take place in May.

Your devoted   Manuel de Falla

STRAVINSKY TO FALLA

"Les Rochers"
Biarritz
February 27, 1924

Granada

My dear Falla,

Thank you for your lovely letter, which was forwarded to me in Biarritz and thus reached me only yesterday.

From March 7 to 20 I will be in Barcelona, where I must conduct in three concerts at the Liceo.

Koussevitzky wrote to me from Madrid saying that they wanted me to conduct there after my Barcelona concerts. But I do not know from whom the invitation comes or for what date. I suppose it is the Filharmónica.

I must tell you that, after Barcelona, I will have very little time to complete my Concerto, which I am supposed to play with Koussevitzky in Paris on May 15.

I will probably be at the Hotel Ritz in Barcelona, where I hope to receive

---

[11] Picture postcard of an *"étude d'expression,"* entitled "La Douleur."

good news from you, my dear Falla. In the meantime, I send my most devoted affections.

Igor Stravinsky

FALLA TO STRAVINSKY

Antequeruela Alta
Granada
March 1, 1924

Biarritz

Very dear one,

Your note just arrived. Our friend Miguel Salvador, . . . who is the president of the Orquesta Filharmónica, would like to have you come to Madrid, as I suggested. I am writing to him now to convey the contents of your letter, as well as your address. It would be a joyful occasion if this could be arranged. We would see each other in Madrid, since I must conduct my *Retablo* [*de Maese Pedro*] there at the end of March.

Affectionately yours,   Manuel de Falla

FALLA TO STRAVINSKY

Alhambra
Granada
April 20, 1925

Maison Pleyel
Paris[12]

Very dear friend,

I have had the *Retablo* sent to you through [J. & W.] Chester. I want you to have this work in memory of our old friendship and because of my profound devotion to your astonishing work.

I learned that you are now going to Barcelona, and at this point I would like to do everything possible to induce you to come to Granada! If that plan interests you, send me your address, so that I can keep you up-to-date on my endeavors.

Very affectionately yours,   Manuel de Falla

FALLA TO STRAVINSKY

Granada
[January 1927]

167, blvd. Carnot
Nice

Despite your obstinate silence, I still think of you and of your miraculous art.

In addressing to you my best wishes for a beautiful new year, I embrace you in devoted friendship.

Manuel de Falla

---

[12] Forwarded to Nice.

STRAVINSKY TO FALLA

167, blvd. Carnot
Nice

Antequeruela Alta
Granada

February 3, 1927
[Postcard] [13]

My silence is most certainly not to be interpreted as a sign of indifference toward you, my dear Falla, since I love you very much and am happy that you think not only of the composer Stravinsky but also of the physical man. I embrace you affectionately.

Your very devoted   I. Stravinsky

FALLA TO STRAVINSKY

Granada
[January 1928]
[Postcard] [14]

Nice

My fervent wish is that this new year will witness the radiant rebirth of *Apollo!* I embrace you with great affection.

Manuel de Falla

My greetings to Madame Stravinsky and regards to your son.

FALLA TO STRAVINSKY

Granada
May 6, 1928

Nice

Dear and wonderful Igor,

On the occasion of the Festival of Granada, we plan to give a series of orchestra concerts for the benefit of the Charity Association. We ardently desire to reserve a portion of the programs for you, and *Petrushka* is the chosen work. Unfortunately, the rental fee (250 pesetas, plus postage) would mean a substantial decrease in the potential profits for this charity. We are making all necessary sacrifices in order to benefit the Association as much as possible. Would you like to cooperate as well, by asking your publisher to make an exception—only this once—for the Madrid Orquesta Filharmónica? . . . We would be deeply grateful, and the public would be duly informed of your gesture.

How I regret having missed you in Paris! And in Barcelona! I heard about your great success, which, as always, was foreseeable.

Excuse me, my dear, if I have bothered you with this petition for your mercy. . . . I embrace you in deep friendship.

Manuel de Falla

---

[13] Picture postcard of Debussy and Stravinsky.

[14] Picture postcard of the Alhambra, seen from the Carrera del Darro.

STRAVINSKY TO FALLA

My dear Falla,

I received your kind letter and immediately got in touch with the director of the Edition Russe de Musique, G. G. Païchadze, who told me that he consents to a reasonable reduction for the rental of the *Petrushka* parts. Work it out directly with him: M. Païchadze, c/o S.A. des Grandes Editions Musicales, 22, rue d'Anjou, Paris 9. He will answer you and tell you what to do.

Will we see each other soon? I am here until the end of May. I embrace you in a true and imperishable friendship. May God keep you.

Your   I. Stravinsky

FALLA TO STRAVINSKY

rue Rochechouart
Paris

My dear Stravinsky,

Thank you for the nice letter and for your kind response to my plea on behalf of the Charity Association, whose directors have asked me to relay their gratitude.

By the same mail I am sending a letter to M. Païchadze, enclosing the Orquesta Filharmónica's request . . . for the parts, since they will now begin rehearsals of *Petrushka* in Madrid to prepare for the Granada concerts.

Unfortunately, I will not be returning to Paris this spring; you should come here instead and conduct your work on June 18! What a joy that would be for everyone, and especially for me!

I embrace you in deep friendship and sincere devotion.

Your   Manuel de Falla

Please excuse the typewriter; because of an eye affliction, which I have had for two weeks now, I am obliged to dictate my letters.

FALLA TO STRAVINSKY

Nice

A few lines, my dear Igor, to tell you that I was congratulated for having initiated arrangements for the performance of your marvelous *Petrushka*. I am happy to say that there was great enthusiasm, and I hope that one day we will have the honor of your presence here in Granada! Do you remember the trip that you missed in 1917? . . .

Yours truly,   Manuel de Falla

Excuse the typewriter, but this is still my only way of writing.

FALLA TO STRAVINSKY   *January [?], 1929*
    [Postcard] [15]

Very dear Igor Stravinsky,

I am sending you my Piano Concerto by registered mail, in memory—very much alive in my mind—of our encounter in London.

By any chance did you keep the article that I published in Madrid on the occasion of your first trip to Spain? I would be grateful if you would let me borrow it for a few days to make some copies.

I embrace you with sincere affection, and all my best wishes for the coming year.

Manuel de Falla

STRAVINSKY TO FALLA   *Nice*
    February 12, 1929

My very dear Falla,

On my return from Dresden, where I conducted *Oedipus,* I found your delicious Concerto[16] on my table along with your note—many thanks. Unfortunately, it has been impossible for me to find your article [about me], even though I know that it is here in my house somewhere. Above all, do not think that in *not* sending it to you I found any "antipathy" for my music in your kind dedication. I embrace you, my old friend, very affectionately.

Your   I. Stravinsky

Please send me a reproduction of Picasso's drawing of you. I want it because I like it very much—as I do you.

FALLA TO STRAVINSKY   *Granada*
    March 18, 1929

My very dear Igor Stravinsky,

I have—finally—found the one good copy that I have of Picasso's drawing, and this I send to you with joy, by the same mail. My joy would be multiplied to infinity if, in turn, you would send me one of the portraits that Picasso made of you (perhaps I would prefer the simplest one). . . .

How I long for the opportunity to chat with you at length and about myriad things. . . . We have not seen each other for almost two years, and, once again, it seems that I will not be coming to Paris this spring. I have such a desire to hear your new works, and conducted by you!

I embrace you with all of my great affection and devotion.

Your   Manuel de Falla

---

[15] Picture postcard of the gardens of the Generalife.

[16] Stravinsky conducted Falla's Harpsichord Concerto at Dumbarton Oaks in 1947, and

STRAVINSKY TO FALLA   *Nice*
                                                Semana Santa
My very dear Falla,   *March 25, 1929*

What pleasure you have given me in sending me your portrait. Naturally, and
with the greatest haste, I will send you my portrait, also by Picasso, as soon as I
receive it from Paris, since here I have only one copy, which belongs to my family. I will write immediately to Rosenberg, the picture dealer. Thank you, too,
for the dedication: I am bewildered, moved, and profoundly touched.

Is it true that you will not be coming to Paris in May or June? In this case, I
do not know when we will see each other again.

Have you heard my recordings (Columbia) of *Petrushka* and *Firebird*
(under my direction)? They are very well done.

We do not forget you, dear Falla. I have a great and true affection for you.
May God keep you.

Your   I. Stravinsky

FALLA TO STRAVINSKY   *Granada*
                                                    [?] 1929
Nice   *Pascua Florida*[17]

It is a great joy for me, as well, to have Picasso's portrait of you, and, in particular, to receive it directly from your hands. . . .[18] I like this portrait even more because it evokes memories of the era when it was drawn. It reminds me of our
strolls together around Madrid and Segovia . . . which would have continued on
to Granada but for your sudden change of plans. . . . And how rare and touching it is to have such pure memories, with no taint of bitterness!

The period in question is also that of the article, which, unfortunately, we
did not find, and which I would like very much to reprint. In the meantime, I
busy myself with another one, to relieve my afterpains (*desfacer entuertos,* as
Señor Luis Hoffe would say).

But we will not see each other in Paris this spring either! My work
has been terribly delayed because of the illness I suffered last year (and thanks
to frequent trips, etc., as well). I am obliged—which I deeply regret—to
stay in my corner, except during the festival days (which are unbearable in
Granada).

No, I have not yet heard your recordings of *Petrushka* and *Firebird,* but I
intend to get them.

Please present my respects to Madame Stravinsky (whom I was so happy

---

the Stravinsky archives contain his photocopy of the score and his set of parts.

[17] I.e., Easter. Falla drew the sign of the cross.

[18] Seven years later, Stravinsky also sent a photograph of himself as a ten-year-old boy,
inscribed as follows: "To Manuel de Falla, whom this child adores with all his heart,
Igor Stravinsky, Paris, May 17, 1936."

to see again in Paris last year) and my best wishes to your son.

I embrace you with all of my old and sincere devotion.

Your   Manuel de Falla

STRAVINSKY TO FALLA

Chalet des Echarvines
Haute Savoie
August 6, 1929

My dear Falla,

Do you have any idea of what [*sic*] is M. Clement Lozano (if I have made out his signature correctly), who sends me proposals to conduct some concerts in Barcelona, in Valencia, and in a third Spanish city? He writes on stationery of the Concerts Catalonia, Barcelona-Paris-Rome, and mentions my first performance of the *Sacre* in Barcelona in the spring of 1928. I answered, accepting the project in principle, but I would like to have some information about this "concert agency" as well as about Lozano himself, to see if this is serious. Among other conditions, he proposes that I come in March. If you are in Granada at this time and can arrange an appearance for me there as part of this series of concerts, I will do the impossible in order to come, and at an exceptional fee, to facilitate the engagement. Answer me, my dear, at the above address. I embrace you.

Your   I. Strav.

FALLA TO STRAVINSKY

Granada
August 12, 1929

Chalet des Echarvines
Talloires

My dear Igor,

Overjoyed at the possibility of your trip to Granada, I will start this minute to look into the arrangements, but I must ask you to send precise information to help me carry out this wonderful project.

Also tell me (as soon as you know) on what day (approximately) in March you would be able to come, so that I can make certain to be in Granada at that time.

So far as I know, Clemente Lozano (Concerts Catalunya) is the *only* agent in Barcelona. I have known him personally for a long time and have no objections to his work, which I find competent. Until three or four years ago he was the music critic for *La Vanguardia*.

I embrace you with the old affection.

Your   Manuel de Falla

FALLA TO STRAVINSKY   *Granada*
                                                    August 22, 1929

Talloires

Very dear Igor,

I was deeply moved by the death of Diaghilev and must write to you before anyone else.

What a great loss for you! He did many wonderful things, but the foremost
was to discover you. We owe that to him, above all. Without you, moreover, the
Ballets [Russes] would not have been able to exist.

Our poor friend is dead. But he did not outlive his work. That is a consolation, since, as I will always remember, he was so afraid that if there were a war,
someone would come to power at its termination and obstruct his pursuit. We
have seen that his fears were in vain. . . .

And now I must ask you a favor: to offer my condolences to those who are
the core of the Diaghilev ballet, since I no longer know anyone, and no one
could receive and convey our sympathy with more tenderness than you, my
dear. I embrace you with all of my old and sincere affection.

                                            Manuel de Falla

I hope that you received my last letter. This one I am sending by registered mail
to guarantee that it will be forwarded to you.

FALLA TO STRAVINSKY   *Granada*
                                                            [1930]
Very dear Igor Stravinsky,   *[Postcard]* [19]

Despite your silence, my thoughts are always with you, and to begin this new
year I address my best wishes to you.

                        Yours truly,   Manuel de Falla

I still await word from you regarding the wonderful project in Granada.[20]

STRAVINSKY TO FALLA   *Nice*
                                                    January 8, 1930

My very dear Falla,

I am touched and bewildered, for although I assure you that I thought of you at
the arrival of the New Year—you are free to believe this or not, but you know of
the loyal affection that I have for you (to be filled in by the addressee).[21]

    I await the decision from this poor Lozano from Barcelona in order to find

---

[19] Picture postcard of the court of the Cypress Trees, Alhambra.

[20] Stravinsky did not visit Granada until March 1955.

[21] The parenthetical direction is penciled in by Stravinsky.

out if I am going there or not. If the answer is "yes," I will be there to conduct a concert in the last week of February. This time, alas, I have no possibility of coming to Granada, having to go directly to Paris. In a week, I leave for Germany and many concerts (I play my new Capriccio for piano and orchestra, and I conduct programs of my compositions), then to Bucharest, then perhaps to Barcelona.

Do not forget me. I embrace you. May God keep you.

Your   Igor Stravinsky

FALLA TO STRAVINSKY

Hôtel de Bourgogne et Montana
7, rue de Bourgogne
Paris
July 14, 1931

Maison Pleyel
Paris

Very dear Igor Stravinsky,

Is it possible for us to see each other? I send you kind regards. I will come to fetch you at Pleyel for lunch on Friday, Saturday, or Monday, as you choose. Meanwhile, I await word from you.

With all my heart, your   Manuel de Falla

FALLA TO STRAVINSKY

Granada
[January?] 1932

Nice[22]

Very dear Igor Stravinsky,

In spite of the hurt I felt at your failure to respond to the note I sent to Pleyel when I was last in Paris[23]—a sad stay also because of my health—I wish to tell you at the beginning of this new year that my friendship and devotion remain solid, as always. I address to you my wishes for peace and justice, which we all need more than ever.

Your   Manuel de Falla

STRAVINSKY TO FALLA

Voreppe
February 4, 1932

My very dear Falla,

You must not take my silence as a sign of indifference. I love you very much, I have always loved you, and I will continue to love you as long as I live.

Very touched to know that you are thinking of me, I too send you all my

---

[22] Forwarded to La Vironnière, Voreppe, Isère.
[23] Stravinsky had not been in Paris but in Voreppe.

wishes for the peace of your spirit (but not my wishes for "justice," since I do not believe that it exists in *this* world), and of health for your body.

I have not lived in Nice since last autumn. I am at Voreppe (Isère, 14 kilometers from Grenoble), where I moved with my whole family in September, and where I ask you to send me more ample news of yourself and of what concerns you. May God keep you. I embrace you.

Your   Igor Stravinsky

FALLA TO STRAVINSKY

Granada
December 27, 1932

Very dear Igor Stravinsky,

The *Sacre* performance conducted by [Fernández] Arbós in Madrid was a great success.[24] I am overjoyed, and proud of my compatriots for the reception that they gave to your absolutely extraordinary work. . . . This piece is for me reminiscent of the first years of our friendship, which, thank God, is still alive.

I also want to offer you my most sincere wishes for a Happy New Year, in the hope that it will bring peace and justice to this world, which is suffering so in their absence.

I embrace you in all devotion.

Yours truly,   Manuel de Falla

STRAVINSKY TO FALLA

Voreppe (Isère, where I have lived
for a year)
December 31, 1932

My very dear Falla,

I am very moved by your lines and by your affection. I send you all my faithful friendship and the immense tenderness (weakness) that I reserve for you and your art. May the New Year be good for you in every way, and may God keep you, my very dear friend.

Please send this [enclosed] card to the good Arbós, who sent me a very nice telegram about the success of the *Sacre* [in Madrid].

I embrace you very fraternally.

Your   Igor Stravinsky

---

[24] G. G. Païchadze wrote to Stravinsky that same day: "I just received the following cable from the old master Arbós in Madrid: '*Sacre* triumph moving. Splendid performance. Audience delirious. Please transmit Orquesta Sinfónica's congratulations to Stravinsky for his work of genius. Arbós.' And this I do with pleasure."

FALLA TO STRAVINSKY

Granada
November 22, 1933
[Telegram]

c/o Fernández Arbós
calle Mayor 91
Madrid

Deeply regret my absence at your concerts in December. Hope to see you in Barcelona, where I will arrive soon. [I] embrace you.   Falla

STRAVINSKY TO FALLA

Voreppe
August 14, 1933
[Postcard] [25]

Alhambra
Granada

I embrace you, my dear Falla, with all my heart. With you.

Igor Stravinsky

FALLA TO STRAVINSKY

Granada
August 24, 1933
[Postcard]

Voreppe

Overjoyed by your card, I embrace you, very dear Igor, and address to you, as well as to your dear sons, all of my devoted thoughts.

Yours, with all my heart,   Manuel de Falla

I recently heard a beautiful performance of your marvelous *Petrushka* in Palma. I am sending [Domenico de'] Paoli a note in Milan.

FALLA TO STRAVINSKY

Casa Mulet B. de Génova
Palma (Baleares)
January 3, 1934

Voreppe[26]

All best wishes for a good year for you and yours, very dear Igor Stravinsky, and, once again, all of my regrets at not having been able to go and see you—and hear you—in Madrid, as I would so love to have done. . . .

I know that your Symphony [of Psalms] had a veritable triumph and made a profound impression in Barcelona. I am very eager to hear it! And I also know that those very moving thoughts and words you shared during your visit to Spain spring from your affection for me.[27]

---

[25] Picture postcard of a view of Voreppe.
[26] Forwarded to 21, rue Viète, Paris.
[27] Falla is alluding to comments that Stravinsky made to interviewers in Barcelona.

I have returned this year to Palma (as last year), in search of the silence and calm lacking in Granada.

I embrace you in great affection and devotion.

Your   Manuel de Falla

21, rue Viête (for this winter)
Paris
January 8, 1934

STRAVINSKY TO FALLA

Thinking of you with all my heart, my very dear Falla. May God keep you in this new year of 1934 as He has done until now and as He has preserved you until now from the wickedness of platitudes and the great stupidities in this beautiful little world here below.

Very touched and moved by your affectionate thoughts. I love and admire you with all my heart.

Your   I. Stravinsky

STRAVINSKY TO FALLA

Paris
January 1936
[Postcard][28]

Antequeruela Alta 11
Granada[29]

My best wishes for health and strength in the New Year, my dear Falla.

Your   I. Stravinsky

A pity what is happening in Spain. Thank you for your telegram.

STRAVINSKY TO FALLA

Mexico City
August 2, 1940[30]
[Postcard][31]

c/o Dr. Quiroga
Color 472
Córdoba
Argentina

It is ourselves[32] again (me) who are thinking of you with permanent affection. Send me a note, my dear Falla, to 124 So. Swall Drive, Beverly Hills, California, U.S.A.

Your Stravinskys, Igor and Vera

---

[28] Picture postcard of the Palais de Luxembourg, Paris.

[29] Forwarded to Mulet Barrio de Génova 6, Palma de Majorca.

[30] Marked by Falla: "received November 28, 1940."

[31] Picture postcard of the Cathedral of Mexico.

[32] The postcard is also signed by Salazar, Rosita Bal y Gay, and others.

FALLA TO STRAVINSKY

Villa del Lago
P. de Córdoba
Argentina
[November] 28, 1940
[Postcard] [33]

Very dear Igor Stravinsky,

I, too, am with you wholeheartedly since the joyous event of receiving your note from Mexico (after an incredible delay!). Will you come here? Last year there was some talk of it. I would be so happy!

Present my respects to Vera. I embrace you.

Your   Manuel de Falla

FALLA TO STRAVINSKY[34]

"Los Espinillos"
Alta Gracia
Córdoba
[January 1945]
[Postcard] [35]

My affection and devotion to you are still very much alive, and I wish you the best possible new year, in this time of misery and ugliness. All my respects to Vera.

Yours truly,   Manuel de Falla

---

[33] Picture postcard of the Bear, in Los Gigantes, Sierras de Córdoba.

[34] Stravinsky preserved this card in an envelope that he marked: "Last card I received from Manuel de Falla in 1945." Falla died in Argentina on November 14, 1946.

[35] Picture postcard of the Cerro de la Cruz in Los Gigantes.

LETTERS FROM

1914 ~ 1919

JACQUES RIVIÈRE

JACQUES RIVIÈRE[1] TO STRAVINSKY

Editions de la
Nouvelle Revue Française
35 & 37, rue Madame
Paris
[February 1914]

My dear Stravinsky,

It has taken me much too long to express my thanks. But I have had you in my thoughts during these past few days, in which I have begun to put some ideas about *The Nightingale* on paper.

You were very kind to have sent those two letters, to Gallimard and to myself. We greatly enjoyed them.

I intend to go to your concert on Saturday [*sic*],[2] and perhaps I will have the opportunity to shake your hand.

Be assured, my dear Stravinsky, of my friendship and appreciation.

Jacques Rivière

RIVIÈRE TO STRAVINSKY

15, rue Froideveux
Paris
May 25, 1914

Dear sir,

Would it be terribly indiscreet of me to ask you for two or three seats for the premiere of *The Nightingale*? I take this liberty only because I noticed last night that there was an exceptionally large number of complimentary tickets. And you can imagine how much I want my wife to have the chance to hear a work to which I myself look forward with such pleasure. If this [favor] is not possible for you, have no qualms about refusing.

If you could give me seats to the second performance, I would gratefully accept them, but I would prefer to attend the premiere.

I heard *Petrushka* again yesterday evening and was profoundly moved.

I beg you, dear sir, to excuse my importunity and to accept the assurance of my deep appreciation.

Jacques Rivière

---

[1] Jacques Rivière (1886–1925), writer, editor of *La Nouvelle Revue Française*. French is the original language of all the letters.

[2] Pierre Monteux's concert performance of *Petrushka* at the Casino de Paris.

RIVIÈRE TO STRAVINSKY   *[May 26 or 27, 1914]*

Dear sir,

You are infinitely kind to have thought of me, and I thank you wholeheartedly. Unfortunately, I had just left when your telegram arrived. For that reason I did not take advantage of the seat you offered me in your loge. I did squeeze into the Opéra on my own, but I heard *The Nightingale* under such miserable conditions that I cannot yet pass any judgment on it. What I managed to glimpse promises me some beautiful surprises at the next performance [on May 28].

      Thank you, again, dear sir, and I beg you to be assured of my fondness and admiration.

                                                        Jacques Rivière

RIVIÈRE TO STRAVINSKY   *avenue de Frontenex*
                                                        Geneva
My dear Stravinsky,   *June 20, 1918*

I expect to receive orders to return to France any minute. Thus you should now send me whatever I need to take care of the errand you discussed with me, which I shall do with pleasure. Would you please give this matter immediate consideration?

      I regret that my trips to Lausanne were so brief that we were not able to see each other at leisure. That we shall have to leave for a later date, in Paris.

      I shake your hand affectionately.

                                                        Jacques Rivière

RIVIÈRE TO STRAVINSKY   *Geneva*
                                                        [June 21, 1918]
Morges   *[Postcard]*

My dear Stravinsky,

Your friend came to see me this morning. I will wait for you tomorrow, Saturday, from 2 to 3 o'clock, or, if you cannot come then, from 5 to 6:30. And if you do not make an appearance tomorrow, I will wait for you again on Monday from 2 to 4. (But I have a class at 4:30 and thus will not be free later that day.) I will be very happy to be able to talk with you for a while.

      Dear Stravinsky, be assured of my best wishes.

                                                        Jacques Rivière

RIVIÈRE TO STRAVINSKY   *June 29, 1918*

My dear Stravinsky,

These are not banal thanks (inspired by no more than politeness) that I wish to address to you for the invitation you sent me. You cannot even imagine the pleasure your little pieces gave me. I shall speak candidly: I have been separated from the world of the living for so long that I had lost track of my aesthetic values; thinking back to what I admired before the war, I wondered if I had not been mistaken. I had become horribly skeptical of my own views.

You have restored my confidence in them. Now I am again certain, and more than ever, of your stature. I beg of you, conserve for us that spring of pure music that is in you, the only real one I know of in the entire contemporary world.

In the program of this concert you were framed by French-Swiss, German-Swiss, and Italian-Swiss music. Oh well! You did not take long to put all of that in the shade.

You avenge many things for us, notably that irritating, sentimental rhetoric in which Germany would like to submerge us. I like the electric allure of your pieces, and the way you have of moving, in a moment, at all costs, and at 100 kilometers an hour, in a very well-chosen direction—though a few toes may be crushed in the process.

I understand that you were hoping very strongly that the Russian front would be restored. You yourself are [a Russian front]. You make Germany go to the rear. You help us, aesthetically speaking, to maintain [Germany] in that state of profound nothingness into which it has fallen. With one jab you [rupture] their false genius, you perforate the enormous balloon of their slight artistic inclinations. For you and for us, [Germany] is nothing. Keep it up. From this moment on, you are rendering us a greater service than you could even guess.[3]

---

[3] On September 26, 1914, Stravinsky had written to Romain Rolland: "My dear colleague, I hurry to respond to your noble appeal to protest against the unprecedented barbarism of the German hordes. Barbarism! Is this really the word? What is barbarism? It seems that the word implies another conception of culture from ours. And that, as well as being something completely different from ours, it does not exclude a value as great as ours. But Germany today cannot be considered the bearer of a new culture. This country is a part of the ancient world, and its culture is as old as that of the other peoples of Western Europe. And for this reason I must affirm that a nation which in time of peace constructed a series of monuments such as those on the Sieges Allee in Berlin, and that in time of war sends hordes to destroy cities such as Louvain and monuments such as the Reims Cathedral, is a nation to be ranked neither among the barbarians nor among the civilized peoples. If by these means Germany seeks to renew itself, would it not be better to begin with the monuments in Berlin? It is in the greatest common interest of all nations who feel the need to breathe the air of their

I do not mean that I see absolutely nothing more to be desired from your music. One day, when I have more time, perhaps I shall explain to you what I would like to see emerge from you in the future. But there is no rush. For now the essential thing is that the voice be left open, singing promises that you will one day fulfill. The essential thing is that a relentless and direct music like yours exists somewhere. The essential thing is that there is someone like you who forces sensitive people to cover their ears.

I shake your hand affectionately.

Jacques Rivière

If you want to reply, you may do so in Russian, but on condition that you form your letters very carefully.

RIVIÈRE TO STRAVINSKY

Nouvelle Revue Française
35 & 37, rue Madame
Paris

My dear Stravinsky,

April 6, 1919

Auberjonois, to whom I entrusted this message, has undoubtedly told you that your letter gave me great joy. Again, I thank you heartily.

Today I must discuss a different matter. Perhaps you have already heard that my friends have decided to give me the editorship of the *Nouvelle Revue Française,* which will reappear on June 1. I am proud of this honor, but it is, at the same time, a great responsibility and the cause of some serious anxieties for me.

I intend to direct the attention of the review to the anti-impressionist, anti-symbolist, and anti-Debussyist movement, which is becoming more and more manifest and which wants, it seems, to assume the form, and the force, of a vast current. I would be extremely happy if you were able to set forth for us, in an article whose length you yourself would decide, your current ideas on music and the significance of the pursuits to which you are devoting yourself at this time.

Do not think that you are forgotten here. Everyone I see speaks of you. The influence of your *Petrushka, Sacre,* and the recent works is evident in the young musicians. Everyone would greet an article by you with curiosity and appreciation.

To accommodate yourself, you could write in Russian. If you do not have someone at hand who could translate [the article], I could do that myself, if the

---

healthy and ancient culture to place themselves on the side of the enemies of Germany and to attack all those who share the spirit of this colossal and obese Germania, threatened with fatal symptoms of moral decay. My dear colleague, please accept the expression of my profound admiration and greatest artistic sympathy. P.S. In these terrible and great days through which we are living, I have found your appeal, *'L'union fait la force!,'* a source of strong encouragement."

manuscript you send me is *very clearly written*. I would then submit my translation to you for correction, of course.

Needless to say, you would be properly recompensed for your work, although I cannot promise mountains of gold.

Please excuse me for having neglected some of the errands you requested of me during our last meeting in Geneva. Most of the people you asked me to see were not in Paris when I arrived. And I myself was away from Paris for so long that by the time I returned, these errands had already been overtaken by events.

I await your reply, which I can only hope will be favorable. With this conviction I beg you to be assured, my dear Stravinsky, of my fondest wishes.

Jacques Rivière

Please do not fail to convey my best regards to Ramuz and Auberjonois. If you decide to address your manuscript to me in Russian, advise me; I will have someone I know facilitate the delivery, after the necessary authorization has been obtained.

RIVIÈRE TO STRAVINSKY

Morges

Paris
April 21, 1919
[Postcard]

My dear Stravinsky,

Of course your letter, depriving me of your collaboration, saddened me, but it thrilled me as well, because I think, as you do, that the true creator should not waste his time discoursing on tendencies and experiments. His work will explain everything on its own.

Nevertheless, should you be struck by the desire to write not only about yourself but about others, Debussy, for example, or contemporary Russian music, or any other subject, keep me in mind, and remember that our pages are always open to you.

Fondly yours,   Jacques Rivière

What is the new *Firebird* Suite? A ballet?

CORRESPONDENCE WITH

1917 ᴧ *1932*

E. ERRAZURIZ & B. CENDRARS

EUGENIA ERRAZURIZ[1] TO STRAVINSKY

60, avenue Montaigne
Paris
January 13, 1917

Cher maître,

I asked Jacqueline[2] to transmit the monthly 1,000 francs I promised you. I was looking forward to seeing you in Paris, and I cannot tell you how sorry I am to hear that you are ill.[3] You have all of my best wishes for this new year; may it bring you peace and health.

Your postcard gave me immense pleasure, and you do not know to what extent I am your admirer and devoted friend.

Eugenia Errazuriz

P.S. My regards to Madame Stravinsky. Do not forget to send news. I have become a savage and wicked beast, but I still hope to preserve our friendship, which is very precious to me.

ERRAZURIZ TO STRAVINSKY

February 20, 1918

Pardon me, pardon me, dear *maître* and friend, for having neglected to tell you that I received the piano pieces[4] and the Etude [for Pianola]. I have been ill and suffering and am discouraged. I humbly beg your pardon.

---

[1] In 1916, after Stravinsky met Eugenia Errazuriz, she began to send him a stipend of 1,000 francs a month. French is the original language of all the correspondence.

[2] Countess Jacqueline Rehbinder. She had telegraphed to Stravinsky, December 10, 1916: "Have sent money through my bank at Madame Errazuriz's request. Friendly greetings."

[3] In December 1916 Stravinsky had intercostal neuralgia, which prevented him from coming to Paris to conduct *Les Abeilles,* the ballet based on his *Scherzo fantastique.*

[4] On December 18, 1917, Stravinsky had written to Alfred Cortot, then undersecretary of the Ministry of Arts, Paris: "Some time ago I asked a friend of mine (M. Gustave [?], Morges, Vaud, Switzerland), . . . who is well known by the Customs authorities, to take charge of some packages of music that I sent to Paris. I have just learned that, unfortunately, they were seized by the Customs officials, who said they would see that the contents were delivered to their destinations after examination by the censor. Since I do not know whether they were ever received, I would like to ask you, if possi-

I gave Misia [Edwards] 1,000 francs, which I asked her to transmit to you. Is it impossible to see you in Paris? I talk to Picasso about you; we, your friends, all share tremendous sympathy for you. But you have one friend who is too stupid to express . . . all of her thoughts and devoted admiration.

Your   Eugenia Errazuriz

STRAVINSKY TO ERRAZURIZ

March 23, 1918
[Telegram]

Thank [Arthur] Rubinstein warmly. I will compose an important piano piece[5] especially for him. Soon I will send you a ragtime recently composed for you. Your   Stravinsky

ERRAZURIZ TO STRAVINSKY

[April 1918]

. . . I am disappointed that you did not come [to Paris] . . . and sorry to learn that you have . . . suffered moments of sorrow. . . . Your beautiful music gives me immense pleasure. I am very proud of the magnificent sketchbook, which I

---

ble, to intervene and find out whether the packages were lost or destroyed. A new composition, Etude for Pianola, was contained therein. One of the packages was to be sent to Madame Errazuriz, 60, avenue Montaigne, Paris, the other to André Gide, *Nouvelle Revue Française,* Paris. The first contained the manuscript of the Etude for Pianola and a sketchbook for my Five Easy Pieces (4-hands), the second the Five Easy Pieces and a sketchbook for the Three Easy Pieces (4-hands). Would it be possible for you to determine whether these manuscripts are still being held by the censor? If so, please establish once and for all that what they contain is indeed music, and testify that you know the sender and that he is not a suspicious character. I thank you in advance."

Cortot answered on December 27, 1917: "I am very happy to inform you that your works arrived safely at their destinations. I have been unable to reach Madame Errazuriz until today, which explains my delay in replying to you. Furthermore, your letter was not delivered to me until the 24th! It gives me great satisfaction to be able to reassure you. While I am awaiting the joy of reading some of your new works, please accept this expression of my most sincere devotion." Stravinsky telegraphed his acknowledgment: "Just received your very nice letter, dear sir. Accept my sincere thanks. Igor Stravinsky." Nearly forty-five years later, on May 21, 1962, Cortot wrote to Stravinsky, "c/o Boulez," to wish a happy eightieth birthday to "the greatest composer of the twentieth century." Stravinsky, then in the middle of a concert tour, received the letter in Paris. Back in Los Angeles, he placed it in an envelope on which he wrote: "Letter from Alfred Cortot . . . which, owing to my numerous displacements, I did not have time to answer. A few days later I learned that he had died. I. Stravinsky."

[5] Rubinstein commissioned what became the Piano-Rag Music. The dedication to him in Stravinsky's sketchbook for the work (the pianist's name with a frame drawn around it) antedates all of the musical notations. See Manuel de Falla's letter to Stravinsky of May 1, 1918, in the present volume; see also Appendix D.

guard avariciously while awaiting your arrival. I had [Misia] Edwards play [the piece] for me, and it inspired great admiration in us both, but we will not present it here until you come. Picasso loves you, and I admire you enthusiastically. . . .

It was at the suggestion of Errazuriz that Blaise Cendrars first wrote to Stravinsky, on April 29, 1917. Cendrars had been given the direction of a new publishing house, Editions de la Sirène, 12, rue La Boétie, Paris. Apollinaire, Cocteau, Picasso, Matisse, Derain, Satie, and others had agreed to entrust certain works to the company. Endeavoring to assemble the "genuine works of our generation," Cendrars wanted to include pieces by Stravinsky. Cendrars, in his first letter, requested the score of Renard,

right away, so that it will be printed by the time the Princesse de Polignac presents the work. Is it available, or have you already promised it elsewhere? Please give me your terms, etc. Satie has promised me the score of *Socrate,* which also belongs to the Princesse de Polignac. If all of these, among other modern works, were published by the same house, they would constitute a beautiful and forceful collection.

Your work would be printed according to your wishes and taste, and I would oversee the printing personally. . . .

Apart from this, do you have an album of songs that could appear even before *Renard?* . . .

In principle, I would be willing to take all of your works, which cannot be found in Paris. Couldn't the *Sacre* be reprinted, for example? . . .

When Stravinsky informed Cendrars that Renard *had already been published, he replied:*

. . . [We] are eager to print the unpublished works, . . . nos. 22, 23, 24 of your prospectus, as well as the *Ragtime* dedicated to Madame Errazuriz that you mentioned, which is not listed in the prospectus. We could even begin with the latter.

Please send me your terms. . . . If we reach an agreement about these pieces, the Editions de la Sirène would like to start negotiations about the purchase of the pieces you had printed in Geneva, and especially *Renard.* [May 14, 1918]

CENDRARS TO STRAVINSKY   *Editions de la Sirène*
                                          July 10, 1918

Dear sir,

Please excuse me, first of all, for taking so long to reply to your letter. I have endeavored to fulfill all of your conditions. Unfortunately, this is impossible for me. Our whole enterprise just is not feasible at the moment because of the tragic events [of the war] that we are undergoing. . . .

At any rate, here is what I have managed to arrange for you: [We] will . . . begin engraving [the *Ragtime*] immediately, so that it will appear before Christmas. This edition would be sold at 6 francs, and La Sirène offers you 600 French francs for the first thousand copies sold and 750 French francs for each additional thousand, and 10 percent of the gross profits, all rights reserved, except in Russia. . . .

Les Noces villageoises interests us enormously, and I beg you to reserve it for us. . . .

Let me repeat that the *Ragtime* would be printed with the utmost care. . . . Picasso will provide the portrait he made of you last winter. . . .

Blaise Cendrars

STRAVINSKY TO CENDRARS *Morges*
August 7, 1918

Dear sir,

I am very sorry not to be able to accept the conditions proposed by your review . . . because I have never agreed to such a low honorarium, . . . which, moreover, is in contradiction to the increase in the cost of living, i.e., for the same reasons that La Sirène cannot accept *my* conditions. If I add that composition is my only livelihood and that I spent two months composing the work in question, clearly you will understand my refusal.

I send you, dear sir, my most cordial regards.

Igor Stravinsky

CENDRARS TO STRAVINSKY *Nice*
August 17, 1918

Dear M. Stravinsky,

. . . I am personally determined to publish your work at La Sirène, and I am equally intent upon paying you your just fees. I have already insisted on this to the management of La Sirène. With your permission, I will commence negotiations anew, and I am certain that you will be satisfied, the dreadful military circumstances allowing. . . . You are well aware of how difficult it is for you and other poor artists to obtain equitable remuneration, especially in Paris. . . .

Blaise Cendrars

CENDRARS TO STRAVINSKY   *October 28, 1918*

Dear sir,

Your letter, finally received two days ago, had not yet arrived when M. [Carlo]
Placci visited me. In accordance with your letter, M. Laffitte[6] is going to send
you the contract to sign. I am very pleased. . . .

    Unfortunately, Madame Errazuriz is in London, and we must wait until
her return. . . .

                          Blaise Cendrars

CENDRARS TO STRAVINSKY   *Monday*
                                                     Editions de la Sirène
Dear sir,

Arriving back in Paris, I still had not received word from you. I became anxious
about the *Ragtime* and managed to convince M. Laffitte . . . to accept your
terms for the premiere. It is done. Please let me know whether you now
agree. . . .

                          Blaise Cendrars

STRAVINSKY TO CENDRARS   *Morges*
                                                     November 11, 1918
Paris

Dear sir,

I received your kind letter of October 28, and I am willing to have Editions de la
Sirène handle my piano reduction of the *Ragtime*. In order to avoid further misunderstandings, I will repeat my terms, in the form of a contract proposal.

    I cede to the Editions de la Sirène my rights to reproduction and sale of *one
thousand copies* . . . of my piece entitled *Ragtime*—in all countries except Russia in its territorial entirety (that is, such as it was before the war . . .). In exchange, I ask the Editions [de la Sirène] for 1,000 Swiss francs. I reserve for
myself all rights for performance, arrangement, transcription (for whatever instruments), and mechanical reproduction. In addition, I submit the following
conditions to the Editions de la Sirène: (1) to procure a copyright in the United
States and to return it to me, showing this phrase on the cover and the first
page of music: "Copyright 1918 by I. Stravinsky"; (2) to include the following
phrase in the same way: "All rights of performance, reproduction, arrangement
reserved in all countries, including Denmark, Sweden, and Norway"; (3) to indicate that the orchestra score (for eleven instruments) of this work is for hire
(in case of a rental request, La Sirène would address itself to me); (4) to advise

---

[6] Paul Laffitte, director in chief of Editions de la Sirène.

me or my heirs as soon as these thousand copies (the object of the present contract) are sold; (5) to furnish me with ten author's copies of the work in question.

There you have my terms, dear sir. I would be grateful if you would remind Picasso of his promise to design a cover for my pieces. I would be pleased if he were to make one for the *Ragtime*.

While I await your amicable reply, dear sir, please be assured of my best wishes.

Igor Stravinsky

CENDRARS TO STRAVINSKY

Paris
November 30, 1918
[Telegram]

Received contract [from Laffitte] today. Letter follows.   Cendrars

STRAVINSKY TO PAUL LAFFITTE   *December 19, 1918*

Sir,

Enclosed I return a copy of our contract[7] with my signature; the other copy I will keep. I wish to draw your attention to point III, where you have forgotten to mention that the rights of reproduction, performance, etc., are reserved in Sweden, as in Norway, Denmark, South America. I hope that this omission will not create any future misunderstanding between us. On the other hand, I am in complete agreement regarding the second edition, which you had wanted, under the present contract, to reserve for yourself.

I will send you the copy of the piano score of the *Ragtime* in a few days. While I await the pleasure of your letter, please accept, sir, my best wishes.

Igor Stravinsky

STRAVINSKY TO CENDRARS

February 2, 1919
[Telegram]

I returned contract with my signature December 20. Did you receive it? Stravinsky

---

[7] Stravinsky signed the contract for *Ragtime* on December 19, 1918. On February 5, 1919, he cabled to Cocteau (10, rue d'Anjou, Paris): "Thank you for your new book. Please ask Laffitte whether he received *Ragtime* contract. Friendly greetings, Stravinsky."

Morges
February 18, 1919

STRAVINSKY TO CENDRARS   *[Telegram]*

Did you receive *Ragtime*? Please send honorarium without delay to Lieutenant Raymond,[8] Adjunct to the Military Attaché, United States Legation in Bern.   Stravinsky

On February 27, 1919, the Librairie Kundig in Geneva sent Stravinsky a check for 1,000 francs, by order of the Editions de la Sirène. Three months later the proofs were given to Alexandre Cingria,[9] who, according to a letter from Cendrars, was to deliver them to Stravinsky in Morges.

CENDRARS TO STRAVINSKY

Today I gave the proofs of *Ragtime* to M. Alexandre Cingria, who leaves for Switzerland on Friday. I hope you will be pleased with them. The lettering is large and quite beautiful. Please tell me if you have suggestions for the cover— would you like it on blue paper?

I would also like to ask you to contribute an article about music to *La Rose Rouge* [a weekly literary review], of which I am sending you several issues. Also, please ask M. Ramuz if he would contribute something. . . .

Blaise Cendrars

By August 29, 1919, the Ragtime *still was not printed. According to Laffitte's letter of that date, the printing house that had begun the task for La Sirène had gone out of business, and another printer willing to finish the* Ragtime *had only just been found. Furthermore, Picasso had not yet submitted the cover ("He made one but was not happy with it and wanted to redo it").*

Finally, in December, Laffitte informed Stravinsky that the Ragtime *would be finished and released for sale at the beginning of January 1920. On December 19, Laffitte sent two copies of the piece to Stravinsky and, at this late date, mentioned that the copyright might be precarious. The composer acknowledged receipt of the music a few days later:*

---

[8] Antonin Raymond, one of Stravinsky's first American friends, though he was of Czech origin. His mother-in-law, Marie Brooks, 600 West 114th Street, New York, contributed money to the 1919 Stravinsky rescue fund. In July 1919 Raymond was transferred to the American Embassy in Paris. He and his wife corresponded with Stravinsky for some years following the war.

[9] The brother of Stravinsky's close friend Charles-Albert Cingria.

STRAVINSKY TO LAFFITTE

Received two completely crumpled copies *Ragtime*. Indispensable immediately to correct frightful error in dedication to Madame Errazuriz.[10] To avoid such surprises [I] had explicitly asked you to send me the last proof, which you failed to do.   Stravinsky

In the meantime, Cendrars, now editing La Rose Rouge, *had proposed a cinematographic enterprise to Stravinsky:*

CENDRARS TO STRAVINSKY

Dear sir,

I spoke to my friend Abel Gance about using your music for films. He is looking for a musician, and although this is not exactly in your vein, I think that the two of you could reach at least a tentative understanding. Gance would be thrilled to work with you. He has big projects and begs you to begin negotiations with him on this subject. Write to: Films Abel Gance, 9, avenue de l'Opéra, Paris.

As for me, I would be very happy if this affair could be arranged. It would be a good beginning. I think he has *Don Quixote* in mind. I am ready to assist you in this transaction.

Nothing new at La Sirène.

Yours truly,   Blaise Cendrars

STRAVINSKY TO CENDRARS

Dear M. Cendrars,

I received your note of October 7 concerning the Gance films, and I thank you very much. I would be very pleased if this company were to make me an interesting proposal—one *in keeping with my temperament*. The question of *Don Quixote* disturbs me because it has nothing to do with my concept of cinematographic spectacles—do you remember our discussions on this subject? Nevertheless, I await a note from M. Gance.

And La Sirène? Will they ever decide to publish my *Rag*?

Best to you,   I. Stravinsky

---

[10] Editions de la Sirène had spelled the name "Errasuri."

CENDRARS TO STRAVINSKY

Café de Paris
Nice
October 24, 1919

My dear friend,

I relayed the contents of your letter to my friend Gance, and here is his reply: "Ask M. Stravinsky if he could not conceive of a visualization of the *Sacre* or *Firebird* in our music halls . . . employing visual themes according to his inclination. I would respect his guidelines and would make a sort of visual and original transposition that he would surely like. . . ." Does that interest you? Gance has a big project in mind . . . and you might want to begin discussions with him now. . . . He will write to you. He just bought a hotel, place de la Concorde, with a big hall where he intends to present films and concerts and exhibit all sorts of new and avant-garde art. . . . Incidentally, he has 100 million in capital.

Please send me a note in Paris. . . . I return there on the 31st. . . .

Blaise Cendrars

Thirteen years later, Cendrars suggested another project to the composer:[11]

CENDRARS TO STRAVINSKY

[August 1932][12]

Igor,

Don't forget to come to lunch at the Comtesse de Lastries' [?]. The Mestcherskys are expected as well.

My good hand,[13]   Blaise

CENDRARS TO STRAVINSKY

Poitiers
September 18, 1932

Voreppe

My dear Igor,

Forgive me for not having written to you sooner. The last days of vacation have been so magnificent that I have had no desire to do anything.

Yesterday I had lunch with my American agent. I was talking about you, and he asked if you had thought of writing your memoirs. . . . If this were of interest to you, he says you could make a pile of American dollars. (I am relating the proposition to you in the same brutal language he used.) I think you might like the idea, and, in collaboration with Vera, who has some inclination to write, you could make a beautiful book, open your heart, and reveal your life, your creations, [even] the four truths. Would you like me to give your address to Mr.

---

[11] By this time the two men had become close friends, and in this and the following letters, Cendrars addresses Stravinsky with the familiar *"tu."*

[12] Note left at the Hôtel du Palais, Biarritz.

[13] Cendrars had only one arm.

W. A. Bradley, 5, rue St. Louis-en-l'Ile, Paris 4, so that you could begin negotiating with him directly? I think you could reach an agreement quite rapidly. . . .

Blaise

You will receive the books next week.

CENDRARS TO STRAVINSKY   *September 23, 1932*

Voreppe

My dear Igor,

Yesterday I telephoned Mr. Bradley and relayed your idea for a book of polemics. He said he was enchanted and will write to you. I would be happy if this plan were realized. An odd aside: Mr. Bradley is an honest American businessman.

You should have received a package of books from Grasset, and I am going to send you another package from a different publisher. . . .

Blaise

CENDRARS TO STRAVINSKY   *Chez Danbas, Antiquarian*
                                          Biarritz
Voreppe   *October 4, 1932*

My dear Igor,

I am writing to you from Biarritz—which is to say that I am retracing our trip backward: Ste.-Radegonde to Poitiers, St.-Michel-des-Lions to Limoges . . . and St.-Suaire.[14]

I found Eugenia [Errazuriz] very well and calmer than I have seen her in a long time.

I received your little photographs. . . . You should receive some others from me, which I will inscribe to you one day when I pass through Voreppe. That was not possible for me this time.

I plan to spend a month here and finish a book for Bradley.

Where will you be at Christmas? . . .

Blaise

---

[14] In June 1932, Stravinsky and Vera Sudeikina had driven to Frankfurt to hear a performance of *Mavra* conducted by Hans Rosbaud (June 23). In mid-August they drove to Biarritz, by way of Tarascon, Aigues-Mortes, Arles (June 17–19, Hôtel Jules César), Les Baux (20th), and Carcassonne, arriving at the Hôtel du Palais, Biarritz, on the 21st. During the next two days, Stravinsky rehearsed the Casino orchestra for a con-

CENDRARS TO STRAVINSKY

Voreppe

Chez Danbas, Antiquarian
Biarritz
October 6, 1932

My dear Igor,

Upon receipt of your letter ([reminding me] of all of the good things I enjoyed just last month), I wrote to our friend Bradley to ask him what had become of your negotiations. I hope that you will have a quick reply. Bradley is punctual, but I heard that his wife is seriously ill at the moment.

Last night I saw our friend Mestchersky,[15] and we spoke of you at length. Everyone here sends you best wishes.

Blaise

CENDRARS TO STRAVINSKY

Voreppe

Biarritz
December 28, 1932
[Postcard]

I am still in the city of our summer triumphs. Eugenia is in Paris, and I am glad you finally received the package of books about which I registered a complaint three months ago! I wish you all the best and a good year.

Blaise

---

cert on the 25th. The couple spent part of that day at the country home of a friend, the Marquis Pierre d'Arcangues, and on the 27th and 28th they visited the Marquis Lur-Saluces (Château-Yquem) in Gavarnie. On September 1 and 2, the Cendrars, Stravinsky, and Vera Sudeikina returned to Paris by way of Bordeaux (Château Montre), St.-Emilion (Château-Biron), Périgueux (Eglise de Dorat), Limoges (Château de Jouxtens; L'Albi Jouxtens wrote to Stravinsky, October 9, 1933, asking whether a musical son "should go to the Juilliard School in New York"), Poitiers (Hôtel du Palais), and Chalon-sur-Saône (Grand Hôtel Moderne). After spending the night of September 2 at Chartres (Hôtel de France), the party reached Paris on the 3rd.

[15] Mestchersky, one of Stravinsky's close friends, wrote on October 18: "I have had no news about you except for Blaise's stories. He has been here for two weeks now, staying with old lady Errazuriz."

A LETTER FROM

1 9 2 2

FRANCIS PICABIA

FRANCIS PICABIA TO STRAVINSKY

Hôtel Continental
Paris

14, rue Emile Augier
Paris
May 26, 1922

Dear M. Stravinsky,

I am sending you the scenario for *Les Yeux chauds*.[1] Excuse me for not having typed it, but that would have taken even more time. I look forward to dinner on Wednesday evening.[2]

Very truly yours,   Francis Picabia

Hot Eyes

A room is plunged into darkness for *30 seconds*. Arrange six white-light projectors around the room and attach black discs, with holes, to them. The discs are spun around very fast, giving the audience the illusion of black and white movement. This lasts *15 seconds*. Then comes a film projection of pink light on a white curtain. Meanwhile, the authors grimace at the audience. This lasts *15 seconds*. Stop the film projection and raise the curtain.

An invisible line stretches across the front of the stage. Suspended from the line are huge gold numbers in the form of a division. Behind the line, on the left, is a very large, transparent, pink ball, lighted from the inside by electric bulbs; the ball must measure about four meters in diameter and should be mounted on rails. At each of the two ends of the stage is a woman dressed in a tight, black-and-white-striped leotard; one woman's stripes are horizontal, the other's vertical. The women will send the ball to each other three times, then

---

[1] William Camfield (*Francis Picabia* [Princeton, 1979]) states that a secretary of Stravinsky wrote to Picabia saying that the composer was interested in this scenario, the existence of which had been announced in *Comoedia* and elsewhere. Vera Sudeikina was the link between the composer and Picabia, whose ex-wife, Gabrielle Buffet, shared an apartment with Madame Sudeikina beginning a few weeks later. The text published here may be the unique copy of *Les Yeux chauds*.
[2] Stravinsky has written on the envelope: "Wednesday evening unless advised to the contrary."

the ball will return to center stage and stop. The time elapsed to the moment the ball stops is 4 *minutes*.

Three sides of the set consist of white curtains on which black circles have been traced. A few gulls make spinning passes. Five women enter from each side (pink leotards give the impression of total nudity). They stand on either side of the ball and greet the audience in the manner of acrobats. The middle woman of each group climbs a rope and disappears. This lasts 4 *minutes*. While the women are disappearing, at the front of the stage a white curtain descends, upon which a film projection casts pictures of a butterfly emerging from its cocoon. This lasts 30 *seconds*.

The curtain is raised, revealing the stage without decor, but rather littered with the usual mess of backstage apparatus. At center stage are five stuffed animals: a parrot, a monkey, a gull, a wild boar, and a deer. They are lighted by two projectors, one green, the other red. Off to the side, an accordion player accompanies a woman who sings as she walks around the animals. This lasts 2 *minutes*, and is followed by a film-projected apparition of the two authors (15 *seconds*). The show ends, as it began, with black and white lighting. This lasts 15 *seconds*.

Total duration: 12 *minutes*.

II

THE NIGHTINGALE IN RUSSIA

Correspondence with Sanine, Struve, and Siloti

In Copenhagen, November 25, 1925, Stravinsky told an interviewer:

What I like most about Denmark is that it is H. C. Andersen's home-
land. . . . Whenever I come to Denmark, I dream of being able to read his
fairy tales in Danish. Quite possibly the original versions contain a few profound truths and psychological insights that are lost in translation.

Andersen's "The Nightingale" was the story Stravinsky chose for his first
opera, and the same author's "The Ice Maiden" provided the plot for the ballet
Le Baiser de la fée. *George Balanchine, aware of Stravinsky's fondness for An-*
dersen, proposed yet another tale of his as the basis for a ballet, which, how-
ever, was eventually inspired by a very different moralist, La Fontaine, and
which became Jeu de cartes.

In Chroniques de ma vie, *Stravinsky recalls that Rimsky-Korsakov had*
seen and approved the first sketches for The Nightingale, *but since these are*
dated from November 1908 through the end of January 1909, Stravinsky must
have confused them with sketches for Fireworks. *After having composed* Firebird, Petrushka, *and* Le Sacre du printemps, *he regarded the single act of the*
opera as an autonomous work that he would not, or could not, extend. He even
had it published—announcing this as a fait accompli in an interview in the
Petersburg Gazette, *October 19, 1912 ("I published the first scene as a separate*
piece"), though the parts were still at the printer's in February 1913—and he
managed to convince the Moscow Free Theatre to perform the 18-minute score.

On February 17, 1913, Alexander Aksimovich Sanine, stage director and
Stravinsky's neighbor on the Kriukov Canal in St. Petersburg, wrote to the
composer:

My dear, kind Igor Fyodorovich!

"Alea jacta est." . . . What I was discussing with you in hypothetical terms in
Paris has come to pass. An artistic-musical institution called the Free Theatre is
being founded in Moscow, and this statement is reliable, since almost all of the
practical arrangements have been made. . . . The initiator of the project is the
famous director Konstantin Alexandrovich Mardzhanov,[1] who feels confident

---

[1] Konstantin Alexandrovich Mardzhanov (1872–1933) was director of the Moscow Art
Theatre, renamed the Mardzhanov Theatre after the Revolution.

that he can lead us out of the almshouse. . . . The theatre itself is located in Moscow and has been rented for a three-year period. . . . I will be moving back to Moscow with my whole family, after an eleven-year absence. . . . The aim of the Free Theatre is to cultivate a wide variety of artistic interests, comic opera, operetta, melodrama, mime. . . . No limits will be imposed, and we must find the form and means to realize all of this. At the moment, we are working out a repertory and selecting the troupe accordingly. . . .

I want to approach you personally, my very dear Igor Fyodorovich, with an official request. Help us. Share your music with us. My greatest dream is to show you off to Moscow, to St. Petersburg, indeed to all of Russia. Mardzhanov agrees; he would like to commission a three-act piece from you that would make up an entire evening's program. You need not limit the character or form; employ prose, opera, dance, and mime all together as you wish in a single work. . . . Mardzhanov is prepared to send you a certain sum immediately as an advance and to draw up an agreement with you right away concerning the purchase of the piece. We will meet all financial and artistic terms. I know that you work slowly. But you mentioned something to me about your *Svadba* [*sic*].[2] . . . Evidently you have been giving thought to that work for a long time now. . . . If you are not taken with the idea of a three-act piece, we will count on your *Svadba*.

I will be here in St. Petersburg until I go to Paris, May 9, so I will keep in touch with you, as well as with Mardzhanov. We begin rehearsals on July 1 and will rehearse through the summer, opening in October, if everything works out. Should this be too little time for you, we will move Stravinsky farther back on the calendar. I would like to know what *Svadba* is in more detail: its character, its length, the number of performers involved. . . . Perhaps you will be generous and, in addition to *Svadba*, give us a little piece of mime. . . . Perhaps something will "occur" to you. . . . But first of all, let me know *right away* what your financial terms are so that I can present them to Moscow. Remember that the theatre will be pleased and glad to work with you and for you.

Your fond [admirer],   A. A. Sanine

Kriukov Canal,
house 9, apt. 8

Stravinsky proposed the one-act Nightingale *in his reply, describing the piece as*

lasting about 18 minutes. . . . The music is with the printer right now, and in the summer my publisher will be able to give you all the parts, which you should examine with final proofreading in mind. *The Nightingale* will be published by the Russischer Musik Verlag (Berlin, Dessauerstrasse 17; address yourself to Nikolay Gustavovich Struve, the director there).

The Nightingale, a high coloratura, sings offstage, the cook-girl is a soprano, the fisherman a tenor, and you already know about the others. For a cer-

---

[2] This seems to be the earliest reference to *Les Noces*.

tain sum, I could offer the Free Theatre exclusive performance rights in Moscow for a number of years. You will have to make arrangements for the advance with my publisher. . . . I shall probably stay here until I go to Paris [for the *Sacre*], so write to this address.

I composed *The Nightingale* in the period of my infatuation with birds (at any rate, when I was at my bird-best). The subject and scenario are simple, very much in the Andersen lyrical style. I worked on the libretto together with my friend . . . Stepan Stepanovich Mitussov.[3] The action takes place in the woods by the sea. The opening: a fisherman is sitting on the shore, singing his song, with recitative. He is waiting for the Nightingale to sing, but is frightened away by people who have come on orders from "His Highness the Chinese Emperor" to find the remarkable bird. The people are courtiers (a small male chorus), a Chamberlain, a Bonze (one a deep bass, the other a baritone), and a "cook-girl," who leads them to the woods. She tells them: "Every day, this is where I hear the Nightingale; listen now, for he will begin to sing." Suddenly, far away, a cow begins to low. The courtiers, in raptures, cannot praise this wonderful song highly enough, but the cook-girl insists that this is only her cow and that the Nightingale will be heard shortly. Then frogs croak, and again the courtiers mistake the sounds for the Nightingale and beg the cook-girl to call the bird, promising her such rewards as an opportunity to watch "how the Emperor dines" and a promotion to the title "cook-in-ordinary." At this moment the Nightingale finally does sing, unaware of the absurd conversation about his singing, which the courtiers discuss in whispers. The cook-girl appeals to the Nightingale on behalf of the courtiers and invites the bird to come to the palace for a court festivity, because "His Highness" desires the Nightingale's presence. The Nightingale replies that it is best to hear his songs "in the green woods at dawn" but yields to the monarch's will. At this point, the Chamberlain extends a lengthy invitation to the Nightingale to come to the palace, after which courtiers follow, pleased with their success, while the Fisherman remains behind, alone, looking sadly after the Nightingale as he moves into the distance. The Fisherman, returning to his work, resumes his old song, and the curtain slowly descends in complete silence.

Sanine answered on March 14:

My dear, charming Igor Fyodorovich,

. . . Of course we will take *The Nightingale,* and you may consider it already bought. Thank you also for all of the details and particulars. . . . We will be putting it on with Alexandre Nikolayevich Benois, who has a good grasp of the tale, of Chinese colors, and of you as a composer and poet. I have one great and urgent request, though, and if you have the slightest fondness for me, you will grant it. Since you already have a beginning, you will be able, without great difficulties, to write one more scene in order to give the tale the Andersen conclu-

---

[3] 1879–1942.

sion. Make this scene as brief as the first one, even briefer, but [portray] the death of the Great Khan. The toy nightingale sings, then the true one. Do this any way you wish, following your inspiration. But this is essential, if your creation is to be complete.

We had been dreaming about *Svadebka*, but I see now that this will have to be postponed. In my conversations with Sergei Pavlovich I sensed (this is confidential) a certain jealousy toward you. But S. Pavlovich is going to South America, so Russia will have a chance to see and hear the *real* Stravinsky. Perhaps you are saving *Svadebka* for Sergei Pavlovich? . . . But, then, *Svadebka* is still in the making and has yet to be born, while *The Nightingale* is already living!!! . . .

If you consent to write another "bird" scene (Benois says that you will be masterful and yet concise in the Great Khan's death scene), we will prepare the first scene, while you work out the second and send it to us later. When the libretto is ready, you can give me the outline. . . . Both Benois and I will be in Paris, where we will be able to make whatever arrangements you would like. . . . Anyway, this is what I suggest: If you agree to complete *The Nightingale* and to honor us with the privilege of introducing the real Stravinsky to Moscow and St. Petersburg, cable us, or me, at the Free Theatre, state your terms, and we will send you an advance. Then I will go to Paris around April 20. On the way, I will stop off in Berlin to see Struve. . . . If you cannot get to Berlin, then I will make a detour on my way from Berlin to Paris and meet with you in Clarens. . . .

I kiss you most affectionately and await an affirmative reply, my kind, gentle, and dearest [friend] !!

On March 17, Stravinsky received a telegram from Sanine: "Anxiously await positive answer by cable Free Theatre." Stravinsky telegraphed: "Answer too complex, will write letter." When another telegram came on March 27, reiterating the request for the extra scene, the composer answered that same day: "Absolutely impossible. Details by letter. Warmly, Stravinsky." But later that day he sent a second telegram: "Have changed my mind. Two more scenes should be written. Since all summer tasks will have to be postponed, a commission will be necessary." And also on that same day, he wrote to Sanine:

The issue is this: the scene that I completed from Andersen's "The Nightingale" is well rounded, entirely finished, and stands alone. By adding to it, however, we could reduce the monotony, not only of the libretto, but also of the music. As it is, the scene lacks a middle; also, there is a conspicuous absence of any musical contrast. The nucleus of the Andersen story is the rivalry between the artificial nightingale and the authentic one. I therefore plan to compose two more scenes and to give the story greater fullness. I will describe both of them briefly. Second scene—"Festivity in the Garden": prelude, interlude, curtain. The porcelain palace of the Chinese Emperor. A servant sweeps the floor, and the gossip about the Nightingale who will sing this evening before the Emperor is endless. (A minor but significant detail: the palace is very drafty, and when the doors are opened, the bells that adorn the walls begin to ring.) Later the Chamberlain appears and chases everyone away, for the Emperor is coming with his entourage. The procession of the Chinese Emperor. The Nightingale is brought out, the Emperor commands him to sing, and when he does, the Emperor's eyes fill with tears. The courtiers also weep. Suddenly the Japanese ambassadors arrive bearing a gift from their Emperor, an artificial nightingale. This is immediately wound up to sing. Deeply offended, the real nightingale flies away, unnoticed until the Chinese Emperor demands that both nightingales sing together. Then the Emperor angrily denounces the real nightingale as worthless, compared with the artificial nightingale, who will sing as often as is desired. The Emperor bestows the title "Court Singer on the Left-hand Night Table of His Highness" upon the artificial nightingale. As Andersen adds, even the Chinese Emperor's heart is on the left-hand side, and thus, in the eyes of the law, this side is considered the more important. So it began, and so it would have ended, except that the Emperor, in his greed, orders the toy nightingale wound up again. It starts to sing, but the music stops abruptly, the cylinders turn, hum, squeak, and the machine falls silent. Great commotion! An alchemist is summoned to fix it, and after much tinkering it is finally repaired; but the alchemist announces that the bird can sing only very rarely and must be handled with great care. Although acutely disappointed, the Emperor commands that the nightingale be placed on the indicated night table and orders his followers to their bedchambers. Everyone retires.

The third scene, divided into two parts, takes place in the Emperor's bedchamber. In the foreground is an anteroom, through which courtiers dart from time to time to ask the Chamberlain whether the Emperor has died. He lies on the bed in spiritual torment. Death sits upon him, watching him, and the evil deeds he has committed hover around him. He wants to be comforted, calls for help, and asks his artificial singer to sing for him, although "there is no winder to wind you up." Unobserved, the real nightingale flies in from the garden, perches on a windowsill, and begins to sing. After one song Death, who has curled himself into a shroud, moves away and disappears, flying out the window. As the Nightingale sings on, the ghosts of the Emperor's evil deeds also vanish, and he falls asleep. The Nightingale finishes, and the Emperor awakes. He sees the little bird in the window and begs him to stay in the palace forever. The bird refuses, but promises to fly to the Emperor to inform him of the sufferings of the poor and of all that goes on in his Great Kingdom. The little bird flies away. The courtiers, thinking the Emperor already dead, approach on tiptoe; but the Emperor meets them, dressed in royal robes and carrying his orb and scepter, which he clutches to his heart. In the dawn light, he says "good day" to the dumbfounded courtiers.

This is all. I actually worked on this scenario before composing the first act. I await your reply. As you can see, a great deal of work is involved, and in order to complete it I will have to apply myself to it steadily after the Paris season. We will discuss the details when we meet in Paris. All that remains for the present is to establish that I will work on these two scenes and try to have them ready by the opening of the Theatre. Frankly, I doubt that I will finish them before January. You say that I work slowly. This is not so: I work quickly, but I do not rush, and I would rather spend time working than worrying about time. I will grant the Free Theatre exclusive rights to perform *The Nightingale* in Moscow for a few years: three years, for instance. I should say in advance that, owing to the intense nature of this work and the fact that I will have to turn down several jobs that would be financially advantageous to me, I will be obliged to charge the management of the Free Theatre a rather large sum. I shake your hand warmly.

Your   I. Stravinsky

Stravinsky received Sanine's reply on March 31: "Welcome [your] change of mind. Hurrah. Will purchase three scenes Nightingale. Work all summer on this. Telegraph me immediately Free Theatre [regarding] terms, advance. Sanine." The composer telegraphed in reply:

I am selling exclusive rights for stage performances in Moscow to the Free Theatre, advance of 3,000 rubles to the Bank of Montreux, 3,500 after the second scene, the same after the third scene. Reach an agreement with Struve about the rest. Greetings,   Stravinsky

On April 12, Stravinsky received another telegram from Sanine, stating that the details of Mardzhanov's terms would be arriving by registered mail. Sanine cabled again on the 19th: "Mardzhanov [will be in] Berlin [on the] 25th. Will make arrangements [with] Struve. . . . If impossible cable [your] final terms. Regards, Sanine."
    Finally a letter arrived from Sanine:

Please understand why it took so long for . . . Mardzhanov to give you a definite answer. Our theatre is still in a formative state, and thousands of things have to be done . . . though the orchestra has already been assembled, along with such first-class artists as Benois and Roerich. . . . There is money, but it is not unlimited, and we cannot exceed the budget.
    What artistic delight and satisfaction your libretto gave when I read it aloud to those who were present. After all, this will be the first time that Moscow—indeed, Russia—meets Stravinsky as an opera composer. . . . Konstantin Alexandrovich has asked me to tell you that he agrees to everything, and he can pay you 10,000 rubles, but he does not want anyone but you to know. . . . Then a second condition: we are purchasing *The Nightingale* for *three years*, for *Moscow* and for *St. Petersburg*, since every year we will be on tour in St. Petersburg for two months (April and May). Now the terms for payment of fees. Konstantin Alexandrovich is prepared to pay you immediately a 2,000-ruble advance. Then 2,000 more when you give the Theatre the whole piece. But he sets the

condition that you give it to us no later than September 20, 1914. The next payment date is that of the first performance of *The Nightingale*: the day after the premiere you will receive 3,000 rubles. The performance is supposed to take place sometime between January 15 and February 1, 1914. In the event that it does not take place then, you will still be paid 3,000 rubles no later than February 1, 1914. Konstantin Alexandrovich promises to pay you the final 3,000 rubles on May 1, 1914. . . . The Theatre wants to put on *The Nightingale* one hundred times in Moscow and Petersburg over a period of three years. . . . Mardzhanov himself will be in Berlin (he has other business with Max Reinhardt) on April 25 and 26 (New Style). He always stays at the Russischer Hof, and it would be nice if you could go there for these two days to see him and to make all the arrangements. . . .

Stravinsky received the following telegram from Mardzhanov on April 27: "In light of difficult conditions [involved in] purchasing score [I] propose either leasing [it] or [that you] reduce fee by 7,500 rubles. Please cable Berlin Russischer Hof. Regards, happy holiday. Mardzhanov." The composer replied: "Can make no concessions except payment by installment because [I have the] option to write either opera or ballet for Diaghilev. Cable. Happy holiday. Stravinsky." On April 30, Mardzhanov wired Stravinsky accepting his terms. Mardzhanov added that he was returning to Russia to arrange the details and to send the advance. His next two telegrams, arriving in Morges on May 30, contain almost identical messages, to the effect that 2,000 rubles has been sent to the composer's account[4] and that Mardzhanov considers the matter "settled."

Sanine's next letter (undated) came from London and consists of an encomium about the English. His next communication was a note addressed to the composer at his nursing home in Neuilly (postmarked Paris, June 12, 1913). On June 22 Stravinsky received a telegram from Mardzhanov: "Very glad [about] your recovery. Do not worry about work. Do it when [you are] well. I shake your hand affectionately." At the end of June, back in London, Sanine wrote that on his return to Russia, he intended to stop in Paris expressly to see Stravinsky. The composer answered, but by this time—early July—Sanine had already been recalled to Moscow.
    Meanwhile, the news had spread that Stravinsky intended to extend his opera. On June 26, Maximilian Steinberg wrote to Stravinsky from Lyubensk: "Is it true that you are going to finish The Nightingale? *I will be delighted if you do, for until now I have regretted that this wonderful work remained incomplete." On October 2, Steinberg wrote again: "I am dying to hear the continuation of* The Nightingale. *Will it be given in Moscow this winter? And if in*

---

[4] Mr. Tertsberg of the Azov-Don Commercial Bank in Rovno wrote to Stravinsky on May 21 that 2,000 rubles had been received from K. A. Mardzhanov, Moscow.

Moscow, at the Bolshoi?" On November 4, Steinberg again inquired about Stra-
vinsky's progress on the opera:

All I know is that Stepan [Mitussov] has sent the whole libretto to you. I am
impatient to become acquainted with the music, remembering the first scene
with the greatest fondness. Is it true that the opera will be performed in Paris
next spring and in Moscow now? The acoustics of the new Moscow Theatre are
somewhat suspect, and in *The Fair at Sorochinsk* the music sounded as if it
were in the background.

On October 30, Diaghilev came to see Stravinsky in Switzerland, to hear the
first act[5] and the nearly completed second, and to discuss the projected per-
formances of the opera by the Ballets Russes in Paris and London in the spring.
On his way to Russia, Diaghilev completed arrangements for this with Struve
("On Saturday Diaghilev dropped in on us; that evening I went with him to his
hotel to discuss everything." [Letter of November 23, 1913]) On November 4,
Stravinsky informed a surprised Sanine of Diaghilev's plans—since Sanine
had not fully understood that he had bought exclusivity only for Moscow:

Dear Alexander Aksimovich,

I am finishing the second act. In a few days I will begin the third. I am working
like a convict. I wanted to finish yesterday but had a terrible migraine and could
not manage: I will devote today and tomorrow to the final, irrevocable ending,
which is perhaps the most difficult part. Not much remains to be done, however, since the second act was the most complicated. I still plan to attend the
premiere in Moscow, and I await this moment with the greatest impatience and
joy. Diaghilev has made me very happy by changing his attitude about *The*
Nightingale: he really likes it now. I say that he has changed, because he had
said that the first act was vague and left him indifferent. Now, having heard the
first and second acts together, he has completely reversed his opinion and intends to present the opera in Paris in May and in London in June.[6]

---

[5] Struve wrote to the composer, October 11: "We received the piano score of the first
act on the 9th and sent it to the engraver the same day. After thoroughly discussing
the matter with Röder [the Leipzig printer], we decided not to have the German text
engraved for the time being and to leave only enough space for the French. The German text is not necessary for the performances in Russia and in France. Besides, I fear
that Feivel, who is consistently late, would not have it translated in time, which would
then hold up the urgent publication of the Russian score. . . . I await *The Nightingale*
with feverish impatience."

[6] Diaghilev's performances took place in Paris, May 26 and 28, 1914, and in London on
June 18 and 19, July 14 and 23, 1914. (On June 19, the *Petersburg Gazette* reported:
"After the success of *Nightingale*, Stravinsky plans to compose another opera on the
subject of life in ancient Rome.") Sanine staged the Diaghilev production together
with Boris Romanov, who was responsible for the choreography. Stravinsky was dissatisfied, but years later he wrote to Païchadze: "Romanov is not exactly a genius. Still,

Tell me, my dear friend, what is happening with Roerich?[7] Has he done any work on *The Nightingale* yet? Shall I send you something in the meantime? The first act is already printed; would you like to have it now? The publisher is working extremely quickly in order to avoid any delay, and in a few days the second act will be engraved.

Always yours,   I. Stravinsky

P.S. Although I am not personally acquainted with Mardzhanov, I still send my sincere greetings to this attractive and energetic figure.

Sanine wrote from Moscow on November 14[8]:

On October 24 I received your letter, and on the 25th I wrote to you that I was enormously pleased that your work was progressing so rapidly. We have already set a time and place for *The Nightingale* production, so I am thirsting for the composition. As for Diaghilev's wish to mount the opera, this is the first I have heard of it. . . . Congratulations, but it is essential that the work be given in Russia first. The reason that we are so anxious to have your music is that

---

he has done some quite remarkable productions; besides, he is not all bad as a person, and to work with him is agreeable. If we made the crossing [to Buenos Aires] together, we could plan all of the arrangements for everything related to the *Sacre.*" (February 14, 1932)

[7] At this date, Nicolas Roerich was to have designed the sets and costumes, though Stravinsky did not want Roerich for the opera and the two men had drifted apart after the *Sacre.* Diaghilev was not beholden to Roerich, however, and the impresario announced in the *Petersburg Gazette,* November 28, 1913, that Benois would design the Paris production of *The Nightingale.*

After the death of Catherine Stravinsky, Roerich wrote to the composer from "NAGGAR, Kulu, Punjab, Br. India": "Dear Igor Fyodorovich, The plane from Paris brought us the sad news of your tragic loss, your wife's death. Please accept our deepest condolences. Despite the great distances that have kept us apart for so long, we often think of you and of your whole family; thus this sad news is all the more sorrowful to us. Many friends from our generation have already died, and of late it seems that we have been receiving such sad bits of news more frequently. God keep you well, in service to your great talent. With warm regards from all of us. You are with us in our hearts." (March 22, 1939)

[8] Struve wrote to the composer that same day: "A copy of the second proofs of Act I was sent to Calvocoressi for translation; but Diaghilev told me that *The Nightingale* will be done in Russian both in Paris and in London." Four or five days later, the publisher wrote again to Stravinsky: "On Monday we sent a second copy of the proofs of the first act to the Free Theatre, along with our conditions for signing. . . . In your agreement with the Theatre, did you discuss the question of the actual production? Do you retain the right, if you are dissatisfied with the production, to withdraw *The Nightingale* from them and give it to another theatre? Otherwise, you might find yourself in a tight situation, for the opera could lie around untouched for three years. . . . Diaghilev still has not returned the contract we sent him to sign and has not settled the account."

Roerich has not started yet. We must have the music now and become fully acquainted with it. . . . Such is the mood of impatience here that, after I sent you my letter, Konstantin Alexandrovich still wanted to cable you . . . thus the telegram that puzzled you so much.

Mardzhanov had simply cabled (from Moscow, November 19): "Please send The Nightingale *as soon as possible."*

A week later (November 26) Mardzhanov sent another telegram to the composer:

Excuse me, but Sanine sent you a letter explaining [that] it is very important [that] you begin work . . . since I already announced [my intentions] to Struve through the Edition Russe. For God's sake, send everything that you have immediately. Accept my best regards.

On December 4, Struve wrote to Stravinsky from Berlin:

I am leaving today for Russia. . . . I will go first to Moscow. The behavior of the Free Theatre worries me. Having come to an agreement with us about the *Nightingale* material, the number of performances, and the payment, they are now, at the last minute, shying away from concluding a contract with us. I still do not know any reason or the details. The Free Theatre did not reply to our inquiries about how many piano scores they will need and when they propose to begin rehearsals. From reading in the newspapers about the Theatre's unsuccessful productions, I wonder if the Theatre has perhaps decided that they cannot handle *The Nightingale* right now and to postpone it. I have also heard that the Theatre's resources are mediocre, that disagreement and misunderstanding are rife within their management. Now I shall see everything for myself, set things straight, do everything that needs to be done, then get in touch with you. Diaghilev has just returned the contract, which he has signed, for *The Nightingale* scores, parts, and performances, but he has still not paid the money that he owes and promised. I must ask you to remind him again. It is very important that he pay the money before the end of this year.

Struve wrote to Stravinsky again on January 6, 1914:

Our contract with the Free Theatre is still with the notary and still unsigned by the Theatre. After my conversations with Mardzhanov, he apologized a hundred times and assured me that all of our terms have been accepted and that *The Nightingale* will be performed this season. But Mardzhanov twice failed to show up at scheduled meetings that would have concluded the business.

Then, on January 12, from Berlin, Struve informed the composer:

I regard the Free Theatre's preparations with great skepticism, unless they arrange some association with Diaghilev. But first they should settle accounts with you, sign the contract with us, and perform *The Nightingale* in Moscow. It is too early to think beyond that.

On January 26, 1914, Stravinsky, informed Struve that André Messager would be conducting the opera in Paris, and Emil Cooper in London. The composer requested that "something from the first two acts be sent to Messager, c/o the Paris Opéra, so that he can have some idea of them." In a letter of February 3 to Struve, Stravinsky acknowledged receipt of the final proofs of the orchestra score of Act I and promised to send the completed orchestra score of Act II "tomorrow or the day after." The reorchestration of the first act had placed an added burden on Stravinsky, whose time was extremely limited.

Struve wrote to Stravinsky on February 16 indicating for the first time that negotiations had begun with Alexander Siloti for performances of the opera in St. Petersburg, at the Maryinsky Theatre:

Since the business with the Free Theatre may fall through in the end anyway, owing to a lack of money and various disagreements, I felt that it was essential not to let Siloti's proposition slip away. . . . If I have a favorable reply from him, you must immediately telegraph to Mardzhanov in Moscow and pose the question point-blank, also demanding a written statement to the effect that the Free Theatre will perform *The Nightingale* this fall. . . . But I think that the Free Theatre, in its present state, will not get around to signing the contract.

Struve wrote again on February 20:

Things with the Free Theatre are really in quite a bad way. Today they inform me that they are still operating, but will be forced to shut down any day now. True, Mardzhanov is proposing to open another opera theatre . . . but no one knows what will come of that. . . . What a mess. . . . I was skeptical about this whole undertaking from the first. We are still waiting for a reply from Siloti.

On February 22, Stravinsky wrote to Siloti at the Hotel Bristol in Vienna:

Nicolas Struve wrote that you had asked him about the possibility of conducting *The Nightingale* next season at the Maryinsky Theatre. I prefer to discuss the matter with you personally, and certainly it would be quicker that way. But first of all, I must tell you about the situation regarding the work itself. The piano score of the first and second acts is already engraved and is being printed. Also, the French translation has been completed, and the orchestra parts for Act I have been extracted. I am composing and orchestrating Act III now, and I hope to send it to the publisher in a month. My obligations are as follows: The Moscow Free Theatre commissioned me to finish the opera—of which Act I was composed and orchestrated just before *Firebird*. I confess that I accepted the commission reluctantly, not having thought about the opera for such a long time and having other ideas in mind. But the financial side of the transaction made it unrefusable, and, accordingly, I finished the opera, adding two acts. I had an advance of 2,000 rubles, and the Free Theatre must now pay me 10,000 more, which they promised to do soon, in installments. Diaghilev has purchased exclusivity from the publisher for Paris and London. That is all I can say. . . .

My impression is that the Free Theatre will probably close, since even now the contract between the Theatre and the publisher has not been signed. If Telyakovsky wishes to assume responsibility for *The Nightingale* from the Free Theatre, I will immediately write to the director of the Free Theatre to ask why they have not signed the contract; and if I do not receive a satisfactory answer, I will write to Struve instructing him to break off relations with the Free Theatre and to give the material to the Imperial Theatres.

Struve is demanding a minimum of ten performances, five in Moscow and five in St. Petersburg. Also, as for sending the piano score to Telyakovsky, I must frankly say that if I do not play it myself and someone else does, he will say "nonsense," as the late Nikolai Andreyevich [Rimsky-Korsakov] used to say about Debussy and Strauss: "Nonsense fortissimo." It would be preferable for me to play the piece for Telyakovsky myself when he comes to Paris, which he does every spring. He has never come to any of my performances, incidentally, so if he is afraid of acquainting himself with the music, it would be good for us to see each other in person. I would be so happy to play *The Nightingale* for you, and you are the only one for whom I could play it with pleasure.

Siloti wrote from Vienna on February 26, but not in reply to Stravinsky's February 22 letter, which appears to have been forwarded to him in St. Petersburg (see Siloti's letter of March 18, below).

You are *not* right in sharing Debussy's surprise and concluding that I *do not want* to play your works, and that I do not support you anymore. Perhaps Debussy did not know, but you at least should have remembered that I never stand in line to play new things and novelties. . . . I played all of your works until you started publishing with Koussevitzky, who, understandably, started performing them *himself* (or, rather, promised to, as was the case with the *Sacre*). My personal taste has nothing to do with it, and my attitude toward you has not changed. For my part, I was wondering what happened to my *old* relationship with you, from before *Firebird,* when absolutely no one wanted to play your works. You can remind Debussy that long ago I played everything and I do not mind helping him to promote himself now, though indirectly. But he insists upon "selling himself" like a harlot on the Nevsky, choosing to go where he can get the most money and forgetting that I played *all* of his new pieces at the time when Koussevitzky would not touch them. Well, there is no sense in talking about it anymore: as a man, Debussy is veritable scum; you cannot even swat him across the snout, because you will never get your hand clean again. I am glad that he had a chance to see my letter, for now he knows what I think of him as a man. . . . I have no desire to know him personally, but I will always play his works. I am sure that he could not forget having seen me at all of the scandalous Russian concerts. But forgive me for writing so much about this loathsome creature, who is now fit only to be spat upon. . . . Yes, that would be one of the most satisfying moments of my life.

Regarding *The Nightingale,* I want very much for it to be presented by the Imperial Theatres; after all, these popular "music-dramas" and "free theatres" are not, in essence, worth much; the ideas are sound, but to realize them is another matter! In the end, it is more *practical* to do business with the Imperial Theatres. In conformity with what I understand to be your terms with the Free Theatre, I am enclosing what I suppose might be your terms with the Imperial Theatres. Make any changes that you think necessary, and return this paper to me. Why wait until the spring? One must strike while the iron is hot. I am thinking of doing the following: next Monday I will go to Struve's (to find out his terms) and will take a copy of the two acts back with me to Russia (where I hope to be by March 16), to play them for Telyakovsky and Coates.[9] T[elyakovsky] will make his decision then. You can play the whole thing for him again in Paris, with the third act. . . .

Struve told me that your wife has tuberculosis. You should take her to St. Petersburg, where there is a young Russian doctor who works on lung patients, curing tuberculosis with Roentgen rays. He has just cured Gorky.

Stravinsky was extremely late in delivering the third act to the publisher. Nevertheless, Struve asked him not to send the piano or the orchestra score in sections, since this "really does not speed up the engraving, the copying, or the proofreading, but, on the contrary, complicates matters. I still have questions concerning The Nightingale *to discuss with you, and we will still have to translate Act III into French." [February 28] Stravinsky promptly left for Berlin to resolve these questions. On returning to Clarens, he received another letter from Struve (March 16), saying that Diaghilev had just been in Berlin and had demanded "all the chorus parts of the first two acts within a week, threatening, otherwise, to cancel; Röder managed to produce the vocal score in three days, sending thirty copies to Diaghilev in Petersburg."*

On March 18, Siloti wrote to Stravinsky from St. Petersburg: "I am going to play The Nightingale *on March 29, so you can expect a wire from me then. Coates backs* The Nightingale *most enthusiastically!" Four days later, Siloti wrote again:*

I just received your long, kind letter, and I hasten to answer it. I know that Coates liked *The Nightingale* very much when I showed it to him and undoubtedly wanted to present it. Knowing Telyakovsky as I do, I anticipated that he would not respond right away to Coates's first letter, following the premiere, since he considers a single, i.e., a first, impression little to go on. I knew that he

---

[9] Albert Coates (1882–1953), English conductor and composer born in St. Petersburg, where he was appointed conductor at the Imperial Opera in 1911.

would wait to see how Coates reacted in the winter, when the "magic" of the first impression might have worn off. So if Coates still wants desperately to produce *The Nightingale* after the fall, then it will probably happen. In my opinion it will not be this year, owing to the fire in Moscow that destroyed all the sets. New sets will have to be built for so many of the current (repertory) shows, and I fear that even the decision on new stagings may be delayed for a while. Bakst, for example, the "dirty swine," was not able to prepare the material for *Orpheus* because of illness, and the set now is still unusable! I will, without fail, speak with Coates when he comes to St. Petersburg; if his desire for *The Nightingale* has not weakened, I myself will intervene to straighten out this affair somehow. I doubt whether Coates's opera will be presented here. In any case, I would oppose it, because he is supposed to come to the Maryinsky Theatre only *if he is successful* there, and not the other way around. If the opera failed in the Maryinsky Theatre, the ballet master's position would be ruined, and that would not be desirable for him; I will dissuade him. Since your brother[10] is now on the staff of the Maryinsky, we will not forget your *Nightingale!*

Struve wrote to Stravinsky on April 4:

I am leaving for Moscow today. On Monday you promised to send the piano score of Act III, but today is Saturday and we still have not received anything. The music of the alto chorus was lithographed the day after we received your manuscript, and I sent ten copies to Diaghilev through Monteux. . . . We are not going to print the Russian libretto separately, because it has to be censored for Russia, but we need the French text for the Paris and London performances. . . . Diaghilev has left Berlin for Paris without informing me of your situation regarding rehearsals or your trip to Russia.

Then, on April 24, Siloti wrote again to Stravinsky:

In light of the fact that *The Nightingale* lasts only 45–50 minutes, Telyakovsky says that 10,000 rubles is out of the question; he thinks about 4,000 is appropri-

---

[10] Gury Fyodorovich Stravinsky (July 30, 1885–July 21, 1917 [Old Style]). According to his passport, his contract with the Imperial St. Petersburg Theatre extended from September 1, 1914, for one year and was renewed on September 1, 1915, but he could have been employed by the Maryinsky in March 1914. He sang in the Narodnyi Dom in Petrograd before joining the Maryinsky. Gury's obituary in the *Central Committee News,* written by his cousin Yevgeny Yelachich, is the chief source of information about Stravinsky's younger brother. Gury left the Maryinsky and became a member of the Land Union in Lvov. In 1917 he was transferred to the all-Russian Land Union in Rumania, where he died of typhus at Iasi. His passport contains visas for Kazan and Lublin, 1910, 1911, and 1913.

ate! Telyakovsky and Coates will be in Paris to hear *The Nightingale;* if necessary, they will have you play it for them on the piano. I like that idea, because I have not been able (owing to lack of time) to "learn" the score and would consider it unconscientious to "approximate" it for Telyakovsky. I have already shown it to Coates, who likes it *very much* and really wants to mount it! Telyakovsky always gives serious consideration to Coates's wishes. Thus, if you change your views regarding the fee, the whole affair may turn out very well.

Stravinsky cabled Sanine on April 27, threatening, if the terms were not accepted, to "compose a ballet for Diaghilev."
    Finally, a letter from Struve in Berlin, May 19, 1914—only a week before the Paris premiere—informs Stravinsky that

the vocal score was sent to the printer on Monday, and Röder will just barely manage to have the copies ready in time for the performance. Not until Saturday evening will any of them be ready, and since I am planning to leave for Paris Saturday night for the premiere, I will have to take all of the copies with me. The rush last week was incredible: express letters, telegrams, and the proofs from Calvocoressi received only on Saturday. Of course, they are not entirely error-free, but this is understandable if you bear in mind the great number of proofreadings, changes, and corrections, and the fact that the word "urgent" was on everything.

After the premiere on May 26, 1914, Struve wrote from Berlin complaining of the many mistakes in Calvocoressi's French translation:

What kind of Frenchman is Calvocoressi that he would allow such a mistake on the title page as *"Rossignol"* instead of *"Le Rossignol"*? Our French is not so poor here that we would fail to notice that *"Rossignol"* and *"Le Rossignol"* are not the same. . . . He made absolutely no changes either in the piano score or in the French libretto! . . . [June 16]

The publisher adds that the first edition of the vocal score has already been distributed, that a second edition during the summer is a likelihood, and that he anticipates "a more sensitive and serious interest in the opera in England, and not just words and compliments, as we have had in France."
    Sometime between late March and the fall of 1914, Stravinsky received a letter from his younger brother, Gury:

Gimura,

This is a business letter. Soon we will begin work on new operas for the coming season. Albert Coates desperately wants to do *The Nightingale.* I have to know whether you have any agreements concerning *The Nightingale* with Diaghilev or with the Free Theatre, or is it available? . . . Write to me without delay and let me know what I can say in your name (but without the breathy voice) when and if I speak to the director of the Imperial Theatres about the matter. A. Coates has asked me to contact you about this. Just tell me what your wishes are.

I won't write very much now because I must be at the theatre soon; tonight I am singing *May Night* for the second time. On Wednesday the 28th I will be doing *Prince Igor* again; I sang it recently and everyone (even Tartakov) responded with praise. Mama will write to you about all of this in more detail. Generally everything is fine, except for some pains in my head where I had the concussion; these are worse when the weather is cold or changing, and [illegible] all by themselves.

We think about you constantly, and our hearts are filled with love for you. We are concerned about all of you.

God keep you, our dear loved ones. . . . I kiss you most affectionately.

Gury

On February 19, 1915, Stravinsky telegraphed to Siloti agreeing to his terms. The composer gives his address as "La Pervenche," Clarens, and Siloti's as Kriukov Canal, Petrograd. On March 13 Siloti telegraphed, committing the Maryinsky to pay 6,000 rubles and guaranteeing thirty performances. These terms were repeated in his letter of March 28:

Yesterday I cabled you about *The Nightingale*. So the conditions are not 10,000, as you wrote then, but 6,000 rubles for three years*; figuring on ten performances per season = thirty guaranteed performances; payment: when the contract is signed, 3,000, then, in a year, the remaining 3,000 rubles. Send me a telegram indicating your agreement (even if only one word, "accept"); then I will ask the office to send you the contract. In addition to this, there is yet another matter that I would like to arrange. In a year your contract with Diaghilev for *Petrushka* will expire. Following that expiration date you ought to give the Imperial Theatres performance rights (in Moscow and St. Petersburg); such an arrangement would not hinder you abroad at all! Since I am already certain that you will be willing to do this, let me know what your terms are, and I will arrange the whole affair without fail! . . .

P.S. I will try to send you the contract right away, acting as though you had given me your power of attorney; otherwise the correspondence will take a very long time.

* From August 1915 through July 1918.[11]

---

[11] The letter arrived while Stravinsky was in Milan, and Catherine telegraphed the news to him there on April 2.

Stravinsky answered Siloti from Lausanne on April 6:

Thanks ever so much for your tireless efforts in arranging performances of my works in the Imperial Theatres. I already sent you a telegram consenting to the last set of terms for *The Nightingale,* and am now waiting for the contract to arrive, along with the first 3,000 rubles. But is there no way to avoid losing 1,300 francs in the exchange? That is a significant sum for me these days! Perhaps the offices of the Imperial Theatres can figure out something more advantageous for me. Regarding *Petrushka,* thank you very, very much for your desire to organize performances in the Imperial Theatres. Before stating any conditions, though, I must know whether M. M. Fokine has performance rights to this work. I seem to remember that Diaghilev's contract with him stipulated that he did not have performance rights to any ballet that he did with Diaghilev for a period of *five* years after the termination of the contract. Since the contract that I have in mind . . . expired, to my recollection, in May 1912, Fokine cannot perform *Petrushka* again until May 1917. Everything now depends on this. You must find this out from Fokine himself. In the event that such terms exist in their contract, Diaghilev will naturally exercise his rights, all the more so since *he* wants desperately to work in Russia.

Apart from this, another consideration ought to be mentioned concerning *Petrushka.* . . . When my *Petrushka* contract with Diaghilev expires, in the spring of 1916, if Sergei Pavlovich finds my terms acceptable, he has the option to extend it. Since I know that he is counting on performing my works in Russia, undoubtedly he will take advantage of this opportunity. Consequently, . . . I find myself between two enterprises, i.e., the Imperial Theatres and Diaghilev, the former proposing to perform *Petrushka* on the termination of my contract with Diaghilev. Thus I must put an official question to the latter as to whether he is willing to continue to perform *Petrushka* through the period during which the Imperial Theatres would like to perform it. If he answers affirmatively and is also willing to meet my financial demands, I will have to cede the work to him. If not, I will turn it over to the Imperial Theatres. I shall demand 9,000 *rubles* for a three-year period of performances of *Petrushka* in Petrograd and Moscow, demanding also a guarantee of thirty performances (i.e., ten per year), and stipulating that it *must be performed in both cities.*

On May 14, the St. Petersburg Financial News *published a lengthy article about* The Nightingale, *announcing the opera for the forthcoming season at the Maryinsky Theatre, quoting the text of the Fisherman's song, and summarizing the libretto. The article says that "Stravinsky will be returning to Petersburg in the fall and will direct the performance."*

Siloti telegraphed on June 5, promising to send the Nightingale *contract in ten days. On July 23, Prince Argutinsky, in Paris, telegraphed to Stravinsky: "Your opera parts arrived [from Switzerland] only on Monday. [I] will be able to send them on to Petrograd in two weeks. Are you sure you have a copy of* *these parts . . . ?" On October 4, Telyakovsky sent the contract, with this note:* "Enclosed herein are the terms for the production of the opera* The Nightingale *in Petrograd and Moscow; the Petrograd Office of the Imperial Theatres humbly requests that you, dear sir, return this document to the office when you have signed it."*

Stravinsky wrote to Siloti on October 15:

I have finally received the ill-fated contract from the director of the Imperial Theatres. Point three of this contract reads: "The director guarantees me, Str., etc. . . ."

All of this would be wonderful if I had a separate copy of the libretto of my opera in Russian. Not only do I not have it in Russian, but I do not even have the French edition, which came out last year at the same time as the piano reduction of the opera. I learned from N. G. Struve's last letter that the Russian libretto of *The Nightingale* was supposed to be engraved in the middle of September (Old Style). Thus, when you read this letter, the Russian libretto should already be available, so please obtain a copy from Struve or from the shop and send it on to the director in my name.

The contract does not indicate that the director made an agreement with the representative of Russischer Musik Verlag concerning the right to use the material. I hope that this question has already been settled between the director and Struve. If not, it would make little sense to send a contract for my signature.

The scores of my musical and dramatic compositions published by the Russischer Musik Verlag are not for sale but, instead, are rented for a specific period of time and for a specific percentage per performance—as has so far been the case with Diaghilev's enterprise. There are various reasons for this procedure, one of the most important of which is the vulnerability of Russian works in countries that as yet have no copyright agreement with Russia. The orchestra scores of these works come under this same publisher's ruling and are not for sale either. . . . I also wanted to ask you whether you have received my letters, one written at Easter, another sent from here during the summer, i.e., from Morges, where I now live. In the second letter, I wrote to you about the money that I was expecting along with the contract from the director of the Imperial Theatres. Just in case this letter was lost, I repeat its contents in brief: I requested that this money, i.e., 3,000 rubles, be sent to me through the Minister of Foreign Affairs, since that way I would receive 250 francs for 100 rubles; otherwise I would get just 200 francs. The difference is enormous; on the entire sum I would lose 1,300 francs. At a time like this, every kopeck counts. Recently I wrote a letter on the same subject to Prince Argutinsky in Paris, asking him to arrange this for me as well. . . . I would be extremely grateful to you.

Well, enough! You have a lot to do, and so have I, and by now you must be quite fed up with me.

On October 23, Argutinsky telegraphed to Stravinsky: "Your package was sent to the management of the Imperial Theatres and should be there. Letter follows with documents to be examined." In this letter the Prince wrote to Stravinsky:

I do not understand anything anymore! I enclose copies of two telegrams—one that you sent from Paris requesting that the Foreign Office furnish the Imperial Theatres with the box containing your orchestra score, and the other, the Baron's reply, stating clearly: *"parvenue destination,"* i.e., that the Imperial Theatres received the box!

I suggest that you cable your family and tell them to get in touch with the director of the Office of Foreign Affairs directly. Have them mention the cable he sent me stating that the box with your score had been sent to the Theatre, and add that the Theatre did not receive it.

I can do nothing more from Paris! Say in your telegram that the box was sent by courier Sorokine on July 21. The box is probably lying around somewhere at Telyakovsky's!

Five days later, Stravinsky's mother cabled to him from Petrograd: "The opera score and parts were finally found at the Foreign Ministry." Evidently the libretto still had not been delivered by December 7, though, since Siloti telegraphed explaining that for this reason he could not yet send the money. This message did not reach Morges until January 2, 1916. On the same day, Stravinsky's mother sent a telegram (opened by the censor) to Prince Argutinsky, 7, rue François Ier, Paris: "Siloti telegraphs [that it is] impossible to send [the] money because the libretto has not turned up yet." But, in the meantime, the libretto had been found, and Siloti telegraphed to the composer on December 30: "Everything in order. I hope to send the money in ten days, since we are waiting for a favorable exchange rate!"

On February 11, Stravinsky informed Siloti that he wanted to make further changes in the score before the Maryinsky performance.[12] *Not until almost*

---

[12] The score that Stravinsky had sent to Petrograd in the summer of 1915, a copy, no doubt, of the 1914 Paris original, does not conform to the score as printed in 1923. In September 1981, London Weekend Television, in Moscow, recorded the Chinese March from Act II and found that the orchestra parts differed significantly from the Boosey & Hawkes edition of the score. For example, the trumpet parts in measure 4 of **66** were given to bassoons in the Moscow parts; the flute and clarinet music at 2 measures before **67** was scored for horn, tuba, and piano; and the tutti at **68** was entirely different. In the 1923 score, the piano replaces the Moscow-version celeste at 2 measures before **71**, bassoons replace trombones at **73**, the contrabassoon replaces the tuba at **75**, and at 6 measures after **75**, violins replace the harps. Finally, at 4 measures before **76**, the piano replaces the trumpet melody. The revisions were probably introduced in 1917, while Stravinsky was preparing the tone poem *The Song of the Nightingale,* and in 1919, when he was copying a new set of parts for Beecham's revival of the opera.

a year later, January 3, 1917, did Stravinsky telegraph requesting the other 3,000 rubles. Finally, in May 1917, Siloti telegraphed asking Stravinsky to choose a designer for the opera. Stravinsky answered the same day naming Benois, but Siloti wrote on June 22, explaining that

there was a scandal here about Benois's [i.e., Diaghilev's] producing *The Nightingale.* Your contract makes no mention of the author's right to select the designer, and, as it turns out, Telyakovsky made arranagements a long time ago to give the production to Golovin! . . . Since all of this took place before I was appointed, I have no recourse . . . but there is one consolation: without me, *The Nightingale* would not have been done this year either. . . . Coates will be conducting.

This letter gives January 9, 1918, as the planned date for the premiere, but the performance—the first of any work by Stravinsky in his native city after the Revolution—did not take place until May 30, 1918, when the opera was staged by Meyerhold, designed by Golovin, and conducted by Coates.[13]

    A revival of The Nightingale *at Covent Garden planned for June 1918 finally took place more than a year later, because the unique set of parts could not be retrieved from Petrograd during the Civil War and new ones had to be extracted from the manuscript. Eugene Goossens conducted the five performances (November 2, 18,[14] and 28, and December 3 and 18, 1919) for the Beecham Company.*[15]

---

[13] See Konstantin Rudnitsky, *Meyerhold the Director,* translated by George Petrov (Ann Arbor, 1981), pp. 250–51.

[14] Roerich wrote to Stravinsky from London after the second performance: "Your part of *The Nightingale* went very well. It was enormously successful, and the orchestra sounded wonderful. The visual aspect was poor, and the third scene took place in the tent from *Tristan,* but everything at Covent Garden is a mess, and, in general, Beecham's enterprise is a pigsty, not to use a stronger word. To work with him is intolerable, and the only good element is the orchestra: the composer is really in the best position. I derive great satisfaction from the knowledge that your music is so far superior to and beyond that of those Frenchmen to whom Diaghilev showed it. . . . Diaghilev must see all of this now and understand it."

[15] Otto Kling had written to Stravinsky on May 14, 1918, requesting the parts for *The Nightingale,* "because Sir Thomas Beecham wishes to present the opera in June." On June 1 Stravinsky cabled that the only parts were at the Maryinsky Theatre, but he offered to have a new set copied. This task could not be completed in time for Beecham's summer season, and a year passed before the decision was made to prepare the new set. On April 6, 1919, Stravinsky explained the situation to Struve: "Zingel [the publisher's representative in Berlin] does not even have a copy of the piano score. I have the manuscript score. . . . Last year, when Beecham was planning to do the opera, I ordered chorus parts in French, for which I did not have any authorization from him, so I am stuck with them." Nevertheless, Stravinsky always felt beholden to Beecham for a gift of money during the war. Madame Khvoshchinskaya wrote to the composer,

Although Stravinsky completed the symphonic poem The Song of the Nightingale *on April 4, 1917, the premiere did not take place until nearly two years later, on December 6, 1919, in Geneva. Since* Le Sacre du printemps *had not yet been performed in that city, the music of* The Song of the Nightingale *created a tempest, as is evident in a cartoon entitled "La Réponse au Rossignol" in* La Suisse Musicale *(December 20).*

January 12, 1916: "I heard from Beecham that he sent you 10,000 francs via Sergei Pavlovich. I was very pleased by this news, and I hope that you have the money by now."

Henry (Harry) Kling, son of Otto, visited Stravinsky in Morges, July 3, 1919, and the following day wrote to the composer asking him to have the parts copied in Switzerland, since this would be much less expensive than in England. Seven days later the publisher acknowledged receipt of the string and chorus parts; and letters from both Henry and Otto Kling, dated August 6 and 15, 1919, and January 27, 1920, show that Stravinsky sent the scores for each act separately and, in one parcel, the

On April 6, 1919, Stravinsky wrote to N. G. Struve:

In 1917 I composed a symphonic poem for medium-sized orchestra (fifty-five musicians) based on Acts II and III.[16] I have the manuscript and Diaghilev has the copy, because he wanted to choreograph this poem.

The new instrumentation is remarkable above all in that only three years had elapsed since Stravinsky had completed the original score of the same music (as compared with nine years between the original Firebird *and the 1919 Suite) and in that the orchestra of* The Song of the Nightingale *is smaller than that of the opera by only six instruments: flute, clarinet, bassoon, trumpet, mandolin, and guitar. The reduction in size is less significant, therefore, than the elimination of the vocal parts.*

Between the first performances in Geneva and Lausanne (December 1919) and in Paris (February 1920) and the publication of the score in February 1922, Stravinsky revised The Song of the Nightingale *only slightly. But some editions do not indicate the correct relationship of tempi at 79, where ♪ = ♪ does not refer to the metronomic marking ♩ = 116–120 at 73, but to ♩ = 76 at the beginning of the Chinese March. (Stravinsky's recording at 79— doppio valore, new ♪ = old ♪ —is wrong.)*

In July 1968, Stravinsky's manuscript notebook for The Song of the Nightingale *was sold at auction for several thousand dollars by Sotheby's. The piece was a favorite of Béla Bartók's, and in a letter to Stravinsky, January 17, 1943, the conductor Fritz Reiner says that his performance with the New York Philharmonic earlier that week may have been one of the best the work had ever received, and that Bartók, who was in the audience, agreed.*

---

brass, harp, celeste, piano, and percussion. A letter from Stravinsky to Struve indicates that the composer took Kling's advice: "At the moment, the lithographing of the string parts of the opera (ten complete sets), for which I am paying, is being completed in Lausanne. Please speak with [Adolph] Bolm ... about payment for the orchestra scores, which will be very expensive (from 1,000 to 1,500 francs each)." (August 20, 1919) Bolm had wanted to stage the opera in America.

[16] At the time of composing this arrangement, Stravinsky wrote to his local publisher, Adolphe Henn, asking for assistance in finding a harp. Stravinsky wanted to purchase the instrument, no doubt to study and learn to play it himself, as he had done with the cimbalom.

FIREBIRD

A Publishing History in Correspondence

From the most popular work that Stravinsky ever wrote, Firebird, *he received the least income. Even worse, he was forced to spend a fortune on litigation in which the composition, and his and others' arrangements from it, involved him. The present chronicle traces the unprecedented legal difficulties that the Russian Revolution raised for the composer as a Russian national living abroad. The correspondence also distinguishes between the ballet and the three suites, since the general public (like, it seems, many musicians) is unaware of the differences.*[1]

According to the memoirs of Stravinsky and Fokine, Diaghilev invited Stravinsky to compose Firebird *after Liadov failed to make any progress with the ballet score. In a BBC radio talk, November 19, 1977, Alexander Tcherepnin claimed that his father had been the first to suggest to Diaghilev, "Why not try the young Igor?" and it is true that a close relationship had existed between Stravinsky and Tcherepnin, in whose St. Petersburg home the fledgling composer had often played his music.*

G. P. JURGENSON[2] TO STRAVINSKY   *Moscow*
                                                   July 9, 1912[3]

Ustilug

I am sending 200 rubles as an advance on the 500 that will be due you when the 500 copies of the piano score of *Firebird* are sold (though I do not imagine that this is likely to occur for another two or three years).[4] From my brother's cor-

---

[1] As late as July 28, 1965, Stravinsky's so-called personal manager, who for five years had been negotiating concert programs that included *Firebird*, wrote to a representative of the BBC: "As I recall, the complete *Firebird*—as [Stravinsky] conducts it—lasts about 28 minutes." The complete *Firebird*, never conducted by Stravinsky in concert, lasts 45 minutes.

[2] On January 25, 1911, at Beaulieu-sur-Mer, Stravinsky had signed an agreement with Jurgenson giving him exclusive world rights to "my composition, *Firebird*," including royalties from "phonograph, gramophone, and all other mechanical instruments." Russian is the original language of the letters to Jurgenson.

[3] The dates of most of the letters sent from one Russian address to another are Old Style, but the dating of international correspondence is inconsistent.

[4] Stravinsky's first piano score of *Firebird*, completed March 21, 1910, was published by Jurgenson in July 1911 (plate 34908; but in a letter of January 10, 1927, Stravinsky

respondence with you, I understood that the 50 rubles that Diaghilev is required to pay our company for each performance is for the rental of parts, rather than a performance fee. This payment is partly to guarantee Diaghilev's exclusivity and partly to reimburse us for the printing. But your last letter contradicts this, suggesting that the payment is a performance fee and therefore should be equally divided between the composer and the publisher. Could you send us a copy of your agreement with Diaghilev, since only from reading this will we be able to determine our rights? We have received requests for the full score of the ballet from London and Paris, but we declined them, citing Diaghilev's exclusivity. Legally, we are not obligated to do this, but we do not know the extent of your commitment to him. If we were to sell even one score abroad, the ballet could be presented in spite of Diaghilev's exclusivity.[5] (Russian composers and publishers are not protected in England, for instance.) And if this were to happen, Diaghilev could refuse to pay the 50 rubles per performance.

G. P. JURGENSON TO STRAVINSKY

Moscow
July 30, 1912

Ustilug

I regret that you were not able to send me a copy of your agreement with Diaghilev. Upon rereading your letter on this subject, I noticed a discrepancy in certain details, and one ambiguous point: precisely what does the "printed material" comprise: only the full score, or the parts as well? Diaghilev can refuse to recognize our right to charge a rental fee for the parts, since not all of them were engraved and printed. . . . How long are we obliged to wait for Diaghilev to pay, or even just to reply, and how can we free ourselves from his exclusivity? Certainly you have the right to approve all productions of the ballet, but it seems to me that you are mistaken in supposing that you have empowered us to safeguard these rights. I found no mention of this in the correspondence. Rather, the contrary is indicated: . . . you, as author, can safeguard our rights as publisher and demand that Diaghilev fulfill the terms, but we cannot do the same. . . . Our authority consists mainly in the right to sell or rent the parts at the price we set *after* the termination of your agreement with Diaghilev, i.e., after January 1, 1915. I am not optimistic that we will succeed in making Diaghilev cooperate.

You wanted an explanation why (1) the price of the orchestra score is printed on the piano score, along with (2) the statement that inquiries concerning the rental of the parts should be addressed to our company. The pur-

---

says that a piano score was published in 1910). Stravinsky completed a second, much revised piano score on December 6, 1918, and dedicated the transcription to Vladimir Vasilievich Yuzhin. The manuscripts of both scores are in the Morgan Library, New York.

[5] The full score (plate 34920) was also published in 1911.

pose of the first was to ensure that the score would be sold for private use only (to a library, for instance), and not for stage performance; the second was to make the score available only from us, after Diaghilev's term of exclusivity.

Breitkopf & Härtel, London, asked for two copies of the score for their clients. I refused, and they then assured us that the score would not be misused, and, under these conditions, I consented. I gathered from your letter that you would *not* have agreed to this, whereupon I sent a telegraphed order to stop these scores from being mailed. Please let me know as soon as possible whether you are indeed opposed to this sale.

G. P. JURGENSON TO STRAVINSKY   *Moscow*
                                                August 20, 1912
Ustilug

In view of your fear that the *Firebird* scores might be used for a stage production, creating problems for us both, I wrote to Breitkopf today requesting the return of the scores. The 900 rubles (or 2,400 francs) that Breitkopf promised for eighteen performances would have been very agreeable, but, unfortunately, it is impossible to copyright *Firebird* for America. Despite the absence of a copyright convention between Russia and France, Russian authors' rights have always been respected there. . . . For the moment, we are not going to release the score for sale. V. Derzhanovsky told me that you are planning to come to Moscow; if you do, we would discuss everything at that time. . . . I would be very happy to become better acquainted with you.

P.S. Diaghilev should make the payment out to the company's name: P. Jurgenson, Moscow.

B. P. JURGENSON TO STRAVINSKY   *Moscow*
                                               September 14, 1912
Ustilug

I do not know why you propose to exclude America from the countries in which we have rights, but this we deem unsatisfactory, because it would deprive us of any defense against American reprints. If a legal American edition, endorsed by you, were to appear, it would be in direct competition with ours in England and all other countries having no official agreement with Russia. . . .

Will you be in Ustilug much longer, and where will you go from there? . . . Could you give me Diaghilev's address? My brother said that Diaghilev wanted to pay us for *Firebird,* but so far we have not had so much as a word from him.

B. P. JURGENSON TO STRAVINSKY

Moscow
October 31, 1912[6]

I discovered that Diaghilev had been in Moscow only after his departure. A few days ago I sent him a cable, with a prepaid reply form, requesting that he send the money, but neither a reply nor payment has followed. Your wishes concerning the score of the ballet will be fulfilled.

Poster for a Ballets Russes performance in Budapest, December 27, 1912. The ballets are Firebird, Les Sylphides, *and* Carnaval. *Béla Bartók attended this performance, Stravinsky that of January 4. Stravinsky had orchestrated the first and last numbers of* Les Sylphides, *in which Nijinsky danced.*

B. P. JURGENSON TO STRAVINSKY

Moscow
January 11, 1913

Ustilug

I have sent the score of the *Firebird* Suite[7] to Oskar Fried.[8]

---

[6] On November 2, 1912, Maximilian Steinberg wrote to Stravinsky: "I gave the *Firebird* score to N. G. Struve, who took it to Berlin!" This was Stravinsky's manuscript.

[7] Published in March 1912, this ill-considered choice of excerpts concludes with the Danse infernale, thereby making little sense to audiences who might have been expecting the suite to represent the form of the ballet as a whole.

[8] Oskar Fried (1871–1941), German conductor and composer. He became a Soviet citizen in 1940.

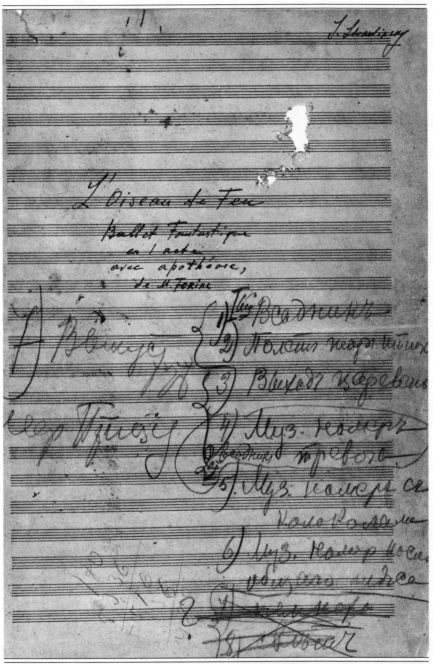

Stravinsky's notes for the scenario of Firebird on his draft of the title page of the score, autumn 1909. The Russian titles may be translated as follows: (1) The first horseman. (2) The flight of the Firebird. (3) The entrance of the Princesses. (4) Musical alarm; the second horseman. (5) Second musical alarm. (6) A musical piece with bells. (7) and (8) Darkness and light [crossed out]. (7) [left side of page] Release of the Firebird. This page reveals that Fokine's conception of Firebird did not include the coronation-scene ending, which was Stravinsky's idea.

B. P. JURGENSON TO STRAVINSKY

Today I wrote to Diaghilev in St. Petersburg, at the address you provided. . . . Back in October he had cabled: "I will pay next week." Three months have now gone by without so much as a gesture from him.

B. P. JURGENSON TO STRAVINSKY

We find ourselves in an idiotic position, powerless to collect what is legally and rightfully ours. I refer to Diaghilev and his failure to pay for our orchestra score of *Firebird*. Although you repeatedly assured me that he would pay, and he repeatedly confirmed this, absolutely nothing has happened. You recently informed me that he would be in St. Petersburg and Moscow, and I sent a reminder to him at both addresses. The letter reached him at his hotel in Moscow, but his response was complete silence. I am extremely indignant about this, since it proves that his word is unreliable. Incidentally, I know that here in Moscow he distributed about 20,000 *in advances* to various people. This does not facilitate matters for us. You obliged us to print the score and parts of the ballet, and now Diaghilev will not live up to his agreement, while we, in the meantime, do not have the right to rent or sell to anyone else. In short, we spent several thousand rubles to engrave and print the orchestra score so that Diaghilev could use it gratis. . . .

You wrote that Diaghilev's exclusivity would be forfeited if he failed to pay. But to enforce this would be at least as difficult as collecting the money he owes us according to the agreement—since *he* has the agreement and we do not. What do you intend to do?

B. P. JURGENSON TO STRAVINSKY

I have just received 1,000 rubles from Diaghilev. Also, in accordance with your letter, I sent a copy of the *Firebird* score to Mr. [Edwin] Evans, in London.

Had Diaghilev simply informed us that he was unable to pay by the fixed date and set another one, we would not bear him any grudge. His negligent attitude has greatly disappointed me, though.

B. P. JURGENSON TO STRAVINSKY

Recently I sent you a copy of some pages of the *Firebird* score. While proofreading the parts, we noticed an inconsistency, either in the position of the piano and celeste parts (one on top of the other, then the other way around), or in the designation of these parts. How shall we correct it?

B. P. JURGENSON TO STRAVINSKY

We will gladly print the *Firebird* Finale that you propose to arrange for a concert edition, as well as the Berceuse.[9] . . . Since we are now at the end of the year, I wonder if you would remind Diaghilev about paying us for the use of the orchestra score of *Firebird* for [1913], as stipulated by our agreement.

STRAVINSKY TO B. P. JURGENSON

In April 1915 I will conduct a concert in Queen's Hall, London. I am thinking of conducting excerpts from *Firebird* (the Berceuse and Finale have never received a concert performance). I wrote to you before about arranging the Berceuse and Finale but decided to put it off until a more convenient time. Now that I am considering doing the arrangement this summer, I ask you to send both the Berceuse (the orchestra score separately) and the orchestra score of the entire *Firebird*. I will reorchestrate the Finale for small orchestra, as I have done with the Berceuse. Thus excerpts from *Firebird* will be accessible to orchestras that do not have the necessary instruments to present the work in full.

B. P. JURGENSON TO STRAVINSKY

You were bound by our agreement with Diaghilev concerning *Firebird* until 1915. This agreement must have terminated by now, and we may therefore consider ourselves free to rent the orchestra parts to others. We should come to an agreement regarding the terms. . . . If we receive inquiries from the Imperial Theatres, for example, what should we do?

   Will you write to Diaghilev? We have heard nothing from or about him, except that he is in Italy, and despite our reminders, he has yet to pay us for 1913 and 1914. Furthermore, he still has the full orchestra score of *Firebird;* he was supposed either to return this to us upon termination of the agreement or to propose an extension of his rights on the same or new terms.

B. P. JURGENSON TO STRAVINSKY

I heard from S. S. Prokofiev that you had extended your agreement with Diaghilev for *Firebird*. I do not want to believe this, because it will mean that you have made arrangements for something that no longer belongs to you. Naturally, on the termination of your first agreement with Diaghilev, the right to make any further agreements regarding the orchestra score reverted to us.

   When we acquired this ballet for publication, we could not foresee that

---

[9] The Berceuse, *Firebird*'s most popular movement, was published by Jurgenson in 1914 in Stravinsky's reduced-orchestra arrangement with a concert ending.

you would obstruct the exercise of our rights as publishers. We had to reconcile ourselves to your first agreement with Diaghilev, but to extend it reduces the possibility of earning a profit from the piano as well as from the orchestra score. It would really have been gratifying if Diaghilev had paid us on time. Furthermore, the crucial fault in the first agreement was that Diaghilev was legally obligated only to you, not to us, thus preventing us from making demands of him directly, and forcing us to deal through you, which obviously entailed as many inconveniences for you as it did for us.

B. P. JURGENSON TO STRAVINSKY   *March 24, 1916*

I have received your letter of February 10. On January 23 I received the money and a cable from Diaghilev, but having had no letter from him yet, I will write to him myself, asking if he would consent to a production of *Firebird* in Moscow, by the Imperial Ballet, and pointing out that, under the present conditions, a production here would in no way be injurious to him. . . . As I already wrote to you, Emil Cooper and the directors are very excited at the prospect of such a production.[10]

They would like to prepare a libretto of the ballet, and, of course, I replied that nothing can be done without your permission. But we would not want to cause any difficulties, in view of Diaghilev's extension of our agreement.

STRAVINSKY TO N. G. STRUVE   *April 6, 1919*

I have just finished the enormous task of reorchestrating the *Firebird* Suite.[11] . . . Sections of *Firebird* have already been published in pirated editions in America and even recorded.[12] Do you know whether the Bolsheviks have begun to reprint those compositions of mine published by you and Jurgenson, respectively? My mother writes that they were planning to do so.

---

[10] On March 10, 1915, the Petrograd *Stock Exchange Register* published the following notice: "Regarding an article that we published recently concerning the inclusion of the ballet *Firebird* in the repertory of Moscow's Bolshoi Theatre, the composer's mother, [Anna] Stravinskaya, has informed us that she has no knowledge of any negotiations between the composer and the directors of the Theatre about this production, and thus Igor Stravinsky could not have presented the directors with his terms, especially not 'minimum' terms."

[11] The manuscript score is signed and dated "Morges, February 11, 1919" at the end of the Dance of the Firebird, and "Morges, February 16, 1919" at the end of the Khorovod. The manuscript score, now in the Bibliothèque Nationale, Paris, lacks the Berceuse and Finale.

[12] I.e., not on pianola rolls.

OTTO KLING TO STRAVINSKY[13]   _July 10, 1919_

Morges

As for _Firebird,_ I regret to inform you that to mention "Moscow-Leipzig" is not
sufficient protection for the work in England or any country included in the
Bern [Copyright] Convention. As long as a work is published and _printed_ in
Russia, there is no recourse.

<table>
<tr><td>O. KLING TO STRAVINSKY</td><td align="right">_J. & W. Chester Ltd._
9–11, Place de la Fusterie
Geneva</td></tr>
<tr><td>Morges</td><td align="right">_March 5, 1920_</td></tr>
</table>

I regret not being able to undertake the publication of your new version of _Fire-_
bird, partly because of the terms you impose (18,000 francs) and partly because the original of this work, which, ethically, should belong to one publisher,
is already in the hands of many people. In short, you wish to sell our company a
new orchestra suite whose commercial value is diminished for the above-mentioned reason and over which I would not have real exclusivity, as I do for your
other works.

Even if we are able to reach an understanding on the latter question, the
total costs (which are on the rise in these difficult times), including engraving
and printing, would be exorbitant. Commercially speaking, 18,000 francs is, in
my humble opinion, much too steep.

Nevertheless, given our history of excellent relations, and to demonstrate
my strong desire not to abandon this matter, I propose to pay you 10,000 Swiss
francs for exclusive ownership of this new Suite. In exchange, I request a document from you freeing me from all responsibility vis-à-vis Jurgenson and his
eventual successors in respect to the original version. I also request all rights to
the piano score of the _Ragtime,_ of which [Editions de] la Sirène of Paris has
published 1,000 copies under a special license.[15]

O. KLING TO STRAVINSKY   _Geneva_
                                                         March 23, 1920
Morges

I am pleased to inform you that if we do publish a new edition of the _Firebird_
ballet, piano reduction only, . . . we would agree to pay you 10 percent of the net
amount earned from copies sold; the net price is 50 percent of the retail price,
and, according to current practice, seven copies count as six. . . .

Please send me confirmation of this, along with an official letter freeing us

---

[13] French is the original language of the correspondence with Otto Kling.

[14] See Stravinsky's correspondence with Blaise Cendrars in the present volume.

of all responsibility vis-à-vis Jurgenson or his successors regarding the new version of the *Firebird* Suite.

DESBAILLETS[15] TO STRAVINSKY   *Geneva*
                                                      July 28, 1920

Carantec

By the same mail, we are sending you the proofs of the full score of the new *Firebird* Suite; we would be grateful if you would return them to us with your corrections as soon as possible. M. Pychenov has just returned the parts, which he corrected from the parts that M. Ansermet delivered to us.

   We would also be grateful if you would immediately send the letter of release vis-à-vis Jurgenson; we await this document, which is very important for us.

   Thank you in advance.

STRAVINSKY TO O. KLING   *Carantec*
                                                August 14, 1920

London

The new *Firebird* Suite,* which you just acquired as director of Chester Ltd., is a work composed from the *Firebird* ballet, published ten years ago by the Russian company P. Jurgenson in Moscow. The ballet was the property of [Jurgenson] but is no longer, thanks to the altered concept of private and intellectual property espoused by the new Russian order, of which I am a victim, as is P. Jurgenson.

   Because I am unable to sell this work through P. Jurgenson, which would be the usual method, I have decided to cede it to your company, as I have done with all of my works composed in the last six years. . . .

   I hope that these few explanatory lines accompanying the surrender of my rights are sufficiently clear.

* I spent six months composing [the new Suite], October, November, December 1918, and January, February, March 1919.

                                                Berlin
E. A. OEBERG[16] TO STRAVINSKY   *May 31, 1922*

While in Leipzig I learned that Jurgenson has empowered his representative, Forberg, to defend his rights to *Firebird,* and requested that Forberg reprint the work. This task is now under way. Moreover, the Edition Russe de Musique is to be his representative in France and London. Bessel is responsible for this.

---

[15] Director of the Geneva branch of J. & W. Chester.
[16] Following Struve, Oeberg was director of the Edition Russe de Musique, until his death in Paris in December 1925. He was succeeded by G. G. Païchadze.

Forberg is reprinting only the _Firebird_ Suite, because he possesses neither the full score nor its piano reduction.

JURGENSON TO STRAVINSKY

Moscow
June 25, 1922

I am addressing myself to you, or rather to Diaghilev (whose address I do not know) through you. I never received the money that he owes us for the use of the orchestra score of _Firebird_ during 1917 and 1918. A considerable sum must have accumulated for use during the intervening years, and this would be most welcome right now. I hope that you will explain the matter to Diaghilev, since for me to do so from Moscow would be much more difficult. Once you have determined the amount, let me know . . . how much it is and through whom it can be obtained. . . . Recently I received a letter from J. & W. Chester in London informing me that they have acquired a new _Firebird_ Suite. Has there been some misunderstanding?

STRAVINSKY TO O. KLING

London

Pleyel
22, 24, rue Rochechouart
Paris
November 21, 1923

I leave for Biarritz next Saturday, and I beg you to send me . . . the orchestra parts (with the duplicates of the strings: 4, 3, 3, 2, 2) of the _Firebird_ Suite, along with my orchestra score.* . . .

* Your son took this with him to copy the page connecting the Danse infernale with the Berceuse.

STRAVINSKY TO O. KLING

London

November 30, 1923

If you would send me my score and parts of the _Firebird_ Suite as I requested in my last letter, I would be grateful. . . . Please pardon my insistence, but I need this material: the concert in which I am to conduct this suite is rapidly approaching.

STRAVINSKY TO HENRY KLING[17]

London

Pleyel
Paris
January 17, 1924

Unfortunately, the _Firebird_ Suite—immensely successful in Antwerp under my direction on January 7, at the Nouveaux Concerts d'Anvers—is full of errors. It is my duty to tell you so.

[17] Henry Kling became the director of J. & W. Chester when his father died on May 6, 1924. Harry died twelve years later.

ROBERT FORBERG TO STRAVINSKY

Recently Mr. Oeberg visited me here in Leipzig. In my capacity as representative of the P. Jurgenson Company, Oeberg made certain proposals to me regarding Jurgenson's editions of your works.

I am writing to you now at the request of Mr. Boris Petrovich Jurgenson. First, I would like to tell you that Mr. Jurgenson and I are both of the opinion that a reworking of your compositions for simultaneous appearance at another publishing house would do considerable harm to the earlier editions that we distribute. A copyright arrangement for your works would of course be desirable for us; but this would be possible only if you were to become a naturalized French citizen or if you were to employ a non-Russian to rework the compositions for you. Certainly nothing prevents this, and your works do not need to be given to another publisher.

I would be interested and grateful to have your opinion. Please write to me about it, also suggesting the amount that you and the Edition Russe de Musique in Paris would deem to be appropriate compensation, should Mr. Jurgenson agree to surrender his rights as publisher.

STRAVINSKY TO GEORGES VRIAMONT

Brussels

In response to your letter of the 17th, allow me to inform you that the orchestra parts of my ballet *Firebird* cannot be located at present. In Russia all parts necessary for performance are undoubtedly available, but I am convinced that you will not find them anywhere in Europe.

I possess my own copy of the large orchestra score of the ballet, and if the Royal Theatre of Antwerp would negotiate with me for the performance rights, which belong to me, I would give them this copy, from which they could make their own and thus mount the work.

In effect, I would like to arrange a rental agreement with the Theatre, asking a certain sum for each performance of the work, on condition that they return the copy, which would remain my personal property, after its use. [*Original in French*]

---

[18] On January 29, 1927, Stravinsky sent this letter and the one *to* him *from* Vriamont (July 17, 1925) to Ludwig Strecker of B. Schotts Söhne, as proof that Forberg did not have any score or set of parts of the *Firebird* ballet. The composer's letter mentions a visit to Strecker from G. G. Païchadze.

G. G. PAÏCHADZE TO STRAVINSKY   *November 8, 1926*

I have discussed the author's rights for *Firebird* with Diaghilev. . . . The meeting was not an easy one. Diaghilev started out by declaring that the issue could not even be discussed, because "he knows very well that you had ceded [*Firebird*] to Jurgenson, and that, consequently, you were not supposed to receive any rights at all from it." I had difficulty responding to this, since I am not well informed on the matter, but I managed to base the discussion on his *"bons rapports"* with you. When Diaghilev asked me what he should tell Jurgenson if he were to try to reclaim his rights, I told Diaghilev to refer Jurgenson to you. I had to convince him in any way possible. Finally, we agreed that for each performance [Diaghilev] must pay you £30.[19] I beg you to send him . . . a confirmation. Also, a thank-you is never superfluous.

SUBMITTED TO THE LEIPZIG TRIBUNAL   *December 2, 1926*

Trial date: February 9, 1927, 9 a.m.
Leipzig, December 2, 1926
County Court, 3rd Civil Chamber
Presiding: [signed] Reerink

Complaint

Of the firm Robert Forberg in Leipzig, Talstrasse 19, plaintiff, represented by the attorneys Dr. Hillig and Dr. Bruener, Leipzig

AGAINST:

(1) the firm B. Schotts Söhne, Mainz
(2) the composer Igor Stravinsky, Nice
(3) the firm J. & W. Chester Ltd., London

THE CHARGE:

The work *Firebird,* by Igor Stravinsky, first appeared as a piano arrangement in Leipzig, end of July 1911, from the publishing house of P. Jurgenson, whose firm is registered in the business registry of the police court, Leipzig, and which also has a branch in Moscow; the suite for orchestra also appeared there, end of March 1912; and the premiere of the ballet took place in Paris, June 25, 1910. The performance was announced in the commercial newspaper of the German book trade.

---

[19] The contract stating that Diaghilev was to pay Stravinsky £30 per performance of *Firebird* in London was signed in Paris on November 17, 1926, and bears the signatures of Stravinsky, Païchadze, Diaghilev, and Walter Nouvel.

Proof: (1) the enclosed piano arrangement;
      (2) the commercial newspaper (*Börsenblatt*) for the German book trade (*Deutscher Buchhandel*) no. 142, June 22, 1911, p. 7482, and no. 83, April 11, 1912, p. 4520;
      (3) letter from the publisher P. Jurgenson, May 15, 1926;
      (4) copy of the business registry of the police court, Leipzig, concerning the firm P. Jurgenson.

Thereby the conditions are fulfilled on which the protection of the said work in Germany . . . and in all the countries of the Bern Convention . . . depends.

II

With his letter of August 27, 1918, the publisher Jurgenson has yielded exclusive rights to the publishing company Robert Forberg, the plaintiff, to publish all works by Russian composers, particularly Igor Stravinsky, which were [formerly] published by the firm P. Jurgenson, and to distribute and sell them in all countries except Russia.

Proof: letter of August 27, 1918, from Mr. Jurgenson to the plaintiff.

III

For some time the work for orchestra by Igor Stravinsky, "Suite from *Firebird*," has been distributed in Germany and also in other countries of the Bern Convention. The firm J. & W. Chester Ltd. of London signs as the publisher. The distribution in Germany is done through the firm B. Schotts Söhne, Mainz, branch office in Leipzig, Lindenstrasse 16/18.

Proof: attached exhibit (sample).

The work is identical with the one of the same name that belongs to the plaintiff, its publisher, even though the author of the new edition attached the inscription "reorchestrated by the composer."

Proof: the enclosed evaluation of the instructor at the Music Conservatory in Leipzig, Mr. Max Wünsche.

Thus there is a violation of the publishing rights of the plaintiff. After identifying the reprint, the plaintiff protested to the composer Igor Stravinsky and to the firm Chester in London by telegram, October 29, 1926, and by letter to the Leipzig branch office of the firm B. Schotts Söhne, Mainz, October 29, 1926. Stravinsky referred the plaintiff to the firm Chester. The firm Chester dismissed the claim, referring to their publishing rights acquired in 1919 and to the fact that the matter concerns a revised edition.

    The plaintiff therefore finds himself forced to assert his rights by way of a suit.

    The competence of the County Court, Leipzig, bases itself, in regard to the accused of points (2) and (3), on paragraph 32 ZPO, and in regard to the accused responsible for (1), also on paragraph 10 ZPO. The Leipzig branch office of the accused in (1) has transmitted to the plaintiff the copy that was passed and has also delivered the work to others here.

In the name of, and with power of attorney for, the plaintiff, I invite the accused to oral negotiation about the disputed rights before the County Court of Leipzig, 3rd Civil Chamber, at a time to be designated by the honorable presiding officer, with the suggestion to charge with their representation one of the attorneys admitted to this court, and to disclose immediately through an attorney in writing to the court and the plaintiff possible objections and proofs against the assertions of the suit.

I will move for the judgment:

I. The accused will be ordered to stop the printing and distribution of the work appearing under the designation "Suite from the *Firebird* by Igor Stravinsky (reorchestrated by the composer in 1919)."

II. To destroy the unlawfully produced and distributed copies of the work designated in I, as well as the apparatus exclusively designed for the unlawful reproduction, such as plates, recordings, lithographical stones, stereotypes, etc. The plaintiff is empowered to charge a sheriff with this destruction.

III. The accused as collective debtors are sentenced to reimburse the plaintiff for all damages resulting from the unlawful manufacture and distribution, and to this end to inform the plaintiff about the number of the unlawfully manufactured or distributed copies, and

IV. to bear the cost of the suit, as collective debtors.

The request for IV is justified because the accused of (2) as composer was grossly negligent when he allowed his work, given to the publisher at another time, to appear through a different publishing company, even if with small changes.

The charge of negligence applies also to the two publishing firms, the accused in (1) and (3), who are, of course, obligated by their profession to exercise special care in the publishing and distribution of musical works. The publisher is obligated to research the availability of a work. This also concerns foreign works that are protected in Germany. See Goldbaum, commentary to authors' rights, remark to paragraph 36, 37, particularly page 232.

Leipzig, November 1926.[20]

H. KLING TO STRAVINSKY   *London*
                                                 December 20, 1926
167, blvd. Carnot
Nice

You have been informed of the measures taken by Forberg-Jurgenson regarding the *Firebird* Suite, which you ceded to us in 1920. Today we were advised

---

[20] The attorneys for Robert Forberg redrafted their statement on December 10, 1926, extending the motion to include "public performance or public reading, including radio renditions, but excepting stage presentations."

that a process will be served and the cause pleaded before the tribunal on February 9. It goes without saying that we will defend our rights, and, in the meantime, I would very much like to know with what attitude you intend to approach this affair.

STRAVINSKY TO H. KLING   *December 23, 1926*

London

Forberg-Jurgenson affair: The [suit] is news to me. I was not even aware of any problem until a month and a half ago, when I received a telegram from Mr. Forberg recommending that I stop all exploitation of the new *Firebird* Suite. He declared that he owns Jurgenson's rights and that the exploitation [of this piece] is therefore detrimental to him.

Since I am neither the proprietor nor the exploiter of the edition, I referred him to your firm. . . . That is all.

You ask me what attitude I intend to assume; I have very little to say in response, because I play no role in this affair, which is between your company and Jurgenson's.

LUDWIG STRECKER[21] TO STRAVINSKY   *January 4, 1927*

Forberg bases the suit on the transfer of your works, by a letter of August 1918, a date shortly before the nationalization of the Jurgenson publishing company. First of all, we will challenge this transfer, which was surely fictive. The contract probably was drawn up at a much later time and simply backdated. Nevertheless, we ask you for the following information:

1. Did you ever receive notice from Forberg or Jurgenson that this transfer had been effected, and, if so, when?

2. Before the publication of your [new] suite, were you in communication in any way with Forberg or Jurgenson, and can you prove (a) that both of these publishers have done nothing for you in the meantime, and (b) could not do anything for you?

Do you know personally whether the orchestra parts of your ballet were in Leipzig, and whether a contract was made for even one performance during that period?

Finally, I request any further details that could be brought forth in this case, and in French, since this is easier for you; on the same basis, I ask your forgiveness for dictating in German.

Furthermore, I request your signature on the enclosed power of attorney for the suit. Since the publisher Forberg has remitted a temporary disposition against Schott, to be argued on January 13 in Leipzig, please reply as quickly as possible.

---

[21] Director of B. Schotts Söhne; older brother of Willy.

Paris
PAÏCHADZE TO STRAVINSKY   *January 9, 1927*

I read Schott's letter carefully, and to me his position seems very weak. At any rate, the matter is disagreeable, and you are entirely correct that you must be circumspect in your answers and actions.

I will attempt to analyze Schott's letter point by point. I consider empty the question of whether or not the date of transfer rights from Jurgenson to Forberg is fictive. The whole question is one of whether or not Jurgenson lost his rights abroad after the nationalization of his publishing house in Russia and whether or not he had rights abroad. I believe that nationalization is valid only within Russia and cannot extend to foreign rights. In that instance, what relevance does this or that date have? If Jurgenson does possess foreign rights, then he could have transferred them even yesterday, and the transfer would be valid. It is a different matter if Forberg's adversaries show that Jurgenson never had the rights to *Firebird* abroad and that, since it was published in Russia, the work is not protected by the Bern Convention. Then the suit should end automatically, but you will have to say good-bye forever to *Firebird* and your other works in the Jurgenson catalogue, for anybody who is not too lazy will be able to publish them. Since the work will be unprotected, you will lose all control over stage presentations. This, of course, is not advantageous for you, but you and I are powerless in this regard. During the course of the suit, the question will come to light inevitably and automatically.

Now I turn to Schott's questions:

1. Your letter to me gave me to understand that neither Jurgenson himself nor Forberg notified you directly of the transfer of rights over your works from one to the other. Indeed, you should answer in this way, saying that you never knew and do not know even now the nature of the relationship between Jurgenson and Forberg. This point is important, and our adversaries have clearly made an error here.

2. The second question in regard to Jurgenson is simple; you can say that since the war you have had no direct contact with him at all and could not have had any, for reasons known to all. As for Forberg, from your answer to the first question it follows logically that since you had no idea that he was to be considered your publisher, you obviously would have felt no compunction to contact him.

To point (a) you can answer further that Jurgenson did nothing for you (although this question seems strange to me and incomprehensible); and to point (b) you can answer that you thought that Jurgenson could not do anything for you in terms of publishing your works, since he was cut off from Europe and you had no precise knowledge about the transfer of rights to Forberg. Again, this answer follows logically from your answer to the first question.

In support of this reasoning one can also declare that the mere fact that certain works listed in the Jurgenson catalogue also appeared in Forberg's publications could in no way indicate to you that rights had been transferred to him, since other foreign publishers, such as Idzikowski in Warsaw, print works from the Jurgenson catalogue in their own house by appending the note "Jurgenson, publisher." This, too, is an important fact, which should be brought to Schott's attention. Schott agrees that one must regard Forberg simply as a repository of Jurgenson's items. [Schott] asks where, to your knowledge, Forberg possesses the orchestra parts of the ballet. . . . Your answer, of course, must have a conjectural character; but . . . you must stress . . . the fact that while your other works have been mounted many dozens of times . . . over a number of years, such a burying alive of your work by Jurgenson causes you, as the author, great harm. This circumstance must be your main argument, since it shows the ethics of *your* position. . . .

In short, here is the scheme:

1. You were cut off from Jurgenson during the entire period;

2. you knew then and know now nothing about the transfer of rights to your works to Forberg and therefore did not consider him your publisher then and do not now;

3. the handling of the *Firebird* ballet by Jurgenson did not predispose you to give him a new work, the impossibility of contacting him aside;

4. you therefore agreed to a publication of this work by another publisher.

As you see, in my arguments I attempt to clarify and justify your position and your actions, since the fate of the suit in regard to Chester, I must admit, does not interest me much. My first thought was that if the suit is lost, Chester could bring a suit against you for selling them a work over which you had no right and could therefore demand that you cover all losses not only from the suit but from the edition. Having considered it, though, I think there is no danger of this, since Chester knew that the basic music belonged to Jurgenson, and it was Chester's duty as the publisher to find out whether they could buy the revised version from you. By the way, how is your contract with Chester worded? Does it indicate that this piece is your property, and that you can dispose of it at will?

I do not think that you should sign the power of attorney, for you might regret it later (the Germans have a knack of entangling people). Thank God you are not a party in this case, but only a witness. Write to Schott about this, tell them that as a witness you will support them fully, within the framework described above. This, of course, you must agree to do. I hereby return Schott's letter and the power of attorney.

STRAVINSKY TO STRECKER   *Nice*
                                                    January 10, 1927
Mainz

I am . . . giving you the details about the surrender of my rights to the new *Firebird* Suite to J. & W. Chester Ltd. in 1919, so that you will be fully aware of this affair. . . .

1. The attached copies are the only documents that I have received from Mr. Robert Forberg since he has been . . . the representative of P. Jurgenson.

No other document informing me of the transfer of Jurgenson's rights to Forberg was ever delivered to me.

2. At the time I was working on the orchestration of the above-mentioned suite, I was never able to make contact with Jurgenson (and naturally not with Forberg, whose name was completely unknown to me), given the absolute impossibility of commercial relations with this nationalized publishing company, as with any other establishment in the Soviet Union.

3. As for your inquiry about the orchestra parts and performances in Leipzig during this period, the question, to my knowledge, never even arose.

A FEW LINES CONCERNING THE SURRENDER OF MY RIGHTS TO THE WORK
IN QUESTION TO THE COMPANY J. & W. CHESTER LTD.

Given the absolute impossibility, as I stated before, of entering into relations with Jurgenson for the sale of my new *Firebird* Suite for orchestra (on which I worked five months), I began negotiating with the Chester company, which had just acquired a series of my works. Since this publisher was already the British representative for many Russian publishers, [Chester] knew perfectly well that the work belonged to Jurgenson; furthermore, I took care to inform Chester of this at the moment we began negotiations and later by a special letter, written at their request.

I would also like to draw your attention to the following fact: I have before me two copies of the piano reduction of the ballet *Firebird*. One appeared in 1910 with no copyright; the other appeared later, with the indication on the cover "all rights reserved" and *"prix de 9 roubles"* (in the new Russian orthography).

Along with these lines, I send you the "Prozess Vollmacht" with my signature, as well as the copy of Forberg's letter and his telegram with my answer, which I mentioned above.

You understand that I replied to Forberg in this manner because in no way am I the *"Verbreitung"* of the suite in question; and it was not in my power to obstruct his *"Verbreitung."*

Please tell me whether . . . there is anything else I should do for the moment, because I just received the *Klage* from Drs. Hilling and Greuner, Leipzig (Markgrafenstrasse, 4/II). I am not sending you this document, because you and Chester should have received it too.

STRAVINSKY TO STRECKER   *January 12, 1927*

In my last letter I forgot to tell you the following: since I did not know, as Forberg claims, that Jurgenson had transferred his rights, I certainly could not have concluded it from the fact that several works from the Jurgenson catalogue are found in the Forberg catalogue. I must also tell you that another foreign publisher, notably Idzikowski in Warsaw, prints works belonging to Jurgenson, simply by stating "Jurgenson, publisher" [on the cover].

O. KLING TO STRAVINSKY   *London*
                                                  January 14, 1927

167, blvd. Carnot
Nice

I cannot tell you how surprised and hurt I was to learn of the attitude you have adopted toward the *Firebird* Suite; it seems to me that, far from playing no role in this, . . . you, as the composer of the work, are precisely the one most deeply affected by the dispute!

For our part, we purchased this suite from you in good faith, and if we have the misfortune of losing this case, we naturally will have no recourse but to ask you for our rightful compensation. Furthermore, Forberg accused you, too. By now you should be aware of what is happening, from the letter (January 4) from Schott, our German representative. After this letter, I do not doubt that you will reconsider the matter in its true light. I would like to believe, *mon cher maître,* that we can count on your complete support. Thus I await news from you impatiently.

STRAVINSKY TO H. KLING   *Nice*
                                                  January 15, 1927

London

In confirming my last letter, of December 23 (the response to which I still await), I inform you that I, too, received notice of a proceeding against Schott, you, and myself [to take place] on February 9.

In the meantime, a letter arrived from Mr. L. Strecker, who proposes [that Schott] undertake the defense of my interests (as he did for your company), which I have just authorized.

I think that the case was supposed to have been heard at a tribunal in Leipzig last Thursday. . . . Have you had any news?

So, in awaiting your answer I send you my wishes for success and victory in this affair.

PAÏCHADZE TO STRAVINSKY   *January 16, 1927*

I received your letters and documents and carefully familiarized myself with them all. . . . For God's sake, do not worry and do not take it so much to heart. My departure was delayed, so I will not leave here before Thursday, but that will not matter, because the suit will undoubtedly be postponed. Postponements are inevitable in German courts. I will gladly follow your wish and make a detour to Mainz to see Strecker, and in Leipzig I will certainly see Forberg. . . .

Your letter to Chester concerning the sale of the *Firebird* Suite to them is another piece of evidence to be added to those I presented in my letter to you.

PAÏCHADZE TO STRAVINSKY

I talked in depth with Strecker about everything. . . . I pointed out to him a few facts of which he was not aware and which are essential to justify your position—and, simultaneously, to sink Forberg. The matter will evidently see a peaceful ending, for I impressed upon Strecker that neither for you, nor for him, nor for Chester, nor for Forberg would it be advantageous to prove that *Firebird* is unprotected and that anyone . . . could print it. I imagine that . . . Forberg will see the weakness of his position, that the parties will eventually come to an agreement, and that the issue will die down. In particular, your position does not worry me; you should go on working calmly and stop thinking about this.

PAÏCHADZE TO STRAVINSKY

I have just returned from Leipzig and found your letter. . . . I met with Forberg, or, rather, with the company's present owner and director, Von Roebel. After my discussions with Strecker, though, we concluded that I ought not to speak to [Von Roebel] directly, because he could misconstrue this as a sign of weakness on our part. Therefore, I conducted myself very diplomatically, directly addressing only those issues that affect the two publishers. Still, I managed imperceptibly to turn the conversation to you, and I have the impression that he will take a firm stand. . . . Kling has really become impudent. In relation to you, it would behoove him to use a different tone in his correspondence.

STRAVINSKY TO H. KLING

London

Firebird Suite: I persist in declaring my complete lack of involvement in your personal proceeding with Mr. Forberg, and I fail to comprehend how you can attribute any responsibility to me. The "good faith" to which you refer cannot have applied to your transactions with me, but rather to the position you took vis-à-vis Jurgenson in accepting the work in question. Moreover, you assumed this position voluntarily. You can argue "good faith" before Jurgenson, but you have no right to use it against me. My letter of August 14, 1920, written at your father's request, informed him of the exact conditions under which I was giving him the NEW *Firebird* Suite. Thus [your father] was perfectly conscious of his position vis-à-vis Jurgenson when [Chester] undertook to print this work and to free me of all responsibility in the affair. I add that as Jurgenson's representative [in England], you should have known better than I what must be done in respect to that firm.

SCHOTT TO J. & W. CHESTER   *February 17, 1927*

London

Only today did we receive the reasoning behind the judgment. Unfortunately, we must inform you that the preliminary disposition went against us and that we are forbidden, under harsh penalty and until further notice, to distribute the 1919 suite. The reasoning for this judgment, which will also be sent to you (we have so far received only a preliminary copy), examines all of the points—except one—in great detail and is, we regret to admit, unobjectionable, as far as we can see. The court takes the view that Jurgenson to this day owns the author's rights because the Leipzig branch made the public announcement of the transfer in time. In the court's view, the Russian expropriation plays no role, since Jurgenson acquired the German publishing rights independently even before the war, and thereby also in the other countries of the Bern Convention. Under these circumstances, the legitimacy or illegitimacy of the transmission of publisher's rights to Forberg is a secondary concern.

But, strangely, the judgment has not considered one point at all, the fact that both Jurgenson and Forberg have violated their duties as publishers toward Stravinsky. Of course, to a certain extent they were not able to fulfill them properly. This point, which we see as our only weapon, could win an appeal against the judgment. The reasons for the court's failure to investigate this point remain incomprehensible to us, especially since our lawyer here pointed it out expressly in his prepared written statement.

PAÏCHADZE TO STRAVINSKY   *Paris*
                                           February 22, 1927

Schott sent you . . . a copy of his letter to Chester, from which we learn that the court has halted the sale of the new suite under penalty of law until further notice. I conclude from this that the court has not yet made a categorical decision about the core of the matter, and the remainder of Schott's letter is therefore incomprehensible to me. . . . They write that their sole weapon now is to prove that Jurgenson did nothing for your works as your publisher. I do not understand from which angle this could interest the court—and if Schott is counting only on this, the situation is very bad.

In every lawsuit the lawyer is only a juridical instrument, manipulated by businessmen, and in your case this instrument obviously is not misused. Therefore, if you succeed in seeing the Germans from Mainz, and if my letter arrives before your meeting, try to hammer into their dull heads that they are preoccupying themselves with questions of secondary interest. What is of the utmost importance is that it was physically impossible for you to contact Jurgenson, and since Forberg did not complete the formalities after Jurgenson's rights were transferred to him, it did not even occur to you to contact him, and you sold your new piece to another publisher. . . . All else is insignificant.

Schott's letter fails to mention any court ruling about you; in fact, your name hardly appears. [I think] . . . a meeting with Schott would be desirable. You must insist on being excluded from this matter, based on the fact that you are responsible only to Chester. I sent Strecker a letter yesterday, written the way you and I agreed. . . . Regards to Vera Arturovna.

SCHOTT TO STRAVINSKY   *February 22, 1927*

To our disappointment, the court has taken the position that Jurgenson's Leipzig branch is legitimate, that Forberg lawfully acquired the German publishing rights, and that he has them still. The question of transferral to Forberg therefore plays only a secondary role, and a whole network of defense arguments is precluded. Nevertheless, we have submitted an appeal and will endeavor to contest this point as well.

Our main weapon will be the fact that neither Jurgenson nor Forberg was able to fulfill his obligations as a publisher in regard to you. Inexplicably, this very strong argument was not taken into account in the verdict, although it was presented in our written plea. The one thing we must ask you to do is, please, to write to us again in detail:

1. Was an orchestra score printed from the Jurgenson suite at that time (1910), or perhaps just a piano arrangement? (I.e., was the score available only in copy form, and therefore did it appear in Germany at all?)

2. How close are the Jurgenson and the Chester suites, and what distinguishes them from each other? Such an evaluation by you would constitute an appropriate basis for a third-party evaluation.

In conclusion, we would like to reassure you that nothing will be overlooked in our attempt to illuminate all points of view. We will send you the written presentation that we are preparing for the court of appeals.

SCHOTT TO STRAVINSKY   *Mainz*
                                                            February 23, 1927

After the civil suit, no possibility exists of excluding you from the case. The accused has the right to involve you, because in his opinion you have violated the author's rights under consideration. . . . Still, we will examine this question with our lawyer once more; but we do not anticipate a different result. That you originally dealt only with Jurgenson and that Forberg is the one suing today makes no difference. This is precisely the backbone of the lawsuit. We are also contesting the authority of Forberg, but the court maintains its first judgment that Forberg is the legal heir of Jurgenson.

What could be of some import is whether you reworked or recomposed the Chester suite from the ballet of the Jurgenson version. In the judgment, there is talk only of the piano arrangement of the Jurgenson suite, which supposedly appeared first in Leipzig. . . . If we could prove that either the suite or the ballet score did not appear first in Germany, then the lawsuit would virtually be won. . . .

Dr. Strecker will call you on Friday between nine and ten o'clock as agreed.

STRAVINSKY TO SCHOTT   *February [24?], 1927*

I reply first to the question of particular interest to you ... whether my new suite was made from the old one or from the ballet version.

Allow me to express my shock that this question is posed now, after the hearing, when your lawyer clearly should have [discussed] this before the judgment of that date (how else could he defend me?).

Above all, the lawyer should know that the new suite consists of the following numbers:

1. Dance of the Firebird
2. Khorovod of the Princesses
3. King Kastchei's Infernal Dance
4. Berceuse and Finale

The old suite ended with King Kastchei's Dance and contained two different numbers:

1. The Firebird's Supplications
2. Scherzo of the Golden Apples

which do not exist in the new suite, as you see; and since number 1 did not exist in the old suite, I could not very well have taken it from there, but only from the ballet itself.

The *Klage*'s affirmation that the phrase "reorchestrated in 1919" does not free the accused from responsibility is essentially wrong. Moreover, he has only to ask any conductor who has conducted both suites to know that this is not a simple reorchestration but a veritable recomposition.

Several days ago I described this grotesque proceeding and the incompetence of the experts to Oskar Fried, who offered to present his competent opinion before the tribunal.

The old suite never appeared in a piano reduction, but only as an orchestra score, and soon after the publication of the complete orchestra score of the ballet. This last was published in Moscow, which was always Jurgenson's base, while Leipzig was the subsidiary branch: just the contrary of what the *Klage* declared.

I am astonished that your lawyer did not take advantage of an overwhelming piece of evidence against Forberg, the letter he wrote to me in 1925, of which I sent you a copy, and to which Païchadze drew your attention once again in his last letter.

Did you read it carefully? In the [1925] letter, Forberg first calls himself the representative *(Vertreter)* of Jurgenson and, in the end, says that he will consult [Jurgenson] about the proposition submitted to me in the letter. I think this could destroy their case.

Now for the issue of my own responsibility. . . . The case is directed against the owner and *Vertreter,* not the composer of the work. I shall persist in trying to convince you to separate me from this purely commercial affair. Logically, I cannot be responsible before Chester, . . . who knew perfectly well what was being purchased from me. Thus I want to be judged in Paris, where I am a resident.

Furthermore, I must tell you that I was not officially informed that since 1918 Jurgenson belonged body and soul to Forberg. The fact that Forberg, as I recently heard, reprinted several of my little pieces from Jurgenson's catalogue does not imply that Forberg is the proprietor of Jurgenson, since everyone knew that Jurgenson was nationalized and that, therefore, anyone could take advantage of the situation.

Also, the Forberg edition of these little pieces certainly appeared after I had ceded the [*Firebird*] suite to Chester, which is to say after the summer of 1920. Thus I request that Dr. Strecker examine that letter carefully before telephoning me tomorrow morning. . . .

N.B. In that 1925 letter Forberg refers to himself as *Vertreter,* which means representative, as I told you. In the court decision he calls himself proprietor since 1918—which to believe?!

STRECKER TO STRAVINSKY   *February 25, 1927*

The February 9 statement was only a temporary disposition, and only the most prominent features of the case were treated. Our lawyer here was so certain of our victory that he did not bother to instruct the corresponding lawyer in Leipzig down to the last detail. That the suit is conducted in Leipzig greatly complicates things, of course. Tomorrow (Saturday) we will have a meeting among our lawyers here for the first time—with the Leipzig lawyer and myself, that is—and consider all points thoroughly. I will send you a copy of the written defense so that you may yourself ascertain that nothing has been omitted.

On that occasion I will ask your attorney for his view as to whether the complaint against you is justified. He will probably have a simple answer. Since this is a civil lawsuit, the issue probably has a simple answer.

I am still confident that we will win; the disadvantageous outcome of February 9 is only bad luck and inconsequential for the appeal.

SCHOTT TO STRAVINSKY   *February 26, 1927*

1. If you have a 1910 piano arrangement of the ballet, send it by registered mail for us to use as evidence. If correspondence exists concerning the arrangement

and proving its appearance in the year 1910, this would be helpful as well. We possess only a later arrangement, but if we could establish that the piano arrangement of the ballet appeared in 1910, the lawsuit would practically be won.

2. Dr. Strecker asks you to obtain Fried's opinion immediately. Dr. Strecker will write to you in greater detail and inform you of the result of the negotiations.

We would also like to request once more a copy of the 1925 letter from Forberg in which he identifies himself as representative rather than proprietor.

H. KLING TO STRAVINSKY   *London*
June 29, 1927

c/o Edition Russe de Musique
22, rue d'Anjou
Paris

The unfortunate *Firebird* affair is of such significance, not only for our publishing house but also vis-à-vis the shareholders of our company (to whom we must fulfill certain obligations), that I felt I must submit your arguments to our counsel and lawyer. I regret that I also am the one who must now inform you that they deemed your viewpoint inadmissible.

In short, it is incontestable that, according to the 1920 contract with us, you sold our company the copyright for a work that no longer belonged to you. The accompanying letter that you wrote to my father is irrelevant.

PAÏCHADZE TO H. KLING   *July 18, 1927*

London

Before his departure, Mr. Stravinsky shared the contents of your June 29 letter with me and brought me up-to-date on the details of this affair. He also requested that I answer you, which I will gladly do. As far as I can tell . . . you and Mr. Stravinsky take opposite views of the issue.

In your letter you claim that the Forberg dispute has not only caused you material harm but, more important, has damaged the prestige of your company. Since your house had been the British representative of Jurgenson for a long time, you could not have been unaware that the original music of the *Firebird* ballet belonged to Jurgenson. Moreover, Mr. Stravinsky informed you of this by registered letter on August 14, 1920, and he has kept your acknowledgment of receipt of this letter. This indubitably fulfills the stipulation in the contract.

Under these circumstances, and after receiving the aforementioned letter, you should either have renounced the publication and canceled the contract, or published the suite, assuming responsibility yourselves before the original publisher for all possible risks. . . .

I do not see where or to what extent you can hold Mr. Stravinsky responsible.

As for the damage to your prestige, it seems to me that your company, an old and important publishing establishment, ought necessarily to be more conscious of current laws and practices ruling this domain than Mr. Stravinsky, who is simply an artist. You should know better than he what you can and cannot do.

In your letter you ask Mr. Stravinsky to make you a proposal. Please be so kind as to explain what kind of a proposal you are expecting from Mr. Stravinsky, since he does not understand this, nor do I.

H. KLING TO PAÏCHADZE   *August 12, 1927*

It is with regret I note the disinclination on the part of Mr. Stravinsky to make any proposal to indemnify my Company upon the question of *Firebird.* . . . It is indisputable that Mr. Stravinsky received from my Company a considerable sum of money as the purchase price of something which he had no right to sell. Under the contract dated March 22, 1920, he, describing himself as Proprietor, assigned to my Company a copyright which did not belong to him, and the personal letter written by him to my father, five months after the contract was made but for some reason dated back to March 22, 1920, has no bearing on the subject at all. Referring to the paragraph of your letter wherein you make allusion to Mr. Stravinsky's ignorance of legal matters, I have too much admiration for Mr. Stravinsky's knowledge in this domain to doubt for a moment that he was perfectly well aware of his status in the affair and that he also realizes his legal position at the present moment. . . .

My Company has had to pay very heavy legal expenses in respect to the Forberg case. The decision having gone against us, we have to refund to the plaintiffs a heavy percentage of all receipts from the work in the past and pay a percentage in the future; it follows, therefore, that a most valuable asset in respect to the copyright of *Firebird* is lost to my Company.

Therefore, although the amount which we are legally entitled to claim from Mr. Stravinsky is far in excess of the sum mentioned, we are willing to accept the sum of Three Hundred Pounds (300) sterling, if paid at once in full settlement of our claim, or alternatively to take a new work from Mr. Stravinsky, free of any charge to us, of the same extent and value as *Firebird.* [*Original in English*]

LONGSTAFF AND FENWICK   *October 27, 1927*
TO LOUIS GALLIÉ[22]

Our clients, Messrs J. & W. Chester Ltd., have consulted us in the matter of their claim against your client, Igor Stravinsky, and have handed us your letter to them dated September 3, but only received by our clients on the 5th.

We can tell you that we have very carefully considered the circumstances of our clients' transaction with yours in the early part of 1920 and have advised them that their claim to be refunded the amount then paid to your client and to be indemnified in respect of damages sustained by them by reason of your client's misrepresentations is undoubtedly sustainable.

Our clients, however, tell us that they are desirous of maintaining, if possible, the amicable relationship that has always existed between your client and themselves, and trust that litigation may even yet be avoided.

If, unfortunately, our clients are forced to seek the assistance of the courts to sustain their claim, we shall advise them in due course as to where those proceedings shall be instituted.

We are afraid that you have not been correctly instructed as to the facts in this matter, and we will now deal with the points as they arise in your letter.

1. The property acquired by our clients under the contract of March 22, 1920, was not "the author's rights" in the new version of the works you mention, but comprised "all the copyrights and rights of publication, representation, and performance," which your client, as beneficial owner, thereby assigned to our clients.

2. The amount of 300 pounds referred to in our clients' letter of August 12 to G. Païchadze was the sum that our clients were disposed to accept in satisfaction of their claim to be refunded a part of the 500 pounds that your client received for rights that he was not in a position to assign. Of course, if our clients are compelled to take legal action, they will have further claim beyond a proportion of the 500 pounds referred to, by way of damage sustained by them following upon your client's misrepresentation.

3. A report of the proceedings brought against our clients will be found in the music trade papers published in Germany and England. It is a fact that our clients were ordered to discontinue publication of the work in question, and they have, in addition, had to pay a large sum to satisfy the plaintiff's claim for their performance and sale of the work since its publication. It is true that they have come to an arrangement with the plaintiff under which they are continuing to sell the work, but they have to pay 60 percent of the proceeds to the plaintiff and also bear the cost of production.

4. With regard to the damage suffered by our clients by reason of your client's misrepresentations, and in addition, of course, to the sum paid to him for the copyright in the work, we need only mention that by reason of your client's default, they have had to assume very heavy legal expenses; they have had to

---

[22] Chester's lawyers and Stravinsky's lawyer, respectively.

refund to the plaintiff a considerable sum, and, in addition, the damage suffered to their prestige and reputation is hardly measurable.

5. With regard to the concealment and misrepresentation we have referred to, our clients have in their possession undoubtable evidence that your client stated that the original work was not the subject of copyright, whereas he must have known that the contrary was the truth. Before the date of the assignment, your client was pressed to give ours an indemnity against any claim that might subsequently be made by any third party, and promised to do so, but it was five months after your client had obtained the 500 pounds before he wrote a very evasive letter enclosing a statement of facts, which he antedated to March 22, 1920, which happened to be the date of the contract.

There are other matters which, at the moment, we refrain from commenting upon, for our clients still think that your client desires only to act rightly and does not wish to avoid his responsibilities, and, entirely without prejudice, they instruct us to repeat the offer to your client contained in their letter to Mr. Païchadze of August 12.

They are, however, eager to have this matter disposed of without undue delay, and we must accordingly ask you to be good enough to let us hear from you as soon as possible.

In our opinion, our clients' offer is an extremely generous one, and as we have before stated, it is made in the hope of maintaining an amicable relationship between the parties.

LONGSTAFF AND FENWICK   *November 10, 1927*
TO GALLIÉ

We duly received your letter of the 3rd inst. You may take it that we know our clients sufficiently well to be able to assure you that they have not concealed from us any material facts whatever.

With regard to what you describe as the two essential questions, our remarks thereon are as follows:

1. What our clients derived from the new version of the work which is the subject of controversy does not concern your client in any way. As a matter of fact, they have had to refund the profit gained to Messrs Jurgenson. We should also point out that our clients are not, at the moment, seeking damages from your client in respect of such refund and other loss sustained, but are asking him to repay some proportion of the purchase money paid by them to your client for something your client was not in a position to sell to them.

2. It is true that our clients were agents in this country for the firm of Jurgenson, but in that capacity they had no responsibility or control whatever over the publications of that firm. You refer, under this head, to "the right to publish." We are anxious to make it quite clear that the right to publish or even "the author's rights," which you referred to in your previous letter to us, were not the only rights which your clients purported to sell to ours. What he did as-

sign to them was all the rights of publication, performance, and copyright and any other rights in the new version.

We can tell you that we are also convinced that our clients have a very well-founded claim against your client, and must now ask you to be good enough to let us know, without delay, if your client is prepared to accept the offer our clients have made to him.

STRAVINSKY TO CHESTER   *September 10, 1928*

I inform you by the present letter that, according to an act of March 2, 1928, duly filed in Berlin, I have ceded to the Edition Russe de Musique all author's rights to all of my works without exception published in diverse editions. By virtue of this act, the above-mentioned rights become the property of the Edition Russe de Musique, with whom all questions concerning the author's rights for my works published with you must be settled.

STRAVINSKY TO STRECKER   *Nice*
                                                          April 25, 1929

Mainz

Diaghilev will probably present *Renard* (which he is doing in Paris and London) and *Firebird* in his performances at the Berlin Staatsoper Unter den Linden (June 18, 19, 20, 21). I want you to know that Diaghilev never rented the *Firebird* parts from anyone, since he had them before Jurgenson bought the work from me. He pays me only my author's rights, as agreed between us, of 30 pounds per performance. So please collect the monies for me during his *Gastspiel* in Berlin.

STRAVINSKY TO STRECKER   *Nice*
                                                          January 8, 1930

Mainz

I received a letter from the Westdeutsche Konzertdirektion in Cologne (copy enclosed) requesting—in incomprehensible French—information about the *Firebird* Suite, which I intend to conduct in my Düsseldorf concert on February 6.

The suite in question is Jurgenson's (not Chester's), published shortly after the ballet, i.e., in 1910. You or Forberg should have this suite, since the Forberg proceeding was based precisely on the supposed damage to the old suite caused by Chester (as a result of the publication of the new suite).

I have had the orchestra score of the old suite in my possession for a long time, but, having no desire to cart this voluminous material along on my extensive tour, I prefer that you send it to Düsseldorf.

Please send both this *and* the Chester suite to Düsseldorf, because I am going to add the Berceuse and Finale of the latter to the former, which does not contain these two numbers.

I will stay here until January 17, when I leave for Berlin.

STRAVINSKY TO STRECKER

Wiesbaden

Voreppe
February 20, 1932

Since January, Edipho has been attending to my affairs regarding mechanical rights, and difficulties have flared up again with Chester over *Firebird*. These bandits pretend to own my mechanical rights to the suite that I sold them in 1919, as if they had not lost *all* rights to it in losing the Forberg case. What was the tribunal's decision on this subject? Did Chester surrender all rights to *Firebird,* including the mechanical rights (which, unfortunately, they had possessed previously), or does [Chester] still have those rights? I do not think so. I must tell you that in 1925 Pleyel ... bought my account from Forberg for all mechanical rights to my works published by Jurgenson, worldwide and forever. By what right could Chester solicit sums for mechanical rights? Is this not a new provocation on their part? Could I ask you to procure a copy of the tribunal ruling for me? I want to put an end to these intrigues once and for all.

I would be especially grateful if you would help me, because I am sick of Chester and would prefer never again to think of these ignoble bandits who have martyred me for thirteen years already.

STRAVINSKY TO PAÏCHADZE

Voreppe
February 26, 1932

You will probably be in Leipzig and see Forberg, so please clear up a little matter for me, one in which he can offer me useful and sensible advice once he has spoken with you. The problem is that Chester is demanding rights in full from Edipho for the recordings of *Firebird*, claiming that I sold him the suite *including* mechanical rights. My objections are as follows: In the first place, Chester's suite became Forberg's property, did it not? In the second place, in losing ownership of that suite, Chester lost the mechanical rights to it, did they not? In the third place, in 1925 Pleyel acquired from Jurgenson-Forberg all mechanical rights to all of my compositions published by Jurgenson, and in 1928 they completely surrendered their purchase to me for a certain sum. I am enclosing a copy of the conditions of the agreement concluded between Forberg and Chester, about which Strecker has written to me. Of course, it is in my interest to have this letter to show to Edipho, but it would be even more useful to have that excerpt from the court decision pertaining to Jurgenson-Forberg's restoration of their rights to *Firebird,* and consequently to the suite that Chester published in 1919 as well.

I will have to disentangle all of this when I come to Paris, around March 9 or 10. But the whole matter is even further complicated because that wretch Robert Lyon[23] has lost (and Pleyel cannot find) a very important document, a transaction that he made with Chester in 1925. By virtue of this document, Chester shares with me the profits from the mechanical rights to the *Firebird* Suite, published by them. . . . Without the document, and in the event of the failure of my arguments—which I do not necessarily anticipate—I would forfeit the profits from recordings of the *Firebird* Suite made by Stokowski and others, which would be a ghastly development. My recording is of the old suite, except for a few transitional measures that served as an introduction to the Kolybelnaya; i.e., only eight measures were taken from the Chester edition.

On July 18, 1933, Schott purchased the Firebird *ballet and the 1919 suite from Forberg, but Stravinsky's trials with the work, literally and figuratively, were not over.*

On February 28, 1936, a representative of the Société de Droit de Reproduction Mécanique (Paris) sent Stravinsky a document summarizing the essential features of the exploitation and deformation of his Firebird *in a film of the same name. According to this statement, Warner Bros. had not only used fragments of* Firebird *illicitly but had also injured the character of the work:*

First, the music is employed as a seduction motif in a detective drama, an obvious abuse, since the music was written for the ballet. Second, the music of the final dance [Infernale] is rendered as an overture to the film. Thereafter, fragments of the original score are introduced and interrupted at random, according to the caprices of the plot. Finally, the title of the film was stolen, and at one point in the dialogue one of the characters even makes mention of "the famous *Firebird* by Stravinsky."

Stravinsky retained a lawyer, Albert Le Bail,[24] who wrote to the composer, March 25:

I have contacted one of the lawyers for Warner Bros. and explained our situation. I think that an agreement could be reached with this firm, but we must proceed very energetically. . . . To have the film seized by an agent of the Commissaire de Police could present certain dangers. . . . In my experience, I have learned that one must veritably pound the notion of artistic propriety into the American skull to achieve any result. . . . I conclude my letter with what may be a somewhat indiscreet request: . . . I would like to have a signed photograph of you.

By May 19, Le Bail was less optimistic:

---

[23] Director of Pleyel until about 1930.
[24] Le Bail had been retained in the suit concerning Chaplin's use of a copyrighted song in his *Modern Times*.

We now have no option but to take Warner Bros. before the Civil Tribunal . . . but, unfortunately, we will have practically no chance. Thanks to your agreement with Forberg, we can only contest your ethical [not material] right to the confusion surrounding the title.

Six months later (November 10), Le Bail wrote to remind Stravinsky that "legal proceedings in America are subject to very long delays." The case was to have been heard at the end of November, but Le Bail decided to seek a postponement. On March 20, 1937, he informed the composer that the case would come before the 3rd Chamber of the Tribunal on May 3. On May 4, Stravinsky's counsel wrote again:

Contrary to what we had thought, the case could not be heard yesterday at the Palais [de Justice]. A new judge has just been named in the Chamber, and therefore no cases were heard yesterday. I managed, nevertheless, to fix a date before the judiciary holidays; thus, the case will definitely be pleaded on June 28. . . . Please be so kind as to send me some newspaper clippings related to the triumphant premiere of *Firebird*.

On May 19, Simone Debreuilh published an article in Paris-Soir *entitled "A Sensational Suit: The Composer Igor Stravinsky Claims 300,000 Francs in Damages from an American Firm." The newspaper quotes Stravinsky:*

This work, so important in the history of music, is completely disfigured in the film. Random fragments were taken and carelessly cut. . . . For example, the Danse infernale, at the end of the ballet, is used as an overture, and other fragments are embellished with Viennese waltz motifs.

Susan Blum, the counsel for Warner Bros., had reported the history of the case to Madame Debreuilh as follows:

In 1932, [Warner Bros.] acquired rights for sonorous adaptation of fragments of several masterpieces, including *Coq d'or* and *Firebird* . . . to be used in films. At the same time, a certain Lajos Zilahy wrote a detective play entitled *Tuzmadar (Firebird)*, which was presented first in Budapest, then in London, with about 125 performances in each city. Stravinsky registered no complaint. The success of this drama inspired the American company to purchase cinematographic rights to *Firebird* from Lajos Zilahy. The film appeared shortly thereafter, starring Verree Teasdale, Ricardo Cortez, Lionel Atwill, and Anita Louise. The film follows the story line of the play: . . . the musical fragments excite the young heroine to rebellious and frenetic actions, which are crucial to the unfolding of the plot.

On June 29, Le Bail informed Stravinsky of the progress of his case:

Your case was heard yesterday for about two hours. The judge is young and knows little about these issues, which is annoying because they really require a specialist. Furthermore, this judge is provisional and will surrender his position to an older one, no doubt to our advantage. . . . The tribunal requests to see the film.

Nevertheless, on August 5 the Société de Droit de Reproduction Mécanique wrote:

M. Le Bail has just informed us of the judgment in the *Firebird* case. The tribunal maintained that the only damage you suffered was in the placement of a Viennese aria immediately after a Stravinsky aria, and thus awards you a token 1 franc.

In August 1940, Stravinsky took out first papers for United States citizenship; later that year he became a member of ASCAP. On August 27, 29, and 30 he conducted Firebird (the 1919 suite) *in the Hollywood Bowl, presented as a ballet with choreography by Adolph Bolm. On August 27, Michel Fokine, then living at 253 North Broadway, Yonkers, wrote to Stravinsky:*

Nobody ever bought the libretto from me, not Diaghilev, nor you, nor any publisher (unlike *Daphnis and Chloe,* which Durand purchased). That is why I was so surprised to read that all rights belong to Jurgenson. . . . Now I read that my choreography will be replaced with a completely new one by Bolm. But it cannot be absolutely independent of mine, because (1) the choreography is linked to the music, the music to the subject, and (2) Bolm, having seen my ballet performed for many years, cannot wholly erase it from his mind. . . . Igor Fyodorovich, I have no doubt that if you re-examine these questions, not from a commercial point of view, but, rather, from the perspective of a man's just rights over his own creation, you will feel the injustice of taking from me something that is actually a part of me, and that I so gladly and trustingly shared with you. [*Original in Russian*]

Stravinsky and Bolm replied by telegram:

Producing not entire ballet but symphonic suite logically requiring new choreography. . . . As to ethical questions we are more than surprised by your lack of confidence in us. Program notes mention you as author choreography of original ballet. [*Original in English*]

Nevertheless, the altercation inspired Stravinsky with the notion to arrange yet another Firebird Suite, *one that could be used both as a ballet and a concert score,*[25] *and one whose copyright he would finally be able to secure, though the noncopyrighted versions could not be withdrawn from circulation. On April 20, 1945, Irving Deakin of Hurok Enterprises wrote to Stravinsky proposing a new* Firebird *ballet with choreography by Adolph Bolm and offering a $500 advance before "commencing the work of supplying the necessary bridges between the existing suite and the additional numbers from the original* Firebird *score." Deakin said that Hurok was prepared to guarantee twenty performances annually for two years at $15 each, adding that if the ballet were filmed, the composer and Hurok would receive 50 percent each. On the same day, April 20, Stravinsky wrote to Aaron Goldmark, of the Hollywood branch of Leeds Music Corporation, reporting on a conference with Lou Levy, the company's president, and promising that the new suite would be completed early in the summer and the copyright taken out in the fall. Stravinsky sent a second letter to Goldmark that same day authorizing him to negotiate with Hurok in respect to ballet productions. Aaron Sapiro, Stravinsky's attorney, answered Deakin for the composer in a letter dated April 24: "[Since Hurok] is reaping the prosperity he deserves . . . I assume that this will warrant a generous attitude in reference to the labor and genius of Mr. Stravinsky."*

On May 7, Stravinsky agreed to sell to Leeds Music Corporation "a certain heretofore unpublished musical composition . . . entitled 'The New Firebird *Suite' . . . an original work . . . [for] an orchestra of 55 players, of a duration of 26–27 minutes." In fact, the 1945 suite is the 1919 suite, expanded by five numbers, which are reorchestrated from the original ballet score: Pantomime I, Pas de deux, Pantomime II, Scherzo: Dance of the Princesses, and Pantomime III. On June 7, Stravinsky sent his manuscript of the 1945 suite to the Leeds office in New York.*

On July 27, Helen Jacobson, of Leeds's New York office, telegraphed Sapiro, reminding him that Eugene Weintraub of her company had talked to Stravinsky "at least four weeks ago suggesting that since Hurok is in California, [Stravinsky] should speak with Hurok directly about negotiations for conducting the ballet." Sapiro replied on August 3 that the contract for Firebird *and other works was discussed*

in the presence of Mr. Stravinsky, Mr. Goldmark, Mr. Stein and myself and [I] made it clear that Mr. Stravinsky did not want to have any direct relationship with Mr. Hurok. . . . [When] Mr. Levy was here, the statement was made in his presence that the Hurok deal would probably be $850, with $30 a performance for a minimum of thirty per season, together with $1,500 for two personal appearances by Mr. Stravinsky as conductor.[26]

---

[25] Rarely performed in concert, the 1945 suite has been used for the New York City Ballet's *Firebird* since 1949.

[26] Sol Hurok had been very successful in presenting Stravinsky as conductor of *Petrushka* and *Apollo* in Ballet Theatre performances, and Stravinsky had received high

Ballet Theatre agreed to give thirty performances during the coming season, with the condition that the $30 per performance be applied against an advance rental fee of $850, but no agreement was reached for Stravinsky to conduct. Sapiro's letter also informs Jacobson of a meeting at Stravinsky's home on June 23, with Messrs Levy, Goldmark, Tansman,[27] and Sapiro, during which Mr. Levy stated that he was negotiating for Stravinsky's Ballet Theatre appearances. Sapiro accused Leeds of bad faith and appended his regrets at the "mishandling of the Levy, Jacobson, Weintraub group of New York." Sapiro sent copies of his letter to Tansman and, for reasons the present writer cannot discover, Darius Milhaud.

The new Firebird, *with decor by Chagall and choreography by Bolm, was first performed on October 24, 1945, at the Metropolitan Opera House.[28] The next day, Jascha Horenstein, who had conducted the premiere, telegraphed Stravinsky: "Orchestra parts simply horrible. Manuscripts done by nonprofessional copyists. Worse than anything ever experienced." Stravinsky wrote to*

---

fees—for which reason he granted the WNYC interview at the Metropolitan Opera, transcribed below. In 1943, Stravinsky conducted *Petrushka* on January 27 at the San Francisco Opera House, on February 8 and 13 at the Los Angeles Philharmonic Auditorium, and on April 2 and 12 at the Metropolitan Opera. On April 25 and 26 and on May 9, in New York, he conducted *Apollo*. The Stravinskys, who stayed at the Ritz Towers, March 31 to May 10, also attended several ballet performances, and at one of them, on April 10, Stravinsky gave a brief intermission interview:

WNYC As we promised you earlier in the program, we are bringing to the microphone the greatest of modern composers, Igor Stravinsky. We have located him in the audience and brought him here. He is just entering our studio now. . . . How do you do, Mr. Stravinsky?

I.S. How do you do?

WNYC Mr. Stravinsky has come from his home in Hollywood to be a guest artist with the Ballet Theatre, to conduct his own ballet, *Petrushka.*

I.S. It makes me feel very happy to have my works performed by such a fine ballet company. The first performance of *Petrushka,* which I conducted last week, was an experience I shall never forget. It is thirty-two years since the first performances of *Petrushka* were presented . . . and now, in 1943, it was given with my old colleagues from the Diaghilev days, Léonide Massine and Adolph Bolm.

WNYC When are you conducting again, Mr. Stravinsky?

I.S. I will conduct *Petrushka* again on Monday night. And now, although I am a guest conductor of the Ballet Theatre, if you will excuse me, I will become a guest at the performance this evening and return to my seat. It is nearly time for the next ballet to begin. *Au revoir.*

[27] Alexander Tansman, a cousin of Sapiro.

[28] Vittorio Rieti reported to Stravinsky: "Chagall's designs are too anecdotal and too numerous. Moreover, they fail to evoke the atmosphere of the story; also, they 'eat' Bolm's choreography, which is otherwise either nonexistent or deplorable." (October 27)

Leeds on October 27, complaining of the unsatisfactory state of the orchestra parts and declaring that he was particularly upset because he had scheduled twelve performances of the new suite in his forthcoming concert tour and had also made arrangements to record the work for Columbia. He sent a copy of this letter to Goddard Lieberson, adding "Poor Hornstein! [sic]."

On October 30, Weintraub wrote to Bruno Zirato, Stravinsky's concert agent, explaining that

a 114-page score arrived here Saturday at 8:00 p.m. All good copyists were either busy or refused to work on Sunday. The question became this: Should I deliver bad parts or have the Ballet Theater cancel their proposed premiere. . . . Although the Ballet have already given three performances with this material . . . we are going to great expense to copy a new set of parts.

Three days later Weintraub wrote to Stravinsky: "George Balanchine, who is to visit you soon, will bear out what we have to say about the conductor's lack of cooperation with regard to . . . The Firebird."

On November 8, Leeds conveyed a request by Fritz Reiner to give the concert premiere of the new suite. Stravinsky refused in a telegram of the 11th. Then, in January 1946, Weintraub wrote to the composer saying that his Firebird score had come unbound but was nevertheless being sent to the Hollywood office, from where "I hope that by this time Goldie has sent it to you." If "Goldie" is Aaron Goldmark, what Stravinsky received from him was a letter in which an offended Goldmark reveals that it was he who had suggested the title for the Ebony Concerto: *"I consider myself very close to you and might convey my disappointment to Mr. Goldfarb in not even receiving at least an acknowledgment of the fact that he received this work." The composer wrote in the margin: "What cheek! How do you like it, dear Mr. Sapiro?"*

In April 1946, an argument broke out between Jacobson and Sapiro concerning the rental accounting, the lawyer warning Jacobson that if this were not corrected by May 3, the matter would be taken to court. By May 16 nothing had happened, and on that date Stravinsky wrote to Weintraub blaming the arduous work of correcting the proofs on the circumstance that the Leeds copyist had used two different orchestra scores, one of which "was revised and corrected by me, the other (or others) was the uncorrected and unrevised Kalmus [pirated] score. . . . The quantity of mistakes was too numerous to [fit] all I had to say in the margins, and I decided to correct everything myself." On May 17, Sapiro received a letter from Leeds that confirmed "our telephone conversation with Hyman O. Danoff, Esq. of your office [;] it is understood that in the action entitled 'Igor Stravinsky versus Leeds Music Corporation,' No. 513891 in the Superior Court, defendant may have until May 25, 1946 in which to plead to plaintiff's complaint." Stravinsky wrote to Weintraub on May 30 insisting that the instruments given on the proofs be followed, and, finally, on July 1 an attorney for Leeds forwarded a check to the composer, along with a request that Sapiro "discontinue the legal action that has been set for trial on July 26."

On September 26, a less ruffled Goldmark sent a conciliatory note express- ing his "best wishes for a Happy New Year."

Not until October 1947 did Stravinsky actually sue Leeds Music Corpora- tion, because of the publication of the melody of the Rondo from Firebird *as a popular song, entitled "Summer Moon." Stravinsky lost the case in March 1949 (New York* Daily News *headline: "IGOR MORTIS"). Less well known is the com- poser's statement, of which he made copies for distribution. A brief excerpt must suffice:*

These vulgar Broadway people . . . had the idea of extracting melodies from *Firebird,* to be arranged as popular songs, . . . and of commissioning someone to write words, packaging the little *cochonnerie* under the title "Summer Moon." . . . The intent was to attract the "juke-box trade" (a one-penny machine found in drug stores). [November 9, 1947]

Finally, on May 19, 1953, Schott purchased the 1945 Firebird Suite *from Leeds.*

Stravinsky's troubles with Firebird *persisted. On January 7, 1949, the* New York Times *published a review by Olin Downes of a* Firebird Suite *performed by Eugene Ormandy and the Philadelphia Orchestra. The "original full scoring" was used, according to the critic, not the "instrumentally truncated late ver- sion." But since Downes felt that some listeners might have "craved a broader pace for the great chords of the conclusion," the reader cannot tell which* Fire- bird *suite actually was performed. The original (1912) suite does not conclude with broadly paced chords, and the 1919 suite, which does end this way, em- ploys the same reduced orchestra as the 1945 version. Stravinsky underlined and questioned the review but did not send a rectification.*

On October 15, 1950, the Times *printed a Downes editorial heralding a new, pirated edition of the complete ballet score that would make accessible to the public "the original instrumentation of Stravinsky's first poetical master- piece, before he began to monkey with it in successive orchestral versions of the suites from his ballet score." The 1945 suite is referred to as the "third, badly curtailed and dehydrated edition." This time Stravinsky protested in a letter to the* Times, *dated October 19, explaining that the "new* Firebird Suite *is not a curtailed but, on the contrary, an augmented edition of my previous [1919] Suite." Stravinsky's letter was not published until November 19, however, at which time it was chaperoned by a second Downes article, assaulting the com- poser's explanations and even ridiculing his English.[29] Downes's argument*

---

[29] Downes's attacks had begun to irritate Stravinsky since the mid-1940s, when the composer referred to the critic in a letter to Merle Armitage as a "famous ass." It should be said that since the 1949 review, Stravinsky had rebuffed two overtures from Downes. In a lengthy letter, February 10, 1949, the critic explained to the composer that he need not concern himself with the commentator (Downes) during two

that a reduction in the number of instruments implies a loss of quality in instrumentation is as weak as his statement that the new suite, "almost in its entirety, is practically [sic] contained in the first two Firebird *suites of 1912 and 1919." The respective durations of the three suites are circa 21 minutes, circa 20 minutes, and circa 27 minutes, and the music making up 4 or 5 of the additional 6 or 7 minutes in the 1945 suite is found in neither of the earlier two suites.*

Downes also declared that the revisions of form and substance had not benefited the music. But since the revisions of form consist principally in concluding with the Berceuse and Finale, omitted in the 1912 suite, and in including the Dance of the Firebird, the most stunning piece in the ballet, but also omitted in the 1912 suite, the form of the later suites is closer than that of the earlier one to the form of the original ballet. As for changes of substance, the only one that most listeners would remark is the absence in the ballet and in the early suite of the trombone glissandos in the Infernal Dance. But to compare any part of Kastchei's Dance in the orchestrations of 1910 and 1919 is to discover that in every instance the later version strengthens the musical ideas. For only one example, 6 measures after the change of meter following those trombone raspberries (14 in the 1919 suite), the violas and cellos play an ascending scale in sixteenth notes in the original version. In the 1919 version the same scale is played by all of the violins, and each note is harmonized as well, forming a complete seventh chord—a revision of substance. The original version sounds feeble in comparison. The 1919 score also adds sustaining horns in the measures before, and other horns double the lower strings. (Incidentally, Stravinsky similarly altered the horn parts in his 1960 recording of the original ballet, Columbia MS 6328.) The 1919 score doubles cellos and violas instead of rotating them, and it introduces thirds in the woodwinds in the last measure on the page, versus the unharmonized octave of the original. The 1919 score also doubles the piccolo with piano and makes more effective use of the basses. It should also be noted that in the 1945 suite, Stravinsky removed the low C in the flute, in the interests of a clear attack on the second eighth note. That these changes are the result of an ever-increasing orchestral mastery is evident.

    Was Stravinsky right, on purely musical grounds, to extract a suite from Firebird? *The complete ballet score is now performed in concert almost as frequently as any of the suites, no doubt because the music between the set-pieces of the suites contains some of the most interesting in the work—at the Death of*

Monday-morning broadcasts of Stravinsky's Boston Symphony rehearsals. Downes's second letter, February 22, 1949, asks Stravinsky for an interview, offering him complete control of "correction or certification." Stravinsky acknowledged the first letter in a terse telegram and ignored the second. When Downes died, in the summer of 1955, the Pacific Coast Music Festival in Santa Barbara asked Stravinsky for permission to perform his Mass under Stokowski, "In Memoriam Olin Downes." Stravinsky refused (letter of September 5, 1955), saying "it would be an unkind irony."

Kastchei, for example, who is characterized (see 191) by figures similar to those associated with the Moor in Petrushka, *and in the Dialogue of Kastchei and Ivan Tsarevich (see 110–111), music that might be mistaken for Pe-*trushka. *Certainly these passages, and that of the Capture of Ivan Tsarevich (98–107), are more powerful and "forward-regarding" with respect to Stravinsky's development than the insipid music for the Princesses with the Golden Apples, which the composer selected for both the 1912 and 1945 suites, or the Schéhérazade-like Supplications of the Firebird. Yet the complete ballet is not wholly successful in the concert hall for the reason that too much music, particularly between the beginning and the Dance of the Firebird, remains tied to stage action. By the same token, the 1945 suite is not a satisfying substitute for the complete ballet score. Finally, of the later suites, the 1919 is a better concert piece than the digressive 1945 score.*

A few years later, Ernest Ansermet added his voice to Downes's: on December 23, 1957, the Gazette de Lausanne *published a letter from Ansermet deploring Stravinsky's "recomposition a few years ago of* Firebird *and* Petrushka, *on grounds that the original orchestrations were not good." In the letter, Ansermet vows never to conduct these new versions, and asserts, "Fortunately . . . when a musician has published his work . . . his judgment over it no longer has any authority." A certain André Gaillard of Lausanne clipped and sent Ansermet's letter to Stravinsky together with a note: "I know that history has sometimes contradicted the judgments of the greatest composers on their works, but is history really the only criterion of judgment?" Stravinsky answered Gaillard on January 8, 1958:*

E. Ansermet was the first to conduct . . . my *Firebird* Suite reorchestrated in 1919 for a smaller ensemble than that of the original score. As E. Ansermet well knows, this suite is the one that is now played throughout the world. Concerning the 1945 suite, to which E. Ansermet refers, the ensemble is the same as that of 1919.

Then, turning to the question of the supposed termination of a composer's authority as a judge after the publication of his work, Stravinsky says that the statement is meaningless:

If . . . E. Ansermet is now inclined at all costs to deny the value of my revisions, he must find more substantial arguments than those that he proposes.

III

CORRESPONDENCE WITH

The Composer as Moneylender, Mortgagee, Landowner, Vodka Distiller

G. P. BELIANKIN

Whether or not Stravinsky's letters to bankers, brokers, lawyers, and estate agents provide sufficient documentation to diagnose a "split personality," the concentration, logic, and concern with minutiae that he devoted to business affairs are awesome, at any rate in a great musician. In this chapter devoted to the composer as businessman, Stravinsky's mind seems to divide almost equally into musical genius and moneylender. After finishing Le Sacre du printemps *on a November morning in 1912, he apparently spent the afternoon writing letters about investment properties.*

Stravinsky's fears concerning money were probably inherited from his parents. In any case, they developed into a powerful neurosis, for even at the worst of times—1916 to 1919, when his income from Russia ceased—he was far from poor. True, he wrote to his publisher, N. G. Struve, April 6, 1919:

For the last two years I have lived by the generosity of certain kind people. . . . My cost of living is 2,500 Swiss francs per month, but before the war I was earning approximately 4,000 rubles from the Edition Russe, which was equal to 11,000 francs. . . . Our property [Volhynia] has been under enemy occupation since 1915, and thus I have been deprived of my only source of income. . . . Unless you cable my monthly payment immediately, I will have to part with my wife's last family valuables.

Shortly after sending this letter, however, Stravinsky received large gifts of money from the United States. And since 1916, he had been collecting a monthly stipend (and supplies of tobacco) from Madame Errazuriz;[1] commissions from the Flonzaley Quartet, the Princesse de Polignac, and Werner Reinhart; advances from publishers; performance rights from Diaghilev (the Ballets Russes had given Firebird *thirty-three times,* Petrushka *thirty-nine times, in the United States alone); royalties; performance fees from England, Spain, Italy, and Switzerland; fees for conducting; money from the sale of manu-*

---

[1] On June 16, 1916, Madame Errazuriz, in Paris, wrote to Stravinsky at the Hotel Ritz, Madrid, asking if he had received the tobacco she had sent. Stravinsky was slow to send receipts for the money, and in at least three letters she asks for acknowledgment: on January 13, 1917, she mentions having sent him 1,000 francs through the Hottinger Bank; on January 18, 1918, she refers to a recent check for 2,000 francs; and on March 17, 1919, she sends "a check for two months, to avoid future difficulties."

scripts; gifts of money from such friends as Thomas Beecham and Princess Vio-
lette Murat (4,000 francs on January 12, 1917). In the United States, March
14, 1925, Stravinsky signed an agreement with Brunswick to record four sides
a year, and he soon received $8,000, for 1925–26 and 1926–27, though the eight
sides were never completed. Stravinsky had already made forty-four rolls for
Pleyel before October 29, 1924, but on that date he signed a seven-year contract
with the Aeolian Company Ltd. of Connecticut (!) to make twenty-eight more
for the "Duo-Art reproducing piano," for either $2,000 or $4,000 annually (the
higher fee would obtain if the recording took place in America). Aeolian ceased
to manufacture the Duo-Art two years before the termination of Stravinsky's
contract, yet he was paid for 1930 and 1931. Eight thousand tax-free dollars in
1925 is the equivalent of $100,000 today. In that year Tanya, Stravinsky's
niece, temporarily living with the composer's family in Nice, wrote to her fa-
ther (Stravinsky's brother, Yuri) in Leningrad: "Uncle said that he would very
much like to help you, but that right now his affairs are hanging by a thread."

Grigory Pavlovich Beliankin,[2] who in 1901 married Lyudmila Gavrilovna Nos-
senko, the sister of Stravinsky's first wife, seems to have been irrepressibly at-
tracted to business ventures for which he had no ability. Graduated from the
Marine Architecture Institute in Philadelphia, Pennsylvania, at the end of the
nineteenth century, he built Stravinsky's Ustilug house, constructed an infir-
mary in the town, and managed his wife's estate there. In the two years prior to
World War I, before Beliankin's ineptitude had been exposed, Stravinsky en-
trusted the management of his properties—as well as that of his mortgages on
land he had sold—to him, and with disastrous results. Neither the composer
nor his wife's brother-in-law seems to have possessed the slightest foresight
with regard to the political upheavals in Russia during the war, and the conse-
quent economic ruin to themselves. It seems that during only one short period,
1935–36, was Beliankin able to earn a living. As Catherine wrote to Igor, Febru-
ary 6, 1936: "I have been praying diligently for the Beliankins for more than a
year, and it is true that since the trip to Ustilug things have gotten better, and
Grisha has been supporting himself." He was employed briefly in the early
1920s as an extra in a stage or film production,[3] in the mid-1930s at the Café de
la Paix (in charge of Russian cuisine), then as a clerk in the Russian depart-
ment of a bookstore, then in the yogurt business—though this, his own invest-
ment, soon failed.

At the beginning of World War I, Beliankin; his mother, Anna Ivanovna
("Baba Anya"); and his wife, daughter Ira, and son Gavril (Ganya) were liv-
ing in Kiev. When the Germans invaded the Ukraine, the Beliankins fled to

---

[2] Grigory Pavlovich Beliankin (January 19, 1873–1949?).

[3] A letter from Irina Terapiano to Catherine Stravinsky, dated July 29 but without the
year, describes "a chance encounter on stage with Grigory Pavlovich Beliankin, who
was making the rounds as an extra and whom I had not seen since leaving Russia."

Poltava, and eventually (1915) to Odessa. Grigory was stationed in Moscow for a time in 1915 but rejoined his family after the collapse of the Russian military forces. After the Armistice, the Beliankins crossed Germany to Switzerland, reaching the border at Lindau (Hotel Bayrischer-Hof) on November 20, 1918. On the 28th, Grigory went to Berlin for a week to ask the Ukrainian diplomat D. I. Dorotenko for help in obtaining Swiss entry permits for him and his family. Meanwhile, to the same purpose, Stravinsky approached everyone of influence that he knew, and posted a cash bond in Bern. A letter from Alexander van der Briggen in Bern (December 3) informed Stravinsky that certain "independents" in the Ukrainian Mission there were "very much against having Beliankin here," and that "in Berlin both the secretary and the ambassador came out against him." The letter reveals that Beliankin had hoped to find a position in the Bern Mission and that the Ministry of Foreign Affairs rebuffed him on the grounds that it was "already overpopulated." Nevertheless, the Beliankins were admitted to Switzerland, and they reached the Stravinsky home in Morges on Christmas Day. A year and a half later, in June 1920, they accompanied the composer and family to Carantec (Brittany), and thereafter continued to live in France, with or near the Stravinskys, as well as, largely, at the composer's charge.[4]

In 1924, with money borrowed from Stravinsky and a few others, Beliankin opened the "Restaurant Château Basque" in Biarritz. After many difficulties, the establishment flourished, but only for a short time; in 1930, the first summer of the Depression, with the state of the economy drastically reducing his American clientele, Beliankin declared bankruptcy. The Biarritz season is short, moreover, and Beliankin had been extravagant, with an overhead that included seven cooks and two orchestras. From the first, and repeatedly thereafter, Stravinsky was obliged to come to the rescue, which he did for his wife's sake, because of his fondness for Ganya (who was afflicted with petit mal), but primarily, perhaps, because Ira Beliankin[5] *had become a close friend of Vera Sudeikina.*

Before the death of Ira's mother, in February 1937, an event that resulted in Ira's conversion to the Church, Catherine Stravinsky's letters to her husband do not express much sympathy for her ("Ira puts on airs and changes her family name to Belline"), unlike his letters about his niece.[6] *But thanks to*

---

[4] Stravinsky also helped other in-law victims of the Russian Revolution, especially his wife's Yelachich cousins. A letter from the Comptoir d'Escompte in Lausanne, August 22, 1920, reveals that 500 Swiss francs were wired to "Madame Yelachich at the Military Hospital in Belgrade, February 27, 1920," a transaction carried out by Beliankin. In September 1929, Sergei Yelachich wrote to Stravinsky from Harbin, China, asking for assistance, and the composer promptly sent $150.

[5] Born March 17, 1903, in Ustilug, died in Marrakesh in August 1971. Cecil Beaton wrote her obituary for the London *Times*.

[6] Stravinsky wrote to Mikhail Nikolayevich Semenov, August 23, 1937: "[Vera Arturovna and I] will write to you about everything from Venice. For now, I just want to

*Ira's cold beauty—her face became famous from advertisements as the "Eliza-
beth Arden woman"—and her enterprise, she managed to support her father
and brother after her mother's death. When Beliankin died—in France, after
World War II—Ira migrated to Tangiers, where she opened a successful, fash-
ionable boutique. Barbara Hutton became her patron and friend, and Ira's later
years were spent in homes in Tangiers and Marrakesh that had been given to
her by the American heiress.*

*The first part of the correspondence that follows concerns Stravinsky's in-
volvement with the Château Basque. The second part is devoted to Beliankin's
role in seeking to expropriate money from Poland for the sale of Stravinsky's
home in Ustilug and from the composer's mortgages and Nossenko family
assets, and to Catherine Stravinsky's loans—and therefore Igor's as well—to
her Nossenko relatives and the payment of interest thereon. If it could be fully
explained, this second part would constitute an interesting chapter in international law. When the Treaty of Versailles fixed the border between Poland and
the USSR at the Curzon Line, approximately 100 miles to the east of the border
established by the partition of Poland, Stravinsky's Ustilug home was in Polish
territory—until 1939, when Russia reannexed the land. Stravinsky wished to
sell Ustilug and his other formerly Ukrainian properties, and he entrusted the
task to his pre–World War I lawyer, Alexander Abramovich Gliklikh—and to
Beliankin. New laws had been enacted, however, and the Polish-Soviet Treaty
of Riga limited the rights of former Russian landowners. Beliankin worked for
eleven years, 1924–35, to realize these objectives, ultimately with some success,
since after returning from Poland, January 19, 1935, he was able to repay
$5,000 on his debt to Stravinsky—who was himself fortunate in receiving $3,000
for Ustilug, as well as collecting some percentage of his old mortgages.*

*But the first part of the story is that of the Château Basque. Here Stra-
vinsky seems to have been remarkably generous and to have controlled his
anger at Beliankin—until the bankruptcy, when the composer refers to him as
a "naive wretch."*

L. G. AND G. P. BELIANKIN TO STRAVINSKY

Biarritz
January 1, 1924

We, the undersigned, Lyudmila Gavrilovna and Grigory Pavlovich Beliankin,
certify that we owe Ekaterina Gavrilovna and Igor Fyodorovich Stravinsky

---

ask you to shelter my niece, Irina Beliankina, who will be with us on this trip through
Italy, but who will go directly to Positano. She is very dear to me, this girl. . . . She
works hard (she has a *maison de couture* in Paris) and only allows herself two weeks
of vacation. Write to her directly if there is anything you can do for her. She is in Paris:
Maison Ira Belline (as she is called), 19, rue Clément Marot, Paris 8. Please excuse my
'indiscretion,' but I regard you more as family than simply as a kind and like-minded
acquaintance, even though for some reason you judge me to be a 'leftist.' Those who
know me well also know that I go my own way in this world."

forty-three thousand (43,000) francs, received from them on various occasions. We are obligated to repay at the first possible opportunity.

G. P. BELIANKIN TO STRAVINSKY   *Biarritz*
                                                 June 5, [1925?]

Dear Gima,

It . . . shames me to have to ask you once again to come to our rescue. I allow myself to do so only because I know that you have an interest in our welfare, since our ability to pay our debts to you hinges on this. The detestable weather we had this spring ruined us once and for all. Today I will pay the rent on the apartment, which will leave only about 1,000 francs in the account, while a number of other payments are due on the 20th of this month. We begin work on July 15. The season promises to be a very good one, with an awful lot of Americans: all of the hotel rooms are already booked and the villas rented. But the question is whether we will survive until then. Don't think that I have not tried to raise the money elsewhere. I received a cable from my mediator to the effect that Couesnon will be sending $1,000 at the end of the month, but, if I know *him,* it will not arrive until the middle of July, and I need it now. . . .

Our business has been evaluated at 700,000 francs, and we have not decided whether to sell it outright or in shares, with a view to opening up a shipping business in the south or in Paris. These projects take time, though, and if word leaks out beforehand, our stock will not be worth a cent.

I am writing to you as frankly as I can about our business. We need 10,000 francs to keep it from folding. I can guarantee you a return of this money in full at the end of July. If Couesnon sends me the money at the end of June, as he is supposed to do, then I will return your money in the first week of July. I enclose a formal I.O.U. in case you decide to accept. If for some reason you cannot send the money, just return the I.O.U. to me. Telegraph immediately one way or the other.

Forgive me for turning to you like this, but I have no other recourse. . . .

BELIANKIN TO STRAVINSKY   *June 15, 1925*

I, the undersigned, Grigory Beliankin, owner of the Restaurant Château Basque in Biarritz, declare to have received from M. Igor Stravinsky, resident at the Maison Pleyel, 22, rue Rochechouart, Paris, the sum of ten thousand (10,000) francs in the form of a loan which I promise to repay to him on the day he requests it and with 10 percent interest annually.

BELIANKIN TO STRAVINSKY   *June 18, 1925*
                                                        [Telegram]

22, rue Rochechouart
Paris

Infinite thanks. We embrace you and send our warmest wishes for your birthday.   Beliankin

BELIANKIN TO STRAVINSKY   *February 1, 1926*

Dear Gima,

Once again we are experiencing critical times. As early as last fall we had decided to sell the business, but because we were ignorant of the customs and
procedures here, we put the task into Dupuy's hands. Unfortunately, he turned
out to be inept, and in the end we had thrown away a few thousand francs on
him. When I abandoned all hope of settling the matter through him, I consulted a large firm, which deals with the artistic world;[7] after that I tried another agency as well. We have established a price of 700,000 francs, but I suspect that it is too high, since no one has taken our bait. Now a new project is
under way, to organize a small corporation with a capital of 600,000 francs,
20–50,000 of which we own from the business, and the remainder of which we
hope to obtain from shareholders. We will not participate in the enterprise, except that I will be a member of the administrative council, for which I am supposed to receive a percentage of the stock . . . at 8 percent per share, like all
shareholders. We are not counting on that percentage, nor on the dividends; we
hope simply to sell the business for 550,000 francs.

An excellent attorney . . . has been hired . . . to handle the matter, a specialist in these matters. But it takes more than one day to do all of this. Circumstances seem very favorable for the realization of our plans—the [Shomberka]
. . . will not be opening up this year, so we will be the only one; even Sasha's
Pavillon Royal is failing; they had a deficit last year of 400,000 francs.

Our concern for now is to make ends meet. At the close of the month we
will have to pay the rent on the apartment, and if we fail to do so, they want to
sell Belsa [?]. Fortunately, they cannot do that under our contract, but we have
only 3,000 left in the bank, and small expenses are accumulating. . . .

I have sent Jenson four telegrams, asking him to send the money in advance for delivery April 20, but to no avail; he promises and promises, but the
money does not arrive. I cannot force him or threaten him, since he is not
obliged to make the payment until April 20. . . . Having lost hope of obtaining
the money from him in advance, I turn to you, however much I regret it. Perhaps you could arrange a short-term loan for us from Pleyel, as you did last
year. . . .

---

[7] Why Beliankin should have consulted an artists' agency for the sale of his restaurant
remains unexplained, unless he was trading on his relationship with Stravinsky.

Now a question about reimbursement: according to our agreement, Jenson is supposed to make the payment in Biarritz by April 20, but I suspect that he will only make it *on* April 20. Consequently, and in order to avoid miscalculations, I do not count on having it until about May 10. I therefore request a 12,000-franc loan for a three-month period, from February 10 to May 10. I will gladly pay a percentage, but because time presses, I am sending you a receipt forthwith.

Please forgive me for troubling you again with such a request. I approach you only after having exhausted all other possibilities. Oh! When will we see that blessed moment of freedom from such situations—[Milochka's] nerves are frayed, and even mine are beginning to act up. If we can just remain patient and healthy until things are successfully concluded, which I hope will be at the end of the current year, thanks to . . . Ustilug, then we will bid adieu to the Château Basque. . . .

P.S. Please be sure to send me a brief reply right away as to whether or not I can count on this money from you.

STRAVINSKY TO BELIANKIN

167, blvd. Carnot
Nice
February 4, 1926
[Telegram]

Biarritz

Have cabled Pleyel and received affirmative reply. Wait a few more days. Letter follows. Affectionately, Igor

BELIANKIN TO STRAVINSKY   *February 10, 1926*

I, the undersigned, Grigory Beliankin, owner of the Restaurant Château Basque in Biarritz, declare to have received from Igor Stravinsky, resident of 167, boulevard Carnot in Nice, the sum of twelve thousand (12,000) francs with _____ percent annual interest. I promise to reimburse Mr. Stravinsky—or whomever he may indicate—for this sum with interest on May 10 next.

BELIANKIN TO STRAVINSKY   *February 16, 1926*

On February 16, 1926, during a meeting in Biarritz, it was established that the sum of the debt owed by G. P. and L. G. Beliankin to I. F. and E. G. Stravinsky was as follows:

For January 1, 1926, the debt and the interest was to be 42,056 [French] francs and 95 centimes, which, it had been agreed, would be converted to Swiss francs before being returned, and at the exchange rate of January 1, 1924.

Also, it was agreed that 2,000 additional francs would be paid, and that these too would be converted to Swiss francs, at the January 1, 1925, rate of exchange.

The present account supersedes all other accounts that the Beliankins may have drawn up earlier, except for the sum of 12,000 French francs given on February 10, 1926, which were to be converted into English pounds before repayment.

G. Beliankin
L. Beliankin

There are two existing copies of the present statement. February 16, 1926

BELIANKIN TO STRAVINSKY   *May 4, [1926]*

Dear Gima,

I received a telegram from Couesnon today saying that he has the money ready but that it will be difficult to send. I proposed that he come to Biarritz, if I am able to obtain a visa for him. I have already procured the visa, and he has wired that arrangements are being made for his passport.

I write to you about this because I fear that he may not arrive by the 10th, in which case my payment [to you] will not be effected on time, but will be a few days late. Please let [Robert] Lyon [of Pleyel] know of this delay so that he will not think ill of me for my tardiness or bear me a grudge.

We believe that the Easter season has been a success. Diaghilev was here a few times, and he even came by on the day of his arrival. He did not spend very much (he drank beer and some coffee), but it was great publicity for the restaurant.

The sale of the business has not progressed much, so I plan to go to Paris myself and see what I can do. I shake your hand affectionately and send hugs and kisses to all.

P.S. Taxes gave me a rude surprise and devoured all of my Easter profits; this is why we await Couesnon's arrival with such anxiety.

BELIANKIN TO CATHERINE STRAVINSKY   *May 21, [1926?]*

Dear Katichka,

In the pre-concert hustle and bustle, Gima must have glanced over my letter without giving it sufficient attention. We have postponed everything that we could. I may have been wrong in failing to enclose the promissory note in the letter, as I have done previously. I am making it out for three months but am hoping to pay back part of it before then. It is very unlikely that Milochka will go to Paris; she still finds it exhausting just to go outside. I am sorry that I had to trouble you and Gima with such a request, but I was really in a tight spot. You were surprised that the sale fell through. Alas, a fellow whom Milochka and I had come to consider a friend played a dirty trick on us. . . . I am sending you the promissory note for Gima in the hope that, as before, this will make it easier for him. I embrace and kiss you and all your loved ones affectionately.

[*On the reverse, from Lyudmila*]

Kisinka,

I was about to send off a letter to you when yours came. How terribly unfortunate that Grisha's request came at such an awkward moment for Gima. The problem is that July 1 is approaching very rapidly, and we begin work then; June is as quiet as May. July is always the most difficult time.

Perhaps Gima will be free after the concert and will be able to meet with Robert Lyon and arrange this loan for us, as he did before.

Forgive, forgive, dear ones, that we continue to turn to you. I think that things will finally change in the fall. I embrace you warmly.

Milochka

BELIANKIN TO STRAVINSKY   *May 25, 1926*

Dear Gima,

I enclose a check for 6,659 francs on the 12,000-franc loan of February 10, 1926, the total of which is equivalent to 90.10.2, and half of that is 45.5.1. The exchange rate today is 146 francs for one pound sterling, leaving 6,594.50 outstanding, to which we will add 3 percent. For simplicity, I have calculated that figure for four full months, rather than three months and eighteen days. An accountant from Lloyds Bank made these calculations. . . . One way or another I will repay the debt. . . .

P.S. The money arrived in Biarritz on Wednesday,[8] so I made the bank transfer on [Thursday].

BELIANKIN TO STRAVINSKY   *November 29, [1926]*

Dear Gima,

Upon receipt of your telegram I mobilized all of my [capital] to effect the transfer.

I hope that Pleyel will not be angry about the inevitable delay. Business is going well, but I have hardly any strength left. I get very tired and have a lot of nervous afflictions. Once again, thank you very, very much for your help. I kiss you affectionately.

P.S. Don't neglect to send me a receipt.

---

[8] This money would seem to be from Couesnon.

L. BELIANKINA TO STRAVINSKY   *June 3, 1929*

Dear Gima,

Once again, I thank you ever so much for coming to our rescue by lending us the money to survive during this difficult time before the season begins.

I had already begun to worry that Grisha would be late, while my own resources were dwindling, and the deadlines for bills were drawing closer; suddenly your 15,000 arrived, at an opportune time. Thank you very much.

I embrace you, my dear. Warm regards to V[era] A[rturovna].

BELIANKIN TO STRAVINSKY   *June 22, [1929?]*

Dear Gima,

I thank you from the bottom of my heart for your aid in this difficult moment. In July I will pay back the 5,000 francs that Katya has lent us. Milenka has all of her clerical work in order and will determine the precise equivalent in Swiss currency, interest included.

Things are still busy here with us, thanks to the exhibition. I suspect that we will begin work on July 15. We are still recruiting personnel. Of the seven cooks that we need, so far we have only one. . . . Is this not a noble profession? I eagerly await the Americans [tourists]; indeed, all of Biarritz is counting on them. . . .

BELIANKIN TO STRAVINSKY   *Biarritz*
                                           May 12, [1930]

c/o Madame V. Sudeikina
22, rue du Ranelagh

Dear Gima,

Ira told me on the telephone to write you an official letter requesting your assistance, as though I were writing to a bank.

This I have done. Milochka has put together an accounting (which I enclose) based on the documents in her possession. If you find something incorrect or confusing, write to us.

I kiss you affectionately, not at all officially.

P.S. Regards to the Ira-Bosset firm.

[*Enclosure*]

Dear sir,

Having payments to make on the 15th of the current month, I beg of you please to discount my debt of 15,000 francs, payable in Biarritz upon presentation, until October 1, 1930.

At the same time I beg you to allow me to delay payment on the sum of 2,000 francs that I owe you from the month of April, as well as on the interest for all of the amounts lent. The blank bill with my signature is in your hands.

Please be assured, dear sir, of my best wishes.

[*Enclosure*]

Regarding the receipt we gave you on February 16, 1926, during your last stay in Biarritz, the sum of our debt to you, including the percentage accumulated since January 1, 1925, was 42,056 French francs and 95 centimes. According to the same receipt, this sum, converted into Swiss currency, based on the January 1, 1924, rate, as well as 2,000 French francs, which would also be converted to Swiss currency, based on the January 1, 1925, rate, we have determined, based on all this, our debt as of January 1, 1930, to be as follows:

For January 1, 1926

	42056 fr., .95		2060 fr.
% % for 1926	1261–70	+	61–80

For January 1, 1927

	43318–65		2121–80
% % for 1927	1299–45	+	63–65

For January 1, 1928

	44618–20		2185–45
% % for 1928	1338–54	+	65–56

For January 1, 1929

	45956–74		2251–01
% % for 1929	1378–70	+	67–53

For January 1, 1930

47335 fr., .44	+	2318 fr., .54
Based on January 1, 1925, rate		Based on January 1, 1924, rate

G. G. PAÏCHADZE TO STRAVINSKY   *June 3, 1930*

Cher maître,

According to the statement we received from you, I confirm a bill of 15,000 francs, owed to you by G. Beliankin, payable on September 1, 1930, in Biarritz.

We will present this bill to M. Beliankin through our bank on the day it comes due and will transmit the sum to you, minus the fees for postage and handling.

Be assured, *cher maître,* of my best wishes.

PAÏCHADZE TO STRAVINSKY

Dear Igor Fyodorovich, . . . I have not seen Beliankin, and I do not understand the phrase in your letter stating that I can give him the promissory note myself when I see him. I am supposed to present him with the promissory note for payment through the bank by September 1, but I can only give it to him personally if he is prepared to pay me the sum in full. Apparently you have come to some agreement with him.

STRAVINSKY TO
THE ÉDITION RUSSE DE MUSIQUE

Paris

Explain the use of the incorrect term "promissory note" in this Beliankin business. It was simply a request that the letter be given to him personally, as it should have been, [instead of being] sent by Païchadze to Beliankin in Biarritz. . . . Have you sent it, and, if so, may I have a copy?

PAÏCHADZE TO BELIANKIN

Biarritz

Dear Grigory Pavlovich,

I have the honor of informing you by this letter that, in accordance with I. F. Stravinsky's instructions, our publishing house will present you with a promissory note, which you have already accepted, in the amount of 15,000 francs, on September 1, 1930, in Biarritz.

Please keep in mind that we will turn this promissory note over to our bank for collection, and that it will then be presented to you for payment on the above-mentioned date.

I. F. Stravinsky has asked that I explain to you that the amount of this promissory note consists of the following sums:

12,000 fr. sent to you by cable on May 31 of this year.
2,000 fr. that you owe for the April transaction.
500 fr. in unpaid percentages on last year's promissory note.
500 fr. in percentages and expenses for the litigation in May (transfers, cash conversion, expenses, stamps for the promissory note, etc. . . .).

Please be assured of our sincere respect.

Païchadze

PAÏCHADZE TO STRAVINSKY   *September 2, 1930*

Dear Igor Fyodorovich,

I hope that our bank had enough time to recall Beliankin's promissory note
from Biarritz. . . . If not, the fault will be Beliankin's own, since he was late in
sending me the letter about the postponement. I gave our bank instructions as
soon as I received your cable. . . .

BELIANKIN TO STRAVINSKY   *September 11, [1930]*

Dear Gima,

That the promissory note was not purchased on time is *in no way* my fault!! You
told me very clearly that you would handle it *in a French bank,* arranging to
have it sent from Paris to Biarritz, registered in Biarritz, and then paid. Such arrangements have existed and, indeed, continue to exist: I pay 200,000 francs
yearly by this procedure. That the promissory note was contested is also no fault
of mine, and this is as unpleasant for me as it is for you, because it will have a
detrimental effect on my credit.

I was not worried when it was not presented to me promptly on September 1, since the bank accountant, or the bank itself, is frequently late. . . . I will
telegraph your money to you immediately, return receipt requested.

So you see, you are angry with me and reproach me in vain. I kiss you,
Katya, and the children.

PAÏCHADZE TO STRAVINSKY   *September 23, 1930*

Dear Igor Fyodorovich,

I want to warn you that I have great doubts as to whether Beliankin will pay his
debts. In accordance with his request and your telegram, I asked for the return
of the promissory note, simultaneously informing him that I had recalled the
note and that it would not be presented. Consequently, I requested that he
send me a new statement showing his accounts so that I could calculate the
percentage on the note for the additional month and ten days (which he suggested), and also figure in the expenditures for the return and for the stamps,
in order to present him with a new promissory note for a new amount due on a
new date.

I received no reply to this letter and therefore conclude that he is probably
not disposed to pay and is assuming that the promissory note has been voided
since it was not presented on time. I find no other explanation for his silence.
He might have thanked me, at least officially, for postponing the date.

If he is assuming that the promissory note was nullified, he is in for a surprise. I extended the old note and submitted it to the bank today for exaction,
along with instructions to protest his failure to pay, as is the common practice. I

repeat, however, that I doubt very much that he will pay the promissory note.

I wanted to explain this to him and to warn him that I will be absent from Paris—for him, at least—during the entire month of October. In case he attempts to seek a new postponement, I will not be available.

PAÏCHADZE TO STRAVINSKY   *October 28, 1930*

Vera Arturovna has told me that you are worried about what I have done with regard to Beliankin, since you would not want me to take any action that could have a negative effect on his situation. As I told you, I protested his promissory note. That cannot possibly have caused Beliankin any harm, for other creditors have surely registered their protests as well. Until we turn our protested expenditure over to court authorities for exaction, Beliankin will be left alone.

I think that you had to protest, even though the protest cost you 16 francs, 10 centimes; otherwise the promissory note would have become void. Then, in the event that one of the creditors were to declare him bankrupt and demand a court's legal liquidation, your claim would not have been entered as one of Beliankin's outstanding debts. As it is now, you will be able to present it on the same basis and with the same proper claim as the other creditors. Yesterday I received a long circular letter from Beliankin: it is thoroughly incoherent, and if he ran his business as incoherently, I am not at all surprised that he went broke.

No specific mention is made in the letter about a creditor's proposal, nor is there any clearly stated request, so I fail to understand what agreement he is attempting to exact from his creditors. I believe he wants us to reply that we will agree to a postponement and only a partial settlement of their claims, while we will retain freedom of action if one of the creditors goes to court.

Read Beliankin's letter anyway, and let me know what you think (but return it to me). I am very sorry to bother you, but there is a certain business aspect to this, aside from the family considerations, which only you can judge. My regards to Vera Arturovna.

STRAVINSKY TO PAÏCHADZE   *Wiesbaden*
                                                            October 31, 1930

Dear friend,

I hereby return the circular letter from the naive wretch [Beliankin]. It is a pity, and I am disappointed and sorry for him. I positively do not know how to act in such instances, and I therefore leave it to you to attend to this. . . .

L. BELIANKINA TO STRAVINSKY

Dear Gima,

Your letter and money touched us deeply and, frankly, also embarrassed us. We are already so eternally grateful to you, and now, once again, you have increased our indebtedness to you; so great is it at this point that we are almost unable to carry its moral weight. It is dreadful to think that the years are slipping by, leaving us less and less time in which to pay our debt to you, both financially and morally. I suppose this is why the situation becomes increasingly difficult to accept. It was easier before, when it seemed that if you extended a helping hand to us today, tomorrow it would be our turn to help you. But fate has dictated that the burden of help is to fall on one side only. I am still hoping that God will grant us the comfort of being of some assistance to you in your old age. For now I embrace you, my dear, ever so gratefully, and wish you and your loved ones the greatest blessings and happiness for the New Year. Grisha and Ganya thank you and embrace you as well.

BELIANKIN TO STRAVINSKY

Dear Gima,

Ira recounted the substance of your conversation with her and also told me of your reproaches. . . . In fact, I wrote you a five-page letter in reply but thought the better of sending it. I will say only that you are right on many points, and I understand your . . . annoyance at having to devote time to business correspondence and money matters, especially when this detracts from the time you have for your principal occupation, composition. And now we are bothering you with yet another request. All of this is true, but you are mistaken in a few details, which I will explain when we meet again. I hope to be able to correct any errors that may exist in our accounts. In all fairness, though, I must say that you cannot imagine how frequently we find ourselves in a desperate situation: life is very difficult for us right now.

Let me thank you once again from the bottom of my heart for agreeing to bail us out. I hope that my official letter arrived in time. I also hope that you will have time to consider the promissory note that Ira gave you and to act on it soon after May 25 so that we might have the money by June 1, since on that date we must pay rent, debts, personnel, and promissory notes.

I embrace you affectionately.

In April 1935, Stravinsky received 20,000 French francs on the Beliankins' debt.

The second part of this chapter exposes the feudal social background against which the modern-spirited artist was composing his masterpieces. The viewpoint of both Stravinskys, and of Catherine's relatives, is amazingly reac-

tionary: they can see only the injustice to the former Russian landowning class. The correspondence does not include any of the extensive exchanges between Stravinsky and his banks in Russia from 1912 until the Revolution. It also omits any example of the numerous letters in which Stravinsky asks for advances from publishers, impresarios, patrons, and performance organizations—documents that contrast strikingly with the letters from people asking him to pay overdue bills, as when one of his concert agents, Zborovsky, writes to say that another agent, Madame Bouchonnet, "told me that you are intending this month to pay the remainder of the sum due to me for your tour in South America [a year ago]." Finally, this chapter does not examine any of Stravinsky's dozen or so ill-advised lawsuits, since this would require too much space. But the reader should note that in the week of rehearsals before the first performance of Le Sacre, *Stravinsky spent time with lawyers discussing proposals for payment of a suit that he had won on May 2, 1913.[9] The reader should also bear in mind that during the time of the letters that follow dating from the 1920s and 1930s, Stravinsky was involved in litigation against the impresario Firmin Gémier, a case that dragged on for years and that produced extensive documentation but little else.[10]*

BELIANKIN TO STRAVINSKY   *November [?], 1912*

Dear Gimura,

Everything is almost set about Moisei's mill. They agree to give you 4,000 rubles cash, which is to say that you will have 4,000 after deducting insurance and taxes. They ask that one rolling machine, which costs about 1,800 rubles, be installed in the peasant mill. That is fair enough, since the machine would remain yours. Also, the extra money for it will be partly made up by the taxes you will receive from them and partly by the installment payments. In short, there is no particular point in arguing over the percentage.

I am sending you a power of attorney to study. If you decide to send it to me, do so in your name through the consul, and include a bank check, not specifying the date of payment; then I will close the transaction. Right now I am not

---

[9] In 1912, Stravinsky had lent 10,000 francs to a M. and Madame Miquel Alzieu, and a M. Alzieu (father of the aforementioned). When the loan was not returned, Stravinsky retained the Paris lawyer Maurice Fanet, who won the case. The tribunal did not fix a date for the reimbursement, however, and the Alzieus approached an intermediary, the lawyer Charles Bonnet, to arrange to delay payment. On August 1, 1913, the Alzieus agreed to pay "not before October." Stravinsky was obliged to pay Fanet 350 francs and to give him two tickets for the first performance of the *Sacre* (note from Fanet, May 28, 1913: *"demain, Jeudi, pour Mme Fanet et moi"*). Between May 22 and 29, Stravinsky met with Charles Bonnet to consider plans of action in the event that the adversaries would appeal.

[10] See Appendix H.

insistent, because they might agree to my terms, [but], not having power of attorney from you, I could fall between two stools. In any case, do not refuse me the power of attorney (Milochka's), because I need it very much.

To sum up:

The mill will cost 25,000 rubles.

You pay 15,000, 10,000 with % a year later. The profit margin for the first year that you may figure is 15,000 rubles.

You receive a deposit (how much has not been decided, probably 1,000 rubles, as we did with Trosyl [?]), which you reinvest into the mill for the rolling machine, which means you are 800 rubles short. Also, since you are making this installment payment, you lower the %, but do not forget that you are increasing the value of the mill.

Expenses for the deed of title are one-half.

The mill is already insured; hence you make money on that and do not have to pay so long as you do not change the term of insurance. The insurance can probably be lowered from the 800 rubles, probably to 700 rubles, so there is 100 rubles in your favor. The whole thing seems to make good sense.

The mill in Vladimir Volynsk is hardly worth it.

When you agree and send the power of attorney, I will go to inspect Moisei's mill personally and complete the agreement.

Bakst was sent out of Petersburg at midnight as a Jew.[11] Here the Russian ballet company, "Shéhérazade," from Moscow, actually appears to be American. Ganya seems better; there has not been an attack for two whole days. I expect to go to Ustilug today.

BELIANKIN TO C. STRAVINSKY

Ustilug
Wednesday, November [20?], 1912

1. I am terribly worried that something might happen to your money in the Rovlenskoe Mutual Credit Bank and that, instead of recouping your investment, you will end up with a pocket full of buttered figs. Owing to the fear of war, we have entered a crisis here such as you cannot imagine. People are declaring bankruptcy and going broke, and the banks are suffering in consequence. The Credit Bank has had a loss of 50,000 rubles, i.e., practically its entire capital. I wanted to send you a telegram but decided against it, thinking that it would only alarm and confuse you. My sincere advice to you is to withdraw from the Credit Bank. I suggest that you send a check in my name (we

---

[11] See Bakst's letter to Stravinsky of November 17, 1912, for the painter's own account of this episode.

probably will not receive the money right away); I will fill in the date and amount and deposit the money in the Azov-Don Commercial Bank, Rovno Branch, and in the Russian-Merchant Industrial Bank, Kovel Branch. You will probably receive only half, but at least it will be real money.

2. Yesterday I finished the business with the vodka distillery.[12] These are the final terms: the rent is 4,800 rubles a year (800 for insurance and other such expenses), one-third of which must be paid in advance. (If you wish, I could negotiate for one-half when the agreement is signed.) They will give a down payment of 3,000 rubles (the down payment plus the % they receive from the banks, i.e., the money that the bank will pay on 3,000 rubles during the fall). Repairs are their responsibility. The mill is already insured until May, so you save 300 rubles there. (On the signing of the deed they will want 15,000 rubles, then 10,000 in installments.)

I sent you the power of attorney, but you sent it back. Can you really not have thought to make a copy of it, just in case? . . . You forgot to take into consideration that the appearance of a 1,000-ruble promissory note [would cause a stir?] . Luckily for you, the owners have told me in no uncertain terms that they will not accept your promissory note, because they do not know you. I will issue one myself, however, if it is owed to them. The deed will state that you have paid all money in full . . . (half of the expenses by the time the deed is signed). The agreement on the lease of the house will [have to be done at the same time] , because to do it later will not be possible. . . . I wrote about that when I sent you the power of attorney.

Although I gather from your letter that Gima is very busy, I am certain that he finds time to write to Diaghilev on business, and despite the very painful toothache.[13] I am no less busy than [Gima], yet I have managed to take care of more than a little of his business. The moral is, if you plan to do something, do it. I want to point out that I will be home on November 25, leaving again for Milochka's probably at the beginning of December. The letter containing your check must arrive in Ustilug by December 1. Once again, I advise you to withdraw from the Rovlenskoe Mutual Credit Bank. . . . Do not delay in sending me a check in my name. . . . To expedite things, I will send this letter to Berlin,[14] to the [Edition Russe de Musique] , and if Gima is not in Berlin, they will forward it to you. The power of attorney is *not* necessary.

---

[12] In a lively and valuable article in *La Revue Musicale Suisse,* Zürich, May 1942, Paul Budry, a friend of Stravinsky during World War I, recalls that he "possessed vast lands in Poland, on which he had a distillery producing enough vodka to intoxicate an entire province. One day he announced to us, nonchalantly, that the Bolsheviks—whom he loathed—had redistributed these lands and emptied the vodka reserves, flooding the village and drowning several children."

[13] Stravinsky finished the composition of *Le Sacre du printemps* on November 17, 1912, "with a terrible toothache."

[14] Stravinsky was in Berlin for the Ballets Russes performances of *Petrushka* and *Firebird.*

Well, I kiss you affectionately, also Baba Sonia, the children, and your very busy husband.

[*On the envelope*] Vartov [?] is on his way to Clarens.

S. V. MASTREVICH TO STRAVINSKY   *Rovno*
                                                       November 22, 1912
Dear Igor Nikolayevich [*sic*],

Yesterday I received a check from you for 13,900 rubles. I will deposit this money in a current account in the Azov-Don Bank, at the same time putting part of it in the Credit Bank; otherwise all the interest that is due you will be lost, for they begin charging extra on December 31. On January 2, I will let you know how much extra they have charged you, and then you can send me a check for the remaining sum, which I will transfer to the Azov Bank. I could not obtain the money today, because you gave November 23 as the date. I hasten to answer you, (1) because I want to reassure you, and (2) because I was already planning to write to you when I received your most timely letter.

   They (Zhukovski) intend to give you, as security, a property—located on the line (near the cemetery, 10.3.zh.d. [?]), and in a very good place—under a second mortgage, for 20,000 at 9 percent, or under the first for 45,000. This property was just sold for 72,000 or 75,000, but it is certainly worth no less than 80,000 rubles. The purchaser will arrange the deed at the same time as the mortgage. If you find this proposition suitable, write to me immediately, because the date for closing the deed and mortgage has been set for December 4.

   If you give 20,000 for a second mortgage, then a debt of only 25,000 to the Land Bank will remain from the first mortgage. If you agree, write to [?], for I think he has your power of attorney; he could then sign the mortgage, and do not worry about it: I will hand it over only when I receive the mortgage, but I must have it by the time of the deed and mortgage closing.

   If you agree, wire me and Grigory Pavlovich; perhaps he will want to examine the property. If you do not agree, write me a letter to that effect, for I must notify the purchaser in time.

   Personally, I consider this to be a sound deal. So tomorrow I will send you verification of the opening of an account in your name in the Azov-Don Bank. In the meantime, I thank you sincerely for your show of trust.

                              Most respectfully yours,   Mastrevich

MASTREVICH TO STRAVINSKY   *Rovno*
                                                       November 23, 1912
Dear Igor Fyodorovich,

First, let me ask your forgiveness for confusing your patronymic. I did not realize I had done so until today.

   The Loan and Credit Society credited 13,896 r. and 85 kp. to your account, having deducted postal or some such expenses. I withdrew 13,800 by check but left the remaining 96 r., 85 kp. in the account to keep them from closing it before January 1, 1913. At that time they will inform me of the interest that has accumulated, and you can then send me a check for that sum and return the check and account book.

If you want to pay the mortgage from the money that you have in the Azov-Don Bank, using the entire 13,800 rubles, then return to me the account book with your signature on the side marked "Paid," leaving a blank space above. If you want to leave part of the money in the account—no less than 100 rubles, according to bank rules—send a notice to the Azov-Don Bank stating the time and place and the following: "Upon receiving this, I request the Rovno Branch of the Azov-Don Bank to pay 13,700 rubles (written out) to S. V. Mastrevich, from my current account (signature)." You must send such a notice in any case.

I shake your hand affectionately and send you my very best wishes. I bought your four études in Kiev, but as yet I have not been able to find a musician who can perform them for me; apparently they are extremely difficult. I myself do not play at all, but I am very fond of music in Scriabin's genre and in yours.

Yours,   Mastrevich

Where is Clarens? I could not find it on my map of Switzerland.

STRAVINSKY TO BELIANKIN   *Leysin*
                                               February 9, 1914

Dear Grigory Pavlovich,

Please examine this statement to the Land Bank of Kiev and, if you think it properly worded, forward it to the bank. You will notice a slight change from the original. I have asked them to let me know if Yarotsky fails to pay the interest on time, something you did not mention in your draft of the "statement." I do not know whether or not the bank will try to collect this money, but it will not do any harm to ask. Please do not bother to send me the bank's letters when you receive them; just read them yourself. I think that I will have to give you power of attorney for the whole [affair]. Tell me what you think it will cost.

Please pay my gardener for the holidays, if you have not already done so.

[*Enclosure*]

To the Land Bank of Kiev
from the landowner Igor Fyodorovich Stravinsky

STATEMENT

Since September 9, 1912, I have been a mortgagee of property belonging to M. V. Yarotsky in Rovno, the Volhynia District. As an interested party, therefore, I humbly request that the directors of the bank notify me—in "Ustilug, Volynskaya District"—each time that an interest-bearing loan is not paid and the property is threatened with sale. I also humbly request to be notified each time that a mortgagee fails to pay his interest on time.

I have given instructions for a copy of the mortgage to be sent directly from Ustilug to Mr. Martinenko at the bank.

Igor Stravinsky
February 1, New Style, 1914
Leysin, Switzerland

S. I. DOBROV TO C. STRAVINSKY   *June 23, 1914*

Dear Madame Ekaterina Gavrilovna,

By this letter I have the honor of confirming that today I have received the power of attorney that you granted me and that was presented on June 20 by the Russian consul in Lausanne. I also received four letters signed "D. Nossenko" . . . that open with "My Dear Chizhik" and "Chizhik my dear. . . ." [I understand that I am empowered to] conduct negotiations with Mr. D. A. Nossenko[15] concerning the settlement of your financial accounts with him, i.e., of your loan to him involving some 80,000 rubles in government securities, or, if peaceful settlement of the matter is not possible, to present Mr. Nossenko with an appropriate suit in your name.

The fee that you intend to pay me for this work will be 1,000 rubles in advance, then 2,500 rubles when the above-mentioned settlement with Mr. Nossenko has been peacefully arranged, or else, in the event of a suit against Mr. Nossenko, when this has been settled. . . . All expenses incurred in the suit, including my traveling expenses, should any be necessary, will be charged to you.

Please accept assurances of my sincere respect.

STRAVINSKY TO DMITRI KHOLODOVSKY[16]   *[1913 or 1914?]*
                                                [Draft]

Dear Mitichka,

I deeply regret that such a misunderstanding has developed; it is not my "youthful enthusiasm" that is to blame, but rather the vagueness of your letter. Not once did you mention anything about 50–60,000 in land; instead you sim-

---

[15] Dmitri Andreyevich Nossenko (1849–1929; Soviet dictionaries wrongly give the date of his death as 1927). His wife was Olga Ivanovna (1849–1942). Their children were Olga ("Lyulya") Dmitrievna Schwarz (1872–1953) and (Dr.) Vera Dmitrievna Nossenko (1882–1969).

[16] Cousin of Stravinsky's mother. Dmitri ("Mita") Kholodovsky died in São Paulo on December 3, 1936, according to a letter from Tatiana Alekhina, who lived with him there, to Catherine Stravinsky—though Catherine says in a letter to Igor that she first heard the news from Georgi Yelachich (who lived in Paris and had approached Stravinsky in December 1925 for help in finding a job with Pleyel). Dmitri Kholodovsky

ply stated that you thought I would receive 50–60,000. Further on you say, "if your capital becomes limited, you will have only yourself to blame," and you advise me to agree to the more advantageous arrangement you propose. According to the latter, you state that I would have freedom of action and security, and this remark is what finally led me to understand your letter. Although I confessed surprise, I told you that it was of a pleasant kind. Well, what else remains to be said about it?! I misunderstood you, and if there is no money, that is that. I will inform my attorney that there has been a mistake, but in general he is fully authorized to negotiate with you; indeed, I engaged him for that purpose, not wanting to become involved in the details myself. Thus I hope that my attorney will meet with you and that the affair will progress one way or the other. A whole year has passed since you and I began our correspondence on this issue, which is difficult and awkward for us both.

Why did [S. I.] Dobrov not come to see you in Omelno? I cannot understand, and I hope that he will go to Gatchina. I also do not understand your tone when you say that you are not prepared to go looking for him. Your expression, "that would be too much," is very general, of course, but I never asked you to go looking for him; rather, I simply asked that you let him know where and when you would be able to see him, which you did. Unfortunately, nothing came of that, and I still do not know why.

I received the money from Lyulya a couple of days ago. Next time, please send it to me via the Government Bank; that way I lose substantially less [in the exchange].

L. BELIANKINA TO STRAVINSKY   *November 2, 1924*

c/o Philharmonic, Warsaw[17]

Gima, dear,

Grisha will not be going to Warsaw on business after all; thus your trip comes at a good time. He asks you to do the following:

---

was survived by his wife, Maria ("Marusia") Nikolayevna. In Rome, November 18, 1951, Stravinsky received a note from Nadyezhda Yelachich saying that she was writing from the railroad station en route to Genoa and São Paulo "to visit my stepdaughter, the eldest daughter of your cousin." She gives her São Paulo address as c/o Pronim, Jomandare 710. When Stravinsky stopped briefly in the Brazilian city in September 1960, he told the present writer that he could no longer remember anything about Dmitri Kholodovsky.

[17] Stravinsky conducted the Warsaw Philharmonic on November 4 and 6, 1924, in a program consisting of *The Song of the Nightingale*, *Firebird* Suite, *Pulcinella* Suite, and *Fireworks*. On his second day in the city, he received a note from Gliklikh: "I am writing to you on Grigory Pavlovich's instructions concerning your mortgage in Rovno, which I think may now be recovered. I gave the mortgage to Grigory Pavlovich, and I believe that he turned it over to you."

1. Arm yourself with letters of recommendation from Paris for the French Embassy [in Warsaw].

2. When you arrive in Warsaw, go see Starczewski, Wilcza 53, through the gates on the left. Remember that Starczewski is not our attorney, but just a "friend." Be nice to him, express our gratitude for the interest he has shown in our affairs, and ask for his advice as to how the matter will be won or lost. He will know several days before the session. If he is confident that we have a chance of winning, do not approach the French Embassy, since interference from there would only anger the Poles. If, on the other hand, [Starczewski] feels that . . . the case may be lost, then do not hesitate to . . . exert as much influence as you can.

Starczewski is home around twelve noon and again about seven in the evening.

3. Go to see Zagurski, our attorney: Leszno 27, apt. 60 (the second courtyard to the left), telephone 122-67.

4. The case will be heard on the 6th, at exactly ten o'clock in the morning, by the Medovai Administrative Tribunal, which, I think, is in building no. 22. You can stop by there and find out the result firsthand. Please telegraph.

5. If the case seems to be going badly, which you ought to be able to find out from Starczewski and Zagurski, then, in your newspaper interviews, complain that your land is being taken away because you do not maintain your home in Poland, yet at the same time you are not allowed to live there. Mention, furthermore, that at the time to which the case refers, the land had not even been cleared, and all of the buildings were still occupied, so that there was no place to keep any cattle.

As for your Rovenski business, Grisha will write an express letter to Gliklikh today saying that you are going to be in Warsaw between November 1 and 7, either at the Bristol or the Hotel Europe (the Hotel Europe is better). Grisha will not ask Gliklikh to go there, because he would charge his traveling expenses to you. Gliklikh's address is: Lawyer Alexander Gliklikh, Łuck (for telegrams), and for registered letters add: Yagielloniska 103. If you want to come to Warsaw, cable him as soon as you arrive, or from Paris. . . . That way it will cost you more, but it would obviously be more convenient, too. . . . If you want to avoid the expense, you can obtain a power of attorney (for litigations) in Warsaw and fill it out for Gliklikh. Since you will give [the power of attorney] without any transfer and for reasons of personal business, it will not have to be witnessed by a notary. Then you can send it from Warsaw to Gliklikh in Łuck. When you see Zagurski, you can consult him about this. . . . Or you could telephone Gliklikh; Grisha does not know his number, but Zagurski should. I think that it would be best to act on Zagurski's advice; since you will be talking with him about our business—which is, at the same time, also your business—his counsel probably will not cost you anything.

Warsaw
June 12, 1925

KURGLUS TO BELIANKIN   [Telegram]

Jokhenson supposed to send a thousand end of month. Shall try to comply first opportunity [?].   Kurglus

A. A. GLIKLIKH TO STRAVINSKY   *November 14, 1925*

On this date, I received from Grigory Pavlovich Beliankin, Igor Fyodorovich Stravinsky's mortgage payment for 25,000 rubles on the Yarotsky property in Rovno.

D. NOSSENKO[18] TO C. STRAVINSKY   *November 22, 1927*

All these years I have been struggling with these accursed Polish authorities, with their nonexistent order, their widespread practice of bribery, and their constant nagging of all landowners, especially Russians! . . . Important political figures in the Polish government, as well as former Russian underground members and socialists, have all made up their minds to enlighten and support the peasants . . . but at the expense of the landowners, not of the government. Are you familiar with these new laws? Even in the case of promissory notes and mortgages, we can collect only 10 percent and 25 percent! . . . Furthermore, the courts have the right to discount as much as they wish for "war damages" (whose, when, and where?!). And, finally, the amount is awarded in zlotys, not rubles, and at a predetermined and compulsorily low exchange rate! . . . All of my efforts and appeals have achieved nothing. . . . Damn them all. I hope with all my heart that within a hundred years vile Poland will split for a fourth and final time. . . .

Instead of receiving 30,000 rubles for the land I sold in 1914 (!), the sum will be a little over 3,000, to be converted into zlotys at some appallingly low rate. . . . I am powerless to do anything about this, since I am some thousand versts away from the land in question and too old for such things; I have entrusted the entire matter to the local notary. I hope that he will quickly bring about the liquidation, for I do not want to saddle my daughters with it. Even most men could not handle this, given the vast number of Polish laws and regulations! Moreover, I need the money to pay my debts and compensate my creditors for their patience! . . .

A few days ago I received a little money for the sale of some small lots of land, but how much more will follow, if anything, I do not know. Although you told me in 1924 that you would not mind if I repaid my debt to you in small installments, I cannot decide whether it is even worth sending you such a tiny sum, which explains this clumsy letter. I can give you 1,000 Swiss francs or

---

[18] See Vera Nossenko's letter to Catherine of April 8, 1929, in this chapter.

5,000 French francs—a trifling sum, but until my notary's efforts to sell the land yield something more substantial, I must resort to paying back my debts in change, which slips through the fingers very quickly. . . . If you would like to have even this sum, write to me. Should I send it directly to you, or deposit it in some current bank account here in your name (keep in mind that they pay only 2 percent interest, or even less), so that later, when things improve,[19] some interest might accumulate?

Lyulya has told me that the children plan to come to Lausanne in December. Olga Ivanovna and I would love to see them. It is a pity that their parents will not accompany them: after all, we do not have much time left in this world, so no visit is superfluous. . . . Well, as God wills it.

Keep well, my dear friend, and conserve your strength. Please give our regards to Igor.

D. NOSSENKO TO C. STRAVINSKY   *November 28, 1927*

. . . You cannot imagine how relieved I am, at long last—and this is no longer just talk and vague promises about an uncertain future—to begin repaying my debt to you, even if only little by little. The first payment has one small hitch: I was thinking in terms of a five-to-one exchange rate for French to Swiss francs, and I gave the bank 1,000 Swiss francs, expecting that to be converted to 5,000 French francs. It seems that today's exchange rate favors the French franc somewhat, so the total was 4,899.55 French francs. Since our dealings are to be in the latter currency, we should stick to round figures. Not wanting to trouble the bank with a trifling transfer of some one hundred French francs, I therefore enclose, along with the check for the indicated amount of French francs, an additional 20 Swiss francs, which together should total approximately 5,000 French francs. Let us all hope that this business of the land sale in accursed Poland will finally be straightened out and our hard-earned money returned to us, if only bit by bit. . . . Yesterday we hosted a meeting of Russians here to honor Her Majesty Maria Fyodorovna on her eightieth birthday; everything went very well. . . . May God watch over and restore the Russian Imperial family.

D. NOSSENKO TO C. STRAVINSKY   *December 8, 1927*

I do not understand your motive in requesting a "document" from me to the effect that "I have begun paying you back"—would it not have been more logical to request such a "document" when I was not yet paying you back? With or without such a document, my children and I have always recognized and will continue to recognize my debt to you. Furthermore, Vera [Nossenko] is

---

[19] I.e., the restoration of the Russian monarchy. See the following letter.

thoroughly familiar with all of my affairs and dealings, thus making it irrelevant that we all stand "before God." The only relevant issue is whether we are able to sell the estate properly, and keep the Poles from devouring all of the proceeds in taxes and robbing all of the unfortunate Russian landowners, for I will only be able to pay you once the land is sold—and then only from those particular earnings, should they be sufficient for me to liquidate my debt. In spite of all that, it will still, and always, be done exactly as you wish!

I enclose a document herewith. All calculations are in Swiss francs, and all of the figures are based on the exchange rate for French francs in December 1924 (when you and I determined the general sum of my debt), which is one-third higher than the current rate. I consider this fair and will gladly accept these terms in repaying the sum, though it is twice as much as it would be if we were to obey these Polish laws, for they award the creditor only 10 percent of the original amount of the debt. The total amount of my debt is exactly 150,000 French francs, at the rate of 27:100,* or 40,500 Swiss francs, minus 19,020 Swiss francs already paid, leaving 29,480 Swiss francs outstanding.

I hope that Fate will arrange things in such a way that I will receive enough from the sale of the estate to pay in full. . . . For the time being, I cannot say what will happen, since I do not know myself. One eventuality frightens me: by selling everything off in small lots, my notary may leave me worse off than before, forcing me either to abandon the land or to settle for compensation of next to nothing, just to avoid having to keep a man on there . . . while waiting for hunters to buy it! . . . To sell land in this damnable Poland is no easy task: almost all Russian landowners are liquidating their land because of taxes and the pervasive Polish thievery. . . . A great deal of land has virtually been given away in the market, greatly diminishing the value of land, so that the buyers now make very low offers, have become overly discriminatory, and demand to pay on a multi-year installment plan. . . .

Keep well, my dear friend. I do not know what kind of weather you are having in Nice, but here it is almost as warm as on the Riviera. We have not yet had a single frost! Regards to all of your family.

* The December 1924 exchange rate.

D. NOSSENKO TO C. STRAVINSKY   *January 9, 1928*

I do not know what my notary is up to, what he has managed to sell, or what kind of future awaits all of our projects, but a few days ago I received a little money from him (without a word of explanation), and so I hasten to share it with you. I will send it by money order in Swiss francs. The bank told me that it is difficult for them—from Lausanne—to pay out Swiss francs in Nice, and suggested a check from Geneva instead, which could be converted into Swiss francs in Nice; I am enclosing a money order from Geneva in the sum of 2,480 Swiss francs (to round off the number). If, for any reason, Nice refuses to pay you in Swiss currency, return the money order, and I will make some other arrangement. I do not want to be dependent on the rate of exchange and run the risk of losing more money.

Keep well, my friend. I wish you and all of your family all the best for the coming Russian New Year.

D. NOSSENKO TO C. STRAVINSKY
May 28, 1928

On May 24, following my instructions, the notary Martinovich sent you, in Nice, TWO THOUSAND dollars from Łuck, via the Rolnyi Bank. The money had to be converted into dollars, since all of our transactions are in dollars now, the only stable currency in Poland. It would not have been wise to convert these dollars into Swiss francs, because francs are not in demand here. When you receive this money, therefore, you yourself will have to change it into the currency of your choice; the dollar is welcome anywhere in the world, and when I transferred the Swiss francs to you, I had just exchanged some dollars that I had received. Based on the current rate of exchange (5.18 Swiss francs to the dollar), the $2,000 amounts to *ten thousand, three hundred and sixty Swiss francs,* which I will ask you to deduct from my debt to you. The remainder of my debt will then total *twenty-six thousand, six hundred and forty Swiss francs.* Please inform me when you receive the above-mentioned $2,000, so that I may be certain that my notary Martinovich has followed my instructions to the letter.

At long last we are enjoying a bit of warm weather. It had been freezing, even with the stove on. . . . In a few days Verushka [Dr. Vera Nossenko] will take a vacation, and we will all (separately, however) go away somewhere for a month and a half. She needs a good rest, more than anyone else, because lately she has had a great number of patients, some of whom are very serious cases, and, thanks to the foul weather as well, she has become tense and emaciated.

P.S. If for any reason you are inconvenienced by receiving these checks in dollars, tell me, and the next time I will revert to the original system (i.e., I will take the dollars myself and try to convert them into Swiss francs).

I have also recently learned that, as a result of my dealings with the peasant-buyers, *instead of the 1,000 [rubles]* I was anticipating, I will receive only 200 *zlotys,* i.e., even less than the 10 percent of their debt. Damn these Poles, their fate, and their government; I hope that it will soon be finished off! What can be done with such laws and such courts?

Clinique Flora
Leysin

VERA NOSSENKO TO C. STRAVINSKY
April 8, 1929

. . . I have been named executor of Betiashchka's will, which has already been validated by the Swiss authorities. But the inheritance process in Poland is complicated by all kinds of nuisances, and since I am the property holder, I must perform all of the necessary duties. One of them is to settle our debt to you. I know that poor Papa gave you a document in December 1927 (is that correct?) in which he declared himself in debt to you for some 40,500 Swiss francs. I absolutely must have that document so that I may present it along with all of the other required legal papers in Poland. I do not know whether or not his signature on this document has been notarized; if it has, I think it will be sufficient simply to give me a *notarized* copy, but it must also be notarized by the French authorities, by the Polish Embassy in France, by the Swiss Canton, then by the Federal authorities, and finally by the Polish Embassy in Bern. . . . Send me Papa's document as quickly as possible; I need to have it on hand, so as to avoid any delays.

Well, my Katiushka, I never thought that I would have to initiate any business correspondence with you! Let me know whether you want me to give you a statement of responsibility for the document. . . .

GLIKLIKH TO BELIANKIN
Łuck
June 4, 1931

Dear Grigory Pavlovich,

I hasten to inform you that the appraisal of the estate has dragged on because I have only just received the 400 zlotys from [illegible], which Feigenbaum finally sent me from Warsaw for the court payment. The Jokhensons have declared bankruptcy and stopped their payments, and [illegible] Shulima and the apartment situation [?]. As you see, things are not going very well.

I sent the 400 zlotys to the court, and the appraisal should be completed at the end of June. Regarding Igor Fyodorovich's mortgage, the district court awarded him about $3,500 from the Yarotsky "property," but not from any particular person. I spent about $300 of my own money in this affair. Now it turns out that an appeal is essential, because the bailiff will not be able to enforce this decision.

Besides, the young judge forgot to award a percentage for 1928. In order for all of this to be done, I will need $150 more, which I myself do not have. Ask Igor Fyodorovich if he would send me the money immediately; I would use my own money, but I simply do not have any more.

If I win the July 1 hearing, I will come to see you. Warm regards to all of your loved ones. Please send me a reply immediately.

GLIKLIKH TO STRAVINSKY
July 11, 1931

Dear Sir, Igor Fyodorovich,

In accordance with Grigory Pavlovich's request, I hereby inform you of the details pertinent to your suit over the mortgage of the Yarotsky properties in Rovno. The situation is as follows: Yarotsky died, and his attorney, who handled his affairs while the former was still living, sold the property to three Jews. Beforehand, he liquidated your mortgage of May 24, 1921, by paying the court's deposit of 97,749 Polish marks, which is equivalent to 652 Polish zlotys, or 72 American dollars. A new law regarding prewar debts was enacted in Poland in 1924, and since I had already been to Rovno and gathered all the necessary documents, I presented the deceased Yarotsky and the three Jews with a suit to restore the mortgage. The Jews objected that, under the terms of the Soviet-Polish Treaty of Riga, you could not take them to court, because you are a Russian nobleman. The Rovensky District Court then awarded you 32,308 zlotys "from the property," but forgot to include interest. Simultaneously, the court restored the mortgage and reimposed an injunction on the property of the Jews, a motion I had already sought. Thus the mortgage has been reinstituted and is registered in the mortgage books. 32,308 zlotys is equal to 3,300 American dollars. Since the court made the award "from the property" and without interest, that decision will have to be appealed in the Chamber Court. I have spent $300 of my own money in traveling, incidental, and business expenses, but now, in light of the monetary crisis, it is difficult for me to continue handling the affair on my own account. I have asked Grigory Pavlovich to send me $150 so that I may continue. I may be able to settle the matter peaceably; we will see what the opposition does. Grigory Pavlovich warned me that he has your former attorney's receipt but does not know where it is. I think that this is a fabrication.

Please accept assurances of my admiration and devotion.

STRAVINSKY TO GLIKLIKH

Luck

Voreppe
Isère
March 7, 1932

Dear Alexander Abramovich,

With regard to the recovery of the money I paid on the mortgage of the Yarotsky estate, I hereby empower you to do everything necessary to bring about a peaceful settlement, if that is what you deem suitable to my interests.

Please accept this assurance of my respect and admiration.

Igor Stravinsky

V NOSSENKO TO C. STRAVINSKY

Clinique Flora
Leysin
March 18, 1932[20]

I have news from Omelno that the property-settlement business has become hopelessly muddled, despite the formal injunction against Vanya Martinovich allowing the peasant-buyers to use the land before the deeds are drawn up. Martinovich permitted all of the peasants to occupy the land, but now, because of the crisis, they will not pay for possession of the land and will not get off of it

---

[20] On December 14, 1931, Vera Nossenko paid 4,900 French francs on her debt to Catherine Stravinsky, through the Banque d'Escompte Suisse, Lausanne.

either. After more than a year's silence, Martinovich writes that there is absolutely no hope of completing the liquidation of the property, and that even what was conditionally contracted will have to go for less than half of what was stipulated in the agreements. I have decided to go to Omelno myself this summer to try to clear up this sad state of affairs and to find out whether anything remains of our proprietorship, and what, if anything, can be done to save us from this liquidator who seems bent on ruining us once and for all. It is said that Martinovich is an honest man, but he has not been very decent with us and, I think, has taken advantage of the desperateness of our situation. . . .

I would like to pay you a portion of my debt straight-away, but I want to know whether or not you would be willing to accept bonds, "obligations" of 4 percent from the Crédit Foncier de France for 1931–32 on their actual value. Please send me an answer to this question. . . . I am exhausted, and if I do go to Poland, it will not be any vacation. I hope that Mama's health will allow her to come here and stay with me, when I return from Poland. At her age, of course, she is at greater risk in the mountains. But if she finds out that she should not come because of her health, she will think that she really is in a bad way and then really *will* run a greater risk of falling ill. So I think that she ought to come to stay with me after all, even though I will be worrying about her.

Keep well, my dear Katiushka. I embrace you warmly, as well as Gimusha, Anna Kir., and the children. . . .

Yours,   Vera

V. NOSSENKO TO C. STRAVINSKY

Les Fleurettes
Leysin
December 23, 1932

Katiushka, dear,

My affairs in Omelno are becoming so difficult that I do not know what will happen anymore, or how I will manage with this task, which has fallen into my lap, with no one there whom I can trust. . . . The notary Martinovich has been very careless with all of our affairs, and this discord is entirely his fault. I am also disappointed in the lawyer Gliklikh; even when I stood before him he would not defend my interests with complete honesty (no doubt because he wished to protect Martinovich). . . . But with no further delay, I want to send you 10,000 Swiss francs. The Banque d'Escompte Suisse proposes that I deposit this money in its bank in your name, since, as they say, the transfer of this amount will cause certain difficulties with the French authorities. Please let me know immediately whether you want me to deposit this sum in your name in a current account in the Banque d'Escompte Suisse (rue de Lion d'Or, Lausanne) or in the *carnet de dépôt*, or simply to turn it over to you. The bank will send you its terms and recommendations on what you should do with the money, i.e., either to have it transferred in a single sum or sent in lots to Grenoble. They operate through the Banque Nationale de France. Please reply right away so that I can tell them what to do. . . .

CATHERINE TO IGOR STRAVINSKY   *December 31, 1934*

. . . The Beliankins received a New Year's present. Gliklikh informed me that
the matter has been settled, and he is summoning Grisha to Warsaw. Grisha,
full of anxious anticipation, plans to leave any day now. His friend [Ermanov],
who worked at [the Château Basque,] . . . will fill in for Grisha at the Café de la
Paix. Clearly Grisha will receive at least part of the money right away. Milochka
told me all of this on the telephone. She added that he will also receive our
money now, through a loan from Rovenskaya. I am happy for them and for Ira,
who can appear in public now and become independent. I have prayed for them
continually, and lately to St. Expedite. I am certain that he has helped
them. . . . God has helped them to extract themselves from those difficult situations, which they endured with courage and without complaint.

CATHERINE TO IGOR STRAVINSKY   *January 3, [1935]*

Grisha is petitioning for his passport and still awaits his visa and money from
Gliklikh for the trip. Without them he will not be able to leave.

CATHERINE TO IGOR STRAVINSKY   *January 11, 1935*

. . . Grisha leaves tomorrow, having received his visa, passport, and money for
the trip. . . . They plan not to tell any outsiders that they have received this
money. Please do not tell Dushkin, at least not for the time being. If Ira still
owes him money, she will probably give it to him now, since to pay those debts
that are especially burdensome would be a great relief for her. I think that they
will now return a certain amount to Vera [Nossenko]. Of course, you understand that they cannot pay off everything at once. I regret that so much of their
money must be devoured in paying their debts. . . . Grisha has learned from
Gliklikh that Verochka [Nossenko's] business with Omelno is definitely hopeless, because of the new laws; obviously neither she nor I will receive anything
more. . . .

CATHERINE TO IGOR STRAVINSKY   *January 18, 1935*

. . . Grisha will probably return tomorrow. Everyone at the Café de la Paix is
asking about him, and his assistant Ermanov awaits his return impatiently.
Grisha sent Milochka 3,000 francs for urgent bills and wrote that he had some
success in his endeavors, though of course he wrote nothing about himself in
the letter. He did say that he ordered a new suit and overcoat, since a good suit
costs only 200 francs. Things are so inexpensive there! I am delighted for him
and for them both. . . .

CATHERINE TO IGOR STRAVINSKY   *January 21, 1935*

... Grisha returned. The amount he managed to salvage from his business—
actually the Ustiluzhski business—is 200,000 francs. For our part, 19,115
francs, 35 centimes. He is hoping to receive a substantial sum from the bor-
ough itself and Gogançon [?], not immediately, but in about three years. Grisha wants to write to you, and perhaps he will explain it better than I have done.
Now they are discussing all possible courses and making all possible calculations, but they have so many debts that even now they will not be entirely free.
They therefore will not be making those big repairs on their present apartment,* but will move to a smaller one in the same area instead. I hope that they
will have enough money for everything, especially since business seems to be
going well at the Café de la Paix, and thus Grisha will have some of his own
earnings.

* Which they were keeping for Ira's business.

CATHERINE TO IGOR STRAVINSKY   *February 28, 1935*

... Business is going wonderfully for Grisha and the Café de la Paix. . . . He
earned about 6,000 in two months. I am especially happy for him. He endured
all of his losses without grumbling, and it was not easy for him to let his daughter support him, after all. He appears . . . younger and is taking care of himself.
Now if he would only have some teeth made, he would be a very handsome
man, but I suspect that even if he earned a million dollars he still would not in-
vest in a set of dentures. . . .

CATHERINE TO IGOR STRAVINSKY   *May 19, 1936*

Grisha is feeling well and will continue in his job. They feared that the Russian
department at the bookstore would be closed, but evidently that department is
more profitable than the French one, so it will remain open.

CATHERINE TO IGOR STRAVINSKY   *February 2, 1937*

The yogurt business is going well. They are making more than a hundred pots
from ordinary milk now, which is a lot better.

CATHERINE TO IGOR STRAVINSKY   *February 11, 1937*

We have to give 3,000 to the Beliankins [for Milochka's funeral expenses].

CATHERINE TO IGOR STRAVINSKY   *October 27, 1937*

Ira writes that Grisha is dropping the *"yugurtnoe"* business, and she is very
happy about this.

"DEAR SAMSKY"

Stravinsky and Samuel Dushkin

Soon after becoming a touring concert artist in 1924, Stravinsky realized the desirability of creating a violin and piano repertory that would enable him to participate in as many as four or five joint recitals in the time required to rehearse a single orchestral concert. His first transcription for this combination, a five-movement suite from Pulcinella, *completed August 24, 1925,[1] was intended for the violinist Paul Kochanski, whom the composer had known before World War I.[2] But the work was first performed instead by Stravinsky and Alma Moodie (Frankfurt, November 21, 1925).[3] Partly in compensation to Kochanski, Stravinsky made three transcriptions for him from* Firebird *(Prelude, Ronde des princesses, and Berceuse[4]).*

The first of the transcriptions for Dushkin was a new version of the Berceuse (contract with B. Schotts Söhne, August 2, 1931). Next came the Russian Dance from Petrushka *(completed April 17, 1932) and a new version of the* Pulcinella Suite, *with, apparently at Dushkin's request, a "Scherzino"[5] (completed July 18, 1932). At this time, too, Stravinsky transcribed the* Firebird Scherzo *(contract with B. Schotts Söhne, September 11, 1932), the* Nightingale *"arias"[6] (August 1, 1932), and the Chinese March (August 3, 1932). The arrangement for violin and wind quartet of the "Pastorale" (1907)[7] was made*

---

[1] The manuscript of the Gavotte and Two Variations is inscribed: "I. Stravinsky to Paul Kohansky [sic], London 1921."

[2] They had been introduced by Arthur Rubinstein in London, in June 1914. One of the links in the friendship was Stravinsky's New York doctor, A. L. Garbat, and it was in Kochanski's apartment that Stravinsky met Gershwin. After Kochanski's death, in 1934, Stravinsky and Vera Sudeikina became close friends with his widow, Zosia.

[3] See the correspondence with Werner Reinhart in S.S.C. III.

[4] On May 3, 1929, Stravinsky signed a contract with B. Schotts Söhne to publish the Prelude and Berceuse.

[5] The title is misleading, both because the transcription is of the Presto tenor aria and because *Pulcinella* already has a Scherzino. (Stravinsky's transcription provides an introduction in a rhythm remarkably similar to that found at **106** in Act II of *The Rake's Progress*.) Dushkin wrote to Stravinsky in 1932 (undated letter): "Kochanski is delighted that the new version of *Pulcinella* is dedicated to him."

[6] Actually one aria, a conflation of the Nightingale's first and last arias in the opera.

[7] Stravinsky wrote the transcription on a copy of the 1924 version for voice and wind

shortly before the recording of the opus (May 6, 1933), but the transcription of this for violin and piano ("an arrangement of the arrangement but twice as long," as Stravinsky wrote to Strecker, July 31, 1933) was not completed until September 1933. The transcription of the Divertimento from Le Baiser de la fée[8] dates from the fall of 1933, when Stravinsky spent a week with Dushkin in Fontainebleau. In April 1937, in New York, Stravinsky transcribed the Chanson russe from Mavra,[9] the last of his works in this genre until the collaborations in the 1940s with Sol Babitz[10] and Jeanne Gautier, and the Dushkin version of the Tango.[11]

What, besides advice on fingering and bowing, did Dushkin contribute to the transcriptions? The full answer would require an examination of each piece, since his participation in some of them was more extensive than in others. In several cases he made suggestions for the better exploitation of the instrument, but the substantive alterations attributable to him are rare and minor. For example, he wrote to Stravinsky, August 30, 1932, asking permission to add the notes G, D, F, and B flat to the beginning of the violin figure on the last beat of measures 16 and 20 in the Berceuse, and to make changes in measures 35 and 36 in the Russian Dance. Stravinsky incorporated both suggestions (though a mistake survives in the first published score in measure 35 of the Russian Dance), but he did not follow Dushkin's notion concerning the violin rhythm at 14 and 10 measures from the end of the piece. An indication to play ponticello (rather than pizzicato), a change in figuration, and many dynamic markings are in Dushkin's hand on Stravinsky's manuscript of the Russian Dance, as well as in the published score; this transcription was made while the two men were together. Similar verbal suggestions in Dushkin's hand

---

quartet, giving some of the vocal part and some of the oboe part to the violin, changing registers and figurations, rearranging the wind parts, and pasting in sixteen entirely rescored measures.

[8] In the original version, Part Three begins with the Ballade (beginning on page 24 of the proofs), but Stravinsky did not include this movement in the published score. The transcription corrects errors that survive in every edition of the full score of the ballet. See, for example, the measure before 74 in the latter, with its C-major triad in the first three horns, and the corresponding place in the transcription, where this is rightly given as G major.

[9] In his letters, Dushkin refers to the piece as the "Maiden's Song." Stravinsky recorded it with Joseph Szigeti, in Hollywood, May 9, 1946.

[10] The 1945 arrangement of the Valse and Polka from Three Easy Pieces is signed in Stravinsky's hand: "By Sol Babitz and the author."

[11] Strecker wrote to Stravinsky from New York, November 19, 1955: "I am mailing a photostat of Sam Dushkin's transcription of your Tango, in case you feel inclined to orchestrate it for a bigger orchestra after all. This violin version, which Sam tells me you worked on together, is a little longer than the original and contains certain parts that might lend themselves better as a basis for an orchestration." Earlier in the month Strecker had been in Los Angeles concluding a contract with Gertrud Schoenberg. He was at the Stravinskys' for lunch on November 5.

are also found on the first-draft score of the Divertimento.[12] *But a study of all of the manuscripts does not uncover any change of real significance by Stravinsky's partner (unlike the cello part in the Suite italienne,*[13] *much of which was apparently the work of Piatigorsky*[14]*). For this reason, perhaps, Stravinsky rebelled against the credit line for Dushkin first proposed by Willy Strecker. Stravinsky wrote to him, May 4, 1931: "I consent to have the printed copies [of the Violin Concerto] read: 'Edited and with fingerings by Samuel Dushkin,' and I prefer this to the phrase you proposed. Two days ago, Dushkin and I spent the afternoon determining the bowings and fingerings for the first part."*[15] *Later, however, Stravinsky changed his mind: "I agree to the phrase 'Violin part in collaboration with Samuel Dushkin,' but you are to print it only on the violin part." (July 2, 1931)*

Dushkin's initial exclusivity over the Violin Concerto, the Duo concertant, and most of the transcriptions, and his less-than-front-rank standing among the violin virtuosos of the time, have been blamed for the slow acceptance of the music. Critics have argued that if Heifetz, rather than Dushkin, had first performed and recorded it, the music would have become popular much more quickly. But Stravinsky could not have worked on violin parts with Heifetz, let alone performed with him. As the correspondence makes clear, Dushkin was the only possible collaborator for Stravinsky.

That Samuel Dushkin (1891–1976), the Russian-born American violinist, did not leave a diary of his concert tours with Stravinsky is greatly to be regretted. The two men were compatible friends from the first, close ones to the last. They were not far apart in age, and they came from the same tsarist Russia, albeit from different social, religious, and cultural backgrounds. They spoke Russian between themselves, though their correspondence is in French; and in England and the United States, Dushkin was Stravinsky's translator. While concertizing they were alone together for weeks at a time, crossing thousands of miles of sea and land in each other's company, sharing the same hotel rooms and train compartments, enduring countless receptions and music-club luncheons together, facing audiences from the same platform. More important still, they spent many hours not only practicing together, but also working on violin parts. And, finally, Dushkin understood the two masterpieces that Stravinsky composed for him.

Gentle, self-effacing, and considerate, Samuel Dushkin was a counterpart to the fiercely dynamic, egotistical, and combative Stravinsky. In fact, much of the success of the friendship must be attributed to the violinist's wholly unag-

---

[12] This sketch is written on a published copy of the *Baiser de la fée* piano score.

[13] This title was not used for the violin-piano version of the music until 1935.

[14] The explanation for this is simply that Stravinsky had had less experience in writing virtuoso cello parts than in writing solo violin music (*Histoire du soldat*).

[15] The third proof of the Violin Concerto, dated June 17, 1931, contains a large number of changes in the third movement.

gressive nature, as well as to his rich sense of humor—so different from Stra-
vinsky's essentially sarcastic kind, examples of which Dushkin much enjoyed
repeating. His Russian-Jewish jokes could break Stravinsky's most ominous si-
lences and dourest moods. Dushkin deeply loved the man beneath the musical
genius, the original character, the inexhaustibly inventive mind, the creature
of often outrageous and idiosyncratic behavior.[16]

Stravinsky's "Dushkin period" was brief, consisting of some seventy joint ap-
pearances between October 1931 and March 1937, with three performances of
the Violin Concerto, conducted by Stravinsky, in the winter of 1941, for Balan-
chine's ballet Balustrade.[17] *The violinist and the composer did not see each*
other at all in 1936, and in January 1937, because of "illness,"[18] *the violinist*
canceled his appearances with Stravinsky at the New York Philharmonic, thus
requiring program changes.

Stravinsky's relationship with Dushkin was inevitably altered after his
marriage (January 13, 1936) to Louise Marion Rorimer, who traveled with the
two men during their 1937 American tour. After Stravinsky took up residence
in California, meetings were rare, but when the Stravinskys were in New York,
Dushkin never failed to visit with them and to help them in countless ways—
meeting their trains, "babysitting" with the composer when his wife was ab-
sent, and carrying his scores, towels, eau de cologne, and other liquid emolu-
ments to rehearsals and concerts. When the Stravinskys moved to New York, in
1969, Dushkin remained one of their most faithful visitors.

Since most of Stravinsky's correspondence with Dushkin is concerned with the
logistics of concert tours and with details in the music they were performing,

---

[16] The present writer owes a considerable debt of gratitude to Sam Dushkin in the
years 1948–49, especially for advice on how to weather Stravinsky's tantrums, and for
warnings against drinking from a glass that the composer had used, for Dushkin believed that Stravinsky was still an active carrier of TB at that time. In the 1950s and
1960s, Dushkin and the present writer became good friends.

[17] This was presented by Hurok in the Fifty-first Street Theatre. Since the ballet was a
critical failure and never revived, the following excerpt from a letter to Stravinsky from
Pavel Tchelichev, who designed the set and costumes, should be of interest: "Dear
Igor Fyodorovich, Forgive me for not coming to your rehearsal Tuesday, but I had a
high fever and was afraid of passing it on to you. I am sorry, too, that I was not able to
attend the performance, and I hope that my absence did not ruin things for you and for
Balanchine. I have become so familiar with your Concerto that I cannot get it out of my
head. It is a wonderful piece, as remarkable in its 'every centimeter' [Stravinsky's ex-
pression] as it is as a whole. Dear friend, do not think ill of me, but I cannot produce a
ballet for Denham. Just thinking about all those 'ballets russes,' invoking poor Sergei
Pavlovich, makes me feel sick. I am sure that Diaghilev would never have formed his
company if he had known what his precedent would lead to." (January 23, 1941)

[18] Nerves? In December 1941, Dushkin wrote to Stravinsky: "I do not have many concerts, but enough to keep me nervous and thin," and by 1948, when the present writer
made Dushkin's acquaintance, he had stopped performing altogether.

the seven letters given here were chosen for the personal view of the relationship that they offer. A paternal side of Stravinsky is revealed here as in no other correspondence with friends. On August 26, 1933, Dushkin wrote: "Cher Monsieur Stravinsky, . . . I need to see you again to recover my courage."[19]

The letters are preceded by a calendar of the Stravinsky-Dushkin concerts, but since the repertory was so similar from one to another, the programs are given only in exceptional cases. Occasionally Dushkin played a Bach, Beethoven, or Brahms sonata, Stravinsky one of his solo piano pieces or the second part in his Concerto per due pianoforti soli. But generally the programs consisted of the Duo concertant, the piano and violin reduction of the Violin Concerto, and the transcriptions from the four ballets, from the two operas, and of the Pastorale.

1931

Stravinsky and Dushkin met in Paris at the beginning of February 1931 to establish a schedule for the year. Dushkin visited Stravinsky in Nice twice, from about April 15 to about May 8, and from September 12 to about September 22. The only piece in their programs for the year was the Violin Concerto with orchestra.

OCTOBER 23. *Berlin. Premiere.*[20]
NOVEMBER 9. *Frankfurt. Besides the Violin Concerto, Stravinsky conducted the* Petrushka *Suite with Erich Itor Kahn*[21] *as piano soloist.*
NOVEMBER 16 and 17. *London.*
DECEMBER 1. *Cologne.*[22]
DECEMBER 14. *Hanover.*
DECEMBER 17. *Paris.*

1932

In mid-April 1932, and again at the beginning of August, Dushkin worked with Stravinsky on the Duo concertant in Voreppe. On August 18, Blair Fairchild[23]

---

[19] Though the letter mentions that "Madame Sudeikina came to see us yesterday, which deeply touched us," Stravinsky gave it to his wife to answer. Writing on August 28, she reveals an uncertainty as to how to close the letter, striking out a *"Bien amicalement"* and a *"Mes amitiés."* The draft does not indicate her final choice.

[20] In a letter to Stravinsky, November 2, 1931, Dushkin complains that in the Berlin performance, "the violin solo was drowned out by the trumpets."

[21] Erich Itor Kahn (1905–56), composer, pianist, Samuel Dushkin's accompanist, and the first musician on relatively close terms with Stravinsky who knew the music of Schoenberg, Berg, and Webern.

[22] It should be mentioned here, if only for the reason that Stravinsky's *Chroniques de ma vie* is vague about dates, that he heard the oratorio *Das Unaufhörliche* (music by Hindemith, text by Gottfried Benn) in Mainz on November 28.

[23] Blair Fairchild (1877–1933), American composer. Stravinsky had corresponded

wrote to Stravinsky from the Grand Hotel Bürgenstock (near Lucerne): "Sam has shown me the last movement of the Duo. . . . Such beauty! . . . The transcriptions are also completely successful and will make a great addition to the violin literature, something precious indeed." Four days later, Dushkin wrote from the same hotel, acknowledging Stravinsky's card from Carcassonne and adding: "In the last two weeks Milstein and Piatigorsky have had fifteen concerts canceled in Germany, and, for the same reason (Hitler), Horowitz does not play at all."

In September, writing from Avon, Fairchild's home at 48, rue de la Cloche, Fontainebleau, Dushkin informed Stravinsky that their only forthcoming appearances in Germany would be those in Berlin[24] and Danzig, but the violinist expresses a feeling of relief, "since there are too many Nazis and not enough money." The same letter reveals that Florent Schmitt had opposed the Société Musicale Indépendante's sponsorship of the Paris recital that was to have introduced the Duo concertant, for which reason Dushkin suggests that he and Stravinsky give the concert on their own. "I have corrected and returned the proofs of the Berceuse," he adds, and he implores the composer to come to Paris in time to rehearse together. In still another letter, Dushkin complains that Stravinsky has sent the manuscript of the new Pulcinella Suite and asked him to have it copied:

It is not simply the problem of finding a copyist, but also of practicing while the copyist has the music. . . . I have already rehearsed the piece with a pianist, and the only difficult movements for the piano are the Tarantella and Finale. Otherwise the piano part is the same as in the original [1925] version,[25] so you can work on these two movements without losing any time. . . . In December, in Paris, I can help you correct the proofs. . . . I would like to look at certain details with you again, also in the Duo. It would be better to play everything with you several times, or at least wait until the first performance is behind us, before giving the proofs to Païchadze. I will be in Paris on Wednesday, and I hope to find out the free dates at the Salle Pleyel for the first two weeks in December. I will telephone you Wednesday evening.

On October 15, Dushkin sent the Scherzino—"so that you will have a few days to learn it"—but Stravinsky did not come to Paris much before October 22, on which day he dined at Nadia Boulanger's with Dushkin and Willy Strecker. After the Paris concert, Dushkin wrote to Stravinsky: "I am returning the Nightingale *arias and the Chinese March, since you asked for them. The Duo is*

---

with him since 1919, when he was president of the Society of American Friends of Musicians in France.

[24] Stravinsky had been invited to attend an evening of contemporary arts in Berlin, in the Nordböhmischen Gewerbemuseums, on September 8, featuring his Suite for violin and piano, Brecht's *Hauspostille,* and Hindemith's suite "1922."

[25] This is not true; the piano part differs from the original version in every movement.

already in Païchadze's hands. . . . I will write to Madame Courtauld before returning the contracts to Tillett."[26]

MARCH 27. *Florence. Violin Concerto, with orchestra.*

MARCH 29. *Milan, Teatro del Popolo. Recital. Dushkin played a Bach solo violin sonata and Stravinsky played his Piano Sonata. The concert began with the* Pulcinella *Suite (1925 version) and concluded with the piano and violin reduction of the Violin Concerto.*

OCTOBER 28. *Berlin. Recital. Premiere of Duo concertant and of the "new Pergolesi Suite."*

NOVEMBER 2. *Danzig. Recital.*

NOVEMBER 7.[27] *Paris. Recital at the Princesse de Polignac's.*

NOVEMBER 8. *Paris. Recital in the Grande Salle Pleyel.*

1933

At the end of January 1933, Dushkin joined Stravinsky and Madame Sudeikina in Wiesbaden and journeyed with them to Munich, where Dushkin and Stravinsky gave a recital on February 2. The next day, Dushkin returned to Paris, and a few days later Stravinsky and Madame Sudeikina went to Italy. At the end of February Dushkin wrote to Stravinsky:

Madame Sudeikina telephoned today, and I know from her that you are back in Voreppe. . . . I had hoped to be able to give you more cheerful news of M. Fairchild. He is a little better some days, but, unhappily, the general situation is the same.[28] His temperature is always 38 or more in the evening, and he is very feeble. . . . Our hearts go up and down with the thermometer. . . . The doctor told us that he has the use of only a quarter of his lungs, but that this is enough to sustain life. . . . Mrs. Stephen Courtauld has invited us to stay with her in London. I would like to make the trip with you, but that depends on M. Fairchild. . . . I hope that everything went well for you in Italy. Tomorrow I will send the corrected part of the Duo.

The BBC recital took place on March 13, and a recital in Winterthur on March 25, but an eight-city tour in France in May was canceled after Fairchild's death on April 23. Here are excerpts from two of Dushkin's letters, the first written before, the second after this event:

Friday. Madame Sudeikina must already have written to you about the sad situation here. Yesterday we received new hope, and I anxiously await the doctor

---

[26] Pedro Tillett, music-program director for the BBC.

[27] On November 4, Stravinsky had played his Capriccio in Königsberg, while, at the same time, Dushkin had played the Violin Concerto in Munich. See the interview with Stravinsky by Claude Dhérelle in *Paris-Soir*, December 6, 1932, reprinted in *Stravinsky: Etudes et témoignages*, edited by François Lesure (Paris, 1982).

[28] Fairchild was suffering from tuberculosis.

tomorrow to see whether this is simply the result of the opium injections, or whether the rapid decline has been stopped. But the doctors know nothing and can predict nothing. . . . The change in M. Fairchild's condition came so abruptly. . . . It pains me that, because of me, you are in a state of uncertainty as well. . . . I received a letter from Erik Schall, who described your adventure in Munich with Hitler's fanatics.[29] What a sad time. . . . I have finished the corrections in the proofs, but many mistakes remain, and I have many questions to ask you. The metronomes, and even some measures, are missing in the first Eglogue.

On Tuesday, April 25, Dushkin telegraphed: "Monsieur Fairchild died on Sunday." He wrote to Stravinsky on Wednesday:

To hear your voice last evening on the telephone comforted me very much. I saw Ysaye[30] today, and he was very kind and humane. He had lost his father recently and understood. M. Fairchild became terribly feeble in the last days, but he did not want to be an obstacle to our work. During this feebleness, and perhaps because of the opium, he asked us to come to him, above all at night, and to talk to him, which was very difficult. . . . The future frightens and paralyzes me.

A memorial concert took place at the Salle Gaveau, May 18, 1934, for the benefit of the French-American Society for Convalescence from Tuberculosis, of which Edith Wharton was the president. Four pieces by Fairchild were performed, as well as Bach's "Christ lag" cantata, conducted by Nadia Boulanger, and Stravinsky's Three Sacred Choruses, conducted by the composer.

Shortly thereafter, Dushkin went to America, and he did not return to France until the end of August 1933. That autumn he participated in two concerts with Stravinsky in Barcelona, playing the Concerto on November 16 (with the Orquesta Pau Casals) and, on November 21, a recital program in the auditorium of the Residencia de Estudiantes that included the piano, violin, and clarinet (played by D. Aurelio Fernández) version of five movements from Histoire du soldat.

1934

FEBRUARY 22. *Manchester, Hallé Orchestra. The Violin Concerto with orchestra and a group of violin and piano pieces.*

---

[29] The incident took place on February 3, 4, or 5, 1933.

[30] Théo Ysaye, of the concert agency Kiesgen and Ysaye, had organized the tour for May. But this had already been canceled on April 19, when Ysaye wrote to Stravinsky that Dushkin had been to see him and enclosed a copy of the letter of cancellation that describes Dushkin as Fairchild's adopted son since infancy. "The doctors say that M. Fairchild could live one more day, or possibly as long as three weeks or more," Ysaye says.

FEBRUARY 23. *Liverpool,*[31] *Rushworth Hall.*

FEBRUARY 26. *Cambridge.*

FEBRUARY 27. *London, Queen's Hall. The program included the trio version of* Histoire du soldat *with Reginald Kell playing the clarinet part.*

FEBRUARY 28. *Oxford.*

MARCH 14. *Turin, Istituto Fascista di Coltura, Sala del Liceo Musicale.*

MARCH 24. *Kaunas.*

DECEMBER 11. *Liège. Orchestral concert. The Violin Concerto; Stravinsky also conducted the complete (!)* Petrushka, Fireworks, Suite No. 2, *and* Firebird Suite.

DECEMBER 12. *Strasbourg, Salle Hector Berlioz.*

DECEMBER 13. *Mulhausen.*

DECEMBER 15. *Toulon.*

DECEMBER 16. *Monte Carlo, Casino.*

DECEMBER 17. *Marseille.*

DECEMBER 18. *Lyon.*

On December 27, Stravinsky and Dushkin sailed from Villefranche-sur-Mer on the S.S. Rex. They arrived in New York on January 3, 1935.

1935[32]

JANUARY 10. *New York, Plaza Hotel Ballroom (Morning Musical). The program (shared by others) consisted of the Divertimento, "Pastorale,"*[33] *and transcriptions from* Firebird *and* Petrushka.

JANUARY 21. *Minneapolis, Cyrus Northrop Auditorium.*

JANUARY 23. *Toledo, Peristyle, Museum of Art.*

JANUARY 25. *Pittsburgh, Carnegie Music Hall.*

JANUARY 27. *Indianapolis, English Theatre. Stravinsky and Dushkin performed on the second half of the program only.*

---

[31] Stravinsky had written to Wilfrid Van Wyck, July 29, 1933: "In my entire life as a performer, the Liverpool fee is the lowest I have ever been offered, but I accept because it amuses me to establish a record." Liverpool paid £47, however, whereas the receipts from Oxford and Cambridge came to only £12 and £8, respectively.

[32] Since Dushkin did not appear in Stravinsky's orchestra concerts in America, all of the joint appearances were recitals. In the Chicago Arts Club, January 13, Stravinsky conducted his Octet in a chamber-music program without Dushkin. Stravinsky conducted the Chicago Symphony in Milwaukee on January 14, and in Chicago on January 17, 18, and 22. After the Indianapolis recital he returned to New York, and on February 3 he led the Radio City Orchestra in an NBC broadcast concert, which he introduced with a sixty-eight-word speech in English. On February 21 and 22, he conducted the Los Angeles Philharmonic, and on March 14 and 15 the Boston Symphony.

[33] In a program note written at the time of the first performance of the version for voice and four woodwinds, Stravinsky wrote that he had "always had the intention to give this piece an essentially *champêtre* character in substituting a small ensemble of wind instruments for piano accompaniment."

FEBRUARY 10. *St. Louis, Municipal Auditorium. Stravinsky conducted the St. Louis Orchestra for three parts of the program, and he and Dushkin performed a group of duos for the fourth.*

FEBRUARY 13. *San Francisco, Opera House.*

FEBRUARY 14. *Palo Alto, Stanford Pavilion.*

FEBRUARY 16. *Carmel, Sunset School Auditorium.*

FEBRUARY 28. *Los Angeles, Philharmonic Auditorium.*

MARCH 3. *Colorado Springs, Broadmoor Hotel.*

MARCH 4. *Denver, Broadway Theatre.*

MARCH 6. *Fort Worth, Central High Auditorium.*

MARCH 24. *Washington, D.C., National Theatre.*

MARCH 27. *Winnetka, School of Musical Arts and Crafts.*

MARCH 29. *Chicago, Orchestra Hall.*

APRIL 9.[34] *Washington, D.C., Library of Congress.*

SEPTEMBER 27. *Oslo, Aula.*

SEPTEMBER 29. *Oslo, Aula.*

OCTOBER 2. *Stockholm. Violin Concerto, with orchestra.*

OCTOBER 5. *Malmö.*

OCTOBER 7. *Stockholm.*

OCTOBER 11. *Göteborg.*[35]

OCTOBER 12. *Helsingborg.*

OCTOBER 14. *Copenhagen.*

On October 28 and 29, at the Salle Pleyel, Paris, Stravinsky and Dushkin recorded the Violin Concerto for Polydor. Then Dushkin left for New York.

1937

Stravinsky and the Dushkins arrived in New York on December 23, 1936, on the S. S. Normandie. José-Maria Sert was also on board, and the Edward G. Robinsons. Stravinsky conducted the Toronto Symphony on January 5, 1937;[36] the New York Philharmonic on January 14, 15, 17, 21, 22, and 24 (national broadcast); the General Motors Symphony (Detroit) on February 14; the Los Angeles Philharmonic on March 12 and 13; and the San Francisco Symphony on March 23.

JANUARY 8. *Worcester (Massachusetts).*

JANUARY 25. *Montreal, Auditorium du Plateau.*

JANUARY 27. *New York, Town Hall.*

FEBRUARY 8 and 9. *Columbus, Capital University, Mees Hall.*

---

[34] On April 13, Stravinsky sailed from New York for Le Havre on the S.S. *Ile de France*, and arrived on the 20th.

[35] While in Göteborg, Stravinsky received Greta Torpadie, who had sung in three chamber-music concerts with him in the United States in 1925.

[36] The program included Brahms's Fourth Symphony, conducted by Sir Ernest Mac-Millan.

FEBRUARY 16. *New York, Brooklyn Academy of Music.*

FEBRUARY 24, 25, and 27. *Cleveland, Severance Hall. Stravinsky conducted the Cleveland Orchestra in all three concerts. In the last two, Dushkin played Mozart's "seventh violin concerto in D," as well as the Stravinsky Concerto. Stravinsky also conducted the orchestra on tour, February 18, 19, and 20, and included Tchaikovsky's* Pathétique *Symphony in all three concerts.*

MARCH 3. *Winnetka, Dushkin School of Music.*[37]

MARCH 4. *Winnetka.*[38]

MARCH 16. *Santa Barbara, Lobero Theatre.*

MARCH 30. *Tacoma, First Baptist Church.*

MARCH 31. *Seattle, Metropolitan Theatre (Ladies' Musical Club).*

Stravinsky returned to New York in April to conduct the first two performances of Jeu de cartes *(with* Apollo *and* Le Baiser de la fée*) at the Metropolitan Opera House, April 27 and 28. He left New York on the S.S.* Normandie, *May 4, arriving in Le Havre on the 11th.*

STRAVINSKY TO SAMUEL DUSHKIN   *25, rue du Faubourg St.-Honoré*
                                                November 2, 1935

My dear Samsky,

I am sending you two typescripts of the second volume of my *Chroniques.* Take one copy with you to New York for Simon & Schuster (386 Fourth Avenue) and please give the other one to Gollancz (Victor Gollancz Ltd, 14 Henrietta St., Covent Garden, WC2). A brief note from you will be very useful and assure me that these two errands have been carried out. Thanks!

Madame Bouchonnet[39] has just telephoned me that Barcelona, with which she is negotiating for the spring, proposes March 12 and 15 as the only possible dates. Both concerts are to be conducted.[40] You see my embarrassment in knowing nothing definite about my engagements in America, even their exact time. I will wait for news of you from New York with doubled impatience, because it would not make any sense to lose these two very well-paid concerts.

Willy Strecker wrote to me that he leaves today for Mainz; the check in question was enclosed with his letter. He saw [Edward] Clark, who wants to come to Paris for the premiere of the new Concerto. If you see him (in Lon-

---

[37] The school had been founded by David Dushkin, Samuel's younger brother, and the program included a Beethoven sonata played by Dushkin and Beveridge Webster, and Stravinsky's Concerto per due pianoforti soli played by the composer and Webster.

[38] The program included the Brahms Sonata in D minor played by Dushkin and Webster, the Concerto per due pianoforti soli, the "Pastorale," the last movement of the Violin Concerto, a "madrigale" (?) from *Perséphone,* and the Scherzo from *Firebird.*

[39] Nadyezhda Dmitrievna Bouchonnet was Stravinsky's Paris concert agent at the time.

[40] In other words, the concerts would not include Dushkin.

don), tell him that he will be welcome, give him my address, and greet him for me. Awaiting a word from you (please include some tender expression), I send you, my sweet heart, my best greetings.[41]

Your   I. Str.

Bouchonnet has telephoned me again begging me to ask you to cable from New York whether or not I can accept the Barcelona dates. Do it, my darling, I shall pay you all the expenses.[42]

STRAVINSKY TO DUSHKIN

Paris
November 16, 1935

My dear Samsky,

Very nice of you to have cabled. Now I can write to you what I think of all of the unfortunate circumstances and give you a little preview of my attitude toward this tour that poor Kavenoki[43] is trying to rescue. I hope that these lines will reach you before the telegram promised "in eight days," which is to say before his trip.

Above all, I must tell you that I will be busy here in Europe in March (England and Spain); therefore do not count on me during this period.

To get to the core of the matter, everything that has happened is certainly not reassuring, and I ask you if it would not be preferable and more reasonable to postpone until next year the few appearances that have already been contracted. According to the list I have in front of me, only Rochester (January 9), the Chicago group (January 25, 28, 30, and 31), and Philadelphia (January 21)—where I do not know whether or not the engagement is for conducting—are in question. This is all. The other appearances are either pending or else the amount of the honorarium is marked "approximately" (Washington). As for the engagements with you, only two are worth considering: February 10 in Columbus and February 13 in East Lansing.

I strongly doubt that Kavenoki will be able to offer me much more than that; hence it is more practical to ask Madame Bouchonnet to find some concerts for me here in Europe in January and February, and, as I said, to postpone these three or four engagements until next year. Above all, I must not lose time waiting for news from America and thus lose the concerts that Madame Bouchonnet can obtain for me.

Conclusion: I will come only in the event that the American concerts are advantageous, and not only from the pecuniary side but also from the artistic one (i.e., conducting works that interest me, such as *Perséphone*, and conduct-

---

[41] The last six words are in English in the original.

[42] The last eleven words are in English in the original.

[43] Severin Kavenoki was an assistant to Alexander Bernardovich Merovich, who had been in correspondence with Stravinsky since August 1933 concerning the 1935 American tour.

ing at least one concert with an interesting program at the New York Philharmonic).

I have just spoken to the people at Polydor. They have sent you the test pressings of the Concerto, which I too am about to examine. I will write soon telling you what I think and indicating my choices.

I am impatient to have news of your primary concern. I do not ask useless and perhaps also indiscreet questions.[44] May your wishes be granted for *your* good and, as you know (still better, as I know you), above all happily.

Your   I. Str.

STRAVINSKY TO DUSHKIN

25, rue du Faubourg St.-Honoré
Paris
January 8, 1936[45]

My dear Samsky,

I hope that you have my cabled reply as well as my card, which replied (a little more substantially than the cable) to your first wire (which crossed with your second). I was in Switzerland when you cabled the first time, which explains the delay of the reply, and for which please excuse me.

Toward the New Year, Madame Bouchonnet forwarded a proposal, cabled from Hurok (manager of the Ballets de Monte Carlo, which at this moment is performing at the Metropolitan Opera House), for concerts in October and November 1936. The total fee is $6,000. I have asked Madame Bouchonnet to tell him to go take a walk: first, I have no confidence in his type; second, the autumn was never a good period in the United States; and third, I believe I can do better than that with you alone in January and February 1936. It is with reference to this question that I answered in my cable to "accept in principle" the question discussed between us many times and resumed in the "conclusion" of my letter to you of last November 16. I will agree to a tour in the United States in January, February, and, if necessary, March 1937, if this tour can offer sufficient artistic and material guarantees. From my point of view, this season would unfortunately have given me nothing of either: *Perséphone,* so brilliantly launched by me last year in Boston, was given to others (New York Philharmonic) to conduct in my presence. The symphonic programs that I had to conduct contained, to put it bluntly, nothing new and interesting but always the same things, *Firebird* and *Petrushka!* So much for the question of artistic satisfaction. As for material satisfaction, you understand yourself that a sum of $4,000, which, according to you, I can count on as a result of three months' work, does not, in my eyes, seem a sufficient profit for me to decide to abandon everything, my composition, my family, and all that is dear to me. The relative artistic and material success of my last tour led me to hope that, with the re-

---

[44] Stravinsky is referring to Dushkin's forthcoming marriage.

[45] Dushkin apparently did not receive this letter until after his honeymoon at the Fort Montagu Beach Hotel, Nassau, whence he wrote to Stravinsky on February 18.

newal of your activity in your country, something much more interesting than this would result. The unfortunate turn of events regarding Merovich[46] and his management are undoubtedly the major cause, but I think that even if Merovich's proposals had been materially attractive, the artistic considerations would not have changed in my favor. In any case, the $4,000 for three months that you and Kavenoki offer me cannot serve as an acceptable basis of a guarantee for our projects next year. If these are to become a reality, whoever is in charge of my tour must find a series of valuable engagements for me, one that offers me advantages both artistic and material. The one without the other—and you know better than anyone what I want—is not worth my while.

Here, for the moment, everything is calm. At the end of January my wife will return to the mountains, probably in Switzerland, to gain strength (I hope). In March it is Spain and England for me, with Nini [Soulima], and in April–May probably Argentina (also with Nini). I will be very happy to have the news that you obstinately do not want to give me. Out of discretion I do not ask you the reason and simply embrace you with all my heart.

Your   Igor Fyodorovich[47]

STRAVINSKY TO DUSHKIN   *Château de Monthoux*
                                        August 8, 1937
My dear Sam,

With all my heart I greet the great news[48] that you announced to me and that took place under the best conditions for Louise. May this be for you a source of permanent happiness. I want to hope that this great event will strengthen the good relations with your in-laws, so much desired by you and your wife. Have a good and happy trip, good and happy returns to three—or perhaps four (do not misunderstand me, I am referring to Beveridge [Webster]).

Now let us turn to business, since your letter authorizes me to speak of it. First, here is the check for the sum that "S. Dushkin paid to Customs" for the photographs from Mrs. Bliss,[49] which are as magnificent as they are useless. Since I pronounce them useless, please do not send them to me but simply give them to Païchadze, if you are in his neighborhood, or else leave them with your

---

[46] On November 26, 1935, Dushkin had written to Stravinsky: "Merovich is insane and is now in a sanitarium in Minneapolis. . . . He committed criminal acts and has become violent. The conductor of the ballet tried to kill himself." On January 5, Dushkin wrote that Merovich "is still in the sanitarium."

[47] The original of the signature is in Russian, perhaps as a gesture toward Dushkin and his forthcoming marriage, which was the news that Dushkin did not want to give, because he knew that Stravinsky did not approve.

[48] The birth of the Dushkins' first child, several weeks earlier.

[49] Mrs. Bliss had sent Dushkin, in Paris, a number of large photographs of her Dumbarton Oaks home. Dushkin returned Stravinsky's check (for 37 francs).

concierge, where they can be picked up in your absence. Still thinking of use-less things, I very much hope that Mrs. Bliss has not forgotten to deposit in my account at Bankers Trust Co., New York, the first installment, which I con-sider, and she too, to be something useful. Meanwhile, I have heard nothing, but it is true that one is never in a hurry with money.

And not only with money but also with a simple polite reply such as, for example, the reply from Charles Chaplin that I still await. (I sent him a regis-tered letter—airmail from New York—on June 8.) When you are back in America, could you find out the reason for this silence? Perhaps E. G. Robin-son* could telephone Chaplin and ask him if he has received my letter—to which, nevertheless, I would like to have an answer. (Robinson's address: 910 N. Rexford Drive, Beverly Hills, California.) So there, my dear Sam, is a little errand that I ask you to do for me when you are there, or, if you wish, before. Write to Robinson and send the letter airmail from New York as soon as you ar-rive—August 21, if I am not mistaken.[50] Also inform Copley,[51] if you see him there, that I have received the telegram from his office announcing the arrival in Europe of Morros,[52] on the *Ile de France,* August 3 or 4. Copley saw him in Los Angeles, and he still does not have anything definite.

Here, for the moment, everyone is together, a very large family with four generations at table. That is happy. Unhappily, my wife is not brimming with health, as had been hoped, given the summer weather, the rise in morale, and the elevation of more than 600 meters, from which she has benefited these past weeks. One day, two days, she is better, then three days less good, and this more than a month after we left Paris. It is a long story. Ask Vera (Jas. 64–40), who is fully informed of all that is happening.

Myself, I compose; and if the health of my wife were not always so uncer-tain and upsetting, this would be a very good summer for me in all senses. My health is very good,[53] with, from time to time, intestinal troubles that are very disagreeable to overcome.

---

[50] Dushkin wrote to Stravinsky from New York on October 4 saying that Mrs. Edward G. Robinson wrote to the effect that she and "Eddy" had been to lunch at Chaplin's, who said that he would "write to Stravinsky himself."

[51] In January 1935, on Dushkin's recommendation, Richard Copley became Stra-vinsky's American concert agent, succeeding Merovich. Stravinsky's first English-language correspondence was with Copley.

[52] Boris Morros, who later became famous for his activities as an American secret agent during World War II, had known Stravinsky in Russia before World War I. Morros was in charge of the music department at Paramount Pictures at the time of his negotiations with Stravinsky to compose music for use in a film, *The Knights of St. David;* Morros had already recorded Schumann's *Davidsbündlertänze,* some Debussy songs, and Ravel's *Chansons madécasses.* (Letter from Alexis Kall to Stravinsky, April 13, 1937)

[53] Stravinsky was suffering from active tuberculosis during the 1937 tour. Alexis Kall wrote to him at Easter 1937: "Don't worry about your tuberculosis. It is a lot worse for young people than for those of your age."

To finish this letter, and while I await a few lines from you, promised before your departure to America, would you ask the Copley office to convey to the mother of the poor Guerschvin [Gershwin] my most sincere sympathies in her great sorrow. I do not know her address. I embrace you very affectionately.

Your   I. Stravinsky

* I suggest this method of approach, believing that without it I will never get a result, since E. G. Robinson has access to Chaplin and was responsible for introducing me to him.

STRAVINSKY TO DUSHKIN

Paris
October 24, 1937

My dear Sam,

Finally news of you! Thank you. How much longer will you be in New York? It is two weeks since I sent a letter to Copley, in answer to his asking me to entrust him with the organization of my concerts for the 1938–39 season.[54] I spoke to him only about symphonic engagements. Since he also had our joint concerts in view, I have to tell him frankly that I have renounced them.[55] Our last conversations on this subject with you in New York clearly showed me that the financial side of these concerts did not give you the satisfaction that you want, which is unfortunately something that, as I answered you very directly, I cannot remedy. My apprehensions seem to have been confirmed, and what you say in your letter is the proof. You may well believe that it is very painful for me always to feel that you are diminished because of me, though this is inevitable, unfortunately. I will tell you more, though you know it very well yourself: I too am not very satisfied with the meager rewards that these concerts bring me. Still, I have a very strong impression that these joint concerts do not seriously compromise your career as a soloist.

I have an agreement this time with Madame Bouchonnet, since, of course, the miserable Van Wyck[56] has succeeded in nothing concerning the Australian project (with Nini). At this time Australia seems rather a good choice, but the period is not yet decided, and the dates must not overlap with the American ones (January–March). Also, the Australian project should not take place either immediately before or after America, because in this case I must count on a loss of at least eight months from composing and from my family.

---

[54] This tour did not take place, owing to the death of Stravinsky's elder daughter in November 1938 and the declining health of his wife.

[55] Stravinsky had written to Copley on October 10: "For certain reasons, I would prefer not to appear in joint concerts." Copley answered on November 2: "As yet, I have not notified Mr. Dushkin that there will be no joint concerts." Nor did Copley ever notify Dushkin, who wrote to Stravinsky on December 23: "I am not satisfied with Copley as a salesman." Copley died suddenly in February 1939.

[56] Wilfrid Van Wyck, Stravinsky's concert agent in London.

Thank you for writing to Robinson, but still nothing from Chaplin, unfortunately. I enclose a copy of the registered letter that I sent to him last June 8. I will be very grateful to you if you would send it through Robinson, asking him to deliver it with his own hands to Chaplin. Without that I will never have the assurance that it did not fall into the hands of his secretaries or of others (his wife?[57]) and that he ever read it.

The first installment from Bliss has finally been received. The delay was due to a distraction on the part of Nadia [Boulanger], who did not send the letter of agreement until after her return from a vacation. The first part of the Concerto is composed and orchestrated. There will probably be two more movements. Nadia told me that Mrs. Bliss asks me to advance the completion of the work for performance in May 1938. I will write to her one of these days to tell her that this is understood.

Unfortunately, the family is not together. After having struggled through bad health all summer, my wife was obliged to go back up to Sancellemoz, where she is now. Recently we have had the impression that she has improved. I will be with her in the second half of November. This week I go to Amsterdam (*Jeu de cartes*), then for a symphony concert in Naples (Tchaikovsky's Third, *Jeu de cartes, Firebird*). I have just returned from London, where the two performances of *Jeu de cartes* had an immense success, though, as usual, the press was absurd. For example: "The three deals of the game of poker may be made amusing on the stage, and no doubt the music contributes to the amusement." Another masterpiece: "Its success last night was principally a personal one for the composer"; this unhappy critic should have consulted, one by one, the three thousand people who applauded me.

A thousand good wishes to Louise, to whom I will reply in English when I am a little less busy. My knowledge of the language is getting better and better.[58] Meanwhile, I embrace you very affectionately.

STRAVINSKY TO DUSHKIN   *Paris*
                                                    January 4, 1938
Sulgrave
New York

My dear Sam,

After two and a half months of silence, a letter from you! Better that, certainly, than three months of silence. But what astonishes me in your letter is that you do not mention having received mine of October 24, which was a reply to yours of October 9.

---

[57] Paulette Goddard, later Mrs. Erich Maria Remarque. The Stravinskys, the Remarques, and the present writer dined together in Berlin in September 1961.

[58] On January 4, 1937, Stravinsky told an interviewer for the *Evening Telegram* (Toronto): "I study English in Paris and I can read it quite well. . . . Hemingway's last book I have been able to read for myself in English."

I send you a copy [of my October 24 letter] with, as always, a copy of this unfortunate letter to Chaplin, the fate of which continues to be unknown to me. I insist on this, perhaps out of stubbornness, because, in truth, I no longer expect anything from Hollywood, or from the collaboration with Chaplin. The proof that I very sincerely wanted it is my registered letter to him. But he very sincerely remains silent, even after Robinson's friendly intervention. Read these old letters, my dear, and please return the yellow copy to me (my letter to you), of which I no longer have a copy. (It takes time to copy letters!) [59]

Very happy with your success at Carnegie Hall and also very happy to know that you and Beveridge will participate in the Bliss concert in Washington under the direction of Nadia, who will conduct the *Soldat* Suite and the new Concerto. She will come to see me one of these days to have the exact tempi of the *Soldat* as well as what is already composed of the Concerto (first and second movements). In two or three days Strecker will send me the proofs of the first movement.

In memory of the holidays that we spent together so agreeably last year, I sent a cable of greeting to you and to Louise's parents. An unbreachable wall has already sprung up since then. For all of this not to seem so unhappy, it is necessary to look ahead and, so far as possible, never backward, even though the future does not exist. There you have it, a little philosophy that you can apply as you see fit.

How is Louise, and how is she taking her condition? I want to believe that everything is going normally, since you tell me nothing except that she expects the child in March. [60] I mention this, nevertheless, wanting to know how she is. And Mrs. Rorimer? [61] Is she over her illness?

I send you this little clipping from *L'Intransigeant*, [62] which asked me to say something—not these insignificant things—about Ravel on the very morning of the day of his death. I could not refuse, and I telephoned these few lines to the newspaper. I went to see him before his body was placed in the coffin. He was stretched on a table covered with black drapery, with a white turban around his head (he was shaved for the trepanning of the cranium), dressed in a black suit, hands in white gloves, arms by the sides of the body. His face was pale (with very black brows), but with an expression of seriousness and majesty. I went to his interment. Lugubrious spectacles, these civil burials, at which everything is banished except protocol.

---

[59] Dushkin answered on January 31: "Robinson is in New York, and I talked to him on the telephone. Mrs. Robinson says that Chaplin told her he never received the letter, but Eddy says that Chaplin is a liar. Eddy advises you to drop the matter and not to insist on it. . . . What astonishes me is that the proposal came from Chaplin." The remainder of the letter is devoted to an explanation of the Sibelius craze in the United States. The Dushkins returned to France in May, but they rarely saw Stravinsky.

[60] A daughter was born on April 12.

[61] Louise Rorimer, Louise Dushkin's mother. James Rorimer, onetime director of the Metropolitan Museum of Art in New York City, was Samuel Dushkin's brother-in-law.

[62] For the text, see *S.P.D.*, p. 74. (The journal is misidentified in *S.P.D.*)

I embrace you, my dear Sam, very cordially, you and Louise.

Always your

STRAVINSKY TO DUSHKIN

1260 N. Wetherly Drive
Hollywood 46, Calif.
My dear Sam,   *December 29, 1941*[63]

How kind of you to occupy yourself with the elephants and with the polka that Balanchine would like me to write for those respectable quadrupeds. In a telephone conversation with him (more than a month ago) I told him that to accept any commission at this time would be difficult, since I am preparing a rather important piece—it will be twice the size of the *Dumbarton Oaks* Concerto—for the end of February. *Danses concertantes* is the title, and the work employs 24–25 instruments. I will conduct the premiere on February 22, here in Hollywood, with the Werner Janssen chamber orchestra, which seems to be quite a good ensemble of about forty players.

I have heard nothing from Balanchine since his telephone call. I also told him that if he was not in a great hurry, I could undertake to do this composition in March; that he should give me the time; that the polka must not be long; and that he would have to see that I am paid very well. Why is Balanchine once again without my address? What has happened to him?

In a week we go to San Francisco, where I conduct my Symphony (and the Divertimento, *Firebird* Suite, and my "Star-Spangled Banner") on the 9th and 10th. Will you ever hear this Symphony? You missed the only opportunity last year, in Boston.

Speaking of Boston, Koussevitzky invited me to Tanglewood for the months of July and August 1942, including an appearance with his orchestra in the same period. I will work with a small group of students (young composers), as I have been working here since last April with a single composer[64] (who is far from young, but who tries to acquire good manners in composition by watching how I rewrite his symphony from top to bottom).

I think this is sufficient for today. I still have many things to do. I embrace you affectionately, my dear Sam, and I wish all three of you a Happy New Year.

---

[63] Dushkin had written to Stravinsky on December 24: "About eight days ago a man telephoned me saying, 'I am Mr. Balanchine's manager. Can you give me Stravinsky's address? Mr. Balanchine wishes to get in touch with him.' . . . Two or three days ago, in Town Hall, Lincoln Kirstein approached me and said, 'I saw Mr. North recently. He is the manager of the Ringling Brothers Circus and he wishes Balanchine to do a polka for the elephants and Stravinsky to write the music.' "
[64] Ernest Anderson. See *S.P.D.*, p. 359.

COCTEAU, BALANCHINE,

AND JEU DE CARTES

On August 11, 1935, Nicolas Nabokov wrote to Stravinsky from Kolbsheim (Lower Rhine):

Dear Igor Fyodorovich,

I am here in Europe for a few weeks and will be passing through Paris around the 26th or 27th on my way to Le Havre. I would like very, very much to see you in Paris. Balanchivadze has asked me to speak with you about the ballet . . . as well as to find out what you think of his proposition. [*Original in Russian*]

Stravinsky's papers do not indicate whether or not any meeting took place, or even if he answered the note, and Nabokov's autobiography, Bagazh, *makes no mention of his letter. While in Paris, Nabokov may well have discussed Balanchine's proposition with G. G. Païchadze, however, since Stravinsky mentions this publisher in a letter to Balanchine.*

On September 20, 1935, Jean Cocteau wrote to Stravinsky from an undisclosed address near Dijon:

My very dear Igor,

A friend who goes back and forth [to Paris] looks after my mail, while I am completing a large decorative work near Dijon. Immediately after this I must survey the work at St.-Mandrier.

What I must tell you is that I consider your genius to be infallible. Whatever your mind conceives, whatever you decide, the result can only be marvelous. Change my text [as you see fit]. Simply to work together with you is the recompense for my labors. Deal with Abramovich as if you had consulted me. I approve everything in advance in both areas, art and business.

In case I must leave here, write to me in care of the hotel, as intermediary.

> Hotel Vuillemont
> 15, rue Boissy d'Anglas
> Paris

I embrace you, I love you, and I ask you to tell Catherine how much my heart wants her to be able, finally, to live with all of you.

Your Jean

None of the two dozen Cocteau biographies consulted sheds any light on this collaboration or mentions his work near Dijon and at St.-Mandrier (near Toulon) or his agent Abramovich. The reference to the return of Stravinsky's wife (from Sancellemoz to her family in Paris), which took place on September 11, suggests that the composer had written to Cocteau at the end of August or in early September.

That Cocteau's text, whatever it may have been, was in any way related to the ballet that was to become Jeu de cartes is mere speculation, except that Stravinsky wanted Cocteau to write a scenario, and ten months later, even after a third or more of the music had been composed, appealed to him for help. Another note from Cocteau to Stravinsky, July 14, 1936—shortly after the composer's return from a South American tour, the poet's from a world tour—promises a meeting soon. This must have taken place on or after July 23, when Catherine Stravinsky wrote to her husband: "I hope that you can get Cocteau to fix up your scenario and think up what is missing." When nothing came of the discussion with Cocteau, Stravinsky turned to Nikita Malayev, a friend of Soulima Stravinsky. Soulima wrote to his father from Montredon: "Malayev is terribly excited at the idea of helping you, and if you need him immediately, he will leave for Paris right away. He awaits your letter and will do whatever you decide." But the prospect of this collaboration alarmed Catherine: "Is Malayev qualified for that kind of work?" she wrote. (July 29, 1936) Nevertheless, Stravinsky telegraphed Malayev in Marseille on August 13, and he arrived in Paris on the following Thursday.

In an interview in Le Jour, March 4, 1938, Stravinsky recalled that the card-game subject of the ballet had come to him while he was riding in a fiacre, but he did not reveal when this had happened. In other memoirs, he says that the motif with which each of the three parts, or deals, begins, composed December 2, 1935, was associated in his mind with gambling casinos in German spas. In any case, Stravinsky enjoyed playing poker, and the choice of theme would have been natural for him. No doubt the "definite and fully intelligible subject" with "some light intrigue" mentioned in his letter to Balanchine of June 30, 1936 (see below), refers to a card-game plot, and by this date Stravinsky could have asked Cocteau to provide no more than a variant on the subject. But what was the text that Cocteau had sent in September 1935, before Jeu de cartes had taken shape in the composer's mind? What did Stravinsky ask Cocteau to do? And how did Stravinsky refuse Cocteau's collaboration, after having requested it?

On November 25, 1935, Stravinsky wrote to Balanchine,[1] at 400 East Fifty-seventh Street, New York:

---

[1] This seems to be the first letter from Stravinsky to Balanchine after the latter's note to the composer following the first series of performances of *Apollo* in Paris and London in 1928. ("Dear Igor Fyodorovich, I consider it my duty to tell you about the success of *Apollo*. All of the performances, with a single exception, went brilliantly. Lifar, as always, [?]. I hope that in the next season the public, en masse, gets a chance to

Dear friend,

Here is the letter that you asked me to send through Païchadze to confirm your authority in the production of *Apollo*. I do this gladly and with confidence that you will be able to meet my musical requirements.

Païchadze also told me about the proposal of your company to commission a classical ballet from me. The idea is most appealing, but I must warn you that if the project is to be realized, I must be notified immediately so that I may begin work as soon as possible and make appropriate arrangements for other people to assume my other responsibilities.

For various reasons, most of them of a personal, familial nature, I have decided to cancel my trip to North America [in 1936], especially since I will be going to Argentina in May. Owing to this last trip, as well as to a whole series of European concerts, I would like to have now, or very soon, some precise dates for your project, to which I might then devote the remaining free months of the next year.

If I begin work sometime in the near future, you could expect to have the piano score of the ballet by next fall.

I am prepared to negotiate my terms with you as soon as I receive a reply to this letter. In the meantime, dear friend, I send you sincere and warm regards.

Yours,   I. Str.

Stravinsky began work exactly a week later. Then, on January 4, 1936, he cabled to Samuel Dushkin in New York: "Balanchine asks Païchadze renew proposition compose ballet. Ask discreetly reasons for silence since he wrote November accepting in principle. Reply, time pressing." Dushkin answered on January 7 that "Balanchine is so eager to have a ballet from you that he plans to earn the money from the Ziegfeld Follies in order to pay you."

Catherine Stravinsky wrote to her husband from Sancellemoz on January 17: "I am so happy when I think about your present composition; I liked what you played for me immensely." How much of the score she could have heard before leaving Paris a day or two earlier is difficult to determine, since the only date in the sketchbook—April 7–8, next to the music at 45—marks the beginning of the two-month South American interruption. By that time much of the First Deal was ready, part of the Second (including the theme and some of the variations and Coda), and bits of the Third, among them sketches for the music at 193. Meanwhile, Balanchine wrote to Stravinsky on February 29:

Dear Igor Fyodorovich,

Please excuse me for not answering your letter right away. I still have not entirely clarified the question of the *Apollo* production or of the new ballet we are

---

enjoy this work and give it the appreciation it deserves. Very respectfully yours, G. Balanchivadze.")

planning, and I did not want to pester you prematurely. Apparently you did not receive my postcard thanking you for your letter. The suggestions you made were very helpful to me in the production of the ballet.

As soon as something more definite is established between my partners and the directors of the Metropolitan Opera, I will immediately write you a detailed letter about our plans. For now, I am genuinely glad that you have been so receptive to our idea. My letter will probably be written in French, since I would like to share its contents with my colleagues.

Once again, I thank you very much for your kind letter and valuable suggestions, and beg your forgiveness for my delay in replying.

Most respectfully yours,   G. Balanchine

Stravinsky was back in Paris in June, and Balanchine wrote again, on the 11th:

I will make every effort to raise the money needed. . . . I like the idea of a classical ballet with a small orchestra, which would make the ballet easier to perform on tour. But I would not want the work to be strictly entertaining in character. I have been entertaining here [New York] for two years already, and now everyone has begun to copy me. That is why it would be very good to have a fantastical subject. . . . Do you remember Andersen's tale "The Flowered Ball"?

Stravinsky answered on June 30, indicating for the first time that he had a subject in mind:

I have just returned from South America and found your letter of June 11. Thank you, dear friend, for your good and kind words. My wife's health is better, thank goodness, but the scars [on her lungs] are not yet healed.

In regard to the ballet that I am preparing for next season, I must tell you that I have never before composed ballet music without knowing the subject beforehand or having done a preliminary examination of the sequence of episodes of action, consistency, and structure. This is absolutely essential for the general musical structure, and I was therefore surprised by your proposal of Andersen. In addition, let me assure you that . . . the ballet I am in the process of composing is not a "divertissement," at least not in the sense against which you warn me. My ballet has a definite and fully intelligible subject with some light intrigue. A normal orchestra is required, a few solo male and female dancers, a single set, and some simple costumes for effect. The length of the piece is between 20 and 25 minutes. The ballet must be produced in the classical style.

I agree to grant performance rights to your company for one year, under the following terms: (1) a payment of $3,000 to me for the world premiere; (2) a guarantee of a minimum of five performances, at $100 each—this is for royalties and rental of the score; (3) a payment of $700 to me for each of the first three performances that I conduct, i.e., a total of $2,100; (4) payment to my son Theodore (who has designed the set and costumes) of $500 for reproduction rights.

I continue the composition of the ballet, which should be finished by the fall, when I will prepare the piano part and begin extracting the orchestra parts.

I am sending this letter on the *Queen Mary,* which leaves Le Havre tomorrow. With sincere regards.

Devotedly yours,   I. Str.

On August 2, Samuel Dushkin transmitted the American Ballet's answers to Stravinsky's terms:

My dear Igor Fyodorovich,

. . . I had two long conversations with Warburg[2] and Balanchine, and I would like to advise you to accept their offer. They noted three difficulties:

1. Theodore—the union here forbids the collaboration of an artist who is not a member. The same problem arose with Tchelichev. . . .

2. Warburg cannot guarantee that you will conduct three performances, because the Stravinsky evening would take place at the Metropolitan on Tuesday, necessarily, since there is no opera then. . . .

3. [Warburg and Balanchine] cannot promise you $100 a performance five times because there may not be five performances. . . . I suggested that they offer you $5,000 for performance rights for one year, with you conducting two performances, since in this case you would have the $5,000 even if you did not conduct. Warburg and Balanchine accepted this. . . .

Stravinsky answered on August 12:

My dear Samsky,

Thank you for your nice and careful letter. Also thanks for taking my interests to heart; I am very touched. I will try to be as brief as possible in replying to you about the new proposals, which is to say to the counterproposals that you very clearly set forth in the postscript of your letter of August 2.

I am in agreement to give the American Ballet my new ballet (the title will be established later) for the duration of one year beginning at the date of delivery of the orchestra parts (approximately toward the end of 1936). I give to this

---

[2] Edward M. M. Warburg, the banker and Harvard classmate of Lincoln Kirstein who commissioned the ballet and served as "director" of the American Ballet. In some marginal comments on Edwin Evans's "analytical notes" for *Jeu de cartes,* Stravinsky denies that the work *was* commissioned. "Completely false," he writes, striking out the word in Evans's text. "I simply sold the performance rights for the period of a year and for America, without exclusivity."

company the right of theatrical dance performances according to my scenic and musical directions for an unlimited number of performances strictly within the indicated period of the year. After this time the company must return the orchestra parts and piano reduction to me. If the company should wish to continue to give the ballet after the stated period, the company must advise me a month in advance. This extension will be subject to a new contract between the American Ballet and my publisher, the latter in the event that my ballet will have been published. The proposed payment of $100 per performance will serve as a basis for the negotiations in question. In addition, I declare myself to be in agreement to give my ballet for the coming year (1937) for the proposed sum of $5,000, but with absolutely no deduction for taxes. The payment will be made in three installments: the first on signing the contract, the second on receipt of the piano score, the third on receipt of the orchestra parts. The agreement for said ballet is for the territory of the United States only, and, I repeat, for one year only and exclusively for staging. Exploitation by the company does not include the right of radio transmission or the right of retrocession. I consent, in addition, to conduct, without a supplementary fee, the first or the first two performances of the new ballet, if my presence in the United States so permits.

A few days later, Stravinsky sent part of the music to his publisher, Willy Strecker (not to Païchadze: the Edition Russe de Musique was scarcely functioning by this date), whose positive response provoked a telegram: "Very happy you are so enthusiastic about my new ballet." (August 22) Strecker was less pleased about plans for the staging. As he wrote to Stravinsky:

With an American Ballet tour, you might . . . spoil the chance of your ballet's having the great artistic impact on which I was counting. I could secure the premiere in Hamburg, Frankfurt, or Dresden, then approach the Staatsoper in Berlin (if they would guarantee to use the right collaborators). I would much prefer to see the German premiere take place in the provinces than in Berlin, to gain experience before it reaches the capital. But if the American Ballet company tours Germany presenting your work, possibly with a bad orchestra and insufficient rehearsals, then all future possibilities are ruined. My feeling is that the Americans should decide which cities they wish to reserve in Europe outside of Germany.

But the company that had commissioned the ballet lacked the resources for more than two performances, let alone a European tour. On September 16, Warburg sent a letter of agreement to Stravinsky, which the composer returned on October 6, with a few changes concerning possible additional performances. Stravinsky received the revised contract on October 22 and forwarded it the same day to Strecker for his approval. Later, on January 19, 1937, after Stravinsky's arrival in New York, Warburg revised the financial terms to the extent of paying a per diem to Stravinsky during the rehearsal period.

Stravinsky must have decided on the title of his ballet in late September or early October. In any case, he refers to the piece by name in a letter to Strecker, October 22:

Yesterday I saw Kahn[3] and examined his [piano] reduction of the first tableau (First Deal). . . . A good job, but much too complicated. I pointed out . . . numerous passages that had to be redone. He argued that these changes would require supplementary hours of work, but I paid no attention, since he agreed to do the piano score [to my satisfaction]. . . . The ballet master and the piano accompanist are currently in need of it. I enclose the contract signed by Warburg, but not initialed by him. I suppose he was distracted. But I am not anxious, because [the] Morgan [Bank] informs me that the [first] installment has arrived.

On December 2, the day before he finished the composition, Stravinsky sent Strecker

the synopsis of the action in French and the scenario in French and English, to be translated into German, in case you need them for the piano score and orchestra score. If you also need the English translation of the synopsis, let me know, and I will send you a copy. The English is very well done (with Old English verses for the epilogue by La Fontaine), but, unfortunately, I do not have a single copy.

In fact, the English is very badly done, except for the La Fontaine, and does not say the same things as the French, which states that the work was "inspired" by a game of poker, whereas the English says that the ballet represents an actual poker game. On December 5, Strecker acknowledged the receipt of both texts and suggested that while the synopsis could be printed

in the front of the piano arrangement and the score, the whole scenario should be offered only to theatres, since it is not feasible to print so many pages of text along with the music. This text is hardly of any concern to the amateur and might even be a disadvantage in concert performances of the work.

In truth, the scenario is a straitjacket for the choreographer, describing the action corresponding to the music throughout, positioning the dancers, and even prescribing the colors of their costumes. When Balanchine read, for example, that "during the five measures of 33, the Joker leaves the stage, still threatening

---

[3] Erich Itor Kahn (1905–56), composer and pianist, transcribed almost the whole of *Jeu de cartes* (to 183), but received no credit for his work on the published piano score. On October 27, Strecker wrote to Stravinsky: "As soon as Kahn does part of the piano arrangement, please send it . . . immediately."

his opponents," the great choreographer must have felt like leaving the stage as well.

It is difficult to believe that Stravinsky could have accepted this inflexible script, copies of which survive in his papers, with numerous changes in Malayev's hand. Yet Stravinsky defended the scenario to Strecker, who wisely saw that it would constitute a major obstacle to stage performances. Stravinsky wrote to Strecker, December 10, 1936:

The ballet is about 20 minutes long. I took my verses for the synopsis of *Jeu de cartes* from La Fontaine's fable "Les Loups et les brebis." Try to find an Old German translation of La Fontaine of the same type as the English one. That is better than attempting to make a modern translation. . . . The string section . . . should consist of twelve first violins, ten seconds, eight violas, six cellos, six basses.

On the same day, Strecker wrote to Stravinsky that "the [German] title should be Das Kartenspiel: *this is better and does not sound translated." Two days later, Strecker returned to the question of the synopsis:*

I have had more of a chance to become acquainted with the work and am enchanted with the music all the way down to the seventh chord at the end. But I have reservations about printing the synopsis even at the beginning of the piano score. So far as I know, neither *Petrushka* nor *Firebird* includes a synopsis. With a little imagination, one can grasp the approximate nature of the subject from the cover illustration. Furthermore, changes will quite possibly occur during the actual collaboration with the ballet master, and if another choreographic solution were more effective, this first interpretation would then be an obstacle. . . . I therefore propose either to omit the argument of the ballet or to print it in a limited number of copies.

On the day before sailing on the S.S. *Normandie for New York, Stravinsky played* Jeu de cartes *for Vera Sudeikina. Two days before that, on December 15, he had written to Strecker:*

I am not entirely in agreement with you about the synopsis. The one I sent you (in French and English) is the summary of my libretto, and as such it cannot be changed. What might undergo changes eventually, and this is difficult to foresee at the moment, is the scenario, but we had decided not to publish this in either the piano or orchestra score. How do you expect me to dispense with the few lines of the synopsis, in which my libretto is so effectively condensed, and which, with those beautiful verses from La Fontaine, I consider a successful [introduction] ? Furthermore, dear friend, you are making an error when you say that *Petrushka* has no synopsis. *Petrushka, Apollo,* and *Le Baiser de la fée* all have synopses in the piano scores, to guide stage directors, and this one cannot be omitted. I ask you to publish it, as agreed, in the piano score and, to complete the German text, to find a good translation (from the right period) of the La Fontaine verses. I will send all of these back with the corrected proofs of the orchestra score.

Writing to Strecker from Los Angeles in early March 1937, Stravinsky affirms that he wants the text of the "Vorwort" *(i.e., the synopsis) as well as that of* "mon argument," *ending with the excerpt from La Fontaine, to be published. He also expresses a doubt that Klemperer, "whom I see here every day," could convince his board of directors to pay a large sum for a concert performance.*

The story of the Jeu de cartes *rehearsals has been told elsewhere.[4] It will suffice to add that two musicians involved in the preparations later became well known: William Schuman, who received $81.20 from Stravinsky for proofreading the orchestra parts, and Leo Smit, who was the rehearsal pianist. Back in Paris, Stravinsky wrote to Strecker:*

I have clippings that my agent, Mr. R. Copley, wanted me to give you. The press in New York was rather inconsequential, because newspapers there never send music critics to the ballet, and of course these gentlemen, who loathe music, and my music in particular, were delighted to spend an evening in the country instead. The audience filled the enormous hall of the Metropolitan twice and demonstrated great enthusiasm for my work. I did not like the decor and the costumes,[5] but I deeply admired Balanchine's dances. [May 20, 1937]

Long before the premiere, Stravinsky had expressed his delight in Balanchine's choreography. ("Beveridge [Webster] told me that you were pleased with Balanchine's work," Soulima Stravinsky wrote to his father before the performance.) Soon after the premiere on April 27, in a letter to Warburg, Stravinsky singled out "the wonderful direction of Mr. Balanchine." (May 3) When the dancer Theodore Koslov wrote from Los Angeles on July 28, asking Stravinsky for permission to choreograph Jeu de cartes, *since "the work can be approached entirely differently from the way it was done by the American Ballet," he answered that the American Ballet had exclusivity until January 1, 1938, and that "I will be very glad if [your] results are as successful as Balanchine's and mine."[6] (August 19)*

---

[4] Lincoln Kirstein's now-classic description of Stravinsky at the rehearsals is reprinted in Minna Lederman, *Stravinsky in the Theater* (New York, 1949), pp. 136–40.

[5] By Irene Sharaff.

[6] Stravinsky had known "dear Fyodor Mikhailovich" Koslov, as the letter begins, since early Diaghilev days, and the composer offered "to send models to give you an idea of how I conceive of the production." Koslov, who was well known as a painter, lived in Woodstock, New York, in his final years and was a friend there of Serge Sudeikin. When Koslov died in 1956, his effects included masks and costumes from the original production of *Le Sacre du printemps*.

*The last phrase accounts for Stravinsky's disavowal of the scenario. He
and Balanchine must surely have jettisoned it and, as was to become their
practice, choreographed the ballet during rehearsals. After the premiere, in a
complete reversal, Stravinsky wrote to Warburg:*

In the program of the premiere of *The Card Game*, I find the following sentence: "Libretto in collaboration with N. Malayev." I do not know how this sentence found its way into the program; it is quite incorrect and I must positively insist that it be omitted from future programs. Also, in the program annotations of *The Card Game*, the whole first paragraph . . . is likewise incorrect. It mentions, again quite unnecessarily, the name Malayev.[7] [*Original in English*]

The first concert performance of Jeu de cartes *took place in Venice, September
14, 1937,[8] conducted by Stravinsky, who then led the piece in London, Amsterdam, Naples, and Paris. He wrote to Strecker from Paris on October 22:*

The performance and the [audience] reception in London were brilliant. Only the press was incompetent and malevolent, as usual, but without affecting the audience's opinion in the slightest; the day after the reviews appeared, I was given a veritable ovation [at the second performance]. . . .

One hour before I received your letter, P. Monteux paid me a visit and expressed his desire to conduct the Paris premiere. . . . Too late now, though; in ten days he leaves for San Francisco, where he plans to include it in his programs. Actually, I am glad that it worked out this way, because I intended to give the [Paris] premiere myself; furthermore, I will not be going to America this year, and I would not like to deprive [Monteux] of the pleasure of presenting one of my new works.

Strecker replied on October 26:

I have reserved the Paris premiere for you. . . . Tomorrow evening (Wednesday), Ansermet's radio concert will be broadcast. Perhaps you will be able to tune in to it. The next concert performance in Germany is scheduled for November 15 in Munich, under Clemens Krauss.

*Stravinsky's experience with the piece in Naples was painful. He reported to
Strecker on November 7:*

---

[7] On December 6, 1937, Malayev signed a statement, at Stravinsky's request: "I was reimbursed by Mr. Igor Stravinsky for the work that I did in connection with the ballet *Jeu de cartes,* and I renounce all author's rights."

[8] On September 15, Stravinsky and Vera Sudeikina had gone from Venice to Rome for a day, then to Positano, where the weather was poor. After a few days, and a trip with the Hindemiths to Paestum, Stravinsky returned to Paris by way of Rome—where he dined at Ranieri's on the same evening as von Ribbentrop; visitors to the restaurant are still shown the two signatures on the same page of the guest book.

As I had anticipated, the very uncultivated Naples audience was too stunned by *Jeu de cartes* to react consciously. . . . In contrast, the Tchaikovsky Symphony (Third), the Cherubini overture (*Anacreon*), and *Petrushka* triumphed. The musicians, a mixture of conservatory youths and their professors, lacked all discipline and experience; in consequence, the orchestra, though not without a few redeeming elements, was very difficult to conduct, and it took a lot out of me to give a decent performance. Naturally, the critics, incompetent as always and blatantly hostile, did not have the courtesy even to mention the performance.

Stravinsky was not to see Jeu de cartes *staged in France. He wrote to Strecker, January 24, 1938:*

I just saw [Jacques] Rouché . . . and declined his offer to mount *Jeu de cartes* [at the Opéra], for the reason that he wants Lifar, in whose choreographic creations I have no interest. I await a better opportunity. It really would be a pity to spoil something as subtle as *Jeu de cartes* because of him. I hope that this work will not have to wait twenty-seven years before seeing the footlights of the Opéra.

IV

CORRESPONDENCE WITH

1952 ~ 1967

ERNST KRENEK

ERNST KRENEK TO STRAVINSKY[1]

Cher maître,

2177 *Argyle Avenue*
Los Angeles
June 17, 1952

A little late, I am afraid, but nevertheless from the bottom of my heart: a million good wishes, and many happy returns.

As always, devotedly yours,

Ernst Krenek

STRAVINSKY TO KRENEK

Dear Krenek,

Los Angeles
[November 1952][2]

Many thanks for your thoughts.

Cordially,   I. Stravinsky

---

[1] English is the original language of all the correspondence, except where indicated. Krenek (b. 1900) had visited Stravinsky in Nice in 1925, but the two composers seem not to have met again between that time and an ISCM concert in Los Angeles around 1950.

From 1955 to the early part of 1960, nearly all of Krenek's letters were addressed to the present writer, but they were intended for Stravinsky as well and are included here as a record of Stravinsky's relationship with the only composer in the Los Angeles area who interested him. (Stravinsky was on friendly terms socially with Mario Castelnuovo-Tedesco, Erich Korngold, Eric Zeisl, Miklos Rosza, and others, but music did not enter into these associations.) Stravinsky was present at every meeting, dinner, concert, and recording session that Krenek mentions, and Krenek's comments on his *Sestina* and other pieces were avidly read by Stravinsky. Both as a theorist of serial techniques and a scholar of Renaissance music from Ockeghem to Monteverdi, Krenek exercised an influence on Stravinsky that heretofore has not been acknowledged. See Stravinsky's description of Krenek in *Dialogues and a Diary* (New York, 1963), pp. 51–3.

[2] On September 27, 1953, after dinner at the Stravinskys', Krenek played recordings of his Seventh Quartet, his Concerto for piano, violin, and thirteen instruments, and his *Lamentations of Jeremiah*, this last in a fine performance by the Hamline chorus. Stravinsky was much impressed by all of the music, but especially by the *Lamentations*.

KRENEK TO STRAVINSKY

2177 *Argyle Avenue*
Los Angeles
December 22, 1953

Dear master and friend,

Your beautiful Christmas present moved me deeply. It was very good of you to think of me on this occasion in so generous a manner.

Please allow me to present you with a little score of mine which I wrote three years ago for the Radio Italiana.[3] It has a few intricate touches which might interest you. A little later I shall take the liberty of sending you a brief explanation and analysis, which unfortunately is not yet ready at this moment. We wish you and Mrs. Stravinsky a Blessed Christmas and a Happy New Year.

As always, devotedly yours,

Ernst Krenek

Gladstone Hotel
New York
January 7, 1954
[Telegram]

STRAVINSKY TO KRENEK

Your wonderful present and letter have just reached me here during my continuous touring. Thank you heartily. Hope you will let me have your analysis when back home. Best wishes and greetings to you both.   Igor Stravinsky

KRENEK TO ROBERT CRAFT

May 22, 1955

Dear Bob,

I wanted very much to talk to you after yesterday's rehearsal at Ojai, but I knew you were rushed with the afternoon concert coming up on the heels of your exhausting rehearsal, and we had to return to Los Angeles without delay.

You may guess that I, of course, find the work by Monteverdi a masterpiece of extraordinary proportions.[4] I was somewhat acquainted with it, but had not studied it closely, nor did I ever hear it. And I am full of admiration [for] this perfectly magnificent choir which, in my opinion, was as well prepared as anybody could wish.[5] The soloists, too, were, on the whole, up to your and Monteverdi's demands, which is saying a great deal.[6] The instrumental ensemble lived up to the customary Los Angeles pattern of the flesh being willing but the spirit sometimes weak (—or is it the other way around . . . ?). Just the same, the effect was overwhelming and the experience something I shall not forget soon.

---

[3] *Parvula corona musicalis.* The score is dedicated "To Igor Stravinsky and Mrs. Stravinsky with all good wishes for Christmas 1953 and a Happy New Year 1954 Ernst Krenek." This work had a considerable influence on Stravinsky.

[4] *Vespro della Beata Vergine* (1610).

[5] The Pomona College Chorus conducted by William Russell.

[6] Marilyn Horne was the soloist in *Nigra sum.*

There are many questions I should very much like to discuss with you if you find time for it: for instance, the relation of the Redlich adaptation to the Malipiero edition, which *prima facie* one would assume to be a sort of "original," and your decision to rearrange the whole thing the way you did. Also: where did the two pieces come from which were MSS? I was unable to check quickly whether they are in the Redlich score at all, and in what shape, if so. Finally, what is uppermost in my mind is the question of the rhythmic and metric style of the interpretation with reference to the significance of the bar lines. I could go on right here blossoming out in a whole essay on this point, especially if I had a score—but I think it would be better to talk about these problems if you have time for it. Will you call me one of these days? The number is still Hollywood 5-6087.

Once more, compliments and congratulations, and all the best, yours,

Ernst

KRENEK TO STRAVINSKY

2177 Argyle Avenue
Los Angeles
June 5, 1955

Cher ami,

It seems that in English, unlike French, there is no distinction between *"théologal"* and *"théologique."*

I have consulted several religious encyclopedias, and in all of them faith, hope, and charity are listed as "theological virtues." This is all I could find out.

Once again, many thanks for the beautiful evening that we recently had at your home. We hope to see you here with us in July.[7]

All the best, as always, affectionately your friend,

Ernst Krenek

KRENEK TO IGOR AND VERA STRAVINSKY

Cologne
December 12, 1955
[Postcard]

1260 North Wetherly Drive

Frohe Weihnachten und viel Glück im Neuen Jahre, and may God bless you. So far we have had a very nice, though naturally extremely busy time. Perhaps we might see you here in Europe before we go back to America (next July).

All the best, as always, from both of us, affectionately,

Ernst Krenek

---

[7] This sentence is in German in the original.

KRENEK TO CRAFT   *March 4, 1957*

Dear Bob,

I understand that Pierre Boulez will be in this area for some part of next week, and I assume you will be in close contact with him. Since we should very much like to see him and possibly to contribute to making his visit pleasant, I would appreciate if you would call me as soon as possible so that we may see what arrangements can be made. I am writing to you since I don't know how to reach you by telephone.

All the best, until soon, as ever yours,

Ernst Krenek

KRENEK TO CRAFT   *Princeton University*
                                                        Princeton, New Jersey
Dear Bob,   *May 6, 1957*

I should like to congratulate you upon the Webern album. I was lucky enough to get a copy—it seems they are selling rapidly. So far I have played only the Symphony, which I found not only very clear, but also intense and sinewy, in welcome contrast to the pseudo-ethereal style that has already become a kind of convention for Webern's music. I am eagerly looking forward to playing the whole set.

Your study on Webern is excellent in its fresh approach to a subject which in my opinion those who were too close to it have so far found too touchy to deal with intelligently.

A tiny footnote to the translation of the poetry (who made it?): in the first poem on p. 23, *"der Nagerlstock"* is not "the wanderer's cane," and no Tannhäuser-miracle is hinted at. *"Nagerl"* is Austrian for *"Nelke,"* which is "carnation." I was always intrigued by this association of the carnation flower with *"Nagel"* (nail), because it also exists in English, though not with reference to the flower, but to the spice, which is called "cloves," this obviously being derived from the Latin *"clovis"* (nail). The spice actually looks like little nails.

My seminars are going well. I am holding forth on serial music—what else? In New York I heard a recital by David Tudor and a four-piano display of "randomized" music (as Milton[8] calls it). This I could do without, I am afraid.

I hope very much we will see you at our house when I return (end of May). Please give my respects to the master.

All the best, as always,

Ernst

---

[8] Milton Babbitt (b. 1916), the composer and theorist.

KRENEK TO CRAFT   *June 3, 1957*

Dear Bob,

Here is my attempt at translating those lines:[9]

> Enlighten us, God of mercies, by the sevenfold grace of the Paraclete so
> that, through it, liberated from the darkness of sin, we may partake of the
> glory of life.

The only word I am not sure of without the aid of a dictionary is *"delic-
torum."* I have just guessed at its meaning. Within a few days I might be able to
check on it, if you can wait that long.

In the tradition of the Church, the Holy Ghost has always been associated
with the figure "seven" (this is, by the way, why in my electronic piece I have
based the music of the "Spirit" on a seven-tone pattern). The source of it seems
to be Isaiah XI, 2, where the "seven gifts" are attributed to the Spirit of the
Lord.

All the best from both of us,

                                                    Ernst

KRENEK TO CRAFT   *November 21, 1957*

Dear Bob,

I hear that you are back in town from your adventures and I hope to see you
sometime soon and to get a first-hand report on your observations. It is good to
have you around again.

You may have heard that we had a performance of my piece for cello and
chamber orchestra, of which I was entirely satisfied. I had excellent cooperation
by the group of musicians so that everything went very smoothly. The soloist
was remarkable in every respect.

Right now I have a little problem in which I should be much obliged for
your advice. Perhaps you have heard about it from Paul Fromm, who wrote me
that he was in correspondence with you. The point is this: I wrote a piece for
voice and instrumental ensemble, commissioned by the Fromm Foundation. I
am expected to conduct it in New York on March 9. The problem is to find a
singer for this piece.

Paul Fromm wanted to engage Patricia Neway, but she found that the
piece was beyond the range of her voice and that she could not do it. In his letter of yesterday he suggested that I get in touch with you for advice. He thinks
of Marni Nixon, and so did I in the first place. I found her work in your Webern
recordings excellent, and I feel that she would be a good choice for my piece.

---

[9] The translation is of one of the Gesualdo Sacrae Cantiones.

But I was a little discouraged when I heard from Lawrence[10] that she was not any longer interested in this type of music since she apparently wanted to establish herself as an interpreter of more conventional stuff.

My question at this point is whether you think this to be true to such an extent that it would not be worth the effort to approach her in this project, and if this were the case, whether you would know of anybody else in this area who might qualify for the world premiere of a very exacting work in New York. The performance is to be followed immediately by a recording for Columbia.

The work is called *Sestina*. I wrote the poem myself (in German) according to the pattern used by Petrarca, Dante, and their predecessors in the Provençal School of the twelfth century. In it I have musically tried my own brand of "total determination," and the piece surely presents a number of unusual problems. The item which will interest any singer in the first place is the range. It goes from [low G] to [high D]. In other words it takes a singer who can do *Herzgewächse* and is not bothered by problems of intonation no matter what happens around her. The piece will take 15 minutes.

Would you be so good as to give us "the benefit of your thought" on this problem (as the Madison Avenue jargon has it . . .)? Please do so as soon as you can, for time is running short, as it always does. Will you call me at Florida 3-1378? Sunday noon would be a very good time, or Monday morning, or 6 p.m.

Thank you ever so much—and I hope to see you soon. All the best, as always,

Ernst

P.S. Please give our love to the Stravinskys.

KRENEK TO CRAFT   *November 29, 1957*

Dear Bob,

Unfortunately the plan of having Marni do my piece in New York has gone awry. I talked to her after I had conversed with you, and she seemed to be very eager to do it. I immediately sent a wire to Paul Fromm advising him to engage her. About the time he must have had the wire, I received a special delivery letter from him from which it transpired that he had instructed Milton Babbitt to engage Bethany Beardslee if she wanted to do it. I immediately called [Fromm] in Chicago to stop this move, but it was too late. The only comfort to be derived from a slightly embarrassing situation is that Fromm's agents are very efficient indeed and that whoever is asked to do my piece seems to jump at the occasion without a moment's hesitation. I told Fromm that it would be for him to explain things to Marni, which he did immediately by telegram. He called me right away and wept a little on my shoulder. I feel sorry for her because it would have

---

[10] Lawrence Morton (b. 1904), then director of the Monday Evening Concerts and the Ojai Festival.

meant a sort of comeback for her and I think she would have done a very good job, but apart from Paul Fromm's impatience which caused the transcontinental signals to get mixed up, it is unfortunately somewhat her own fault (that is, someone else's—we know whose), for if there had not been these disconcerting rumors about her changed attitude, I would have approached her much earlier. Well, this is now so much water under the bridge.

I don't know whether she would feel at least slightly compensated if she would be able to do this piece out here. Of course, the glamour of the "first" performance and the Columbia recording would be missing. But apart from what she would feel, I would of course very much like this piece to be done here. Thus I am looking forward with much anticipation to your visit, when I can show you the score and we may talk things over.

Next week all evenings are free, except Saturday (December 7). Thursday night is not too good, but available if necessary.

All this could be talked over by telephone, but I know that you are very rarely at your place, and I hesitate to disturb the peace of the Stravinsky household. So please call me as soon as you can (Fl. 3-1378).

All the best as always yours,

Ernst

KRENEK TO CRAFT   *January 14, 1958*

Dear Bob,

A few days ago I had a lengthy telephone conversation with Paul Fromm through which I learned that you had not gone to New York after all because you had been sick with that damned flu, about which I am sorry. But he told me that in the meantime you had gone to Houston,[11] which pleased me, for apparently you were well again. Now I hear that you are back here and busy with rehearsals, so everything seems to be in good shape.

Paul told me that everything in New York was under control so that I should have no trouble in preparing the *Sestina* when I get there on March 1. He also told me, and this is very important, that if you would plan an L.A. performance of the work we can count on his full cooperation. Would you be good enough to take the matter up with Lawrence [Morton] as soon as possible so that a date could be visualized during the second half of next season when we both will be back from Europe? I feel it would be best to leave the management of this affair to you.

So to Europe, I have written to both Hamburg and Cologne, also regarding the possibility of bringing Marni over there, but so far I have not had any re-

---

[11] Stravinsky had concerts in Houston and Mrs. Stravinsky an exhibition of her paintings, but the present writer did not go with them. The Houston sojourn is described by Paul Horgan in *Encounters with Stravinsky* (New York, 1972), pp. 93–123.

plies. Please keep me posted on whatever may develop on your end. I am negotiating about still other possibilities, but it may take a little more time.

Paul talked to me also about the Princeton project as if it were settled for good.[12] I hope he is right. More power to him. I certainly should be happy to join forces with you at the Ivy League.

At any rate, please talk to Lawrence and let me know what gives. We hope to see you soon. Please give our love to the Stravinskys.

All the best as ever yours,

Ernst

KRENEK TO CRAFT   *January 20, 1958*

Dear Bob,

I am happy to hear that Lawrence wants to put on the *Sestina* next year under your direction. Of course it would be much better if Paul Fromm would not have to help financially in this project, and I agree that this should not be necessary. Certainly some sort of "moral" association with the Fromm Foundation would be mutually helpful. I will call Lawrence and discuss the matter with him.

As to New York, I have asked for 9 rehearsals, one for the 3 wind instruments, one for violin, guitar, piano, one for the two percussion groups and piano, one for piano and voice, one for groups 1 and 2, one for groups 2 and 3, and three for the whole ensemble. This would be in the time between March 3 and 9. Of course, I hope that Milton [Babbitt] will be able to do a little preliminary work, about which I am going to write to him. If you should be able to drop in at some of the sessions, I certainly shall appreciate it.

I too wrote to Cologne and Hamburg about the *Sestina* and Marni and heard from Cologne about the same as you did, that is, that nothing could be decided before a little later. But the man who wrote me mentioned that they were exploring the possibilities for Marni. These outfits are taking on a Pentagon-like texture. (For instance, I've never met Mr. Winkler,[13] who has written to you.) With these octopuses (or octopi, octopodes) one never knows which πούς may have developed in a minor sub-head of dubious competence while you were looking the other way. Anyway, I am watching developments closely— whatever that means.

I know Schmidt-Isserstedt since we studied together in Berlin in 1921 or so, but I'm afraid he is a lazy blockhead.

I shall be happy to get the Gesualdo record. I am playing over the music which you left with me, and it is truly amazing. I'll have to talk to you about a

---

[12] Paul Fromm sponsored a seminar in contemporary music at Princeton in the summer of 1959.

[13] Eric Winkler, of the Westdeutscher Rundfunk in Cologne, was a concert agent for Stravinsky in the early 1950s.

few details, and I should like to know more about the sources of these transcriptions.[14]

I am not sure that I will be able to decipher Bo Nilsson's[15] esoteric runes, but I will try my best to be of assistance to you.

Certainly I want to listen to the Boulez recording sessions, no matter how tedious they might be. Did I read correctly that they will take place on February 4 and 7? Please call me about this and everything else (Florida 3-1378).

All the best from both of us, as ever,

Ernst

P.S. I am glad you found my guitar piece interesting, and that Norman[16] is going to put it in circulation—but where?

KRENEK TO CRAFT   *February 5, 1958*

Dear Bob,

I am sorry that we had to sneak away the other night so suddenly. Gladys has to get up at 7 a.m. these days, and you know how long a drive we have to get out here.

We were not just impressed, but even slightly appalled at the amount of work which you expended during that session.[17] In fact, Gladys worried that you were working yourself to a frazzle, and [was] concerned about your well-being. Well, I am sure you know what you are doing, and I know that being really engaged in a project one can do more than seems humanly possible.

As to the business under consideration, it is difficult for me to distinguish clearly between the problems of the composition and those of its rendition. Off hand, I feel that some of the composer's dynamic specifications remain somewhat theoretical. I wonder whether it is actually possible for the performers to carry out so many dynamic nuances, especially in a fast tempo. Frankly, I am not sure that I was able to make out whether all dynamic prescriptions were carried out completely, in spite of the numerous repetitions. This causes me a slight headache because there are many instances in my *Sestina* in which the same problem has to be faced. I'll know more about it four weeks from now—so we hope. . . . I was also slightly disappointed with the percussion. Most of these "traps" to me seemed to sound very much alike. I believe that this is the fault of the composition—there is simply too much of it, to my taste, at least.

Anyway, it was a most instructive and exhilarating session. Curiously

---

[14] The transcriptions, from the Library of Congress copy of the 1611 score book, were the work of Lawrence Morton and the present writer.

[15] Swedish composer much in avant-garde vogue at the time.

[16] Theodore Norman, Los Angeles musician, performed the guitar parts in works by Schoenberg, Webern, Boulez, and Stravinsky in the 1950s and 1960s.

[17] The first of the two recording sessions of *Le Marteau sans maître*.

enough, the work sounds much less like "Punktmusik" than I thought, and frequently rather "romantic" and "impressionistic"—whatever that may mean, if anything.

I'm sorry I can't be there for the Friday session. But please do let me know as soon as possible when you do the [Stockhausen] *Zeitmasse*. I want to hear that by all means. Also I should very much like to see you at least briefly before you and I go to New York.

All the best, as ever, your friend

Ernst

KRENEK TO CRAFT   *February 10, 1958*

Dear Bob,

Would it be possible for you to let me know as soon as possible the definite date of your Stockhausen recording session? I want to make sure that I don't miss it since I'd like to hear it by all means, and there are a couple of other dates I have to make around that time, so that I should like to be sure of the date as soon as I can. Please call me, would you?

I forgot to tell you that I conferred briefly with Bill Kraft[18] about the Nilsson score, trying to answer some of his questions. As I remember it, some of the problems were: metronome markings. They are indicated on top of the score, and they frequently change from one bar to the next. How to make such changes as from 80 to 82.5 to 67.5 and similar for just one bar, I don't know and I hate to think that this should be my problem. . . . The abbreviation "Hz" means "Hertz," which is the German term for fragments (cycles, i.e. pitches, after the physicist Hertz). In other words, this is how [Nilsson] wants his bongos, or whatever they are, to be tuned. 440 Hz indicates the normal A, and so forth. *"Pedalbecken"* is the sort of cymbals which the jazz-bandits operate by footwork. I imagine that ♫ just means hitting the two cymbals which are mounted one on top of the other together. ♬ then should probably mean hitting another pair of higher pitch. I imagine this will mean as much headache to Craft as footache to Kraft. . . . These are the problems I seem to remember. If you think I may be able to interpret any more of the tricky Eskimo's directions,[19] please ask me about it at the Stockhausen meeting.

Please let me know about this as soon as you can (Fl 3-1378).

All the best, as ever,

Ernst

---

[18] The composer William Kraft (b. 1923) was at this time the leader of the percussion section of the Los Angeles Philharmonic.

[19] Bo Nilsson was born in the Arctic circle.

KRENEK TO CRAFT   *February 14, 1958*[20]

Dear Bob,

Many thanks for your note. If I don't hear from you, we'll be Friday the 21st at 7 p.m. at the same place as the last time to get our time properly measured.[21] I do hope you won't call it off, since I don't want to miss this application of the "roadhouse" [?] treatment by any means. Looking perfunctorily at the score I could see that the problems are staggering. In comparison my *Sestina* is a rather primitive exercise. I am now in the process of putting together a few short pieces for chamber ensemble which I might produce in Darmstadt next fall. They will be perhaps a little more tricky than the *Sestina,* but even then the conductor will have a comprehensive job. I've never believed that outrageous difficulty is a token of superior quality, as some people seem to do.

I am sorry that the "Boo"[22] piece is disappointing. Two years ago his *Frekoenser* was one of the more attractive pieces in Darmstadt. From what you mention about Boulez, I gather that all these people seem to have got caught in the "roadhouse" and don't see how to get out of it. [Stockhausen's] *Gruppen* idea is not even particularly novel—Charles Ives dreamed of several orchestras working away on various hilltops.

What I wanted to ask you is whether anything further has developed in your plan to bring Marni to Europe. Recently I had an inquiry from Radio Cologne whether she was actually coming. This was in connection with a possibility of doing the *Sestina* there, in which case they would perhaps arrange an additional recording session with her. The whole thing may come to naught, since I had previously settled for the European premiere of the *Sestina* at the Berliner Festwochen (end of September) and the date which was offered in Cologne lay before that, so that I could not accept it. But there may be still a change of mind (and dates), and I should like to know what to say about Marni in such a case. Of course, two engagements in Cologne would not be enough for her, but I wondered whether you might have arranged something else in the meantime. Incidentally, in Berlin they want to try for a German singer. I hope we will soon hear whether she can make it. If not, I would recommend Marni, provided she could be sure that she will be going to Europe. So please advise me on what the situation is at this time.

I admire your highly educational envelopes, though I should like to ask those mapmakers how a person looking onto the earth from a point above the North Pole can see objects below the equator. Some problem!

All the best, until soon, as ever,

Ernst

---

[20] Stravinsky gave a party for the Kreneks on February 16, after the premiere of *Sestina.*

[21] This refers to the recording session of *Zeitmasse.*

[22] The first name of Bo Nilsson is pronounced "Boo." The present writer conducted a piece by him in one of the Monday Evening Concerts.

KRENEK TO CRAFT   *March 8, 1958*

Dear Bob,

I am sorry I missed you and your concert here.[23] I'm sure Milton [Babbitt] told you that I had just arrived and had to get a little organized so that I was not quite prepared to sit through this lengthy service. I was equally sorry to hear that the occasion caused you some anguish and disappointment. I hope that by this time the balmy breezes of the Pacific have wafted away your chagrin.

You might be interested in hearing that the *Sestina* so far has gone admirably well (keep fingers crossed). It seems that the piece is much less difficult than it appeared to be. I had separate rehearsals with four different groups, five with combinations of such, and two full rehearsals which took much less than the scheduled time (I cancelled one of the planned rehearsals). In fact, I think that after rehearsing the separate groups singly, two full rehearsals are entirely sufficient. Actually, this style is easier to do than much of the traditional stuff, because there are practically no problems of phrasing, precision being all that is necessary. Once everybody is made to play on time, everything else falls in line (such as there is . . .), continuity, discontinuity (or what have you) being an inevitable result (you might say "chance" result) of the construction. I might say that I am myself amazed at the piece. In a sense, it transcends my own power of perception in that it produces musical situations which I would hardly have thought up had I not somehow blindly relied on the constructive mechanism which I set in motion. Of course, arriving at this and no other mechanism was a soul-searching affair, and it is not easy for me at this point to determine exactly what prompted my choice, for the results at any given point were practically unforeseeable. Saying that an act of faith was involved would probably be an oversimplification which would stand in need of further analysis. For this I am not yet ready by a long shot.

At any rate, I am fortunate in working with a group of excellent musicians who went with me without raising an eyebrow. In fact, we had a wonderful time all the way through. Especially the percussion players, who had to deal with some novel assignments, plunged into it with real enthusiasm. Bethany is doing a marvelous job too. But so will Marni, and I am even now looking forward eagerly to your doing this piece a year from now.

Paul Fromm arrived today, and discussions of the Princeton project are beginning. This is going to take some talking, discussing, maneuvering, organizing, and what not. I'll tell you all about it as soon as I get back to L.A.   Monday and Tuesday I'll record the *Sestina*. Next weekend I'll spend in Princeton. On the 17th I am to give a lecture at Amherst and on the 19th I plan to fly back to L.A. We must get together very soon.

All the best now, as ever yours,

Ernst

P.S. Please give my love to the Stravinskys.

[23] New York. The present writer had conducted a Stravinsky concert (Symphony of

KRENEK TO CRAFT   *April 28, 1958*

Dear Bob,

Here is the map—which looks more involved than it is—by which, as we hope, you will come with the Stravinskys to our place next Saturday.[24] I hope this time there will be no inundation so that you may have smooth sailing. Just the same, allow about 50 minutes driving time.

Looking forward, and good luck, as always,

Ernst

KRENEK TO CRAFT   *May 10, 1958*

Dear Bob,

I have read the Webern papers, and I'll be glad to talk to you about them. They raise a number of points of a more general nature which I should very much like to discuss with you. Please give me a ring (Florida 3-1378, best time about 5:30 p.m.) so that we may make a date for dinner and protracted conversation.

As always yours,

Ernst

KRENEK TO CRAFT   *June 10, 1958*

Dear Bob,

As it turns out, Gregg Smith's concert at the Immaculate Heart College is actually scheduled for Monday night, and I think I'd better be there. I am very sorry about this coincidence and regretfully return the tickets to you.

Please be good enough to let me know if and when there is a sort of dress rehearsal for *Mavra*[25] and the other items on your program and if I would be permitted to attend it. I certainly would love to do so. Please call me at your convenience (5:30 p.m. seems to be the best time).

As ever yours,

Ernst

Psalms, Symphonies of Wind Instruments, etc.) on March 2. The organizers were Lincoln Kirstein and George Balanchine.

[24] The dinner actually took place the next day (Sunday). On May 22, the Kreneks dined at the Stravinskys'. Five days later, Stravinsky wrote to the Burgess Publishing Company in Minneapolis: "Dear Sirs, Dr. Ernst Krenek showed me the two volumes of the Hamline Studies in Musicology published by your company in the 1940s. I am very much interested in acquiring these volumes for my library. Is it still possible to have [them] from you and if not will you tell me please where can I get them."

[25] Stravinsky conducted a staged performance of *Mavra* at Royce Hall, UCLA, June 16, 1958, in the Los Angeles Music Festival.

The text is the beginning of the famous Psalm 70 (71 in the Protestant count-ing):[26]

    1. In thee, O Lord, do I put my trust: let me never be put to confusion.
    2. Deliver me in thy righteousness . . .
    3. Be thou my strong habitation . . . to save me. (The translation, espe-cially of the first verse, does not even approach the majesty and beauty of the Latin rhythm, but it's King James . . .)

The next verse must be taken from a different psalm which I cannot identify. It goes approximately like this:

Thou shalt free me from the snare which they have hidden from me,
    for thou art my protector.
Glory to the Father and the Son and the Holy Ghost.

My humble suggestion for the first verse would be:

In thee, O Lord, have I set my hope:
I shall not be confounded in all eternity.

Ernst

KRENEK TO CRAFT   *July 4, 1958*

Dear Bob,

I was sorry to hear that you had to give up your New Mexico engagement[27] be-cause of your being so fatigued by the recording work.

    It is just the recording business about which I wanted to ask you for some advice. I am to do a recording of *Jonny spielt auf* in Germany next November for the Vox Company. My question is whether it is customary for the conductor of such a recording to receive royalties from the sales of the records apart from his fee for the conducting job? I should think that this must be so, for how else would Elvis Presley make his millions from record sales? So far I have not been offered any contract—just promised a certain not very impressive fee for the conducting—and I should like to know what I am up to, being unfortunately somewhat ignorant of these things, as the opportunity has not occurred before. Would you be good enough to let me know what your own or Mr. Stravinsky's

---

[26] The text is that of Gesualdo's "Psalm of the Compline," which the present writer had recorded.

[27] Conducting Verdi's *Falstaff*. Instead, the present writer directed a concert (that in-cluded the *Eroica* Symphony) and the next day joined the Stravinskys' train from Los Angeles to New York.

Theodore Stravinsky, Vera Sudeikina, and Lyudmila ("Mika")
Stravinsky, St.-Germain-en-Laye, June 1933. Photograph by Stravinsky.

With (left to right) Samuel Dushkin, Vera Sudeikina, Blair Fairchild, and Beveridge
Webster, at Fairchild's home, Avon (Fontainebleau), July 1931.

With (left to right) Willy Strecker, Paul and Gertrud Hindemith,
and Vera Sudeikina, Berlin, October 1931.

Berlin, June 1929. Photograph by Vera Sudeikina.

Left: With (left to right) G. G. Païchadze, Prokofiev,
and Koussevitzky, Combloux (Mégève), 1928. Right: With Alfredo Casella
and Vera Sudeikina, at the railway station in Rome, May 27, 1935.

With (right to left) Jack Hylton, Ansermet, sound engineer, and two of the Hylton Band's
saxophonists, London, January 25, 1931.

Haarlem, May 24, 1930.

In the Hemenway Hotel, Boston, after his marriage, March 1940.
Photograph by Vera Stravinsky.

With (left to right) Mme and M. Blaise Cendrars and Eugenia Errazuriz, Biarritz, August 1932. The portraits of Mme Errazuriz and Stravinsky are by Picasso.

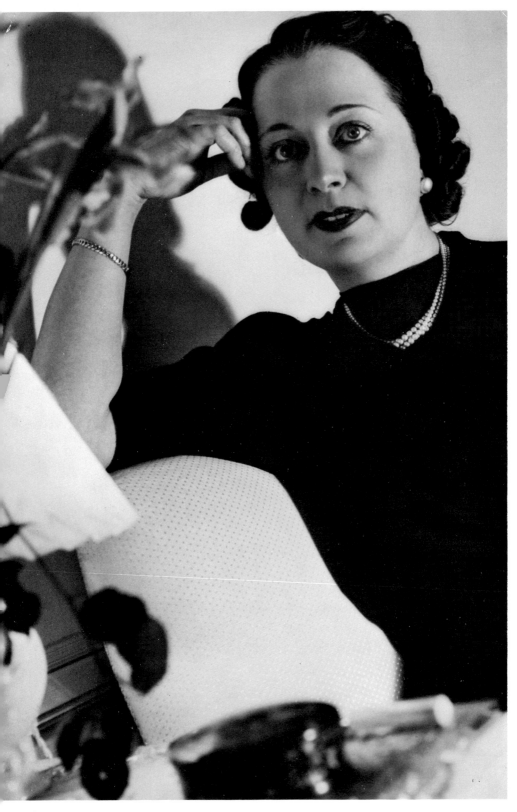

Vera Sudeikina, Paris, 1939. Photograph by George Hoyningen-Huene.

דריי באַרימטהייטען פון דער מוזיק-וועלט, ביי אַ אינטימען צוזאַמענקונפט אין
סאַן פראַנציסקאָ. — רעכטס איז איגאָר סטראַווינסקי, דער הױסיγער קאָמפאָ-
זיטאָר, וועלכער איז נאָסט-דיריגענט פון סאַן פראַנציסקאָ סימפאָני אָרקעס-
טער. אינמיטטען זיצט פיער מאָנטע, דער פראַנצױזיישער מוזיקער. וועלכער איז
דער שטענדיגער אָנפיהרער פון יענעם אָרקעסטער. לינקס איז וינסענט לאָפעז,
פאָפולערער דיריגענט פון דזשעז-אָרקעסטערס.

Top: With Pierre Monteux (center) and bandleader Vincent Lopez, Palace Hotel, San
Francisco, December 1939. Above: Publicity photograph for *The Card Party* (*Jeu de
cartes*), New York, April 1937. Edward M. M. Warburg is at left, Balanchine at right,
and William Dollar, who danced the Joker, has his back to the camera. The four
Queens are (left to right) Hortense Kahrklin, Leda Anchutina, Ariel Lang,
and Annabelle Lyon.

At the Disney studios, Hollywood, December 1939. Walt Disney is at far right,
and Balanchine (in dark jacket) is at center.

With Florent Schmitt, American Embassy, Paris, October 1957.

Stravinsky's piano, 1260 North Wetherly Drive, Hollywood, 1960s.

Before speaking at an eightieth-birthday celebration, Hamburg, June 18, 1962.

With Pierre Boulez, Robert Craft, and Frau Heinrich Strobel, after a recording session at the Südwestfunk, Baden-Baden, October 1957. The manuscript is that of Boulez's Third Piano Sonata.

Robert Craft with Ernst Krenek at a recording session of Boulez's *Le Marteau sans maître*, Hollywood, February 1958. (Stravinsky was in the control room.)

With Mayor Willy Brandt,
Nicolas Nabokov, and an unidentified man, Berlin, September 1961.

With Nicolas Nabokov, Dolder Grand Hotel, Zürich, October 1968.

The Stravinskys leaving the Berkeley Hôtel, Paris, May 1963. Nicolas Nabokov
and Robert Craft are at far right.

experience is in such cases? I should be much obliged to you for your information.

We shall be out of town from July 8 to 11 approximately—I have to attend some sort of convention at Asilomar (near Carmel). After that we'll be here until July 15 or so, when we plan to take off for a few days in the desert.

All good wishes for you, and all our love to the Stravinskys, as ever yours,

Ernst

KRENEK TO CRAFT   *May 27, 1959*
                                                      [Postcard]
Dear Bob,

Many thanks for your message from Japan. It was good to hear from you. How now? When will you be free to come, and when will the Stravinskys? Please call very soon so that we may coordinate dates, since we will be out of town for a few days at the end of June and in July. We tried to reach you, but I think you can reach us more easily (Florida 3-1378).

All the best, as always,

Ernst

KRENEK TO CRAFT   *June 1, 1959*
                                                      [Postcard]
Dear Bob,

Saturday, June 6, is perfect. Come as early as you can and bring the tapes as well as Lawrence. We have already notified him. So please arrange the rest with him. Looking forward eagerly,

Ernst

KRENEK TO CRAFT   *June 7, 1959*

Dear Bob,

Last night it suddenly seemed to go so fast that I did not get around to talking to you about a few things I had in mind. Needless to say that we thoroughly enjoyed the evening. It was only too short.

Anyway, #1, about your own schedule: When are you going to Santa Fe and are you coming back here before you go east?

#2: What is the Stravinskys' schedule? Are they going to stay here now for a while?[28]

---

[28] The Stravinskys were in Santa Fe, briefly. On July 12 Stravinsky conducted *Threni*

#3: Who is in charge of this opera business in, or near, Santa Fe? Are they interested in anything besides Donizetti?

#4: Who is doing *Threni* in Santa Fe? (I mean, what agency, and who are the performers?)

#5: I remember that in your card from Japan you mentioned that some people were asked to write memorial pieces for the Prince of Donaueschingen. Do you know who was asked, and by whom?[29]

#6: On July 5, Bill Kraft expects to do a new percussion piece of mine, "Marginal Sounds," at the Immaculate Heart College. Will you be here at that time? It would be so nice if you could hear it (I'll conduct it). I had in mind to show you the score, but there was not enough time.

I am sorry that my machine did not respond to your tapes. The Stockhausen tape is on a reel which the European radios use; it can't be used in this country. The BBC tapes were double track ones, which are unfamiliar to me. Unfortunately, I am no expert at this business.

Please call me, or drop me a line about these things. We'll see you at the [Franz] Waxman affair, I hope. And give our love to the Stravinskys, and my affectionate thanks for the dedication of the book.[30] All the best, as ever yours,

Ernst

KRENEK TO CRAFT   *January 5, 1960*

Dear Bob,

Assuming that you are back here from your travels, I'd like to inform you about a detail of the Monday Evening Concert of February 1, of which you are in charge, as it seems.

When the program was announced with my 4th Piano Sonata, I wrote to Lawrence [Morton] before he left for Europe that it might be of some interest to play instead my new piano pieces *Sechs Vermessene* since they are not yet known here. He referred me to the pianist, Pearl Kaufman. I sent her a copy of the pieces (when I returned from Princeton) and waited to hear from her. After a lapse of time I tried to call her, but could not get in contact. So I wrote her a note. When, after another lapse of time, I did not hear from her, I called Leonard [Stein] for advice. He referred me to Mr. Holt, who seems to be a sort of coordinator of the show.[31] I tried to reach him over the phone, without any better result. So I wrote a note to him. Again no reply to this day. Maybe I'll have

---

on a program in which the present writer conducted Bach's *Trauer Ode* (with the left arm, owing to a multiple fracture of the right elbow).

[29] Heinrich Strobel, director of the Südwestfunk in Baden-Baden, asked, among others, Stravinsky, who wrote his Epitaphium for Flute, Clarinet, and Harp "for the Tombstone of Prince Max Egon von Fürstenburg."

[30] *Conversations with Stravinsky.*

[31] Henry Holt, opera conductor at the University of Southern California in Los Angeles,

better luck with you. Of course I have no objection against the 4th Sonata's being played, only made a suggestion, calling attention to a more recent piece of music.

We hope your trip was pleasant and profitable. I was happy to notice that Stravinsky's concerts in New York came off well, which happily indicates that he is well. Please give these friends our love and sincere wishes for the New Year.

Hope to hear from you soon. With all good wishes for yourself, as ever,

Ernst

P.S. On the 13th I'm going to Oberlin for a few days to participate in their Contemporary Music Festival (I'll play there those 6 pieces). I expect to be back on the 18th or 19th.

KRENEK TO CRAFT   *March 5, 1960*

Dear Bob,

I hear you are back here—welcome. I am sorry we could not come to the last Monday Evening Concert. Something had come up here which made it impossible.

At this moment your schedule is not quite clear in my mind, but I understand that you will be here at least until April 4, a date which was mentioned to me as a substitute for the Fromm concert of February 1. It also seems that you have some control over that program. (I am sorry that my information sounds so hazy; nobody talks to me, and whatever I hear about the Monday concerts comes from New York in roundabout ways.) Anyway, some piano work of mine is supposed to appear on that program. On February 15, Mr. Holt told me that Pearl Kaufman was going to play my new pieces, that he was to see her immediately and put her in contact with me so that I could instruct her. So far, nothing has happened. Now what? Perhaps you would care to look into the matter.

Another question: Has Stravinsky's piece for piano and orchestra which was presented in New York been published, or, if not, is there some way for me to see the score? I have been asked tentatively whether I would consider conducting this piece in one of my concerts in Europe next year. Of course, I would consider it a very special honor if the master would entrust me with this task. But I should like to see the score so that I may decide whether I may be able to do it.

Please let me hear from you. As always,

Ernst

---

succeeded Lawrence Morton as director of the Monday Evening Concerts while Morton was on a sabbatical in Europe.

STRAVINSKY TO KRENEK

1260 North Wetherly Drive
Hollywood
March 8, 1960

Greetings to Ernst Krenek!

I certainly would be very glad if you decide to conduct the enclosed score of Movements [for Piano and Orchestra]. The Swiss pianist Margrit Weber, who played it in New York under my direction, has the exclusive rights for one year in Europe (and two years in the Americas) from the day of its first performance, i.e., January 10, 1960. The score will appear very soon at Boosey & Hawkes.

   Hope will see you in the nearest future. All best, cordially,

I. Str.

STRAVINSKY TO KRENEK

Hollywood
April 16, 1960
Easter Eve

10424 Pinyon Avenue
Tujunga, California

Buona Pasqua, dear friends!

Sorry I didn't see you [after the] last Monday Evening Concert to tell you how much I liked your piano music and enjoyed your performance, your wonderful performance. Cordially as ever,

I. Stravinsky

KRENEK TO STRAVINSKY

Roberts-at-the-Beach Motel
San Francisco
June 22, 1960

Mes très chers amis,

We are very sorry indeed that we were not able to see you recently. This seems to be a very busy period for all of us (I wonder whether there are any other periods . . .). Thus we also had to miss the opening of Madame's exhibition, since we had to leave before that. I am attending here a composer's meeting, where I have to lecture and conduct. We shall call you before you leave to wish you bon voyage.

   At any rate our best wishes are with you, and we greet you affectionately as ever,

Ernst Krenek

KRENEK TO STRAVINSKY

10424 Pinyon Avenue
Tujunga, California
November 3, 1961

Carissimo maestro,

We have been away, in and out, and as we noticed from the papers, you have been traveling a great deal too. I do not know whether you are here at this time. But if so, we would be very happy to have again contact with you.

Last year I had the honor of conducting your Movements in Winterthur, and it was a great pleasure too. This beautiful work did not seem to me to be terribly difficult. I think the performance was better than satisfactory. At any rate, it was very successful.

With all good wishes—and may God bless you—to both of you, from your devoted friends, as always,

Ernst Krenek

KRENEK TO STRAVINSKY

Cher maître,

10424 Pinyon Avenue
Tujunga, California
January 21, 1962

Your telegram for the New Year gave us great pleasure, and I wish to thank you most sincerely for this token of your friendship.

A few days ago I saw your letter to Mr. [Albert] Goldberg in the Los Angeles *Times*.[32] Since we were in and out of town a great deal, I did not see the USC production of your opera, and as we do not read the local newspapers (such as there are left) regularly, I was not quite aware of what went on. As I mentioned in a letter to Lawrence Morton some time ago, the function assigned to me by this community seems to be that of taxpayer and consumer of gas and groceries, and I am playing the part.

Naturally, your angry refutation of Goldberg's misstatements is entirely justified, and so is your exasperation with his general attitude toward new music. Unfortunately, the vagueness of the subject matter and the standards prevailing in our society make it very difficult for the artist to take exception to unfair criticism because the critic can always claim that his judgment was based on subjective opinion (which Mr. Goldberg predictably has done immediately). That, again unfortunately, reduces the controversy in the public eye to a conflict of disadvantage because the artist is suspected of having an axe to grind, while the critic is basking in the light of the (however unwarranted) assumption that he is unbiased. Thus it usually is a thankless task for the artist to reply to his critics. Perhaps silent contempt is the best punishment, although one's patience frequently is taxed to the breaking point.

In the last *Melos* I read with keen interest large portions from the German edition of your *Conversations*. Especially your remarks on the sociological aspects of new music are very relevant and much to the point, though not exactly encouraging. But, then, what is?

We hope that everything is well with you and yours and that we shall see you sometime soon. Meanwhile, with much love from both of us to you and Mrs. Stravinsky, as always affectionately yours,

Ernst Krenek

---

[32] This letter is reprinted in *Themes and Episodes* (New York, 1966), pp. 82–84.

STRAVINSKY TO KRENEK   *February 7, 1962*

Best greetings to the Kreneks!

Back home—am plunged again in my composition after ½ a year of interruption. Your good letter gave me much satisfaction. I share your attitude towards the critics and if I did not keep silence this time it is because I wanted to help the young generation to act. I have nothing to lose with the Goldbergs of the world: too old for that.

Hope to see you both very soon. Affectionately as ever yours,

I. Str.

KRENEK TO STRAVINSKY   *June 7, 1962*

Cher maître,

All our best wishes—may God bless you—with love from both of us.

Ernst Krenek

> *I*gori, carissimo amico,
> *S*apientissimo magistro, qui
> *T*am gloriose peracta inventute
> *R*aro vigore ac mente indefessa
> *A*peruit sibi
> *V*ias novas
> *I*ste canon octoginta (pro tantis annis celebrandis)
>   verborum acrostichida eius nominis formantium
> *N*ovo modo
> *S*eriali
> *C*onstructus supra seriem dodecaphonicam
>   ita inventam ut intervallorum eius summa aequet iterum
>   octoginta semitonia eiusque dimidia inverse
>   ac retrorsum eandem figuram perhibeant, crescens
>   in temporis distantia, ut indicet amici crescentem
>   fortunam, atque perpetuus
> *I*n imagine perennitatis fortunae optimae dedicatus
>   est cum admiratione et amore per
>
>   Ernestum

To Igor, dearest friend, wisest master, who, after his youth so gloriously accomplished, with rare vitality and untiring mind has found for himself new ways, this canon of eighty words (for so many years to celebrate) which form an acrostic of his name, constructed according to new serial techniques over a

twelve-tone row so invented that the sum of its intervals equals eighty (again!)
half-steps and its two halves show the same shape in inversion and retrogres-
sion, growing in distance of time to indicate the growing fortune of the friend,
and perpetual as a symbol of the durability of his excellent fate, is dedicated
with admiration and love by

Ernst

STRAVINSKY TO KRENEK   *New York*
July 2, 1962

10424 Pinyon Avenue
Tujunga, Calif.[33]

Dearest Ernst Krenek,

Longing to see you and embrace you and thank you for this incredible acrostic-canon you composed for my 80th birthday. I cannot tell you how happy you made me to possess this treasure. 100,000 thanks, your

I. Stravinsky

KRENEK TO STRAVINSKY   *December 27, 1962*[34]

Dear friend and master,

Let us reciprocate most heartily your good wishes from our house to yours. May God bless you and yours in this New Year to come. As ever, devotedly and affectionately yours,

Ernst

STRAVINSKY TO KRENEK   *Beverly Hills*
December 31, 1962
[Telegram]

10424 Pinyon Avenue
Tujunga, Calif.

Just returning from tour received your kind letter. Hope see you soon. Very best New Year wishes. Cordially,   Stravinsky

---

[33] Forwarded to 4132 Oakhollow Drive, Claremont, California.
[34] Written on the back of a photograph of the Kreneks' garden with their house in the background.

KRENEK TO STRAVINSKY   *10424 Pinyon Avenue*
                                                        Tujunga, California
Cher maître,   *March 1, 1964*

We tried to communicate with you, but the telephone did not produce any information. . . . All best, always affectionately,

                                                        Ernst K.

STRAVINSKY TO KRENEK   *[March 1964]*

Dear friend,

So much thanks for your article (which I will try to get in English).

Your CANONS in my honor are beautiful. I heard them ½ hour before the performance. I cannot stand any more concerts where I feel as if in a streetcar surrounded by strangers. In a few days flying to Cleveland (one of the best orchestras in U.S. with that of Chicago) and for 2 or 3 days after to Cincinnati where Vera has her show. All best, cordially yours,

                                                        I. Str.

Only for you my telephone is CR 1-4858.

KRENEK TO STRAVINSKY   *10424 Pinyon Avenue*
                                                        Tujunga, California
Cher maître et ami,   *March 5, 1964*

We are sorry we missed you last Monday when you came to the choir rehearsal. The exquisite bottles were passed on to us by Lawrence [Morton], and we wish to thank you heartily for this thoughtful present. I think the choir did very well by our little pieces. I am glad you could hear my *pièce de hommage*.

With all good wishes, always affectionately,

                                                        Ernst

KRENEK TO STRAVINSKY   *Palm Springs, California*
                                                        June 16, 1967
1218 North Wetherly Drive   *[Telegram]*

On this blessed day[35] our thoughts of friendship and heartfelt wishes are with you as ever. Affectionately,   Ernst and Gladys Krenek

At Christmas 1968, the Kreneks sent Igor and Vera Stravinsky one of Ernst's water colors of a desert scene near the Kreneks' new home in Palm Springs.

---

[35] Stravinsky's eighty-fifth birthday.

LETTERS TO

1957 ~ 1963

PIERRE BOULEZ

According to Peter Heyworth's New Yorker *profile of Pierre Boulez (March 24 and 31, 1974), "of all of the composers who have emerged since the war, Boulez, both as a man and as a musician, was for years the closest to Stravinsky." But Elliott Carter, whose reputation dates from after the war, was closer to Stravinsky, and for a far longer time. Heyworth goes on to say that "Stravinsky and Boulez had first met at a party in Virgil Thomson's apartment in New York in 1952. . . . It is inconceivable that [Stravinsky] could have been unaware of Boulez's assaults on his neoclassic music." What really is inconceivable is that Stravinsky would have attended the party if he had been aware of Boulez's role in these assaults. Stravinsky was fully informed of the controversy surrounding a festival of his music in Paris after the liberation, but the dossier that he kept on the affair, with clippings and letters from Nadia Boulanger, Manuel Rosenthal, Marcelle de Manziarly, and others, does not mention Boulez.*[1] *That Stravinsky understood Parisian musical politics at the time is evident in his correspondence, for example, in a letter to Manuel Rosenthal, who had conducted* Four Norwegian Moods, *dated January 12, 1946:*

> [The] sincere and spontaneous manifestations against the *Sacre* in 1913 [were] comprehensible because of the violent character of this score. . . . But one doubts the spontaneity of a howling manifestation against the *Norwegian Moods,* the elements that could provoke boisterous protestations being totally absent.[2] . . . Unless I am mistaken, it seems that once the *violent* has been accepted, the *amiable,* in turn, is no longer tolerable. [*Original in French*]

---

[1] Stravinsky was familiar with only one name connected with the controversy, René Leibowitz, thanks to a letter about him from André Schaeffner, September 1, 1946. In spite of Schaeffner's disparagement, Stravinsky granted an interview to Leibowitz in Hollywood in December 1947, which seems to have revived the composer's interest in Schoenberg, or so one deduces from Stravinsky's order to Broude Bros., Inc., New York, shortly afterward, for a copy of Schoenberg's *Models for Beginners in Composition* (!).

[2] In a letter to Rosenthal, August 18, 1945, Stravinsky criticized the French version of the title, *Impressions norvégiennes:* "That is not it at all. By *Mood* I mean *Modus* (in Latin), as in, for example, *In modo antiquo.*" Writing to Stravinsky, June 23, 1949, Igor Markevitch describes the Oslo orchestra's spontaneous reaction to the *Four Norwegian Moods:* "At the first rehearsal, the players' smiles came as a surprise [to me].

In June 1953, six months after the meeting with Boulez in New York, Stra-
vinsky read the new two-volume Musique russe, *edited by his former friend*
Pierre Suvchinsky. The composer was jolted by Boulez's contribution, "Stra-
vinsky demeure . . . ," but more so by that of Suvchinsky. The Rake's Progress
had received its French premiere on June 18. In a letter to Stravinsky com-
menting on the performance, Nadia Boulanger referred to Suvchinsky's very
enthusiastic reaction to Boulez's polemic. Stravinsky answered on June 27:

Those who informed you that I was upset over Boulez's article have in any case
a decided gift for invention. On the one hand, I learned of it only a week ago,
and therefore no one could have known my reaction until then; on the other,
one has only to read in the middle of page 221 to be certain that I do not run the
risk of being charmed by Boulez, any more than he does by me.

If you have the time, I suggest that you look also at Suvchinsky's article:
page 21 [and 22]: ". . . the aspirations of the young contemporary music, above
all the great works of Stravinsky like *Le Sacre du printemps, Les Noces, Le Ros-*
signol."

Salon careerism continues!!! . . .

But by 1956, Stravinsky appears to have forgotten the articles in Musique
russe. *In November of that year the present writer effected a reconciliation be-*
tween Stravinsky and Suvchinsky, and Boulez called on Stravinsky in the Rote
Kreuz hospital in Munich. Not until March 1966 did Stravinsky read every-
thing that Boulez had written about him, thanks to Pierre Suvchinsky, who
sent Stravinsky a copy of Boulez's Relevés d'apprenti. *On March 28, Suv-*
chinsky wrote to Stravinsky:

The person who collected, edited, and put together the volume of Boulez's articles was P[aule] Thevenin. . . . She seems to go everywhere and at the moment
has impressed Boulez with her literary connections. She spends weeks on end
with him in Baden-Baden and edits, with his knowledge and consent, everything he writes. This *"perenositsa"* ("mother nurse," Leskov's[3] expression) is
a terrible gossip and meddler who causes everyone to quarrel with everyone
else. . . . Of course I did not know about the reprinting of the articles. That was

---

Most of the elements, which you borrowed either from their folklore or their composers, were familiar, but the musicians were astonished to find these elements in a
context so remote from the sentimental one in which they are generally expressed.
Some performers were furious and refused to play, imagining that you were mocking
Norway! I had quite a time persuading them that you had no such intention and that,
on the contrary, they should be proud of this charming homage. . . . At the same time,
I became somewhat anxious about what the public reaction would be. Nevertheless,
from rehearsal to rehearsal the musicians entered into the spirit of the music more and
more and developed such a taste for it that they played the concert superbly."

[3] The writer Nikolai Semyonovich Leskov (1831–95), known for his innovative use of
Russian. The libretto for Shostakovich's *Lady Macbeth of Mtsensk* is based on a story
by Leskov.

arranged by her. . . . It is all very sad. Boulez has become unapproachable, behaving like a dictator. As soon as he finds something not to his liking, or if you say anything at all critical of his opinions or actions, nothing more is to be done. [*Original in Russian*]

Stravinsky wrote on the title page of Relevés d'apprenti:

Les rares mots de sa dialectique m'épatent de moins en moins. Pourvu qu'il n'arrive pas à la même chose avec sa musique. I. Str.[4]

He also attached a clipping from Le Monde *(March 29, 1966) to the cover of the book, a blurb describing the contents as* "les écrits du plus grand musicien et penseur de la musique d'aujourd'hui," *underscoring the words* "plus grand" *and* "penseur" *in red pencil and placing large question marks next to them.* Relevés d'apprenti, *even more than the disastrous presentation of* Threni *in Paris in 1958, was the underlying provocation for Stravinsky's subsequent comments on Boulez and for the 1970 "public withdrawal" (as Heyworth characterizes it) of what Stravinsky himself termed his "earlier 'extravagant advocacy.'"[5]*

The older composer first heard Boulez's name and encountered his music in Baden-Baden in October 1951, when Heinrich Strobel played a tape of Hans Rosbaud's Donaueschingen performance of Polyphonie X. *The next encounters occurred the following year at a concert in the Petit Théâtre des Champs-Elysées, May 7, 1952, when Boulez and Olivier Messiaen[6] played an installment of the former's* Structures, *and on May 23, in the Salle de l'Ancien Conservatoire, when Stravinsky, with Nadia Boulanger and the present writer, attended an evening of "musique concrète" that included Boulez's* Etude à un son.[7]

---

[4] "The obscure words of his dialectic thrill me less and less. As long as he doesn't reach the same point in his music."

[5] Stravinsky's letter to the Los Angeles *Times*, June 23, 1970.

[6] Stravinsky had been familiar with Messiaen's music since the end of World War II but did not meet the composer until 1958. At the request of Suvchinsky, Stravinsky cabled the following fiftieth-birthday greeting to Messiaen from London, December 11, 1958: "My warmest greetings to the great French musician for a new half-century." For Stravinsky's eightieth birthday, Messiaen sent a "Strophe of the *'grive musicienne'* [musician-thrush], collected for Igor Stravinsky, May 25, 1962, at the edge of the forest, Olivier Messiaen." The music, one-voice only, consists of about a dozen short figures, most of them repeated three, four, and five times. The range is three octaves and a fifth, and no instrument is indicated.

[7] Stravinsky made a note about this two months later: "*Musique concrète.* A session that took place in Paris in May 1952 in the Salle de l'Ancien Conservatoire. Endless pieces whose substance was a mélange of sounds and noises. . . . The participants were professional composers, very antipathetic, and amateurs, 'revolutionaries,' rather sympathetic. A lady next to me raged in the intermission, declaring that this 'music'

*In September 1952, Stravinsky attended several rehearsals and a perform-
ance of* Polyphonie X *in Hollywood. But between Virgil Thomson's party, in December of that year, and November 9, 1956—when Boulez, Stockhausen, and
Luigi Nono called on the composer of the* Sacre *in the Rote Kreuz hospital in
Munich—Stravinsky and Boulez were not in communication. A few weeks
after the hospital visit, Stravinsky, stopping for twelve hours at the Ritz Hotel
in Paris between trains from Rome to London, attended recordings of two of his
works for Boulez's Domaine Musical. The two musicians met again in London
a few days later.*

*On January 4, 1957, Boulez wrote to Stravinsky[8] from Paris saying that
an invitation had come from Lawrence Morton of the Monday Evening Concerts in Los Angeles to conduct* Le Marteau sans maître *there in March.[9] Stravinsky urged Boulez to accept and arranged for him to stay in the Tropicana
Motel, a few blocks from the Stravinsky home. In Hollywood, Boulez spent considerable time with the older composer, and on March 8, Stravinsky attended a
symposium at UCLA in which Boulez, Lukas Foss, Paul Des Marais, and the
present writer discussed the state of contemporary music. Then, at the concert,
March 11, Boulez delayed his performance until Stravinsky's mislaid score had
been found, whereupon many in attendance surmised that he was the only
member of the audience who mattered.*

Back in Paris, Boulez wrote to Stravinsky, March 23, asking him to conduct
Agon *there, under the auspices of the Domaine Musical. (Boulez sent a longer
and more detailed letter to the present writer on April 8.) Stravinsky answered
by cable on April 11:*

Agree conduct for $1,500 European premiere *Agon* Paris October 12 Südwest-
funk Orchestra prepared by Hans Rosbaud. Notifying Roth. Details Craft's letter. Greetings.

*Boulez cabled his agreement on April 15, but since the Domaine Musical did not
have a concert bureau, Stravinsky was obliged to write, on June 29:*

My dear Boulez,

I will leave Hollywood in eight days and would really like to clarify the question
of how my fee will be paid for conducting *Agon* in Paris in October. I will ask
you to make arrangements so that the payment will be made in U.S. dollars, or,

---

was horrible. I had . . . a great desire to ask her: 'But how do you know, Madame?' Was
she acquainted with other examples [of *musique concrète*] that were not so bad?"

[8] This is the first of Boulez's fifty letters (including a few postcards) to Stravinsky. The
only years not represented are 1964 and 1965. French is the original language of all of
the correspondence.

[9] This was not Morton's idea, but the present writer's. At this time Morton was deeply
skeptical of Boulez's intentions vis-à-vis Stravinsky.

if absolutely necessary, in Swiss francs in Switzerland, or in marks in Germany.

Once again, thanks to you and to Stockhausen for remembering my birthday and for your message. Answer me here without delay; it will be forwarded.

Very cordially,

I. Str.

Stravinsky wrote again, on July 15, this time from Santa Fe:

Dear Boulez,

Thank you for your letter of July 9, although its contents have disappointed me a little, since you will not come to Dartington. Too bad, we were counting on it so much. This note to reply to two things: (1) Dr. E. Roth of Boosey & Hawkes just informed me that the orchestra score of *Agon* will be at the disposal of the Südwestfunk at the very beginning of September, and a letter from Strobel tells me the same. (2) M. Worms[10] still has not paid anything, neither the $100 for the "36 questions," nor the $80 for the photos, in spite of the contract that I signed and sent airmail a good month ago. My best wishes go out to you. Good work.

Boulez wrote to Stravinsky in Dartington, August 7, 1957, and in Venice, September 20, 1957. According to plan, Stravinsky arrived in Baden-Baden on October 8 by car from Munich—where he had conducted a concert the night before—and rehearsed Agon *on the 9th and 10th with the Südwestfunk Orchestra. (Between rehearsals, he heard Boulez record his Third Sonata.) On October 11, Stravinsky left for Paris on the night train and, in the morning, led an acoustical rehearsal of* Agon *in the Salle Pleyel. The concert that evening was a great success, and, in commemoration, Boulez gave Stravinsky a copy of Jacques Scherer's* Le "Livre" de Mallarmé, *inscribing it "En souvenir d'Agon et du concert du Octobre 11. Avec mon amitié." Many hours were spent discuss-*

---

[10] Gerard Worms, of Editions du Rocher, Monaco, who had commissioned from the present writer *Avec Stravinsky*, published in 1958. In lieu of contributing a preface to the book, Stravinsky suggested that he touch on a variety of subjects in question-and-answer form. The result, "Answers to Thirty-six Questions," was written largely during Boulez's visit to Los Angeles in March 1957. Boulez had agreed to translate the text into French and to check the French version of the rest of the book. On May 13, 1957, Stravinsky wrote to *"cher Boulez,"* enclosing "the definitive version (which I succeeded in finding) of the last sentence of 'Thirty-six Questions.' I believe that it is good now. Please add it to the others. I hope to have the French proofs soon. When you send them, do not forget to tell us when and how the little honorarium, concerning which Deborah Ishlon was to have spoken to you, will be sent. . . . I believe it was $100. And a few lines about yourself. *Agon* is finished, full of erasures. . . . It is cold, the sky is dull, and we have no spring, though it is already May 13, *parbleu!* I. Stravinsky." (Deborah Ishlon, of Columbia Records, had been entrusted by Stravinsky with the preliminary editing of his manuscript.)

*ing both the "Livre" and Paul Klee's theoretical writings in the days thereafter,
with the participation of Alberto Giacometti, who made his first drawings of
Stravinsky at this time.*

*According to Peter Heyworth, however, Boulez "achieved his greatest coup
when he persuaded Stravinsky himself to conduct the first European performance of his most recent work,* Agon, *at the Domaine Musical. . . . Today Boulez
likes to quote a remark attributed to Lenin that not every compromise is a con-
cession." Unhappily, this confirms the suspicions held by most of Stravinsky's
friends at the time that he was the compromised party.*

The Paris Agon *was a German import: an established and well-subsidized
German orchestra played the piece, after having been thoroughly rehearsed by
Rosbaud. When Boulez invited Stravinsky to Paris again the following year to
conduct his* Threni, *the performers were to be recruited locally, a shaky arrangement even if Boulez had fulfilled his promise to prepare the work himself.
That he did not find time to do so is explained, though hardly excused, by his
efforts to finish a composition of his own,* Poésies pour pouvoir, *for the 1958
Donaueschingen festival. Well aware that Paris did not have a chorus capable
of singing* Threni *and that employing a pickup orchestra for this music would
involve myriad hazards, Stravinsky had urged Boulez to make an agreement
with the Rundfunk of Cologne, as he had done in October 1957 with that of
Baden-Baden. Boulez wrote to Stravinsky in New York on November 6, and in
California on December 1 (from Cologne, during rehearsals of* Le Visage nuptial) *and on January 9, 1958. Shortly thereafter, the score of* Le Visage nuptial
arrived, and Stravinsky acknowledged it:

Boulez, what a beautiful present you have given me! So happy to have this gigantic and very beautiful orchestra score, which I long to hear, and concerning
which Suvchinsky, after hearing it in Cologne, wrote to me with much enthusiasm. On that subject, what has happened in the negotiations with Cologne? I
would like so much for you to succeed in this, and to do *Threni* with their choir
and ensemble in Paris. A word from you on this matter (especially positive) will
be very welcome. My very sincere affections take to the night air. [January 25,
1958]

*On February 26, Stravinsky wrote to Suvchinsky, saying "I am beginning to
understand D. H. Lawrence, who fled from Paris," and asking him to inform
Boulez of the death of Alessandro Piovesan: "Not having received any answer
from Piovesan, the director of the Biennale di Venezia, [Boulez] got angry and
refused to take part in September." In another note to Suvchinsky, March 29,
Stravinsky reveals that he has finished* Threni *and inquires about Boulez's*
Doubles *for orchestra, just performed in Paris.*

*Boulez's next letter, April 10, 1958, was forwarded to Stravinsky in the
Clift Hotel, San Francisco, and the one after that came on Stravinsky's birthday. He answered, June 20, 1958:*

Upon receiving your letter, I sent the following note to Dr. E. Roth in London: "Pierre Boulez beseeching me to ask you to send him IMMEDIATELY full score and chorus parts of *Threni*. I am doing that without delay. Boulez is a serious man, and if he is asking something in this manner, he means it. I hope that you can do it without delay, and (let me add) for a gracious rental fee. . . ."[11] I gave him your address. Be assured, dear friend, that I understand your difficulties very well and that I sympathize with you entirely. I send you and Madame Tézenas[12] my most sincere friendship.

The following day, Stravinsky wrote to Suvchinsky:

Along with this letter, I am sending my sketch of the orchestra score of *Threni* to you and to Boulez so that you may become acquainted with it. In accordance with Boulez's request, I asked London to send the chorus parts and score to him immediately. . . . But if he has already left for Baden-Baden, I do not know how all of this will work out.

On July 26 and on September 5, Boulez wrote to Stravinsky assuring him about the preparations for the concert. But finally Threni *was so badly sung and played—at the Salle Pleyel, November 14, 1958—that the audience received it with jeers, and when Boulez tried to maneuver Stravinsky into taking a bow, the humiliated composer curtly refused and swore that he would never again conduct in Paris, a vow that he kept.[13]*

A "coup" of a different kind awaited Stravinsky that same night when he learned that a new book, Rencontres avec Pierre Boulez, *by Antoine Goléa, had been sold in the foyer during the* Threni *performance. Luckily, Mrs. Stravinsky spirited these* Rencontres *away before her husband could read the first page of the text, which described the Boulez-led demonstration against Stravinsky's "neoclassic" music during the* Norwegian Moods *concert in Paris at the end of World War II. On November 25, Stravinsky wrote to Boulez from the Hotel Hassler in Rome, without showing any reservation toward him or even directly referring to the concert:*

---

[11] Quotation in English in the original.

[12] Suzanne Tézenas, patroness of the Domaine Musical, to whom Suvchinsky had introduced Boulez.

[13] Stravinsky wrote in his diary that night: "My concert (*Threni*) at Pleyel (unhappiest concert of my life!)." Back in California, Stravinsky attached a note to a packet of Boulez's letters: "All this correspondence resulted in the scandalous concert in Paris on November 14, 1958." Stravinsky made known his resolve never to appear in Paris again. He wrote on a letter from the International Music Council, December 7, 1959, inviting him to conduct in Paris in October 1960: "Responded December 13, 1959: Decision never again to appear in Paris after the reception accorded *Threni* last year."

My dear Boulez,

Just a note to find out if you have heard anything from New York in respect to the $1,500 which was to have been credited to my account at Bankers Trust Co. (Park Avenue and 57th Street). I am anxious to have that money in New York at the beginning of December for tax and accounting reasons. I would greatly appreciate it if you would expedite this payment, in case it has not yet been effected. Thank you.

A thousand kind regards from all of us, and see you soon. Your

I. Str.

Back in California, Stravinsky wrote to Suvchinsky:

The New York concert of *Threni* on January 4 went sensationally. Beautifully conducted, it met with loud approval. The ovations were endless. Still, even after hearing such a performance, I do not think that the attitude of Paris toward *Threni* and toward me would be any different from the one shown me on November 14. . . . I will not recall what I went through in Paris with any feeling of gratitude to Boulez. . . . He did not have enough courage to admit his own negligence and to say "mea culpa." [January 25, 1959]

This is the first documented indication of Stravinsky's true response to the experience. Another was to follow a month later, when the periodical Das Musikleben *published a poisonous review of the concert by, of all people, Boulez's biographer, Goléa. Stravinsky drafted, in French, a letter to the editor, part of which follows:*

Your reviewer of the Paris concert in which I conducted my *Threni* in November 1958 (your February issue, pages 79–80) . . . is guilty of a vicious injustice. The responsibility for the failure of the concert [rests with] the Domaine Musical. As the author of a book that is in part a history of that organization,[14] your reviewer is close enough to it to know the truth, which is that the Domaine Musical did not prepare the concert as promised.

Stravinsky delayed sending this until he could discuss the matter with Suvchinsky, to whom the composer wrote on March 9, referring to Goléa as "Boulez's lackey" and adding:

I received two letters from Boulez.[15] In one, which I send to you . . . he does not excuse himself for the absence of any kind of preparation of *Threni* . . . but he

---

[14] Stravinsky is guessing at this, not having read the book. The pages of his copy, a gift from Suvchinsky, were never cut.

[15] Actually four letters since the beginning of the year.

does complain about [Goléa's] phrase. This, however, does not concern me in the least, but only Boulez himself and his *"coup de publicité."* When he finally refers to *Threni*, it is only to express regret about the lack of resources in Paris for performing such pieces. But what is new about that? As you yourself can see, the possibility that he will admit his own guilt is slight . . . and I therefore hold no hope of receiving a satisfactory answer. If I send the letter that you suggested (threatening to pass my letter on to the press, if he refuses to accept the blame), it would simply make him bitter and complicate my position further. . . . All of this has put me on edge. How unpleasant it is. How I would like to kill it all with the unyielding silence of the beast, the horse, the cat.[16] I will make an effort, and perhaps succeed. . . .

Boulez's second letter concerns only himself, the orchestra, the chorus, and the soloists in the Munich *Threni*.[17] Loaded with useless details, the letter . . . is designed to give me the impression that he was very busy with the music, which, in itself . . . probably interests him very little. Still . . . a higher professional attitude is demanded than the one that he showed me in Paris.

Meanwhile, on March 10, Stravinsky had written directly to Boulez:

In one of your letters (February 26) you express regret at not having noticed, in time to have it omitted, a phrase employed by [Goléa] in reference to his book about you. He attributed to you certain intentions. Obviously such an interpretation of your actions (that publicity was your only motive in inviting me into the young organization) could only come from someone fundamentally hostile to my musical activity. I can imagine how much that must have offended you, and I thank you for reassuring me of your true intentions, which I never doubted.

Since this is the case, it is your place, in my estimation, to answer the journalist's insolent article in *Das Musikleben* about our unfortunate concert. . . . Were it left to me to answer him, I would have to blame the Domaine Musical for being poorly prepared, for the complete incompetence of a group of singers, for the lack of rehearsals. . . . This journalist would hardly dare to claim ignorance of all these circumstances. The article is so vicious, so vile, so unfair, that you, not only as organizer of the concert and the one responsible for [my] appearance, but also as the subject of his book, should feel morally obliged to reply. I go further: I feel that it is your duty to contest him. I await that gesture from you.

Already it is March 10 and I am astonished still to have received nothing about the March 6 concert in Munich. We fly to Japan on March 25 and return

---

[16] This is an idiomatic expression in Russian.
[17] Boulez had conducted *Threni* in Munich on March 6. Stravinsky added this paragraph on March 11 or 12.

here around May 9. Is there a chance that we will see each other again in Europe soon, since I will be in Copenhagen on May 21–26?[18]

Stravinsky wrote to Suvchinsky on March 19:

Yesterday I received your letter of the 15th and was glad about the reconciliation that I sensed with Boulez. I hope that your interpretation of his repentance is not mistaken. I am now awaiting a letter from him about Goléa's article, and from you about my demand that Boulez refute it. . . . I only fear that Boulez will delay in giving me an answer. . . . I would like to erase this entire affair.

I told Bob about your impressions from your conversations with Stockhausen, but Bob continues to affirm that, in private, Stockhausen refers to me, to Schoenberg, and to other composers of the older generation in a totally negative fashion. Bob simply does not believe what was said to you. And this leaves me skeptical. I fear that Bob is not completely wrong: after the rehearsal in Baden-Baden, where Stockhausen, Boulez, and Rosbaud were conducting their triple orchestra [for *Gruppen*], I personally had rather a bad impression of Stockhausen, as of an arrogant Nazi, also in his treatment of the musicians he was conducting.

At the end of the rehearsal, the musicians of Boulez's group applauded him, while Stockhausen's group remained silent. That's just one thing: another is his attitude toward me. Just recall his article for the book *Avec Stravinsky*. That article is not, as you say, written by someone who really understands and appreciates [my music] but rather by someone who, out of necessity, wrote an article. . . . Reread it and you will see that I am right. Love can be neither bought nor sold, but I regret only the lack of reciprocity, for *his* music does interest *me*.[19]

On March 23, Stravinsky wrote to Boulez:

Thank you for your letter of March 19 and the review of *Threni* in Munich. In opening the letter, I expected to have your answer to mine of March 10, addressed to "Mr. Pierre Boulez, c/o Dr. H. Strobel, Musikabteilung Südwestfunk, Baden-Baden, Germany." Did you receive it? I hope so. Now you can answer me at the Imperial Hotel in Tokyo, where I will be on April 6 (going via Honolulu, Manila, and Hong Kong).[20]

---

[18] On May 25, Stravinsky received the Sonning Prize (50,000 Danish kroner) between performances of his Octet and *Firebird* Suite, conducted by him in the Tivoli Concert Hall. The program began with the overture to Carl Nielsen's *Maskarade*.

[19] In December 1960, at Stravinsky's request, Stockhausen sent tapes of four of his compositions. On February 15, 1963, Stravinsky wrote to Alfred Schlee of Universal Edition, Vienna: "I am most eager to see the score of Stockhausen's *Momente*. Do you have one you could sell or lend to me?"

[20] Boulez wrote to Stravinsky in Tokyo on April 10 and 27, and in California on May 9.

I repeat what I wrote to you on March 10 about our travels, which is to say that we will be returning on May 9 and that we fly to Copenhagen on SAS, May 20. I conduct there on the 25th, and on the 26th we fly back to Los Angeles. I think you will be in Scandinavia at that time, and we would be happy to see you in Copenhagen. Say yes. Excuse the hastiness of this note before the trip.

Your devoted   Igor Stravinsky

Boulez came to Copenhagen, armed with his answer to Goléa. Stravinsky made a copy of it and sent another copy, with his own additional comments, to Suvchinsky from Hollywood on May 29.

While in Copenhagen, Boulez asked Stravinsky for the European premiere of his Movements for Piano and Orchestra. He answered on June 6:

My dear Boulez,

The two premiere performances of Movements have been set by Rolf Liebermann for June 17, 1960, in Cologne, and June 27 in Hamburg.[21] Since you had intended to give the Domaine Musical concert with my Movements before June 28 (as you told me in Copenhagen), and since Margrit Weber is the only possible pianist (she has a one-year exclusivity for the work in Europe), you would be obliged to squeeze the concert and rehearsals into the tight space of one week, between June 18 and 25. This would permit Madame Weber to rejoin me in Hamburg on the 26th for the dress rehearsal of the concert on June 27. I hope that you will be able to manage this; if not, you will probably postpone this concert until autumn 1960. You would be very kind to inform me of your decision.

How did it go in Vienna? I was happy to see you, and how nice it was of you to have come to Copenhagen! Thank you. Best regards.

Boulez wrote on July 4 and 20, and, in reply, on July 23, Stravinsky persisted in the matter of the answer to Goléa:

I see that the June issue (VI) of *Musikleben* has appeared and that your answer to Antoine Goléa still is not published. Is this bad faith on the part of the review? Do you intend to respond?

---

[21] Stravinsky wrote to Suvchinsky on August 24: "I have finished my Movements for Piano and Orchestra earlier than anticipated and will therefore not wait until next June but will conduct the premiere in New York at Christmas or immediately after the New Year. The piece turned out to be quite difficult, not so much for the pianist as for the conductor, because of the rhythmic, and even metric, complexity. I am worried about this work . . . but perhaps should not be after the success of *Threni* everywhere except in Paris!"

By August 15, Stravinsky was once again doubtful of Boulez's sincerity and motives:

I received your letter of August 11 along with the typewritten letter in German. You know the German language well enough to realize that this is not a translation of the article you gave me in Copenhagen, but an abridged German version (one-third as long as the French), smoothed and sweetened beyond recognition from the original, which you sent to the *Neue Zeitschrift für Musik* in Mainz. [Your intentions have been distorted in the process] because, as you yourself state in the article, your aim was "above all to set straight a flagrant injustice." This important phrase, like so many others, was not translated, and the result is that, contrary to your wishes, the injustice has not been "set straight."

I am surprised by all this, because I expected a very different attitude from you, given our friendly, cordial relations. For this reason I sign this letter with much grief and disappointment.

On August 16 Stravinsky sent a copy of this letter, together with the "abridged" and "sweetened" version of Boulez's article, to Suvchinsky, and on August 29 Boulez wrote, promising Stravinsky that the Copenhagen version would be printed. Stravinsky acknowledged this new pledge:

Just a note before our departure for Europe (in two days) to let you know that your letter of August 20 reassured me, and I thank you for it sincerely. Thus we have only to await the appearance of your letter in German in the next *Musikleben*. [August 24]

On the same day Stravinsky wrote to Suvchinsky:

Boulez writes that my letter grieved him very much and that he sent a letter to Strobel with a request for permission to translate the text as it is into German, and to send it to *Das Musikleben*. We will see what happens, and whether or not [Boulez] is conniving.

Five months later, however, Stravinsky was still writing to Suvchinsky:

I received the December issue of *Das Musikleben*, in which, as in the preceding issues, Boulez's answer to that *govno* Goléa was conspicuously absent. I wrote to Boulez about this. You might stress the point to him also, but I fear that the affair is hopeless. [January 23, 1960]

In fact, the Copenhagen version was never published, but eventually a letter did appear.[22] *Stravinsky described it in a letter to Suvchinsky, February 23, 1960:*

---

[22] Boulez had written to Stravinsky five times in the interim, September 18 and October 10 and 28, 1959, and January 13 and February 12, 1960.

[The letter was] printed in the usual type and in the same, never-changing place. Boulez did not remove the phrase *"contre-coeur,"* which he could have done if, as you say, he has begun to treat that *govno* Goléa with contempt, though nobody could ever do this strongly enough . . . except perhaps the Soviet dogs who threw themselves on poor Pasternak,[23] and they would do it for the wrong reason: Goléa's "devotion to progressive music." Well, explain that to the American optimists who applaud Khrushchev.

Strangely, Heyworth's New Yorker *article does not mention the* Threni *episode and its aftermath, noting only that "in the middle sixties, relations grew less cordial, and after 1967 there was no further contact between the two men." Actually, relations grew more, not less, cordial when the efforts toward a professional association ended. For Stravinsky's eightieth birthday, June 18, 1962, Boulez sent his manuscript score of* Domaines.

The Paris performance of Movements *that Boulez had planned for June 1960 did not materialize. After the first performance of* A Sermon, A Narrative and A Prayer, *in Basel in February 1962, Stravinsky received a program autographed by several musicians, including Boulez. Stravinsky wrote to Suvchinsky:*

It would be interesting to know what Boulez's reaction *really* was, since it is impossible to tell from his *"mersi bokou voo noo mankie bokoo esper voo voir bentoe"* style.

The two musicians met only four times after that, in Paris in May 1962, in Los Angeles in March 1965[24]—at which time the older composer heard Boulez rehearse his Eclat—*in Paris on June 6, 1965,[25] and in Stravinsky's Hollywood home in May 1967. The last communications were two postcards to Stravinsky, May 29 and August 18, 1967; two cables, a birthday greeting ("O saisons O châteaux votre plus haute tour") and an appeal (October 5) to protest the kid-*

---

[23] On January 28, 1960, Stravinsky wrote to Suvchinsky: "I read *Dr. Zhivago* in Russian, and, with sadness, I confess my disappointment. Of course it is real *peredvizhnichestvo.* How strange to read such a novel in the age of James Joyce."

[24] During this visit, Stravinsky was being filmed in his home, and Boulez had been invited for lunch. After the meal, he opened the score of *Les Noces* to the last page and tried to convince the composer that the two measures of rest between 134 and 135 were a mistake; one measure, according to Boulez's calculations, was the correct number. Stravinsky, slightly inebriated, agreed. All of this can be seen in the Rolf Liebermann/Richard Leacock film *A Stravinsky Portrait.* In December 1965, at a recording of the work, Stravinsky restored the second measure of rest.

[25] Boulez's recorded performances of *Renard, Les Noces,* and the *Sacre* had so upset Stravinsky in the early 1960s that he did not attend a program of these three works led by Boulez at the Paris Opéra, June 5, 1965. Yet the two musicians dined together the following day. A year later, Milene Marion wrote to her father, June 15, 1966: "Vera wrote to me that you intended to spend your birthday with Boulez in Baden-Baden."

napping of the Korean composer Ysang Yun (Stravinsky had already responded to the same request from Luigi Dallapiccola); and a note on a program for a concert of Zvezdoliki, Requiem Canticles, *and the* Sacre *that Boulez had conducted in London, August 1, 1968:*

Bien cher ami,

How we are missing you these evenings! We think of you very affectionately. I greatly hope to see you in Los Angeles next January. Friendly greetings to Vera and to Bob.

Stravinsky did not receive Boulez in January 1968, but Mrs. Stravinsky and the present writer saw him, at the home of his then-intimate friend Lawrence Morton, who had vacationed with him in Yosemite and Mexico, and been his house guest in Baden-Baden and in France.

Several weeks after Boulez's May 1967 visit, Stravinsky had read a Boulez interview with Janeslav Buxga in Prague, published in Melos, *in which the French musician stated that "Stravinsky's Variations contain nothing new, or nothing that Webern had not done already."[26] The following letters from Stravinsky to Boulez date from the comparatively untroubled period after* Threni *and before the* Melos *interview.*

STRAVINSKY TO BOULEZ
[Hollywood]
August 24, 1959

The composition of Movements is finished, and because this was not anticipated, I have had to redistribute my time (spring and summer 1960) completely. I wrote to [Rolf] Liebermann on this subject, but he had already set the date of the world premiere for June 17 in Cologne. In Hamburg, Movements was to be done . . . on June 27. Now I will change these dates and give the premiere in New York (Christmas or the beginning of January), without waiting the additional ten months. I await Liebermann's reply to find out whether he will keep the Cologne and Hamburg dates, in spite of the New York premiere. If so, I do not think that it will be possible for you to count on June 24, since Mrs. Weber, who possesses the exclusive performance rights [for one year in Europe], will probably be busy with rehearsals for the June 27 concert in Hamburg.

That is all for today. I hope to have news from you in London or Venice. Write to me c/o Boosey & Hawkes Ltd., 295 Regent Street, London W1, until September 14, then in Venice at the Bauer-Grünwald. Best greetings.

Cordially,

---

[26] The textures of the twelve-part variations are actually remote from Webern and quite new.

STRAVINSKY TO BOULEZ   *[New York]*
                                                      January 13, 1960

My dear friend,

We will not give the January 23 concert (too expensive). We have finished our
three concerts, with Movements (the other two were the *Noces* and the *Sacre*).
All three were a great success (even in the press), but they cost me a fortune!
So it is with choirs and orchestra! Imagine that even [when] Bernstein's Philharmonic [is] entirely sold out, [the] cost [to] the sponsors [is] $250,000 a
year.

   Madame Weber had a great triumph before the New York audience (and
the press), and I now wish to make the recording of Movements with her in
Hollywood this June (Columbia). This will satisfy me in a way that a concert
cannot do, thanks to all the tension of a "premiere" and a pianist who, although
having memorized the piece, is wholly unfamiliar with the style of the music. I
have heard that she will play it in Cologne in June with Schmidt-Isserstedt.

                                                      [New York]
STRAVINSKY TO BOULEZ   *September 14, 1960*

Thanks, dear Boulez, for your lines. We fly on September 17 to Italy. I conduct
at the Biennale on the 17th and will be at the B [auer]-Gr [ünwald] all of October. The exclusive rights of Madame Weber for Movements end January 10,
1961. Will be happy to hear from you soon.

                                                      Cordially,

STRAVINSKY TO BOULEZ   *Hollywood*
                                                      May 11, 1961

Kapuzinerstrasse 9
Baden-Baden

Dear friend,

Would you give me a present for my birthday: the tape of *Pli selon pli?* I am determined to have that and the orchestra scores as soon as they can be purchased. Say yes.

   Will we see you in Europe this summer? Perhaps your Brussels *Wozzeck*
will coincide with our dates there for a concert at the Radio (October 6–11)?
Will be happy to have news from you, and in the meantime, I embrace you affectionately.

STRAVINSKY TO BOULEZ   *August 23, 1961*

My dear Boulez,

I have just received your letter of August 17. Thank you. The program you describe is good. I regret only the absence of Movements, which you had pre-

viously planned to give despite the "retrospective" character of the concert.[27]

As for my dates, here they are: tomorrow we fly to New York. September 1 we sail on the *Kungsholm* to Scandinavia. On the 12th, I conduct in Helsinki, and from the 15th to the 25th we will be in Stockholm with a radio concert of the *Sacre*. From the 27th to the 30th, God willing, in Berlin. From October 1 to 18 in Zürich, at the Hôtel Baur-au-Lac, and from the 19th to the 31st at the Savoy in London, where I conduct for the BBC. We fly to Cairo on the 31st for five days, then to Bangkok for three days,[28] then continue the flight to Australia and New Zealand. After all these concerts, we rest in Tahiti for five days and arrive in Los Angeles in the first week of December.

What a pity that I will already be in London during the three days that you will be in Basel, and that we will not see each other this year! I should like to have news from you in Stockholm (Grand Hotel), or in Zürich, where I conduct *Histoire du soldat* at the Opera, following *The Nightingale* conducted by someone else.

STRAVINSKY TO BOULEZ   *Hollywood*
                                                   January 8, 1963
Kapuzinerstrasse 9
Baden-Baden

My dear Boulez,

Thank you for your letter of December 17. Just this note in great haste to tell you that the second program you suggest seems to me the better one, because (1) you will use the choir in two compositions, and (2) you would conduct the Paris premiere of *A Sermon, A Narrative and A Prayer,* and better that it be done by you than by some incompetent.

Your letter gave me real pleasure, and now we have only to be assured that your negotiations with the Théâtre des Champs-Elysées end in a definite agreement.

We will stay here until spring, probably the end of March, for which reason I unfortunately have very little hope of seeing you soon. Your good lines reached me at the same time as the announcement (from Zürich) of the death of Hans Rosbaud.[29] I am overcome.

Affectionately yours,

---

[27] "Retrospective" meant, in effect, Stravinsky's popular Russian pieces, whereas he wanted Boulez to play the late works. Stravinsky wrote to his friend Adriana Panni in Rome, January 13, 1965: "Do not think that I disapprove of your choice of Boulez to conduct my *Abraham and Isaac.* On the contrary, I am delighted that you invited him to do it."

[28] Planning to go to Angkor Wat, Stravinsky had obtained a Cambodian visa in London and made arrangements to charter a small airplane, but the trip had to be canceled because of lack of time.

[29] Stravinsky wrote to Suvchinsky, January 19: "Hans Rosbaud is dead. . . . I cannot

Stravinsky's next news of Boulez came from Suvchinsky, who wrote on December 16, 1963:

Wozzeck [at the Paris Opéra] fills the house and is a real triumph. Boulez conducts magnificently, but the sets and production (J.-L. Barrault) are very poor. And Boulez is to blame for this, for, as always, he was very slow to understand. He gave a very shocking explanation to his colleagues of the intent, the essence, and—most unfortunately—of the concept of this amazing work. Now he acknowledges all of the inadequacies of the production. What a strange person he is. . . . If you could only see what happens on stage.

Three days later Suvchinsky wrote again to say that on December 18, Boulez was invited to lunch with de Gaulle, and returned "awkward but pleased."

After Stravinsky's death, Boulez told an interviewer, Célestin Deliège, that his view of the composer of the Sacre *had not changed since 1949. In the same book,* Conversations with Deliège, *Boulez refers to the visit of the Südwestfunk Orchestra to Paris in 1957 without mentioning Stravinsky—whose participation had been the reason that money was found to pay for the event.*

---

rid myself of the idea that contemporary music has been orphaned. His death had a profound effect on me." Yet Stravinsky had written to his wife from Baden-Baden, May 18, 1954: "I have just attended a rehearsal of the Symphony in Three Movements conducted by Rosbaud. Very clear, but somewhat mathematical and lifeless."

LETTERS TO

1929 ～ 1967

NICOLAS NABOKOV

In June 1928, Stravinsky's niece Ira Belline appeared in Diaghilev's production of Nicolas Nabokov's[1] oratorio-ballet Ode,[2] but whether or not it was this that brought about the association of the two Russian musicians the present writer cannot say. In any case, Nabokov's first letter to Stravinsky, November 1, 1928, reveals that they were already on friendly terms, and in an October 1929 post-card to Ansermet, Stravinsky comments approvingly on the younger man's music.[3] Little more than a month later, however, Nabokov was in disfavor, and the next exchange of letters was to be the last for fourteen years. In an article entitled "The Life and Work of Serge de Diaghilev," published in the November 15, 1929, issue of the Paris review Musique, Nabokov wrote that Petrushka "seems to have been Diaghilev's idea, not Stravinsky's," and that "certainly Diaghilev gave Stravinsky the first idea for Liturgie, which is to say for that which became Les Noces." Since both claims are untrue, and since Robert Lyon, the director of the magazine, was also Stravinsky's business manager, one wonders why the composer was not asked to verify them. The answer may simply be that, biographical facts of this kind not yet being available in 1929, Nabokov's information was assumed to be true.

Nabokov, in his article, says that "for Diaghilev, Stravinsky was the great-est genius of our era, and what attracted Diaghilev to Stravinsky was the enigma that surrounds every great creator." Nevertheless, Stravinsky wrote to Marc Pincherle, editor-in-chief of Musique, tersely correcting the misinforma-tion without so much as mentioning Nabokov's name.[4] Nabokov sent an apol-ogy to Stravinsky (December 5) and persuaded Jacques Maritain to intercede (letter of December 6[5]). But Nabokov's letter is maladroit, blaming Diaghilev for the errors and insisting, "I have never wanted to hurt you or to anger you." Stravinsky pounced on this—"That would be the last straw!"—and his an-swer, though polite, is dismissive. A note from Nabokov to Stravinsky in the summer of 1935, requesting an audience on behalf of Balanchine apropos of a

---

[1] Nicolas Nabokov (1903–1978), composer, author, teacher, classical scholar. French is the original language of the correspondence except where indicated.
[2] The first performance, June 6, was on a program with Les Noces.
[3] See S.S.C. I, p. 200.
[4] See S.P.D., p. 294.
[5] See S.P.D., p. 293.

new ballet (eventually Jeu du cartes), *seems to have been ignored, as well as an announcement of the wedding of Nabokov to Constance Holladay (Minneapolis, March 23, 1939), and Nabokov's name does not reappear in Stravinsky's correspondence until 1943.*[6]

During World War II, Nabokov taught at St. John's College, Annapolis, and at the Peabody Conservatory in Baltimore. In the spring of 1945 he was appointed to an important position in the American Army of Occupation in Germany. He was uniquely qualified for this, speaking German and French as fluently as Russian and English, and possessing a knowledge of European culture ranging far beyond music. (Stravinsky used to refer to him as "the culture generalissimo.") Moreover, as a member of a prominent family in the Russian liberal movement, Nabokov was at least as informed about East-West politics as were the leaders of the Allied governments. While in Berlin, he served as political intelligence adviser to General Lucius Clay. At the same time, Nabokov was made responsible for the reconstruction of German musical life, and he appointed the directors of the opera houses, radio stations, and symphony orchestras that were to determine the artistic continuity and development of the country after denazification. He proved to be so able an organizer and administrator that in the 1950s and 1960s the U.S. government financed arts festivals that he presented in Paris, Rome, Tokyo, and Berlin. All of these featured the music and the presence of Igor Stravinsky.

In July 1944, Nabokov published an essay, "Stravinsky Now," in Partisan Review.[7] *For a time thereafter, Stravinsky seems to have thought that he had found a champion in the largely hostile American press, but Nabokov's next Stravinsky article, a description in the* Atlantic *of Christmas 1947 in Stravinsky's Hollywood home, failed to please,*[8] *albeit for reasons that remain obscure: the account of the Stravinsky residence and of the mode of living of its inhabitants is perfectly accurate, and an invitation* had *been extended the year before.*[9]

"Christmas with Stravinsky" had not yet been published when its author and subject next saw each other, in Washington, D.C., April 3, 1948. By this time Nabokov had taken a new wife, Patricia Blake, an action of which the Stravinskys disapproved, not for any personal reason but simply because they

---

[6] Soulima Stravinsky wrote from Paris to his father in Hanover, December 8, 1931: "Nabokov, Markevitch, and Sauguet are saying that Ansermet did a terrible job with the *Sacre*, but I found it brilliant."

[7] On May 15, Nabokov had written to Stravinsky that *Partisan Review* "is a rather leftist magazine of literary character à la N [ouvelle] R [evue] F [rançaise]. I managed to offset the leftist association by dedicating my essay to Maritain."

[8] See p. 375.

[9] On November 20, 1947, Nabokov wrote to Stravinsky that when Balanchine said he was going to California, "I decided I would like to go, too, but only if it would be convenient for you."

were not sympathetic to the instability in Nabokov's marital relationships and disliked having to adjust to new spouses.[10] *(Here it should be said that the Stravinskys reacted the same way to the wife changing of their other friends, and opposed their bachelor friends' marrying at all; and though Stravinsky was always hospitable to newly acquired friends of friends, his possessiveness was such that the older link in the relationship often broke.) An accidental encounter between the first and the third wives on the stairs to the green room at Town Hall, New York, April 11, 1948, kept the newlyweds from seeing the Stravinskys, though a note Nabokov sent that same night gives a different reason: "We wanted to join you backstage, to kiss you and thank you for the joy ... you gave us with your concert. . . . The Symphony in C is worthy of Mozart. . . . But there was such a crowd."*

Stravinsky and Nabokov saw each other briefly in New York in February 1949. By December 1950, Nabokov's role in Stravinsky's life had become, as it was to remain, that of an entrepreneur. As the letters show, it was Nabokov who arranged the premiere of The Rake's Progress in Venice, Nabokov who presented Stravinsky in the Paris festival of the following spring, and Nabokov who made Stravinsky the focus of the Rome festival of 1954. The 1952 Paris appearance was Stravinsky's first since the summer of 1938, and he and his music, together with the Vienna Opera's Wozzeck, were the main attractions in this celebration of "the arts of the twentieth century."

Though on a smaller scale, the festivities in Rome proved to be more consequential for Stravinsky, leading to the commission for the Canticum Sacrum, and, through Nabokov, those for Threni, the Movements for Piano and Orchestra, and Abraham and Isaac. The commission for Threni, effected through Nabokov's friendship with Rolf Liebermann, director of the Hamburg Opera, led to conducting engagements for Stravinsky there and in four Swiss cities (in 1958, and again in Hamburg in 1962 and 1963), as well as the composer's participation in Los Angeles, Hamburg, and London in a film portrait of his life (1965). Finally, it was Nicolas Nabokov, through his friend Arthur Schlesinger, Jr., who prompted President Kennedy to fête Stravinsky in an eightieth-birthday dinner at the White House.

During Nabokov's fourth marriage, which, in name at least, lasted from May 1953 through the 1960s, the relationship with the Stravinskys was less intimate, partly because their interests and those of the new wife, Marie-Claire, were so dissimilar. But other reasons existed for the distancing, above all Stravinsky's renewal of a long-suspended connection with Pierre Suvchinsky, a Russian émigré whose political views were fundamentally opposed to Nabokov's.[11] Stravinsky and Suvchinsky had avoided each other in May 1952, and the reconciliation did not begin until August 1957—following a brief meeting

---

[10] Natasha Shakhovskoy, Constance Holladay, Patricia Blake, Marie-Claire Brot, Dominique Cibiel.

[11] Just before flying from New York to Paris, June 1, 1945, Nabokov wrote to Stravinsky: "I am going to try to see everyone I can, especially Pyotr Petrovich Suv-

*in Paris in December 1956. Nabokov and Suvchinsky became increasingly jeal-
ous of each other's position and influence vis-à-vis their great compatriot; but
on this question the correspondence reveals almost nothing.*

*Stravinsky enjoyed the company of both men, though he saw Nabokov
much more frequently and in many different places throughout the world, and
saw Suvchinsky, with few exceptions, only during trips to Paris. It must also be
said that Stravinsky did not completely trust either of these friends, being fully
aware of Suvchinsky's tendency to blow hot and cold, and of Nabokov's habit of
making fun of him behind his back—as Nabokov did of all of his friends,
though the victims accepted this as a natural peccadillo.[12]*

*Stravinsky's music and presence were the feature of Nabokov's Berlin fes-
tival of October 1964. (Stravinsky's 1956 Berlin appearance had been negotiated by Nabokov, the one in 1961 partly by him.) On this occasion, however,
Nabokov was not in his best form. He sent a letter of apology to Stravinsky,[13]
but until the reunion in September 1965, in Hamburg, the friendship was at a
low ebb.*

*After that, and beginning in Zürich and Paris in October and November
1968, the connection became, and was to remain, closer than ever before. The
two men were together in New York in April 1969. And from November 1969 to
February 1971, Nicolas and Dominique—his last, and, as many of his friends
believed, most suitable wife—spent as much time with the composer in his suite
at the Essex House as any of his friends. Stravinsky had always responded to
Nabokov's "Russian" warmth, his sense of the ridiculous, his parodies of accents and speech. In the last months of Stravinsky's life, these qualities and
gifts gave him more pleasure than ever before, and in this final period he did
not have a more faithful friend. At the funeral in Venice, April 15, 1971, Nabokov stood by Mrs. Stravinsky's side during the ceremony and at the cemetery.*

*The Stravinsky-Nabokov correspondence offers only pale reflections of the rela-
tionship that was so vivid whenever the two were together. Fortunately, one of
their typical meetings—the present writer witnessed nearly all of them—in
Stravinsky's hotel room in Hamburg in May 1963, has been preserved on film.
As a raconteur and mimic Nabokov was unrivaled, but these talents depended
on live performance and did not show to advantage in print, where, in addition, he could not exploit his linguistic gifts, his humor, and his immense culture. The Russian letters of both men are richer and more intimate and affectionate than those written in French (which, on Nabokov's side, were nearly*

---

chinsky." But on December 23, 1950, writing to Stravinsky about mutual friends in
Paris, Nabokov remarked that "the best, the purest, the most loyal and incorruptible of
all . . . is Nadia Boulanger. . . . The Suvchinskys proclaim the 'genius' of M. Pierre
Boulez, who writes notes, not music."

[12] That Stravinsky did not excuse this habit is shown in a 1965 letter to Adriana Panni;
see fn. 81 on p. 417.

[13] See p. 416.

always dictated), largely concerned as they are with Stravinsky's conducting fees, schemes for tax avoidance, program planning, rehearsal schedules, and travel itineraries. But the letters as a whole form a framework for Stravinsky's 1950s and 1960s European activities that is offered by no other correspondence with a friend.

Nabokov's first letter to Stravinsky refers to "what you said to me that day in the café ... that a chord properly done ('placed') contains within it the elements of uncompromising and eternal religious laws." If Stravinsky answered, he did not keep a copy. His first letter follows the one to the editor of Musique.

STRAVINSKY TO NICOLAS NABOKOV   *Paris*
                                                December 8, 1929
Dear Nika Dimitrievich,

I have received your letter of December 5 and must tell you that, reading your "open-hearted" confession, I was completely surprised to learn that you did not wish to "hurt" or "anger" me. "That would be the last straw!," one feels the urge to cry out. So to lay this question to rest, I will accept as an explanation what you call your "inadvertent error." I have no right to refuse to forgive someone who confesses to me so frankly; so I forgive you. But I must add that you did not hurt me with your blunder so much as you injured Truth, and that in order to redeem yourself, it would be appropriate for you to admit publicly that the "facts" published in the latest issue of *Musique* have been found to be inaccurate. This should be done by publishing my letter in the editorial section of the coming issue. Only through such action can your mistake be redeemed and Truth established.* This would be more effective than the most sincere private confession, since the public, misled by the inaccuracies, would not benefit from your private clarification. This is all that I wanted to say to you in reply to your letter.

* (which is undoubtedly what you want as well) [*Original in Russian*]

STRAVINSKY TO NABOKOV   *Hollywood*
                                            September 8, 1943[14]
Annapolis

Dear friend,

Just these lines to tell you how much pleasure I had in reading your letter and brilliant articles on Prokofiev (*Atlantic*, July 1942) and Shostakovich (*Harper's*, March 1943). It is gratifying to see that these American reviews

---

[14] In a letter to Stravinsky, September 2, Nabokov had outlined the points he wished to make in an article on Stravinsky's music: "Technique in the classical tradition is not an external adornment, but the very essence of music; if one tries to isolate technique

take an interest in a mentality such as yours. In inviting you to write an article about my music, they made an excellent choice, as you did in choosing my most recent compositions as a theme. That obviously requires a more solid cultural competence on the part of the critic and a very different approach from those that, alas, we witness so often.

I will immediately inform Mr. Hugo Winter of the Associated Music Publishers, Inc. (25 West 45th Street, New York), that he should put at your disposal the orchestra scores of my last Symphony, *Norwegian Moods, Circus Polka, Danses concertantes,* and *Ode* (recently composed to the memory of Natalie Koussevitzky—for the Koussevitzky Foundation).

Very sincerely yours,

STRAVINSKY TO NABOKOV

Hollywood
October 5, 1943

My dear Nabokov,

Yesterday I sent you a cable in order to save you some time and difficulty regarding my Symphony [in C]. Why not simply borrow it from Reginald Stewart[15] for a few days, since he now has the score?[16] Unfortunately, I have only one photocopy, which I cannot let out of my sight even for a short time. I hope that you will manage to reach an agreement with R. Stewart or H. Winter on this subject.

With regard to the *Ode,* tomorrow or the day after I will send you a photostatic copy of the orchestra score, which you should have by Monday, October 11, at the latest. Listen to the broadcast of the Koussevitzky concert in Boston, where it will be played for the first time on October 8 or 9. Remember that only the first half of the program will be broadcast, on Saturday, October 9. I hope my *Ode* will be included in this half and that Koussevitzky will be faithful to my tempo indications. I enclose this short note, which I sent the other day to Mr. John N. Burk (who is in charge of the program [notes] of the Boston Symphony) to provide you with a little more information about the *Ode.*

Norwegian Moods:[17] Not as *Stimmung* or temper of mind, but as mode,

---

from the musical fabric, music becomes an academic matter. . . . Your music is crucial in this regard, since it brings technique and artistic meaning together again, after the estrangement brought about by the hubris of the nineteenth century."

[15] Reginald Stewart, conductor of the Baltimore Symphony Orchestra 1942–52.

[16] The original score of the Symphony in C had been in the Library of Congress, but as Nabokov's letter to Stravinsky of September 30 explains, the Library had sent the manuscript to a secret basement vault for the duration of the war and had not kept a photocopy in Washington. In a letter of November 5, 1943, Nabokov says that he has borrowed the score from Reginald Stewart and studied it " *'daskanale'* [thoroughly], as the Poles say."

[17] In his September 30 letter, Nabokov had asked: "Did you call the suite 'moods'—

i.e., form, manner, or style. Each part of my suite joins together various tunes from a selection of Norwegian folklore,* authentic (except for their esthetic presentation, of course, which is by Grieg, Sinding, Svendsen & Co.). Very true, your remark about my attitude regarding the Haydn tradition in the treatment of folklore.

Dumbarton Oaks was never recorded. As for *Danses concertantes,* we made a tape of it (under the pretense of obtaining a souvenir) during the V. Golschmann[18] rehearsals in April of this year, in the last concert of the Serenade [Museum of Modern Art]. Not a very good recording, indeed: the dynamics were not well regulated (microphonic insufficiency), and the tempi were often too nervous and unsteady (fault of the conductor, probably owing to the fact that our friend Golschmann is not familiar with my recent compositions). I give you, nevertheless, the address of the company that made this imperfect recording: Mary Howard Recordings, 37 East 49th Street, New York. The orchestra score of *Danses concertantes* was just released by Associated Music Publishers, Inc.

I think that I have answered all of your questions. If you have more, do not hesitate to ask me. If I have time (not always the case), I shall answer you willingly.

Cordially to you,

* I found W. Hansen's edition, from the beginning of the century, in the Public Library here.

On January 10, 1944, Nabokov wrote that Harper's *had rejected his article on Stravinsky as being too technical. The letter is signed "Bien à vous, Nicolas Nabokov."*

January 12, 1944
[Telegram]

STRAVINSKY TO NABOKOV

Kindly send copy your article [to] Ritz Towers where [I] will be only one day, January 17. The broadcasted part of my [Boston Symphony] program changed as follows: Symphony, *Norwegian Moods*, [Circus] Polka. Please advise Reginald Stewart, as he intends [to] perform it.

'*nastroynya*'—only for thematic considerations, or did you have other reasons?" In a letter of October 13, he says: "I had understood moods to mean mode, but then it occurred to me that perhaps you had intended a more Platonic meaning—mood = mode = moral or ethical condition, soul-form. But I may be trying too hard, and your definition (form, manner, style) is quite enough in itself."

[18] Vladimir Golschmann (1893–1972), conductor of the St. Louis Symphony Orchestra 1931–58. He and his wife were good friends of the Stravinskys in their American years.

On January 15, Nabokov replied that he had telephoned Stewart and that at the moment no copy of the article was available; hence Stravinsky should give an address to which the text could be sent. Stravinsky answered Nabokov's next letter (of May 15, 1944) from Hollywood.

STRAVINSKY TO NABOKOV   *May 20, 1944*

My dear Nabokov,

These few lines in great haste to thank you for the interesting letter [of May 15]. I have very little time at my disposal right now (and until mid-July, probably) to compile the chronological resume (two pages long!!) you requested. I would like to assist you, nevertheless, so I propose that you type up a questionnaire and let me answer, if only briefly, each question. . . . Leave enough space for my replies, and type it double or triple spaced.

I am very happy that you liked the Sonata for two pianos,[19] and I find the idea of playing it for your students very agreeable. But do not play it publicly, since it has not yet been published.

As for the two copies you requested, address yourself to Hugo Winter, Associated Music Publishers, 25 W. 45th Street, New York 19, N.Y. Not long ago, I sent him my manuscript of transparencies (for provisional reproductions). Only one copy remains here. . . . That is all for today. I shake your hand very cordially. A thousand best wishes to your wife.

Stravinsky and Nabokov met in March 1945, for the first time since 1942, the second time since 1928.

Nabokov's next letter, June 1, 1945, was posted from a New York airport just before his departure for Europe. The letter after that, March 22, 1946, is stamped "Office of Military Government for Germany (U.S.), Office of the Director of Information Control, APO 742." Here Nabokov writes that he has found and is sending an old program "that belonged to my father and that contains the name of your father." He says that he expects to be in the United States in a fortnight and hopes to see Stravinsky then, because of a plan to write "a kind of commentary on the Poétique musicale," *the purpose of which would be to counter "the musical ordure coming from the USSR, the United States, and the young French school." Nabokov says that he is weary of Berlin: "I have had enough of discussions with representatives of the Soviets, of telephone calls from the Soviets—though the telephone ceases to function every*

---

[19] In the letter of May 15, Nabokov says that he had heard the Sonata at Marcelle de Manziarly's, that he especially liked the variation movement, and that he wanted to analyze the piece with his students at Peabody and in Annapolis. Mlle de Manziarly, assistant to Nadia Boulanger, was a close friend of the Stravinskys, especially during the 1940s.

time Mr. Churchill makes a speech that the Russians do not like—and enough of banquets with Marshals Zhukov and Budennyi." The letter concludes:

In the tragic world in which we live . . . only a few encouraging, reasonable, and beautiful things remain. One of these, and for me the most important, is your art, with all of its nobility, beauty, and intelligence. . . . It is in thinking of the Symphony in C that one begins to see clearly, and to feel again the meaning of homo sapiens.

STRAVINSKY TO NABOKOV   *April 1, 1946*

c/o Mrs. Constance Nabokov[20]
St. John's College
Annapolis

My dear friend,

May this note express my joy in receiving your letter (of March 22, 1946) and your promise to come here soon. Come, come, we await you impatiently. You can stay at our house, on the same floor and under the same canopy where Nadia Boulanger spent her nights when she came to Hollywood. As you probably know, she has been in Paris (36, rue Ballu), since mid-January. The whole time that we were in New York (January–February) we waited for you, to no avail. George Balanchine read us a letter that he received from you and Natasha, and he gave us news of you from time to time. Reginald Stewart (whose Baltimore Orchestra I conducted in the beginning of February, also giving a lecture there) spoke of you as their guest professor for next year, but that is all I have heard about you. Now, finally, I have direct news of you. From the bottom of my heart, I hope for your return and your visit here. In this, the most *deaf* period we have ever suffered, it is good to see each other. After the few lines (concerning your experiences and observations) I declare with pleasure that we speak the same language—which I had doubted. So know that you are welcome, and do not forget to confirm your visit.

   Very cordially to you.

On June 9 Nabokov wrote that he had been to Paris and had seen Boulanger, Desormière, Sauguet, and others "of a group of people who admire your recent music"; that he was grateful to Stravinsky for a package of food sent to Fyodor Vladimirovich Weber (of the defunct Russischer Musik Verlag); and that a certain Anatole Memorsky, an interpreter for the Russians in Berlin, sends compliments "to Vera Arturovna and to you." Nabokov says, too, that he received a

---

[20] Acknowledging a postcard from Stravinsky, Nabokov wrote, January 12, 1945: "I cannot come to your concert in New York on the 27th . . . since my wife will be there for the week and I must stay here in the role of governess."

letter from Anna Akhmatova in Leningrad, and that Prokofiev found Lev Kar-
savin in Vilnius, working as a professor, and, after five years of silence, tele-
graphed this news to Suvchinsky.

STRAVINSKY TO NABOKOV   *December 8, 1947*

Dear friend Nika Nabokov,

The airplane ticket is ordered for you on December 27. We expect you and
George Balanchine on the 21st, and we will meet you at Pasadena station, the
last stop before the Los Angeles station (20 or 30 minutes from the "ter-
minus").[21] Inform us immediately of the exact time of arrival in Pasadena, and
the name and number of the train. On the "Chief," I hope. Bring me three
albums of the *Dumbarton Oaks* Concerto, which they still do not have here in
the stores.[22] Tell this to Sasha Schneider, who so zealously defends the Keynote
Corp. We await you.

                                         Sincerely yours,   I. Str.

I was not able to hear the Krenek symphony.[23] . . . Did you know that Sokolov[24]
is in the Algonquin Hotel in New York? He's playing in *Crime and Punishment*.
[*Original in Russian*]

Nabokov left Hollywood on December 27 and wrote from New York on the 30th,
thanking the Stravinskys for "the love, the kindness, the tender and touching hos-
pitality that you showed me during those, in all senses, splendidly sunny days."

STRAVINSKY TO NABOKOV   *January 2, 1948*

Dear Nika Dmitrievich,

Although there isn't time to write a letter, I could not fail to acknowledge your
kind message.

---

[21] On December 13 Nabokov wrote saying that his train does not stop at Pasadena, but
only at the Los Angeles station (at 11 a.m., Sunday, December 21).
[22] The Concerto had been recorded in New York between April 27 and 30. See *S.S.C.* I,
p. 332.
[23] Nabokov's letter of November 30 deprecates a symphony by Krenek, performed in
New York by Dimitri Mitropoulos. In the same letter Nabokov says that he is bringing
some bottles of Eau de Genièvre; asks "Vera Arturovna to reserve a plane ticket for my
return to New York on the evening of the 27th"; and says, "I do not know Robert
Craft, but recently I heard something about him to the effect that he is a serious fellow."
[24] Vladimir Sokolov, the actor. His wife, Lisa, was co-owner with Mrs. Stravinsky of an
art gallery in Hollywood. An invitation to stay at the Sokolovs' Hollywood home came
through Nabokov's first wife, Natasha.

What a disgrace that we will not hear your *Elegia*. What a lot of sh——
this is anyway, all of this K.[25] Neither him, nor a mother with a hundred asses,
nor the French word *con* can describe him in Russian any other way than with
[the letter] K.

New Yorker: You must agree. It would be good if you would mention there
and in *Life* just how amused I was by the sensation raised in the press over the
transcription—attributed to me—of *Firebird* melodies for jazz, an arrangement
I did not even see until it had come out. Please do that for me; I will be very
grateful to you.

I will write to Ralph Hawkes[26] about you, without fail; he will be back soon.
But to tell the truth, your idea to go off to Europe for two whole years grieves us.

Having had nothing but promises from the agents of the ocean liner, we
secured places through influential friends on the S.S. *America* (for May 12).
This will take us directly to France without having to stop in England, which
would mean a loss of two whole days for us, to say nothing of all the baggage
and fuss.

Every night I read a little, three or four pages, of Lev Shestov's wonderful
book on Kierkegaard. There is no time for more than that, and, with this accessible memory of mine, I carefully pack away all that I read. When one thinks
about what Sartre did with Existentialism, one cannot help recalling the anec-
dote about the peasant woman who saw a camel for the first time in Soviet Moscow.* "Lov, keesses."

Of course I want Handel's *Caesar,* but later; right now I am still waiting for
the Mozart. Don't you have the *Così fan tutte* piano score?

* "Look what the Bolsheviks have done to horses!" [*Original in Russian*]

Nabokov married Patricia Blake on March 21,[27] and on the 26th the Stra-
vinskys sent their "heartiest wishes and congratulations" to the newlyweds at
the Hotel Gladstone, 114 East 52nd Street, New York, which was to be Stra-
vinsky's residence, when in New York, from late November 1951 to January
1960.

STRAVINSKY TO NABOKOV   *September 23, 1948*

Dearest Nika Nabokov,

I was glad to exchange a few words with you over the telephone, but I still want
to tell you that although your answer to this twelve-tonal obscurantism and to

---

[25] Koussevitzky (i.e., ka-ka).

[26] Ralph Hawkes (1898–1950), director of Boosey & Hawkes.

[27] While still in California, Nabokov had told the Stravinskys about his relationship
with Miss Blake, though the Stravinskys already knew about this from Alexander
Schneider in his letter of September 23, 1947.

the impudent René Leibowitz is worthwhile,[28] I think that the *Partisan Review* will not stop with this, but will give him its pages to continue his bad-mouthing. I have the impression that Leibowitz has definitely gained a certain prestige and even authority in the eyes of the musically ignorant editorial staff; otherwise they would have inserted a qualifying remark when publishing one of his articles to the effect that the editorial staff does not necessarily endorse his statements and conclusions, but leaves him personally responsible for them. . . . Exactly when will your answer appear? Will you send it?

Svetik [Soulima] told me of his concern about your other article too. Has it still not been decided where and when this will be published?

Svetik played the Mozart concerto "beautifully," in the word of Abrasha [Alexander] Schneider, only it is a pity that Antonini, the conductor, could not see any reason for not playing Mozart with a Strauss arrangement of instruments. This Antonini is evidently a pretty primitive gentleman. Additional rehearsals would also have been useful for him.

What, Lifar still has not had his ears boxed?

Sincerely yours,

[*Original in Russian*]

On December 10, 1949, Nabokov sent a long, nostalgic letter to the Stravinskys, saying how he "envies Balanchine and Craft their opportunities to see and be with you," and how sad he was "to hear from Genya Berman[29] that you did not like my article, for I had written it with love and admiration." The letter describes Messiaen's Turangalîla *(performed by the Boston Symphony) in unprintable terms and says, "I have been relishing the impressions of Perséphone, Orpheus, Firebird, and Mavra. . . . I am especially grateful to Craft for his concerts, which he conducts with such energy and urgency."[30]*

STRAVINSKY TO NABOKOV   *December 15, 1949*

Dear friend,

Thank you for your letter. I am completely immersed in writing the opera, working at the moment on the third scene of the second act. Everything to there is orchestrated. If I can get as far as the part of the orchestration that you saw at Auden's, I will send it to you for the holidays.

---

[28] Nabokov had enclosed his answer to Leibowitz's article, "Schönberg and Stravinsky" (*Partisan Review,* March 1948), in a letter to Stravinsky dated September 2, 1948. Nabokov's article, "The Atonal Trail: A Communication," was published in a subsequent issue.

[29] Eugene Berman (1899–1973), stage designer, was one of the Stravinskys' closest friends.

[30] Stravinsky underscored this sentence in red pencil.

I heard Prokofiev's Sixth Symphony: Nothing justifies its dullness.[31] Moreover, it demonstrates neither esthetic nor technical novelty. This is clear to everyone except Comrade Olin Downes.[32]

All week here I've listened to Aunt Britten and Uncle Pears, but we will discuss that later. Britten himself makes quite a favorable impression, and he is very popular with the public. He undoubtedly has talent as a performer, especially at the piano.[33]

As might be expected, Merle Armitage's little book[34] testifies only to his good relationship with me, which, of course, is not enough. It was absurd and stupid to feature the article by Scriabin's brother-in-law.[35] . . . What rubbish of the Russian intelligentsia this exhibits.[36] The general appearance of the book, with its importunate, cheap, and provincial illustrations and vignettes, is as unacceptable as the price of six dollars.

Concerning your own article,[37] I regret that Berman got to you before I did, for I wanted to talk to you about it myself. I think that your impression of my opinion of it would have been different from the one that was formulated after your conversation with him. I am postponing this until our meeting, I hope in March, since to write about these things is complicated and lengthy. I will say that I am a bit puzzled by the conclusion that you draw from my critical attitude toward the article. For some reason you suspect "affected self-esteem," even some "offense," in the motives for my criticism, and use this excuse yourself. This is nonsense. The truth is a lot simpler: I am not in agreement with the contents of the article and with the way in which you use it. That is all. Why go into this business of "self-esteem" and "offense"?

---

[31] Nabokov had written to Stravinsky, May 15, 1944: "I have heard Prokofiev's new music, and I fear that in these latest works he has begun to fall into a kind of bourgeois infantilism. And Shostakovich's Eighth Symphony is simply impossible to listen to. Such *merde* is imposed on the naively stupid, apathetic, and profoundly uncultivated American public by orchestra conductors who are themselves *canailles* and who exploit the stupidest emotions of the people in this cultural desert."

[32] In a letter of October 13, 1943, Nabokov had asked Stravinsky to send him "any particularly stupid reviews that you may happen to have, Downes's for example."

[33] When Stravinsky and Britten were jointly awarded the Erasmus Prize (100,000 guilder) in November 1965, Stravinsky tersely declined. "How tactless these Dutch," he wrote to his publisher, November 18, 1965.

[34] *Igor Stravinsky*, edited by Edwin Corle. This was a revised edition of the 1936 symposium, edited by Armitage, who also designed both books.

[35] Boris de Schloezer.

[36] The low caliber of the "Russian intelligentsia" is a theme of Stravinsky's correspondence, but the reader is shocked to find Nabokov replying, September 27, 1948: "I am reading Herzen and finding more and more that the Russian liberals were really feeble-minded dilettantes."

[37] Nabokov's "Christmas with Stravinsky" article had been included in the Armitage book.

I will close now. It is already one o'clock in the morning, Friday, December 15, 1949. We kiss you both.

I'll be happy to hear your new music—the ballet and cantatas. Regarding Fedya's book,[38] I will write to him *without fail*. I myself have not had a letter from him in two months. [*Original in Russian*]

A year elapsed before Nabokov's next letter (December 23, 1950), which contains an account of his involvement with the "Congress for Cultural Freedom," of the European musical and literary scenes, of a visit with "an old friend of mine, Isaiah Berlin," and of a meeting in Rome with Mario Labroca, director of music for the Italian Radio. It was then that Nabokov convinced Labroca, in principle, to secure the Rake *premiere ("Bob has kindly given me some news of Act III") for Venice and to give Stravinsky $20,000 for conducting the opera.*

STRAVINSKY TO NABOKOV   *January 2, 1951*

Very dear friend,

It was a great pleasure to have your letter, especially after so many months of silence. I was not at all up-to-date on your activities, and my surprise, therefore, on reading your addresses, covering many countries, from [Italy] to Iceland, was that much greater. I would love to talk to you about it at length, but for the moment am forced to limit myself to a few lines.

Infinite thanks for having defended my interests vis-à-vis Labroca. I just wrote to him, and we will see what comes of it. In effect, I ask $20,000, payable here, and the guarantee of an excellent, professional, English-language performance. Otherwise I indicate my preference for La Fenice.[39]

Thank you also for the wonderful Soviet clipping, which would make Karl Marx laugh.[40] I return it to you, attached.

As for the Bach-Casals, it delights me. Finished with Bach-Busoni and Bach-Stokowski. Now we have Bach-Casals-Schneider, if the Soviets authorize it. I keep this letter as a treasure. Pardon my haste. A good year to both of you from both of us.

On January 5, Nabokov wrote that the Baltimore Orchestra would be playing the Symphony in C in New York on January 17, and that "if Bob is in Los Angeles, ask him to put some program notes together and send them to me." On March 7, Nabokov reported having "heard from Bob that the Fenice arrangement came through. . . . I miss you so much that if I had $300 I would come and visit you for Easter."

---

[38] Theodore Stravinsky's *Le Message d'Igor Strawinsky* (Lausanne, 1948).

[39] Stravinsky had understood that Labroca wanted the opera for Rome.

[40] The illustration, from the Soviet magazine *Ogonyok*, shows Marx writing *Das Kapital* with, on the wall next to him, a portrait of Stalin.

STRAVINSKY TO NABOKOV

1260 North Wetherly Drive
Los Angeles
March 9, 1951
[Telegram]

1350 Madison Avenue
New York

Too bad cannot find 300 dollars in my purse but only 220 to offer you air coach round trip via American or TWA. Will you accept to fly that way and be my guest next weekend? Do you want check now or here? Love,   Igor Stravinsky
[*Original in English*]

STRAVINSKY TO NABOKOV   *March 16, 1951*

1350 Madison Avenue
New York

Very dear friend,

Here is the check. . . . We are thrilled that you accept our invitation. Our only regret is that you will have so little time. I say nothing else, because I have just returned from Cuba and have many things to liquidate now, but we will talk when you come. Advise me of your exact arrival time (which flight?). If the hour is not outlandish, we will pick you up at the airport (Vera and I . . .).

STRAVINSKY TO NABOKOV   *March 30, 1951*

1350 Madison Avenue
New York

Dear Nika,

Thank you for the letter. How fortunate that you have recovered your score!! . . . What a story!!![41] Also, thank you for the names of the singers. For the time being I hold them in reserve, because, before all else, the issue is to keep the Venetian gondola afloat. Right now everything depends on the realization or nonrealization of my agreement with La Scala, because, aside from the prospects of a Ghiringhelli–Boosey & Hawkes lawsuit, it is certain that if La Scala is

---

[41] Nabokov had stayed in the Stravinsky home from Thursday, March 22, to Monday, March 26. After returning to New York, he telegraphed that he had lost a music manuscript and hoped it might still be at the Stravinskys'. On the 28th he wrote that it was found in a copy of *Life* magazine on the TWA airplane that he had taken to New York. The letter thanks the Stravinskys "for those splendid four days, for the music, for Bob, for Huxley, for Isherwood, for the conversations, even for the gastritis."

On March 28, Stravinsky had written to Willy Strecker: "Nicolas Nabokov came to see me at Easter and played me his recent compositions. . . . I had the idea to recommend him to you, and since in a month he must return to Europe on an official mission, he can use the opportunity to visit you and to enter into contact with you directly.

not satisfied, Ghiringhelli will arrange to torpedo Labroca directly (and at the same time the Biennale).[42]

Tell me if you still want me to send you the first two acts of the *Rake;* you don't confirm that for me in your letter, and I wonder if you still want them.

Thank you very much for the small check. In the meantime I hope that your health is recovered. I am better, but now it is Bob's turn to run to the bathroom.

On April 3, Nabokov wrote, "I desperately want [copies of] the first and third acts . . . and I also want some Huxley glasses, since I cannot go on playing the trombone from a telephone book."[43] *On April 13, Stravinsky sent a copy of his manuscript of the opera, and on April 27, Nabokov thanked him: "It is all so masterful, so clear, so infinitely beautiful, and so pleasing to the mind. 'Die schöne Musik muss auch klug sein,' Hanslick wrote. . . . Regards to Bobónok." Also on April 27, Nabokov flew to Paris, and his next letter came from there, dated May 12. He had heard Igor Markevitch conduct the* Sacre *"very cleanly and honestly. . . . In my opinion, out of a scoundrel has grown a real man, intelligent, musically honest, and knowing his business."*

STRAVINSKY TO NABOKOV   *May 17, 1951*

My dear Nika,

Thank you for your nice letter of May 12 from Paris. As you can easily imagine, your vivid impressions and observations interest me. I still do not know anything and am sending a third telegram to Ballo[44] right now in the hope of eliciting some sort of response. He telegraphed on the 9th:

> Premiere *Rake* in Venice almost definite with Intendente Teatro La Scala. Meeting Friday the 2nd. Definite details follow [in] letter.

I cabled twice to find out the result of that meeting of the 2nd and to press him to negotiate with the singers, but I have received no reply. I hope that the situation will have been resolved by the time of your arrival in Italy. . . .

The Berman, Balthus, Ebert, Strehler question[45] is important but for the

---

Nabokov is a serious composer, and one of value, who certainly merits publication and performances more than many many others today."

[42] Antonio Ghiringhelli (d. 1979) played a large role in re-establishing La Scala after the war.

[43] Huxley's "glasses" were celluloid goggles with several perforations, the size of pinholes, through which the eye was forced to exercise and avoid staring.

[44] Ferdinando Ballo was director of the Venice Biennale in 1951.

[45] Of who was to direct and design the *Rake*. Carl Ebert was Stravinsky's choice to direct. The sets were by the Italian painter Gianni Ratto. (See the correspondence with Auden in *S.S.C.* I, pp. 316–20.)

time being enters into my worries only in the background, much behind the problem of recruiting singers. If we continue to drag, we will find no one suitable. . . .

Thank you for the good intention of sending me your check, but you must have forgotten to slip it into the envelope; I found no trace of it. . . .

Nabokov wrote from Paris on June 8, saying that he had heard an excellent performance of Stravinsky's Mass at the Sainte-Chapelle, sung by a boys' choir. The letter announces a festival in Paris in May 1952, sponsored by the "Congrès pour la Liberté de la Culture." For this occasion, Nabokov wants to "re-create the Sacre, with new choreography by George Balanchine."

STRAVINSKY TO NABOKOV   *June 13, 1951*

Congrès pour la Liberté de la Culture
41, avenue Montaigne
Paris

My dear Nika,

Received your letter of June 8; thank you for the always-welcome news. . . . I expected to hear from you from Rome because you told me that you had to be there at the beginning of June.

As for the *Rake*, . . . I was counting on you to clarify the picture, because what goes on behind the scenes in Italy is pretty mysterious. . . . Ten days ago I received a note from Ballo announcing his capitulation to Ghiringhelli, while preserving appearances. Following this La Scala should proceed with the preparation of the *Rake*. . . . But since Ballo seems to act like a very small boy before Ghiringhelli, terrorized by him, he has begged me to make direct contact with Ghiringhelli on the question of rehearsals, dates, etc. That is what I did, immediately, by cable, but at the present hour the ogre-dictator of La Scala still deems himself sufficiently important not to deign to answer me. I do not know how much longer this will go on, because I do not intend to run humbly after him.

. . . For my part, I will conscientiously execute my contractual engagements and, as foreseen, debark at Naples from the *Independence* on August 15. I hope that by then the Italian burlesque will have decided what to do with me.

Your project with the League of Composers does not appear to me to have died, as you thought. I received a note from Miss Louise Talma, who spoke of organizing a concert of my works conducted by Mitropoulos and asked if I could attend, since it would be on the occasion of my seventieth birthday. As you see, since the question of my participation is not raised, they seem to have abandoned your idea. I replied that I could not assure them of my attendance. Musical activity interests me, but worldly activity does not. If Mitropoulos can be paid, so can I, just as easily, and that would be a better way of marking my birthday than offering me a cup of tea and a hollow speech. . . .

P.S. The death of Koussevitzky stunned us. The event created a lot of fuss, press, radio, etc. In order not to refuse *Time* magazine, and to join Copland and others there (Hindemith was not asked), I wrote these few lines on the subject: "That Serge Koussevitzky was a great celebrity, everybody knows, but that many careers were created by his generosity, very few know. When a man passes away, those wishing to pay tribute to his memory recollect his good deeds, the things he did most ostensibly [*sic*]. Let us dwell today on those things that Serge Koussevitsky did for others without telling anyone about it. And for those things let him be rewarded manifestly."

I think that my homage, limited to what is true, is also more sincere than many of those that have so far been published.

Nabokov wrote from Paris, June 27, that Balanchine was

stupefied but also pleased by the proposition to choreograph the *Sacre*. He wants to do a non-Russian version, with Picasso, but naturally, after the recent antics of Comrade Picasso, and the unpardonable canvas on the massacres of Korea, he is out of the question for us. . . . Who, in your opinion, could honor the score of the *Sacre* and the choreography of Balanchine? Would it be worthwhile to ask Tchelichev? Or old Matisse?

STRAVINSKY TO NABOKOV   *July 3, 1951*

Very dear Nika,

I was happy to read your letter of June 27, and to see that the Italians have begun to move. I have been officially informed that La Scala and the Biennale have finally reached an agreement. I think that they have approached all of the singers that I recommended and that they were still available.

Now to your proposition for Paris next year. The project seems to have grown, since it was originally a question of conducting the *Rake* at the Opéra. . . . As for the *Sacre,* I suppose that you will give a complete program of my ballets, the *Sacre* alone being too short for a whole evening. Evidently Picasso would have been the most desirable had he not been deemed "undesirable." But why not ask Tchelichev? He can always be counted on to do something unexpected and admirable.

For the concert, I suggest my Symphony in C (28 minutes) and my Symphony in Three Movements (23 minutes); we will see about an ending. We leave Hollywood for New York on July 30 and stay at the Lombardy, 3 East 56th Street, August 2–7. On the latter date we will depart on the *Constitution* (instead of the *Independence*), in order to arrive in Naples on August 15. I would be pleased to hear from you again before my departure.

Nabokov had written on July 3, describing a seminar on new music that he had held in the house of Baroness Hansi Lambert in Brussels. He wrote again on July 17, asking Stravinsky, while in New York, to discuss the matter of the new Sacre *with Balanchine or Lincoln Kirstein: "I wrote to George . . . but with him one never knows, since he puts letters in his pocket without reading them. . . . In Glyndebourne I saw an excellent* Idomeneo *staged by Ebert. . . . In London I heard rumors that Auden himself wants to direct the* Rake.[46] *. . . [Elisabeth] Schwarzkopf and Jennie Tourel have been engaged for the opera."*

After attending the premiere of the Rake *in Venice, September 11, Nabokov returned to Paris by train. On October 12 he came to Baden-Baden, where Stravinsky had a concert with the Südwestfunk Orchestra, and there, at the Brenners Park Hotel, Nabokov signed a letter of agreement with Stravinsky concerning his participation in the 1952 Paris festival.*

On November 13, Nabokov wrote to Stravinsky at the Excelsior Hotel, Naples, that Denis de Rougement had reported that Stravinsky wanted to conduct Oedipus Rex *(not the* Sacre*) in the Paris festival. (Stravinsky and de Rougement had spent an evening together in Geneva two weeks before.) The letter is signed* "Je vous embrasse tous les deux de tout coeur et j'envoie mon biggest hug à Bob."

Nabokov's next letter, December 29, was written on stationery of "L'Oeuvre du XXe Siècle, Paris, mai 1952, Exposition Internationale des Arts" and addressed to Stravinsky in California. The contents are concerned with the performance of the Rake *in the festival.*

Stravinsky answered on his first full day home, January 2, 1952, but his letter is entirely concerned with the Paris Rake, *which was not to take place. Nabokov's reply, January 17, says that the death of the Maréchal de Lattre de Tassigny has affected all government agencies, including the Opéra, and hence the meeting with Maurice Lehmann, its director, has only just taken place. Nabokov also says that his organization cannot employ Roger Desormière[47] to conduct the* Rake, *because "he is an active member of the Communist Party"; and Nabokov promises to send a design for* Oedipus Rex, *"as Cocteau conceives it." Stravinsky's answer again discusses the* Rake *and concludes: "It is too bad that Cocteau is not acceptable [to direct] the* Rake. *. . . In any case, I am pleased to know that he will participate in* Oedipus Rex, *though I regret that Theodore will once again be left out of it."[48] (January 22)*

Nabokov wrote on January 29, enclosing "a letter from Anna Kallin, who runs the Third Program of the British Broadcasting Corporation. She is a Russian yevreiskaya dama, quite nice and very bright. I know that you hate speaking on the radio, but I also know that the BBC would pay you quite a lot of money for it. Why don't you ask them for $5,000." On January 30, Nabokov

---

[46] The rumors were true. See Auden's letter to Stravinsky of July 25, 1951, in *S.S.C.* I.

[47] Desormière (1898–1963) suffered a stroke early in 1952 and never recovered.

[48] Stravinsky had wanted his son to design *Oedipus Rex* for its premiere in 1927. (See the correspondence with Cocteau in *S.S.C.* I, pp. 95–111.)

*sent the schedule of Stravinsky's rehearsals and concerts. Stravinsky's answer,
February 5, is confined to questions of rehearsals and travel and hotel arrangements. He wrote again on the 9th:*

I write to you today after having seen the prospectus that your organization
published announcing "The masterpieces of the Twentieth Century, April
29–June 1, 1952, Paris."

   This prospectus was sent to Bob Craft by Walter Alford, the press agent of
your committee, which asked me for photographs and other material that I had
given to Bob. I see that Bob was asked for a note on the Symphony in C, though
I had chosen the Symphony in Three Movements.

*In the remainder of the letter, Stravinsky shows his concern about the contents
of the program that was to mark his reappearance in Paris after fourteen years.
He insists on presenting* Oedipus *alone, with a 10- or 15-minute intermission
between its two acts: "I did it like this in Dresden, before Hitler, and believe me,
my dear Nika, it is better this way, because opera and theatre audiences are not
the same as those for symphonic concerts. The mixture of the two would mean
that the Symphony would be sacrificed." He goes on to say that in the ballet
programs he will not conduct* The Cage *(String Concerto), but only* Orpheus,
"a work created entirely with my collaboration."

   *On February 13, Nabokov wrote that he had engaged Hans Rosbaud to
prepare* Oedipus *for Stravinsky and to conduct a second performance of it the
day following the composer's, but the letter does not mention that this other
program would include Schoenberg's* Erwartung. *The surprise in the letter was
the news of the postponement of the* Rake *until autumn, for the reason that the
Opéra had decided to mount Rameau's* Les Indes galantes, *which, as Nabokov
says, "has waited 250 years to be staged there, and, as I observed to no avail,
could surely wait a few more months."*

   *On February 15, Nabokov wrote that "what was acceptable to the Dresden
public twenty years ago is no longer the case today, when audiences are used to
long concerts." He proposed to precede* Oedipus *by* Scènes de ballet, *and on the
19th, Stravinsky cabled his agreement. Stravinsky's letters of February 22 and
March 7 are limited in subject matter to questions of payment, program arrangements, and travel schedules. Nabokov responded on March 19, asking the
Stravinskys to come a few days before the festival and commissioning them to
write to Huxley and Isherwood to participate in the writers' discussions. Nabokov's letter of April 2 reveals only that "the brilliant and wise Mr. Rabenek of
the ehemaliger Russischer Verkussevitzkyverlag[49] came to see me, to discuss a
proposal to televise* Oedipus. . . . *I have asked Bob to conduct* Façade *and Ioni-
sation."*

   *After the festival, Nabokov did not write for nearly three months. Then, on
August 10, 1952, he sent a note from the Chalet Waldegg, Gstaad, Switzerland,*

---

[49] Koussevitzky was the founder of the Russischer Musik Verlag.

the home of Hansi Lambert, "a very kind lady of the Belgian Rothschilds," as Nabokov describes her. Stephen Spender and Samuel Barber were there with him, and he had been to Rome and the sulphur baths at Aquae Albulae.

STRAVINSKY TO NABOKOV   *August [14?], 1952*

My dear Nika,

Thank you for the news of yourself; I have waited some time for it and wondered about the meaning of your prolonged silence. I am happy to know that you are in Gstaad and relaxing after the hardships of Paris and the heat of Rome.

Briefly, here are my plans: I will stay here [Hollywood] until the beginning of December, then go to Cleveland for a week (December 8–15) of guest conducting and recording for Columbia—Symphony in C and *Pulcinella* (the whole piece, with singers). From Cleveland I go to New York and probably install myself at the Gladstone Hotel until March. The *Rake* should be done at the Met at the beginning of February, perhaps a little later, but not *after* February. It would of course give us great pleasure if you were in New York at that time.

It pleases me that you have taken up composition again after the long interruption because of your administrative responsibilities and the Paris festival.

About Paris, and between the two of us, Bob Craft still has not been paid. I suggested that he write to you, and I hope that you will be able to intervene in his behalf. I am sorry for him, because he is in straitened circumstances and hasn't a sou.

Do not leave me too long without news.

Love, kisses,

Nabokov did not answer until November 25, because of personal problems, as he explains (the breakup of his marriage to Patricia). He outlines a new festival, to take place in Rome in the autumn of 1953 (it eventually took place in the spring of 1954), and implores Stravinsky to accept the presidency of the Music Advisory Board.

STRAVINSKY TO NABOKOV   *December 3, 1952*

My dear Nika,

Happy to have news of you, finally, since I had begun to ask myself what had become of you. I am sorry to hear that you have had troubles, and I hope that the consequences will not be upsetting.

Here we have also had some excitement. Three weeks ago Vera had to undergo major surgery, long if not serious, an operation on the thyroid. She was in the hospital for eight days and is now recovering. She will join me in New York on December 20.

I leave for Cleveland the day after tomorrow. . . . On November 11, I conducted a very interesting concert here that included the premiere of my new

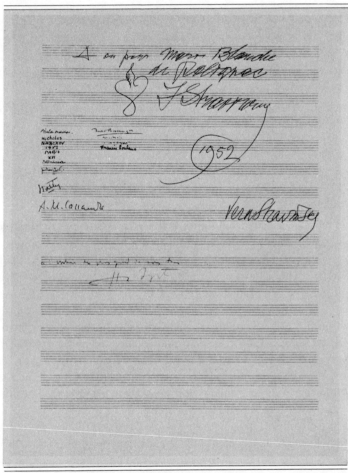

The guest book of Countess Marie-Blanche de Polignac, signed by, among others, Stravinsky, Nicolas Nabokov, Patricia Nabokov, Henri Sauguet, Nadia Boulanger, Georges Auric, Francis Poulenc, and Vera Stravinsky. Stravinsky was in Paris from May 2 to May 18, 1952.

Cantata (for soprano, tenor, and small female chorus, accompanied by five instruments), also my Concertino in a version for an ensemble of twelve instruments. I will repeat these two works in my concert at Town Hall, New York, December 21, and record them the next day. Hugues Cuénod sang the Cantata and will sing it again in New York, where the soprano will be Jennie Tourel.

We will be happy to see you in New York. I do not know the exact date of the *Rake.*

To turn to your new project . . . The "presidency" that you propose does not interest me at all. A trip to Rome and a holiday there are always agreeable, but I cannot lose the time and would come only if I had a small concert tour.

Stravinsky then enumerates the terms under which he would accept the presidency and concludes by referring to his wife as "Madame la Présidente." Nabokov replied on December 15: "I was very surprised by your news about Vera Arturovna's operation and have had more details in a charming letter from Bob." Nabokov invites the Stravinskys to a concert by the Boston Symphony Orchestra in New York on January 17, in which "[Charles] Munch will beat time to my Vita nuova." *Nabokov promises to obtain conducting engagements for Stravinsky after Rome.*

STRAVINSKY TO NABOKOV   *March 18, 1953*

My dear Nika,

I have just received a letter from Denis de Rougement—copy enclosed, also the copy of my reply. To tell the truth, and between the two of us, I do not understand the necessity of his message and of all this confusion of "Committees" and "Centers," which have nothing to do with me. In accordance with the agreement between us, protect me from all of this epistolary activity.

I take this same opportunity to inform you that after my European tour was announced, Corti[50] wrote to ask me to conduct at the Accademia di Santa Cecilia. He did not give me any details, and no date, and he asks me for the premiere of my next work. I answered that I do not have any new work for symphony orchestra, that my new pieces are a cantata and a septet, and that he must put himself in direct contact with you for any concert that he wishes to present, since you have organized my appearances in Rome. Confidentially, and between ourselves, I have nothing against Corti and the Santa Cecilia, but I would much prefer that you obtain the greatly superior orchestra of the Rome Radio. See what you can do; perhaps it would be possible to have the radio orchestra for Corti's concert. As a member of the Accademia, I find it awkward to ignore their proposal. At the least, I should do a concert there, to please them, and a second concert, with the radio orchestra, to please me. . . .

I will be in Havana, Hotel El Presidente, from March 29 to April 7, then in New York, the Gladstone Hotel, until April 30, then in Boston, c/o the Opera Workshop, Boston University, until about May 20, to conduct the *Rake.*

Affectionately to you,

---

[50] Mario Corti, director of the Accademia di Santa Cecilia.

Nabokov's letter from Rome, March 25, is entirely filled with details of business and concerts, as is Stravinsky's answer from Havana, April 6—except for the final sentence: "So Prokofiev no longer exists; the death of Stalin did not succeed in erasing the impression of this other disappearance."

Gladstone Hotel
New York
April 29, 1953

STRAVINSKY TO NABOKOV

Returning from Caracas, I am here in New York for a few days before going to Boston for the *Rake.* Unfortunately and unhappily, I caught a virus on my arrival here, and I must stay in bed until it passes before I can go to Boston to begin my strenuous work there.

I am harassed without let-up and from all sides, including South America, about engagements for next year. I must know first of all what has become of the Rome project, and whether or not it will take place. Please answer me without delay, telling me if your Rome conference is definite, exactly what the dates are, and if we are in agreement on terms, which is to say, the budget.

Write to me at the Hotel Sheraton-Plaza, Boston.

In his next letter, May 5, Nabokov announces, "the day after tomorrow I will marry Marie-Claire Brot, whom you met in New York. She has a ravishing home near Chantilly,[51] where we will live next year, and where we hope to invite you."

Hotel Sheraton-Plaza
Boston
May 10, 1953

STRAVINSKY TO NABOKOV

. . . First of all, I wish you, also your wife, whom I had the pleasure of meeting in New York, a very happy new life. . . .

The programs of the Italian concerts must be worked out with Labroca and company. But already I can tell you that *Renard* is impossible, because of a French text[52] that has no value as song and deprives the work of its literary value. For 60 minutes of music, I propose *Oedipus Rex* or *Perséphone,* but I must have an ensemble such as I heard at The Hague last year.

Nabokov replied on business matters, May 26, and on June 25 he wrote about the Paris performance of the Rake, *saying that "the translation[53] is awful, regardless of what Nadia Bulochnikova [Boulanger] thinks of it." On July 10, he sent a formal letter of agreement, which Stravinsky rewrote and forwarded on July 20.*

---

[51] Verderonne, in Liancourt (Oise).

[52] By C.-F. Ramuz. See the correspondence with Ramuz in *S.S.C.* III.

[53] By Abdré de Badet.

STRAVINSKY TO NABOKOV

I have just had indirect news of you: the Guggenheim Foundation sent papers asking my opinion concerning your candidacy. I answered recommending you in the warmest terms—obviously—but it was a surprise for me to learn that your project is *Rasputin*. I believe that this is an excellent subject, and I wish you, as well as [Chester] Kallman, good luck.

I have signed contracts with Rome and Turin. Also, I am looking for reservations on a boat, which are not so easy to obtain. We prefer to go by sea, resting some days, rather than flying and arriving tired. I still plan to arrive on April 5, but you have never confirmed this.

Ten days or so ago I wrote to Labroca, asking him to try to arrange one or two concerts for Bob, who wants to make the trip on his own account. I hope that Labroca can arrange something for him, either with the Rome Radio or with the [Florence] Maggio Musicale.

To you and your wife, our friendly greetings.

Nabokov wrote from Rome, November 17, to say that he and Kallman had blocked out a libretto on the subject of Rasputin:

I am expecting to receive the first scenes of his libretto, but, alas, Kallman is not very reliable as a *foutriquet,* neither as a correspondent, nor, I believe, as a worker. At any rate, I have not heard from him since he left Rome about four weeks ago. . . . Would you ask Bob if he would like to conduct that bluffy piece *Intégrales* by Edgard Varèse? If he does, then perhaps we may have something for him. If Bob would like to get in touch with Vlad,[54] here is his address: Roman Vlad, rampa Mignanelli 12, Rome. Matrimonially I'm very happy. Please keep your fingers crossed.

STRAVINSKY TO NABOKOV   *November 21, 1953*

I have just received yours of November 17. In the same mail I am answering a letter from Labroca, and I attach a copy. Before having an answer on these questions of timing, I do not want to discuss anything else. I will be on tour in the United States from September 20 to February 2, returning to Hollywood after that until February 23. Then I will go to Portland and Seattle until March 20.

(. . . I remind you that I will need your payment of $5,000 no later than March 1. . . .)

---

[54] Roman Vlad (b. 1919), Italian composer, author of *Stravinsky* (Turin, 1958; third English edition New York, 1978). He was artistic director of the Accademia Filarmonica Romana, which participated in Nabokov's festival.

Thank you for what you did for Bob, who will write to you directly. Enough for today; I have too much to do.

Love,

Stravinsky's next letter, December 5, is entirely concerned with the contents of the programs for Rome. Nabokov wrote on December 19 that the program of April 15, 1954, would not include works of "the competition,"[55] but only works by Stravinsky: "I am looking after Bob's affairs and will write to him shortly. Best regards to Vera Arturovna and yourself, and Merry Christmas and a Happy New Year!"

Stravinsky sent a telegram to Nabokov on December 22, 1953, from the Hotel Warwick, Philadelphia; "I need to be enlightened." On January 15, 1954, he wrote to Nabokov: "Bob has informed me that you wrote to him directly asking him for my addresses and decisions about programs. . . . Do not speak to me anymore about changes in the programs. I return to Hollywood on February 3 . . . [and by whatever route] we will be in Rome on April 3 or 4."

Nabokov replied on January 21: "What disturbs me is the huge overload of concerts that you have in America. Bob wrote to me that you had the flu twice but still must do about fifteen concerts before you leave for Italy."[56]

On February 6, Stravinsky wrote from Hollywood that he had returned "safe and sound," and on the 10th Nabokov answered that he would be in New York for ten days, "staying in the apartment of Charles Jones, 311 East 58th Street. I will . . . call you from New York. What is the best time of the day to get you?" In a Russian postscript, Nabokov says that "[Julius] Fleischmann[57] has had a heart attack, and they are trying to keep it quiet."

STRAVINSKY TO NABOKOV   *February 15, 1954*

My dear Nika,

. . . Since you leave Rome on the 23rd, I suppose that you will be in New York the 24th, which is to say the same day that I must fly in the evening from here to Portland. I have concerts in Portland and Seattle, and I will be at the Hotel Multnomah, Portland, from the 24th, just before midnight, until the morning of March 4, then until the morning of March 10 in Seattle (Olympic Hotel). I return here March 10 and leave for New York (by air) Saturday, March 13, morning, staying at the Hotel Gladstone until the 19th, when we leave [for Naples] on the S.S. *Saturnia*. . . .

---

[55] A prize, awarded for a piece of music, was presented by Stravinsky to Mario Peragallo on April 9 for his violin concerto.

[56] Stravinsky was conducting the Philadelphia Orchestra on tour.

[57] Julius Fleischmann of Cincinnati, heir to the Fleischmann gin fortune, was the chief sponsor of Nabokov's Congress for Cultural Freedom.

The simplest and surest means of obtaining the parts for the Septet is from Boosey & Hawkes in New York. . . .

Telephone me in Portland (Hotel Multnomah), and not here, Thursday, February 25, in the morning between 9 and 11 (noon–2 p.m. New York time), or in the evening between 11 and midnight (2–3 a.m. in New York).

Nabokov wrote on February 18, complaining that suddenly the Rome Radio had informed him that it could not transmit a concert of profane music on Good Friday; hence Stravinsky's April 15 concert had to be switched to the 14th.

In his first letter after the festival in Rome, dated April 29 and written on stationery of the American Academy in Rome, Nabokov says, apropos of the broadcast of Stravinsky's concert (Violin Concerto and Perséphone) in Turin: "The older I become, the closer I grow to all that you do. I read the Septet again yesterday. . . . It is absolutely remarkable."

Nabokov's letter of July 6 describes an ear operation that he had undergone in London and the "preparations for the arrival of a baby, for which reason we will be moving in a week or two to our new house near Chantilly." On Monday, August 16, the Stravinskys sent a cable to the newly born Alexander Nabokov: "Welcome to you. Wishing you most successful life. Love to you all."

STRAVINSKY TO NABOKOV   *November 22, 1954*

Dear Nika,

. . . Bob has informed me that you were going to India, but meanwhile I wrote to you in Paris. Here are my plans for Europe in 1955: March 15 we fly from New York to Lisbon (Aviz Hotel), where we will stay about four days to rest before [driving] to Madrid (Ritz Hotel, concert March 25). On March 31 we arrive in Rome, Hotel Hassler, RAI concert April 6. We leave Rome on April 17 for Baden-Baden (Brenners Park Hotel, concert on the 22nd), then go to Lugano (Radio Monte Ceneri, concert April 28), then to Stuttgart (concert May 3). On May 4 we leave for Copenhagen, and fly to Los Angeles on the 5th or 6th, on the new SAS Polar route. . . . A pity that we have not seen you here this year. . . . A thousand best wishes to your wife and your newborn.

STRAVINSKY TO NABOKOV   *December 30, 1954*

Dear Nika,

. . . I will be traveling here and there in the United States in January, but write to me here, and your letter will be forwarded. I am very curious to have your impressions of India and to have news about your projects.

Nabokov wrote from Paris, February 7, 1955, promising to see the Stravinskys at the Hassler Hotel in Rome.

I have arranged it so that Marie-Claire, and I with Ivan[58] and the baby, will spend most of April in Rome at the American Academy. . . . I heard that you have finished *Agon;* is that true? I also heard that you are writing a Passion for St. Mark's in Venice. . . . When is the opening of Vera Arturovna's Rome show? Please ask Bob to write me the exact date.

STRAVINSKY TO NABOKOV   *February 11, 1955*

Dearest Nika,

. . . I have just returned from a month-long concert tour, and I will be on the road again on March 5: Pittsburgh, Lisbon, Madrid, Rome. Vera's opening is on March 29. I will be so happy to meet you in Rome (Hotel Hassler).

Thus far I have composed barely half of *Agon.* . . . Kirstein, Balanchine, and I have set the premiere for February 1957. . . . It would not work out sooner.

Regarding the "Stastye St. Mark," the contract with the Biennale still has not been sent. I think that the money has not been found yet, but they are rushing, rushing, and have asked me to begin work. I answered that I will not begin without having signed a contract. . . . We are living through difficult times here: Poor Maria Huxley is dying from cancer. Poor, nearly blind Aldous, his whole life revolved around her! This year he was sixty. It is just horrible. I embrace you warmly. [*Original in Russian*]

Nabokov answered from Paris on February 27: "Alas, I shall miss Vera Arturovna's opening, for I am leaving here only on the 2nd and will arrive in Rome by car only on the 6th, the day of your concert." The scene in Paris is "dominated by Suvchin-ism and Boulezovism," he adds, and he offers to help with arrangements for the St. Mark's affair: "What should be done is to have the Patriarch[59] get the money; he is a very kind man and is very fond of music."

In his next letter, sent from Bangkok on November 22, Nabokov asks Stravinsky: "Is it true that your new work is a Vesper Service based on the Gospel according to St. Mark, and that certain parts are written in serielnaya technique?" From Bangkok Nabokov flew to Japan on the 23rd, then went to South India before returning to Paris for Christmas. His next letter (from Paris) is dated January 26, 1956: "I wrote to Bob, but, probably to punish me for my silence, he has not answered, and I am very sad. . . . [In February] I will be in Louisville (Kentucky), where the orchestra plays a new work of mine . . . Symboli Christiani.[60] . . . If you only knew how much I would love to have you, Vera Arturovna, and Bob spend some time with us in our beautiful home in the country near Paris!"

---

[58] Nabokov's eldest son.
[59] Cardinal Roncalli, the future Pope John XXIII.
[60] Dedicated to Stravinsky.

On February 14, Stravinsky telegraphed to Nabokov in Louisville, and on
the 17th Nabokov sent a card from New York saying that the piece had enjoyed
a "thundering success."

On March 23, Nabokov wrote from Paris, reporting on "yesterday's Suv-
chinsko-Boulez concert" and on the "artificiality of Boulez's Masterless Hammer." On April 7, he wrote from Rome, sending the Athens address of Dr. Dox-
iades, physician to the King of Greece, and the address of "Mr. Korakas (it
means crow)." Stravinsky was ill in Athens (July 1956), and required the services of both men. The next letter, August 1, addressed to Stravinsky in Venice,
asks him to lend his name to an honorary committee for a Paris concert by the
Boston Symphony in memory of Georges Enesco.

Nabokov attended the premiere of Canticum Sacrum *in Venice, September*
13. Two weeks later, in Berlin, he was with Stravinsky every day, and the two
men saw each other again in December in London. On November 26, Nabokov
had written an especially affectionate letter to Stravinsky in Rome, begging
him to stop exerting himself: "We all need you so much. . . ." The next letter
came from Gstaad:

I heard from Ivan that you enjoyed conducting *Perséphone* in New York and
that your health has improved. I hear from Pavlik Tchelichev that you are composing *Agon* and that George is returning to America in the fall to produce
it.[61] . . . I have had a very serious intestinal infection, contracted in India, and
could not leave the bathroom for ten days. [March 10, 1957]

STRAVINSKY TO NABOKOV   *Hollywood*
                                                      March 15, 1957
Dear Nika,

Thank you for your letter. I hope next time to have better news regarding your
health. For my part, there is little to say—I am continuing my blood treatment[62]
and am recovering quickly, although I am not quite back to normal yet. I stay at
home and read or compose, longing for a cigarette even though I gave up smok-
ing at the beginning of December.

Boulez was here working all last week; he read a remarkably interesting
lecture at the University [Royce Hall, UCLA] and conducted his splendid
"Molot bez Mastera"[63] for our Monday Evening Concerts. All of us, as well as
the musicians he was directing, who presented him with some cuff links, were
extremely impressed with him as a musician and a man.

---

[61] Balanchine was living in Copenhagen, where his wife, the ballerina Tanaquil
LeClercq, was in a hospital with polio.

[62] Phlebotomy, for Stravinsky's polycythemia.

[63] *Le Marteau sans maître* (*The Masterless Hammer* of Nabokov's letter of March 23,
1956).

I heard today that Balanchine has returned to New York. Kirstein and I have been anxiously awaiting his return, naturally. Regarding my plans, I have to finish the composition of *Agon,* and it is going slowly. Kirstein is planning a festival of my ballets in November and December, though whether he actually arranges it is another matter. In any case, I have promised to conduct a number of times, and so I will be in New York in November and December.

I have not had news of Mildred Bliss[64] in ages, nor have I seen her in New York.

My three concerts of *Perséphone* in New York went very well, and despite the fact that I also made a recording of *Perséphone,* I did not feel at all tired.

It would be *wonderful* if you could come to Hollywood, even for a couple of days. Try to convince your committee.

I close this letter, for want of more space and time. With a warm hug, sincerely,

Igor Str.

[Original in Russian]

Nabokov wrote, in English, June 17, 1957, the day of the premiere of Agon, *at Royce Hall:*

How I should have liked to have been in Los Angeles and heard the first performance of *Agon.* . . . Here is the gist of the proposal that I indicated in my cable: Rolf Liebermann, Music Director of the Zürich Radio, and, as you know, a very good friend of mine, has now been appointed Music Director of the Hamburg Radio, which has become one of the most important in Europe. . . . Would you accept a commission from Hamburg to write a work of a duration of approximately 20 minutes or longer, for a first performance by the Radio in September 1958 under your direction? Liebermann and I thought that we would ask you to conduct this new work, but that the rest of the program would be conducted by Bob, in order not to put any unnecessary strain on your health. You and Bob will of course plan the program to your own satisfaction, but it would be nice if Bob could include the performance of a work by Boulez.

---

[64] Mrs. Robert Woods Bliss had commissioned the *Dumbarton Oaks* Concerto (Concerto in E flat), named after the Blisses' Washington, D.C., home. Stravinsky's Symphony in C had been commissioned jointly by Mrs. Bliss ($2,500) and Mrs. John Alden Carpenter ($1,000). At a dinner party for Stravinsky at the Colony Club, given by Elizabeth Sprague Coolidge after Stravinsky's matinee concert at Town Hall for French War Relief, March 14, 1940, Mrs. Bliss told the composer that $1,000 of the $2,500 was to be considered as the purchase price of the manuscript, which she planned to donate to the Library of Congress.

STRAVINSKY TO NABOKOV   *Hollywood*
                                                        June 21, 1957

Dear friend,

. . . In spite of your precise and definite proposal I am embarrassed not to be able to give you any definite answer today. I prefer to speak with you about the matter in Dartington, where I firmly hope to see you.

Indeed, I am embarrassed because I do not know if I will have time enough to write a twenty-minute piece. . . . I already started a composition promised a long time ago, and I must interrupt it for six months. I am going to Santa Fe for the *Rake's Progress* where Bob is conducting it, then at the end of July to New York and, on the 29th, sailing to Plymouth (*Liberté*). August—Dartington, September vacation (Italy, France, Switzerland?), October concerts in Munich, Paris, Rome. End of October with the same *Liberté* back to New York. In November (between the 10th and 17th) Balanchine's premiere of *Agon*, which I have to conduct. December at home, in January two concerts in Houston (money question), and only in February continuing my interrupted work. Too bad I do not feel able to compose interesting music at Mozart's speed.

I am here until July 7th. [*Original in English*]

Nabokov answered from Liancourt, June 28, 1957, and included an account of the premiere of Poulenc's Dialogues des carmélites: *"Like you, I cannot abide religious subjects on the stage, and when the guillotine finally began lopping off heads, I was relieved and glad." In Zürich, October 20, Stravinsky met with Nabokov, Liebermann, and Alessandro Piovesan, director of the Biennale, to conclude arrangements for the premiere of* Threni *in Venice in September 1958. Stravinsky arrived at the Hotel Baur au Lac, Zürich, on the evening of the 19th, having conducted* Agon *in the afternoon in Donaueschingen. After the meeting on the 20th the Stravinskys flew to Rome, to be there for the birthday of the present writer, who was conducting a symphony concert on October 21 in the Teatro Eliseo.*

The subject of Nabokov's letter of February 12, 1958, is his work on his opera (Rasputin's End). *He adds, "I learn from Bob that* Threni *is 35–40 minutes long."*

STRAVINSKY TO NABOKOV   *February 19, 1958*

Dearest Nika,

Thank you for your letter of February 12, though it arrived late.

I hope that by now you have completed your opera and that you are more at ease. I feel that you will not be coming to the performance in Louisville—so far away and a considerable expense—and that we will see you only in Europe. On July 29 we are taking the *Cristoforo Colombo* from New York, and we will arrive in Cannes or in Genoa twelve days later. Where do you propose to be at this time?

In connection with your opera, you probably are in contact with Stephen Spender,[65] and it occurred to me to ask you to tell him that for a long time and with some impatience I have been waiting for two photographs (taken in Monte Carlo with Diaghilev, Nijinsky, Benois, etc. . . .) sent to him a year ago for the illustration of an article and never returned. I would be very grieved at their loss. He must find them.

We are trying to convince Aldous Huxley [to come to Venice]: Bob is not losing hope. We will see.

The composition of *Threni* is slowly coming to an end, but the length of what is already composed is not as great as Bob tells you, for he always tends to exaggerate.

From April 13 to 20, we will be in San Francisco, where I am conducting three concerts. April 14 is the golden wedding anniversary of Mildred and Robert Bliss; do not forget to send them a telegram in Washington.

Something must be done about Piovesan: Boulez has already canceled because of Piovesan's failure to answer letters. Now the solo singers in *Threni*, who were supposed to take part in Bob's Gesualdo and in the works of other old masters, cannot get an answer from him. In all likelihood he has neither the money nor the power to draw up terms and contracts. What a disgrace!

I/we congratulate you on your own home, and I/we send you our warmest greetings. [*Original in Russian*]

On February 28, Nabokov wrote to tell Stravinsky of the death, at the age of forty, of Alessandro Piovesan. (The letter goes on about Stephen Spender: "The disorder of Stephen is equaled only by that of Wystan [Auden]; we were together in Gstaad recently, at Hansi Lambert's, and Stephen went off with four or five of my shirts, which I cannot get back from him.") On March 3, Nabokov wrote that he had spoken to Labroca, but "he did not know the cause of Piovesan's death and indeed seemed very disturbed and distracted." On March 5, Nabokov said that he had telephoned to Count Cini in Venice, but that he was away, at Bernard Berenson's. "Bob knows Piovesan's family. I do not know them. . . . If you have his widow's address, please let me have it. . . . [Emilia] Zanetti told me that in Italian bureaucratic circles people behaved terribly toward him precisely because he was such a good man. . . . He was the one astonishingly decent, intelligent, and kind person I encountered in this dark mire of musical 'slick dealers.'" On March 6, Nabokov wrote again: "It is awful about Piovesan. . . ."

---

[65] Stephen Spender (b. 1909). The English poet and critic was the librettist of *Rasputin's End*.

STRAVINSKY TO NABOKOV   *March 8, 1958*

Dear Nika,

Today I received your second letter (of March 5), following the untimely death of poor, dear Piovesan. I am extremely grieved by this event, and I am especially overwhelmed that, immediately following it, I received the news of my dear Willy Strecker's sudden death. Perhaps at our age it is natural to pass away like this; nevertheless, my reaction is one of pain.

What you write about the reactions of people like Labroca and Cini is as expected as it is terrible.

I personally received the news of Piovesan's death from Malipiero, since the widow of the deceased asked him to inform me. It seems that poor Piovesan's family is in great need. I do not know her address, but I think I will find it out soon, since I sent her some financial assistance through Malipiero.

We also do not know the details of Strecker's death: I hope to learn them from Strobel, who is writing to Bob about this sudden and unexpected death.

Can it really be true that Liebermann is going to have to refuse the Biennale because of the carelessness of the idiots who survive Piovesan?

How marvelous that you were able to drag the photographs out of Stephen. Thank you. I am waiting for them. Do write.

                                                    Yours,   I. Str.

[*Original in Russian*]

                                                    Hollywood
STRAVINSKY TO NABOKOV   *March 10, 1958*

The photograph has arrived. Thank you, my dear Nika. But where is the original picture that belongs to me? There was another picture besides this one, me with Diaghilev. Where is it? Both of these pictures were on cardboard backings, and I took them out from a very valuable album especially for reproduction. Please make one more effort and request both of these originals from Spender—they are not his, but mine. What kind of a man is he, anyway? What impudence.

I am glad if, after all, there is some hope of seeing you here.

                                                    Warmly yours,

[*Original in Russian*]

Nabokov wrote on March 11:

I was so shocked by the death of Piovesan that I completely forgot to ask you a question that was put to me the other day: Would you be prepared (after finishing *Threni*) to write a piece for piano and orchestra, or a group of instruments of your own choice, for an excellent young Swiss pianist? The length should be approximately 15–20 minutes, and it would be commissioned by a Swiss industrialist who owns several hotels in Arosa. His name is Weber. If you were interested, this gentleman would be prepared to pay $15,000 for exclusive rights during a season (i.e., roughly six–eight months). I am confident that this sum would be tax-free. The only condition he makes is that during this period he is to hold exclusive rights, and only you or Fricsay[66] could conduct the work.

STRAVINSKY TO NABOKOV   *Hollywood*
                                                              March 16, 1958

Dear Nika,

In answer to your letter of March 11 . . . Now listen: I agree in principle to the proposal of the industrialist Weber, and to the condition of a six- to eight-month period of exclusive performance rights for the Swiss pianist (what is his name?), and to my conducting, or Fricsay's, during this period. I am relying on your recommendation, and for the moment I can only tell you: "I consider it." Also, I have my own conditions: not a word is to be said about this, nothing is to be given away; this is very important to me, as I will explain later. Is the pianist French-Swiss or German-Swiss? Is the pederast Weber really taking on some serious expenditures? As for the sum of money you quote, it should be deposited in my bank in Basel—Société des Banques Suisses—in my name or in Vera's: the question about the tax, as you see, has already been answered. The clients should also know that my publisher, Boosey & Hawkes, which prepares the parts for performance, always charges a rental fee, and that this is very significant. I cannot change this condition, and do not wish to. The composition will take me no less than one year.

    Regards and kisses.

                                       Yours,   I. Str.

[Original in Russian]

Nabokov replied on March 21 that he had written "a stern letter" to Spender, that

scatter-brained *"Tante Bourda."* . . . The pianist is not male but female, Weber's wife, and he is apparently not queer at all, but a Swiss who owns some colossal hotels in Arosa, Venice, Saint-Moritz, etc. . . , and who has a good collection of paintings. Fricsay says that he is an extremely modest, kind, and cultured man. . . . I will be going to Venice on Tuesday, the 25th, to set everything straight . . . then to New York on the 5th, then to Louisville from the 13th to the 17th, then back here.

---

[66] Ferenc Fricsay (1914–63), Hungarian conductor.

On March 24, Nabokov wrote that "Liebermann, who is sitting here while I am dictating this letter, sends his warmest greetings and asks me to tell you that he has already paid half of the commission into your Swiss bank account. . . . Piovesan was supposed to send Liebermann the music of the Ferrara-Venetian School—Missa Ercole of Josquin des Près—but he died before he had a chance to do so."

STRAVINSKY TO NABOKOV

Hollywood
March 26, 1958

Dear Nika,

A few words in answer to your letter of March 21. Keep in mind that I will not be in Hollywood from April 10 to 20, but will be conducting in San Francisco during this time, and it will be very difficult to reach me by telephone. If you can, call on April 7, 8, or 9 from New York.

Did Fricsay call you on the 23rd, as you had asked him to do? If he wants to conduct the premiere of my future concerto—then fine, if he thinks that he can do this better than I can. With whom shall I conclude the contract?

I impatiently await your letter about Liebermann's visit and how everything came out with the Biennale. Between Mortari and Labroca, I think Labroca is probably the better. Whom did they choose?

I finally received the photograph from Spender, along with a letter of which I cannot make out a single word.

I wait for news, and do tell me whether or not the rehearsals of your opera have been rearranged according to your orders.

With sincere greetings, and a kiss,

Yours,

[*Original in Russian*]

STRAVINSKY TO NABOKOV

Hollywood
March 27, 1958

Dear, kind Nika,

No sooner do I send you a letter than I receive yours of March 24. Thank you.

Threni is finished. The music lasts longer than I had thought, not 20 minutes, but 35, and my program must be changed: to listen to *Threni* twice in a single sitting would be exhausting. I substitute the Bach Variations[67] for the Mass, though I performed the Bach Variations in San Marco two years ago. The Variations are appropriate, and they lighten the program by their pace and instrumental ensemble. That they were played not long ago should not mean anything: my Mass, too, was performed not long ago in Venice. I am writing to Liebermann about all of this. The new program, Symphonies of Wind

---

[67] Chorale Variations on *Vom Himmel hoch da komm' ich her.*

Instruments, [*In Memoriam*] *Dylan Thomas,* Bach Variations, and *Threni,* is harmonious and of a proper length—63 minutes of pure music is quite enough, considering its concentration and the unavoidable fatigue of listening.

This, like yesterday's letter, you will probably read when you have returned from Venice, where you are now. I await your answer.

Yours cordially,

[*Original in Russian*]

Nabokov wrote on March 29: "Liebermann says that Weber's wife plays the piano very well indeed and that Weber himself is a very decent fellow. . . . I saw Piovesan's widow. How difficult for her, with two children. Poor Piovesan died, you see, a year and a half before pension age."

STRAVINSKY TO NABOKOV   *Hollywood*
                                                        April 3, 1958

Dear Nika,

Glad to have yours of March 29.

Now awaiting your call from New York. From the question in your letter about my Venetian program I conclude that you have not yet read my letter of March 27. There you will find all the answers. I shall say today only that my new program, sent to Liebermann, has already been acknowledged by him.

We are going to San Francisco on the 10th by car and starting my rehearsals on Sunday the 13th. Your premiere on the 16th coincides with my first concert in San Francisco. Wishing you a great success, I am sending you, dear Nika, my love and kisses.

I. Str.

[*Original in English*]

STRAVINSKY TO NABOKOV   *April [7], 1958*

Dear Nika,

In my attempts to talk to you on the telephone I completely forgot to ask you— or you forgot to tell me—whether or not you had seen Fricsay before his departure for America. I still have received nothing from him and would like to know how to act in this matter, because of several answers that are pending and that I soon must give, and because of the time, which must be carefully distributed; otherwise you will not get out of the muddle.

Write to me, good friend, at the Clift Hotel in San Francisco, where I should be on Saturday evening, April 12.

Sincerely yours,

[*Original in Russian*]

On May 31, Nabokov wrote from his rue Jean-Goujon apartment in Paris describing an automobile accident in which he and his son Alexander had been
involved. Nabokov discusses the Venice program and both refuses and accepts a
10 percent commission from Stravinsky for the piano and orchestra piece,
Movements. The letter also mentions the Paris visit of the Bolshoi Ballet: "Everyone is delighted with Prokofiev's horrible Romeo and Juliet score. . . . Shostakovich is also staying here, and Auric and Poulenc fuss over him like children
with a new toy."

Nabokov telegraphed from Louisville, April 15, and Stravinsky telephoned
to Nabokov in New York, April 21, to discuss the commission from Weber.

STRAVINSKY TO NABOKOV   *Hollywood*
                                                  June 8, 1958
Dear friend,

What news! Thank God that all this is over and in the past. I can imagine what
you went through!

The money has already been sent to your New York bank, and not a thousand, but fifteen hundred dollars, i.e., the 10 percent commission I promised
you.

I am declaring this money to the tax collector *not* as a percentage for the
commission of the Piano Concerto [Movements]—I shall remain completely
silent about that—but rather for your procuring concerts for me in 1958
(London, Paris, Rome, Switzerland, etc.), which amounts to approximately
$15,000 to the tax collector as income for this year. Please do not mention
Weber; in fact, forget about him completely, otherwise I shall never extricate
myself from an incredible muddle.

I regret that the commission has already become known in New York to
Balanchine and Kirstein. You must have told them the secret, since they could
not have learned anything from Hans Ericmann, with whom I came to an
agreement about the matter: he returned immediately to Zürich.

I am supposed to meet with Weber in Zürich at the end of September. At
that time a date will finally be set; meanwhile, September 1959 is the target,
though this seems to me too near, and I will probably haggle with Weber about
changing the date to September 1960. I do not want to rush, and besides, tricks
are impossible with composition. What is this idea of yours that you say will be
very "lucrative" for me? I am very curious.

We are leaving for New York in the middle of July and taking the *Cristoforo Colombo* on the 29th, landing in Genoa on August 7 (Savoy Hotel). We will
spend two days in Genoa, then go by car to Venice.

Let us hope that all goes well so that we may meet you in Genoa.

With warm greetings.

Yours,   I. Str.

[Original in Russian]

STRAVINSKY TO NABOKOV   *Hollywood*
                                                      June 16, 1958

Dear Nika,

Through absent-mindedness and inattentiveness, I made a big mistake in my letter of June 8. Rereading the letter, I noticed in my sentence—"when you declare these 15 thousand dollars to the *fisc*," but of course I meant not 15 *thousand*, but the 15 *hundred* that I paid you. So take this into account.

Another thing that I wanted to say is that Hamburg refused the $750 to Bob, offering him only $500. With this money he must pay for the trip, Venice to Hamburg, and two weeks there (food and hotel). Because these terms seem to me very poor, I asked you on the telephone from San Francisco to try to influence Liebermann, and you very kindly promised to do this. Is it possible that Liebermann did not agree to the increase, or that you forgot to ask him? In any case, Bob was turned down. I told him that I would write to you about it, and if this does not bring results, I will pay him the $250 from my own pocket. He is doing this Hamburg business only for me and, what is more, would be paying for it himself.

I will be glad to hear from you. I kiss you.

                                                      I. Str.

[Original in Russian]

On July 2, Nabokov wrote from Paris thanking Stravinsky for the $1,500 commission. The letter explains that Fricsay is offended, however, since the idea of the commission originated with him, and

he thinks that you have pushed him aside. . . . I called him from Hamburg and assured him that you had nothing to do with it and that Weber wanted you to conduct. . . . Balanchine told me that he and Lincoln plan to commission a ballet from you, and I asked him why he could not base his ballet on this concerto, but George was not pleased with the proposal.[68] . . . Between the two of us, your Marion[69] must have written to Liebermann an excessively sharp or dry letter. . . . Be good enough to write him a personal note, tell him that you heard from me that they had a son (he is going to be a rabbi), and congratulate them. . . . How I would like to come to Genoa to meet you on the pier. . . . How did Vera's exhibition go?

STRAVINSKY TO NABOKOV   *Hollywood*
                                                      July 7, 1958

Dear Nika,

Thank you for your long letter of July 2. Because of the complete lack of time, I am putting off everything about which you write—and which I

---

[68] Balanchine eventually did choreograph the Movements, in 1963.

[69] Andre Marion, Stravinsky's son-in-law, served for a time as his secretary in the 1950s.

would like to discuss in detail—until our meeting in Venice. For now, just two things:

1. You are mistaken, it was not a "sharp or a cold" letter that "my Marion" wrote to Liebermann, but rather one of the "dear sir," business type in which he requested the establishment of the payment of still unpaid sums for *Threni*, all of the parts having already been delivered to Hamburg by my publisher. There was no answer to this letter of June 21, and I learn from you that Liebermann took offense. If anyone is to be offended, I should be the one, is that not so?

2. To your claim that "they do not pay more than $500 to European conductors," I answer OK, but they are demanding a different, not independent, work from Bob, rehearsals that take, let us say, four days, and then difficult work for two more weeks. Besides this, they require him to attend all of my Swiss concerts in the event that something happens to me. You yourself will agree that this is not very lavish.

Today I am rushing about madly just because of this. Write to me about whether I should think about Japan in April 1959, for, if so, I must arm myself now with reservations, which are bought up very quickly for April, which is their season.

I congratulate the Liebermanns on the birth of their son. I kiss you.

[*Original in Russian*]

On August 12, Nabokov, in Kolbsheim, Bas-Rhin, sent his itinerary: "Tomor-row to Salzburg, then three or four days with the Hofmannsthals (Schloss Prielau, Zell am See)." From Schloss Prielau, Nabokov wrote (on the 20th) to ask, "Is Bob already in Hamburg, then?" On his return to Paris the same day, Nabokov wrote to say that the festival in Japan had to be postponed but that Stravinsky could conduct his concerts there in the spring of 1959 anyway.

On August 27, Nabokov wrote to say that he had talked at length with Oscar Fritz Schuh of the Cologne Opera "about the project I outlined to you in a previous letter. He is most interested and would come to Venice to discuss the whole matter with you, Bob, and myself, if you would like him to do so. Please either drop him a line, or send him a telegram saying that you would be in-terested in seeing him in Venice."

STRAVINSKY TO NABOKOV   *August 30, 1958*

Dear Nika,

Many thanks for yours of August 27. What is the matter with Oscar Fritz Schuh? You mentioned his name in one of your last letters, but you never told me what the project was or the proposition. You understand that in this case it is very embarrassing for me to write or to wire him. *Un mot s.v.p.* to explain the situation.

Liebermann told you in Zürich that "so far all is well." Maybe, but what is not well is his—Liebermann's—obstinate silence: he doesn't answer our letters at all.

A thousand best wishes. Cordially as ever,

I. Stravinsky

[*Original in English*]

On September 1, Nabokov again wrote at length about the proposition from Schuh, and ten days later Nabokov was in Venice. His next letter, December 16, is concerned with arrangements for Stravinsky's Japanese tour. The postscript says: "I have had no news, neither from Lucie [Lambert] nor from her mama. I am worried about Lucie's health. Are they [Mlle Lambert and the present writer] getting married, and when?" On December 22, Nabokov wrote to Stravinsky at the Gladstone Hotel, New York, advising him about Japanese cultural politics.

STRAVINSKY TO NABOKOV

6, rue Jean-Goujon
Paris

Gladstone Hotel
New York
December [26?], 1958

Dear Nika,

I received today your letter of December 22 with enclosures: (1) two copies of your answers (December 11 & 19) to Mr. Katsujiro Bando and (2) your draft for my letter to him. Thank you.

When I received some days ago your two letters (from December 16 & 19) with enclosures (copies of Muriyama's letter of December 13 and your answer to her of December 16), I cabled to Miss Muriyama: "Accept two concerts Tokyo one Osaka same orchestra same program my fee 4500 dollars taxes your charge please cable answer I.S." The next day I received her answer: "Accept 4500 dollars net for total three concerts same program stop regards Muriyama Osakfestival Tokyo."

I hope that this answer means that the three concerts are two in Tokyo and one in Osaka, and not only with the same program but also, as mentioned in my cable, with the same orchestra (in order to have only one set of rehearsals), and that these concerts follow each other closely.

Now as the thing seems to be settled with Muriyama I do not think I have to write to Katsujiro Bando (your draft) but simply a word to Broadus Erle[70] telling him exactly what you suggested to me in yours of December 12. But I have to write now to Muriyama to confirm by letter this engagement and to ask for the date on which we have to fly. (We decided to cancel the boat reserva-

---

[70] American violinist, who had made a counterproposition to Stravinsky for a tour with another orchestra.

tions—too long!) As soon as I will have her answer (her dates) we will decide the date of our flight and let you know immediately. Are you staying in Paris for a while now?

Our Atlantic trip was all right although the sea was pretty rough the first three days. Here—very cold, no snow, and an ideal blue sky. Happy new year.

Cordially, as ever,

Here—until January 11. Afterwards—Hollywood.
[*Original in English*]

Nabokov answered on January 13, saying that he planned to be in Japan at the same time as the Stravinskys.

STRAVINSKY TO NABOKOV   *Hollywood*
                                                        February 16, 1959
Dear Nika,

In a great rush. Only this: we are flying to Japan through Honolulu, Manila, Hong Kong, arriving Tokyo April 6.

We arrive in Manila, Pan American, 6 a.m., March 29 (and leave April 1). Will it be possible to stay at the Embassy and have their car at our disposal to see the country? Will it be possible, I mean, and also avoid parties, black ties, official dinners, obligations, etc., etc., etc.? Can you write Bohlen[71] and ask him to give *eine recht aufrichtige Antwort?* Thank you in advance.

My three concerts will be: One in Osaka on May 1, two in Tokyo on May 3 (or 4) and May 5 (or 6).

Please answer by return mail when you are coming.

Love,   I. Str.

[*Original in English*]

Nabokov answered on February 23, asking Stravinsky to write to Bohlen directly, and adding: "Perhaps they would wish to give one (repeat 'one') reception for you, so as to enable you to meet some of the inmates of the Manila Zoo, which, I understand, consists of eight hundred American generals and colonels (with their wives, children, drugstores, and liquor black markets)." Nabokov wrote again on March 2: "Bohlen's name is Charles. Everyone calls him 'Chip.' I call him 'Chiparidze,' because his accent in Russian is like Georgian. . . . George Balanchine is here for a few days, and the Liebermanns too. Markevitch played his new composition yesterday. Where will you be living in Tokyo?"

On April 7, Nabokov wrote saying that he expected to be in Tokyo on the

---

[71] The Stravinskys stayed a few days in Manila and spent much of their time with Ambassador and Mrs. Bohlen.

14th. He joined the Stravinskys and the present writer in Kyoto, and several days and nights were spent very enjoyably together in that city, in Osaka, and in Tokyo. On May 11, Nabokov wrote from New York to say that he would come to Copenhagen, where Stravinsky was to receive the Sonning Prize. Nabokov's next communication after this meeting, from Liancourt, August 10, 1959, simply stated that his next address was "c/o Baroness de Rothschild, Hesselagergaard, Hesselager, Fyn, Denmark." On September 3, he wrote from his Paris apartment that on September 16 he would come see the Stravinskys in Venice "for three days." He added: "I have terrible news from Pasternak. . . . He thinks that they are preparing to try him for high treason."

Nabokov's postcard dated March 13, from Khajuraho, India, says that he has been there for eight days, after ten in Japan, three in Hong Kong, and two in Siam, and that he will be back in Paris on the 17th. A letter of April 5, from Paris, contains scarcely any information, but a postcard from Berlin on June 25 reports on events in Cologne: "I heard Boulez's new piece and am not impressed by it." A Christmas letter promises a trip to America in March, and the next note came from the Chelsea Hotel, New York, February 24, 1961: "I will be leaving for Paris in a few minutes, but after Tokyo apparently I will be returning to Paris via the United States, and I would like to know whether you and Bob are going to be in Hollywood in May, and, if so, whether I might come to visit you. . . . I hear that Bob is giving a concert here next week. Wish him success." Stravinsky acknowledged this on February 26, saying that he expected to be home in May.

But on May 10, Nabokov wrote from the Miramar Hotel, Hong Kong, that he was obliged to return to Europe via India, and that until he reached Paris, May 27, his address would be c/o the Administration Générale des Beaux Arts, Teheran: "The festival in Tokyo went very well—a pity that neither you nor Bob was there."

STRAVINSKY TO NABOKOV   *May 21, 1961*

Dear Nika,

Thank you for your letter of May 10. It is a pity you are not coming.

Our plans: In July I am conducting in Santa Fe (*Oedipus* and *Perséphone*). In August, at home. At the beginning of September we sail from New York to Scandinavia—Helsinki, Oslo, Stockholm—from there to Berlin, where I will conduct (*Oedipus* and *Perséphone*) with the Santa Fe company; I will do the same in Warsaw[72] [both] for the State Department. From there to the BBC, London. At the end of October we fly from London to Cairo, Karachi, Bangkok, New Zealand, and Australia (to conduct concerts), and from there to Tahiti (to rest for a short week), then home. With God's help, I hope to get through it all.

---

[72] This was later changed to Belgrade.

Recently here in Los Angeles a terrible fire burned poor Huxley's house to the ground. Great treasures were lost in the fire: his journals, his correspondence, the famous letters of D. H. Lawrence. . . . It is terrible.

I will be glad to hear from you. Write to me here; everything is always forwarded.

A friendly kiss,

I. Stravinsky

[*Original in Russian*]

Nabokov answered this on June 12, saying that in ten days he would have to go to Switzerland for a hernia operation, and enclosing an announcement from Le Figaro *about Stravinsky's visit to the USSR the following year. Nabokov's next note, sent from the Cecil Clinique Générale in Lausanne, presses for an explanation about the Russian visit. Stravinsky seems not to have answered, and Nabokov did not write until August 4—from the Denmark home of Baron Philippe de Rothschild—asking for information about Stravinsky's forthcoming Berlin appearances conducting* Oedipus *and* Perséphone. *The two friends were in Berlin together for a few days in September, where they watched the erection of the wall. Then Stravinsky started on his trip. Nabokov had arranged high-level receptions for the composer in Cambodia and Thailand (Prince Kukrit Ramoz in Bangkok), but both visits had to be canceled because of a delay (airplane trouble) in Cairo. On December 26, Nabokov wrote asking Stravinsky to compromise on his refusal of Mrs. Kennedy's invitation to a reception at the White House, and to suggest alternate dates.*

Nabokov spent a few days with Stravinsky in Washington in January 1962, and several more days with him in Hamburg in June.

On January 3, 1963, Nabokov cabled from Vienna asking Stravinsky to write to Khrennikov in Moscow.

STRAVINSKY TO NABOKOV   *January 14, 1963*

I have not written anything to Khrennikov yet because unfortunately circumstances have changed, and there has been a shift to the right in the realm of the arts. By recommending you, although you are not unknown [in the USSR], I would obviously be putting Khrennikov in an awkward position, since it is not within his powers to change the official attitude toward new art that has emerged following Khrushchev's sharp criticism of abstract art. We are awaiting Hurok's return from Russia and will find out from him what the circumstances are regarding you. I told him of your wish to go to Russia and asked him to help, which he promised to do, if he could, but he was not certain that this was the right time.

I must close this letter, for I have many more to write. . . . I embrace you.

Hans Rosbaud has died. It is a heavy blow (to those who knew him and love music . . .).

[Original in Russian]

Nabokov's next note, from London, February 3, is written on a notice inserted in a Festival Hall program:[73]

Dear Igor Fyodorovich and Vera Arturovna,

We are writing to you from a concert by Sviatoslav Richter, who is playing Bach and Schubert brilliantly. He is a flaming fag. I had a number of writers from the Soviet Union over. They say that Khrushchev's speech is not as important as we make it out to be. Still, it would be good if you would confirm with Khrennikov that I wrote to him at *your* suggestion. I am afraid that I cannot go this year, but still, if you can, write. I embrace and kiss all three of you. Yours, Nika.

To this is added:

We are sitting here, coughing. Richter is playing very "excitedly" in the Dos-toevsky-Rozanovsky-Pasternak tradition. Only the Germans do this well, of course, since they discovered the *"âme slave."* I am very sorry that I will not be able to get to California before December, but I hope that you will come here in May. (I will be in Moscow in April.) Warm regards to Vera Arturovna and Bob. Isaiah Berlin.

Nabokov wrote to Stravinsky from Berlin, September 2, 1963:

How are your trips, your recordings, your performances, your work? I also would like to hear once in a while from Bob, who is surprisingly silent. Why? . . . I want to come through with the offer I made to you and also to Bob last autumn: could you and would you *please* come and spend a month or two

---

[73]   PLAIN MAN'S GUIDE TO COUGHING

There are two ways of coping with a cough during a concert.

One is to suppress it entirely—as the artists invariably manage to do during per-formances.

The second way—when complete suppression is not possible—is to muffle the cough by the discreet use of the handkerchief.

There is a third way, but since this is distracting to both the artist and the audi-ence it is unlikely to find favor with Festival Hall patrons. It is to open the mouth and use it as a sounding board for projecting the cough into every part of the auditorium. A single unrestrained cough of this character released during a quiet passage of music can effectively ruin the enjoyment of three thousand listeners, on whose behalf this homily is published.

(or even three if you want) here in Berlin, in comfortable surroundings, in a beautiful villa (overlooking a lake), which the City of Berlin will put at your disposal free of charge? You will have a staff of servants to look after you. Vera will have her studio and you yours to work in. This is how it would happen: Willy Brandt, the mayor of Berlin, would send you an official invitation to come and spend several months here. . . . We will have a number of symphony and chamber-music concerts. . . . The center of our musical program will be dedicated to your work of the early, the middle, and the present periods. And now comes my unexpected and rash question: would it be possible for you to consider making an orchestral arrangement, or rather a transformation and adaptation for voice and orchestra (in the way you did so beautifully of Bach), of two, three, or four Negro spirituals? I have just returned from Salzburg, where I heard and saw my dear old friend Leontyne Price. She would be delighted and honored to sing these adaptations of Negro spirituals here, either under your direction or under somebody else's. I would like to commission you to do this. Thus we would have *"eine Uraufführung"* of a work of yours in our program. Thus, too, you would, I think, greatly help the cause of emancipation of the American Negro and at the same time earn the gratitude of the Negro people all over the world. . . . Bob promised to send me your schedule but did not. I know from Signora Panni that at the end of October you will be going to Sicily, and later to Rome. I will be there, of course, and then we can discuss the details.

On February 13, 1963, Nabokov wrote from the American Academy in Rome:

I am next door to the [Elliott] Carters and surrounded by all of our friends: Mrs. Plum [Panni], Signor Labroca, and the dear Vlads. . . . Khrennikov still has not given me a reply, so I decided to drop the matter for now. But we will talk about it when you come to Europe. I will meet you in Hamburg, at Rolf's, for the premiere of *The Flood* on April 30. . . . I have Denisov's score and notes to Volkonsky's music.[74] It is all pretty poor and hopeless, a hybrid of Webern and early Hindemith, but it is also touching, when you think about the conditions under which this music is being written. The reproductions of the abstract artists also tell a story. . . . You get a sense of the same helplessness, an imitation of yesterday's Western prototypes. . . . I embrace and kiss you, and send warm regards to Bob Bobinsky.

On February 17, 1963, Nabokov wrote from the Hotel Grand Excelsior in Catania, describing the premiere of his opera there. Then on March 31 he sent a new itinerary, of a trip to Israel, returning to Berlin on April 16, and, sometime between the 26th and the 28th, coming to Hamburg for the premiere of The Flood. *On September 2, Nabokov wrote from Berlin that because of mastoid*

---

[74] Edison Denisov (b. 1929) and Andrei Mikhailovich Volkonsky (b. 1933), Soviet composers.

*trouble he was unable to come to the festival in Brazil, where Stravinsky con-
ducted.*

STRAVINSKY TO NABOKOV   *October 6, 1963*

Dear Nika,

I have waited so long not only because I had hoped to receive the "spirituals"
and to give you an opinion about the possibility of an orchestration or arrangement . . . but also because Vera has been ill, first with flu and then with food
poisoning, and the time has been unpleasantly occupied since our return from
Brazil.

Though your festivals have always been the most intelligently planned and
the most capably executed, and though they have always shown the greatest
devotion to me and my work, I loathe festivals. Even more, I loathe most of the
people they draw, the Stuckenschmidts, the Bornoffs and the thousand other
cons from Italy to everywhere. Therefore, please reserve our concert for the end
of the festival, or for a time when the white trash will have cleared out.

You asked in Hamburg about programs and conductors. I would like the
concert of my later music to be conducted by Dorati (who has just done *The
Flood* in London), with the program: *A Sermon, A Narrative and A Prayer;*
Movements; *Abraham and Isaac;* Interval; *The Flood.*

Why should it only be myself or Bob to conduct these difficult newer
works? Dorati has at least shown interest in them, and *none* of the other star
conductors has. For the piano soloist in Movements I can recommend the gentleman from Zagreb.[75]

For *our* program, myself and Bob, I would like to do *Les Noces* and *Renard,*
and a staged *Histoire du soldat* by [Ingmar] Bergman, who is doing it already
in Stockholm; this *I* would conduct. I do not want Scherchen for these pieces;
or Boulez, whose only aim is to be faster than anyone else.

For the rest, we would like to come in August and stay as long as we find
convenient. The important thing is that I have a *muted* piano and a quiet room.
And servants [for] we are less and less elastic.

I do not know what I can do with a "spiritual": I had to give up the idea of
orchestrating some Mussorgsky songs recently because the music is so far from
me now. But I will study the "spirituals" when they come, and I am attracted
by the idea.

We will stay here until sometime in the first half of November, then to
New York (Pierre Hotel), but I hope to hear from you before. And I hope to
hear, above all, that you are well again.

                                                        Love,

[Original in English]

---

[75] Yurica, who had played it there with the present writer conducting.

Nabokov answered on October 24, from Donaueschingen:

I am delighted to hear from Bob that you feel better, and I will certainly do my best to come and see you in Rome. . . . I will be most happy to invite Tony Dorati to conduct your new works, and, in fact, if you do not wish to conduct during the festival, please do not. We could have your concert after the festival is over. . . . I will try to get Ingmar Bergman to come, but I doubt that he will. He does not want to come to Germany in general, and to Berlin in particular. But maybe he would if you were to ask him.

STRAVINSKY TO NABOKOV   *November 2, 1963*

Dear Nika,

Thank you for your letter. Hope you will allow me to reply to it in person in Rome, November 24–25. We fly back to New York on the 26th. We will be in Rome ca. November 13–14 too, but I do not advise you to come then as we will be exhausted and upside-down from the trip, and we will be leaving for Palermo perhaps already on the 14th.

As for Berlin, do not count on what I am composing now. Besides I do not like to speak about music I am composing which is not a commission and which is not yet finished. As for the Scherchen concert, that is of no interest to me and I will surely not attend. A concert by Dorati of my late works no longer attracts me either, after reading all the unfavorable comment on his apparently disastrous performance, in London, of *The Flood*. And unless I do at least one concert myself, my tax lawyer will not permit me to come to Berlin. But we can talk about all this in Rome.

In a hurry but affectionately, yours as ever,

I. Str.

[Original in English]

On December 14, 1963, Nabokov wrote from Berlin:

How are you, how is your health, how is Vera's exhibition coming, or has it already started? How are your engagements with Philadelphia, and how is Bob Ivanovich Bobinsky? Here everything is arranged, and everybody is delighted at the prospect of your coming next year. An official invitation to you by the mayor of Berlin is now on its way. . . . After having talked to you and to Bob, I told the mayor that you would like to come around September 1 and stay a month or a month and a half. But if, during that time, you want to make trips, you are entirely free to do so. During September I hope that there will be other friends around, such as George Balanchine and Wystan Auden and Stephen Spender. But, as I said before, if you do not want to see anybody, you will not.

Nabokov wrote from Tel Aviv on February 12(?), raising the questions answered in Stravinsky's next letter.

STRAVINSKY TO NABOKOV   *February 17, 1964*

Dear Nicolas,

Sorry not to cable a reply, but I have too much to say.

1. *Abraham and Isaac* is to be sung only in Hebrew, as *Oedipus Rex* is sung only in Latin. It was composed this way and cannot be translated. I know no more about Hebrew than Fischer-Dieskau, but can't he read the phonetics?

2. I have received and answered the Mayor's letter.

3. I will not conduct *Abraham and Isaac* in Dorati's concert.

4. The programming of *Abraham and Isaac* is a matter of some concern to me because it must have sympathetic neighbors. What is Dorati's program?

5. And the other concert, *Renard*, the two concertos, *Noces*. This has too much piano music. The Capriccio would be enough, and the Piano Concerto could be replaced by *Abraham and Isaac*.

6. We will appeal to the Ford Foundation for our transportation, but can we make reservations now and then ask for the money?

Hope the India trip was successful for you. All best as ever,

Yours,   I. Stravinsky

[Original in English]

Nabokov wrote on February 24, 1964:

Could Bob get in touch with Mr. Joe Slater of the Ford Foundation, 477 Madison Avenue. It is with him that I negotiated for your transportation, and he agreed that the Ford Foundation could pay for this. . . . My trip to India was very successful, and we had a very funny, rather absurd conference, where the Indians made Mioumiou and we made Wouwou.

STRAVINSKY TO NABOKOV   *February 28, 1964*

Dear Nicolas,

Answering yours of February 24. The program seems to me very good, only please do not announce now who is to conduct which pieces.

I would hope that Fischer-Dieskau could record at the time of the concert or rehearsals, but I will leave that to Columbia, who, incidentally, have no difficulty with his other recording contracts. I hear from Aaron Propes[76] that you

---

[76] Director of the Festival of Israel during Stravinsky's two tours there, in 1962 and 1964.

will be in the U.S. in April. Know only that we are with the Cleveland Orchestra March 8–15, otherwise here.

Yours cordially as ever,   Igor Stravinsky

[*Original in English*]

Nabokov's next letter, April 10, 1964, is addressed to the present writer:

Forgive me for taking so long in replying to your postcard, but it takes me a week to decipher your writing and two weeks to meditate about it. . . . I was most pleased when I heard that I. S. is writing a piece on a poem by Auden.[77] . . . Unfortunately, dear old Varèse has been very sick and is not able to finish his piece for me.

STRAVINSKY TO NABOKOV   *April 18, 1964*

Dear Nika,

Glad to have your cable and letter, for *we* had begun to worry about *you*.
  Our schedule is:

1. Ann Arbor, Michigan, with the Philadelphia Orchestra, April 29–May 3.
2. Toronto (recording), May 4–7.
3. New York (recording), May 8–20 (Pierre Hotel).
4. Home.
5. Minneapolis—concert June 1–3.
6. Home.
7. Denver—concert June 8–12.
8. London (Savoy Hotel)—June 15–July 5 (recording and Oxford concert).
9. New York-Chicago concerts in July, then Bob to Santa Fe to conduct *Lulu,* ourselves to Los Angeles.
10. August 15—to Israel.
11. August 22—to Paris and then Berlin.

The Kennedy *Elegy* turned out so much different than expected, a tiny (2 minutes) piece for solo voice and three clarinets, that we cannot do it in Berlin or in any orchestral concert.
  Will you, I hope, come to London? Perhaps on June 18th if you can manage.

As ever yours,   I. Str.

[*Original in English*]

---

[77] *Elegy for J.F.K.*

STRAVINSKY TO NABOKOV   *April 28, 1964*

Nika, dear friend,

This is in reply to your telegram of the 27th regarding the *Elegy*.

I have decided to hold off with this short epitaph, which, I think, has come out very well, until such a time as I can hear the music; that would be in November, at a concert that Bob and I, along with Berio's wife, Katya Berberian, are planning for Town Hall in New York. It is a difficult piece to include in a concert program: it would go very well with the Epitaphium, for example, or with the Dufy canons, Dylan Thomas, my Cantata with female choruses, or the Shakespeare songs,[78] but these things do not make up a concert program. Well, we will discuss it again before November, but I wanted to warn you now so that you do not count on this *Elegy* for your own concerts.

Tomorrow morning we are flying to Ann Arbor (Michigan), where we have a rehearsal of our January Philadelphia concerts—including *Perséphone*—in a matinee concert on May 3, after which we will go to Toronto by limousine for the *Mavra* recording (in Russian) with Columbia. Then to New York for twelve days of recording, again with Columbia, and on May 20 we will fly home for a few weeks of rest. I will tell you about our further plans later, when I have more time. Now I have to pack, but before that, I embrace you.

Yours,   I. Str.

[Original in Russian]

On May 6, Nabokov wrote to Stravinsky at the Pierre Hotel, New York: "It now seems doubtful that I will be able to come to London to spend your birthday with you on June 18, for the City of Berlin is asking me to go to Japan to plan una stagione giapponese next year in Berlin." Nabokov wrote from Berlin, June 9, to Stravinsky at the Hotel Savoy, London, about plans to be in Moscow for four days on his way back from Tokyo, and the suggestion of the Soviet ambassador that Stravinsky write a note to Madame Furtseva "introducing me as an old friend of yours."

On June 19, Nabokov wrote that he had received a visa and was going to Moscow, but by way of Tokyo. On July 11, he wrote from Berlin, explaining that he never reached the Russian capital and that his flight from Tokyo had landed five times before finally touching down in Karachi; that since he was obliged to pass from the cold within the plane to the tropical heat outside (Manila, Hong Kong, Phnom-Penh, Bangkok), he had heart spasms on his arrival in Karachi and was taken to a hospital; then, after thirty-six hours in a hotel bed, he flew

---

[78] Epitaphium for Flute, Clarinet, and Harp ("for the Tombstone of Prince Max Egon von Fürstenburg"), 1959; Double Canon for String Quartet (Raoul Dufy in memoriam), 1959; *In Memoriam Dylan Thomas*, 1954; Cantata, 1952; Three Songs from William Shakespeare, 1953.

to Frankfurt and Berlin. As if to add to these problems, Stravinsky cabled from Hollywood (on the 22nd) that he had an ear infection and was not permitted to fly for several months. On the 24th, Nabokov cabled for permission to perform Abraham and Isaac *with another conductor.*

STRAVINSKY TO NABOKOV   *July 24, 1964*

Dear Nika,

This is in reply to your telegram—do not worry yourself about my health: it is just that I have to stop flying for a while because of the ear infection I contracted in London in June. The doctors here have helped, but I still will not be able to fly for another three months.

Israel is desperate—not surprisingly, since they have sold everything at enormous prices for the benefit of the hospitals and have built the entire festival on *Abraham* (the sacred ballad), which lasts 12 minutes and is dedicated to Israel. Bob was supposed to conduct (and I the Symphony of Psalms). They have not been able to make any secret of the fact that the whole festival (which depends on my concert) was put together on my name and not on that 12-minute piece of serial music which is both unintelligible and uninteresting [to them], except for the dedication. They sent Bob (who was supposed to conduct) a telegram asking whom I would prefer to see conducting the piece, Bernstein or Stokowski, to which Bob replied that both were excellent, almost adding the suggestion of Pablo Casals, but then thought better of it because he was not sure they would see the irony.

God, how revolting, how insulting it is to see one's name associated with all of these "celebrities," and how distressing is the indifference (and I am thinking about Boulez, too, and his indifference) and more often the hostility (which I frankly prefer) with which the music I am now composing is greeted, as well as having my name linked to these festivals all over the world. Do not be angry with me for this. You know how fond I am of you, and also that *I* know why you arrange these festivals (which are better and more intelligent than any others) and how *it is a requirement of your nature to experience hundreds of cultures in so many different parts of the world.* . . . What I have written is not directed against you but is rather said in my own defense and in defense of my rights, which few people recognize, much less respect.

Berlin will be able to perform *Abraham,* as will anyone else, after the premiere in Israel at the end of August. It would be a shame if Fischer-Dieskau did not perform *Abraham* because of the *required* Hebrew text, but, since I composed *Abraham* in the old Jewish language, I will not allow it to be performed in anything else. I would like Bob to conduct *Abraham* (he has learned it all from me—what to do and how).[79] Invite him. He is in Santa Fe (New Mexico),

---

[79] The program of the September 22 Berlin concert was as follows: *Renard* (Stravinsky

Hotel La Posada, preparing a production of *Lulu* by Alban Berg. Bob is the only person whom I can trust to perform *Abraham* well. I pray to God for your well-being. I miss you.

Fondly, your loyal friend,

[*Original in Russian*]

STRAVINSKY TO NABOKOV
Hollywood
July 29, 1964

Dear Nika,

Thank you for your cable. Our schedule is still not quite definite, because I am still expecting a letter from Propes, which will tell me how many days have been set aside for our [Israel] performances.

Whatever the case, Vera and I will be flying from New York to Paris on August 17; we are planning to rest there for a day or two (the 18th and 19th), and that is all we know for now. As soon as we learn the dates of my three performances in Israel (one in Jerusalem and two in Caesarea), and where we will be stopping off on the way home—i.e., in Rome or in Paris—I will let you know.

I am sending a cable today to Willy Brandt expressing my deep regret that I will not be able to be present for the Berlin festival because of the condition of my ear, and that, therefore, I will not be able to accept his hospitality.

That is all for now. Keep well yourself. I embrace you.

I. Str.

[*Original in Russian*]

Stravinsky cabled to Willy Brandt on July 30. Nabokov did not see the Stravinskys in Paris, but he wrote to them in Hollywood, saying that the Berlin festival had programmed twenty-two Stravinsky pieces. After an exchange of a half-dozen cables and calls, the Stravinskys finally went to Berlin. Nabokov wrote to them, October 5, after the festival:

Forgive me. . . . I promise in the future to deal only with *business*. . . . I will write to Bob separately. . . . Did you get the statement that I released to the press concerning Bob's work? Did you get a copy of my little book?[80]

Nabokov wrote again on November 1, from Zagarolo, Provincia di Roma:

---

conducting), *Noces* and *Abraham and Isaac* (the present writer conducting), and Capriccio (with Nikita Magaloff as soloist, Stravinsky conducting).

[80] *Igor Strawinsky* (Berlin, 1964).

I came here partly to rest, partly to recover from the festival commotion, but principally to work. Alas, as soon as I arrived I was driven to bed by a foul angina virus. . . . Today I am up and about, but after all of the antibiotics I feel like an *"apukhtinskaya"* fly. And how are you? How is your health? How was the move to the new house? How is your work going? What is Bob doing? Did he get my letter? Please ask him to write to me here. . . . If there are any errors in my book, please tell me what they are so that I can correct them for the second edition. The British firm Collins now wants to publish the book [in English], so I would like to put everything in order and in accordance with your criticism. I have written this book *entirely* as an act of friendship. . . . I am feeling bored and wretched. If only you and Vera were nearer. . . . God keep you. . . .

After returning to Paris, Nabokov wrote again, on December 12:

It has been nearly two months since I have had any news from you. I heard that you were in New York and that you had a concert there on the 6th featuring your new Cantata and the epitaph for Kennedy. . . . Spender told me that you had an abscess or some kind of cyst under your truss and that it was causing you a great deal of pain. . . . On January 9 I will be going to Japan for two weeks on Berlin festival business. After that I will return here and, if convenient for you, will fly from here to California to visit you at the beginning of April. . . . I hope that you are not overworking yourself.

New York
December 29, 1964
[Visiting card]

STRAVINSKY TO NABOKOV

Happy New Year. We will not be home in April.[81]

[Original in Russian]

Nabokov wrote from Berlin on January 9, 1965:

I heard *Abraham and Isaac* in Paris, an excellent performance.[82] . . . On the following day I left with Marie-Claire for the south of France to visit some Greek friends who live near Arles, so I did not read the reviews. . . . My health is better than it was when you last saw me, but the heart spasms seem to be coming

---

[81] Stravinsky's frigidity here is explained by his letter of January 11, 1965, to Adriana Panni in Rome: "I have just heard about the very unpleasant things that Nicolas Nabokov told you on the subject of my last appearance in Berlin conducting *Renard* and the Capriccio. It is enough to say that this is not the first time he has talked behind people's backs in such a fashion. But this time it has greatly astonished me."

[82] Conducted by Maurice Le Roux, with Derrik Olsen.

more often. . . . Tomorrow morning I fly to Japan (Hotel Okicha, Tokyo) and will be there until the 23rd, then to Paris for two days, then back to my kennel in Berlin, where I will finish the ballet [*Don Quixote*] for George. When exactly will he be producing your Variations?[83]

On January 18, Nabokov wrote from Kyoto, and on March 17 from Berlin, the latter note on behalf of Mstislav Rostropovich, saying that he wanted to commission a piece for cello and that "he sincerely loves and admires your present style. We went together in Paris to hear Abraham and Isaac, *which . . . was very well done."*

STRAVINSKY TO NABOKOV   *March 21, 1965*

Thank you for your letter of March 17, dear Nika. It is a good sign that you do not say anything about your health: it must mean that you are well.

As for Rostropovich and his instrument, to be quite frank, I am not terribly interested, and in any case I am up to my neck in work; in July I will begin composing the symphony I promised the young Princeton orchestra so long ago.[84] But Rostropovich has no cause for anger—I have heard from many people that he is a brilliant performer, but when I think about Russia, where all of my works are played free, from illegal photocopies, I do not feel any inclination to write for Russia or for a Russian performer.

I spent this whole week working for television with Liebermann,[85] and although it was exhausting, with him and his remarkable team it was also a pleasure. He has gone to New York for a few days and will go to Hamburg from there.

I am glad that you are finishing your ballet and that you have interesting work ahead of you with Balanchine in New York, but I am sorry that I will not be there at the time.[86] God grant you great success, my dear friend. I kiss you affectionately.

Yours,   I. Str.

Despite all of my work I have still managed to read very thoroughly your excellent book about me. I did find a number of things, however, that ought to be corrected. But we must wait until we see each other. Where and when might that be? I do not want to return the book to you with my pencil marks in the

---

[83] Variations for Orchestra (Aldous Huxley in memoriam). The ballet was first performed on March 31, 1966. Balanchine rechoreographed the Variations for the 1982 New York City Ballet Stravinsky festival—his last choreography.

[84] *Requiem Canticles.*

[85] Filming *A Stravinsky Portrait.*

[86] Stravinsky saw *Don Quixote* in New York on September 30, 1965.

margin, since a few quite complex points require explanation. But write to me about this. In nine days—a week from Tuesday—we fly to Texas for a few days.

[*Original in Russian*]

Nabokov wrote from Bonn on April 5 on the subject of his book about Stravinsky:

I will do everything that you want, according to your directions. (I will definitely enter your corrections in the second German edition.) After all, the book is written in English, though I am purposely delaying the release of the English edition, which is being put together by the brilliant editor Anna Kallin of the BBC; she has been very active in this. As soon as the edited English version is typed, I will send it to you. . . . I will convey your decision to Rostropovich, and I am in full agreement with you. . . . My health and morale are significantly better than they were last autumn. I am going to Berlin now for ten days but will be returning from there to Paris for Easter.

The next Nabokov communication came from Mount Kisco, New York. He did not see the Stravinskys until September, in Hamburg. The remaining five letters are from Nabokov to Stravinsky. On April 20, 1966, Nabokov wrote from Berlin:

What Balanchine has done with your *beautiful* . . . Variations is most *remarkable*. It is all so intelligent and compels people to listen to the music. Balanchine is really a musical phenomenon, and the better the counterpoint, the more condensed and complex the structure (like yours), the better *his* Variations are on the stage.

On December 9, 1966, Nabokov wrote from Paris:

According to rumors, your health is considerably better now. . . . I also heard that you have written a new piece, apparently a Requiem, and that you yourself are going to conduct the premiere in Edinburgh.[87] . . . Later I heard that you wanted to spend the spring here in Europe, partly in Rome, partly in Paris. Finally, I was told that Bob is going to conduct in Cologne. . . . I myself am planning to come to America on January 15 to stay in Princeton for three months, as I did last year. . . . I have some very interesting scores from young Russians that I would like to show you. But it is possible that you already have them, since Blazhkov, the young director from Kiev, says that he is corresponding with you. . . . I am reading Chekhov's letters (surprised at their beauty), as well as

---

[87] Peter Diamond, then director of the Edinburgh Festival, had visited Stravinsky in California and invited him to Edinburgh. That Nabokov did not know the *Requiem Canticles* had been performed in Princeton two months earlier indicates how far apart the friends had drifted.

some brilliant stories by Gorky.[88] . . . I embrace you and Vera most affectionately and kiss you both tenderly on all four cheeks. . . . I also embrace Bob Bobovich ("Silov"[89]).

The next letter, dated May 5, 1967, was sent from the Century Association, West 43rd Street, New York:

Dear Igor Fyodorovich and Vera Arturovna,

I was not able to visit you after all. First there was Oppenheimer's slow and painful death.[90] . . . Then I got into various scrapes in connection with the Congress for Cultural Freedom and the fact, which simply stunned me, that Fleischmann was a plant of the C.I.A. . . . I finally found a temporary post for next year lecturing at the City University of New York, right here downtown. I tried to call you for Russian Easter, but your number was busy the whole day, so I sent you a telegram. On the 7th, I am going to Berlin, where I will remain until the middle of June. Then I will probably go to Russia after all, and, after that, in July, to Paris, and in August I will be taking my youngest son north to Germany and Norway. . . . I was just at Dr. Lewithin's[91] and he told me that the two of you had spoken yesterday on the phone, and that you will be going to Toronto on the 11th and then coming here to New York. It is a pity we will miss each other again. . . . Now that Madame Stalin—Alliluyevna—is here, I think one should start to look for Hitler's son and, when they find him, put them all together on a Tolstoyan farm and raise holy, nonmilkable Indian cows. Svetlana has already received more than a million dollars for her book, which, except for George Kennan. . . , no one has read. . . . I have listened and listened and listened to your *Canticles* and developed an infinite love for it. It is absolutely beautiful music, concise, intelligent, or, rather, wise, and so fully alive.

The next letter, dated July 17, 1967, came from the home of the Baronne de Turckheim, 18, avenue Président Wilson, Paris:

I have just returned from Russia and am a bit worn out from the traveling. It was all very good and a bit sad. I saw many people, including Furtseva and Khrennikov, as well as some youngsters. On Blazhkov's behalf I sent you a spiritual book and a record of the bells of Rostov. What a muddle the Soviet Union is in!! As you say, who needs it?! I forward regards from everyone, Furtseva (an extremely kind and intelligent lady) to mad Yudina.

---

[88] Stravinsky had also been reading Chekhov and Gorky.

[89] *"Silovyi"* is an adjective describing force or power—a play on the German *Kraft*.

[90] On the day of J. Robert Oppenheimer's death, Nabokov called Stravinsky, who was in Miami, to say that Oppenheimer had left a request to have Stravinsky's *Requiem Canticles* performed at a memorial service.

[91] Leon Lewithin was Stravinsky's physician in New York at the time.

The final note, August 8, 1967, comes from the same address as the first one, forty years before—Kolbsheim, Bas-Rhin:

I have not written because I was utterly worn out after Russia. Next to India it is the most exhausting country I have been to, full of such funny people, like, on the one hand, the old ladies Yudina and Lina Prokofieva, and, on the other, Blazhkov and all of the young composers, who do everything to imitate Xenakis, Cage, Stockhausen. . . . St. Petersburg's beauty angered me. All façades . . .

APPENDIXES

Stravinsky at the Musée d'Art Moderne

"Igor Stravinsky: La Carrière européenne," the title of the catalogue[1] of the Stravinsky centenary exhibition at Paris's Museum of Modern Art, is an impossible premise, since the composer's European and American careers cannot be separated by drawing a Maginot Line through the year 1939. If his American concert tours prior to this date might be overlooked, the same is not true of the transatlantic commissions, *Apollo,* the Symphony of Psalms, *Jeu de cartes,* and the *Dumbarton Oaks* Concerto. Nor can a sufficiently comprehensive presentation of Stravinsky conclude with the beginning of World War II. Moreover, the Paris homage was further confined to theatre pieces, little or no account being given of most of the concert music.

The catalogue's introductory statement by François Lesure, "This exhibition . . . is limited to the European years of the composer's activity," is bald-facedly untrue. For one thing, the catalogue ignores Stravinsky's work in Europe in the 1950s and 1960s, though parts of *Agon, Threni, Abraham and Isaac,* and other pieces were written in Venice. For another, a large portion of the materials dates from the post-1939 period, including half of the portraits in the section "Visages d'une vie," a gallery of twenty-six photographs, drawings, and paintings.[2] Likewise, half of the photographs in "L'Héritage sonore d'I. Stravinsky," a stunning mix-up of pictures and captions,[3] show him in New York between 1947 and 1965 (*not* 1966, the catalogue's choice of year for a snapshot with Benny Goodman).

Since the 1939 boundary is also violated by the art on exhibit, notably in Tchelichev's decor for *Apollo* (Buenos Aires, 1942) and in two Giacometti

---

[1] By François Lesure and Jean-Michel Nectoux (Paris, 1980).

[2] "1950(?)" is given for a view of Stravinsky in a "Columbia studio," though he recorded exclusively for RCA at that time, and "1956(?)" is the date attached to a picture of him said to be conducting the Mass in Venice, though he never led that work there.

[3] The photograph reproduced in the catalogue as no. 356 matches the caption of no. 354 (except that the record company is Keynote, not Columbia), while photograph no. 354 fits no caption, though obviously intended for that of no. 353. This caption reads that, *"très probablement,"* the picture is of Stravinsky recording his Octet (which actually took place in May 1932). What the often-reproduced photograph *does* show is the composer recording the end of the first tableau of *Petrushka*. The same picture was reproduced in *L'Intransigeant,* February 4, 1929, with the caption "Stravinsky conducting *Firebird*."

The true story can be pieced together from the report in *L'Instrumental,* January 1929, of the Columbia Records Gala at the Théâtre des Champs-Elysées, December 15, 1928. On that occasion, a film was shown of Stravinsky "in a sweater" conducting

drawings, one wonders why Marino Marini's red-ink drawing and bronze heads of the composer (New York, 1950 and 1951) are excluded, especially when the only interest in the portraits by Larionov, Bakst, J.-E. Blanche, and Gleizes (no resemblance to anyone) is in the subject. But the iconography is unaccountably poor. Where are the charcoal portrait by Ivan Thiele,[4] Tatiana de Jonquières's sculptured head, and the bust by Fiore de Henriquez? In the main, the stage and costume designs are holdovers from the Bibliothèque Nationale's 1979 Diaghilev exhibition. Of them all, Roerich's colored drawing for the costume of "the third maiden" in Part Two of the *Sacre* would alone be worth the trip to the museum.

The catalogue's category "Amis et interprètes" is astonishing for two reasons, the exclusion of Stravinsky's closest friends of the period and the inclusion of the "interpreters" he most abominated. Thus Pierre Monteux, his name forever joined with the *Sacre,* is not among the conductors, though in that section space is devoted to, of all people, Furtwängler. ("I am not an admirer of this conductor," Stravinsky wrote to his publisher, March 20, 1931, and similar statements abound in the composer's correspondence.) Whatever the reason, the catalogue suggests that Stravinsky had no friends outside of music, though the opposite is nearer the truth. To judge by the correspondence, Mitussov, Argutinsky, and Cingria were at the top with the trusted and elect, yet on them the catalogue sheds no light at all.

Of musician friends, Nadia Boulanger receives the warmest words, though it must be said that her relationship was not so much that of the Egeria of the catalogue's description, as of a prodigious proofreader.[5] But why omit Lord Berners, surely a more genuine and enduring friend than Florent Schmitt? And if Vittorio Rieti, represented by a 1942 typewritten letter from Stravinsky[6]—a strange choice in view of Stravinsky's calligraphy—then why not Arthur Lourié, who was closer to him during the 1920s than any other musician? Fi-

---

Petrushka, while his recording, "perfectly synchronized," was played with the movie. After this, the audience watched an actual, live recording session of Stravinsky conducting *Firebird.* (He chose to record the original Suite, rather than the 1919 version, because the orchestra had been rehearsed for the Ballets Russes performances in Diaghilev's revival of the original work, December 24, 1928.)

[4] Thiele wrote to Stravinsky (in Russian), June 5, 1913, saying that Koussevitzky wanted the portrait. A letter from Thiele years later suggests that he completed the work, but the present writer has not seen it.

[5] Photograph no. 210, of Stravinsky and Nadia Boulanger, dated "Cambridge 1937," was actually taken in the Cambridge home of Edward Forbes in January 1941. (The two musicians are pictured comparing scores of the 1940 Symphony.) The catalogue states that Boulanger was "one of Stravinsky's closest friends from the time of his installation in France." This would mean 1920, but the relationship was not close until a decade later. They first met at the time of the *Firebird* premiere.

[6] The catalogue reproduces the last half of the letter, though the first half, which reveals that Stravinsky had agreed to write a ballet "after" Donizetti (not, as stated in the caption, after Bellini), is the important one.

nally, the iconography of Balanchine, the most important of all of Stravinsky's "Amis et interprètes," consists exclusively of pictures from the American years, photographs of the 1949 *Firebird* and 1957 *Agon,* and designs for the 1941 *Balustrade,* which for some reason conclude the section "Les Années françaises."

The authors of the catalogue deserve much praise for touching on the subject of "Stravinsky et les poètes simultanéistes," even though limiting it to Sébastien Voirol's *"transposition synodique"* of *Le Sacre du printemps.*[7] Stravinsky had attended Ricciotto Canudo's Simultanist functions two years before meeting Voirol, and Canudo's manifesto, "Notre Esthétique: A propos du Rossignol de Stravinsky," had the greater influence. The catalogue states that Stravinsky's connection with Dada was less significant than that with the Simultanists, although it was the Dadaists who developed the Simultanist idea, as is shown by the Dada program for an event in Paris, February 5, 1920, that Stravinsky attended. Moreover, some of Dada's most prominent animators were Stravinsky's friends, among them Tzara, Picabia, Cendrars, and Alice Bailly.

Bailly[8] (the catalogue follows Stravinsky's misspelling, Bally) deserves a paragraph to herself, since the catalogue includes a facsimile of "Les Cris de Pétrouchka," accompanied by a misreading of some of its contents, but not by a single word of explanation concerning the circumstances of the manuscript—

---

[7] The catalogue does not explain the connection between Stravinsky and Voirol, which began on June 24, 1913, when the latter wrote to the composer in his nursing home in Neuilly: "I and my friends, your fervent admirers, have learned that at the very time we were ceaselessly acclaiming your name, you were gravely ill." The letter also refers to a project, surely the " *'Sacre' synodique,"* a poem of fifty-six pages, handwritten in violet, red, blue, and green pencil and ink, and issued in Paris in an edition of fourteen copies; Voirol sent a copy to Stravinsky, November 22, 1913. The lines to be spoken simultaneously, by groups or individuals, are bracketed, but these are not numerous. Stravinsky and Voirol seem to have met for the first time in Paris in May 1914, possibly when Ravel, Casella, and Daniel Chennevière played *The Nightingale* 6-hands (this event was reviewed in *L'Intransigeant*) at the home of Madame Valentine de Saint-Pont (the Futurist dancer and painter, and granddaughter of Victor Hugo, not to be confused with Hugo's daughter, the subject of Truffaut's film). Stravinsky sent a manuscript to Voirol for publication by "Les Editions M. Mouillot," as a letter from Mouillot to the composer, July 14, 1914, confirms. Voirol's last recorded meeting with Stravinsky was at the preview of *Mavra* at the Hôtel Continental, Paris, May 29, 1922.

[8] Alice Bailly (1872–1938), painter and engraver. She and Cécile Cellier, the future Madame C.-F Ramuz, shared an apartment in Paris on the rue Boissonnade, where Ramuz lived from 1910. Stravinsky preserved Alice Bailly's letters to him from 1917, as well as two series of photographs with her, one with Ansermet, Werner Reinhart, Elie Gagnebin, and the publisher Mermod, taken in Winterthur on March 17, 1930, the second with Dushkin and Reinhart, taken in Zürich in March 1933. Reinhart wrote to Stravinsky, January 5, 1938: "I went to the interment of Alice Bailly two days ago. . . . She had been working for two years on the decor for the foyer of the Théâtre de Lausanne. A good friend has disappeared, one who participated in many of your successes in Switzerland and Paris, and at which I was also present."

which is dated *"janvier 28,"* not *"janvier 1918,"* as the catalogue states. In Geneva, on January 27, 1917, the *"samedi dernier"* mentioned in Stravinsky's text, Ansermet conducted a performance of *Petrushka*. Calls for the composer were finally answered, but when he went onstage, saw a group of admirers ap-

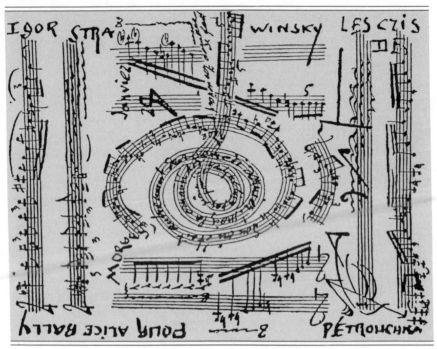

"Les Cris de Pétrouchka," sent to Alice Bailly on January 28, 1917.

proaching with a Petrushka doll, and heard the demonstration of approval increase, the embarrassed composer fled. During the next day's atonement, he wrote and sent the manuscript (reproduced above) to Alice Bailly, and blamed "the cruelty of the public" for preventing "Petrushka" from thanking her *"comme il faut."*

    With only six graphic objects, the section of the catalogue called "Stravinsky et les Futuristes" is woefully inadequate. The historical notes, by Giovanni Lista, state that after Stravinsky's meetings with the Futurists in Rome in February 1915, three soirées in honor of the composer and Diaghilev were held in Milan during *"le mois suivant."* No, these took place in April 1915.[9] Lista repeats Marinetti's story that Stravinsky wanted to present the *bruiteurs*

---

[9] Lista describes Stravinsky's participation in the Milan gatherings from Pratella's memoirs, but Francesco Cangiullo's account is the more convincing. Cangiullo—spelled "Canquillo" in the Bibliothèque Nationale's 1979 Diaghilev exhibition—visited Stravinsky in Milan in June 1963 and invited him to a show, "Cangiullo futurista e passatista." The artist inscribed the catalogue of this event: *"Si ricorda, Maestro, a*

in Paris but did not wish to use their instruments himself,[10] even though Stravinsky was able to travel to Paris at this time only with the help of friends in Russian, Swiss, and French diplomatic circles.

As might have been anticipated, Lista focuses on Diaghilev's production

Portrait of Stravinsky at the piano by Francesco Cangiullo.

of Stravinsky's *Fireworks* (Rome, April 12, 1917) with Giacomo Balla's composition of colored lights moving at different speeds. But much more is now known about this than Lista imparts, thanks to the survival of Balla himself until 1958—by which date interest in the Futurists had revived—and to the re-

---

Roma, a Napoli, con Diaghilev," and drew a picture in which the smoke from Vesuvius spells "Napoli" and the initial "C" forms the Bay of Naples shoreline. (See *Yale Italian Studies,* Spring 1980, for a list of publications by Cangiullo and for the facsimile of his manuscript of *Viva Marinetti!,* in which the "Stravinsky storm" is compared to the storm provoked by Matisse's *Red Dancers.*)

[10] A letter from Luigi Russolo's widow to Stravinsky in Milan, April 21, 1954, reminds him that he had heard and admired the "Russolophone" (in April 1915).

construction of the spectacle in Rome in 1967 and 1968. The premiere of the four-minute opus having been aborted by "a technical accident"—blown fuses?—Lista's appraisal of the event as "a major one in the experimental, avant-garde theatre of the first half of the century" seems slightly exaggerated.

The remainder of Lista's text mentions some of Stravinsky's contributions to Futurist publications. But after the *Fireworks* fizzle, the reasons for the composer's involvement were personal and not owing to any lasting sympathy with the movement. Thus the page from *Noces* reproduced in *La Brigata* (Bologna, May 1917) appeared in an issue dedicated to modern Russian art; Clemente Rebora, the Milanese poet who procured the illustration from the composer, did not even refer to Futurism. Similarly, the publishing of the page of *Renard* in *Noi* (Rome, January 1919) should be attributed to the efforts of Bino Sanminiatelli, who went to Montreux and obtained the manuscript from Stravinsky himself.

Stravinsky's association with the "little mags" of Orphism, Dadaism, and Futurism was in response to appeals from painter and writer friends such as Canudo (the exhibition should have included the crucial May 29, 1913, issue of *Montjoie!*), Severini (*Noi*), Morandi, Chirico, Cocteau, and Ramuz, who wished to publish his and Stravinsky's translations of Russian folk poetry. Lista refers to the "echoes" of *Fireworks* that appeared in the Paris review *SIC* (*Son, Idées, Couleurs*; the magazine was published from 1916 to 1920) but does not say that its founder, Pierre Albert-Birot, and his assistant, Pierre Lerat, were acquaintances of the composer.[11] Claude Artout, editor of another Paris avant-garde *journal d'art*, wrote to Stravinsky "on the recommendation of Cocteau," claiming Picasso, Bakst, and Satie as contributors: "It is known that you work with Ramuz; what we would like is a *'poème musical'* created in collaboration with him." (June 10, 1917) When two of these collaborations, "Chant dissident" and "Le Moineau est assis," were published in *La Revue Romande* (September 15, 1919), the Swiss press ridiculed the second as a specimen of Dada.

Months before the opening of "Igor Stravinsky: La Carrière européenne," its organizers were obliged to announce that the USSR would not participate. The loss was crippling, especially of the costumes and sketches by Roerich for the *Sacre* in the Bakhrushensky collection. To some extent this deprivation was offset by loans from Theodore Stravinsky, the exhibition's largest private source. These included one of his father's early landscape paintings and many photographs. Yet Theodore Stravinsky's greatest treasures were regrettably not

---

[11] Lerat wrote to Stravinsky from Rome, May 4, 1917, asking him to send a manuscript to *SIC*, and a letter from Albert-Birot to the composer reveals that he complied: "Picasso is in Spain, and I have not received any word concerning the manuscript [which you sent to him, rue Victor-Hugo, on May 4]. Just this minute I received the manuscript that you promised me in your last letter. I will publish it in the next issue. Would you give me the full name of the translator Ramous [*sic*]?" The May 1917 issue contained costume designs by Fortunato Depero for *The Song of the Nightingale*.

on exhibit, his father's annotated volumes of Kireyevsky and Afanasiev, from which the texts of *Les Noces, Renard, Histoire du soldat,* and several songs were taken.

What most surprises this reader of the catalogue is the small number of non-French sources—still another sense in which "La Carrière européenne" is a misleading title. Italy could have provided much more than the few items displayed, Belgium more than the single program, and Britain at least a wide representation of pianola rolls, one that would include the *Roi des étoiles,* cut by Esther Willis, Philip Heseltine's protégée.[12] The British Museum alone could have provided a broader selection of manuscripts.[13] (The one of the Capriccio is opened, in the catalogue, to a famous gaffe, the indication "Doppio Movimento"—instead of "Doppio Valore"—at **33**.) But the limitation of the contribution from Germany to some lithographs of Karsavina is baffling. B. Schotts Söhne, Stravinsky's chief publisher in the 1930s, could have stocked several showcases. And is no one among the organizers aware that *Histoire du soldat* and *Oedipus Rex* had triumphed in German theatres before these pieces had been staged at all in France? Yet the celebrated 1923 Bauhaus production of the *Soldat* is not mentioned, while the date of the first and far from acclaimed Paris performance, 1924, is termed "the decisive year" for the opus.[14]

Even so, the greatest disappointment is the absence of manuscripts from French collections, particularly those of the late André Meyer and of Serge Lifar. True, the Musée Picasso in Paris is the source of the chief novelty, a melody for clarinet that Stravinsky composed for Picasso in Rome in April 1917:

But neither the Meyer autograph full score of Part One of the *Sacre* nor the manuscript of the first draft score (complete except for the Danse sacrale, now in the collection of the Paul Sacher Foundation in Basel), both of them indis-

---

[12] Constantin Braïloï's judgment that this piece *"annonce un bouleversement"* in Stravinsky's development might have been the result of listening to the pianola arrangement, probably made around 1915, in addition to studying the score. It should be mentioned that the version of Braïloï's essay that appeared in *La Tribune de Lausanne,* September 24, 1918, was much reduced in length, and that the complete text (unpublished) constitutes a remarkable piece of criticism for its time.

[13] More interesting than any manuscript on view is the set of corrected proofs of *Petrushka* showing "eight measures of the finale." The catalogue identifies the passage as that in which "the Moor pursues Petrushka to kill him: [Stravinsky] made an entirely new *rédaction."* No; the music is that of the concert ending.

[14] By all accounts the most absorbing production of the *Soldat* was that by Pirandello in Rome in 1925, partly because of the superb translation by Alberto Savinio, Chirico's brother, whose qualities as a writer have only recently attracted English readers, in John Shepley's translation of Savinio's essay on Isadora Duncan. (See Savinio's music criticism, *Scatola sonora,* and drama criticism, *Palchetti romani.*)

pensable for the adequate study and comprehension of the work, is mentioned. (In the Sacher score, purchased by him on November 11, 1982, Part Two begins with the music for two trumpets—now after 84—and not with the Prelude as we know it; the E-flat key signature does not obtain at two measures before 22 and the string chord there is written in sharps, thereby confirming that the second violins should play E and not E flat; tempi in several places are faster or slower than in the final score; and the end of Part One is dated February 24, 1912.) Moreover, the original (and only) scores of Stravinsky's orchestrations for *Les Sylphides,* which Lifar unveiled in Strasbourg, May–September 1969, and of the 1913 *Khovanshchina* manuscripts are not listed, though the full score of Stravinsky's final chorus for Mussorgsky's opera is known to be in the *coffres* of Lifar.

The most puzzling section of the catalogue is François Lesure's preface, with its negative characterizations of Stravinsky's music and breathtaking errors of fact. When the composer "fled" Europe *"en guerre"* in 1939, he was forty-three years old, Lesure writes. Stravinsky, fifty-seven, did not "flee" but went to fulfill engagements in America with every intention of returning after them. Nor did he live in a *"luxueuse villa de Hollywood,"* but, for twenty-four of his twenty-nine years in California, in a one-bedroom cottage, and in far from affluent circumstances. Lesure says, too, that Stravinsky's correspondence has not yet been published, which ignores the major selection that appeared in the USSR only one year after the composer's death.

But Lesure's unsympathetic attitude toward his subject is curious, to say the least. He quotes a 1937 Stravinsky letter to Ansermet as an example of the composer's harshness to his interpreters, remarking that Ansermet "had thought he had acquired the right to formulate his observations on [Stravinsky's] new creations." The point at issue, however, is not that of offering "observations" about a new piece *(Jeu de cartes)*, but of performing it, repeatedly and against the composer's express wishes, with cuts. Which composer would *not* have said, with Stravinsky: Play the piece uncut or not at all?

In conclusion, Lesure writes that Stravinsky's music strikes us by *"son ironie, sa colère ou sa crudité."* Irony, surely, anger sometimes, though tenderness—as in the lullabies "by" a feline, for characters in fairy tales, a goddess of spring, an inmate of Bedlam—is a quality that comes as quickly to mind. Of crudity Stravinsky's music has not a particle: on the contrary, his tiptoe lightness, his elegance and grace are unique in twentieth-century music. Finally, what strikes us primarily in his music is its festiveness and joyfulness, the joy in making *(poiēsis)*, joy in belief and affirmation, joy in a circus as well as in a psalm, and, finally, simple *joie de vivre.*

On Premieres of LE SACRE DU PRINTEMPS

This "anthology of music criticism"[1] purports to republish the most significant reviews of the first performances of *Le Sacre du printemps* in thirteen countries, although no critiques, but only dates, are given for Argentina, Hungary, Holland, and the United States (Philadelphia). The introduction, notes, and commentary are in French and English, though not all of the English is intelligible. Viz.:

> The articles are reprinted following the chronological order of performances, country by country, respecting the priority of publication for each one.

This means, the French text reveals, that the reviews are grouped by country, and chronologically within each one. Thus the press coverage for Diaghilev's 1913 London ballet production is followed by that for Goossens's 1921 concert performance there, which is succeeded by two reviews of Koussevitzky's 1914 performances in Russia (albeit in the wrong order, Moscow in actuality having preceded St. Petersburg).

Since the first-city-only format is suspended by the republication of reviews of a premiere in a second German city, Leipzig, and of a third American one, New York, the editor might have mentioned the amazing tally of performances in other German cities, beginning with Dresden (October 13, 1924), Düsseldorf, and Wiesbaden (1925), and, in the next five years, Duisburg, Munich, Karlsruhe, Bremen, Chemnitz, Frankfurt, Essen, and Cologne, the last three also having staged the piece. The justification for including Leipzig is odd: the performance, conducted by Furtwängler, was "all German," whereas the first performance in Germany, in Berlin, was conducted by Ansermet. Yet Monteux conducted the Dutch premiere, and other non-nationals most of those in other countries, including the Spanish, which took place in Barcelona[2] under Stravinsky, while the first "all-Spanish" performance was in Madrid under Arbós.

The United States, Italy, and Switzerland present special cases. Reviews of Monteux's performance with the Boston Symphony in New York are included, but not those from the orchestra's home city, where the piece was first played. In Italy, two performances of Part One were given before the first complete one, in Florence in 1935 (three years after Oslo and nine after Prague, neither of which is mentioned). In a 1924 letter to Juan Mestres Calvet, Stravinsky had

---

[1] *Igor Stravinsky: Le Sacre du printemps, Press-book,* edited under the direction of François Lesure (Geneva, 1980).

[2] March 22, 1928. The press-book does not supply the full date. Stravinsky repeated the program on the 28th.

authorized performances of Part One only and had agreed to conduct it. Nevertheless, the first complete Swiss performance (Zürich, 1929, under Volkmar Andreae) is not listed, but only the incomplete one by Ansermet (Geneva, 1923), concerning which the press-book states that the conductor "was compelled to make cuts in the second part." No! Ansermet played Part One, as announced in the program, and only the Introduction to Part Two, for which Stravinsky had composed a concert ending.

The reviews and interviews are published in facsimile, photographed from the newspapers and journals in which they appeared. This increases both the authenticity and the difficulty for the reader, especially in the case of Karatygin's St. Petersburg notice, some of which is faded and blurred beyond legibility. (Why were translations not provided? If the texts are not meant to be read, what is the purpose of the book?) A more serviceable publication would have been that of T. C. Bullard's dissertation (University of Rochester, 1971) containing the Paris reviews of the 1913 performances; this, at least, can be read by the Franglais public. Since Stravinsky was less interested in the local reviews of the event than in the Russian ones (not included in Bullard or the press-book), he preserved them, and their publication might eventually be expected. Among the worthwhile critiques of the Paris premiere not included in the present volume are those by G. Linor, Jean Chantevoine, Georges Pioch, and Reynaldo Hahn; but then, the most valuable of all the 1913 texts, Stravinsky's interview in *Gil Blas* the day after the premiere, is also absent.

The introduction claims that certain critics who had attended the Paris premiere wrote "repentantly" after the revival there in December 1920, but the book offers no example of pre- and postwar reviews by the same person.

APPENDIX C

The First Scenario of THE NIGHTINGALE
and Some Letters from S. S. Mitussov

Stravinsky wrote the following draft for the *Nightingale* scenario, Acts one and three only, on March 22 (Old Style), 1908, in the home of V. I. Belsky, Rimsky-Korsakov's librettist, though a letter from S. S. Mitussov (Leningrad) to the composer, May 4, 1925, reminds him that "you became pregnant with *The Nightingale* in my apartment at B. Bolotnya 6, Apartment 7, St. Petersburg." Stravinsky began to compose the music on November 16 (O.S.), 1908, and he had made several drafts of the Prelude and the music at 5 by January 19 (O.S.), 1909. The first act was completed in sketch form in the summer of 1909 and in full score—which differs in orchestral color and detail from the published version—the following autumn. Here is an example of the florid style of the Fisherman's aria as originally conceived:

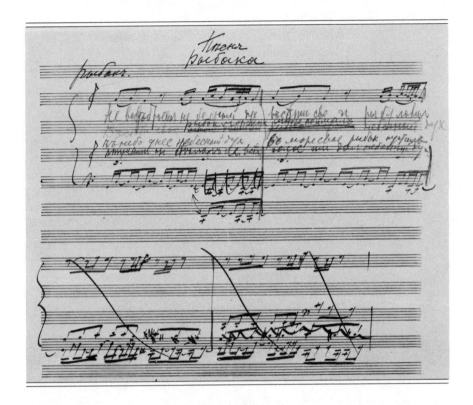

Scene One

The Fisherman is repairing his net and lamenting his fate, his only consolation the singing of the Nightingale. The Nightingale, on the scene, is singing . . . his song comforts the Fisherman.

Cautious steps are heard (someone approaching stealthily). The Nightingale flies away. Enter the Chinese Emperor's kitchen servant, accompanied by the court's chief bonze and the Emperor's closest courtier. A servant turns to the courtier and says that this is precisely the place in the forest where the Nightingale sings his dawn song and that they should be hearing it momentarily.

Just then a lady-bird notices the Fisherman—everyone is delighted*—and the Fisherman, in his turn, notes that it is indeed his lady-bird. . . . The servant affirms that it is a lady-bird and that the Nightingale should begin singing at any moment. But, in the meantime, some frogs have started croaking.

Courtier: What a bird . . .
Bonze Tsin-pei: And such a powerful voice in such a small bird!
Chorus: How remarkable!

> *Bonze Tsin-pei:* How wonderful . . . it is just like the silver bells in our monastery.
>
> *Courtier:* It is as though her throat were lined with silver.
>
> *Chorus:* How beautiful!
>
> *Servant:* No, no, those are just frogs in the marsh; the Nightingale has not appeared yet.
>
> *Courtier:* Listen, Cook, I will show you how the Emperor eats if you will find the Nightingale.
>
> *Cook:* There is the Nightingale singing now.
>
> *Everyone:* Where? Where?

The Courtier asks to be introduced.

> *Cook:* Little Nightingale, the Chinese Emperor's highest courtier wants to relay a request of the Emperor to you.
>
> *Nightingale:* The Emperor's will is sacred to me.
>
> *Courtier:* Tell him[1] that the Emperor would like to see him at the palace and listen to his song—if the Emperor is pleased, he will be rewarded with golden slippers, [?], etc. . . .

The Nightingale agrees and flies down to the Cook's arm. Everyone exits; the Fisherman watches them leave and says that now his only consolation has been taken away from him, that it is fine for them there, but I am here, etc. . . .

Scene Three

The Emperor is lying down.

One can hear the footfall [din] of the "Evil Deeds," as it gradually gets louder and becomes a roar. The Emperor cries out: "Music (climbing down), music!" Big Chinese drums. "I do not want to hear their words! *You* sing, dear, sweet, golden bird. I have given you gold jewelry and hung gold slippers about your neck . . . Sing! Sing! But you are silent. There is no one to wind you up, and you cannot sing otherwise."

(Death appears.)

"Oh! How wretched I am . . . who will save me from this terrible specter who looks at me from his empty eye sockets and nods his head at the words of my Evil Deeds."

(The Nightingale appears.)

Three songs:

1. On the forest, the sunset, and the Fisherman*
2. On the Imperial Gardens**
3. On the cemetery***

---

[1] Beginning with this line, Stravinsky decided that the sex of the Nightingale is masculine.

* After this song: "Sing, sing, dear Nightingale. I recognize you, sweet little bird." (The shadows ripple.)

** "Thank you, thank you, dear little bird! I banished you from my kingdom, and now you have chased that terrible specter away from my bedside. Perhaps you can chase Death away too? Sing, sing, little Nightingale." (The shadows disappear altogether.)

*** Death flies out, leaving behind the saber and the crown.

> *Emperor:* You have saved my life. How can I reward you?
>
> *Nightingale:* I have already had my reward; I have seen tears in your eyes and will never forget it!
>
> *Emperor:* You must stay here with me forever; I will throw away the artificial bird.
>
> *Nightingale:* No, I cannot live in the palace. Let me just come to your window every evening to sing to you. My song will cheer you. Farewell!!!

The Emperor watches him leave, then puts on his imperial robe, sets the crown on his head, clasps the golden saber to his breast, and stands erect in all his imperial greatness. While all of this is taking place, the courtiers steal up from the door, look under the canopy, and, not finding the Emperor there, look at each other, puzzled; then, when they notice him standing at the window, they prostrate themselves.

The Emperor addresses them: "Hail."

FROM STEPAN MITUSSOV'S LETTERS TO STRAVINSKY

Dear Igor,

St. Petersburg
May 3 [O.S.], 1913

A certain young lady, Alexandra Vasilievna Saznovskaya, will be coming to see you and bringing you this letter.

She is a singer in the process of setting up a concert in Paris, the details of which she will give you herself. Be a friend. Do not refuse to do this little something for her: introduce her to Sergei Pavlovich [Diaghilev] and do anything that might benefit her without putting yourself to too much trouble. This is the request I make of you.

I kiss you affectionately, as well as Fedya and Lyudmila. I send my sincere respects to Ekaterina Gavrilovna and kiss her hand.

Yours,   Stepan

Dear Igor, *[Early July 1913]*

First of all, your fear of hurting my feelings is groundless, because everything I write now is in the service of your talent and has nothing to do with me; any questions about pride of authorship are irrelevant. Believe me, I am happy to be able to contribute a single brick to the foundation of the building you are constructing; and if the brick does not fit, I will be more than glad to run off in search of another. Second, listen:

> Shine the lantern over here, here . . .
> Today will be a holiday; how marvelous!
> Who has seen the Nightingale?
>
> We have not seen him.
> Ask the Cook; she has seen him.
> She is now the Resident Cook.
>
> Is it true?
> Look, here she comes herself.
> (Bring the bells over here)
> *some:* Can we ask you, Resident Cook . . .
> *others:* Cook, oh Cook, tell us . . .
> After all, you have seen the Nightingale. Is he big (what is
>   he like?)?
> He is probably huge . . .
> *some:* And he shines like gold . . .
> *others:* And sparkles like a diamond . . .
> *Cook:* No . . . He is a small, gray bird.
> You would hardly see him in the bushes.
> But when he sings . . . everything seems so simple,
> And you cannot keep the tears from coming to your eyes.

The Chamberlain should make his entry at this point, I think. The following is just a suggestion: The servants, having finished cleaning the room, gradually exit in individual groups, and the bustle diminishes. By the time the Cook finishes her story, only a small group remains listening to her. The Chamberlain then comes in and chases them all out. But perhaps that would be odd, and he should ask them whether they have finished cleaning, and not simply chase them straight off.

> *Chamberlain:*   Out!
> Get out!
> The great lords and ladies
> Are coming now
> To await His Highness's arrival.

This is all off the cuff and quite poor. Perhaps it should go like this:

> Get out, here come the great lords
> And ladies to await His Highness.

That is also no good. I suggest:

> Get out, here come the great lords.

And that's all. Then the procession begins.

Now a few minor notes. First, you may or may not want the lanterns and bells. I included them because they are in Andersen's text, because they justify everyone's departure (though the cleaning is done, or nearly done, anyway), and because with a large number of people onstage, it would hardly do to have them all talking about the same thing.

Second, "He is huge and shines, etc. . . ." may be contrived. I would suggest, "He is huge and shines like gold." "No, he is small and gray" provides contrast and a certain style. The courtiers bombard the Cook with questions and make such assumptions as: "He glitters like gold, sparkles like a diamond, he is huge"; "no he does not glitter at all, and he is quite small."

If you write to me, use the S. P. B. Sheletovaya address. I will be leaving here very soon. Oh, Igor, it is so difficult to discuss all of this by letter; there are so many things I want to say and point out, but I imagine that you yourself feel the same way. I will send the song in a few days.

In the event that this scene should prove unsuitable, let me know. I already have alternative versions in mind, but I do not want to send them to you until I have your reactions to this one.

In composing the song, I have made no mention of the roses in Scene Three. The Nightingale only mentions the Imperial Gardens briefly, then mentions the cemetery at the end of the garden, and the willows and the gravestones, then sings a lullaby. As for the night table, I will send something along with the song.

I kiss you. Regards to Ekaterina Gavrilovna, from my wife, too.

For God's sake do not be afraid to speak your mind and to reject anything you do not like, in order that we may do this with a clear conscience. What matters is that you are satisfied. Indeed, if you do not reject anything, I will be offended. On the other hand, do not reject something just to please me. . . . My pleasure is irrelevant.

Ustilug

Oredezh
[July 1913]

Dear Igor,

Concerning your instructions, things are not going well. I am not worried about the [illegible], because I know that you do not need them as much as [illegible: the name of a book], which, at my request, Volodya looked for in all the bookshops but without success. Evidently it is sold out. How are you going to arrange the signs?

I am here in Oredezh and cannot possibly get to St. Petersburg before the 15th of the month. I am sorry. I am also sorry for not having sent you anything; there are many reasons. In the first place, everything I have written seems so weak to me that I am ashamed to send it. In the second place, I received your letter only very late, since they did not know where to send it to me from St. Petersburg . . . to Bologoye or to Oredezh.

But now listen to the Nightingale's song:

> Look into your heart,
> What do you see?
> A fragrant garden
> Of blooming flowers.
>
> In your heart they are warmed by the sun,
> The sun of your love.
> And when the flowers begin to fade
> I will give them life again:
>
> I will sing my song,
> And when you weep
> Your tears, like morning dew,
> Will revive the flowers.

It is short and quite poor, isn't it?! Well, do not despair, my friend. If you do not like it, we will write something else. I have a few other variations, anyway, using different subjects. In Andersen's text, the Emperor does not speak before the Nightingale's song; so we would have to make do with *nods of the head,* which is what I had in mind. As soon as the Emperor sits down on his throne, the Prime Minister says something like:

> Great Emperor
> By your imperial will
> The Nightingale has come,
> And now humbly awaits
> Your command.

Then the Emperor can nod his head, answering his courtier with this gesture, or he can simply say: We are listening.

Well, Igor, I kiss everyone. Write to me in St. Petersburg, since it is difficult to receive registered letters here. I will probably be sent somewhere else from St. Petersburg immediately (on the same day). Regards to everyone I know.

Yours,   Stepan

[*On an attached sheet*]

1) Ah!
    Oh!   If you look into your heart

2)   What do you see?
             beautiful
4)   *Within* bright   flowers
     There wonderful
8)   How to give them life again.
12) You revive the flowers
     (To avoid parallels, literally yourself)
9)   (with the original 8th)
     I will sing my song (so that you do not have "then" without "when")

MORE CHANGES

Ustilug   [*July 1913*]

Dear friend,

I am thinking of making some small changes in the Nightingale's song in the
second act.

The second couplet:

> Oh! Sorrowful heart,
> Dawn mist,
> Transparent tear,
> And the moon, and the tear . . .

The third couplet:

> Oh! Tender heart
> Oh! Blue night sky
> Spring dreams
> And stars and dreams.

"Spring" can be changed, however, to "beloved."

Ustilug   [*July 1913*]

Dear Igor,

Yesterday I dropped in at Koussevitzky's for your romances and *Spring*. Christ!
Wholly unintentionally I made off with the *Japanese Lyrics*. How this happened, I have no idea. Accidentally, in any event. "I am the unwitting thief!"
     You noticed right away, of course, that I have changed the following:

> The blue night
> Is already nearing its end.
> The dawn mist
> Has enveloped the flowers.
> The flickering starlight,

> Fading into the invisible fragrance
> Of the flowers (and grass),
> Shimmers in the air.
> And a white rose-bush
> Stands in tears.

I send a kiss to everyone. I will send you the beginning presently.

Yours,   Stepan

Dear Igor,

St. Petersburg
August 6, 1913

I turned the cabinet inside out but could not find the book of songs. I went to Ilin's store and asked them to send it to you as soon as they get it (they did not have the book). The notary also had an ownership transfer of the libretto for you. We will do the transfer in Russian with a French translation.

I saw Roerich, who will be designing the set for *The Nightingale*. He returned from Moscow recently, where he saw Sanine, Mardzhanov, and some others. He has asked me to write to you so that you should not worry about the dates, because the state of mind in Moscow on this point is one of great flexibility. Everyone there was very grieved to hear of your illness, and everyone is glad now that you have recovered. The Chinese materials are really very interesting (Roerich bought up everything Chinese), at least everything that I saw, which was less than half.

I really do not like the Emperor's phrase, "But what is this, then?" There is something vulgar about it, inappropriate for an Emperor. Would it not be better to change it somehow, for example: "What is this," with the accent on the word "what," and not on "this"; it may be less clear, but accompanied by an appropriate gesture and the right musical expression, these two words might better convey a sense of surprise, surprise beyond description. If you understand what I am saying and approve, let me know so that I can put the matter aside as settled; if you do not like it, we can leave the original version intact or think up something else.

Incidentally, write the words "little Nightingale" into the Emperor's lines after the Nightingale's song, like this:

> How beautifully you sing.
> How can I reward you?
> Speak, . . . etc.

I think it will be better that way. Of course, as you know, *I am worried that the whole thing is poor*, worried in earnest. By tomorrow half of the last act will be finished; I will send it the day after tomorrow.

The first page of the Nightingale's song looks like this so far:

> The blue night
> Is already nearing its end.

> The flickering starlight
> Has faded into the fragrance of the flowers,
> And I do not know anymore
> What is star and what is flower.
> A white rose-bush
> Stands in tears.

Before this, after the Emperor has asked for the drums, the Nightingale flies in and sings:

> Oh! Here, I am here, great Emperor.
> I will sing you praise of
> Your beautiful garden.
>
> The blue night, etc. . . .

Let me know right away whether you like this sort of thing, and if so, I will go on. I embrace you, the children, and Ekaterina Gavrilovna.

Yours,   Stepan

Ustilug   *August [10?], 1913*

Dear friend,

This is how the first verse ("ati-mati") looks:

> We are all your deeds come to remind you
> That you committed us long ago,
> We are all your deeds and thoughts.
> Oh! Remember us,
> Remember.

Unfortunately, I cannot remember the last two. Perhaps some changes ought to be made. I wrote this letter and gave it to the notary. Write to me whether there are supposed to be chains or something. I embrace you.

Stepan

August 12, 1913

The Emperor is lying under a large canopy. Death is sitting on his chest; she has put on the Emperor's crown and is holding the jeweled saber in one hand, while in the other she holds the red flag. From the folds of the canopy, ghosts are looking on . . . they are the Emperor's good and evil deeds.

Ghosts: They sing at the same time as the Emperor and even during the Nightingale's song. Their song is sorrowful and monotonous. They all sing together, almost in a whisper. Against the background of this whispering, individual voices stand out:

Ghosts: (singing-whispering)

> Ati-mati, ati-mati
> Ati-mati, etc. . . .
> Do you remember me?
> Had you forgotten me?
> Do you remember me?
> Do you remember me, then?
> We are your good deeds.
> Oh! Remember me.
> We are your good deeds.
> Oh! Remember me.
> We are your evil, unworthy
> Deeds. Don't you know me?
> We are your good deeds, ati-mati.
> We are your unworthy deeds.
> You are ati-mati.
> Do you remember me?
> Do you remember me, then?
>   etc. . . .

Emperor: What is this? Who are they?

> I do not know you.
> I do not know about you.
> Oh! I do not want to hear any more.
> I want music, play me music.
> The great Chinese drums.
> Oh, sing, *you* sing, diamond bird;
> I have given you gold and precious stones.
> No, you will not sing. You must be wound up.
> But there is no one to wind you up.
> Bring me music, the great Chinese drums.

Nightingale (flies in):

> Oh! Here, I am here, great Emperor, etc. . . .

For God's sake, write to me and tell me what you think about all this; I cannot write any more until you do. My address *now* is: St. Brusovo (Mosk. Vind. Ryb.) "Bratskoye" property. I kiss you and all your loved ones.

Stepan

Ustilug

August [18?], 1913

Dear Igor,

Since I did not receive the answer I wanted from you regarding the first half of the third act (the scene with the ghosts, which I sent you on July 31), I am sending you the conclusion. If you have even the slightest appreciation for my work, telegraph immediately as follows: "needs changes, letter follows"; or, "I accept"; or else, "unsuitable, do again," etc. . . . But please telegraph me.

Here is the conclusion:

> *Nightingale:* . . . .
> . . . .
> And a white rose-bush stands in tears.
>> *Emperor:* How wonderful . . .
>>> *Death:* (angry)
>>> I like listening to you sing.
>>> Why are you silent? Sing (a little?) * more . . .
>
>> * For iambic pentameter.

> *Nightingale:* Give the Emperor his crown
> And the jeweled saber and flag,
> Then I will sing until the very dawn.
>> *Death:* I will give him everything, every-
>> thing, but sing some more.
>> I want to hear you

That is a bit too expansive for Death; here is an alternate variation:

> I have given him everything, everything . . .
> See? I want to hear you, sing some more.
>> *Nightingale:* Oh! Shimmering stars . . .
>> Oh! Flowers! . . .
>> There, behind the white fence
>> There is another garden—
>> The sad garden of the dead.
>> Oh! How quiet is that garden.
>> Even the dew is heard
>> As it falls
>> On the grave moss.
>> On the boughs of blossoming plum trees
>> The fireflies go out one by one.
>> Sad is the moon that shines on
>> The sad garden of the dead.

> *Death:* My garden! My garden!
> What melancholy overtakes me.
> To my garden I hasten, to my garden. (Flies away.)

Emperor: How wonderful, little Nightingale; thank you.
      I feel my strength returning.
      You have chased the terrible specter away.
      But you are not leaving?
      I will make you the greatest member of the court.

Nightingale: No, your tears are your greatest gift to me.
      That is the singer's highest reward.
      I will come to you
      Every evening and sing.
      But tell no one. Now I am away.
      The sun is rising.
      Farewell, great Emperor.

The Emperor should raise himself on his elbow to utter his last words, and as the Nightingale is saying his last lines, the back wall of the set turns pale and dull ("comes to naught," as hairdressers say). The Nightingale sings the words "Farewell, great Emperor" when both he and the Emperor are already out of sight. The sun fills the first room with light. A dense curtain hangs where the Emperor's canopy used to be. The courtiers gather together hastily in fright, but also in silence. Then the Emperor comes in (holding his saber to his chest). . . . Then, the famous "Hail," under the bright rays of the sun.

    Well, my dear friend. I await your telegram.

Yours,   Stepan

I will send you the transfer of ownership of the libretto in a few days.

Hôtel Châtelard
Clarens

My dear Igor,

Imperial Society
for the Encouragement of Art
Morskaya 38
St. Petersburg
October 2, 1913

I will be sending you something in the next few days; but I have already prepared a short conversation to follow the Nightingale's song, as well as part of the song itself. I do not know whether or not the meter is suitable:

              ᴗ–ᴗ–ᴗ–ᴗᴗ– (three times, this line)   couplet
                    ᴗ–ᴗ–   *correct*

properly speaking:

                ᴗ–ᴗ– ⎫
                      ⎬ three times, then: *incorrect*
                ᴗ–ᴗᴗ– ⎭

(four of these; is that too long?).

                ᴗ–ᴗ–   Exactly the same.

Each set of two verses will have to be combined into one, although in terms of the music this is of little significance.

The Nightingale's song is followed by the Emperor's address to the Nightingale

ᴗ–ᴗ–ᴗ–ᴗ– (three times)

ᴗ–ᴗ–ᴗ–ᴗ–ᴗ

more or less like this:

> *The Emperor is deeply moved.*
>
> How wonderfully you sang,
> Little Nightingale; how can I reward you?
> Speak. (To the courtiers) I shall give him
> My golden slipper to wear around his neck

(Or the last two verses without "Speak"?)

> My golden slipper I shall give him
> For his neck.

or:

> Speak. I shall give him, from
> My own foot, this golden slipper for his neck.

I think the last version is the worst (it is the original version). In any event, this is followed by the Nightingale's rebuff:

ᴗ–ᴗᴗ–ᴗᴗ–ᴗᴗ–ᴗ

ᴗ–ᴗᴗ–ᴗᴗ–ᴗᴗ–

ᴗ–ᴗᴗ–ᴗᴗ–ᴗᴗ–

ᴗ–ᴗᴗ–ᴗᴗ–ᴗᴗ–

more or less like this:

> God is all-seeing, and I have been abundantly rewarded for
>   everything.
> I saw tears in your eyes.
> There is wonderful strength in an Emperor's tears.
> What further reward could I want?!

At this point we could put in the phrase, loaded with powerful [illegible]—I do not need any reward (in reference to the slipper)—in order to link the Emperor's words with those of the Nightingale. Then we could have the dawn or—whichever you prefer—the ladies could sing the words: "How lovely; how sweetly and coquettishly he sings!" etc. . . . You may not want to include this at all, even though in Andersen's text it directly follows the Nightingale's song. In any case, it is not terribly important.

Now for the first scene of Act Two. I want you to send me an outline of some kind. The problem is not so much the text as the music, because all of these are separate phrases, exclamations, snippets of conversation, and so on; an outline will make the writing a lot easier. It is also possible here to repeat whole phrases and individual words. Write to me right away about anything that you do not like, so that I can make the appropriate changes . . . otherwise I will have no idea of what to change or how. I will be sending the song along in a day or two.

Now a little news about myself: my daughter suffered a lung inflammation (in both lungs, actually) and very nearly died. There were days when she just moaned and gnashed her teeth, and she is still very ill now. I am afraid it has set me back a great deal.

Well, warm regards to Ekaterina Gavrilovna.

Yours,   Stepan

Have you read any German, and, if so, what?

[Stravinsky inserted the following verses in the letter, in his own hand]

> And I forgot everything in the world,
> Including my own sad fate.
>
> So lovely were these songs.
> So uncommonly beautiful were they
> That in them I found consolation.
>
> Where are you, Nightingale, let me hear you.
> And with your wonderful song
> Relieve the grief of an old man.
>
> Here I am, old man, happy to know
> That in my song
> You find comfort.
>
> I have come to you now,
> As in times past,
> To console you with my song.

Hôtel Châtelard   *[December 1913]*
Clarens

Dear friend,

Here is the Fisherman's verse:

> The sun has risen, the night is over.
> The birds are singing loudly in the reeds.
> Listen to them: the Holy Spirit itself
> Speaks through the birds' voices.

I have seen Diaghilev. He begs you to make the Ghosts' song as short as possible. If you absolutely must have a third verse, perhaps we could shorten the length of them, for example, like this:

> 1. We have caught up with you
>   We are all your deeds
>   Oh, remember us,   oh, remember, remember,
>   Remember
>
> 2. We are here and will not leave
>   We are all your deeds, etc. . . .
>
> 3. We stand here before you
>   We are all your deeds, etc. . . .

Or else two new verses, leaving your version intact, i.e., the third verse would then be:

> Henceforth we will be with you.
> Through the centuries we will be with you.
> We are all your deeds, etc. . . .

or

> Henceforth we will be with you.
> We will be with you through the centuries.

My dear, I fear that I have delayed things. I kiss you affectionately.

Stepan

APPENDIX D

On the Piano-Rag Music

Stravinsky may have begun work on the *Ragtime* for eleven instruments immediately after completing the Etude for Pianola, late in the summer of 1917. The first sketches for the new opus are graphologically identical to those for the Etude, found on the same page of a blue and gold notebook with green endpapers. After the virtual absence of iambics in the Etude, the dotted rhythms in the next sketches surprise the reader. But since the last entry (measures 57 to 60, violin part) in this first group of *Ragtime* sketches is dated October 27, the piece was more likely begun after the completion of *Les Noces* on October 11.

The first of these early sketches is the most interesting:

(first sketch for the music from measure 83)

With the addition of dotted rhythms, this is soon headed in the direction of the motif:

Stylistically, however, the first example is closer to the Piano-Rag Music than to the *Ragtime,* and closer still to the third of the Three Pieces for Clarinet.[1] Stravinsky returned to the *Ragtime,* in either December 1917 or January 1918, finishing the abbreviated full score on February 5. The first sketches for the Piano-Rag Music were written soon thereafter, but these were interrupted by a page of notations for what was to become the opening of the Symphonies of Wind Instruments, and by the Four Russian Songs. The latter were not completed until March 1919, in which month Stravinsky resumed work on the Piano-Rag Music, after a year's interruption. He entered the new sketches, thirty-three pages of them, in a brown notebook with marbled endpapers. (The

---

[1] The dotted rhythms in the sketches for the clarinet piece suggest that it was to be a ragtime in the manner of the dance in *Histoire du soldat.*

"rag" sketches are remarkably voluminous in view of the brevity of the music, those for the Piano-Rag filling twenty pages, the *Ragtime* twenty-eight pages in the blue notebook.)

The *Ragtime* will not be discussed here, except to say that it is repetitive, banal, and greatly in need of tightening: its four minutes seem far too long. One is tempted to conclude that Stravinsky intended it as a parody, though even this would not redeem it. The Piano-Rag Music, on the other hand, is a collage, or composed improvisation, unique in Stravinsky's work, and sixty years have not corroded its idiom. Nevertheless, the work divides into a comparatively formal first half and a "free" second half, beginning with the nonmetered boogie-woogie music. Nor does the piece really end; rather, it pauses in a suspension. The Piano-Rag points to future works, too, as in this passage from the sketches resembling the Concertino for string quartet

(cf. measures 40–41)

and the first of the following two measures, which anticipates the introduction of the Octet; the second measure illustrates an experimental tendency in the sketches, which is seldom manifest in the published compositions:

(cf. measures 79–81)

The first page of the Piano-Rag sketches (blue notebook) exposes, in embryo, the introductory measures of the piece, though not yet in order; in eighths instead of quarters; and in need of some harmonic separation. Stravinsky did not establish the introduction conclusively (first nine measures) until just before finishing the opus; and only shortly before that did he discover the rhythm for measures 10–13 and 15–17: sixteenth-note triplets followed by a sixteenth (versus eighth-note triplets followed by quarters in the earlier sketches—an example of the condensation that is lacking in *Ragtime*). What is most striking in this first sketch is the composer's realization that he could build characteristic "introductory" chords, rhythms, and motifs from the music in the eighth and ninth bars.

The next notation (verso of page 2) is for the music from measures 20 to 32.

The percussion—tambour de basque; large, middle, and small side drums; bass drum—could be introduced in performances today; no doubt Stravinsky did not publish the part because it does not participate in the last section of the piece and would be commercially impractical.

Stravinsky returned to the Piano-Rag in March 1919 (brown book) with this same motif (measure 55), but the Four Russian Songs, composed in the meantime, had left a few imprints, as is evident in this figuration from "Sektanskaya":

and this one from the Rag:

(*cf. measure 14*)

The ink sketches from 1919 in the latter part of the blue book show the music in a more advanced stage than the brown-book drafts of the same passages, most transparently in measures 51–54, and in the nonmetered music:

Large and small side drums without snare

(cf. measure 83, after the 23rd quarter beat)

The sketches for the final portion of the piece, found only in the brown book, begin with notations for the fifths, alternating with single bass notes, in the metered measures. These entries are followed by one for the ending with a three-note pattern in the bass (G-E-G) that some listeners may prefer to the more "classical" published version. Did Stravinsky revise this conclusion in order to avoid the E octave? (In the example below, the music in the upper staff is in the treble clef, marked 8va basso.) When was the change made?

These and other questions might be answered only after all manuscripts and proofs have been collated. The fair copy in the composer's collection is puzzling in many respects. First, the music begins on the lower part of the centerfold, page 5, goes from there to pages 3 and 4, then to pages 1 and 2, and concludes on page 6. Nor is this ordering haphazard: the layout of the manuscript has been perfectly planned, and the writing is flawless. What Stravinsky may have had in mind—and this interpretation is supported by the many double bars and fermatas—is a collage of units, not necessarily to be heard in fixed order or even complete, for the player could begin on page 1. Stravinsky wrote the rag sectionally, after all, and even after dating and signing it in his sketchbook, he added the large segment that fills page 9 and the first score-system on page 10 (published score). Furthermore, the upper part of the centerfold contains three leftover units, not found in the music as published (which also lacks passages). Each of these units is self-contained (by a double bar), and the third ends mysteriously, with a crescendo on a sustained note.

Arthur Rubinstein, who commissioned the Piano-Rag Music, muddles its history in his published memoirs. The pianist cabled to Stravinsky from London, October 15, 1919, requesting a year's exclusivity to perform the Rag. Stravinsky cabled back the same day, ignoring the request, saying that he had already sent the manuscript to New York, in care of a mutual friend and advising Rubinstein to obtain a copy from J. & W. Chester before leaving London. Rubinstein did not understand the music, and he never played it.

APPENDIX E

On the Symphonies of Wind Instruments

By November 1916, the friendship between Stravinsky and Debussy had cooled, at least to judge from a remark in a note from Louis Laloy to Stravinsky, during the latter's brief visit to Paris that month, inviting him to dine with the French master: "Debussy feels that you are avoiding him." If indeed this was the case, the reasons might be that Cocteau had written to Stravinsky, "Debussy says he is 'tired of all these Russians,' " and that Stravinsky's unfavorable opinion of *Le Martyre de Saint-Sébastien*, communicated in a letter of November 21 to Diaghilev in Rome, had been repeated to its composer.[1] There is no evidence to indicate whether or not the dinner took place.

Occasional strains in the relationship aside, Stravinsky's feelings for Debussy were profound and lifelong, as is shown by correspondence, concert programs (in 1935 Stravinsky conducted performances of *Nuages* and *Fêtes*), and Stravinsky's participation in a Free France broadcast on the twenty-fifth anniversary of Debussy's death. Furthermore, Stravinsky seems to have written the so-called bell motif, with which the Symphonies of Wind Instruments begins, on March 26, 1918, upon hearing the news of Debussy's death. After completing the short score of the *Ragtime* for eleven instruments on March 5, and the full score on the 25th, Stravinsky had gone on to fill six more pages of the same notebook with sketches for the Piano-Rag Music. Suddenly he interrupted this work and entered the following notations:

---

[1] See page 31.

Example 1

The graphological and other physical evidence supports the assumption that these entries were composed at the end of March or beginning of April 1918, and so does the chronology of Stravinsky's other work: from April to September he was totally occupied with the composition of *Histoire du soldat;* moreover, the next date in the notebook is in 1918, i.e., *not* in the spring of 1920, when Henry Prunières asked Stravinsky to contribute to a memorial album for Debussy to be published by *La Revue Musicale.*

Stravinsky resumed the Piano-Rag Music in March 1919, finishing it on June 27. The following motif for the chorale, with which the Symphonies concludes, is found toward the beginning of this second series of Piano-Rag sketches, but in another notebook:

Example 2

As in the case of the bell motif, no indication is given that the music may have been intended for another composition. The complete Piano-Rag sketches are followed by a repetition of this motif and twenty-six pages of music, almost all of it used in the Symphonies of Wind Instruments, although the specifications for harmonium and strings are more numerous than those for winds.

Were these sketches written a full year before the piece was composed? The only answer seems to be that Stravinsky is unlikely *not* to have worked on a new piece during the summer of 1919 (*Pulcinella* was not begun until September[2]) and to have given all of his time to the instrumentation of *Noces.* The har-

---

[2] The first group of sketches for the Concertino may have been composed in the autumn of 1919, while Stravinsky was waiting for a contract from Diaghilev for *Pulcinella.* The Concertino was commissioned in a letter from Alfred Pochon, second violinist of the Flonzaley Quartet, August 17, 1919. Stravinsky wrote to Pochon, February 25, 1920: "I am thinking about the music I will compose for you, not only thinking about it, but . . . putting down on paper the things that come to me through my head, my fingers, and my ears." Stravinsky eventually transferred one motif from the Concertino sketches to the Symphonies, that of the flute part in Example 8.

monium part in *Noces,* written during July and August, supports the case for assigning the twenty-six sketch pages to the same period.

One of the few entries consistently designated for winds is a passage for two bassoons:

Example 3

This duet was intended as a response to the following duo for violin and viola, identified for these instruments in several places:

Example 4

That the chorale was the first part of the Symphonies to be completed is explained by the unrefusable request from *La Revue Musicale.* A progression in this little piece contains questionable notes in the second and fourth chords.

Example 5

That the F in the fourth chord should be a natural, and not a sharp, is certain, Stravinsky himself having made the correction in his copy of the Debussy album; also, the F is a natural in Stravinsky's first notation of the progression in his sketchbook, which, in his case, is usually the ultimate authority. In the same chord, the E has a flat in the album, which he erased in the copy of it that he used for the 1945 instrumentation (in which he also corrects the metronome from a quarter equals 100 to a quarter equals 65, pencils in some doublings for the instrumentation, and adds his timing, "2 minutes and 13 seconds"). The E is not flatted in the original sketch and not flatted in the three proofs of the 1920 score. Furthermore, Stravinsky canceled the printed flat in his copy of the 1926 piano reduction.[3]

Emile Vuillermoz, who proofread the album for *La Revue Musicale,* seems to have noticed the mistake.[4] The question is of some consequence, because the three chromatic steps in the bass—requiring the E natural—are established in the first statement of the motif at the beginning of the piece, and because Stravinsky, reorchestrating the chorale on December 11, 1945, from a photostat of the erroneous album reduction, incorporated the mistake. So does the "definitive" 1947 revision of the complete opus, prepared from the first proofs, which Stravinsky received from Paris after World War II.

A second problematical note is the A in the second chord of the same sequence. Should it be A sharp? Not according to the first notation and the first publication in the Debussy album, yet the sharp appears in Stravinsky's hand in another sketch—

Example 6

—as well as in the final proof, having been added to the second proof by Ansermet. On June 30, 1933, Ansermet wrote to Stravinsky asking about the A sharp and the E natural. The composer confirmed (in a margin of Ansermet's letter) that the E should be natural but did not answer the question about the A. (In the Debussy album used in 1945, Stravinsky had penciled in the sharp before the A, then erased it, but imperfectly.) In any event, Ansermet added the sharp, no doubt on the assumption that Stravinsky had intended an exact sequence, parallel to measure 8. Nor did Stravinsky cancel the sharp in the last set of proofs.

---

[3] The publisher's number of this score is RMV 423. The first proofs of the orchestra score are without a number; both the second and third are identified as RMV 459. The differences between the second and third proofs are even more numerous than those between the first and second, but in some places the second proofs are more correct than the third. The discrepancies exist in every category: pitches (compare the chords in the third measure of 16), rhythms, and figurations (compare the flute-in-G music at 17, for variants in pitches as well as rhythms). Not all of the corrections on the proofs were inserted, the second clarinet part, for instance, lacking a flat before the B in measure 4 of 3 in all versions of the 1920 score.

[4] According to a letter to Stravinsky from Henry Prunières, November 17, 1920. By this date, Stravinsky was completing the full score and may already have written E natural.

It should be noted that Ansermet, in his letter, also observes that the penultimate note in the piece is a B in the English horn and first trombone, but a C in the third horn. The right note, of course, is C, but neither scores nor parts have been corrected, and Stravinsky instructed his publisher to withdraw them from circulation.

In another letter, June 27, 1933, Ansermet had asked Stravinsky to verify the A flat (fourth chord, treble) in a progression of chords near the beginning of the piece (presented here in an early sketch):

Example 7

The reader familiar only with the 1947 version will wonder why, in 1947, Stravinsky canceled both the D flat and the C flat in the second chord. But, then, to compare the 1920 and 1947 versions is bewildering from almost every aspect. Why did he change the bass in the first tutti of the piece from F (measure 4 in the 1920 version) to B flat a fifth below (measure 7 in the 1947 version)? Not only is the instrumentation entirely different,[5] but so, too, are some of the pitches and the metrical structure, most of the articulation, some of the rhythmic figuration (of which the most obvious instance is the substitution, at the aforementioned tutti, of an eighth-note rhythm for the triplet rhythm). One very important change of pitch is that of the clarinet D sharp to E in the later score:

Example 8

The first notations of the flute motif in Example 8 are found among the Concertino sketches; the 1920 manuscript of the Symphonies and the three proof

---

[5] Ansermet's June 30 letter reveals that the bass-clarinet part sent by Stravinsky's publisher as a substitute for the unavailable alto clarinet was written to sound an octave too low!

scores require a sharp on the first G, a natural on the second. Furthermore, in the measure before 17 (fourth measure of 40 in the 1947 score) the time value of the A and D chord is a quarter note, not an eighth—surely a conscious change on Stravinsky's part in 1947, but one that destroys the rhythmic pattern. One undoubted oversight in the 1947 score is that the chord on the first eighth in the third measure of 45 (two measures before 27 in the 1920 score) lacks the main melodic note, F.

In Ansermet's opinion (letter to Stravinsky, January 31, 1948), the 1947 version is incomparably more powerful than the 1920 in the section from 51 to 56. Still, the 1920 version should be corrected and performances permitted, if only for the sake of the instrumental colors—the mixed timbres in the chorale, for example, as well as the unmixed ones (the family of four flutes) at 8. The 1945 chorale should also be published, because of differences both in color— the muted brass—and in harmonic emphasis (the major second). The choice of instruments in the 1945 orchestration was determined by the ensemble of the Symphony of Psalms, with which the chorale was to be coupled in order to fill a half-hour CBS broadcast.[6] Clarinets were eliminated, therefore, but Stravinsky had more flutes, oboes, bassoons, and trumpets at his disposal. He chose an ensemble of four flutes, four oboes, English horn, three bassoons and contrabassoon, and he added a fourth trumpet to the brass.

The 1920 and 1947 versions are identical in the strict relationships among the three tempi, the metronome a quarter equals 72, its sesquialtera, and its doppio movimento. In music whose speeds are so strictly controlled, fermatas and rubatos would seem to have no place, yet Stravinsky did not eliminate them in the later version, but merely converted some of them to measured quantities. Thus the final chord in the 1920 score is a whole note with fermata (in a measure of $\frac{4}{4}$), while in the 1947 score this chord is sustained through three $\frac{2}{4}$ measures—which the composer intended the conductor to beat.

A feature of the first drafts of the Symphonies that deserves mention is the frequent absence of meter. In the first part of the following example, Stravinsky had started to pencil in bar lines, but the emphasis provided by the piccolo on every other one of the first nineteen beats disregards weak and strong accents in the phrases of the other lines:

---

[6] On December 8, 1945, Stravinsky wrote to Bruno Zirato, his New York concert agent: "All they [CBS] need from me are an additional few minutes; that is their problem—quite easy—but mine, to fit those minutes to the Psalm Symphony (exact timing, 21 minutes, 30 seconds), is another question. Fortunately I have the solution for it. I will begin with the final chorale of my Wind Instruments Symphony.... In order to avoid extra expenses, I am myself rearranging this short piece (about 2 m. 15 s.) to make it fit the general sound." (Original in English) The Symphony of Psalms was to have been recorded at the time of the performance (February 1946), but the session was canceled because of a musicians' strike.

Example 9

APPENDIX F

On the Chronologies of the Composition of the Octet, Serenade,
and Concerto per due pianoforti soli

Twelve measures of the valse variation in the Octet, starting at measure three
of **35**, were composed in the spring of 1919, while Stravinsky was working on
the Piano-Rag Music. The same passage recurs in one of the first drafts (July
1920) of the Symphonies of Wind Instruments. The first completed section, the
fugato variation, was composed in January 1921, on a subject

derived from one of the sketches of the unfinished "Pour les 5 Pièces monométriques":

Stravinsky wrote the first four measures as they appear in the final score (at
51), except for a single octave transposition and an eighth rest that he quickly
relocated. The next version introduced elaborations, eventually discarded, and

the metronome quarter equaling 116. This was followed by a draft for piano 4-hands of the entire fugato, note-identical to the final score and linearly more distinct in the two measures before 54, where the instrumentation obscures the voice-leading of the middle parts. Instrumental specifications in pencil and red ink were added to the four-stave score at a later date. Still another 4-hand score, a fair copy, displays improvements including phrasing and the reduction in speed to an eighth equals 100. That the music was intended for piano, not for eight winds, is confirmed by a direction, "for the right hand"; by the low register of the bass (which exceeds that of trombones and bassoons); and by the use of nine-note chords.

A five-page draft for the beginning of the first-movement Allegro, written just before or just after *Mavra* (an interval of a year), reveals that at one time Stravinsky had a piano and wind orchestra in mind. The upper stave is marked "orchestra"—though the only instruments identified are two flutes, two trumpets, and timpani—while the lower two staves are reserved for the piano part, the octave style of which anticipates the Concerto of 1923–24. A larger ensemble than the one Stravinsky finally chose would be required, of course, for the twelve- and thirteen-note chords.

The next notation, found in a later sketchbook and dated July 12, 1922, contains the complete treble and some of the bass of the movement's nine-measure ending. This entry is followed by one in which, experimenting with the descending scale of the principal theme, Stravinsky places treble and bass in syncopation, the bass anticipating the pitches of the treble for one measure, then vice versa:

The next two sketches, for the music between 14 and 15, and 6 and 9, are assigned the respective metronomes a quarter equals 84 and a quarter equals 138, which indicates that Stravinsky had not yet perceived the character of the movement as a whole. The two sketch-pages that follow contain the music from 8 to two measures before 10. Then Stravinsky jumps to 14; the missing section, found on a separate sheet, may have been composed after the movement was completed. The next sketch, for the first two measures of 14, is accompanied by a roster of the instruments of the final ensemble. The notations that follow are, first, for the four measures before **16** (but with the bass in D minor!); second, for the music from **5** to **6** and **4** to **5**; third, the four measures before **14**; and, fourth, the music from **19** to **21**. This last segment is dated August 8, 1922.

On August 6, 1922, Stravinsky had attended a corrida in Bayonne. On August 14, he wrote to René Auberjonois, complaining that to compose had become difficult because of a parrot:

> Since you were so kind to have thought of me, I select my prettiest stationery and envelope to thank you and present my news. Now—what to tell you? A *peroquet* that lives across the street interrupts my work with his idiotic cry and imitations. The child who spends all day teaching it stupidities has now taught it a very foul expression, which the wretched bird repeats endlessly. At this time my thoughts go to another *peroquet:* your first painting, which you showed me. That is one *peroquet* I liked immensely. I would so much like to see what you are doing now. To ask questions is useless, because you will not reply. I understand you—nothing is more annoying than such questions. But to hear from you now and then would give me great pleasure, since I still remain your loyally devoted
>
> Igor Stravinsky.
>
> P.S. The word *"perroquet"* is lacking an "r" throughout this letter. Please excuse me.

Despite the psittacine profanity, Stravinsky completed the first movement in abbreviated full score on August 16, though on the cover of the manuscript he describes the contents simply as *"Brouillons."* Two sections have been pasted in: the ten measures beginning at **2** before **10**, and the four and a half measures at **13**. Some instrumentation is indicated, and where the voice-leading is intricate, red ink distinguishes a line or lines; the phrasing in the introduction is marked in pencil.

On August 18, Stravinsky added the fugato to the *"Brouillons"* under the title "II" (second movement). The next entry is that of the aforementioned 1919 valse fragment, slightly expanded. This music coincidentally contains the first intervals of the fugato subject and therefore of the theme, which, on August 23, 1922, he copied into the *"Brouillons."* On the same day, he gave the movement a title, *"Thème avec variations monométriques,"* and divided the first eight measures of the *Thème* into two phrases of four unequal measures each.

The final entry in the "sketchbook" is a draft of Variation D that lacks the last twenty-one measures. (An earlier draft is found on a page of printed music-paper, together with the "Junction of the Infernal Dance and the Berceuse" that Stravinsky had inadvertently omitted from the 1919 *Firebird.*) At this point, Stravinsky postponed the composition and turned his attention to some corrections in *Le Sacre du printemps,* then left for Berlin to await his mother's arrival from Russia. On November 18, back in France, he completed Variation D and added it to the *"Brouillons."* Variation A followed on December 1, Variation B on December 6, and Variation C on December 9. The last page of the "Finale," so titled from the beginning of the flute cadenza, is inscribed "Paris, May 20, 1923."

A little later, Dr. Vladimir Zederbaum, Koussevitzky's secretary, wrote to Stravinsky:

Deeply respected Igor Fyodorovich,

With the greatest gladness I learned from Sergei Alexandrovich that your new Octet will be performed under your direction at a concert on October 18. Your score has already been given to the copyist, and the parts will be ready in time. . . . In accordance with the request of Sergei Alexandrovich, I venture to disturb you and most humbly beg you to send comments that you deem necessary for the program. The first performance of your new piece represents a great musical event, and, as I remember from our conversation in Biarritz, you said that this new work is significant as a new stage in your art.

The persistence of major errors in the revised versions of the Piano Concerto,[1]

---

[1] The revised full score of the 1924 Concerto that Stravinsky delivered to Ralph Hawkes in New York, May 1948, lacks the many corrections, as well as fingerings, that the composer had been entering in his own copies of the piece since its first performance. Among the most important mistakes, still found in the 1949 two-piano and the 1950 full scores, are the following: one measure before 2, third horn, the last note should be C (concert pitch), not D; at 2, the third horn should play C (concert pitch), not E flat; at 7 and 29, the required trumpet parts are 1, 2, and 3 (not 1, 3, and 4); at four measures before 15, piano part, the eighth-note should be E flat (not E) and the first quarter-note F sharp (sustained from the preceding measure); two measures after 38, piano part, the first sixteenth-note in the upper line should be E flat, and the fifth sixteenth-note, upper line, should be E natural (without parentheses); one measure before 47, piano part, upper line, the sixteenth-note E after the comma should sustain through the E in the next measure; one measure before 52, bassoon part, the slur, A flat to G, should be deleted; two measures before 61, first and third basses, the slurs should be deleted.

The manuscript score of the reduction for two pianos, in the Library of Congress, contains the beginning of a list by the composer of his performances of the solo part, followed by "etc., etc.," and "over forty times, all over the world." The copyist's score that he actually used for most of these performances, which contains pasted-in sections in manuscript as well as dynamics, fingerings, and other markings, gives the complete log of all of his performances, numbered by the composer to forty, though the actual count, including two public dress rehearsals, seems to be only thirty-nine. Stravinsky must have compiled the list some time after he had stopped playing the piece, since he scrambled the chronology, offered no precise dates but only years, and could not recall the names of all the conductors. *1924:* First performance, Paris (Koussevitzky); second performance, Paris (Koussevitzky); Warsaw (Fitelberg); a public dress rehearsal, Leipzig (Furtwängler); Copenhagen—Tivoli (conductor not given);

Sonata,[2] Serenade (*1925*), and Concerto per due pianoforti soli (*1935*) is difficult to account for, Stravinsky having sent meticulously corrected copies of these works to his publishers. Yet all three pieces are still performed in wrong tempi, and with wrong notes, articulation, and dynamics. These remarks on the Serenade therefore begin with a selected errata.

In the latest edition of the music, the second chord in the right hand of the

---

Berlin (Furtwängler); Geneva (Ansermet); Lausanne (Ansermet); Marseille (Sechiari); Amsterdam (Mengelberg); Haarlem (Mengelberg); The Hague (Mengelberg). *1925:* Boston (Koussevitzky); a dress rehearsal, New York (Mengelberg); New York (Mengelberg); Philadelphia (Reiner); Detroit (conductor not given); Barcelona (Monteux); Paris (Koussevitzky); Wiesbaden (Klemperer); Frankfurt (Scherchen); Winterthur (Andreae); Zürich (Andreae); Basel (Andreae); Rome (Molinari). *1926:* Amsterdam (Mengelberg); Rotterdam (Mengelberg); Milan—La Scala (Scherchen); Milan, popular concert (Scherchen); Vienna (Dirk Fock); Budapest (Telmányi). *1927:* London—broadcast (Edward Clark); Scheveningen (conductor not given). *1928:* Paris (Bruno Walter). *1929:* Berlin—Kroll Opera (Klemperer); London— Queen's Hall (Goossens); London—Queen's Hall, BBC (Ansermet). *1930:* Paris— Pigalle (Siohan).

[2] The Boosey & Hawkes edition of the Sonata for piano (*1924*) is teeming with errors, but, in the first place, the score does not even mention that Stravinsky revised and fingered the piece in *1947*. Among the mistakes, the following are especially important: In measure 28, treble clef, the eighth-note D, a third below the F sharp, is missing (*"manque le ré,"* Stravinsky wrote in his copy); in measure 46, the parenthetical natural should be deleted before the A (in the first edition it applied to the wrong note, C, a third higher); also in measure 46, the dot should be removed from the quarter-note in the bass part; at the end of measure 119, a comma is missing in the treble part (which should match the bass); in measure 121, Stravinsky added *"ancora meno"* beginning with the second quarter-note. (It may be worth noting that Stravinsky composed the first movement between August 4 and 21, but not from beginning to end; thus measures 135 to the recapitulation were written on August 12, measures 121–135 on the 13th, and measures 83–88 on the 15th.)

The second movement preserves four wrong notes, omits many of Stravinsky's expression and dynamic markings, and in several places confuses the player. In measure 34, second staff, the last thirty-second-note, lowest line, should be C natural (not C sharp); at the end of measure 42, top line, the natural before the G in the appoggiaturas before the first sixteenth-note should be transferred to the G in the appoggiaturas before the second sixteenth; in measure 38, the last note in the top line should be B flat; and in measure 41, bottom staff, the G at the beginning of the second quarter-note should have a flat (and the parentheses should be removed from the natural two notes later). Throughout the movement, accidentals that belong next to notes are for some reason placed in parentheses above them, while other parenthetical accidentals are wholly unnecessary. Whereas the first edition (May *1925*) properly aligns the treble and bass notes on the eighth and tenth sixteenth-notes in measure 2, the *1947* edition moves the bass notes to the right, misleading the player. Measure 27 begins with a ligature in the upper line not connected to any note in measure 26. The composer's "molto crescendo" from the last eighth of measure 32 through the first eighth

"Hymne," second voice, should be C, not the adjacent D, and in measure 28, also in the second chord, right hand, the B should be G.[3] The marking "piano" should begin at measure 30 (not 31); the C sharps between measures 45 and 46 should be tied, as should the first two eighth-note E's in measure 63. In the penultimate measure, the G and B, left hand, should tie to eighths in the final measure.

In measure 15 of the $\frac{3}{8}$ section in the "Romanza," the appoggiaturas on C and B are tied to the notes they anticipate, but this is not the case with the G. Four measures later, the first E in the bass should not have a downward stem. Thirteen measures later, the last bass A should slur to the E in the next measure. Four measures after that, the E and C chord (thirty-second notes) requires an accent, the remainder of the measure a diminuendo. Eight measures before the next-to-last double bar, the right-hand chord should be arpeggiated. Three to four measures before the same double bar, the appoggiaturas (F sharp, A, and D) should not be sustained.

In the "Rondoletto," measure 11, the first two and second two notes should be slurred, by twos, but the slur in measure 12 is a misprint. In measure 51, the second note in the left hand is D (not D flat).

At the beginning of the "Cadenza Finala" (*sic*) the first measure is "MF," the second measure "subito piano." Though the latter dynamic does not change, Stravinsky marked an additional "P. sub." starting with the last eighth-note in measure 35. In measure 75, the last bass note is F natural.

In New York, March 14, 1925, after signing a contract with Brunswick Records, Stravinsky recorded six of *The Five Fingers*: Andantino, Moderato, Allegro, Larghetto, Lento (più mosso at the second theme), and Vivo.[4] He claimed to be attracted by the time limit of composing pieces to fit 10-inch 78-rpm record sides, and he said that the Serenade en la was written to order, its four movements exactly filling four record surfaces. He did not record the Serenade until July 1934, however, and for French Columbia, not Brunswick. His correspondence reveals that more than four movements had been intended, and that the others were not composed because of lack of time. In a remark addressed to an audience in Rosario, Argentina, before a performance of the piece there, May 12, 1936, he compared the Serenade to the eighteenth-century suite "made up of an indeterminate number of pieces." Still another indication that at some point he had had a longer work in mind is his having changed the title of the first movement from "Hymne à l'Introduction" to "Inno" (on the manuscript copy

---

of measure 33, his "subito meno" from the fourth eighth of measure 34, and his "tranquillo" from the third eighth of measure 37 are all missing in the 1947 revised score.

[3] Even in the recordings of pianists who knew Stravinsky personally—Marcelle Meyer, for one—the B is played, and, in measure 46, D on the fifth eighth-note, upper line; the notes are correct in all of Stravinsky's manuscripts.

[4] This seems to have been Stravinsky's first commercial recording.

sent to the engraver) to "Hymne." The three brief succeeding movements hardly warranted an "Introduction" of approximately the same length as each of them.

The name of the opus on the cover of the "engraving" manuscript is "Serenata," and the "Hymne" has a flat in the key signature, the "en la" having been penciled in, probably by one of the engravers of Delanchy, Dupré & Cie, in Asnière (Seine). On the cover of this manuscript, Stravinsky says that the copy was made partly by his wife, partly by himself, though only the "Romanza" and the first fifteen measures of the last movement are in his hand. The engraver's copy omits the fingerings found throughout Stravinsky's original score—for which the staves are drawn with his stylus, except in the "Rondoletto," which he hurriedly copied in pencil on printed music-paper and inserted in the bound book.

On the subject of titles, "Cadenza Finala" seems a strange choice, since by ordinary definitions a cadenza is a "brilliant flourish," often improvised, or improvisatory in character, and usually occurring in the solo-instrument part of an accompanied piece. The "Romanza" contains two short cadenzas of this description, so titled in the sketches, though the word was deleted in the published score, no doubt because of the "Cadenza Finala," an "improvisatory" movement in character but totally devoid of virtuoso effects. Legato from beginning to end—Stravinsky's one essay of the kind—and offering no contrast, whether melodic, harmonic, or rhythmic (a steady, "motionless" succession of eighth notes), the finale could hardly be less cadenza-like.

Stravinsky began the movement on April 11, in units of sixteenths (rather than eighths), and with C naturals in the right hand in measures 5–6. These first notations also contain the music of measures 21–23, and the sketch page is marked by several different flat-key signatures. Here, for instance, is a notation for measures 58–61:

Did Stravinsky recognize the movement as the finale of a piece? The sketches reveal nothing of this and, unlike those for the "Hymne," are remarkable for their similarity to the final version. The fair copy is dated May 19, 1925, the final manuscript the next day, when he also timed the movement to 2 minutes, 50 seconds.

The "Hymne," which required the most extensive sketching, was begun on July 18, with a rough draft of the first fourteen measures and of 36–40½. A notation of the opening melody harmonized in sixths, with an F key-signature, seems to have been written next, on a page that also contains the music from 15 to 21 (first half of the measure), and measures 27–28—this time an octave higher and in the chords as published, though the left-hand part lacks the sixteenth-note figuration (first inserted in pencil on an ink draft of the movement). A further sketch covers measures 20–51. On July 20, Stravinsky completed the music to measure 51 and sketched the subsequent section (sixteenth note figuration in the left hand). The completed manuscript is dated August 3.

The "Rondoletto" was begun on August 13 with the last seven measures of the movement, a notation of the first theme (in G, not A!), some of the intervals of the later sixteenth-note passages, and several six-note chords: he had not yet conceived the two- and three-voice style of the piece. On August 14, he sketched six measures beginning at measure 44; the next day he drafted measures 14–27. On August 17, he continued from the second half of measure 48 through measure 52. He then rewrote measures 11–17, 6–8, and the first twelve measures of the piece—half of them with the bass. He also notated the theme and part of the bass at measure 59 and wrote the upper line of measure 67 $(\frac{5}{8})$.

Measures 47–68 and 79–88 (to the cadence) and measures 92–102 are found on separate but undated sketches. The original manuscript, signed September 26, indicates the interruption, meanwhile, for the composer's Venetian trip, during which he experienced a thumb-healing "miracle,"[5] and, in Genoa, returning to Nice via Florence, the revelation that was to lead to *Oedipus Rex*. No doubt he was impatient to complete the Serenade en la.

A complete draft of the "Romanza" is dated October 10, 1925, but the final score says October 9. In the later draft, measures 37–42 of the $\frac{3}{8}$ "minuet" occur, not in sequence, but at the end of the movement. Of two earlier sketches, the first, for the beginning, resembles the introduction to the Piano Concerto:

In the first movement of the Concerto per due pianoforte soli, the sixteenths in the measure before the $\overset{12}{16}$, in spite of the marking, do *not* equal the sixteenths in the $\overset{12}{16}$; the old $\frac{2}{4}$ measure equals the new $\overset{12}{16}$ (or $\frac{4}{8}$) measure, as the manuscripts and Stravinsky's recording with his son Soulima[6] clearly show. The new "sixteenths" are actually groups of triplets, and three notes, not two, are equiv-

---

[5] See *S.P.D.*, p. 260.

[6] The Concerto was recorded in the Paris studio of Pathé Marconi, February 16, 1938. On March 14, the test pressings were ready, but the album was not issued until March 1951 (by French Columbia: LFX 951-952-953). The matrices had been offered to Columbia in New York in 1950 but were refused on the grounds that the 78-rpm discs could not be transferred to LPs. On May 10, 1951, Stravinsky wrote to Willy Strecker—in New York: Strecker had returned there after two days in Los Angeles—saying that the discs were finally available and urging him to "place them at the disposal of pianists who wish to have an exact idea of the work."

alent to the eighth note in the preceding measures. (Originally Stravinsky gave a slower metronome to the $\frac{12}{16}$.) In measure 18 of the $\frac{12}{16}$ section, the fourth sixteenth-note should be A flat (not A). Similarly, after the $\frac{2}{4}$ and second $\frac{12}{16}$ sections, the sixteenths in the $\frac{3}{2}$ measure, despite the marking, are *not* equal to the sixteenths in the following measure, the correct proportion being three sixteenths equals two sixteenths. In the thirty-first measure from the end of the movement, the last three sixteenths in the lowest line should be D flats.

In measure 82 of the "Notturno," Piano II, the first five thirty-second notes, treble clef, should be B flats (not A flats); in measure 25 of the third movement, Piano II, the first three notes in the treble part should be sixteenths. In the last movement, last measure, Piano I, the E should be D sharp.

Apropos of the Concerto per due pianoforte soli, corrections of another kind are overdue. In *Dialogues and a Diary* (1963), Stravinsky said that he had begun the piece in Voreppe and completed the first movement in 1931; that he had started to compose the "Variations, originally the second movement" after completing *Perséphone* (1934); and that he had performed the Concerto many times in Europe and South America with his son, and in America with Adele Marcus.

Actually, the Concerto was begun in Paris, November 14, 1932, after a concert tour with Samuel Dushkin in Danzig, Königsberg, and Berlin. The first notations, a good example of Stravinsky's jigsaw composing processes, are for measures 77–80, 30–33, and 37–40, in the first movement. On November 15–16, he sketched measures 16–29; on November 20, measures 137–140 and 147–148; on November 21, measures 134–136 and 138–139; on November 26, measures 32–33; and on November 27, measures 37–40 (in more complete form). Because of further concert engagements, he abandoned the composition at the beginning of December and did not resume work until August 1934; the music from measures 134 to 170 is dated August 10, and much of the first part of the movement was written soon after, though the very beginning is inscribed "May 15 (1935), Paris." The Notturno was composed between June 11 and July 13, 1935, and the Preludio e Fuga were completed on August 21. The Variations (actually the third movement) were completed, respectively, on September 9, September 20, November 3, and November 9. Stravinsky had given eight concerts in Scandinavia between September 27 and October 14, and on October 28 and 29, back in Paris, he had conducted recording sessions of his Violin Concerto for Polydor (formerly Brunswick).

Stravinsky performed the piece with his son twelve times, including private recitals at the Princesse de Polignac's on November 21, 22, and 27, 1935; at Prince Pierre's of Monaco on December 1 (?); and at Countess Lily Pastré's on December 5, 1936. Other performances took place as follows: December 17, 1935, Lausanne; April 4, 1936, Baden-Baden; May 12, 1936, Rosario (Argentina); May 22, 1936, Montevideo (Uruguay); November 29, 1936, Naples; February 19, 1937, Milan; March 3, 1937, Rome. The composer first participated in performances of the piece in the United States with Beveridge Webster, in 1937, in Winnetka, Illinois, later playing it with Adele Marcus in Worcester, Cambridge, Boston, and New York City. (According to Charles Joseph's *Stra-*

vinsky and the Piano [Ann Arbor, 1983], Marcus performed the Concerto a total of nine times with Stravinsky, all in 1940.) His final performance was with Willard MacGregor[7] in Chicago in 1944.

APPENDIX G

On the Chronology of the REQUIEM CANTICLES

The movements were composed in the following order:

INTERLUDE

Begun in March 1965. (Stravinsky was in Austin, Texas, from March 31 to April 4, then in Hollywood, and, from the 15th, in Chicago, New York, and Europe, returning home on June 18; from June 28 to July 17 he was on a concert tour in the United States and Canada.) The composition was resumed on July 15 and completed on August 29 (with interruptions to make recordings, August 19–26, and to conduct at Hollywood Bowl, September 2). The dated sketches are for the music at 163–175 (July 25–26), 152–158 (July 28), 161–162 (August 20), and 176–178 (August 29). From September 3 to 5, Stravinsky was in New York, on the 6th in Hamburg (for filming) and on the 10th in London (for a televised concert on the 14th). On September 15 he flew to New York, and on October 10 to Cincinnati (for concerts on the 15th and 16th), returning to Hollywood on the 17th.

EXAUDI

Completed on November 10.

PRELUDE
(*"Preludium"*
in the drafts)

Begun about November 18.

DIES IRAE

December 1965–January 1966. The five pitches in measure 91, eventually the trombone part, were written first, then the choral setting of the words "Dies irae," to which Stravinsky added a reminder in the sketch: "Make the response ["irae"] an echo." In another sketch, on a page from a Savoy Hotel (London) note pad, he repeats the word "illa" in echo, in the same rhythm as the "irae." In

---

[7] MacGregor had already played the Concerto with Beveridge Webster. On December 12, 1943, Stravinsky asked Remi Gassman, who was organizing the Chicago concert, to "tell the pianist who will play with me my Double Concerto, that I will play the second piano as I always do for a good reason to better lead the ensemble." (Original in English)

the full draft, not one but both words, "Dies irae," are echoed. Measures 88–89 were the last composed (on January 24); Stravinsky added them to the complete draft score in light-blue pencil.

TUBA MIRUM   January 1966. On January 7 Stravinsky composed the music from "Per sepulchra" through measure 124. In the full draft of the movement, the music for two bassoons (final version) is scored for harmonium.

REX TREMENDAE   Begun on March 29 and completed on April 6. Stravinsky was at the Eastman School of Music from March 6 to 11 and at the Pierre Hotel (New York) from March 12 to 18.

LACRIMOSA   Completed on April 27. A page from a Hotel Pierre note pad, dated "April," contains sketches for the trombone responses, but in triplets, quarters, and eighths (instead of in eighths and sixteenths). Measures 235 and 234 were sketched separately (in that order), and measure 234 is marked "trombones."

LIBERA ME   No sketch is dated, but all except the last one (Hotel Pierre note pad) were written after the Lacrimosa and before Stravinsky's departure for Europe (May 12). The final sketch, for measures 270–272 and 280 to the end, almost identical to the ultimate version, was composed in Lisbon—on music paper purchased there—in the last week of May.

POSTLUDE   July 26–August 13. The words "beginning and finishing measure" occur at the head of the first sketch for the first chord.

The chronological order of the first notations for the Interlude is puzzling. On graphological evidence, the four measures of Example 2 seem to antedate the series, written three ways (Example 1):

Example 1

Example 2

The two series originated in the following notations:

Example 3 (measures 163–165)

Example 4 (measures 173–175)

Each of the four orders of series II was written on a separate strip of paper, then aligned in chart form and attached below the chart of series I. A third chart, also for series I, reveals that Stravinsky's first plan had been to derive the verticals exclusively from the beta hexachords. Both series occur in early sketches for the Interlude, and both are combined in measures 166–172, where the first flute plays the retrograde of II, the other three flutes the inversion of I. The use of two series simultaneously in the Postlude merits separate study (as does Stravinsky's plan to use the retrograde of the retrograde inversion in the unfinished orchestra piece of 1967).

Measures 163–167 of the Interlude were written before measures 161–162, initially a passage for two bassoons, a link with the middle and final bassoon duets, the first bassoon playing a slow melody, the second an accompaniment figure of repeated seconds similar to that of the third flute at 168–172.

Nevertheless, Stravinsky clearly regarded the series as written in Example 5, and not in Example 3, as the basis of his composition; he placed this sketch first in his notebook, with Examples 3 and 4 on the facing page. The first draft of the Interlude (see Example 6) begins with a version of Example 5, which was composed in several stages: the first five notes; then the D sharp and last C natural; the quarter notes, which he drew in red pencil, at the same time red-penciling over the notes indicated here by circles; and finally the identification "II R " No sketch indicates when he corrected D natural to B, and the second C natural to A.

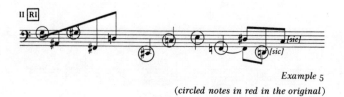

Example 5

(circled notes in red in the original)

Stravinsky's first idea for the beginning of the Interlude later became measures 147–151:

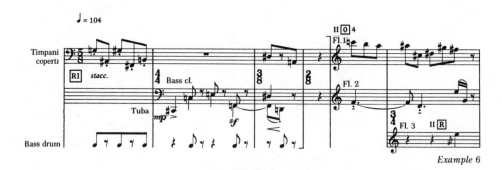

Example 6

But the movement did not as yet have a title. Several stages later, Stravinsky extracted measures 175–196; marked measures 184–192 "Variation of the same" (i.e., of 175–183); added double bars; wrote "flute music" over the beginning; and dubbed the excerpt Interlude.

The first notation for the actual beginning of the Interlude consists of the first two notes, in rhythmic form only (without pitches) and repeated exactly. A second sketch provides the harmony as found in the final score but extends the pitch compass an octave higher. A third sketch, also employing the higher range, surprisingly repeats a rhythm of the Danse sacrale, bass alone on the first crusis of the measure, treble on the anacrusis. Another sketch identifies the harmony in horizontal lines as, treble to bass, O, I, R, and RI, series I. The full draft of the movement indicates that, in addition to horns and timpani, the chords were to be scored for three trombones.

The first two notations for the beginning of the Libera me are not serially derived. Moreover the three-part harmony contains octaves in almost every chord. Each of the twelve chords in the first sketch is different, and the music resembles a chorale more than the fauxbourdon that Stravinsky seems to have had in mind from the first. In contrast, most of the twenty-two chords in the second sketch are repeated, thus establishing the chant style, and long notes are introduced at phrase endings. In the subsequent sketch, Stravinsky assigns the music to the tenor and bass (only), and has the four-part chorus speak the text in the same rhythm in which the two solo voices sing it—which may be the best way to perform the piece. Toward the end of the sketch, the melodic leaps are surprisingly wide. The pitch content is that of both hexachords of O, series

II. Measures 274–275 derive from the fourth form of the alpha hexachord of the inversion of II, measures 276–277 from the beta hexachord of the same.

The music for 280–284, found on one side of another sketch page, is also not serial, and the upper line ascends to the word "miseriae" somewhat in the manner of the climax in the Credo of the Mass. A sketch on the obverse contains the last two measures of the piece almost exactly as in the final score (II, R̄, fourth form, beta hexachord). Still another sketch on this same side, for 270–273, uses both hexachords of II, inverted, fifth form. The final sketch for 270–271 and for 280 to the end is practically identical to the ultimate version. The two chords of 270–276 combine the notes of series II, inverted, fifth form, alpha hexachord (the first three notes of which are triadic). The two chords of 280–284 combine the notes of the alpha hexachords, first form, series II, inverted. Measures 280–286 are constructed from the beta hexachord, third form of the retrograde (the last three notes of which are triadic). Measures 278–288 use only the first, second, and last notes of the fourth form of the beta hexachord of the retrograde (thereby avoiding the triad produced by notes 3, 4, and 5).

The Postlude harmonies of the first four measures are constructed from the original order of series II. The chord in the sixth measure derives from both the original and retrograde forms of the hexachords of series II. The six chords in the next measure combine original and retrograde elements of both series, as follows (upper to lower lines): series II, retrograde; series I, retrograde; series II, original; series I, original. The harmonies in the next two measures derive from the same orders, except that only the beta hexachords are used. The eight-pitch chord in measure 11 and the chords in measures 12–14 derive from the original form of series I, alpha hexachord, and the inverted form of series I, beta hexachord. The final two chords, found in the same sketch-page as the first chord of the Postlude, are derived from series I. The five pitches of the penultimate chord are from the original form. The four pitches of the final chord are from the inverted form, both gamma and beta pitch-collections.

APPENDIX H

The Firmin Gémier Affair

From the beginning of his fame as a composer, Igor Stravinsky was seldom free of lawsuits, a fact mentioned chiefly to deplore the amount of time and energy expended on these largely futile contests. Some of these, against mortgagees in arrears in Russia and defaulting debtors elsewhere, are discussed elsewhere in this volume. The reader need only be reminded that the question of Stravinsky's Russian real estate holdings was not settled until 1935, by which time his properties had become Polish territory. After the Revolution, when he was no longer a landowner, Stravinsky's legal actions were mainly against publishers. It should be mentioned, too, that on more than one occasion in the 1930s, Stravinsky brought unsuccessful suits against film companies for pirating and misusing his music.

After World War II, the composer's principal legal adversary was the U.S. Department of Internal Revenue, which audited him, for the first time, for having deducted his granddaughter's medical expenses in Switzerland. The IRS disallowed any deduction for support of a relative living outside the United States, and he was obliged to make restitution and pay a penalty.

Stravinsky was embroiled in legal squabbles even in his domestic world. In 1930, financial difficulties arose with his wife's brother-in-law, and in 1969 the composer was obliged to sue his son-in-law for the return of manuscripts given temporarily into his custody, but surrendered only after a judge's order.

The most curious of Stravinsky's court battles came about because he did not receive his fee for performing in a concert in Paris in 1928. In February of that year, he had been invited to appear in the "Second International Festival of Dramatic and Musical Art" presented by the "Union Française de la Société Universelle du Théâtre." His concert was part of a "Mozart Cycle," otherwise consisting of performances of five of the operas presented in the Théâtre des Champs-Elysées. The honorary committee could not have been more distinguished: the president of the republic and the ministers of justice, war, education, and fine arts,[1] as well as such luminaries of the cultural world as the Princesse de Polignac and Paul Valéry. In contrast, the working committee listed only four names, none of them well known. The following story is concerned with only two of them: Firmin Gémier, president, an actor and impresario, and Georges Caurier, general administrator. On February 19, 1928, Caurier and Stravinsky signed a contract stipulating that the composer would play his Concerto at the Salle Pleyel on May 19, with rehearsals on the 17th, 18th, and 19th, for the sum of $500, payable on the day of the concert.

On March 2, Stravinsky received a letter from the Comtesse de Ganay, president of the honorary committee, explaining that the proceeds of the Mozart Cycle would be given to a hospital for the treatment of hereditary diseases, administered by a League of Nations department, "Le Terrain Humain et la Maladie." The letter named Bruno Walter as music director, Max Reinhardt and Firmin Gémier as stage directors. Rehearsals had already begun, and world support was assured. Although no further request was made of Stravinsky, even for the use of his name, the letter seems to constitute an appeal[2] to per-

---

[1] Edouard Herriot. In 1925 he had arranged for the words "Russian National" to be omitted from Stravinsky's and Vera Sudeikina's passports, thus making it possible for them to travel.

[2] He might well have responded affirmatively. On February 15, 1925, he had donated

form gratis for this worthy cause. Stravinsky fulfilled the engagement, playing his Concerto on a program that included overtures by Weber and Berlioz, and Mahler's Fourth Symphony.

Stravinsky was not paid, and the next day, telephoning the Société, he received no satisfactory explanation. Instead, a letter arrived exalting his "great talent" and thanking him for the "manner of the perfect gentleman" with which he demonstrated his willingness to help the Société "during this slightly difficult moment." His reply, May 21, a demand for immediate payment, was ignored. He wrote again on June 15—an uncharacteristically long interval, possibly explained by his preoccupation with the Paris premiere of *Apollo*. The answer to this being evasive, he wrote again on the 21st, and was again ignored. On the 27th, he addressed the committee of the Société, enclosing copies of correspondence and documents, and threatening to sue if the fee were not forthcoming by the 29th "at noon."

When nothing had happened by that date, Stravinsky gave the case to his attorney, Louis Gallié, who met with Maurice Meyer of the Tribunal of Commerce. For a July 30 hearing, Stravinsky gave Meyer a power of attorney and copies of all relevant documents, a dossier indicating the composer's unwillingness to spend his time and energy in writing letters, digging out specimen contracts of other engagements, having these papers copied, consulting with lawyers, and fending off journalists—for on July 5, the story was given headline space. One letter *was* worth the effort: Stravinsky's inquiry to the secretary general of the League of Nations, Geneva, requesting the Société's credentials. The reply was that it had none, and that the organization was spurious. Stravinsky's original suspicion that it was operated solely for the profit of Firmin Gémier was well founded.

Meanwhile, at a hearing on October 9, Gémier testified that Caurier had lacked the authority to sign the contract in the name of the Société. Moreover, according to Gémier, payment in dollars would have been illegal. On December 4, the tribunal ruled that the dollar provision did not nullify the contract. The newspapers supported this, claiming that "all great stars of international fame accept fees only in dollars, since other currencies are so unstable." But no matter, since Stravinsky had already agreed to accept his fee in francs.

Gémier introduced such further arguments as that Stravinsky had wrongly sued him rather than the Société, of which he was only an administrator; that Stravinsky was not a French citizen; and that the Tribunal of Commerce was not competent to try the case. Concerning this last, the court ruled that "all enterprises of public performances are considered 'commerce.' " At a hearing on June 27, 1929, Gémier reintroduced the argument that he had no personal responsibility. On April 14, 1930, he maintained that he was an artist, not a businessman, and that he had never agreed to pay Stravinsky the $500. The tribunal ruled in his favor.

---

his services for the benefit of a New York organization for mental hygiene in a recital at Mrs. Vincent Astor's, 840 Fifth Avenue.

But Gémier's attorney, apparently unaware of his client's false pretenses, pleaded diplomatic immunity for the Société as a branch of the League of Nations, whereupon Stravinsky produced the League's denial of any connection. Gallié then displayed contradictory statements from Gémier concerning Caurier's authority to represent the Société. Despite this, Gémier insisted that the debt was Caurier's, not the Société's, and that Caurier was insolvent. Gallié appealed to the court's patriotism: Stravinsky was a great artist of world renown; if Gémier and Caurier were not obliged to pay Stravinsky, he would tell the world how artists are treated in France, and foreign performers would stop coming. Furthermore, Stravinsky had signed a contract partly because the highest officials of the French government, including the president, had given their names as patrons. To condemn Gémier and Caurier was essential to the moral reputation of the nation. Gallié also produced testimony from others who had been tricked in the same way by the same pair, discovering when payment was due that no one was responsible.

On April 12, 1932 (!), the president of the court and the attorney general of France intervened. The press began to speculate: "Will Igor Stravinsky be paid in dollars or in francs?" On April 26, the court ordered Gémier to pay legal costs but absolved him from any obligation concerning Stravinsky's fee, placing it instead on the bankrupt Caurier. On April 28, Gallié wrote that he was preparing to attach the Société's assets. But on June 29, he advised Stravinsky that the warrant to seize the property had not been acted upon, since a declaration of insolvency would result, and in this case the move would be impractical. The story ends here. The dossier was returned to Stravinsky on March 22, 1937. He never received a cent or a centime.

APPENDIX I

"Chantage de Mon Secrétaire Alexis Sabline, 1925"

Alexis Mikhailovich Sabline, Stravinsky's secretary, English translator, and valet in 1925 during his three-month tour in America, returned from the trip with, so it seems, the wherewithal to blackmail the composer. But the tale that Sabline threatened to publicize has never been revealed. He contended that Stravinsky had not paid him a promised $250 monthly salary in addition to his expenses, but Stravinsky denied that he had ever made this commitment, and, in any case, the blackmail was only tangentially related to the salary dispute.

In the winter of 1925, Alexis Sabline was on leave of absence from the French merchant marine. Returning with Stravinsky from America in March of that year, Sabline seems to have followed the composer to Spain, where he had concerts.[1] Sabline mentions Koussevitzky in connection with Stravinsky's Spanish trip, and the conductor was indeed involved. In the summer of 1925, Sabline caused Stravinsky a great deal of trouble because of some mysterious allegations. Whether these were ever spelled out for anyone except the composer is not documented, but Catherine Stravinsky unwisely used the term "blackmail" in one of her letters to Sabline, who then saw a new chance for extortion in a possible suit for slander.

Sabline's letters allude to seriously damaging statements allegedly made by Stravinsky in New York, in the presence of witnesses, about artists'-management tsar Arthur Judson. In what these statements consisted remains too vague even for speculation, but whatever Sabline's story was, he threatened to publish it in "one of the American newspapers." When, through his Paris lawyer, André Aron, the composer threatened to retain an attorney in Nice, Sabline

---

[1] The earliest mention of the name Sabline in Stravinsky's biography seems to occur in a remarkable document, a letter from Vera Sudeikina to Stravinsky's wife describing the composer's departure for America at the end of December 1924:

"Without any unnecessary words, I would like to express my gratitude to you, Ekaterina Gavrilovna, for giving me the opportunity of writing to you. It will be a great relief in this sad and troublesome time, and I am happy that this has happened. It is difficult to talk about all those moments that trouble or touch one and that give meaning to everything. But you will understand, since we have a common language. To whom should I write about what is dear to me except to you? And from whom but you can I receive news that is dear to me?

"I went to Le Havre on Saturday to see Igor off. Although it was decided from the beginning that I was not going, he seemed so unhappy in the last few hours before his departure that I stayed with him until he left. Robert Lyon came along with us, and it was in his name that I sent you the wire saying that Igor had left in good spirits.

"We were in Le Havre from eight to ten o'clock and were allowed to visit the ship and to have dinner on board. Igor's cabin is the best on the ship, in the exact center, and with all conveniences. There was also a piano. Sabline was allowed to come from third class to help Igor install himself and to dress him. I am afraid Sabline will not be much help: he seems slow, sleepy, and not very intelligent.

"On arriving in Le Havre we found that there was a great storm at sea and everything around was shaking and tearing. Because of this, the life on board appeared strange. As soon as the passengers had gone aboard, music started playing, the restaurant and the bar were opened, and the boat looked like a large first-class hotel—all of this, of course, so that the passengers would not think of the stormy night and of the possible dangers awaiting them. That was my impression, but most of the American passengers did not seem to be bothered, and they certainly looked calm—almost too calm.

"The ship was supposed to sail at ten but was delayed because of the storm. Visitors were asked to leave at ten, and we did. Igor stayed below in his cabin and did not come up on deck. He must have felt depressed. The experience of leaving like that can only be balanced by the joy of returning. Robert Lyon left with the night train. I spent the night in Le Havre and listened for the whistles to hear when Igor's boat was leaving, but I could not distinguish them from the whistles of other boats."

seems to have retreated, probably lacking the means to sustain a legal contest.

The only reason for pursuing the Sabline question now is that he may have kept a diary of his three months with Stravinsky. The basis for believing this is that Sabline's lawyers would probably not have accepted him as a client if he had had nothing in writing against so famous and powerful an enemy.

Sabline's letters reveal him as a sleazy character. Why, therefore, did Stravinsky not recognize this from the first? Moreover, how did Sabline know the composer and his family? Sabline must have been socially presentable, and he must have had considerable linguistic skill to have translated for Stravinsky during his rehearsals. The reader is unfortunately prejudiced in Sabline's favor concerning his complaint of having been promised and not paid a salary—if only because Stravinsky had faulted on similar obligations. Sabline's valet's-eye-view of Stravinsky, if it ever comes to light, could be a text of some interest.

ALEXIS SABLINE TO STRAVINSKY[2]

Nice
June 22, 1925

c/o Pleyel
Paris

My dear, esteemed, Igor Fyodorovich,

Forgive me for not writing to you until now and for not apologizing to you, but I have been ill and confined to bed all this time. . . . I was in a daze for the whole trip from America, so dazed, in fact, that I did not even thank you or say good-bye to you. All that I can remember through the fog in my head is that, seeing Vera Arturovna, I ran from her, realizing even in my state of stupor that I was infectious. I finally recovered in the hospital on the day of your concert in Spain, and I recalled with a sense of dread what a terrible orchestra it was . . . and remembered the red-faced Koussevitzky standing there, trying to interfere with your conducting and grabbing the baton you had in your hand.

My intention was not to write to you but to visit you personally when I recovered, but something that happened yesterday made me take up my pencil. Yesterday I was visited by a certain American who had learned my address from Tsiporkin and who asked me to clear up certain details concerning negotiations with Judson about guarantees. . . . The American said that he would be going to Italy tomorrow, and he asked me to write to him there. . . . I don't understand anything in these matters, so I decided to ask you what I should do in this instance. Should I write to him, and if so, what should I write? Perhaps you would be good enough to send me a note or to visit me if you happen to come to Nice. I will be here until July 1. . . . Expecting to hear from you, I send you, Vera Arturovna, and all of your dear family my very best regards.

My address: Asile Evangélique, ruette de Près, Nice (A.M.).

Devotedly yours,   A. Sabline

---

[2] Russian is the language of all the correspondence.

SABLINE TO STRAVINSKY

41, rue Gambetta
Nice
July 23, 1925

My dear, esteemed Igor Fyodorovich,

Thinking that you were in Paris, I wrote to you there at the Pleyel address, but I did not receive any reply. I imagine the letter did not reach you, so I am writing to you at your Nice address. . . . Mr. Weisman, evidently an American, came to see me and asked me to communicate to him by letter the details of certain negotiations made in my presence concerning guarantees, or in other words, to tell him whether his impressions of what took place were or were not correct. He then gave me a very precise account of one of the conversations with Judson. I am supposed to write to Weisman in the next few days, since he returns to America at the end of July, but I do not think it would be correct to write to him without your approval, and so I decided to ask you what I should say about the matter; should I confirm everything he said, should I deny it, or should I not write him anything at all? It is my opinion that those conversations were so insignificant that to conceal them is hardly worth the effort. If you are of the same opinion, do not write me anything, and I will know by your silence that you agree and that the whole affair is not worth a sou.

Devotedly yours,   A. Sabline

SABLINE TO CATHERINE STRAVINSKY

July 24, 1925

Dear Ekaterina Gavrilovna,

Since I have always felt a great respect for you and have always placed great value on your opinion, I was very grieved and surprised to receive your letter in which you write about some act of blackmail to which someone has supposedly incited me. Because of my sincere respect for you, I shall not take it upon myself to enlighten you in this matter, even though I see that it has been represented to you in the wrong light.

I happened to be a witness to a certain conversation, an interesting one in a psychological and ethical sense. A man came to see me, and, for clarification, asked me what had actually taken place. I got in touch with Igor Fyodorovich and, *upon his advice, refused to confirm the truth* (although the truth was not a professional secret), saying simply that I could not remember much. I was asked about this twice more, and each time I replied in the same way. That is the whole affair. What "blackmail" is involved here I cannot understand, since I am not a lawyer and have not had time to speak with lawyers, though if they find a hint of blackmail in my actions, I will offer you my most profound repentance. Yet at the same time, I have heard the word "blackmail" from another source—in a piece of slander that has reached my ears—and I intend to contest this in writing. . . . You may rest assured that I will only write the truth as it can be confirmed by the people I intend to mention, both in America and here. . . .

Devotedly yours,   A. Sabline

SABLINE TO STRAVINSKY   *Nice*
                                                          July 29, 1925

Dear Igor Fyodorovich,

A woman came to see me today on Mr. Weisman's behalf, and, in consequence,
I think that you should come to see me. I will be at home from 1:00 to 4:00. . . .

                                        Yours,   A. Sabline

SABLINE TO STRAVINSKY   *Nice*
                                                         August 5, 1925

Dear Igor Fyodorovich,

Miss Kelly came to see me again on Sunday, and from the details she related I
learned much that concerns me personally. I therefore consider myself within
my rights to address one of the American newspapers, as well as a local paper
here, in order to stop false rumors.

C. STRAVINSKY TO SABLINE   *Nice*
                                                         August 6, 1925

Dear Alexei Mikhailovich,

Igor Fyodorovich has just received your letter. He will be absent for a few days
and has asked me to tell you the following:
    If a certain lady came to see you *on business that was truly your own per-
sonal business,* then of course that could not have anything to do with him. If
this question "of a personal nature," as you put it, does have anything to do
with Igor Fyodorovich (with your service to him during the American trip),
then clearly the question cannot be considered your personal affair; you cannot
publish anything in the newspapers that mentions his name without his consent. Igor Fyodorovich cannot understand your desire to talk about yourself to
the American papers or to the newspapers here merely "to avoid false rumors."
What false rumors are you referring to?
    I close this letter with an expression of hope that you will not fall prey to
the blackmail to which these strangers are inciting you. When Igor Fyodorovich
returns to Nice, he will notify you and help you with his advice. . . .

                              Respectfully yours,   E. Stravinskaya

C. STRAVINSKY TO SABLINE   *August 12, 1925*

Dear Alexei Mikhailovich,

I see from the letter you wrote yesterday that you have misinterpreted my
phrase concerning blackmail, something that I would never accuse you of. I
simply meant by this word to warn you to be careful with people you do not
know, people whose meddling in the affairs of others has caused me to be

alarmed about possible blackmail on their part. For the time being, I cannot be certain that blackmail is their intention; rather, I am simply watching out for it. I am surprised at the persistence of people who meddle in the affairs of others, even though these affairs may not involve any professional secrets. You did not, of course, just happen to be witness to the business conversation with Judson, as you say; you were there in the capacity of secretary and translator for Igor Fyodorovich.

I should confess to you, dear Alexei Mikhailovich, that I greatly value the peace that Igor Fyodorovich so desperately needs for his work, and that I sincerely believe in your good intentions. . . .

Ekaterina Stravinskaya

SABLINE TO C. STRAVINSKY *Nice*
August 13, 1925

Dear Ekaterina Gavrilovna,

I would not think of disturbing Igor Fyodorovich's peace, or of interfering in any way with his work, if it were not for these gentlemen from America who have turned up and disturbed my own peace. I would very much like to see I. F. around the 14th or the 15th, since on the 16th I will be leaving for a time, in order to clear up certain questions and to give him an opportunity to read a letter in which I have taken the liberty of mentioning his name, and to comment on those parts of the letter that he does not like. I will be finished with the translation of this letter for the *New York Herald* today and will put it at I. F.'s disposal for his examination.

A. Sabline

SABLINE TO STRAVINSKY *Nice*
August 15, 1925

Dear Igor Fyodorovich,

In the middle of your visit to me you suddenly jumped up and disappeared, and I cannot understand what happened to you. What you said to Ekaterina Gavrilovna in my presence about the incident with Judson was not entirely correct, and it misses the essence of the question, which, if you will allow me, I will recall for you. When Judson complied with your persistent request to ask Michael [?] about a continuation of the guarantee, and Taylor told you that Michael had refused, you did not stop there, but, when you arrived home, you called several people on the telephone and told each of them: "Judson, who is always trying to make money from me without my permission, asked M. to continue the guarantee." . . . That is what is written in my notebook. Now about the rumors concerning me: I should say that everyone who has known me in one capacity or another will be able to testify to the propriety of my relationship with you and to the fact that I have always protected your interests in any way that I possibly could. As for the generous payment received for my services to you, I must say that *you never fulfilled a single duty or promise to me in this regard. Indeed, you never paid me a salary* and only partly fulfilled your last promise to pay for my medical treatment and my trip to Nice, giving me a small sum with which to pay the hospital. I realized that I had been deceived in all the promises that had been made to me. Nevertheless, I protected the reputation of one who had been close to me, and I would never have seen you again if it had not been for the appearance of this American. Nor would I ever have found out what was being said about me if that lady had not come to see me. Furthermore, Judson obviously still does not know what it was that you said about him, and M. still does not know how you deliberately misled him. It was probably one of those people to whom you so eloquently described Judson's deeds on the telephone who became interested in the affair as a matter of principle. But you can only be angry with me personally for having told you, on the boat, that it is bad business to leave a hotel without paying for the services you received. . . .

I do not want to publish my whole notebook, only the facts that I have revealed above, and I will not draw any conclusion, but, rather, let everyone draw his own.

If you consider anything that I have said here unjust, you can come to see me in person for an explanation, but without Ekaterina Gavrilovna, for it hurts me to expose the truth about these matters in front of her.

A. Sabline

STRAVINSKY TO L. B. DELANEY[3]

Nice
August 25, 1925

8, avenue de la Victoire
Nice

Dear sir,

I am astonished by your letter, and I do not understand what "case of M. Alexis Sabline" you are referring to. Since I will not be here for two or three days, I would be much obliged if you would explain yourself by letter and tell me the substance of the matter. Awaiting your friendly reply, I send you, dear sir, my respectful greetings.

DELANEY TO STRAVINSKY

September 2, 1925

107, blvd. Carnot
Nice

Sir,

I acknowledge the receipt of your letter of August 25. I have been instructed by my client, M. Alexis Sabline, to claim from you the payment of the sum of $750

---

[3] One of Sabline's attorneys.

together with interest of 6 percent up to the time of the full payment of this sum.

You will recall that while my client was your personal secretary in the United States, you did not pay him anything for his services on the sum claimed by him to be due for these services during the period of three months at the rate of $250 a month.

I ask you to send me this money before the end of this week. In default, I will find myself obliged to take such measures as I judge to be appropriate to protect the rights of my client.

L. B. Delaney

STRAVINSKY TO DELANEY   *Nice*
                                                        September 4, 1925

8, avenue de la Victoire
Nice

Sir,

I have received your letter of September 2 and am in complete disagreement with it. I owe nothing to M. Alexis Sabline, and I refuse to give any attention to this matter. . . .

I. Str.

STRAVINSKY TO YOUNG[4]   [*No date*]

My dear Young,

Something very annoying has happened to me. My ex-secretary, Sabline, in the hands of blackmailers, has suddenly become vicious. He claims that the sum that I spent on him during our sojourn in America, a sum we had decided in common agreement would constitute his honorarium, is not what I had agreed to pay. He is now demanding an additional honorarium. I therefore ask a service of you. If by chance the matter gets as far as you, I would like you to help me. . . .

                                                              [*No date*]
STRAVINSKY TO ANDRÉ ARON   [*Telegram*]

Can you recommend a very good lawyer in Nice? The best course would be for you to handle this very delicate matter. Kindly telegraph me urgently. Stravigor, Nice

---

[4] Young seems to have been a legal functionary in Nice.

APPENDIX J

Stravinsky and the Institut de France

On July 8, 1935, Stravinsky wrote to Gabriel Pierné:

> My very dear friend,
>
> Jacques-Emile Blanche told me of your very gracious intention in my behalf. That the initiative to propose my candidacy for the Institut de France comes from you deeply touches me, and I do not need to tell you how happy and honored I would be to become a part of this illustrious group. Believe me, my very dear friend, your sincerely devoted
>
> Igor Stravinsky

The chair in the Institute that Stravinsky hoped to occupy was the one left vacant by the death of Paul Dukas.[1] But though Stravinsky had been influenced (*Fireworks*, 1908) by Dukas, and had conducted a memorial performance of *The Sorcerer's Apprentice* in Rome, these connections cannot have been a factor in the acceptance of the nomination. What, indeed, *could* have persuaded him to allow his name to be put forward, since the prestige attaching to membership in the Institut de France is dubious, and the electoral procedures, which oblige the candidate to call on each member, are degrading (at least for a Stravinsky)? His answer—that members enjoyed certain privileges (including preferential treatment in obtaining visas) that would be useful to him in his concert tours—is unconvincing. What can be said with certainty is that his defeat led to a resolve never to accept any academic honor, and though he could not always escape them, in later years he refused a great many honorary degrees "on principle."

French newspapers soon began to exploit the contradictions in Stravinsky's position. Then the question of his eligibility arose, because of a 1934 revision in the law (of 1927) further restricting the rights of naturalized subjects. (Stravinsky had acquired French citizenship in June 1934.) An expert on this matter, Professor de La Pradelle, citing the most recent opinion (January 24, 1935) by the highest legal authority in the state, wrote to Stravinsky assuring him that his nomination was legitimate for the reason that membership in his case would not involve a pension. But this information was not given to the press.

---

[1] Stravinsky did accede to Dukas's "chair" in the Ecole Normale de Musique. On September 17, 1935, Alfred Cortot wrote to his "dear and illustrious friend" that "Mlle Nadia Boulanger has informed us that you wish to accept the post of *inspecteur* of the course in composition (replacing our great and sorely missed Paul Dukas) and to participate in the analyses of the works of the masters."

Pierné wrote to Stravinsky, October 27, 1935, saying that at a meeting the day before, the election had been scheduled for Saturday, November 23, but that J.-E. Blanche, who could not be present on that date, requested a postponement. Knowing that Stravinsky too would not be in Paris at that time, Pierné seconded the motion. He added: "I feel that, in the circumstances of this double absence, your insufficiently prepared candidacy would not succeed." The election was rescheduled for January 17, 1936, then postponed again to January 25. On January 2, Pierné wrote to Stravinsky advising him to "address the president of the Académie des Beaux Arts directly, since Charles-Marie Widor, the secretary, is ill. Enclose a curriculum vitae and the date of your naturalization, and request a list of the names and addresses of all of the members of the Academy." Pierné asked Stravinsky to pay the necessary courtesy calls, beginning with the musicians.

Methodical as always, Stravinsky compiled agendas of the visits he intended to make, allowing an hour to an hour and a half for each one. The obscurity of most of the "immortals" on his roster, and the third-rateness of the few whose names have survived—Charpentier, the composer of *Louise*—reduces Stravinsky's politicking to a comic level. He began his rounds on Thursday, January 9, at 2:00 p.m., with a visit to the architect Paul Bigot; there followed a visit to the architect Victor Laloux at 3:00, one to Henri Martin at 4:00, Lucien Simon at 5:00, and Marcel Baschet at 6:00. On January 10, Stravinsky was out again from 2:00 to 7:00, visiting the painters Maxence, Devambez, and Desvallières, and the architect Pontremoli. Others among the "illustrious group" on the composer's itinerary for successive afternoons were Monsieur Sulpis, and such musicians as Widor and Henri Rabaud, to whom, under other circumstances, Stravinsky would not have extended his hand. A few members, including the musician Paul Landowski, had to be written to at the Academy in Rome.

Stravinsky's curriculum vitae identifies the sole source of his musical education as Rimsky-Korsakov, and the list of compositions is notable for the absence of the Symphony of Psalms and the four concertos. Stravinsky's letter to the president of the Academy is remarkable in that the name of "my illustrious colleague Paul Ducas" is misspelled, as it is in all of Stravinsky's letters.

On January 9, a secretary of the Academy wrote to Stravinsky asking him to submit proof of his naturalization "two hours before the meeting at the Institute on the following Saturday." If Pierné and Blanche had been informed of this development they might have suspected a challenge to Stravinsky's candidacy, but, in any case, he had already endured a considerable number of visits and written (January 7) to the likes of Alfred Bachelet, director of the Conservatoire in Nancy. Bachelet's answer shows him to have been both embarrassed and deeply flattered, and the same is true of Le Sidaner's telegram in response to Stravinsky's request for an appointment on Wednesday, January 15, "since I will be at St. Germain that day and can easily come to you in Versailles."

As the election approached, newspaper comment increased, inspiring a photographer to write (January 8) asking Stravinsky to pose. An article in *Le Figaro Littéraire* (January 11) seems to have turned the tide against Stravinsky by remarking on "the utter ridiculousness of the composer of *Firebird, Sacre,* and *Noces* applying to enter an Academy in which his fellow musicians are Bachelet, Alfred Bruno, Charpentier, Widor." Whether calculated or not, this statement very likely provoked these and other mediocrities to oppose the composer of *Firebird, Sacre,* and *Noces,* and to organize a movement to nominate Florent Schmitt, who delightedly accepted.

On January 15, Pierné and Blanche sent a joint letter to Stravinsky:

The most recent legal opinion concerning the Code, the Academy, and naturalized citizens is not in your favor. This, together with the regrettable publicity concerning your candidacy, has forced us to the conclusion that the best and noblest gesture would be for you to withdraw.

Pierné added, in his own name, that he would never forget the honor that Stravinsky had paid him by accepting the nomination. Blanche added an angry description of the politics of the affair as "a medieval scandal."

Disregarding Catherine Stravinsky's pleas to follow the advice of Pierné and Blanche, Stravinsky wrote to them the same night.

Returning this evening to Paris after having paid my required visits to Maurice Denis and Le Sidaner, I find your letter. I proposed my candidacy only on your insistence and because you, my dear Pierné, told me that not to do so would be a disaster. Now it seems that I must withdraw in order to avoid "humiliation and a scandal."

The legal question is not within my competence. If my candidacy contravenes existing laws, let these laws be applied. This is not my affair. As for the publicity surrounding my candidacy, you yourselves know perfectly well that I have had nothing to do with that.

I submitted myself—against my convictions, it is true—in order not to derogate customs and formalities. Your encouragement was never lacking until this evening. And now, suddenly, you ask me to withdraw. To do so for reasons beyond my comprehension would be a noble gesture in some eyes, perhaps, but surely the majority would attribute such a move to fear of not being elected, and my dignity forbids me to expose myself to this interpretation.

I infinitely regret, my dear friends, who have touched me with your affectionate and devoted feelings, not to be able to satisfy your request this time. But I am convinced that you will believe in the justice of the reasons that will not permit me to act otherwise. Believe in the cordial friendship of one who loves you.

Blanche answered the next day, saying that he understood Stravinsky's bewilderment and that the president of the Academy had asked to have Pierné clarify the situation for the composer: "Between the two of us, imagine the ridiculous position of the composers in the Institute." Blanche goes on, "This candidacy of a major artist will inevitably jolt all '*Institutards.*' "

The voting took place on the afternoon of January 25. Five ballots were required. On the first one, Schmitt received eight votes, Busser eight, Stravinsky five, Samuel-Rousseau ten. Schmitt was elected on the last ballot with twenty-eight votes to Stravinsky's four. That evening, *Le Figaro* published the results and, in ridiculing them, noted that "the anti-Stravinskyites who went to St.-Cloud to ask Schmitt to oppose the composer chose a man who had mocked the Institute throughout his career." At six o'clock, Pierné sent a note to Stravinsky, who was not in Paris, saying that Nadia Boulanger had promised to communicate the result to him.

Pierné was crushed, but not Blanche, who wrote three days later explaining that "your case was much too extraordinary for the peculiar structure of the Institute," and that "obviously you should have been elected by acclamation—which might possibly have happened if it had not been for the naturalization question." The letter identifies the organizer of the opposition as Rabaud and calls the event "a disgrace for France." Other sympathetic messages began to arrive and to appear in newspapers (notably André Coeuroy in *Gringoire,* January 27, 1936); and on February 13, Blanche wrote: "My dear, great Stravinsky, I have just heard *Oedipus Rex* again. Listening to this music, one of the most magnificent and genuine works of our time, has plunged the other affair into oblivion."

Throughout the campaign, Guermantes, the music critic of *Le Figaro,* had used the occasion to attack Stravinsky, most irritatingly in an article entitled "Le Sacre de l'automne." With the help of Charles-Albert Cingria, Stravinsky wrote a reply, "My Candidacy for the Institute" (*Le Jour,* January 28, 1936).

Much has been said in the newspapers, and the commentaries have been varied. I would like to reply to some of the better of them, as summarized in the article by Guermantes in *Le Figaro,* "Le Sacre de l'automne."

"Monsieur Stravinsky's candidacy for the Institute is indeed astonishing," Guermantes writes. "I realize, of course, that this same question is posed each time that a highly original artist, independent in expression and attitude but approaching his fiftieth year, suddenly discovers the road to the Pont des Arts. . . ."

It would have been indiscreet of me to have answered before the vote of the Institute, but I can do so now. I stood as a candidate for one reason only, because a few of my friends insisted upon it, and because I could not refuse them the gesture of respect for this venerable French institution of which they are members, and as a member of which they believed that I might be useful. I was not soliciting an honor but performing a favor.

Guermantes remarks that until now I have taken pains *not* to display any "visible decoration of this sort." But how could I display any decoration when I do not have one?

As for Guermantes's strange question, "What kind of metamorphosis has occurred, that Stravinsky's talent and spirit could suddenly accommodate themselves to this kind of glory?" the answer is in my music, and in my autobiography, the second part of which, containing my ideas and opinions clearly set forth, has just been published. These are the same ideas that I would have brought to the Institute, where I could have defended and supported them.

Guermantes continues: "I do not say that one ought to despise honors, but only that Stravinsky's works seem to say 'No' to them." It is not for me to decide whether or not my works say "No," but for the Institute to say "Yes"—or "No." I received only five [*sic*] votes out of thirty-two.

Guermantes concludes: "A moment occurs in the life of an artist when he no longer consults his youth."[2] This is true, of course, as well as natural, and to deny it would be to deceive. But I have never forgotten my youth, and I do not regret it. I have not reached the age where, all too often, people live only in the past; I still look ahead with joy. Let us suppose, Guermantes, that a miracle were to occur and make me twenty years younger—something that I am very far from desiring. Would I then be a living anachronism, looking older than I am in reality? Do you see how ridiculous are those wrinkled revolutionaries who did not progress but continued to repeat themselves over and over and to fight blindly for ideas long since dead? I detest artificial youth and plastic esthetic surgery, internal as well as external.

I am not ashamed of my age and am not afraid of it. At my age Bach composed his finest cantatas, Beethoven his last symphonies, and Wagner—which I say for the sake of Wagnerians—his *Meistersinger*. It is revolting to see older people flattering the young when this flattery is dictated only by the fear of being regarded as backward. Do the old ever consider what a cruel disappointment they are preparing for the young when, selfishly, they fail to guide them, but instead flatter them today and drop them tomorrow? Goethe said: "The greatest art in life is to endure." Finally, why does Guermantes give a pejorative sense to "Le Sacre de l'automne"? The season of the harvest is beautiful, the season of Pomona is full of riches, a blessed season, certainly worthy of a *Sacre*.

Charles-Marie Widor died shortly after Schmitt's election, and once again Stravinsky's name appeared in the newspapers as the obvious candidate for the chair of the deceased (*Le Figaro*, March 20, 1937). Questioned about the matter in October 1937 by a reporter, René Simon, Stravinsky said:

I will never undertake another act of candidacy. . . . I have no more taste for "officials" than they have for me. Nevertheless, apropos of Paul Dukas, when he died I was in Rome, where I conducted [one of his] works. This

---

[2] Next to this statement, in the margins of a draft, Stravinsky wrote (in Russian): "I think his real objection is quite different. He obviously deplores that I am not composing any more *Petrushka*s—which he finds more to his liking and to which he attributes all the success of my name. But even if the Octet, the concertos, Psalms, *Oedipus*, *Perséphone*, and *Apollo* do not tell him anything and he still longs for my youth, to which I myself no longer turn, his statement still does not follow."

had, with the Italians, a certain effect. I am still waiting for a word of thanks from a representative of France. [*L'Intransigeant,* October 13, 1937]

APPENDIX K

Walter Nouvel and CHRONIQUES DE MA VIE

To criticize Stravinsky's autobiography[1] for its numerous errors of both commission and omission may be unfair, since he states in a foreword that his wish is to relate important events of his life "according to the dictates of my memory." Yet to offer this skimpy version of his career up to 1933 under a title implying a comprehensive account was, and continues to be, misleading. Another aim set forth in the foreword was to correct "the accumulation of misunderstandings that has gathered about both my work and my person." Stravinsky attributes the distortion of his thoughts and words to journalists,[2] yet his esthetic, philosophical, political and musical opinions expressed in interviews dating from approximately the same period as the *Chroniques* are the same as those in the book—with the difference that his impromptu talk, even in translation, is livelier, more candid, and sharper in imagery. In effect, what the composer succeeded in doing in the book was to multiply the misunderstandings a hundredfold.

At the outset, too, Stravinsky vows to "take great care not to confuse my present reactions with those experienced at other stages in my life." Nowhere has he done this: the perspectives of the *Chroniques* are those of the mid-1930s. For one example, his comments on the choreography of the *Sacre* are those of twenty years after the event, though he tries to give the impression that his crit-

---

[1] *Stravinsky: An Autobiography* (New York, 1936). Originally published as *Chroniques de ma vie,* 2 vols. (Paris, 1935 and 1936).

[2] In one curious instance, a dozen years later, Stravinsky gave an interview on film music to Ingolf Dahl, his musical assistant, and by no definition a "journalist." David Raksin, the musician who had made the band arrangement of Stravinsky's *Circus Polka* and who composed for films (*Laura*), published a rejoinder which mentions that Stravinsky had endorsed Dahl's program notes for the Symphony in Three Movements. Stravinsky wrote to Dahl, February 9, 1948: "I have never expressed my opinion, approving or otherwise, of either the whole or parts of your program notes for my Symphony in Three Movements. If passages from the program notes are used to imply extramusical connotations in my work, I have to disclaim any responsibility for such interpretations." But this is not true: Dahl's notes quote Stravinsky, who approved them before they were published.

Medallion given to Stravinsky by his uncle Alexander Frantsevich Yelachich to commemorate the two first performances, by the St. Petersburg Court Orchestra, of Stravinsky's Symphony in E flat, April 14 and 16 (Old Style), 1907, and a boutonniere from Stravinsky's father, inscribed "Son Igor, January 3, 1901."

icisms do not differ from the ones of 1913. And for another example, here is his description of the milieu of his Yelachich relatives,[3] who were important to him in his adolescence:

> They all prided themselves on their liberalism, extolled progress, and considered it the thing to profess so-called advanced opinions in politics, art, and all branches of social life. The reader can easily see from this what their mentality was like: a compulsory atheism, a somewhat bold affirmation of "the Rights of Man," an attitude of opposition to "tyrannical" government, the cult of materialistic science, and, at the same time, admiration for Tolstoy and his amateur Christianizing.

---

[3] See the genealogical tree at the end of this appendix. Two of Stravinsky's maternal aunts, both older than his mother, married Yelachich brothers.

The "mentality" defined was anathema to Stravinsky in later years, obviously, but how did he feel about it at the time?

The failure of the dictates of Stravinsky's memory is astonishing, and in only one instance does he seem to have referred to his archives—for the story of the Kaiser's reaction to *Petrushka* and *Cléopâtre* in Berlin in 1912: Stravinsky's wording is the same as that of the account in the Russian newspaper *Rech,* no. 326, November 25, 1912. In the entire *Chroniques,* Stravinsky offers only a handful of dates, and most of these, even including that of the premiere of *Le Sacre du printemps,* are incorrect. After stating, "I composed this symphony . . . [and] at this point the period of my adolescence came to an end" (he was twenty-three!), Stravinsky goes on to remark that he graduated from the University of St. Petersburg in the spring of 1905 (it was in May 1906) and that he became engaged in the autumn of 1905 (it was on August 15). Yet the symphony, or most of it, precedes both of these events; the first movement was completed on July 18, 1905, the second on July 21, the third on August 4, and the fourth on September 24.

Stravinsky also recalls that in 1916, "in Geneva . . . I was captivated by the [cimbalom]," and he bought one and "carried it off to Morges." (He had been captivated by a cimbalom in January 1915 and had had one sent to Château-d'Oex.) At one point he pauses to "mention a work which I composed directly after finishing the score of the *Soldat* . . . my *Ragtime* for eleven instruments." (The *Ragtime* was composed before the *Soldat.*) A little later he says that in 1919, "I went to Paris in the early spring . . . , and there I met Diaghilev, whom I had not seen for more than a year." (Stravinsky had not seen Diaghilev for more than two years before this trip to Paris, which occurred in the second week of September 1919.) Stravinsky says that he had "recommended [Ansermet] to Diaghileff to take the place of Pierre Monteux, who . . . had had to leave us to take up the direction of the Boston Symphony Orchestra." (Ansermet became Diaghilev's chief conductor in 1915, while Monteux was in the French army.)

And Stravinsky contradicts himself, again and again, saying on page 202 that he "tackled" (conducted) the *Sacre* for the first time in a concert in Amsterdam, and thirteen pages later that it was in Paris that he was "tackling" the *Sacre* for the first time. On page 102 he is proposing a symphonic poem to Diaghilev that "I had been thinking of making . . . by combining the music of the second and third acts of *Le Rossignol*" for a ballet, adding that the impresario "warmly welcomed the suggestion, and I adapted a scenario from Andersen's fairy story to serve the purpose." (Stravinsky places this meeting in Switzerland in January 1917, but in actuality the ballet was commissioned in Santander in September 1916.) Then a little further on, Stravinsky says: "I had destined *Le Chant du rossignol* for the concert platform, and a choreographic rendering seemed to me to be quite unnecessary." In several other instances the composer clearly means something other than what he says. Thus, in reference to *Les Noces,* he writes, "I . . . found my solution in the form of an orchestra comprising piano, timbals [timpani], bells, and xylophones [*sic*], none of which instruments gives a precise note." (All of these instruments produce exact pitches.)

The *Chroniques* is useful mainly as a guide to the people who were in or out of Stravinsky's good graces at the time it was written (1934–35). Thus Arthur Lourié is ostentatiously absent,[4] while people referred to in the most denigrating terms in the composer's letters of the same period—Lifar, for instance, and Hindemith—are praised. Even Darius Milhaud's *Le Train bleu* earns a kind word, the one inconsistency in Stravinsky's forty-year stream of abuse of that composer.

The best-known story in the *Chroniques,* found at the very beginning, is typical of the book's style and inadequacies:

> One of my earliest memories of sound will seem somewhat odd.
>
> It was in the country, where my parents, like most people of their class, spent the summer with their children. I can see it now. An enormous peasant seated on the stump of a tree . . . simply clad in a short red shirt . . . not a white hair, yet an old man.
>
> . . . The children would gather round him. Then, to amuse them, he would begin to sing. This song was composed of two syllables, the only ones he could pronounce. They were devoid of any meaning, but he made them alternate with incredible dexterity in a very rapid tempo. He used to accompany this clucking in the following way: pressing the palm of his right hand under his left armpit, he would work his left arm with a rapid movement, making it press on the right hand. From beneath the red shirt he extracted a succession of sounds which were somewhat dubious but very rhythmic. . . .

First, the reader would like to know when and where this took place, information that could have been provided by Stravinsky's mother, who was living in his Paris home when he told the story to Walter Nouvel. Second, why doesn't the composer indicate the social class to which the Stravinskys belonged and whether or not the other children were also from this stratum? Third, how did Stravinsky make the determination that the syllables were "the only ones [the peasant] could pronounce"? Fourth, doesn't a contradiction exist in that the peasant is an old man, yet sings in "a very rapid tempo" and works his arm with "a rapid movement"? A comparison with the French reveals that the translator cannot be blamed for the style and the ambiguous pronouns. Finally, the vocabulary is off-target, "dexterity" hardly being the *mot juste* for a vocal exercise, and "dubious" signifying nothing at all: Stravinsky must have meant vague in pitch or bizarre in sonority.

The composer devotes only a few thousand words to his childhood. When

---

[4] In a letter to Stravinsky, September 5, 1935, Lourié complains that whereas, in the past, "it was enough that I simply pick up the telephone to see you, . . . now I have to make arrangements through others and the result is perpetual postponement."

the second chapter opens, he is already in his adolescence, mentioning his dislike of an unnamed school. Four years at the University of St. Petersburg Law School are then disposed of in one sentence. He does elaborate to a degree on two friendships—with Ivan Pokrovsky and Stepan Mitussov—but displays no evidence of the gift for descriptive detail that marked his conversation and his caricatures, while even such figures as Rimsky-Korsakov and Glazunov are seen only from a distance. "I was married in January, 1906," Stravinsky writes at the end of Chapter Two, but he does not disclose his wife's name (the index identifies her as "Mme Igor Stravinsky"), and she is mentioned only twice again, both times simply as "my wife."

In the next chapter, Stravinsky chronicles Rimsky-Korsakov's death, but without any indication of the emotion that this must have aroused. He also refers to Ustilug as "our estate in Volhynia," although at this time, shortly after his marriage, the "estate" was that of his nameless wife's family. And although he acknowledges that the performance of his *Scherzo fantastique* and *Fireworks* "marks a date of importance" for him, he does not divulge it. Diaghilev enters the book unceremoniously (" he commissioned me"), without benefit of a first name, or, indeed, of any distinguishing feature. From there on, the autobiography, as its title claims, is little more than a chronicle of works composed, people met, musical preferences and prejudices, and anecdotes.

Yet the *Chroniques* are remembered for one statement, which stuck to Stravinsky all of his life: "Music is, by its very nature, essentially powerless to *express* anything at all. . . ." The philosopher of esthetics Suzanne K. Langer reached the same conclusion via Ernst Cassirer a few years later (1942), but her distinction between "expression" and "expressiveness" in music had not yet been formulated at the time of the *Chroniques*. Ansermet took issue with Stravinsky's statement and wrote to the composer, April 15, 1935:

> Your war against "expression" seems to me to attribute a meaning to this word that it actually does not possess. All words—talk, gestures—are ex-pression. The issue is that when people speak of "expression," they understand a kind of super-expression, expression added to that which is expression, or a faculty of playing with that expression.

On September 22, 1932, William Aspinwell Bradley, a literary agent in Paris, wrote to Stravinsky in Voreppe, saying Blaise Cendrars reported that Stravinsky had been receptive to a project of Bradley's "to write a book for America." Stravinsky answered immediately (September 24), inviting Bradley to Voreppe to discuss the affair, and adding: "For a certain time I have nourished the idea of writing a book, polemical in character, in collaboration with a friend of mine with whom I am in complete spiritual sympathy." The friend was Diaghilev's and Stravinsky's lifelong companion Walter ("Valenka," "Valechka") Nouvel. Stravinsky, on his return from a Scandinavian and German tour, apparently met with Bradley sometime between October 20 and 26. But though the correspondence reveals nothing more, Bradley's initiative may have sparked Stravinsky to begin the *Chroniques*.

The book was ghostwritten by Nouvel,[5] described by Stravinsky's first wife as her husband's "faithful co-worker" (August 6, 1935), and even as "a member of our family" (January 31, 1936). A note in Stravinsky's hand, a resume of his activities in 1934 prepared for Nouvel, contains the sentence: "Taking advantage of Valechka's stay with us, I began the *Chroniques de ma vie*, and Volume I was concluded just before my trip to America." A letter from Catherine to Igor, March 11, 1935, reveals that Nouvel was to have received one-third of the revenue from the book, a sum later reduced to one-fourth. Fifteen receipts survive, signed by Nouvel, for payments described as "author's rights."[6]

Catherine Stravinsky was not enthusiastic about the *Chroniques*, and when her husband wrote to her that he planned to work on Volume Two during his 1935 American tour, she answered: "It is lamentable that this undertaking will keep you from doing any composing." Writing on July 16, 1935, she asked him to "bring some of the second volume of your chronicle," but added: "What a great pity that I cannot hear what you have already composed of your Concerto, of which I have not heard one note." Stravinsky was in Sancellemoz for one day (July 23; he returned to Paris by car on the 24th), at which time he read the second volume of the book to his wife.

The style of the *Chroniques* resembles that of Nouvel's other "in collaboration with" book, the life of Diaghilev by Arnold Haskell (1935). Unlike that volume, Nouvel's collaboration with Stravinsky was never acknowledged—with unfortunate results, since Stravinsky had to assume the responsibility for the clumsiness of phrasing ("my wife's health . . . decided me to get her into

---

[5] Nouvel also ghosted Stravinsky's article on Diaghilev. "Valechka is writing your memoirs of Diaghilev," Catherine wrote to Igor, March 4, 1935, "and he has already finished about a quarter of it; at first the work went well, but now he feels that it does not contain a sufficient number of anecdotes to please the American public." Stravinsky's contract with Nouvel is dated December 1934: "I, the undersigned, Igor Stravinsky, resident of Paris, 25, rue du Faubourg St.-Honoré, promise to pay M. Walter Nouvel, resident of Paris, 26, rue Pasquier, one-fourth of the sums I will receive as author's rights in all countries from the publishers of my book entitled *Chroniques de ma vie*, this in remuneration for the assistance M. Nouvel gave me in compiling the French text of the work." Stravinsky's wording seems to imply that the book had been written in Russian and that Nouvel simply translated it. But the original text was written in French, not in Russian, though very likely Stravinsky dictated the biographical information (at least) to Nouvel in Russian. To judge from the unverified statements and the lacunae, the book is clearly of the "as told to" variety.

[6] February 1, 1935: 432 francs, 50 centimes; February 25, 1935: 144 francs; April 8, 1935: 675 francs; April 29, 1935: 1,700 francs (one-quarter of the American advance from Simon & Schuster); December 7, 1935: 675 francs; September 17, 1936: 282 francs; November 14, 1936: 271 francs; December 17, 1936: 278 francs, 47 centimes; March 26, 1937: 467 francs; May 25, 1937: 41 francs (from Simon & Schuster); October 14, 1937: 400 francs; November 6, 1937: 200 francs; December 20, 1937: $21.75; January 26, 1938: 250 francs; June 17, 1938: 94 francs.

mountain air"), the stilted and quaint language ("Diaghilev was discountenanced," "Diaghilev besought me," "Ramuz and I got hold of the idea," "the works of days gone by"), and the malapropisms (as when, after the abdication of Nicholas II, Stravinsky says that "nothing could have been more inept [inapt?] than to sing *God Save the Tsar*").

Only four minor corrections in Stravinsky's hand appear in his copy of the French manuscript of Volume One. On page 22 he changed *"le diapason"* to *"l'étendue."* In the margin on page 42, he questioned the description of Debussy's *"liberté"* as *"impressionnante"* and suggested *"impressioniste."* (This change was not incorporated.) On page 119, concerning the duration of his stay in Vaud, he corrected Nouvel's *six mois* to *six ans.* On page 183, regarding the premiere of *The Song of the Nightingale*, Stravinsky changed *"sous la même direction d'Ansermet"* to *"sous la direction du même Ansermet."*

In the proofs of Volume Two, Stravinsky made the following changes. On page 30, in describing Boris Kochno, *"bien du plaisir"* is changed to *"un réel plaisir."* In the discussion of the Piano Concerto on page 60, *"même un simple vacilement"* had been changed by someone to *"une simple vacillation."* Stravinsky circled this, indicated that the original should be restored, and wrote in the margin, *"c'est juste!!!"* On page 72, he inserted the word *"penchant"* after *"l'art musical,"* and on page 83, in discussing St. Francis of Assisi, inserted the parenthetical remark *"(Provençal? Sa Mère était Provençale)".*

A CHRONOLOGY OF *CHRONIQUES DE MA VIE*

1934

November 28. London. Victor Gollancz of Victor Gollancz, Ltd, 14 Henrietta Street, writes:

> ... The book cannot hope to make any appeal to the general public [in England] : it is written with far too much sobriety, and far too great an intellectual and artistic conscience, to have that possibility. The general public here wants gossip, anecdote, intimate "revelations," and so on.
>
> ... There is the further very grave difficulty of length. English people, and particularly English booksellers, detest short books: we consider a really short book [one] of 60,000 words, and yours is 25,000 words only. In view of this idiosyncrasy of our people, this shortness makes it necessary to "deck it out." ... I have designed a page of quarto size, with good large margins, but even so the book will only come to 100 pages. ... I feel it to be absolutely essential to include, not the six plates which you mentioned, but sixteen plates. ...
>
> I can offer you a royalty of 10% the first 2,000 copies, 15% the next 3,000 copies, and 20% on all copies sold thereafter. ...

December 4. Paris. Denoël & Steele sends Stravinsky a contract proposal.

December 6. Paris. Denoël & Steele sends Stravinsky a check for the advance of 2,700 francs.

December 9. New York. Clifton Fadiman of Simon & Schuster writes expressing his publisher's interest in the *Chroniques,* adding:

> We have been particularly successful with biographies of great artists in the past, our most distinguished book in this field being Mme Nijinsky's life of her husband.

December 18. Madrid. Guillermo de Torre, Spanish representative of *Sur,* sends a contract to Stravinsky, adding:

> Since this is your first literary work, [it is difficult] to fix an exact sum, so I shall simply offer you the highest possible advance, the same as M. Paul Valéry requested, 3,000 francs. . . . Please send me the original manuscript so that it may be translated without delay and appear at the same time as the French edition.

According to the contract signed by Stravinsky and Victoria Ocampo, December 19, 1934, the composer was to receive 10 percent of the profits; he also added a clause stipulating that these author's rights be paid every semester.

The Spanish edition was translated by Guillermo de Torre and prefaced by Victoria Ocampo's "Letter to Igor Stravinsky."

<u>1935</u>

September 1935. Buenos Aires. *Sur* publishes Leopoldo Hurtado's review of the *Chroniques:*

> I read that Stravinsky wishes his works to be treated as objects of nature, and therefore beyond all possible criticism. I do not know whether [he] would like this rule to be applied to these "chronicles" as well, but this would certainly facilitate the critic's task, since to declare that a tree or a rhinoceros is "well done" or "badly done" is to adopt an absurd attitude. . . . It is inadmissible to say, "This should have been done differently," in respect to objects of nature, which must be taken as they are, not as we think they should be. . . .
>
> No autobiography is more external, more "from without," as Ortega would say, than Stravinsky's, [which contains less than] a milligram of what could be called "inner life." . . . All phases of artistic growth and development are described meticulously; the rest consists of mere indications of trips and time: "in such and such a year I worked on such and such a composition." Except for the recollections of early childhood, there is not one single detail that could not have been written by a witness. The acknowledgment of passions—loves, hates, ambitions, triumphs, disappointments, hopes—that customarily accompanies the life of a great artist has been rigorously excluded. Instances of passion arise here only for the most

prosaic purposes: because his nurse dies, he has a pain in his side, or he cannot feed his wife and four children.

. . . Naturally no romanticized, supernatural aura surrounds the artist-subject here. But this would be contrary to the Stravinsky spirit. The things themselves are what count, not the atmosphere surrounding them. . . .

This book should be considered for what it contains and not for what it does not contain. Omission has its merits in certain cases, and this is one of those cases. When Stravinsky speaks of his work and not of his loves, he anticipates the nature of the artists of the future. . . . The musical work of the future will be rooted not in a chaotic sentimental experience, but in a plain and full acceptance of a powerful artistic vocation, based on a more secure and perfect technique. . . .

The composer's references to [his] works consist in a succession of tours and dates, between which ballets and operas were conceived, germinated, born, and presented. The reader must imagine the connections among all of these things on his own. Of course, these connections are . . . occult. Stravinsky deliberately leaves us completely in the dark regarding the act of composition, to which he alludes throughout the book. . . .

We do miss a certain intimacy in the *Chroniques;* oddly, other lives of Stravinsky, that of Schaeffner, for example, are more intimate.

September 15. Paris. Stravinsky writes to Gollancz:

I hope to be able to send you the second volume of the *Chroniques* very soon. I would like to know whether the first volume has been translated. If so, please send it to me, since it must be read under my supervision. If you have not begun the translation, I could have it done here (at your expense) by some very cultivated English musicians.

September 25. Paris. Stravinsky writes to Gollancz:

I would like to give Haskell's book on Diaghilev to a friend of mine who was also a friend of his, but who has no means of procuring it. Would it be indiscreet of me to ask you to send me a copy?

October 5. London. Gollancz sends Stravinsky the English translation of Volume One.

October 19. Buenos Aires. Victoria Ocampo writes to inform Stravinsky that she would be happy to publish Volume Two of his *Chroniques.*

November 6. London. Gollancz acknowledges receipt of the manuscript of Volume Two.

December 16. London. Gollancz writes to Stravinsky:

We hope to publish the whole book . . . during the first week of March. I most sincerely hope that it will be possible to prevent the second volume of the French edition being published till then. As you know, the French edition of the first volume has been widely reviewed in the English press, and while this has done no harm (on the contrary it has done a great deal of good) it would certainly do a great deal of harm if the second volume were also reviewed in the English press before our joint volume came out. . . . If it is absolutely impossible to arrange this will you please be very careful not to send any copies of the French edition to England, and . . . see that Denoël and Steele send no copies?

December 24. London. Norman Collins, of Gollancz, sends Stravinsky the translation of Volume Two, with several questions:

On page 16, I am not familiar with the word *"chout."*

On page 17, I do not know whether *"soufflé"* should be rendered as "whispered" or "hummed."

On page 18, should *"carré"* be translated as "square" or "well-built"?

. . . I am particularly worried by the word *"sonorité."* Both "sonority" and "sonorousness" exist in English, of course, but scarcely with this meaning. . . .

. . . On page 51 [of Volume One] I wonder if "vanguard" should be in inverted commas—i.e., if there was a set specifically known as the vanguard, or whether there was a set which had the attributes of a vanguard. And on page 57, as the word "truculent" seems to me out of place in the English, I am wondering whether the word "crude" [or] "barbaric" conveys your meaning. . . .

1936

January 10. Paris. André Coeuroy writes in *Beaux-Arts:*

. . . This second volume [of the *Chroniques*] is much superior to the first: less dry and inhuman, and it reveals . . . certain niches of the musician's profound spirit. . . .

You will find here . . . a Stravinsky who does not solicit your sympathy precisely because he is too self-aware.

January 21. Paris. Stravinsky writes to Gollancz:

. . . I gave your English translation to a very serious person [David Ponsonby]. . . . According to this Englishman, who knows French as well as his native tongue, the translation is, unfortunately, so defective and my text so disfigured at many points that he felt compelled to make numerous alterations. . . .

Not having sufficient knowledge of the English language myself, I had my friend Dushkin, the violinist, review the translation of Volume One when you sent it to me last November. He found the translation satisfactory, but did not compare it with the French. I will send you the revised translation in several days.

January 24. Paris. Stravinsky receives 2,916 francs from Denoël & Steele for author's rights.

January 24. Paris. From Boris de Schloezer's review:

> Many artists have bequeathed us their memoirs, autobiographies, reflecting on their art, and, generally, these writings provoke some surprise, offering us a new image of the man. . . . This is not the case with Stravinsky: between the music and the writing, there is not the slightest variance. Reading his *Chroniques* is somewhat like listening to one of his recent compositions: clean, precise, dry . . . with emotion scattered here and there but in carefully rationed and chosen terms.

January 29. New York. Quincy Howe, of Simon & Schuster, writes requesting the originals of the photographs, since the plates that Gollancz bought from Denoël & Steele "will not give the best results."

February 10. London. Gollancz writes to Stravinsky:

> I received the manuscript back from Mr. Ponsonby, but I am really a little puzzled by his letter. He has done splendid service in the matter of musical and aesthetic terms—but in any case we were of course going to have these checked by a musician (our idea had been to send the translation for this purpose to Mr. Ernest Newman).
>
> But in addition to this Mr. Ponsonby writes: "I have corrected a few mistakes in spelling and made several improvements in the style. From the point of view of the latter the whole work ought really to be retranslated, but we understand that there is no time for this." Of course I will print the work (with an exception which I will come to in a moment) in the form in which Mr. Ponsonby has sent it to me, but I find many of his alternative renderings no improvement, and some of these terms (I give below one which I have chosen at random) quite definitely not so good as those in the original version. For instance:

"so indecent an accompaniment"	has been changed to	"such an indecent accompaniment"
"he told me that I must above all"	" " " "	"he told me that before saying anything else I must"
"it was not its fault that our academy gave birth every year to mediocrities of the Prix de Rome type"	" " " "	"it was in no way responsible for the number of mediocrities of the Prix de Rome type to which our academy gave birth every year"
"to work unhurriedly"	" " " "	"to work without haste"

and one which I have picked out as being worse, in my view, than the original is:

"for the benefit of	has been changed to	"equally intended
those people who		for those interested
are interested in		in my music
my music or me"		and myself"

As to the spelling, he has throughout changed "choreography" to "choregraphy." There is no question that "choreography" is the usual spelling. As you know, the great authority for spelling in England is the New Oxford Dictionary, which is published in a "big" and in a "condensed" form. I have had the word looked up in the condensed dictionary which we have here, and it duly gives "choreography" and doesn't give "choregraphy" even as a possible alternative! I am having the word looked up also in the Big Oxford Dictionary to see if there is any authority for "choregraphy." In any event I shall use the spelling which the big dictionary gives, as the one having the greatest authority.

I mention these points lest you should think I have been careless in dealing with the translation of so important a work. As I say, Mr. Ponsonby has done admirable service in the matter of musical and aesthetic expressions, but in any event these were going to be dealt with by a musician.

February 12. Paris. Stravinsky sends to Simon & Schuster:

3 portraits of me by Picasso
1 portrait of me by my son Theodore
1 portrait of Ramuz by me
1 Picasso design for *Pulcinella*
1 Picasso design for *Ragtime*

These reproductions cost me a total of 75 francs = $5—for which I would appreciate reimbursement. In addition, I would like to call your attention to the existence of an excellent series of photographs of me made by Edward Weston, Carmel (California), from which you could pick one or two to complete the illustrations.

February 20. London. Gollancz sends the contract for Stravinsky's signature.

March 6. Paris. Stravinsky signs the contract for the *Nuevas crónicas de mi vida.*

A list (undated) in Stravinsky's hand shows that he intended to send copies of Volume Two to "C.-A. Cingria, Gab [rielle] Picabia, Roland-Manuel, [Irena] Terapiano, V. [Vera Sudeikina], the Princesse de Polignac, Prince Pierre of Monaco, Victoria Ocampo, André Schaeffner, Arthur Lourié, Nadia Boulanger, Gabriel Pierné, Paul Landormy."

May 1. New York. Emil Hilb, of Simon & Schuster, writes to Stravinsky:

Your autobiography will make a shorter book than we would like to publish, and we therefore think it an excellent idea to add to the book your own guide to your compositions. . . . The book is announced for early fall and will be on the market before you arrive in the United States. The addition should therefore reach us before August 15.

July 6. Paris. Stravinsky writes to Simon & Schuster:

> Unfortunately it is absolutely impossible for me to [make a catalogue now] . . . thus you must abandon this project, which, in any case, is not essential to the success of my book. Moreover, such a guide would . . . be very limited. To guide a reader in understanding my music would require a new book.

July 21. Paris. Denoël & Steele sends Stravinsky's royalty statement but asks if payment might be deferred until the end of September. On September 15, Denoël & Steele sends Stravinsky 1,125 francs, 50 centimes.

September 29. Paris. Stravinsky writes to Gollancz, Ltd., requesting copies of the reviews in the English press.

October 1. London. Norman Collins sends clippings and informs the composer that 1,318 copies have been sold.

November 7. Prague. Stanislas Hanus writes to Stravinsky:

> Last year Denoël & Steele sold the [Czech-language] rights to your *Chroniques* to the Czech publishing house Orbis. I translated the first volume and am now working on the second. Orbis would like to publish Volumes One and Two in one volume.
>
> Given the modest number of copies we can sell here . . . in such a small country, Orbis would like you to accept 1,000 francs for [the translation rights of] Volume Two, which is to say, 2,500 for the whole volume.
>
> My aim is to be your *traduttore* and not *traditore*. I have worked for many years as a co-director of the Czech musical review *Tempo* and I am a writer and poet. . . .
>
> I take the liberty of asking you for some clarifications:
>
> 1. Fernand Chavannes . . . is he a writer, painter, musician?
> 2. Léon Woizikowski? In Czech his name must be written Wojcikowski/Wojzikowski if he is Polish by birth. If he is Russian, we would write Vojcikovskij/Vojzikovskij. Would you clarify this for me, and write this dancer's name in Russian characters?
> 3. Siohan. If I am not mistaken, he is a Parisian conductor? . . .

November 23. London. Gollancz, Ltd., sends Stravinsky a check for £17 16s. 7d.

1937

October 12. Paris. Stravinsky asks Simon & Schuster to deposit the royalties due him, $96.57, in his account at Bankers Trust, 57th Street and Park Avenue, New York.

500

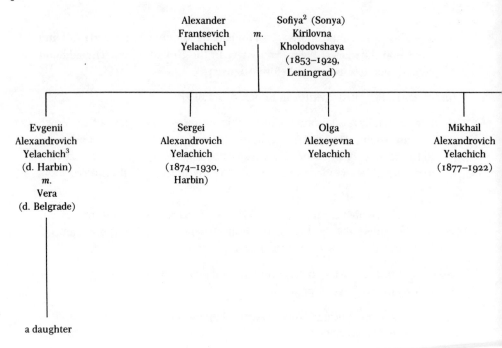

Alexander
Frantsevich
Yelachich[1]
  m.
Sofiya[2] (Sonya)
Kirilovna
Kholodovshaya
(1853–1929,
Leningrad)

Evgenii
Alexandrovich
Yelachich[3]
(d. Harbin)
  m.
Vera
(d. Belgrade)

Sergei
Alexandrovich
Yelachich
(1874–1930,
Harbin)

Olga
Alexeyevna
Yelachich

Mikhail
Alexandrovich
Yelachich
(1877–1922)

a daughter

---

[1] Stravinsky inscribed a photograph of A. F. Yelachich: "My favorite uncle." (His only other uncles, besides Nikolai Yelachich, were his father's brothers, Konstantin and Alexander Stravinsky)

[2] Not to be confused with Sofiya Dmitrievna Vel'sovskaya, who brought up Catherine Nossenko after the early death (1887) of her mother. On June 10, 1913, Stravinsky instructed the Azov-Don Commercial Bank in Rovno to send 100 rubles to "Mrs. S. D. Vel'sovskaya in Kharkov."

[3] Evgenii Yelachich, assistant to General Brusilov in 1917, published an obituary for Gury Stravinsky in the *Central Committee News*, August 1917.

[4] Stravinsky identified N. A. Yelachich on a photograph as "my oldest cousin." He was a pianist, but Stravinsky did not want him to have his Piano Concerto "or any of his other works for that matter." (Letter from Tania Stravinsky, 1925)

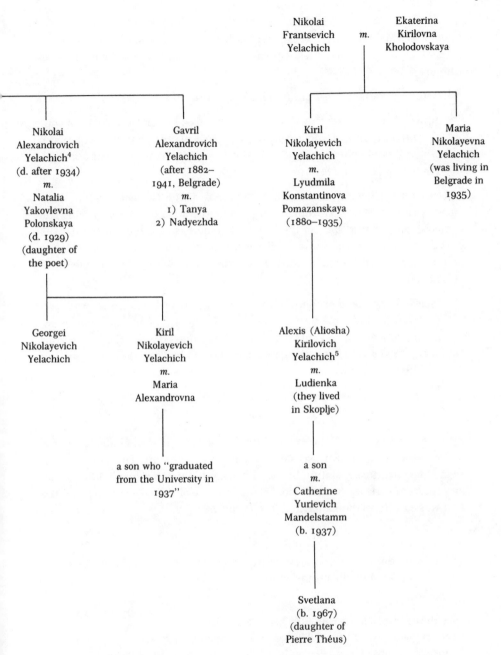

Nikolai
Frantsevich   *m.*   Ekaterina
Yelachich   Kirilovna
                    Kholodovskaya

Nikolai
Alexandrovich
Yelachich[4]
(d. after 1934)
m.
Natalia
Yakovlevna
Polonskaya
(d. 1929)
(daughter of
the poet)

Gavril
Alexandrovich
Yelachich
(after 1882–
1941, Belgrade)
m.
1) Tanya
2) Nadyezhda

Kiril
Nikolayevich
Yelachich
m.
Lyudmila
Konstantinova
Pomazanskaya
(1880–1935)

Maria
Nikolayevna
Yelachich
(was living in
Belgrade in
1935)

Georgei
Nikolayevich
Yelachich

Kiril
Nikolayevich
Yelachich
m.
Maria
Alexandrovna

Alexis (Aliosha)
Kirilovich
Yelachich[5]
m.
Ludienka
(they lived
in Skoplje)

a son who "graduated
from the University in
1937"

a son
m.
Catherine
Yurievich
Mandelstamm
(b. 1937)

Svetlana
(b. 1967)
(daughter of
Pierre Théus)

[5] A. K. Yelachich visited Stravinsky
in Echarvines in late summer 1928
and made an unsuccessful effort to
arrange a concert tour for him in Yu-
goslavia. After another visit to the
composer, in Paris in June 1937,
A. K. Yelachich published an interview with him in *Karporova* (Belgrade), July 29, 1937.

October 21. Mainz. Willy Strecker writes that "the publication [of the *Chroniques*] in Germany has met with much interest and should help to dispel rumors."[7]

November 15. Paris. Louis-Ferdinand Céline writes to Stravinsky:

> It would give me great joy to send you my books. I await the copies [of your *Chroniques*] from Denoël. Did you receive a manuscript for a ballet with which I was hoping to tempt you? But I imagine that prior inspirations already have you in a fever!

November 22. Château de Monthoux. Apropos of the German edition, Stravinsky writes to Martin Hürlimann, of Atlantis-Verlag, Zürich and Berlin. The composer says that in spite of the lack of time he has read the proofs, that the cuts do not always make sense, and that he insists again that in each instance of a change or cut the reader must be apprised of the fact by a footnote. Stravinsky adds:

> Please do not keep bringing up that passage about Bayreuth . . . that you declared inadmissible for contemporary Germany! I can refer you to another passage that you cut which I know would in no way offend the censor or the Nazi reader;[8] it is the passage at the end in which I discuss diminutive Russian names, which Jewish virtuosos have the bad taste to use formally.[9]

1939

February 17. Berlin. V. V. Leontiev of the Petropolis publishing house proposes to Stravinsky to issue a Russian-language edition of the book. The letter was answered for Stravinsky, stating his conditions, on March 15, just before his departure from Paris for Sancellemoz. Nothing came of the negotiations, and the first Russian translation appeared in Moscow in 1963.

1947

The Italian edition of *Chroniques* is published by Alessandro Minuziano Editore, in Alberto Mantelli's translation.

---

[7] See the correspondence with Strecker in *S.S.C.* III.

[8] The complete text was not published in German until 1958.

[9] Stravinsky seems to have been bothered by the customary use of nicknames later in life as well. Thus when the New York publisher E. H. Morris wrote to him, June 1, 1967: "Mr. Mischa Mortnoff has transcribed and edited for piano solo the second movement of Ebony Concerto," Stravinsky wrote next to the name, "Why not Sasha Bolvanoff or Moishe Schneiderson?"

APPENDIX L

Roland-Manuel and LA POÉTIQUE MUSICALE

At the end of March 1939, Stravinsky was officially invited to give Harvard's Charles Eliot Norton lectures for the academic year 1939–40. His in-principle acceptance had been conveyed to the university by Nadia Boulanger months earlier, however, and Stravinsky had undoubtedly turned his mind to the subject matter in the autumn of 1938.

Stravinsky actually wrote only some fifteen hundred words for *La Poétique musicale* (as the published lectures were called), and in verbal note form: not a single sentence by him actually appears in the book of which he is the nominal author.[1] The thirty-thousand-word text was written by Roland-Manuel,[2] with assistance, in the lecture on Russian music, from Pierre Suvchinsky. But to distinguish Stravinsky from his ghostwriter is possible only by examining Roland-Manuel's transcriptions of his discussions with Stravinsky, which may or may not have been preserved.

The aim of the present investigation is simply to translate and publish Stravinsky's own words, leaving the discovery of the ideological differences between his annotations and Roland-Manuel's book to the reader. At the time when both were written (April–August 1939), Roland-Manuel seems to have been preoccupied with Freud, Suvchinsky with Sartre, Stravinsky with Nicholas of Cusa (particularly with the idea of the *coincidentia oppositorum*) and with Nesmielov's *The Science of Man.*[3] Needless to say, the philosophies of the fifteenth-century German and of the nineteenth-century Russian are remote from those of the contemporary Viennese and French writers.

Why did Stravinsky not write the lectures himself? Chiefly because he had begun to compose the second movement of the Symphony in C, and no time remained for any other work. Why, then, did he accept the lectureship? The answer is that he needed the money ($10,000), or at least believed that he did. In countless letters to concert agents of the period,[4] he states his minimum terms for a transatlantic tour as $15,000 after expenses. The money from Harvard, together with fees for conducting the Boston Symphony Orchestra while in residence at the university, would match this figure.

---

[1] Nevertheless, Stravinsky was to write to the Czechoslovakian publisher of the book: "The translation ought to be entrusted to a person thoroughly versed in French ... because of the highly subtle, idiomatic language I used." (February 10, 1947)

[2] Pseudonym of Alexis Manuel Levy (1891–1966).

[3] Stravinsky used the third edition (2 vols.; Moscow, 1905) and wrote extensive marginal commentaries.

[4] N. Zborovsky and Severin Kavenoki, among others. It was Kavenoki who, in 1937, introduced the composer to Max Manischewitz, the wine manufacturer, who became a good friend and who sent a moving letter to Stravinsky after the death of his wife.

The point of departure for the lectures was a polemic by Roland-Manuel[5] challenging Boris de Schloezer's classification of Stravinsky as a Pelagian,[6] "who relies only on himself and on his prodigious technique." The truth, of course, is that Stravinsky's profoundest belief was in the divine nature of artistic inspiration, and in St. Paul's "I know that in me dwelleth no good thing: for to will is present with me! . . ." Stravinsky's struggle to castigate his will was lifelong.

Maurice Ravel introduced Roland-Manuel to Stravinsky in 1911. On May 26, 1913, this future biographer of Ravel sent a postcard to Stravinsky: "From Liège, whither the magical sonorities of the *Firebird* have pursued me, I cannot resist the temptation to remind you of the admiration of Roland-Manuel." A decade later, Roland-Manuel wrote to the composer of *Mavra*, before it was publicly performed, bravely dissenting from his views about the merits of Tchaikovsky. After *Le Baiser de la fée,* a second letter came on the subject:

> *Mon cher maître,* On January 6, 1922, you wrote to me about *Mavra.* . . . What goodness and generosity in that letter . . . which I now see as clearly prophetic. *Le Baiser de la fée* is a success that surpasses success, as do all works marked with perfection. The powerful emotion that it inspires in me results from the unity of substance in the diversity of the objects. Everything that one loves in you is here retained, linked up, synthesized. And how could I deny that the "catalyzing" element in this splendid composition is the very Tchaikovsky that I did not like? In my eyes, *Le Baiser de la fée* justifies all of the [developmental] steps in your art that I was somehow unable to appreciate. This work explains everything to me. I demanded this revelation from your art because of my unshakable confidence in your artistry. . . . Two days ago this marvelous work provided this vision, and so forcefully that I cannot restrain myself from thanking you from the bottom of my heart and with all of my affection. [November 30, 1928]

Then, in 1936, Roland-Manuel's intelligent review of *Chroniques de ma vie* caught the composer's attention, no doubt the following lines in particular:

---

[5] Roland-Manuel's article and one by Suvchinsky—the latter with an epigraph from Sartre—were published in the special Stravinsky number of *La Revue Musicale,* May–June 1939.

[6] After conducting the *Dumbarton Oaks* Concerto at the Salle Gaveau in June 1938, Stravinsky wrote to Vittorio Rieti: "I was very surprised by the success of my new Concerto and not at all surprised by the press: with a few exceptions . . . an attack (Schloezer, *bien entendu* . . .)." When Boris de Schloezer sent his monograph on Stravinsky to the composer (May 25, 1929), Stravinsky seems not to have acknowledged the book and, instead, filled his copy with marginalia: *"Quel sottise!" "Complètement faux," "Quel bavardage!" "Pas si simple que ça,"* etc. Schloezer had inscribed the book: "For Igor Stravinsky, this work of admiration and of profound gratitude for all that his art has revealed, this book, in which I have tried, quite imperfectly no doubt, to discover the secret of his immeasurable work." In later years, Schloezer reversed his views on Stravinsky, writing to the composer, January 18, 1963: "I have just heard *Danses concertantes,* and with what pleasure. . . ."

The more the master of the Symphony of Psalms composes, and the more he expatiates on his art, always concerned to purge it of all that is not purely musical, the more his esthetic resembles an ascesis. . . .

Durus hic sermo. We must continue to point out to our Aristotelian, however, that a piece of music is inevitably expressive. Whether or not its author wishes it to be, it expresses him.[7] [*Courrier Royal,* January 4, 1936]

Stravinsky chose Roland-Manuel rather than Suvchinsky to write the lectures because the former was a professional musician (composer) and author-critic as well as a native speaker of French, the language in which, by stipulation, the *Poétique* had to be written. Suvchinsky's roles were those of adviser on the state of music in the USSR[8] and translator of the Russian words and phrases in Stravinsky's notes. A substantial passage near the end of "The Avatars of Russian Music" was also Suvchinsky's work, and he wrote a seventeen-page draft in Russian for this lecture.

It should also be mentioned that in December 1938, Stravinsky read an essay by Suvchinsky, "Reflections on the Typology of Musical Creation: The Notion of Time and Music," and recommended it to Charles-Albert Cingria with a view to publication in *La Nouvelle Revue Française.* Though a regular contributor to the *NRF,* Cingria wrote to Suvchinsky on January 15, 1939, disclaiming any influence with Jean Paulhan, the editor, and revealing that a similar article by himself, likewise based on the Stravinsky-Scriabin polarity, was already due to appear in the periodical. Cingria explained that Gide and Schloezer, Stravinsky's nemesis among the music critics of the moment, were certain to oppose the essay, whereupon, at Stravinsky's request, Cingria met with Victoria Ocampo in an effort to promote the publication through her. In a

---

[7] "Since I am not a partisan of expressionism in music, I think that the role of music is not to express the meaning of a piece or the meaning of its libretto, and not to create an 'atmosphere' for a spectacle. According to what principle do the play of the music and the action of the spectacle operate? My answer is: according to the principle of independence from each other. Every art is necessarily canonical, possessing laws of its own that rule and govern it. This applies to all theatrical spectacles, and I find no logical reason not to apply it likewise to all cinematographical spectacles." (Unpublished note by Stravinsky, 1932, in the composer's archives.)

[8] Suvchinsky had been to the USSR in 1937, according to his letter from Marseille on his return telling Stravinsky of the sense of relief at being back in France. Suvchinsky had sent Stravinsky the article in *Pravda* attacking Shostakovich, "A Muddle Instead of Music" (January 18, 1936), with the comment: "Obviously written on direct orders from Stalin." Stravinsky wrote in the margin: "The muddle is in the head of the author of this article, who cannot distinguish the valuable and the worthless in contemporary music (*Lady Macbeth*). What an idiot." Stravinsky underscored two statements in the article, one to the effect that Shostakovich "has deliberately turned everything upside down so that nothing will remind us of classical operatic music," the other the claim that the composer "has the ability to express simple and strong emotions."

January 25 letter to Madame Ocampo, Jules Supervielle quotes Paulhan: "Suv-chinsky is too quick to apply what he thinks he has discovered, and, in any event, his piece is too abstract." From Suvchinsky's essay, nonetheless, Stra-vinsky borrowed the word "typology" for the title of his fourth lecture, and the composer's study of Nicholas of Cusa must be attributed to the influence of his compatriot.

In September 1938, Stravinsky visited Roland-Manuel at his home in La Roche Saint-Pierre (Fontainebleau), after which their friendship became more intimate. On November 3, Stravinsky dined with Roland-Manuel at the restau-rant Weber in Paris, and the younger man kept notes on the composer's con-versation. A card from Roland-Manuel, February 20, 1939, informing Stra-vinsky that "I will come to see you on Thursday," helps to date the next batch of notes to have survived.[9] Stravinsky's written notes must date from late Feb-ruary, if only for the reason that he was unable to work for several weeks after his wife's death on March 2. Seriously ill himself, Stravinsky left Paris for San-cellemoz on March 15. A letter from his daughter-in-law to Nadia Boulanger, in Boston, March 23, reveals that he had suffered "a pulmonary incident [lesion] like the one he had in America two years ago. The doctors have warned him that he must take his condition seriously. At first, they foresaw the possibility of having to perform a pneumothorax."

Roland-Manuel wrote to Stravinsky on March 24, and the composer jotted a *pensée* for the lectures on the back of the envelope:

> The musician can approach the words that he puts to music in two ways. First, the word can be treated as sonorous material of expression itself. . . . Second, the word can determine the meaning of the music, [in which case] it is left meaningless without the word. The second approach is the passive one. The active approach is that of the musician who employs the word as sonorous material *only,* taking no account of its literal significance.

Stravinsky's characteristic presentation of his arguments is through such dia-lectical distinctions. Though the use of this form is more manifest in his notes than in their elaboration by Roland-Manuel, he followed the composer's subject outline almost without deviation.

The following chronology of the composition of the lectures has been ex-cerpted from correspondence, including two letters from the composer's mother, of which the one dated May 15 reveals something of the character and critical propensities of this eighty-five-year-old woman.

1939

March 23. Boston. Edward Forbes sends Stravinsky an official invitation to give the Charles Eliot Norton Lectures and describes the terms.
March 24. Paris. Roland-Manuel to Stravinsky: "I have assembled my notes and begun to organize them. This gives me the feeling of being near you and makes

---

[9] In the Roland-Manuel Collection, Paris.

me very happy. I have not forgotten that I must send certain books to you, above all, Dalbiez on Freud and Chesterton's *Chaucer.*"

April 4. Paris. Suvchinsky to Stravinsky:[10] I stopped by at Sauguet's today to ask for the piano score of the *Chartreuse* for you. Recently I had dinner with Cingria. He claims not to have enough money to buy a stamp.

April 11. Sancellemoz. Stravinsky cables his in-principle acceptance to Forbes.

April 25. Paris. Anna Stravinsky, the composer's mother, living at 7, rue Antoine-Chantin since the death of her daughter-in-law, writes to her son: "Today is Radonitsa,[11] but I was unable to go to church, much less to the cemetery. . . . Father Vassily went, and I was sad not to be able to visit our graves to put Easter flowers on them. . . . We have had no news from you for almost a week, my Gimurochka. All that has arrived is a letter from Fedya in which he asked about your shirts, but he does not write about any of you. . . . I seem to remember that you will be x-rayed on Wednesday. No later than Thursday, then, we hope to have a letter from you, which, God willing, will cheer us up."

April 26. Paris. Suvchinsky writes: Roland-Manuel leaves on Saturday morning and will be there by evening. You should be able to accomplish a lot in six days together—enough, in any case, so that you will not have to trouble yourself any further in this matter. The second (and probably the last) trip that Roland-Manuel makes will depend entirely on you. He is free at the beginning of June. He should turn out to be more useful than I because of his French and for a variety of other reasons. I unfolded the plan and character of the lectures to him in general terms. I am happy for you, and for Roland-Manuel, though disappointed that circumstances have made it impossible for me to go in his place.

April 27. Sancellemoz. Stravinsky cables his definite acceptance to Forbes.

April 29. Paris. Suvchinsky writes: I have explained everything to Roland-Manuel—that you will take on the cost of the trip, the stay in Sancellemoz, the purchase of books, up to 10,000 francs. Within a few days you will see whether you can work with him satisfactorily. Whether or not I continue to participate in this affair will depend on your determination.

May 5. Paris. Suvchinsky writes: Sauguet is thrilled that you like his opera. How is your work with Roland-Manuel going?

May 7–17. Paris. Stravinsky is in Italy, conducting in Milan on the 12th, in Florence (*Perséphone*) on the 16th.

May 13. Paris. Roland-Manuel writes to thank Stravinsky for his hospitality during the sojourn. "I will work with Suvchinsky tomorrow or the next day and explain your point of view precisely. . . . The first movement of the Symphony in C is so masterful that it discourages the rest of us from writing our music."

May 15. Paris. Roland-Manuel writes: "I saw Suvchinsky, and we sorted out the difficulties in the lecture on typology. I gave him a copy of the first lecture and of the first part of the second."

May 15. Paris. Anna Stravinsky writes to her son in Florence: "Gimurochka . . .

---

[10] The excerpts from Suvchinsky's letters are paraphrased.

[11] The Tuesday of the second week after Easter.

thank you for your letter-postcard, which I received this morning. . . . I was happy to hear that your health is good, and of the great triumph of your concert. Let us hope that the one in Florence enjoys equal success. The Florence orchestra must be good, too; in fact, you are probably already familiar with the orchestra, so working with it will not be too difficult. . . . I hope, my Gimurochka, that you will write in greater detail about the Milan concert. . . . According to this morning's *Le Matin* . . . '*L'Université de Harvard annonce aujourd'hui que le fameux compositeur Igor Stravinsky a été nommé professeur à l'Université.* . . .' Why '*professeur*'? Is there no more appropriate title? It also seems odd to me that they should say *fameux*—which sounds strange, somehow— ironic—instead of *célèbre;* evidently the translator took the word straight from the dictionary."

May 18. Florence. Stravinsky sends a postcard to Roland-Manuel (a photograph of Pope Pius XII).

May 23. Paris. Suvchinsky writes: I was about to send the material for the last part of the fifth lecture, but, instead, I decided to work on it myself first, to facilitate things for you. If you find the result suitable, I will show it to Roland-Manuel, and we will endeavor to translate it into French before he leaves to visit you. He has shown the first lecture to me. I think it is good, but too much material is presented all at once; some should be transferred to the second lecture.

May 25. Paris. Suvchinsky writes: How happy I am that you liked my text. . . . I am glad that certain things which no one has wanted to state openly will finally be said. How wonderful that you are the person to say them. . . . While preparing for the fifth lecture, I read almost the whole of Soviet musical/critical literature. . . . I will meet with Roland-Manuel today to discuss the translation. . . . Perhaps in the first lecture, where you talk about "artistic appetite," something should also be mentioned about the *presentiment of discovery*. Roland-Manuel will paraphrase my thoughts on this subject to you.

May 25. Sancellemoz. Stravinsky telephones Dagmar Godowsky,[12] in New York, asking her to fix the dates of the lectures with Edward Forbes. (Stravinsky wrote out his four-page telephone message in advance, in German.)

May 30. Roland-Manuel returns to Sancellemoz.

June 3. Sancellemoz. Stravinsky writes to Forbes: "The titles of the lectures have not yet been established, and for me to deliver more than six is impossible."

June 7. Paris. Anna Stravinsky dies of pneumonia at 3:00 p.m.[13]

---

[12] Daughter of the Russian-American pianist Leopold Godowsky. (After Godowsky's death on November 21, 1938, Alexis Kall wrote to Stravinsky: "Not long ago, Godowsky dedicated a new edition of a piece of his to me; I went to the synagogue for his funeral, at which Edward G. Robinson read a beautiful speech.") In Stravinsky's correspondence with Kall in Los Angeles, during the same period, the composer refers to Miss Godowsky as "the dangerous person."

[13] In a letter of condolence, dated Belgrade, July 15, 1939, Stravinsky's Yelachich cousins refer to the deceased by the names "Niuta" and "Niutochka."

June 10. Paris. Stravinsky attends his mother's funeral service, in the Russian church, 32, rue Boileau. (Catherine Stravinsky's funeral had taken place in the same church, on March 4.)

June 17. Sancellemoz. Stravinsky sends the titles of the six lectures to Forbes.

June 18. Paris. Roland-Manuel writes to Stravinsky: "I continue to work on the sixth lecture and to see to the typing of all the texts. I have a typist who knows literary English perfectly and who could translate the summaries."

June 21. Suvchinsky writes: Do not even dream that you have reached a "dead end." In the first place, what is happening to you is a transition from one cycle to another.[14] I have found out from Roland-Manuel that the lectures are finished, and I eagerly await an opportunity to read them as a whole.

June 22. Paris. Roland-Manuel writes: "I met with Suvchinsky this morning, and we have adjusted the last details of the fifth lecture, to which he has added an appendix.[15] The sixth lecture is almost ready." Roland-Manuel acknowledges Stravinsky's payment of 5,000 francs.

June 23. Paris. Suvchinsky writes: It occurred to me that the fifth lecture has no ending, and that perhaps a return to the general questions is desirable. I wrote a conclusion and am sending it to you. . . . Roland-Manuel has made a few revisions in the sixth lecture, some of which, in my opinion, are not quite correct. When I mentioned them to him, he agreed. Thus he wrote *"seminaristes exaltés"* where I think it should be *"paradoxalement athées"*; concerning Tolstoy, he wrote *"de la genèse de la création artistique"* where I think he ought to have said *"de la genèse de toute création"*; and on *Eugene Onegin* he has: *"réaliste et ethnique"* where I would have said *"de moeurs réalistes."* Further on, he writes *"ce fût le contraire,"* but it would be more precise to say *"c'était aussi, etc.";* finally, he wrote *"les différentes cultures régionales se transforment et s'amplifient en s'agglomerant"* . . . where I would have said *". . . et s'amplifient pour s'intégrer."*

June 24. Sancellemoz. Stravinsky writes to Roland-Manuel: "I impatiently await the sixth lecture. When will I have it? Agreed for the English translations of the summaries—a sum of about 500 francs."

June 28. Paris. Suvchinsky writes: This very day I composed the addition [to the fifth lecture] and sent it to Roland-Manuel. He and I have read all of the lectures together, one after the other. I think that this book came out very well. Do you agree that it would be more correct to describe the *"Piatyorka"* as "musical populists" instead of "musical slavophiles"? Almost all of them were *"nevyi's,"* weren't they? And in *Pskovityanka*, the "Gosudari-Pskovichi" was sung by the students as a revolutionary song.

June 29. Paris. Roland-Manuel writes to Stravinsky: "I read the sixth lecture to

---

[14] It would be interesting to know exactly what Stravinsky had written to Suvchinsky, since this statement is so utterly unlike anything the composer ever said. Stravinsky's late-in-life correspondence with Suvchinsky is disappointing, the composer refusing to be drawn out on any important subject.

[15] In the manuscript, the appendix is in Suvchinsky's hand.

Suvchinsky before having it typed, and I showed him the third lecture, which he had never seen. We made a final appendix together for 'The Avatars of Russian Music.' . . . I put the summary of the sixth lecture in the margin, and I am finishing the other summaries."

June 29. Paris. Suvchinsky writes to Stravinsky: Yesterday Roland-Manuel gave me 1,000 francs, according to the terms of our agreement, thus settling the matter satisfactorily.

July 3. Paris. Roland-Manuel writes to Stravinsky: "The work on the summaries is progressing."

July 5. Paris. Suvchinsky writes to Stravinsky: I suggested to Roland-Manuel that he put in a comment about "artistic *effort*" and "chance in the artistic process," since chance is inherent in it and differs from "invention." I will discuss this with him when we meet.

July 17. Paris. Roland-Manuel writes to Stravinsky: "I believe that you have received the sixth lecture. . . . Here is the fifth. I have kept copies in which to insert your corrections. The typist has the manuscript of the fifth, so I cannot rectify what I suppose to be an error on page 22, line 5." The manuscript is a fifty-six-page draft in the hand of Soulima Stravinsky, on which Roland-Manuel has made one hundred and sixty changes (stylistic improvements). On pages 50 and 52 (pages 148 and 150 of the 1969 bilingual edition), Stravinsky has marked the places for inserting the titles of contemporary Russian operas, from a list in Suvchinsky's hand. Beneath this list, the composer has reminded himself, in Russian, to "verify the transliterations."

August 2. Sancellemoz. Stravinsky writes to Cie Transatlantique, Paris: "I need a round-trip ticket, since I will be returning from America in May 1940."

August 9. Paris. Roland-Manuel writes to Stravinsky: "I have the copies of the three lectures that you still lack. The translations of the summaries are under way. . . . I hope that the weather permits you to take walks with Madame Sudeikina . . . and that your daughter's health permits her to leave her bed." (Milene Stravinsky was still in Sancellemoz when Stravinsky and Madame Sudeikina returned to Paris at the beginning of the war.)

August 20. Paris. Roland-Manuel writes to Stravinsky: "I am sending the second and third lectures by the same post. Now you have the complete course. . . . An American painter here tells me that the word *'pompiers'* is understood [in his country] by everyone at all conversant with the arts. . . . I am impatient to hear the Symphony in C."

August 24. Stravinsky acknowledges Roland-Manuel's letter of the 20th and the typescripts of the second and third lectures, encloses a 490-franc check for the copyist, and suggests a new beginning for the fifth lecture: *"Aujourd'hui donc, tout comme autrefois, du temps de Stassoff et de Moussorgsky (musicien de génie, certes, mais toujours confus dans ses idées), l'intelligence rationante prétende assigner à la musique un rôle et lui attribuer un sens totalement étranger à sa vrai mission et dont elle est en vérité fort éloignée."*

August 29. Paris. Roland-Manuel writes to Stravinsky: "I thank you for your letter and for the unexpectedly large check."

September 7. Paris. From Paul Valéry's notebook for this date: "At Nadia Boulanger's, at [Gargenville], Stravinsky. Conversation in the twilight about rhythm. He goes to fetch the texts of the lectures that he has just written and will give at Harvard. He calls them *Poétique,* and his first ideas are more than analogous to those of my courses at the college."
End of September. Paris. Valéry writes to Gide: "Stravinsky read us his future *Cours de Poétique* (he too!) *musicale,* which has analogies with mine—something very curious."[16]

No doubt scholars and cryptographers will someday be able to fill in the blank spaces in the following transcription of Stravinsky's notes, but Roland-Manuel himself encountered difficulty in deciphering many words, to judge by his more legible versions in the margins.

STRAVINSKY'S NOTES FOR *LA POÉTIQUE MUSICALE*[17]

Second part of the first lecture

I am obliged to speak polemically, first to cover the inversion and the transferral into music, and second because the lectures have a first-person perspective. [Illegible] Since the beginning of my career, my musical biography, my work (which is not a passing whim, and I am not about to consider it simply a fortunate coincidence), has, for this reason [polemics], been termed "reactive." This "reactive" [element] is in contact with the musical reality surrounding me, and with the milieu of ideas and people, whose reactions [to me] have been as violent as they have been misdirected. Perhaps one should say that they were misaddressed. Such erroneous reactions are serious, for they demonstrate the vice that resides in the whole musical conscience, and thanks to which all ideas, themes, judgments, opinions about music and art, one of the principal faculties of the human spirit, are falsified. It must be remembered that at the time when *Petrushka, Le Sacre du printemps,* and *The Nightingale* appeared, many things changed, not on the esthetic level but in the mode of expression. The changes to which I refer took place together with a general revision of the basis of the art of music and its primary elements.

The question of the phenomenon of music has begun to interest me personally insofar as it emanates from an integral man, i.e., a man armed with all the resources of our senses, our psychic faculties, and intellectual means.

Above all, I declare that the phenomenon of music is one of speculation (see my interview with [Serge] Moreux), a speculation consisting of sound and time.

---

[16] Stravinsky saw Valéry several times in the two weeks at Mlle Boulanger's before the departure for America.
[17] Stravinsky's quotation marks and italics have been preserved throughout.

The *Chronos*. [In the typescript, Stravinsky has elaborated, in Russian: "An analysis of the elements of time and movement, indicating either Lento or Presto in music."]

1) The dialectic of the creative process in music. The principle of contrast and similitude in music and creation: my attitude toward "variety" and "similitude" (polychromy, monochromy).

2) Meditation in active and passive music (author-listener).

3) Musical emotion (see interview).

4) The limits of the art of music: pure music and descriptive music. (I discuss realizations and give examples in Lecture 4.)

I contend that the general change, begun in the period of [the *Sacre*], continues its development endlessly, and the conjunction of certain concrete facts and events in the musical life that we have all witnessed testifies to this continuum.

I know that a popular interpretation of my development is: Revolution at the time of the *Sacre,* and assimilation of the revolutionary conquests now. This interpretation is wrong.

I admit that my course will be extensive, not in order to defend myself, but rather to defend music and its principles verbally as strongly as I do through my musical compositions.

Now allow me to outline my course. It will be divided into 8[18] lectures, and each one should have a title. (I will then name them.) The first, which has just been given, is nothing more than "Getting acquainted." The second [illegible]. The third [illegible].

As you will see, this *"Explanation"* of music that I undertake before you and with you will, I hope, be a systematic synthesis of views, beginning with an analysis of the phenomenon of music and ending with the problem of performance. I warn you that in this instance I have not chosen the standard method, which consists in developing a thesis using the general as a departure point and finishing with the particular (detail). On the contrary, I plan to follow the method of "synchronization," meaning that I will discuss the general and the particular at the same time, supporting the one with the other, because it is only by virtue of practical necessity [i.e., the particular] that we are challenged to distinguish, discern things, arranging them in purely conventional categories, such as primary, secondary, principal, subordinate, etc.

[Illegible] The real hierarchy of phenomena and things and also the relationship of things takes form, incarnates, on a completely different level. I nurture the hope that this theme will be elucidated, for that is what I desire most from the course.

Second Lecture: The Musical Work (Elements and Morphology)

a) the sonorous scale

b) interval, chord

---

[18] Stravinsky had insisted that he lacked the time to prepare eight lectures, but not until June 1939 did Harvard agree to reduce the number to six.

c) mode, tonality

d) melody, theme, motif; phrasing, period, development, *reprise*. Cite examples: sonatas, cantatas, etc. Do not forget *Variations*

e) harmony

f) modulation

g) movement in time, meter, rhythm

h) sonority: pitch, register, timbre of the sound

i) the instrument producing the sound and the human voice.
The human voice: the word and the syllable. Intonation (keeping in mind the accent, which is to say, sometimes strong, sometimes weak, but not a dynamic element).

j) scheme, form, system (coexistence in a mechanical or organic unit of different forms)

The Phenomenon of Music

a) That which does not constitute music: noises, even the songs of birds. What music *is:* sounds organized by the conscious action of man. I admit that I have no taste for the problem of "origins" and "prehistory." Alas, such an excursion into the depths and shadows of the past, which claims to possess the qualities of an exact science, too often is nothing but an *interpretation* of little-known facts. The interpretation has *its* origin in ideas and points that were clearly preconceived. Example: I am a materialist. Long live Darwinism, therefore, and I search, consequently, for the monkey in question rather than the man.

b) To formulate the origins of music in magic, incantations, etc.

Third Lecture: The Métier of Music, or, rather, "On Musical Composition"

a) The composition of a work: the implication is that the work is a *piece* that is composed.

b) [Taken literally and from this departure point], the term *composer* has a pejorative sense, as a reproach: see my interview with Moreux (artist, artisan, etc.).

c) The invention, the imagination (self-expression), intellectual imagination.

d) The will and the accidental in the creative process.

e) The writing—musical invention (tightened [illegible]: easy or expanding sequences, Wagner, etc.)

f) Inspiration

g) Culture and taste. The culture *of* taste. One searches for good taste, imposes it upon oneself and upon others. That is cultural and traditional. [*In Russian*] I am in the process of creating, and at a certain moment it begins to happen automatically. Rarely can one invent a law about creative processes.

h) Order. As rule and as law; external and internal orders. Order and disorder. The realm of necessity and the realm of liberty. [*In Russian*] Dialectics supposes that art is synonymous with free creation, but this is not so. Art is more free when it is more limited, more finished, canonical, dogmatic.

Fourth Lecture: Musical Typology (that which is established by tracing history) [original subtitle]

Making synoptic, synchronic, and parallel analyses, in order to arrive directly at the problem of *style*, which is very difficult, if not impossible, to define. The question of musical history, the problems of continuity and discontinuity;[19] evolutions [vs.] evolution in history; the determinate and the indeterminate; chance (miracle; the accidental) and genesis (origin; *rapport causal*). Haydn-Mozart are of common origin, but each has his own miracle: the phenomenon is determinate and indeterminate at the same time.

Before discussing such arbitrary classifications as, for example, *Classicism* and *Romanticism,* I would like to expound on the law to which any art must subject itself, the phenomenon of submission and ascendancy, the yielding and the unyielding. [*In Russian*] The subordinate and the independent. Cite Sophocles (from the interview).

Distance [of the classical rules] demands of music things that are beyond its jurisdiction—the principle of illustration imitation (leitmotif). Example of the *negative:* Wagner-Strauss (epigone), *Symphonia domestica;* and the *positive:* Beethoven *Pastoral* Symphony; Verdi, the storm in *Rigoletto; gesetzmässig.* With this in mind, return to the discussion of Classicism and Romanticism. Examples, a slow movement by Haydn and one by Chopin. Then compare two Romantics, Chopin and Weber. Also mention Schumann and Brahms. The commonplace and the platitudinous [illegible].

"Courant": This is the contrary of duration—without limit and without end.

Two words on the subject of "modernism" and academicism. What an ineffectual word, "modernism."

The two academicisms. I have nothing against the good one, which can do no harm and always renders a certain service. Pedagogy. I am not a modernist. *I had always been taken for what I am not.* I am not revolutionary, nor am I conservative.[20]

Fifth Lecture: Russian Music

Why do I suddenly launch into a discussion of Russian music? Not because I am Russian or because I value it more than other music. Also, do not think that I oppose the manifestation of nationalism, since such a thing is of course subconscious. I do not pretend to be a citizen of the world, as the Russian revolutionaries of the nineteenth century fancied themselves.

Folklore and musical culture. Plainchant, sacred and profane music. The Italianisms, the Germanisms, and the Orientalisms of nineteenth-century Russian music. The continuity of Russian culture. The two Russias, the Russian revolutionary and the Russian conservative—the two disorders, which collided

---

[19] [*In the margin*] Cycles: periods with precise beginnings and ends.

[20] Roland-Manuel wrote *"Pulcinella"* here, but Stravinsky struck it out.

tragically before World War I: *Glinka, Tchaikovsky* = order; *Scriabin* = disorder (religious, political, ideological, psychological, and musical).[21] Mussorgsky [is] between the two. [Present-day] Russia as the third Rome, [including] Rozanov's very just description: "Russia lost its colors in three days, if not two."

The new Soviet folklorism: Ukrainian, Georgian, Armenian, Azerbaijanian, etc., and the degradation of values.

Sixth Lecture: On Performance

Being, nothingness, and reality [are] simultaneous in a musical work. Music exists while it is played and exists when it is played again. Between these two moments, the music does not exist (whereas a painting or a sculpture does exist).

Interpretation and execution.

The performers, the listeners, and the public. Presence and absence in respect to the music.

Passiveness and activeness of the public toward the music. The problem of musical criticism, its aberrations, the classical bewilderment. (*"Klassische Kritiken"*: ask Strecker.[22]) And now the Epilogue.

The true meaning of music. Like all the creative faculties of man, music is a quest for unity, communion, union with fellow beings and with Being [illegible word], Monism, the Creator.

Postscript: The Janin Edition of *La Poétique musicale*

On February 12, 1945, Roland Bourdariat, of the Radiodiffusion Française and the publishing firm of Janin, cabled Stravinsky from Paris requesting permission to publish a special edition of the *Poétique musicale*. Stravinsky, at the Hotel Drake, New York, cabled his authorization to Bourdariat after confirming that no copies remained of the 1942 Harvard University Press edition. On February 28, a representative of H.U.P. wrote to Stravinsky and asked for permission to publish an English-language edition. Bourdariat wrote to Stravinsky on April 25 saying that Louis Jouvet, returning from America, had brought a copy of the book,

> which I have just read with great joy and emotion. When I wrote to you about making a French edition, I was not aware that the book consisted of texts by Roland-Manuel and Suvchinsky. . . . Musicians here are divided into partisans for or against Messiaen and the chapel of ridiculous disciples that surrounds him, hypnotized by him, and in which, like Father Divine, he preaches a pseudo-mystical jargon. The religiosity of his sermons cannot

---

[21] Roland-Manuel develops the dialectic of order and disorder but, unlike Stravinsky, does not go so far as to cite Scriabin as the embodiment of this disorder.

[22] This refers to Weber on Beethoven, etc., classics of critical gaffes that Stravinsky quotes in the lectures.

hide an unbelievably vulgar sensuality, as well as false and absurd doctrines. These pupils hail the *Sacre* and *Noces* . . . but create scandals at performances of every other work of yours. Western music does not interest them, but only so-called Hindu rhythms and pseudo-Oriental melodies. . . . For these Messiaenists, the greatest modern composer is Schoenberg. . . .[23] But then, apart from Poulenc and Françaix, we have no musician of value to oppose and resist this current. . . . Turning to the subject of *La Poétique musicale,* the text will be sent to the printer in a few days, and I hope that the work will appear in June.

Bourdariat wrote again on May 16 to ask Stravinsky if he would allow the publisher to omit the chapter on Russian music, since, apart from the "violent polemics that it would certainly provoke, the censor might ban the book; Roland-Manuel and Suvchinsky are of the same opinion." This letter was delivered to Stravinsky in person by Nadia Boulanger, who must have been in accord with the suggestion; she helped to persuade Stravinsky to suppress the "Russian chapter," a decision that he cabled to Bourdariat on June 18. On August 16, Stravinsky wrote to his younger son:

I never received the contract that Bourdariat promised me in his letter of April 25. . . . A month ago, I entrusted the producer John Houseman (who was leaving for Europe) with a gift for Bourdariat, the recording of my *Scènes de ballet* that I made with the New York Philharmonic last February. Was this gift received?

Whatever Stravinsky thought of Bourdariat's report on the musical situation in Paris and of other accounts of the protests—hissing, booing—that greeted *Danses concertantes* at its Paris premiere on February 23, the composer responded with denigrations of Messiaen. Regarding Messiaen's *Petites Liturgies,* Stravinsky wrote to Suvchinsky, November 18, 1946: "Why compose such rubbish, anyway? Who needs it?" But Stravinsky did not comment on Suvchinsky's observation (letter of November 11) hat "the *Poétique* was not properly published in France. It needed one or two more chapters, and a new preface"—or on Suvchinsky's remark, "After much agonizing thought I have decided not to return to Russia." (Could Suvchinsky seriously have considered living in Stalin's Russia?) On September 20, Bourdariat wrote to Stravinsky thanking him for the recording, praising the score, promising that it would be performed at the end of November at the Théâtre des Champs-Elysées, and inviting him to conduct his new symphony in Paris. The letter also said that the proofs of the *Poétique* were due any day, and that the book would be published on or about October 15.

Stravinsky received the contract on October 5 and immediately cabled that it was unacceptable since it failed to specify that Janin's rights applied only to France. Janin settled the matter directly with the Harvard University Press, and

---

[23] Marcelle de Manziarly wrote to Stravinsky from Paris, March 16, 1947: "It is astonishing, the influence that Schoenberg has on all of these young composers."

a new contract was sent by mid-November. On November 8, the critic Claude Rostand wrote to Stravinsky requesting permission to publish two excerpts in a new review—and also reminding the composer that they had been introduced by Poulenc and Sauguet at the Princesse de Polignac's ("I will never forget the day when I had the joy and honor to approach so great a master"). The book was printed by December 7, and a copy was sent to Stravinsky. On the 11th, the widow of Ricciotto Canudo[24] sent a letter to Stravinsky saying that she had worked on the book for Janin, though in fact she appears to have headed the company.

According to a letter from Bourdariat, September 9, 1946, the edition of five thousand copies, which was released at the beginning of March, was sold out in three weeks. This letter also refers to the critical acclaim that the book received, though most of the reviews would be more accurately described as mixed. Meanwhile, the English translation had been entrusted to the Gide expert Marie D. Molles Stein, the wife of Schoenberg's assistant, Leonard Stein. When Mrs. Stein wrote to Stravinsky on December 26 expressing regret that she was too busy to complete the task, Stravinsky asked Ingolf Dahl to undertake it. Dahl agreed on condition that he could collaborate with Arthur Knodel, the authority on Saint-John Perse. By the summer of 1947, Janin had defaulted on the payment of royalties. Stravinsky sued the publisher, who then declared bankruptcy. Stravinsky tried to attach the company's assets, and the litigation lasted until December 1951. In 1952, finally free to issue the book in French through another publisher, Editions le Bon Plaisir, Stravinsky restored the chapter on Russian music. By this date, of course, the cold war had intensified.

---

[24] See *S.P.D.*, p. 522.

INDEX